Taxation of Trusts

Edition 4

2021 Edition

Taxation of Trusts

Edition 4

Wolters Kluwer

2021 Edition

CCH New Zealand Limited
PO BOX 33-270, Takapuna
Auckland 0740
Telephone: 0800 500 224
www.wolterskluwer.co.nz

About Wolters Kluwer

Wolters Kluwer enables legal, tax, finance, and healthcare professionals to be more effective and efficient. We provide information, software, and services that deliver vital insights, intelligent tools, and the guidance of subject-matter experts.

We create value by combining information, deep expertise, and technology to provide customers with solutions that improve their quality and effectiveness. Professionals turn to us when they need actionable information to better serve their clients.

Wolters Kluwer. When you have to be right.

Enquiries are welcome on 0800 500 224.

A catalogue record for this book is available from the National Library of New Zealand.

ISBN 978-1-77547-395-4 (print)

ISBN 978-1-77547-396-1 (eBook)

Published by CCH New Zealand Limited

First published January 2010

This edition published July 2021

Contents

Foreword

Although the law of trusts predates income tax by some six centuries, in a curious way they are intertwined, as the concepts of income and capital inherent in income tax are drawn from trust law. This book, however, focuses firmly on the 21st century. It is a remarkable testimony to both the flexibility and the adaptability of trusts and trust law that the taxation of trusts is a critical part of New Zealand's current tax system.

The reasons trusts are used are varied and include protection against professional liability claims, safeguarding your assets from financial disaster, succession planning for future generations, confidentiality about financial affairs, and reducing the exposure to relationship property claims by future partners. It must be acknowledged that, in some cases, trusts are also used to gain some tax advantages.

Now in its fourth edition, this book deals with important recent cases, such as *Penny and Hooper* and *Newmarket Trustees* as well as other significant developments in such areas as sham, changes to closely held companies, foreign trust disclosures in the aftermath of the revelations caused by the release of the Panama Papers and the increased disclosure requirements made necessary by the introduction of the bright-line test and changes to personal income tax rates.

Vicki Ammundsen's book tackles the hard topics in the taxation of trusts and seeks to answer questions which are critical in practice. It would be surprising if this was not one of the more useful texts in any businessperson's or tax practitioner's library.

Professor Craig Elliffe
Professor of Tax Law, University of Auckland Faculty of Law
Director of the Master of Taxation Studies
Consultant, Chapman Tripp (barristers and solicitors).

About the Author

Vicki Ammundsen BSc, BCom, LLB, TEP and Notary Public, the author of *Taxation of Trusts*, is a director at Vicki Ammundsen Trust Law Limited in Auckland where she specialises in all areas of trust law. Vicki is the author of a number of texts including *The Trustee's Handbook* and *Trustee Liability: What Every Trustee Needs to Know*. Vicki's day-to-day experience with trusts means that she is well placed to appreciate the practical and tax-related matters that apply to trusts. Vicki is also the author of the blog mattersoftrust.

Author's Acknowledgments

In addition to acknowledging the assistance from Wolters Kluwer, I would like to thank Lee Treadaway (Content Manager – Tax and Accounting Portfolio) for her insightful management, support and content assistance. I would also like to thank Reshma Korah (Content Editor – Research and Learning) for her invaluable editing support.

Acknowledgment is also due to Hugh Ammundsen (Solicitor, Vicki Ammundsen Trust Law Limited) for the significant contribution that he has made to this text.

Vicki Ammundsen

Part I

INTRODUCTION

CHAPTER 1

Introduction to Trusts and Overview

¶1-010 Operating principle

A trust has no legal personality. Instead, the legal "face" of a trust, and the person that is liable in the first instance for the trust's tax and legal obligations, is the trust's trustee(s).

¶1-020 Trusts are a common asset and estate planning tool

Trusts, once considered the preserve of the wealthy, are now a commonplace asset and estate planning tool. Trusts can provide a flexible and tax effective means of long-term intergenerational asset ownership.

However, with the proliferation of trusts has also come an increase in taxation legislation targeted at tax advantages previously available to trusts. Further application of avoidance provisions has also meant that arrangements that are permissible for trust purposes can be avoidance arrangements for tax purposes. See, for example, *Krukziener* v *C of IR (No 3)* [2010] NZHC 1714; (2010) 24 NZTC 24,563, *Penny and Hooper* v *C of IR* [2011] NZSC 95; (2011) 25 NZTC ¶20-073. Such measures have new relevance now that the top marginal rate has once again been increased to 39% with effect from 1 April 2021, while the trustee rate remains at 33%.

Trustees are personally liable for trust tax obligations and can be held to account if they fail to meet their tax obligations and/or breach the duties owed by trustee. See, for example, *C of IR* v *Bayly* (1998) 18 NZTC 14,073, *AMP General Insurance Ltd* v *Macalister Todd Phillips Bodkins* [2006] NZSC 105; (2007) 23 NZTC 21,086; (2006) 1 NZTR ¶16-017, *Case* 5/2013 [2013] NZTRA 05; (2013) 26 NZTC ¶2-004 and *Selkirk* v *McIntyre* [2013] NZHC 575; (2013) 26 NZTC ¶21-008. Trusts are also increasingly subject to challenge by creditors, spouses and partners, beneficiaries and other dissatisfied parties. There is also an increase in cases where trust validity is challenged, whether as a sham or some other ground of invalidity (see *Clayton* v *Clayton (Vaughan Road Property Trust)* [2016] NZSC 29; (2016) 4 NZTR ¶26-002, *Webb* v *Webb* [2020] UKPC 22; (2020) 5 NZTR ¶30-011, *JSC Mezhdunarodniy Promyshlenniy Bank* v *Pugachev* [2017] EWHC 2426 Ch). Trustees' actions, or inaction, are coming under greater scrutiny and it can be expected that this will be a continuing trend. This is highlighted in *Official*

Assignee v *Wilson* [2008] NZCA 122; (2008) 2 NZTR ¶18-005 by Robertson J who notes at [92]:

> "Evidence of poor administration of the trust is insufficient, of itself, to establish a sham. This may be evidence of a breach of trust, but the fact that the trustees have acted poorly in managing the trust does not establish an intention that the trust operate as a sham".

Where trust management fails to meet even minimum standards, while this will not by itself lead to a finding of sham, it can provide important indicia as to the parties' intentions. See *Rosebud Corporate Trustee Ltd* v *Bublitz* [2014] NZHC 2018; (2014) 3 NZTR ¶24-025, where a trust settled to provide a structure behind which a bankrupt carried on a business (notwithstanding his bankruptcy), was found to be a sham. Factors that contributed to the sham finding, in addition to the Court's view that a trust was not intended, included the trustee's failure to meet even minimum standards of trust management.

¶1-030 Trustees do not always appreciate their duties and obligations

What the case law continues to demonstrate is that although the use of trusts is increasing, trustees and other involved parties do not always fully appreciate the obligations and duties involved.

Baragwanath J has noted as follows in *NZHB Holdings Ltd* v *Bartells* (2004) 1 NZTR ¶14-009 at [34]):

> "Recent experience in more than one case suggests that the concept of trust is used more often than it is understood. Unlike a company or an incorporated society a 'trust' is not a legal person recognised as distinct from the humans who direct their affairs. On the contrary, trustees can contract only in their own right: either they do so and are personally liable to the extent provided by the ordinary law which the agreement may modify or there is no agreement at all".

Tax and accounting professionals increasingly find themselves confronted with trusts where the documentation is such that it is difficult or sometimes even impossible to establish the trust's full history or how the trustee has discharged the duties owed to the beneficiaries and the obligations owed to Inland Revenue.

Fundamental to good modern trust management is for the trustee to have a good understanding of how a trust is taxed and who is liable for payment of that tax. A lack of appreciation of such factors virtually ensures that a trust cannot be operated in a compliant manner from either a trust law or tax law perspective.

The primary purpose of this book is to consider the various ways in which trusts are taxed, paying particular attention to the rules of taxation that are peculiar to trusts.

However, before embarking on the specifics of how a trust is taxed, it is important to establish what a trust is.

¶1-040 What is a trust?

A trust, in its simplest form, is property that is subject to obligations owed by the property's owner, the trustee(s), to the beneficiaries for whom the property is held.

Fundamental to a trust are the rights of the beneficiaries, as noted by Millett LJ in *Armitage* v *Nurse* [1998] Ch 241 at 253–254:

> "... there is an irreducible core of obligations owed by the trustees to the beneficiaries and enforceable by them which is fundamental to the concept of a trust. If the beneficiaries have no rights enforceable against the trustees there are no trusts".

As a trust itself has no legal personality, it is the trustee that acts personally for the benefit of a trust's beneficiaries. This means that a trustee is liable for the trustee's actions as if those actions were on the trustee's own account. This is the case regardless of whether the trustee is able to personally benefit from the trust. However, as many trustees have no particular training or experience, a full appreciation of these obligations is often lacking.

Although trustees are commonly indemnified against personal liability, either through statute (Trusts Act 2019, s 41) or the terms of the deed, in many circumstances liability in excess of that for which the trustee is indemnified remains the trustee's personal liability. In addition, if a trustee is in breach of the obligations owed pursuant to the trust, any right of indemnity may be forfeited.

¶1-050 A brief history of trusts

In determining the "irreducible" core of obligations fundamental to the existence of a trust, it is helpful to consider the origins of trusts.

The "use" as the early trust was known, has been referred to in writings since at least the early 13th century. The early use came into existence in medieval times to address the inflexibility of the law of the time which provided that land could not be bequeathed by will. Thus, on the death of a landowner, an adult heir had to pay the landowner's feudal overlord a sum to claim the inheritance plus the subsequent profits of the land.

To address this inflexibility, the concept of a separation of beneficial and legal ownership was utilised so as to ensure a legal ownership that escaped the impact of the law of the time, while maintaining a beneficial ownership that met the original landowner's wishes.

Certain aspects of modern trust law are now governed by legislation such as the Trustee Act, the Charitable Trusts Act 1957 and the Charities Act 2005. While a new Trusts Act has been proposed by the Law Commission following a significant review of the law of trusts in New Zealand (see Law Commission *Review of the Law of Trusts – A Trusts Act for New Zealand* (NZLC R130, August 2013), the bulk of the law relating to trusts is still the law of equity that has developed over time alongside the common law on a case-by-case basis.

¶1-060 Definition of a trust

The Trusts Act defines the characteristics of an express trust (a trust) as "... a fiduciary relationship in which a trustee holds or deals with trust property for the benefit of the beneficiaries or for a permitted purpose; and the trustee is accountable for the way the trustee carries out the duties imposed on the trustee by law".

However, it cannot be presumed that the same definition will always apply for income tax purposes. As noted in interpretation statement IS 19/04, "Income tax – distributions from foreign trusts":

> "... it is considered that the word 'trust' in tax law has the meaning that it has under New Zealand general law. This meaning is that a trust is not an entity but a description of an equitable obligation the law imposes on a person holding property to deal with that property in a certain way; namely, for the benefit of beneficiaries or a charitable purpose. Circumstances will be found to give rise to a trust only where there is such a person (the trustee(s)), property that can be the subject of the trust, someone (one or more beneficiaries) for whose benefit the property is held and where the law imposes the required obligation. It is an objective exercise to determine whether a trust exists and a court is likely to take account of the provisions of the Trusts Act 2019 which is intended to align with common law and equity while not being a code".

¶1-070 Essential elements of a trust

The Trusts Act provides that a trust may be created by a person (the settlor) who, clearly and with reasonable certainty (and subject to any formalities prescribed by any enactment):

- indicates an intention to create a trust, and
- identifies the beneficiaries (or classes of beneficiaries) or the permitted purpose of the trust, and
- identifies the trust property.

This definition essentially codifies the "three certainties" set out at common law. See *Knight* v *Knight* (1840) 3 Beav 148 per Lord Langdale at 172, *Kauter* v *Hilton* (1953) 90 CLR 86; 27 ALJ 714 at 97, *Herdegen* v *FC of T* (1988) 20 ATR 24; 84 ALR 271, *Clayton* v *Clayton* [2015] NZCA 30; (2015) 4 NZTR ¶25-001 at [50] confirmed in *Clayton* v *Clayton (Vaughan Road Property Trust)* [2016] NZSC 29; (2016) 4 NZTR ¶26-002 at [111].

¶1-080 It must be certain that there was an intention to create a trust

Certainty of purpose or certainty of trust means that it must be certain that there is or was an intention to create a trust. This can be important where a trust is not settled by deed, as is usually the case, or where a deed is not drafted in conventional form. Although there are no special words necessary to create a trust, commonly there will be a document, usually in the form of a deed, which states that a certain asset or certain assets will be held "upon trust". In the case of a "modern" trust, that asset might only be a nominal sum of money. However, the settlor likely intends to make further settlements onto the trust.

Words alone will not create a trust if this is not what is actually intended: *Solicitor-General* v *Wanganui Borough* [1919] NZLR 763 (CA) at 773, *Clayton* v *Clayton* [2015] NZCA 30; (2015) 4 NZTR ¶25-001 at [50].

¶1-090 There must be a person or people who can benefit

The object of a trust means the beneficiary or beneficiaries who can benefit from the trust. Historically, these beneficiaries are referred to as the "cestuis que trust" meaning, literally, those of the trust, that is the person(s) for whom the trust was created.

It is a fundamental rule of equity that a trust, other than a charitable trust, must be for an identifiable beneficiary or beneficiaries who have the power to enforce the trust. See *Clayton* v *Clayton* [2015] NZCA 30; (2015) 4 NZTR ¶25-001 at [50]. Also see *Davis* v *White* [2016] NZHC 1626; (2016) 4 NZTR ¶26-012, where the trustees were unable to demonstrate what the objects of the trust of which they were trustees were.

¶1-100 There must be property subject to the trust

The subject of the trust is the property of the trust. Any property or interest in property that a person can transfer at law or equity can be settled onto a trust. However, it must be possible to determine this property or interest with absolute certainty. A trust will fail if its property cannot be determined. For example, in *Re London Wine Co (Shippers) Ltd* [1986] PCC 121, a settlor was held to be unable to declare itself a trustee of 20 of 80 bottles of the same wine in a cellar where the 20 bottles in question were not separately identified as the subject matter of the trust. By contrast in *Hunter* v *Moss* [1994] 3 All ER 215, the English Court of Appeal held that a trust could be declared in respect of 50 of 950 identical shares because, unlike in the case of the wine where each bottle could be different, regardless of the fact that each bore the same label, all 950 of the shares were identical and there could be no uncertainty of subject matter. Also see *Clayton* v *Clayton* [2015] NZCA 30; (2015) 4 NZTR ¶25-001 at [50].

Importantly a trust does not commence until a trustee holds property of the trust. See the Trusts Act, s 15(2).

¶1-110 No single trust standard

At its simplest level, what is commonly referred to as a trust is simply a reference to the property that is owned by a trustee or trustees for the benefit of defined beneficiaries.

Matters involving trusts are often confused because there is no standard form of trust. Although standard form precedent deeds are commonplace, other than a requirement that any deed identifies the intention that there is a trust, the trust property (usually the original settlement onto the trust for these purposes) and the persons who are to benefit from the same, there is no particular requirement as to form.

Accordingly, care is required to ensure the terms of each individual trust are drafted to meet the applicable circumstances. It is also important not to presume that the terms of one trust will be the same as another and that each trust is viewed and considered on its own terms.

¶1-120 Lifespan of a trust

The maximum duration of a trust other than a charitable trust, which can last in perpetuity, is 125 years. See the Trusts Act, s 16. The maximum duration also has application to any resettlement, meaning that the maximum duration cannot be extended by resettlement. See Trusts Act, s 17.

¶1-130 The role of the trustee

A trustee, as the legal owner of trust property, is the "public persona" of a trust. Publicly, the trustee is liable, subject to any agreement to the contrary, for the trustee's actions.

Privately, the trustee must carry out the settlor's wishes in accordance with the terms of the deed of trust. However, the trustee owes duties of care not to the settlor, but to each beneficiary and is answerable to each beneficiary for any failure to properly manage the trust property.

¶1-140 Special trust advisor

In addition to "responsible" trustees (ie the trustees identified as trustees and the legal owners of trust property), a trust can also have special trust advisers or (less commonly in New Zealand) protectors. Special trust advisers are a creature of statute, and although trustees may consult with special trust advisers, the trustees are not bound by the special trust advisers whose role is only consultative: Trusts Act, ss 74, 75.

¶1-150 Protector

Some trust deeds make provision for a "protector". Although there is no legal definition of protector, the term is used to describe the role of a person, or persons, who are neither trustees nor beneficiaries, but upon whom a trust deed confers certain determinative powers that would appear to be trustee powers but for clear statements to the contrary in the deed of trust.

The distinction between a special trust adviser and a protector is quite marked as, although trustees may consult an advisory trustee where the deed of trust provides so, the trustees must act when directed by a protector.

As noted in *Kea Trust Co Ltd* v *Pugachev* [2015] NZHC 2412, whether a person holding the position of a Protector under a trust owes fiduciary obligations will require consideration of the "words of the relevant trust instrument, and the objects of the trust that can be gleaned from them and any relevant extrinsic evidence".

¶1-160 Deed of trust

At the simplest level, a deed merely prescribes the rules that the trustees are to operate the trust by. These rules will provide, for example, whether any beneficiary is a beneficiary as to capital and income, or whether some beneficiaries are beneficiaries only as to capital and others as to income. The deed might prescribe limitations that are intended to ensure that the settlor or some other person cannot benefit from the trust.

What is important is that the trustees adhere to the terms of the trust, or when in doubt or if this is not possible, seek advice or directions from the High Court: Trusts Act, s 133.

¶1-170 Taxation of trusts

Trustees, as the legal owners of the trust property, are also the first line of defence vis-á-vis a trust's taxation obligations.

In most circumstances the trustee is liable for the trust's tax obligations, including the beneficiary's tax liability.

It is important to appreciate that the scope of this book is limited to taxation of trusts from a New Zealand perspective and that increasingly there may be obligations in other jurisdictions that also require consideration.

¶1-180 Guide to this book and overview

This book is set out so that each chapter provides an overview of a principle of taxation, followed by commentary and ending with excerpts of the relevant legislation. Given the range and varieties of circumstances that may apply to trusts, the inclusion of the legislation allows a consideration of how the legislation applies to different circumstances. There is, of course, no substitute for considered professional advice, and any trustee who is uncertain regarding any matter of trust law or taxation should seek professional advice.

The chapters are grouped in parts, each part focusing on a different area of taxation that is relevant to trusts, or on trust circumstances that can have tax consequences.

Part I — Overview

The primary income tax provisions that apply to the taxation of trusts are contained in Subpart HC of the Income Tax Act 2007. Other taxation provisions that relate to the taxation of trusts, settlors or beneficiaries are contained elsewhere in that Act, in the Tax Administration Act 1994 and the Goods and Services Tax Act 1985 (GST Act). Please note that all law references in this book are to the Income Tax Act 2007 unless otherwise stated.

As the provisions that relate to the taxation of trusts are not contained in any one section of the Income Tax Act or any other legislation, care is required to ensure that the various taxation obligations of trustees, beneficiaries and settlors are fully appreciated.

Part I contains an introduction to trusts and tax policy regarding the taxation of trusts and an overview of how trusts are taxed by reference to the settlor, which is a fundamental aspect of the taxation of trusts in New Zealand.

Part II — Income and Distributions, Business

Part II focuses on taxation of trustee income and distributions from trusts and issues related to trusts carrying on business.

A trust is not a legal person for tax purposes. Although IRD numbers are issued to trusts and it is the trust not its trustee that registers for goods and services tax (GST), the trustee has personal liability for tax.

Trust income is accounted for by the trustee who derives the income or by a beneficiary who receives a distribution of income. Income derived by a trustee that is not beneficiary income is trustee income. Special rules apply to the taxation of beneficiary income distributed to minor beneficiaries.

Trustee income is taxed at the trustee rate of 33% regardless of whether the trustee is a natural person or a company.

Trustees benefit beneficiaries by making distributions of a trust's income or capital. At the time of every distribution, a trust is classified as complying, foreign or non-complying for tax purposes. This classification occurs for tax purposes only and determines whether certain distributions are taxable distributions or exempt income to the recipient beneficiaries.

Complying and foreign trusts are effectively defined by reference to whether the trust's settlor is resident in New Zealand. If a trust is neither complying nor foreign, it is non-complying.

It is important to appreciate that testamentary trusts are trusts for the purposes of classifying distributions from trusts.

Trustees are permitted deductions for any loss incurred in deriving income or in the course of carrying on a business. However, these losses can only be utilised by the trustee.

Part III — Life Leases and Debt Forgiveness

Part III considers the tax implications that can flow from asset and estate planning activities such as granting leases and debt forgiveness.

Part IV — Special Rules

Part IV comprises a consideration of special rules that apply to trusts, including:

- rules that prevent streaming of imputation credits derived by trustees to the beneficiaries most able to utilise the credits
- modifications of shareholder continuity rules in relation to trustees so that a change of trustee will not usually result in a loss of continuity
- associated persons rules that apply to certain transactions involving trustees, settlors, beneficiaries and related companies.

Part V — Administration

Part V considers the administration and disclosure obligations that arise in respect of trusts, including an increasing range of reporting obligations.

If a trustee derives income, the trust must have an IRD number. A trust can also require an IRD number to transfer or receive property. In addition to statutory administrative and record-keeping obligations, a trustee must maintain trust accounts and other trust records in accordance with the terms of the trust.

Trustees can have various reporting obligations for tax purposes, in addition to disclosure obligations for trust law purposes.

Separately a trustee is personally liable to meet a trust's income tax and GST obligations. Where there is more than one trustee, the liability is joint and several. Importantly this liability cannot be limited by the trust deed.

Part VI — Avoidance

Part VI considers the general and specific avoidance provisions that can apply in respect of trusts.

Trusts are routinely used in asset and estate planning and as a vehicle for operating a business and owning assets. However, due to the ability to limit the tax rate that would otherwise be paid to the trustee rate, there are circumstances where a transaction will be re-characterised for taxation purposes because of the use of a trust or because an existing arrangement is recast to include a trust.

Separately, a specific anti-avoidance rule, referred to as the attribution rule, prevents higher income earners from diverting personal services income to a trust so that income can be streamed to beneficiaries on lower marginal tax rates. If the requirements of the attribution rule are met, personal services income is taxed in accordance with the rule, regardless of whether the arrangement is in fact a tax avoidance arrangement.

Part VII — Goods and Services Tax

Part VII covers the GST provisions that apply to trusts.

A trust must register and account for GST if the trust makes taxable supplies in excess of the registration threshold. The casual nature of supplies made by some trusts, and different valuation methods that apply to associated persons, means that trusts can fail to recognise a GST liability.

Part VIII — Death

Part VIII focuses on testamentary trusts and the provisions specific to tax following a death.

Transfers of property in the tax base at death are disposals and acquisitions for tax purposes. The tax treatment of these transfers is determined in accordance with asset-transfer rules. These rules are modified for transfers to close relatives.

Part IX — Special Cases

Part IX provides an overview of special purpose trusts that have specific tax treatment. For example:

- Gross proceeds from gaming machines operated by gaming trusts for an authorised purpose are exempt from income tax.

- Income derived by funeral trusts, which meets specified requirements, is tax-exempt.
- The tax rules that apply to unit trusts allow a unit trust to be treated as a company and distributions to beneficiaries are deemed to be dividends.
- Exemptions from income tax are available to registered charitable trusts that derive income for charitable purposes.
- Income derived by community housing entities, including trusts and companies, is exempt income.

Part X — Variation, Resettlement and Winding Up

Part X focuses on the taxation consequences that arise from the resettlement, variation and winding up of trusts.

A trust can be varied without tax consequences. However, there may be tax consequences where the extent of variation is so significant that a new trust results.

When trust assets are resettled onto a new trust, the disposition of any property in the tax base must be accounted for. Asset transfer rules will determine the value of depreciable property that is transferred. Any outstanding debts should be novated or otherwise dealt with.

When a trust is terminated or wound up, any remaining property is distributed in accordance with the terms of the deed. The taxation treatment of a distribution on the winding up of a trust is the same as for any distribution made during the life of the trust.

CHAPTER 2

Settlors

¶2-010 Who is a settlor?

When drafting or otherwise reading a trust deed, it is important to consider the role of the settlor and who will be treated as the settlor, whether for trust or for tax purposes.

At the simplest and most obvious level, the settlor is the person named as the settlor in the trust deed. However, due to tax rules and the historic use of nominee settlors, it can be necessary to look beyond the deed. See *Re Hindle* [2012] NZHC 903; (2012) 3 NZTR ¶22-009, where the deed of trust provided that the beneficiaries are the settlor's children and grandchildren. However, the named settlor was in fact the "true" settlor's solicitor, who had drafted the deed, and a number of beneficiaries were defined by reference to the named settlor. The mistake was only identified following the solicitor's death. An order for rectification was required to remedy the error. In the judgment reference was made to "the well-known trap that exists when precedent documents are used of failing to carefully review all the provisions of the document to ensure that those which were appropriate for the original purpose for which the document were used do not require amendment for the current purpose".

Also, as a practical matter, while the trust deed may refer to the original (usually nominal) settlement onto a trust, it is also important to consider subsequent settlements onto a trust by way of gift or sale for less than market value. Outstanding current accounts can also be relevant in this respect. See ¶3-250. Each of these forms of settlement can also have tax implications.

¶2-020 The settlor for tax purposes

New Zealand has a settlor regime for tax purposes. This determines when, how, or the extent to which, a trust comes under the New Zealand tax jurisdiction. The trust rules in the Income Tax Act 2007 interact with the core provisions to tax income derived by the trustees of trusts based on the residence of the settlors, rather than the residence of the trustees. This is a different approach to that adopted in the majority of other jurisdictions which tax trusts by reference to the residence of the trustees. See Chapter 8 – *Migration of Settlors, Trustees and Beneficiaries.*

Accordingly, New Zealand-sourced amounts are taxed in New Zealand regardless of the residence of the settlor. However, foreign-sourced amounts will generally only be taxable in New Zealand where the settlor is resident in New Zealand. For this reason, correctly identifying a settlor (and, by corollary, a settlement) is essential to identify the relevant nexus.

For this reason, the definition of settlor in the Income Tax Act is broad (see s HC 27), and includes a person who transfers value to a trust, provides services for less than market value or provides financial assistance and a beneficiary with a current account of more than $25,000 where interest (if any) is less than the prescribed rate or the market rate. The definition of settlor has relevance for the minor beneficiary rule (see ss HC 35 to HC 37) and also determines who is the settlor of resettlements, who can have residual liability for tax and whether a trust might remain as a complying trust. See s HC 10.

The definition of "settlor" is important in several respects, including:

(a) determining when foreign-sourced amounts derived by non-resident trustees will be assessable income: s HC 25

(b) determining when foreign-sourced amounts derived by resident trustees will be exempt income: s HC 26

(c) determining whether a trust is a foreign trust: s HC 11; also see Chapter 5 – *Taxable Distributions*

(d) determining whether a settlor is liable for the income tax: see ¶2-030

(e) the minor beneficiary rules: see Chapter 10 – *Minor Beneficiary Income*

(f) understanding the associated persons provisions relating to trusts (ss YB 7 to YB 9), and

(g) calculating income for social assistance purposes: s MB 7.

A number of activities that are treated as those of a settlor are set out in s HC 28. For example, a person can be treated as a settlor of a trust if the person:

(a) has a control interest in a company that settles an amount on a trust

(b) is the settlor of a head-trust and a trustee of the head-trust settles an amount on the sub-trust

(c) has control over a trustee or a settlor of the trust.

The following examples from interpretation statement IS 18/01, "Taxation of trusts – income tax" demonstrate when a person has control over a trustee or settlor.

> "Example 8. Control over a trustee
>
> A Hong Kong resident, Jenny, makes an initial settlement of $990,000 on the Dragon Trust, which is a discretionary trust. The trustee of the Dragon Trust, Dragon Co, is a company owned by Jenny. Dragon Co has the power to appoint and remove beneficiaries. Apart from the $990,000 of trust property, Dragon Co does not have any assets. A New Zealand resident, Steve, acquires Dragon Co for $1 million. Steve appoints himself as director of Dragon Co. There is no indication that Jenny settled the trust as a nominee for Steve.
>
> By acquiring Dragon Co and appointing himself as director, Steve has acquired rights or powers over the trustee that enables him to require Dragon Co to treat Steve, or his nominee, as a beneficiary of the Dragon Trust. This is an "effect" of the acquisition of the rights or powers. In addition, the fact that Steve paid $1 million to acquire Dragon

Co, a company that does not have any assets of its own, suggests that the purpose of the acquisition was to enable him to require Dragon Co to appoint Steve, or his nominee, as a beneficiary of the Dragon Trust.

In this example, Steve has not transferred any value to the Dragon Trust and in the absence of s HC 28(6) would not be treated as a settlor. Nevertheless, under s HC 28(6) Steve is treated as a settlor.

Example 9. Acquiring rights under the terms of the trust

The original settlor of the Mete Trust dies and triggers a provision in the trust deed passing on the power to appoint or remove trustees to Grace, the Trust's lawyer. Under the trust deed the power to appoint or remove beneficiaries passes to the trustees. As a result, Grace has acquired rights or powers over the trustees of the Trust. The acquisition of these powers would enable Grace to remove the existing trustees and appoint herself as the sole trustee of the Trust. Grace could then appoint herself, or a nominee, as a beneficiary of the Trust. Grace may have no intention of doing this, but it is an effect of the acquisition that she could require the trustee to treat herself, or a nominee, as a beneficiary.

Therefore, it might appear at first that s HC 28(6) would apply to treat Grace as a settlor of the Trust. However, taking into account the purpose of the provision and the circumstances of Grace's acquisition of the right, it is considered that Parliament would not have intended s HC 28(6) to apply. Grace is in the business of providing trust administration services. The appointment of Grace could have been expected under the terms of the trust as an ordinary incident of the administration of the trust. The circumstances do not suggest that Grace was attempting to avoid settlor status by acquiring rights or powers in relation to an existing trust. Therefore, Grace would not be treated as a settlor in this situation."

Care is required in complex structures to recognise where a person, or multiple persons, will be treated as a settlor. See the following example from IS 18/01:

"2.83 It is possible that more than one person could be treated as a settlor of a trust as a result of a settlement by a controlled company. This is because more than one person may have a control interest of 10% or more in the controlled company.

2.84 In addition, this settlor treatment can apply through multiple layers of controlled companies. A "person" that has a control interest of 10% or more in a controlled company might, itself, be a controlled company. Further, a "control interest" of a person includes direct and indirect control interests as calculated in subpart EX.

Example 6. Settlor—multiple layers of controlled companies Jack has a direct control interest of 15% in Holdings Ltd, which is a controlled company. Holdings Ltd has a direct control interest of 100% in Operations Ltd. Operations Ltd settles an amount on a trust. Jack is treated as a settlor of the trust for two reasons. Firstly, Jack has an indirect control interest in Operations Ltd (via Holdings Ltd) of 15%, which is more than the 10% required to be a settlor under s HC 28(3). Secondly, Jack has a control interest in Holdings Ltd of 10% or more and Holdings Ltd is treated as having settled the trust that was settled by Operations Ltd (because it has a control interest in Operations Ltd of 10% or more). Operations Ltd (who made the actual settlement) and Holdings Ltd (who has a control interest of 10% or more in Operations Ltd) would also be treated as settlors.

2.85 In addition, the controlled company provisions can work in tandem with other parts of the settlor definition. For example, a settlement may be made by a nominee of a company with the result that the company is treated as a settlor. And if a person has a control interest of 10% or more in that company, they may also be treated as a settlor."

¶2-030 Definition of settlor

The features of the definition of settlor are set out in interpretation statement IS 18/01 as follows:

> "2.13 The definition of 'settlor' in s HC 27 has the following features:
>
> (a) the core concept of a person who transfers value to a trust;
>
> (b) a legislative response to the decision in *Re Marshall (Deceased), CIR* v *Public Trustee* [1965] NZLR 851 (CA) (*Re Marshall*) discussed below [2.57] to [2.59];
>
> (c) rules that help in determining whether a transfer or provision has been made; and
>
> (d) exceptions for:
>
> (i) trusts for retirement benefits of employees;
>
> (ii) employee share purchase agreements; and
>
> (iii) contributions to foreign superannuation schemes.
>
> 2.14 A person can also be treated as a settlor under s HC 28. In particular:
>
> (a) a person who has a control interest in a company that settles an amount on a trust is treated as a settlor of the trust;
>
> (b) where a trustee settles an amount on a sub-trust, the settlor of the head trust will also be a settlor of the sub-trust;
>
> (c) a person can be treated as a settlor of a trust, if they have control over a trustee or a settlor of the trust; and
>
> (d) a person can be treated as a settlor, if s HC 28(2), an anti-avoidance provision, applies.
>
> 2.15 Although not part of the definition of 'settlor', a person may be treated as a settlor under s YB 21, if someone else settles a trust as nominee for the person.
>
> 2.16 Finally, as previously noted, the definition of settlor is qualified for the purposes of the minor beneficiary rules and the associated person rules."

Fundamental to the definition of who is a settlor is the concept of transfer of value to a trust, either directly or indirectly. This transfer can be a payment of money, transfer of property, or any other transaction at less than market value. As noted at [2.27] in IS 18/01:

> "... Generally, the market value of something is the price that would be agreed between a willing but not anxious seller and a willing but not anxious buyer. It is important to identify the relevant market for the property or service being provided. Also, in determining the market value, surrounding circumstances that might reasonably be expected to affect the price agreed on must be taken into account. The market value of property or services is determined objectively. The subjective value placed on property or services by the person transferring or receiving the property is not relevant (*Edge* v *CIR* [1958] NZLR 42 (CA); *Hatrick* v *CIR* [1963] NZLR 641 (CA) at 661; *R* v *Islam* [2009] UKHL 30 (HL)). Where the settlement is denominated in foreign currency, the market value will be the value in New Zealand dollars on the date of settlement."

The following examples from IS 18/01 are illustrative:

> "2.28 In the case of a transaction between a person and a trust involving the provision of money's worth in exchange for money, a transfer of value to the trust could arise in two ways:
>
> (a) Firstly, where a person is providing money's worth to a trust, a transfer of value could arise as a result of the trust paying a below market value consideration.
>
> Example 1. Transfer of value – below market consideration
>
> Sara sells her car to a family trust to be used in a business carried on by the trust. The sale price is $6,000, but the market value is $10,000. Sara has transferred value of $4,000 to the trust because she has sold her car to the trust for a discounted price.
>
> (b) Secondly, where a trust is providing money's worth to a person, a transfer of value could arise as a result of the person paying an above market value consideration.
>
> Example 2. Transfer of value – inflated consideration
>
> Erica acquires management services from a trust. She pays $10,000 for the services, but the market value is only $1,000. Erica has transferred value of $9,000 to the trust because she has paid an inflated price to the trust for the management services.
>
> These facts could also raise other issues (involving potential avoidance considerations and the amount of income derived by the trust). However, this example is intended merely to illustrate the operation of the settlor definition."

A transfer of value can also occur where there is a release from an obligation. See IS 18/01 at [2.32] and [2.33].

> "2.32 As well as the general definition above, a 'transfer of value' also specifically includes the release of an obligation to pay money. The release may be by agreement or by operation of law.
>
> Example 3. Settlement made by release of obligation Dory sells her house to a family trust, which was settled by her parents. The purchase price is satisfied by a loan from Dory to the trust. Dory later forgives the loan owed by the trust. By forgiving the loan, Dory has transferred value to the trust equal to the loan balance. Therefore, Dory is a settlor of the trust.
>
> 2.33 There may be situations where the obligation to pay money will have no value (eg, because the trust and trustees are insolvent). Whether this is so will be a question of fact to be determined in each situation. If the obligation to pay money has no value, no settlement will result from the release of the obligation."

Valuation of deferral, or non-exercise, of rights to demand payment is difficult due to the range of potential variables and the inherent difficulty in valuing something that has not happened. This is addressed by the new s HC 31B, which addresses the valuation of financial assistance provided there is:

- an obligation to repay interest or principal on demand, and
- the right to demand repayment is not exercised or is deferred.

New s HC 31B applies when:

- financial assistance is given on an on-demand basis for either principal or interest or both, and
- not demanding the interest or principal gives rise to a transfer of value that comes within the meaning of distribution in s HC 14 or would make a person a settlor of a trust by virtue of s HC 27(2)(b).

The formula provided for in s HC 31B calculates the value of the distribution or the settlement for any period as the amount of interest that would be foregone if the demand had instead been exercised. The value is calculated as the difference between:

- the interest that would be payable on the principal at market rate or the prescribed rate (at the choice of the taxpayer) for that period, and
- the amount of interest accrued for that period on the principal amount owing, including an amount that would have accrued for that period if that amount had been included in a taxable distribution.

The proposed formula is like the calculation of the value of a fringe benefit for on-demand shareholder current accounts and ensures that administration and compliance costs can be minimised when valuing such financial assistance.

The definition of "financial assistance", formerly located in s HC 36(5), is relocated to s YA 1 and applies for the purpose of the trust rules. This amendment clarifies the meaning of financial assistance, consistent with the Commissioner's view, as set out in interpretation statement IS 18/01, "Taxation of trusts – income tax" in *Tax Information Bulletin* ¶307-103 Vol 30, No 7, August 2018.

Application date

New s HC 31B applies to determine the value of financial assistance that would give rise to a distribution or a settlement on a trust on or after 23 March 2020, including financial assistance that exists before 23 March 2020.

¶2-040 Settlor liability for income tax

Nominees are not treated as settlors. Historically it has been common for professional advisers or relatives or other associates or parties to assist in establishing a trust by settling a nominal sum on trust on behalf of another person. Where this is the case, the nominee is not the "true" settlor of the trust but is in effect only an intermediary or functionary. The true settlor is the person on whose behalf the named settlor acted in putting their name to a trust and provided a nominal initial settlement. Section YB 21 treats the person for whom the nominee acted as the settlor rather than the nominee.

> Example 11. Settlement by a person's lawyer—delegated A client of a law firm may ask their lawyer to establish a trust by making a settlement on their behalf. If the lawyer then delegated this request to a colleague, the colleague would be regarded as having settled the trust at the direction or request of the client.

Source: interpretation statement IS 18/01, "Taxation of trusts – income tax" at [2.124].

In light of the new adviser obligations in the Trusts Act 2019, whereby advisers must give advice to the initial settlor of a trust with respect to any modification or exclusion of default duties (see s 39 of the Trusts Act) and must give advice to the settlor regarding the meaning and effect of any liability exclusion or indemnity clause; it is apprehended that nominee settlors will be far less commonly used moving forward.

¶2-050 Settlor liability for income tax

Section HC 29 specifies circumstances where a settlor may be liable for income tax. The section apples to a person who makes a settlement onto or for the benefit of a trust after 17 December 1987 (the date when New Zealand's settlor-based trust regime came into effect). Under s HC 29(2), if a trustee derives income in an income year, the settlor is liable as agent of the trustee for income tax payable by the trustee.

If a trust has more than one settlor, the trustees are jointly and severally liable. (Agency liability does not apply in all circumstances, for example, where the trustees are trustees of a community trust – see s HC 32.) The agency rule applies if the trust has a resident trustee for the full income year or where the first settlement is made during an income tax year or in other specified circumstances (s HC 29(3)–(5)).

However, s HC 29 does not apply where a settlor can establish, through full disclosure to the Commissioner that another person had settled property on the trust and should be liable with respect to those settlements (s HC 29(6)).

¶2-060 Beneficiary current accounts can make beneficiaries settlors for tax purposes

A beneficiary who has a current account will be a settlor of a trust for tax purposes if the amount of the beneficiary's current account is more than $25,000 and the trustee is not paying interest on the amount at a rate equal to the prescribed rate of interest (the FBT rate) or the market rate.

What this means is that beneficiaries could become liable for income tax in the limited circumstances that apply under s HC 29 if there is no resident trustee. While these circumstances will not commonly arise, more relevant for many beneficiaries will be that their status as settlor will need to be taken into consideration when calculating family scheme income for working for families tax credits and student loan repayments as trust income will be taken into consideration for these purposes where a beneficiary is a settlor of a trust for income tax purposes. Also see ¶3-250.

¶2-070 Reporting obligations regarding settlors and settlements

New reporting obligations introduced by the Taxation (Income Tax Rate and Other Amendments) Act 2020 will require reporting with respect to settlements that identify the settlor with information to be provided, such as name, IRD number and date of birth, as well as the amount and nature of each settlement. Further, from the 2021–22 return year, trustees will need to provide names and details of settlors from previous years. See ¶20-020.

By way of background, Inland Revenue has not previously collected information on subsequent settlements on a trust. This has been identified as an information gap, which means that Inland Revenue is not capturing information on the true settlor. It is considered that this is a key piece of information, as New Zealand has a settlor-based trust taxation regime.

¶2-080 Legislation

Income Tax Act 2007

[...]

HC 11 FOREIGN TRUSTS

A trust is a **foreign trust** at a moment in time if no settlor is resident in New Zealand at any time in the period that–

(a) starts on the later of 17 December 1987 and the date on which a settlement was first made on the trust; and

(b) ends with the moment in time.

[...]

HC 27 WHO IS A SETTLOR?

HC 27(1) WHEN THIS SECTION APPLIES

(repealed)

HC 27(2) MEANING OF SETTLOR

A **settlor** of a trust is a person who, at any time,–

(a) transfers value–

  (i) to the trust; or

  (ii) for the benefit of the trust; or

  (iii) on terms of the trust:

(ab) provides, for less than market value, services to the trust or for the benefit of the trust that are more than incidental to the operation of the trust:

(b) provides financial assistance to the trust or for the benefit of the trust with an obligation to pay on demand, and the right to demand is not exercised or is deferred:

(bb) is a beneficiary of the trust who is owed money by the trustee and does not meet the requirements of subsection (6):

(c) is treated as a settlor under section HC 28.

HC 27(3) TRUSTS FOR RETIREMENT BENEFITS FOR EMPLOYEES

Despite subsection (2), a person resident in New Zealand who makes a settlement on a trust as an employer for the benefit of 1 or more employees is not a settlor of the trust if the following circumstances apply:

(a) the trust is established or created mainly to provide retirement benefits to natural persons; and

(b) the trust is neither a foreign superannuation scheme nor a superannuation fund.

HC 27(3B) EMPLOYEE SHARE PURCHASE AGREEMENTS

(repealed)

HC 27(3C) CONTRIBUTIONS TO FOREIGN SUPERANNUATION SCHEME

Despite subsection (2), a person who makes a contribution to a trust that is a foreign superannuation scheme is not a settlor of the trust.

HC 27(3D) RESETTLEMENTS

Despite subsection (2), a trustee of a trust (the **head-trust**) who is resident in New Zealand and settles an amount on a second trust (the **sub-trust**), or makes a distribution to, or on terms of, the sub-trust, is not a settlor of the sub-trust if, when the settlement or distribution is made on or to the sub-trust,–

(a) a settlor of the head-trust exists and each settlor of the head-trust is a non-resident; or

(b) no settlor of the head-trust exists and the last surviving settlor of the head-trust was a non-resident when that settlor ceased to exist.

HC 27(4) INDIRECT SETTLEMENT

A person may make a transfer of value, or provision of financial assistance, referred to in subsection (2) directly or indirectly and by 1 transaction or a number of connected transactions.

HC 27(5) NIL VALUE OF BENEFICIARY RELATIONSHIP

The fact that a person is, or will become, a beneficiary of a trust does not constitute the giving or receiving of value.

HC 27(6) BENEFICIARIES OWED MONEY BY TRUSTEE

When a trustee of a trust owes an amount to a beneficiary of the trust, the beneficiary does not become a settlor of the trust under subsection (2) solely as a result of being owed the amount if–

(a) the amount owing at the end of the income year is not more than $25,000:

(b) the amount owing at the end of the income year is more than $25,000 and the trustee pays to the beneficiary, for each income year in which the amount is owing and by the date given for the income year by section HC 6(1B), interest on the amount at a rate equal to the prescribed rate of interest or the market rate.

HC 27(7) DETERMINING AMOUNT OWED TO BENEFICIARY

For the purposes of subsection (6), the amount of money owing to a beneficiary at the end of an income year is the amount of the debt at that time, adjusted to include the effect of transactions that are–

(a) made after the end of the income year and by the date given for the income year by section HC 6(1B); and

(b) included in the financial statements of the trust for the income year.

HC 28 ACTIVITIES TREATED AS THOSE OF SETTLOR

HC 28(1) WHEN THIS SECTION APPLIES

This section applies for the purposes of the trust rules to describe certain activities of a person that result in the person being treated as a settlor.

HC 28(2) AVOIDANCE

A person is treated as a settlor if, in relation to a trust,–

(a) they act, refrain from acting, or enter into a transaction or a series of transactions; and

(b) what is done or not done has the effect of defeating the intent and application of the trust rules.

HC 28(3) SHAREHOLDERS IN CONTROLLED FOREIGN COMPANIES

A person is treated as a settlor of a trust if a controlled foreign company settles an amount on a trust and the person has a control interest of 10% or more in the CFC–

(a) at the time of the settlement:

(b) for the accounting period of the CFC in which the settlement occurs.

HC 28(4) SHAREHOLDERS IN COMPANIES

A person is treated as a settlor of a trust if–

(a) a company settles an amount on the trust; and

(b) the company would have been a CFC at the date of settlement if it had been a foreign company at the time; and

(c) the person would be treated as having a control interest of 10% or more in the company, if the company were a foreign company,–

  (i) at the time of the settlement:

  (ii) under section EX 1(3), for the accounting period of the company in which the settlement occurs.

HC 28(5) SECOND TRUSTS

A person is treated as a settlor of a trust (the **sub-trust**) if–

(a) they are a settlor of a trust (the **head-trust**); and

(b) a trustee of the head-trust settles an amount on the subtrust, or makes a distribution to, or on terms of the subtrust.

HC 28(6) CONTROL OVER TRUSTEE OR SETTLOR

A person is treated as a settlor of a trust if–

(a) they acquire, directly or indirectly, rights or powers in relation to a trustee or a settlor of the trust; and

(b) the acquisition has the purpose or effect of enabling them to require the trustee to treat them, or a nominee, as a beneficiary of the trust.

HC 29 SETTLORS' LIABILITY TO INCOME TAX

HC 29(1) WHEN THIS SECTION APPLIES

This section applies to a person who makes a settlement to or for the benefit of a trust after 17 December 1987, and the settlor is resident in New Zealand in an income year. It applies whether or not they settled property on the trust on or before that date. Subsections (3) and (4) override this subsection.

HC 29(2) LIABLE AS AGENT

If a trustee of the trust derives trustee income in the income year, the settlor is liable as agent of the trustee for income tax payable by the trustee. For a trust with more than 1 settlor, the liability is joint and several. However, this subsection does not apply to income tax that the trustee is liable for as agent under section HC 32.

HC 29(3) EXCLUSION: RESIDENT TRUSTEE

This section does not apply if the trust has a resident trustee for the full income year or, if the first settlement on the terms of the trust is made during the income year, from the day on which the settlement is made to the end of the income year.

HC 29(4) EXCLUSION: TRUST TYPES

This section does not apply to the settlor of–

(a) a charitable trust; or

(b) a superannuation fund; or

(c) a trust to the extent to which trustee income is derived from the settlor's remitting an amount under a financial arrangement to which section EW 31 or EZ 38 (which relate to base price adjustments) applies.

HC 29(5) EXCLUSION: SETTLOR NOT RESIDENT AT TIME OF SETTLEMENT

This section does not apply if the settlor is a natural person who, unless they make an election under section HC 33,–

(a) is not resident in New Zealand at the time of any settlement on the trust; and

(b) had not after 17 December 1987 previously been resident in New Zealand.

HC 29(6) EXCLUSION: OTHER SETTLOR MORE APPROPRIATELY LIABLE

This section does not apply to the extent to which the settlor establishes, through full disclosure to the Commissioner of the settlements made, that another person who has settled property on the trust should be liable, having regard to the respective settlements made.

HC 29(7) LIMITED EFFECT OF DISCLOSURE

Subsection (6) does not apply to determine whether the tax obligations in relation to the trustee's income tax liability are met for the purposes of section HC 10(1)(a) and (ab) and meeting the requirements for a complying trust.

[...]

HC 31B VALUE TRANSFER BY DEFERRAL, OR NON-EXERCISE, OF RIGHT TO DEMAND PAYMENT

HC 31B(1) WHEN THIS SECTION APPLIES

This section applies when a person (the **creditor**) provides financial assistance to or for the benefit of another person (the **debtor**) with an obligation (the **debtor obligation**) that the debtor could meet, if performance of the obligation were demanded immediately after the time of the provision, by paying an amount (the **debt amount**) and–

(a) the debtor does not pay to the creditor, for a period for which the debtor has the debtor obligation, interest on the debt amount at a rate equal to the prescribed rate of interest or the market rate; and

(b) the debtor obligation is not forgiven; and

(c) the right of the creditor to demand payment of the debt amount under the debtor obligation is not exercised or is deferred; and

(d) the non-exercise, or the deferral, results in a transfer of value by the creditor; and

(e) the transfer of value meets the requirements of–

   (i) section HC 14 for the transfer of value to be a distribution made by a trustee:

   (ii) section HC 27(2)(b) for the creditor to be a settlor of a trust.

HC 31B(2) WHEN THIS SECTION DOES NOT APPLY

This section does not apply to a situation in the application of section HC 27(6) to the situation.

HC 31B(3) VALUATION

The value transferred by the creditor during a period for which the debtor obligation exists is the amount calculated for the debt amount, treated as a loan, using the formula–

benchmark interest - interest paid.

HC 31B(4) DEFINITION OF ITEMS IN FORMULA

In the formula,–

(a) **benchmark interest** is the amount of interest that would have accrued on the debt amount that is unpaid during the period if the interest had been calculated on the daily balance of the loan at a rate that is equal to whichever the debtor chooses of the prescribed rate of interest and the market rate:

(b) **interest paid** is the total of–

(i) the amount of interest that accrues on the debt amount during the period:

(ii) the amount that would have accrued as interest on the debt amount during the period if the amount had not been included in a taxable distribution to the debtor:

(iii) for a period that includes the date on which the Taxation (KiwiSaver, Student Loans, and Remedial Matters) Act 2020 receives the Royal assent (the **transition date**), the amount that is benchmark interest for the part of the period that precedes the transition date.

Part II

INCOME AND DISTRIBUTIONS, BUSINESS

CHAPTER 3

Beneficiary Income

¶3-010 Operating principle

A trust is not a legal person for tax purposes. Trust income is accounted for by the trustee who derives the income or by a beneficiary who receives a distribution of income.

The income earned by a trustee that is distributed to a beneficiary, rather than retained and capitalised, retains its character as income: *Baker* v *Archer-Shee* [1927] AC 844 (HL) and *Syme* v *C of T* [1914] AC 1013 (PC).

¶3-020 Trust income is trustee income or beneficiary income

Income earned by the trustee of a trust is either trustee income or beneficiary income. Income distributed to a beneficiary is, with few exceptions, taxed to the beneficiary at the beneficiary's marginal rate.

The dichotomy between trustee income and beneficiary income is simple in principle. However, in practice, differentiating between trustee and beneficiary income can be less straightforward.

This chapter considers the definition of beneficiary income highlighting areas of practice that are not directly addressed by the definition.

¶3-030 Beneficiary income vests in or is paid to a beneficiary

Beneficiary income is income derived by a trustee in an income year to the extent to which the income:

- vests absolutely in interest in a beneficiary of the trust in the income year, or
- is paid to a beneficiary of the trust in the income year, or by the later of:
  - □ a date within 6 months of the end of the income year, or
  - □ the earlier of:
    - — the date on which the trustee files the tax return, or
    - — the date by which the trustee must file a tax return under s 37 of the Tax Administration Act 1994: s HC 6(1), (1B).

Beneficiary income includes any resident withholding tax (RWT) substitution payment made to a beneficiary under s RE 2(7) if it meets the requirements of s HC 6(1) or is paid on a date referred to in s HC 6(1B): s HC 6(1C).

Excluded from the definition of beneficiary income is income derived by a trustee:

- of a superannuation fund
- to which s CC 3(2) (financial arrangements) applies
- any amount by which a beneficiary RWT tax credit is reduced under s LB 3(6), or any beneficiary tax credit is allocated under s LB 3(5), or
- as a result of s EW 50 (debt forgiveness): s HC 6(2).

Beneficiary income vested in or paid to a person is that person's income: ss CV 13(a), HC 17.

Before the 2009–10 income year, beneficiary income had to be paid within 6 months of the end of the income year. However, the definition of beneficiary income was amended by the Taxation (Consequential Rate Alignment and Remedial Matters) Act 2009 (s 43) to address perceived problems where tax agents were effectively required to prioritise the preparation of trust accounts and tax returns over other accounts and returns so as to meet the 6-month deadline. See *Tax Information Bulletin* ¶221-108 Vol 22, No 1, February 2010 at 25.

However, as it is common for deeds of trust that were drafted before this to include a clause that provides that any income not allocated or paid within 6 months will be capitalised, care is required to ensure that the terms of the deed of trust provide that income is available to be paid or applied outside the 6-month period and, if not, that the terms of the trust are varied to allow this (assuming a suitable power of variation).

When income is paid to a beneficiary outside the 6-month period where a deed contains provision for income to be capitalised if not allocated or paid within 6 months, the income will still meet the definition of beneficiary income for tax purposes. However, for trust purposes, the distribution will represent a distribution of capital. If this occurs, the trustees should maintain separate accounts for tax and trust purposes. Further, in the event the beneficiary is not a beneficiary as to capital, the trustees will have to address whether the payment has been made in breach of trust.

¶3-040 A trustee must account for income that is derived for tax purposes

As a general principle, income is derived when it is received. However, an amount can be deemed to be income that is derived for tax purposes. For example, an amount is deemed to have been derived even though it has not been actually paid to or received by the person or has yet to become due or receivable if the amount has been dealt with in the person's interest or on the person's behalf, such as by crediting it to an account, reinvesting, accumulating, capitalising or carrying it to any reserve, sinking or insurance fund: s BD 3(4). Where the application of rules of derivation only relate to timing of income, no special issues arise for trustees.

¶3-050 Deemed income can vest in a beneficiary in some circumstances

Deemed income is income that may not result in actual cash flow to the trust in a particular income year, or sometimes at all. The incidence of deemed income can cause mismatches between the tax law and trust law treatments. Examples of deemed income include attributed controlled foreign company (CFC) income, foreign investment fund (FIF) income, and look-through company (LTC) income based on an owner's effective look-through interest.

The practical difficulty for trustees where the income is not actually received in any conventional sense is to determine firstly whether there is any compliance with the definition of beneficiary income and secondly how to meet the trust's tax obligations and ensure compliance with the terms of the deed of trust.

Guidance on how to address the distribution of deemed income is provided by interpretation statement IS 12/02, "Income Tax – Whether Income Deemed to arise under tax law, but not trust law, can give rise to beneficiary income" (*Tax Information Bulletin* ¶247-104 Vol 24, No 7, August 2012), which provides that:

- The Income Tax Act does not prevent deemed income giving rise to beneficiary income. However, income must vest absolutely in interest in, or be paid to, a beneficiary before it can be beneficiary income for income tax purposes. For trust purposes, the terms of the trust deed, and general trust law, determine how a trustee may deal with the trust fund.
- For an amount to vest absolutely in interest in, or be paid to, a beneficiary, the trust deed must provide for such vesting or payment, either by express provision in the trust deed or through appropriate powers of the trustee.
- The Commissioner considers that an amount of deemed income cannot automatically vest in, or be paid to, a beneficiary. This is because there is no actual income and the income does not exist for trust purposes. This means that trust must have an actual (non-deemed) amount in the trust fund available to be distributed that can be vested absolutely in interest in, or paid to, a beneficiary.
- It is not problematic of itself if trust law income is the same as, or exceeds, tax law income, provided that an equivalent amount of trust law income is actually vested absolutely in interest in, or paid to, a beneficiary.
- Deemed income will be beneficiary income only to the extent to which is it reflected by an actual amount vested absolutely in interest in, or paid to, a beneficiary by the trustee or under the terms of the trust deed. Whether this is possible will depend on the terms of the relevant trust deed. Accordingly, it will be necessary for a trustee to resolve that the actual amount from the trust fund is being treated as the vesting or payment of deemed income for tax purposes. If an actual amount from the trust fund is used to vest or pay the deemed income for tax purposes, the amount of deemed income will meet the definition of "beneficiary income", and will be taxed at the beneficiary's marginal tax rate.

IS 12/02 also contains examples of 3 types of trust deeds in a situation in which the tax law income of a trust exceeds its trust law income in a particular income year:

- The trust deed does not define income. The tax law income and trust law income of a trust are different. Under the trust deed, the trustee can only vest absolutely in interest or pay income of the trust according to trust law concepts of capital and income. Therefore, trustees will not be able to vest absolutely in interest or pay an amount that equates to deemed income. The deemed income will be treated and taxed as trustee income. This would be the case in any income year.
- The trust deed defines trust law income as income calculated for income tax purposes. The tax law income and trust law income of a trust are the same. Under the trust deed, the trustees can vest absolutely in interest or pay income of the trust to beneficiaries according to tax law. To the extent that there are sufficient amounts available in the trust fund, trustees may vest or pay amounts that equate to deemed income. The deemed income will then give rise to beneficiary income.
- The trust deed defines income using trust law concepts of capital and income, but the trustees have the power to distribute trust capital to income beneficiaries. The tax law income and trust law income of a trust are different, but the trustees have the power to vest or pay amounts that are more than trust law income to income beneficiaries. To the extent the trustees actually vest absolutely in interest or pay amounts equating to deemed income, the deemed income will give rise to beneficiary income.

Now see s 60 of the Trusts Act 2019, which provides that "[f]or the purposes of distribution, and of preparing and completing a financial statement for a trust, a trustee may determine whether a return on an investment is to be treated as income or capital".

Where deemed income can be paid as beneficiary income for tax purposes, the income will be taxed at the beneficiary's marginal tax rate, rather than as trustee income, regardless of the fact that there is no actual cash flow.

¶3-060 Income is trustee income to the extent to which it is not beneficiary income

Income that does not vest in or is not paid to a beneficiary is trustee income. The expression "to the extent to which" income is vested in or paid to a beneficiary is expressed in terms reflective of the classic language of apportionment: *Ronpibon Tin NL* v *FC of T*; *Tongkah Compound NL* v *FC of T* (1949) 8 ATD 431 at 437; 78 CLR 47 at 60. The import of this language reflects the fact that it is possible for only a portion of the trust's income to be distributed and taxed as beneficiary income. Therefore, if only a portion of income is paid to a beneficiary, it is permissible, for taxation purposes, for the balance to be retained and taxed as trustee income.

¶3-070 Income vests absolutely in interest if there is an immediate right of present or future possession

The phrase "vests absolutely in interest in a beneficiary" is not defined in the Income Tax Act.

For the purposes of the definition of "beneficiary income", income "vests absolutely in interest" in a beneficiary where the beneficiary obtains an immediate fixed right of present or future possession of the income. For example, income derived by a trustee will ordinarily immediately vest absolutely in interest in a beneficiary with a life interest in the income of the trust. Income will also vest in a beneficiary through an appropriate resolution, following which the income is the beneficiary's income. See ss CV 13(a), HC 6 and HC 17. A trustee cannot cancel a resolution without committing fraud against the beneficiary (*Re Baron Vesty's Settlement*; *Lloyds Bank Ltd* v *O' Meara* [1951] Ch 209 and *C of IR* v *Ward* 69 ATC 6050).

Income will be "paid" to a beneficiary if the income is transferred to the beneficiary in money or money's worth. It is not necessary that the income be transferred directly to the beneficiary; it is sufficient that the income is placed unreservedly at the disposal of the beneficiary. See *Tax Information Bulletin* ¶15-114 Vol 1, No 5, November 1989, Appendix. (The definition of "pay" in s YA 1 includes "to distribute", "to credit", or "to deal with the amount in their interest or on their behalf".)

Income will be paid to, or will vest in, a beneficiary, if, among other things, the trustees pass a resolution that results in the income becoming the absolute property of the beneficiary.

From a trust law perspective, the payment or application must constitute a valid exercise of a power available to the trustees under the trust instrument.

¶3-080 Income must be paid within 6 months after the end of the income year unless a trustee has a tax agent

Income derived by the trustees of a trust during an income year will be beneficiary income if it is paid by the trustees to or for the benefit of a beneficiary during, or (unless an extension applies: see ¶3-030) within, 6 months after the end of that income year.

Actions that indicate that income has been "paid" to a beneficiary include transferring the income in question to the beneficiary in money or money's worth. It is not necessary that the income be transferred directly to the beneficiary; it is sufficient that the income is placed unreservedly at the disposal of the beneficiary: *Tax Information Bulletin* ¶15-114 Vol 1, No 5, November 1989, Appendix.

Trustees can achieve this by passing a resolution that a defined amount of income is the absolute property of the beneficiary. It is not necessary for actual payments to be made to or on behalf of the beneficiary. Nor is it necessary for the amounts paid to be physically severed from the trust fund or separately invested on behalf of the beneficiary. However, the trustee must not be able to call back, vary or alter the amount allocated to the beneficiary. See *Davidson and Duke* v *C of IR* (1976) 2 NZTC 61,121.

Whether any particular act constitutes payment of income will depend on the facts.

It is also important that the trustees have made a distribution of income to a beneficiary that has commercial and economic reality. Book entries alone may be insufficient to establish this. See ¶22-080.

¶3-090 Beneficiary income can be paid for tax purposes when the amount is not known

Funds can be paid, even if the amount payable is not determined, if there is a formula that provides how funds are to be allocated on application to the beneficiaries.

In *Davidson and Duke* v *C of IR* (supra), the trustees resolved that, unless otherwise determined, the income of the trust should first be applied in payment of certain expenses, with the balance allocated between the beneficiaries in shares of one-third and two-thirds. Whether a later determination could alter the payments made in the meantime was not considered further. Somers J held that this amounted to an application of trust income. He was of the view that to say that the resolution had effect unless otherwise determined meant only that the resolution had effect until a new or other determination was made.

If the trustees resolve to distribute the income of the trust to more than one beneficiary, the resolution must irrevocably provide for a fixed amount or share of that income to be distributed to each of those beneficiaries. Although the entitlement of each beneficiary must be certain, the resolution need not define a specific sum: *Davidson and Duke* v *C of IR* (supra).

Care must be taken when making such a resolution to ensure that the trustee does not inadvertently bind the trustee for the future, trustees generally having no power to fetter future discretion: see *Snell's Principles of Equity*, 26th ed 149, citing *Re Vestey's Settlement*; *Lloyds Bank Ltd* v *O'Meara* [1950] 2 All ER 891, 895. Accordingly, unless authorised by the trust instrument, a trustee resolution allocating all or a share of the income of the trust to beneficiaries, expressed to continue until the trustees resolve otherwise, may not constitute a valid and effective application of income in respect of income derived by the trust in future years.

¶3-100 Income can be distributed before accounts being finalised

It can be necessary to distribute income in accordance with a formula if a trust's accounts have not been prepared within 6 months of the end of the income year or if an extension applies but the deed of trust requires that income is paid within 6 months of the end of the income year.

Where this is the case, it is not uncommon for trustee resolutions to be prepared later than 6 months after the end of the income year, following preparation of trust accounts. Trustees who sign such resolutions risk a subsequent audit finding that beneficiary income was in fact trustee income as the resolution recording the decision to distribute beneficiary income was made more than 6 months after the end of the income year.

However, it is not necessary for the trustees to resolve to distribute an amount calculated by reference to the income as determined in the trust's accounts. It should be sufficient for the trustees to resolve to distribute an amount of income calculated with reference to the taxable income or accounting surplus of the trust. This is different from resolving to apply income if or when the accountant advises.

¶3-110 Beneficiary income can be paid to the beneficiary's parents

Income paid to an infant (minor) beneficiary can be paid to that child's parent or guardian.

In *C of IR* v *Simpson* (1989) 11 NZTC 6,140 (CA), the trustees resolved to appropriate (appropriation is the application of a payment for the purpose of paying a debt: Hinde and Hinde, New Zealand Law Dictionary 3rd ed) the whole of the trust income to 2 infant children. The trust deed provided a good and valid discharge to the trustees if payment was made to their parents and guardians. The income was paid to the parents' joint account. The Court held that the good and valid discharge to the trustees meant that the infants had taken an indefeasibly vested interest in the trust income, which was thus income of the infant beneficiaries.

Also see the Trusts Act, s 62.

¶3-120 A book entry may not be sufficient to effect payment

A book entry, with no supporting trustee resolutions, noting that trust income has been applied to beneficiary expense will not generally be sufficient to provide that income has been paid to a beneficiary: see *Case* S43 (1995) 17 NZTC 7,293.

¶3-130 Distributions to a non-beneficiary cannot be accounted for as beneficiary income

It is perhaps trite to note that beneficiary income that is vested in or paid must be vested in or paid to a beneficiary of the trust that derived the income. However, care must be taken to ensure that the person in whom income is vested or to whom income is paid is in fact a beneficiary of the relevant trust. Where this is not the case, the "distribution" will be of different character and will require to be accounted for accordingly.

¶3-140 It is not clear whether a beneficiary receives beneficiary income derived before the beneficiary's appointment

It is important in the context of allocating beneficiary income to consider at what point a beneficiary must have either come into existence, or have been appointed, before that beneficiary being able to have income paid or otherwise appropriated to it. Consider, for example, the situation in which a beneficiary is appointed after the end of an income year, but before the end of the 6-month period following that income year or, if an extension applies, by the time by which the trustee's return is filed or is required to be filed. Can that beneficiary receive beneficiary income that relates to the previous income year?

There are practitioners whose view is that it is acceptable to distribute income to beneficiaries that were not appointed or not even in existence during the income year in which the income was derived so long as the beneficiary is appointed within the time frame for payment of income that meets the definition of beneficiary income in s HC 6: see ¶3-030.

The definition of beneficiary income provides that income that vests in a beneficiary must do so in the income year. Therefore, it seems quite clear that income cannot vest in a beneficiary who does not exist during the income year.

The position is less clear regarding the payment of income. While it could be argued that the reference to "a beneficiary of the trust in the income year" provides a temporal reference to the beneficiary, it is equally possible to relate the reference to "income year" to one of the applicable payment periods.

In the absence of authority on this point, a cautious approach would recommend that trustees avoid paying income to beneficiaries appointed after the end of the income year in which the income was derived. Limited support for the proposition that the beneficiary must be in existence is also provided by "question we've been asked" QB 15/11, "Income Tax – Scenarios on tax avoidance – 2015", which provides at [71] that "[a]ll beneficiaries of the trust are existing beneficiaries of the trust ...". Where a beneficiary was not in existence at the time the income was earned, questions may also arise as to whether the subsequent appointment of a beneficiary to receive that income could amount to tax avoidance. See QB 15/11 at [93]–[94] where the Commissioner expresses that view that:

> "[93] ... On some facts, it will be arguable that no distribution of income to a beneficiary of the trust was made from a commercial or economic perspective. That is, where it is arguable that, in commercial and economic reality, either:
>
> - the beneficiary was not a beneficiary of the trust, or
> - no distribution of income was made to the beneficiary.

[94] Consideration would need to be given to various facts, including (but not limited to):

- the timing and pattern of the addition or removal of beneficiaries;
- how and when the income was distributed (eg, whether authorised distributions are paid in cash or credited to beneficiaries' current accounts)

  [...]".

Also see ¶22-080.

¶3-150 The standard balance date for a trust is 31 March

Beneficiary income for an income year is determined by reference to "income derived in an income year by a trustee": s HC 6(1). For a beneficiary with a 31 March balance date, "income year" means a year beginning 1 April and ending 31 March.

If a trust has a non-standard balance date, that is, a balance date other than 31 March, any income derived by a beneficiary is treated as being derived in the same tax year that corresponds to the trust's income year: s HC 6(3).

Also see *Tax Information Bulletin* ¶15-117 Vol 1, No 5, November 1989, Appendix, at [8.21], which discusses when income distributed to a beneficiary of a trust should be returned. Note that this view should now be read subject to the amended definition of beneficiary income.

Example

The trustees of a discretionary trust with a 31 May balance date pay the income derived during the year ended 31 May to a beneficiary with a 31 March balance date on 30 November. The trust does not have a tax agent. Will the income constitute trustee or beneficiary income and in which income year should it be returned?

Applying a strict interpretation of the legislation, it would appear the income should be returned as trustee income because it has not been paid to or applied for the benefit of the beneficiary within 6 months of 31 March, that is, by 30 September. If the trust is a complying trust, the distribution to the beneficiary would be received by the beneficiary tax-free.

However, adopting the Commissioner's approach, the income has been paid to the beneficiary within 6 months of 31 May, and it should be returned by the beneficiary as beneficiary income.

¶3-160 Superannuation fund income is excluded from the definition of beneficiary income

Superannuation schemes constituted as trusts settled in New Zealand are generally treated as complying trusts. All of the scheme's investment income is taxed as trustee income and all benefits paid, whether as a pension or in the form of a lump sum payment are received tax-free by the beneficiary members.

¶3-170 Debt forgiveness income is excluded from the definition of beneficiary income

Trustee income may be derived where a debt owed by the trustee has been forgiven and a distribution is made to a beneficiary who is neither a natural person for whom the creditor has natural love and affection nor a registered charity. This is where the creditor is a natural person and the trust was established mainly to benefit natural persons for whom the creditor has natural love and affection, or a charity. The trustee income is derived in the income year in which the distribution is made. See s EW 50 and ¶4-110.

Income that arises from debt forgiveness cannot be vested in or paid to a beneficiary as beneficiary income.

¶3-180 Beneficiary income is taxable regardless of source

A New Zealand resident beneficiary is liable to taxation on beneficiary income that does not have a New Zealand source or any other connection with New Zealand.

This is the case even if the income in question is a foreign-sourced amount derived by a trustee that is not taxable to the trustee in New Zealand: s HC 26.

¶3-190 Distributions from accumulated trustee income and capital gains are not beneficiary income

Distributions made out of accumulated trustee income and tax-free capital gains from complying trusts do not constitute beneficiary income. However, such distributions may constitute "taxable distributions" when made by trustees of foreign and non-complying trusts. See Chapter 5 – *Taxable Distributions.*

¶3-200 Planning opportunities exist where distributions of beneficiary income exceed the accounting surplus

As the definition of beneficiary income is expressed in terms of income, it is possible that amounts distributed as beneficiary income could exceed the accounting surplus and/or taxable income of the trust. This situation could arise if the trust incurs non-deductible expenditure or distributions made by the trustees simply exceed the accounting surplus or taxable income of the trust. There is no tax requirement for the trustees to apply the income of the trust to meet its expenses before making distributions. Unless the deed of trust provides that expenses must be met out of income, the trustees could choose to meet these expenses out of trust capital or corpus.

This gives rise to certain planning opportunities. For example, if the trustees made distributions to charities during the income year, or within a period following the end of the income year that would still meet the definition of beneficiary income, which in total were equal to or in excess of the trust's income, it might be advantageous to treat all of that income as beneficiary income. In this situation, any deductible expenditure incurred by the trustees could be carried forward as a tax loss to the following year.

Similar opportunities could arise in relation to distributions made to non-residents and beneficiaries on lower marginal tax rates. However, see ¶3-140 and ¶22-080.

However, any trustee considering adopting the above approach will need to carefully consider the trustee's obligations at trust law and in accordance with the terms of the trust instrument. In this regard we note that it is a common feature for a trust deed to require that the trustees meet the expenses of the trust before applying income to beneficiaries.

In the absence of a provision in the trust instrument permitting expenses to be met from capital or corpus, amounts distributed as beneficiary income may represent a distribution of capital for trust law purposes if they exceed the accounting surplus of the trust. In practice, this issue is unlikely to cause a problem where the trustees have an absolute discretion to distribute both income and capital to all beneficiaries. However, it could be a problem where there are different income and capital beneficiaries. The trustees will also need to ensure the trust remains solvent following the distribution.

¶3-210 Beneficiaries are not entitled to offset expenses or deductions

A beneficiary who receives a distribution of beneficiary income cannot claim a deduction for any expenditure or loss that a trustee has incurred in deriving that income: s DV 9; nor can a beneficiary claim a deduction against the beneficiary's income when the beneficiary has advanced funds to the trust to meet expenses. See *Brown* v *C of IR* [2014] NZHC 1599; (2014) 26 NZTC ¶21-089. See ¶24-070.

Deeming provisions do permit a trustee to treat beneficiary income as trustee income for the purposes of determining the trustee's deductions for a tax year so that the deductions that arose in earning the beneficiary income are available to the trustee.

Beneficiary income is determined before tax losses carried forward by a trustee are offset against the trustees' current year income. This is because beneficiary income is defined by reference to income derived by a trustee and it is only after calculating the trustees' net income, that is, assessable income less allowable deductions, that tax losses can be offset. However, trustees can pay money to a beneficiary in substitution for RWT credits paid in respect of beneficiary income: ss LB 3(3), RE 2(6).

Before making a distribution of beneficiary income that might otherwise be available to recoup previous year losses, a trustee must carefully consider the trustee's obligations under trust law and in accordance with the terms of the trust instrument.

For example, as a matter of trust law, if there is no contrary provision in the trust instrument, where a business carried on by a trust incurs losses, the losses must be recouped out of profits of subsequent years: *In re Nairn (dec'd)*; *Logan* v *Nairn* [1935] NZLR s134, *Rutherford* v *C of IR* (1964) 14 ATD 32; [1965] NZLR 444 (CA).

¶3-220 Beneficiary income retains same character as when derived by the trustee

Income derived by a trustee retains its character whether the income is taxed as trustee income or beneficiary income: *Baker* v *Archer-Shee* (supra) and *Syme* v *C of T* (supra). This means then that foreign-sourced income derived by trustees retains its character as foreign-sourced income when distributed as beneficiary income; and dividends derived by trustees retain their character as dividends when distributed as beneficiary income.

It is important to keep track of the character of income so that the beneficiary receives the benefit of, for example, foreign tax credits or imputation credits.

Although in certain circumstances the credit may be limited to a certain kind of foreign tax, a beneficiary is allowed a foreign tax credit for foreign tax paid on beneficiary income derived from an overseas jurisdiction: Subpart LJ.

Non-resident withholding tax must be deducted from non-resident passive income that is beneficiary income derived by non-resident beneficiaries.

In certain circumstances, statutory provisions ensure that beneficiary income retains the character it had when the income was derived by the trustees. For example, s HA 16 ensures that an exempt dividend derived by a trustee-shareholder of a qualifying company remains exempt when distributed to a beneficiary as beneficiary income.

In determining whether interest or dividends are resident passive income from which resident withholding tax (RWT) must be deducted, interest or dividends that are beneficiary income are deemed not to be derived by the trustee: s RE 2(6).

¶3-230 Minor beneficiary income is taxed as trustee income

With limited exceptions, income paid to minor beneficiaries is taxed as trustee income, not beneficiary income. See further at Chapter 10 – *Minor Beneficiary Income*.

¶3-240 Foreign-sourced income distributed to a non-resident beneficiary is not accounted for as trustee or beneficiary income for tax purposes

Foreign-sourced amounts derived by trustees of foreign trusts and non-complying trusts can be exempt income, if no settlor of the trust is resident in New Zealand at any time during the relevant income year: s HC 26. Foreign-sourced income that is exempt income can be distributed to a non-resident beneficiary, even if the trustee is New Zealand resident, but such income will be neither trustee nor beneficiary income for New Zealand tax purposes. See also ¶4-040.

¶3-250 Beneficiary current accounts can make beneficiaries settlors for tax purposes

Trustees of many trusts maintain current accounts for beneficiaries and these can have consequences as to whether a person is a settlor for tax purposes. See ¶5-050.

The most common application to beneficiaries can occur where a distribution is made to a beneficiary, but the value is not transferred to the beneficiary and no interest is paid on the outstanding amount.

A recent amendment to s HC 27(6) provides that a beneficiary who has a current account will be a settlor of a trust for tax purposes if the amount of the beneficiary's current account is more than $25,000 and the trustee is not paying interest on the amount at a rate equal to the prescribed rate of interest (the FBT rate) or the market rate, which presently will likely be the less than the prescribed rate.

What this means is that beneficiaries could become liable for income tax in the limited circumstances that apply under s HC 29 if there is no resident trustee. While these circumstances will not commonly arise, more relevant for many beneficiaries will be that their status as settlor will need to be taken into consideration when calculating family scheme income for working for families tax credits and student loan repayments as trust income will be taken into consideration for these purposes where a beneficiary is a settlor of a trust for income tax purposes.

A further amendment to s HC 27(6) was introduced by the Taxation (Annual Rates for 2020–21, Feasibility Expenditure, and Remedial Matters) Act 2021, which introduced a new section (s HC 27(2)(bb)) to clarify that a beneficiary who is owed money by a trust will always become a settlor if the beneficiary does not meet the requirements of subs (6). As such, a beneficiary that is owed more than $25,000 on which interest has not been paid at the prescribed rate or market rate. By way of background to this as set out in the Commentary on the Bill at 92:

> "It was always intended that beneficiaries owed more than $25,000 on which interest has not been paid would become settlors of the trust. However, a beneficiary owed more than $25,000 on which interest has not been paid may not become a settlor if they do not have sufficient knowledge of the amount they are owed or how it is being used by the trustee. While the Commissioner of Inland Revenue can determine the amount owed to a beneficiary and whether interest is being paid, it can be difficult for the Commissioner to ascertain the beneficiary's level of knowledge. Therefore, the Bill proposes to amend the definition of a settlor so that a beneficiary owed more than $25,000 by the trustee on which adequate interest has not been paid, is deemed to be a settlor of a trust, regardless of their level of knowledge".

See s HC 27 and see Chapter 2 – *Settlors* at ¶2-060.

¶3-260 Legislation

Income Tax Act 2007

[...]

CC 3(2) INCOME: TRUSTEE

Income derived by a trustee in the circumstances described in section EW 50 (Income when debt forgiven to trustee) is income of the trustee.

[...]

EW 50 INCOME WHEN DEBT FORGIVEN TO TRUSTEE

EW 50(1) WHEN THIS SECTION APPLIES

This section applies when–

(a) a trust is a debtor; and

(b) the trust was established mainly to benefit 1 or both of the following:

  (i) a natural person for whom the creditor has natural love and affection; or

  (ii) an organisation or a trust whose income is exempt under section CW 41 (Charities: non-business income) or CW 42 (Charities: business income); and

(c) the creditor is a natural person; and

(d) the creditor forgives the debtor's debt; and

(e) a trustee of the trust makes a distribution, including a distribution of beneficiary income, to a beneficiary; and

(f) the beneficiary is–

  (i) not a natural person for whom the creditor has natural love and affection; and

  (ii) not an organisation or a trust whose income is exempt under section CW 41 or CW 42; and

(g) the distribution is made on or after 20 May 1999.

EW 50(2) EXCLUSION

This section does not apply when–

(a) a trust (**trust** A) is a debtor; and

(b) trust A was established mainly to benefit 1 or both of the following:

  (i) a natural person for whom the creditor has natural love and affection; or

  (ii) an organisation or a trust whose income is exempt under section CW 41 or CW 42; and

(c) the creditor is a natural person; and

(d) the creditor forgives the debtor's debt; and

(e) a trustee of the trust makes a distribution to another trust (**trust B**); and

(f) at the time the distribution is made, trust B is also established mainly to benefit 1 or both of the following:

(i) a natural person for whom the creditor has natural love and affection; or

(ii) an organisation or a trust whose income is exempt under section CW 41 or CW 42.

EW 50(3) TWO POINTS ABOUT SUBSECTIONS (1) AND (2)

For the purposes of subsections (1) and (2),–

(a) the debtor's debt includes an amount accrued and unpaid at the time of the forgiveness; and

(b) the means by which the debt is forgiven, whether in a will or otherwise, is immaterial.

EW 50(4) DISTRIBUTION IS INCOME OF TRUSTEE

The distribution is income of the trustee, under section CC 3(2) (Financial arrangements), to the extent to which it is less than or equal to the total amount of the debts of the trust forgiven to it by the creditor.

EW 50(5) DISTRIBUTION SUBTRACTED FROM TOTAL AMOUNT FORGIVEN

The distribution is subtracted from the total amount of the debts of the trust forgiven to it by the creditor as the total amount stands at the time of the distribution.

EW 50(6) TIMING

The income is derived by the trustee in the income year in which the distribution is made.

EW 50(7) APPLICATION OF TAX ADMINISTRATION ACT 1994

Section 22B of the Tax Administration Act 1994 applies to a trustee to whom this section applies.

[...]

HC 6 BENEFICIARY INCOME

HC 6(1) MEANING

An amount of income derived in an income year by a trustee of a trust is **beneficiary income** to the extent to which–

(a) it vests absolutely in interest in a beneficiary of the trust in the income year; or

(b) it is paid to a beneficiary of the trust in the income year or by the date after the end of the income year referred to in subsection (1B).

HC 6(1B) DATE BY WHICH INCOME MUST BE ALLOCATED

The date referred to in subsection (1)(b) is the later of the following:

(a) a date that falls within 6 months of the end of the income year; or

(b) the earlier of–

 (i) the date on which the trustee files the return of income for the income year; or

 (ii) the date by which the trustee must file a return for the income year under section 37 of the Tax Administration Act 1994.

HC 6(1C) [RWT SUBSTITUTION PAYMENTS]

Beneficiary income includes an RWT substitution payment made to a beneficiary under section RE 2(7) (Resident passive income) to the extent to which the payment meets the requirements of subsection (1) or is paid on a date referred to in subsection (1B).

HC 6(2) EXCLUSIONS

Beneficiary income does not include–

(a) an amount of income derived by a trustee of a trust in an income year in which the trust is a superannuation fund; or

(ab) an amount of income derived by a trustee of a trust in an income year in which the trust is an approved unit trust referred to in clause 2 of the Income Tax Act (Exempt Unit Trusts) Order 1990; or

(b) an amount of income derived by a trustee that is income to which sections CC 3(2) (Financial arrangements) and EW 50 (Income when debt forgiven to trustee) apply; or

(c) an amount by which a tax credit of a beneficiary for resident withholding tax is reduced under section LB 3(6) (Tax credits for resident withholding tax); or

(d) an amount of a tax credit of a beneficiary allocated under section LB 3(5).

HC 6(3) DERIVING BENEFICIARY INCOME IN SAME YEAR

When an amount derived by a trustee in an income year is also beneficiary income, the beneficiary is treated as having derived the income in the same tax year as that corresponding to the trustee's income year.

HC 6(4) DERIVING BENEFICIARY INCOME IN SAME YEAR AS TRUSTEE

(repealed)

CHAPTER 4

Trustee Income

¶4-010 Operating principle

Income derived by a trustee that is not beneficiary income is trustee income.

However, in addition to income as defined by reference to ordinary concepts, certain gifts and settlements onto a trust must also be accounted for as trustee income.

Trustee income is taxed at the trustee rate of 33% regardless of whether the trustee is a natural person or a company.

¶4-020 Trustee income includes certain amounts that would not otherwise be accounted for as income for trust purposes

The general rules that apply to determine whether a receipt is income apply to a trustee in the same way as they do to any other taxpayer.

However, receipts that would otherwise be accounted for by the trustee as capital or gifts can also be income to a trustee.

The definition of trustee income for taxation purposes is defined to include:

- income derived by a trustee to the extent that it is not beneficiary income: s HC 7(1)
- minors' beneficiary income: s HC 7(2)
- the market value of a property settlement (less any amounts treated as beneficiary income or distributions during the period): s HC 7(3):
  - by a trustee of another trust to the extent to which if the property were distributed to the beneficiary of the other trust, and that beneficiary was resident in New Zealand, the distribution would be beneficiary income or a taxable distribution to that beneficiary: s HC 4(3)
  - for which the settlor is allowed a deduction: s HC 4(4)

    - that, but for the settlement onto trust, would be:
        - income to the settlor: s HC 4(5)(a)
        - income to the settlor if the settlor was resident in New Zealand at the time of the settlement: s HC 4(5)(c)
- income derived by the trustee of a testamentary trust, whether the income is sourced in New Zealand, that would have been the deceased person's income, had that person not died: ss CV 12, HC 8
- subject to certain exceptions, income derived by a non-resident trustee if at any time during an income year: s HC 25:
    - a settlor of the trust is a New Zealand resident (who is not a transitional resident)
    - the trustee is a superannuation fund, or
    - a trustee is resident in New Zealand and a settlor died resident in New Zealand.
- income that arises when a debt is forgiven to a trustee: s CC 3(2).

In addition to ensuring compliance with the Income Tax Act, a trustee must also act in accordance with the terms of the deed of trust. In the absence of perfect symmetry between the 2, situations can arise in which the correct outcome is unclear due to the deed of trust providing how a particular receipt is to be treated, which treatment may not accord with the taxing legislation.

¶4-030 The principles that apply to differentiate between capital and income apply equally to trustees as to any other taxpayers

The general principle is that income is something that comes in. In the words of Lord Macnaghten in *Tennant* v *Smith (Surveyor of Taxes)* [1892] AC 150 (HL) at 164 "[income tax] is a tax on what comes in – on actual receipts".

This principle is developed further by s BD 3(4), which provides that an amount is deemed to have been derived even though it has not been actually paid to or received by the person or has yet to become due or receivable. The rule applies where the amount has been dealt with in the person's interest or on his or her behalf, such as by crediting it to an account, reinvesting, accumulating, capitalising or carrying it to any reserve, sinking or insurance fund.

However, some amounts, for example, FIF income, can also be income for tax purposes even if neither is received nor dealt with on the taxpayer's account.

These rules apply to a trustee in the same way as to any other taxpayer, regardless of the difficulties this can cause a trustee. See ¶4-060.

¶4-040 With some exceptions, regardless of the trustee's residence, foreign-sourced trustee income is not taxable in New Zealand if there is no New Zealand resident settlor

Foreign-sourced amounts derived by a New Zealand resident trustee in any income year are exempt income under s CW 54 if no settlor of the trust is a New Zealand resident who is not a transitional resident at any time during the year and the trust is not:

- a superannuation fund, or
- a testamentary trust or a trust established during the settlor's lifetime where any settlor of the trust died resident in New Zealand: s HC 26(1).

Example

A non-resident individual establishes a trust with a New Zealand resident trustee. The trustee will only be taxed on income derived from New Zealand and not on foreign-sourced amounts. This is provided that no other settlor of the trust is a New Zealand resident who is not a transitional resident at any time during an income year in which the trustees derive foreign-sourced amounts.

However, if the disclosure rules for a foreign trust are breached, the exemption from New Zealand tax on foreign-sourced amounts will not apply: s HC 26.

¶4-050 Income can be apportioned between trustee and beneficiary income

Income that does not vest in or is not paid to a beneficiary is trustee income: see ¶3-060.

¶4-060 Trust law does not mirror tax law

Sometimes it is difficult for a trustee to reconcile tax and trust law obligations. This is less likely to be an issue when all the beneficiaries are beneficiaries as to capital and income. However, when this is not the case, for example, where there is an income beneficiary and a capital beneficiary, it is necessary to correctly determine trustee and beneficiary income, both for tax purposes and so that the trustee ensures compliance with the terms of the deed of trust and tax law obligations.

The trustee's starting point in resolving such a matter is to refer to the deed of trust. For example, it is common for more modern deeds of trust to reserve a discretion to the trustee to determine whether any sum is income or capital; alternatively, the deed of trust may otherwise provide how any income or capital is to be distributed. See ¶3-050, which discusses the circumstances where deemed income can vest in a beneficiary by reference to the terms of the deed of trust.

Where the deed is of no assistance, the trustee can seek directions from the High Court: Trusts Act 2019, s 133.

¶4-070 Trustee income includes income from financial arrangements

Income from financial arrangements is trustee income and is taxable over the life of the arrangement: Subpart EW.

Exclusions from the financial arrangements rules that allow persons with small interests in financial arrangements to calculate financial arrangements income on a cash basis also apply, with some exclusions, to trustees: s EW 58.

Where a trustee of a bare trust is a party to a financial arrangement, the beneficiary of the trust is treated as the party to the arrangement to the extent of the beneficiary's share in the beneficial interest of the arrangement. In other words, the beneficiary is treated as deriving income or incurring expenditure in proportion to their share in the beneficial interest.

¶4-080 Trustee income includes minor beneficiary income

Minor beneficiaries are beneficiaries that are under 16 years of age on a trust's balance date.

Unless an exemption applies, minor beneficiary income is treated as trustee income for the purposes of determining the tax rate, regardless of the minor's applicable marginal rate.

The trustee is also responsible for paying the tax and providing the income tax return in respect of minor beneficiary income. See Chapter 10 – *Minor Beneficiary Income*.

¶4-090 Certain settlements onto trust are deemed trustee income

An anti-avoidance provision provides that settlements onto a trust that have the effect of avoiding a tax impost are deemed to be trustee income (except to the extent that they are treated as beneficiary income or distributions): s HC 7(3).

Property settled onto a trustee from the trustee of another trust is deemed to be trustee income in the hands of the recipient trustee to the extent that the property would represent beneficiary income or a taxable distribution if distributed to a New Zealand resident beneficiary: s HC 4(3).

Property settled onto a trustee for which the settlor is allowed a deduction is deemed to be trustee income. It is important in this regard for a trustee to be aware of the comprehensive nature of the definition of settlor and settlements for the purposes of the Income Tax Act. See ¶5-050.

Property settled onto a trustee that would, but for the settlement, have constituted settlor income, whether the settlor is resident in New Zealand, is deemed to be trustee income: s HC 4(5)(a), (c).

Property settlements that are deemed to be trustee income are derived by the trustee in the income year corresponding to the settlement, less amounts deemed to be beneficiary income or distributions during that year (s HC 7(3)) and are excluded from the definition of corpus: s HC 4(2).

¶4-100 The trustee of a deceased estate may be a cash basis person if the deceased was a cash basis person

The trustee for a deceased estate will be a cash basis person for financial arrangements in the estate in the income year in which the death occurred and in each of the 4 succeeding income years if the deceased was a cash basis person at the time of his or her death and the estate otherwise meets the cash basis person requirements: s EW 60(1), (2). If the trustee of an estate ceases to be a cash basis person at any time during the 5-year period, the trustee cannot be a cash basis person in any subsequent year: s EW 60(3).

Property disposed of by the trustee of a deceased estate must be valued at cost rather than disposed of at market value: s FC 8.

¶4-110 Debt forgiveness can comprise trustee income

A debt that is forgiven under a gifting program is excluded from the definition of a financial arrangement to the extent that s EW 50 applies.

The exclusion applies if:

- a debt owed by trustees of a trust is forgiven by a natural person, and
- the beneficiaries of the trust include a tax charity and/or persons for whom the lender has natural love and affection.

However, if a distribution is made to a person other than a tax charity or a person for whom the settlor has natural love and affection, income will be derived by the trustees to the extent of the debt forgiven.

Example

The trustees of a trust have had debts totalling $540,000 forgiven by the settlors. The trustees decide several years later to make a distribution of $100,000 to a charity that the settlors have recorded as being of special interest to them in their memorandum of wishes. The charity is not a tax charity that is registered with Charities Services.

The trustees must account for the lesser of the amount of debts forgiven or the amount distributed to the unregistered charity as income.

In this case, the trustees must account for income of $100,000.

However, if using the same example as above, the debts forgiven totalled only $54,000 and the same distribution was made, the amount of income to account for would be limited to the amount of debt forgiven of $54,000.

See further at Chapter 14 – *Forgiveness of Debt.*

¶4-120 The Commissioner can determine trustee income if the trustee does not maintain sufficient records

Trustees are required to maintain records that are sufficient to allow the trustee's income to be calculated.

If a trustee cannot obtain sufficient information to calculate the amount of income derived by a trustee in an income year (s 93B(1)(c)), the Commissioner of Inland Revenue has the discretion to determine the amount of trustee income derived: Tax Administration Act, s 93B(2).

The Commissioner of Inland Revenue will also determine the amount of trustee income derived by a trustee in an income year if:

- the existence of a trust has not been disclosed in accordance with s 59 of the Tax Administration Act: s 93B(1)(a), or
- information is not disclosed in accordance with s 17 of the Tax Administration Act: s 93B(1)(b).

Note that the Taxation (Business Tax, Exchange of Information, and Remedial Matters) Act 2017 amended the Tax Administration Act and introduced new registration requirements for foreign trusts, providing that unregistered foreign trusts are taxable in New Zealand on their worldwide income. See ¶20-070.

¶4-130 A capital gain can be re-characterised if a relevant association exists

Amounts received on the sale of an asset that would otherwise be capital gain, can be income to the trustee due to certain associations. See Chapter 18 – *Associated Persons.*

¶4-140 Time when income is derived depends on the nature of the income

The rules that determine when income is derived apply, with some exceptions, to a trustee in the same way as they do to any other taxpayer.

¶4-145 Treatment of debt from insolvent deceased beneficiary

Care is required to manage trusts to avoid beneficiary current accounts or beneficiary loans that cannot be repaid. While natural person creditors can forgive debts owing by trustees, there is no corollary position for trustees.

That is, trustees cannot "forgive" debts owing by a beneficiary. If trustees do, the trustees will incur "debt remission income" under the base price adjustment required by s EW 31 of the Income Tax Act 2007. That forgiveness does not fall within the narrow exception for debts forgiven in return for "natural love and affection" contained within s EW 44 of the Income Tax Act 2007. Accordingly, if trustees forgive debts or if debts become uncollectible, either is caught: see public ruling BR Pub 99/7, "Debt forgiveness in consideration of natural love and affection" in *Tax Information Bulletin* ¶119-133 Vol 11, No 9, October 1999 at 34.

¶4-150 Dividends are generally derived when paid or credited to the trustee

Dividends, including any imputation credits or foreign dividend payment (FDP) credits, derived by a trustee, which are not distributed to a beneficiary, are trustee income. Any imputation credits or FDP credits can be offset against the trustee's current year tax liability.

Dividends will generally be treated as derived when they are paid to or credited to or for the benefit of the trustee-shareholder.

Where a trust owns shares in a closely-held company and it is intended that a dividend be credited to the trust during an income year, the required director's resolution and solvency certificate should be signed and the dividend should be credited to the trustee-shareholder's current account before the end of that year.

It is not sufficient for the required documentation and journal entries to be completed after the end of the year when the company's financial statements and tax returns are prepared, as is often the case. In the latter situation, the dividend would not be derived until the following income year.

¶4-160 Interest income must be returned on an accruals basis unless the trustee is a cash basis person

Interest income derived by a trustee must be returned on an accruals basis unless the trustee is a cash basis person. See ¶4-070, ¶4-100.

This is the case irrespective of whether that income is trustee income or beneficiary income.

¶4-170 Income that cannot be vested in or paid to a beneficiary can be taxable to the trustee

Regardless of whether income derived by a trustee can be vested in or paid to a beneficiary, it can be trustee income that is taxable to the trustee.

¶4-180 Revenue account property gains are trustee income

Any increase in value of property held on revenue account will be income to a trustee in the same way as to any other taxpayer.

However, care must be taken where a trustee makes an in specie distribution of such property, that is, the property is distributed to a beneficiary of the trust, rather than, for instance, the proceeds of the sale of the same, so as to ensure that the trustee can meet the resultant tax liability absent the receipt of any income being derived from the distribution.

¶4-190 Attributed income is not trustee income

Trustee income excludes income that is attributed to a beneficiary of the trust in accordance with the attribution rules contained in ss GB 27–GB 29.

The attribution rules that apply to trusts prevent a person from diverting income from personal services through a trust so that the income can be distributed to beneficiaries on lower marginal tax rates. The policy intention is to ensure that these taxpayers cannot avoid the highest personal tax rate.

When the attribution rules apply, the amount of income that is derived by the associated entity of a taxpayer who provides personal services is attributed to that taxpayer, after the deduction of allowable expenditure. The amount attributed is deductible to the associated entity in the income year in which the amount is attributed.

These attribution rules apply purely for the purposes of income tax. Transactions between the trustee and any third parties remain unaffected in any legal or commercial contexts. See also Chapter 23 – *Attribution*.

¶4-200 Asset transfers and sales can result in income to the trustee

Income can arise following an asset transfer or sale if there is depreciation recovery: ss EE 44–EE 52. This can be the case regardless of whether consideration has been received, for example, following certain distributions to beneficiaries or resettlements onto trustees of other trusts.

The specific exceptions that apply in respect of certain distributions, transmission and resettlements are discussed in detail at Chapter 26 – *Deceased Estates* and Chapter 33 – *Resettlement*.

¶4-210 Losses are taken into account in determining trustee income

With the exception of beneficiaries of non-complying trusts, who can offset any loss available for carry forward as a deduction from a taxable distribution (s HC 22), trust losses cannot be distributed to beneficiaries, regardless of whether a beneficiary receives income that the losses relate to: s DV 9.

Any losses incurred by the trustee are taken into account when determining trustee income: Subpart IA.

However, the application of those losses may be directed by the terms of the deed of trust. This is because at trust law, but subject to any contrary provision in the deed of trust, where a business carried on by a trust incurs losses, the losses must be recouped out of profits of subsequent years: *In re Nairn (dec'd)*; *Logan* v *Nairn* [1935] NZLR s134, *Rutherford* v *C of IR* (1964) 14 ATD 32 (CA).

Where there is no such prohibition in the deed, the trustees may wish to distribute all of a current year's income as beneficiary income and carry the loss forward.

Whether this is permissible is not entirely clear.

The Commissioner's position is that losses must be utilised by offsetting against current year income: *Tax Information Bulletin* ¶15-117 Vol 1, No 5, November 1989, Appendix, at [8.41]. Only income remaining after the deduction of losses carried forward can be dealt with by the trustee as trustee or beneficiary income.

However, some practitioners are of the view that, for tax purposes, a distribution of the total income can be made to beneficiaries, while the loss is retained to carry forward and offset against future profits of the trust. The basis for this argument is that as beneficiary income is defined in gross income terms, amounts distributed as beneficiary income can exceed the accounting surplus and/or taxable income of the trust. This situation could arise, for example, if the distributions made by the trustees exceeded the accounting surplus or taxable income of the trust. This being the case, there does not appear to be any legislative requirement that the trustees first apply the gross income of the trust in meeting its expenses. In the appropriate circumstances, the trustees could choose to meet these expenses out of trust capital or corpus instead.

Any trustee adopting the later approach should carefully consider the terms of the deed of trust and wisdom of adopting an approach that although technically possible is not in accord with the Commissioner's views.

¶4-220 A trustee is personally liable for income tax

Trustees are personally liable for the income tax on trustee income sourced in New Zealand: s HC 24(1). Trustee income will have a New Zealand source if the income was derived in New Zealand or if a settlor of the trust was resident in New Zealand and not a transitional resident at any time during the income year. This is the case whether any trustee is resident in New Zealand.

A trustee will be liable for the income tax on trustee income that is sourced offshore only if there is a New Zealand resident settlor who is not a transitional resident at any time during the income year.

Trustees are also liable for the tax on any beneficiary income in the trustee's capacity as the beneficiary's agent: s HC 32. The liability as a beneficiary's agent includes the liability to account for income that is beneficiary income that cannot comprise trustee income. An example of such income is foreign-sourced income from a trust that has no New Zealand resident settlor.

The trustee's liability to tax does not derive from the trustee's residence except when a New Zealand resident settlor dies, in which case the trustee will be liable for tax if resident in New Zealand any time during that income year: s HC 25.

For tax purposes, trustees are treated, when they are more than one, as a notional single person. However, multiple trustees are jointly and severally liable to satisfy that notional single trustee's obligations: s HC 2.

A trustee's liability for tax arises regardless of whether the trust is complying, non-complying or foreign. See Chapter 21 – *Trustee's Liability for Tax.*

Trustees may also be liable for taxes incurred in any jurisdiction outside of New Zealand.

¶4-230 Trustee rate is 33%

Trustee income is taxed at a flat rate of 33% (sch 1 pt A cl 3), regardless of the beneficiaries' tax rates. This is the case whether the trust is complying, non-complying or foreign. However, the trustees of charitable trusts only account for income that is not exempt income: s HC 13.

Where a trustee is a company, whether that trustee is the sole trustee, the applicable tax rate is the trustee rate, not the company rate.

Example

The trustees of the Nest Family Trust are Mr and Mrs Nest and the Nest Trustee Company.

The tax rate applicable to any trustee income is the trustee rate of 33%. This would be the case even if the Nest Trustee Company was the sole trustee.

However, where a corporate trustee receives a fee for its trustee services, or any other income, the tax rate that applies to that income is the company tax rate.

¶4-240 A trustee is not entitled to tax credits

A trustee is not entitled to any tax credits. However, tax credits can be converted to a tax loss and carried forward: s LE 2.

¶4-245 Trustee income can be counted as family scheme income

Trustee income that is not distributed as beneficiary income is included in family scheme income for the purposes of calculating working for families (WFF) tax credits. See s MB 7. Unless an exemption applies (see s MB 7(3)), s MB 7 provides that trustee income and income from trust owned companies is attributed equally to a trust's settlor(s) (other than where a person is a settlor by virtue of providing professional services for less than market value in the administration of the trust or the maintenance of the trust property). This attribution is only for the purposes of calculating entitlement to family tax credits and the treatment of trustee income for tax purposes does not change where s MB 7 applies.

A person's family scheme income has been calculated using the following formula:

(trustee income + companies income) ÷ settlor number

where:

- **trustee income** is the net income of the trustee for the income year, reduced to not less than zero by trustee income vested or paid by the trustee as beneficiary income for the year
- **companies income** is the greater of zero, and the total amounts calculated under the formula below for each company in which the trustee and associated persons of the trustee hold voting interests of 50% or more on the last day of the income year, and
- **settlor number** is the number of settlors of the trust who are alive at any time in the income year and to whom s MB 7 applies.

For the item "companies income", an amount to be totalled is calculated for each relevant company using the following formula:

trustee's interest × (income − dividends)

where:

- **trustee's interest** is the percentage voting interests for the relevant company held by the trustee on the last day of the company's income year
- **income** is the net income of the relevant company for that income year, and
- **dividends** is the total dividends paid by the relevant company for that income year.

Example

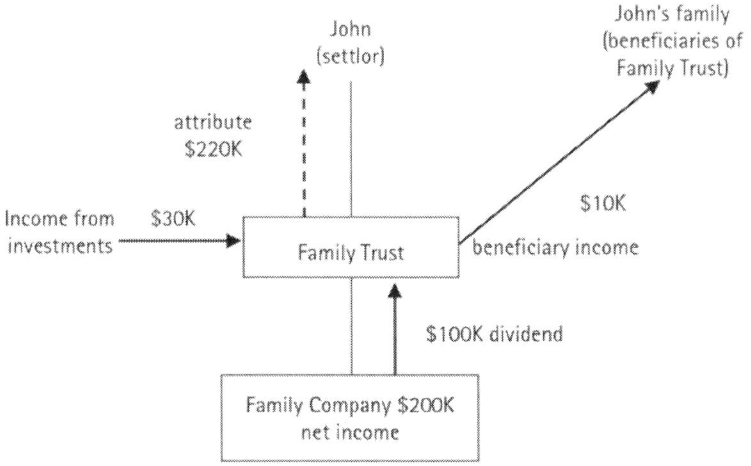

In this example, John is the sole settlor of Family Trust. Family Company is wholly owned by Family Trust. Family Company's net income is $200,000 and it pays an imputed dividend of $100,000 to Family Trust. Family Trust also earns income of $30,000 from investments. Family Trust distributes $10,000 as beneficiary income to John's family.

John's family scheme income for the income year is calculated as follows:

Trustee income	$100,000 dividend + $30,000 debt investment income less $10,000 beneficiary income
	= $120,000
Companies income	100% trustee's interest × ($200,000 net income – $100,000 dividend)
	= $100,000
	(trustee income + companies income) ÷ settlor number
	= ($120,000 + $100,000) ÷ 1
Total	= $220,000

Therefore, $220,000 is included in John's family scheme income for the income year

Previously, the definition of settlors for the purposes of s MB 7 could include people who had gifted property to the trust and since died. The formula was amended by the Taxation (Annual Rates, Foreign Superannuation, and Remedial Matters) Act 2014 so that the attribution of income takes into account only settlors who are alive during the income year. This includes people who were alive for only part of the income year, including the person for whom family scheme income is being calculated.

See *Tax Information Bulletin* ¶264-106 Vol 26, No 4, May 2014.

¶4-250 Legislation

Income Tax Act 2007

HC 4 CORPUS OF TRUST

[...]

HC 4(3) SETTLEMENTS ON OTHER TRUSTS

A property settlement by a trustee of another trust is excluded from corpus to the extent to which, if the property were distributed to a beneficiary of the other trust, and the beneficiary was resident in New Zealand, the distribution would be beneficiary income or a taxable distribution to that beneficiary.

HC 4(4) DEDUCTIONS

A property settlement for which the settlor is allowed a deduction is excluded from corpus.

HC 4(5) INCOME OR DIVIDEND

A property settlement is excluded from corpus if, but for the fact of the settlement,–

(a) it would be income of the settlor; or

(b) *(repealed)*

(c) it would fall under paragraph (a) if the settlor were resident in New Zealand at the time of the settlement.

[...]

HC 7 TRUSTEE INCOME

HC 7(1) MEANING

To the extent to which it is not beneficiary income, an amount of income derived by a trustee of a trust is **trustee income**.

HC 7(2) MINORS' BENEFICIARY INCOME

An amount of beneficiary income to which section HC 35 applies that is derived in an income year by a person who is a minor is treated as if it were trustee income for the purposes of–

(a) determining the tax rate that applies; and

(b) paying the tax; and

(c) providing returns of income.

HC 7(3) EXCLUSIONS FROM CORPUS

The trustee of a trust has, from a property settlement that is referred to in section HC 4(3) to (5) and made in an income year, an amount of trustee income for the income year equal to the market value of the property settlement reduced by the amount of the market value that the trustee treats as beneficiary income, or as a taxable distribution made by the trustee, in the income year.

[...]

MB 7 FAMILY SCHEME INCOME OF SETTLOR OF TRUST

MB 7(1) WHEN THIS SECTION APPLIES

This section applies for the purpose of determining the amount that represents the family scheme income of a person for an income year when the person is the settlor of a trust (the **person's trust**) at a time in the income year, other than solely as a result of providing personal services for less than market value in the administration of the trust or the maintenance of trust property.

MB 7(2) EXCEPTION FOR SOME TRUSTS

This section does not apply if–

(a) the trustee of the person's trust is registered as a charitable entity under the Charities Act 2005:

(b) the person's trust is solely for the benefit of a local authority:

(c) interest and dividends derived by the trustee of the person's trust would be exempt income of the trustee under section CW 45 (Funeral trusts):

(d) the person's trust is a superannuation fund:

(e) the person and the members of the person's family are not permitted to benefit from the person's trust except under an order of a court.

MB 7(2B) INCOME AMOUNT

The amount included in the person's family scheme income is the amount calculated using the formulas in subsections (3) and (5), adjusted, if applicable, by subsections (7) and (8) for main income equalisation account amounts.

MB 7(3) FIRST FORMULA: FAMILY SCHEME INCOME

For the purposes of subsection (2B), the relevant amount is calculated using the formula–

(trustee income + companies income) ÷ settlor number.

MB 7(4) DEFINITION OF ITEMS IN FORMULA IN SUBSECTION (3)

In the formula in subsection (3),–

(a) **trustee income** is the net income of the trustee of the person's trust for the income year reduced, to not less than zero, by the amount of the trustee's income that vests or is paid by the trustee as beneficiary income for the income year:

(b) **companies income** is the greater of zero and the amount given by totalling the amounts calculated by applying the formula in subsection (5) to each company in which the trustee of the person's trust and associated persons hold, on the last day of the income year, voting interests of 50% or more:

(c) **settlor number** is the number of settlors of the person's trust who are alive at any time in the income year, including the person, for which this section applies.

MB 7(5) SECOND FORMULA: COMPANIES INCOME

For the purposes of the item **companies income** in subsection (4)(b), an amount to be totalled is, for each relevant company, calculated using the formula–

trustee's interest × (income − dividends).

MB 7(6) DEFINITION OF ITEMS IN FORMULA IN SUBSECTION (5)

In the formula in subsection (5),–

(a) **trustee's interest** is the percentage voting interests for the relevant company held, on the last day of the company's income year, by the trustee:

(b) **income** is the net income of the relevant company for the company's income year:

(c) **dividends** is the total dividends paid by the relevant company for the company's income year.

[...].

CHAPTER 5

Taxable Distributions

¶5-010 Operating principle

At the time of every distribution, a trust is classified as complying, foreign or non-complying. This classification determines whether the distribution is taxable, and if taxable, what tax rate applies: see Appendix at ¶5-190. See interpretation statement IS 18/01, "Taxation of trusts – income tax" in *Tax Information Bulletin* ¶307-103 Vol 30, No 7, August 2018 for the background to the taxation of trusts regime in New Zealand.

¶5-020 Categories of trust for the purposes of the trust rules

The identification of trusts as complying, non-complying (previously qualifying and non-qualifying) or foreign occurs for tax and reporting purposes only and has no effect for trust law purposes.

¶5-030 Most family trusts settled in New Zealand are complying trusts

Most trusts settled by a New Zealand resident settlor fall within the definition of complying trust in s HC 10, which provides that:

(1) A trust is a **complying trust** in relation to a distribution if–

(a) the following requirements are met for the life of the trust up to the time of distribution:

(i) no trustee income derived includes an amount of non-resident passive income, or non-residents' foreign-sourced income, or exempt income under section CW 54 (Foreign-sourced amounts derived by trustees); and

(ii) the tax obligations relating to the trustee's income tax liability have been satisfied for every tax year; or

(ab) the requirements of paragraph (a) are not met and–

(i) a person makes an election meeting the requirements of section HC 30(2) and the requirements of subsection (2) are met; or

(ii) a person makes an election meeting the requirements of section HC 33(1) and for all income years beginning on or after the date on which the election applies to the trust and before the time of distribution, the trustee's tax obligations relating to the trustee's income tax liability for the trustee income, determined consistently with section HC 33(1C), are satisfied; or

(ac) the requirements of paragraph (a) are not met and the distribution meets the requirements of section HC 30(4)(ab); or

(b) it is a superannuation fund.

[...]

That is, a complying trust is a trust for which the trustees:

- are liable for tax at the trustee rate on all their worldwide trustee income, and
- all income tax obligations have been met.

The life of the trust referred to in s HC 10(1)(a) includes every income year from the start of the income year in which a settlement was first made on the trust up to the time of a distribution.

For the purposes of subsection (1)(a) and (ab) of s HC 10, s HC 29(6) does not apply in determining whether the requirements are met. See s HC 10(4).

Section HC 29, which provides for a settlor to be liable as agent for the income tax liability of a trustee in certain circumstances, was amended as a consequence of the change in s HC 10 to clarify that when a trust becomes a complying trust under s HC 10(1)(ab), a settlor of a trust cannot avoid liability as agent on the grounds that another settlor is more appropriately liable. For all of the trust's income to be taxable in full, the trustee's income cannot include any income that is non-resident passive income, non-residents' foreign-sourced income, or foreign-sourced amounts.

Complying trust income is taxed as:

- trustee income, or
- beneficiary income at the beneficiary's marginal rate.

Distributions of accumulated income, capital gains and corpus from a complying trust are exempt income to the recipient beneficiary and are tax-free: s HC 20.

Section HC 10 was amended by the Taxation (Annual Rates for 2015–16, Research and Development, and Remedial Matters) Act 2016, which clarified that a foreign trust can be treated as a complying trust to the extent allowed by s HC 30 if an election is made and certain tax obligations are satisfied for the life of the trust. The amendment was effective from 1 April 2008. See further at ¶5-060.

¶5-040 Foreign trusts have no connection with New Zealand

A foreign trust is a trust that has not had a New Zealand resident settlor at any time since 17 December 1987, the date on which the current trust regime was introduced. Trustees cannot elect for a trust to be a foreign trust.

A non-resident can settle a trust that has non-resident beneficiaries but has a New Zealand resident trustee. Such trusts can be tax-effective in certain offshore jurisdictions. However, such trusts are not treated as New Zealand trusts because New Zealand taxes trusts based on the residence of the settlor, not the trustee. See Chapter 8 – *Migration of Settlors, Trustees and Beneficiaries.*

Distributions of New Zealand source and taxable distributions to non-resident beneficiaries of foreign trusts are subject to tax in New Zealand.

Taxable distributions from a foreign trust are taxed at the beneficiary's marginal rate.

Trustees of foreign trusts are only liable for tax on income sourced in New Zealand, regardless of where the trustee is resident. New Zealand-sourced income that is non-resident passive income may be subject to non-resident withholding tax (NRWT).

¶5-045 Treatment of foreign trusts when a settlor becomes resident

Section HC 30(4)(a) of the Income Tax Act 2007

Section HC 30(4)(a) provides that if a settlor of a foreign trust becomes resident in New Zealand and is not or stops being a transitional resident; if no election is made for the trust to become a complying trust by the election expiry date, the trust is treated:

(a) as a foreign trust to the extent to which the distribution consists of an amount that is derived by the trustee before the election expiry date and does not give rise on or after the transition date to an income tax liability:

(ab) as a complying trust to the extent to which the distribution consists of an amount derived by the trustee that gives rise on or after the transition date to an income tax liability meeting the requirements of subsection (4B) or section HC 10(1)(ab):

(b) as a non-complying trust to the extent to which the distribution consists of an amount derived by the trustee that gives rise on or after the transition date to an income tax liability that is not satisfied before the distribution is made.

The election expiry date is the first anniversary of the transition date, which is the date on which a natural person settlor:

- becomes resident in New Zealand and is not a transitional resident
- stops being a transitional resident and continues to be a New Zealand resident, and
- the trust would be a foreign trust in relation to a distribution if a distribution were made immediately before the settlor became resident.

See s HC 30(1).

¶5-050 Settlor or settlors must be identified to classify a trust

Complying and foreign trusts are defined by reference to the trust's settlor.

However, care must be taken to accurately identify the settlor or settlors when classifying a trust, as the definition of "settlor" for the trust rules is very wide. For tax purposes, a settlor is not limited to the settlor named in the deed of trust but includes any person who transfers value to a trust. See Chapter 2 – *Settlors.*

¶5-060 Foreign trust can elect to become a complying trust

A foreign trust can become a complying trust before any distribution is made from that trust if an election is made by the election expiry date, which is a period of 12 months (plus an additional 4 years if the settlor is a transitional resident): ss HC 10(2), HC 30 and HC 33.

Once an election is made, for the trust to remain a complying trust, it must meet all the requirements for a complying trust. The election is made on IR 463 (Election to pay income tax on trustee income).

The election can be made by a settlor, trustee or beneficiary.

Once an election is made, the trust is treated as:

(a) as a foreign trust to the extent to which the distribution consists of an amount derived by the trustee before the date of the election and which does not give rise after the transition date to an income tax liability that is paid before the distribution is made:

(b) as a complying trust to the extent to which the distribution consists of an amount that is derived by the trustee–

 (i) before the date of the election and gives rise on or after the transition date to an income tax liability that is paid before the distribution is made; or

 (ii) on or after the date of the election, if the requirements of section HC 10(1)(a) are met for the trustee income derived on or after the date of the election:

(c) as a non-complying trust to the extent to which the distribution consists of an amount that would not be included in a distribution described in paragraphs (a) and (b).

See *Case* Y25 (2008) 23 NZTC 13,270, in which the Court found that although an election was made, all trustee income had not, by application of the relevant definitions, been subject to New Zealand tax.

Section HC 33 provides that a trustee, settlor or beneficiary can elect to satisfy the income tax liability of a trust on its worldwide income.

See Commentary to the Taxation (Kiwisaver, Student Loans, and Remedial Matters) Act 2020, which introduced a number of amendments to s HC 33 to clarify the scope and import of this section.

¶5-070 Non-complying trust is a trust that is not a complying trust or a foreign trust

A non-complying trust is a trust that is not a complying trust or a foreign trust.

Examples of a non-complying trust include a trust that:

- has a resident settlor, was settled overseas with non-resident trustees and has not been liable for New Zealand income tax on trustee income since it was first established
- would be a complying trust but for the failure to meet tax obligations.

Distributions of income and capital gains (other than corpus) from a non-complying trust are assessable to beneficiaries either as beneficiary income (to the extent a distribution is income) or as a taxable distribution.

If a trust is a non complying trust only because of a failure to meet filing or tax obligations, that trust can retrospectively regain complying trust status once the trust's tax obligations have been satisfied.

The payment date for tax on a taxable distribution from a non-complying trust is the terminal tax date of the person liable to pay the tax.

¶5-080 Distributions from foreign and non-complying trusts can be taxable distributions

The concept of a taxable distribution does not apply to a complying trust. The only distribution from a complying trust that is included within a beneficiary's income is beneficiary income. Any other distributions from a complying trust are tax-free.

Beneficiaries of foreign trusts and non-complying trusts pay tax on taxable distributions.

The classification regime operates to ensure that trust income and certain capital gains that can be connected with New Zealand under the trust rules are taxed in New Zealand.

A penal tax rate of 45% applies to taxable distributions from non-complying trusts: sch 1 pt A cl 4. This tax rate reflects that the payment of income tax may have been deferred.

Taxable distributions from foreign trusts are taxed at the beneficiary's marginal rate.

¶5-090 Definition of taxable distribution is more extensive for a non-complying trust than a foreign trust

A taxable distribution from a non-complying trust is any distribution that is not:

(a) beneficiary income; or

(b) a part of the corpus of the trust; or

(c) a payment or a transaction that represents a distribution of the corpus of the trust.

See s HC 15(2).

A taxable distribution from a foreign trust is any distribution that is not:

(a) beneficiary income; or

(b) a part of the corpus of the trust; or

(c) a profit from the realisation of a capital asset or another capital gain; or

(cb) a foreign superannuation withdrawal; or

(cc) a pension; or

(d) a payment or a transaction that represents a distribution of either the corpus of the trust referred to in paragraph (b) or a capital gain referred to in paragraph (c).

See s HC 15(4).

A trustee makes a distribution when the trustee transfers value to a person because the person is a beneficiary of the trust: s HC 14. A transfer of value, which has a corresponding meaning to transfers value, is defined as:

- the provision of money or money's worth
- the provision of money or money's worth for more than market value
- including the release of an obligation to pay money, either by agreement or operation of law.

A distribution that comprises making trust property available at less than market value is a taxable distribution from any trust that is not a complying trust.

Example

Making trust property, such as a family home, available rent-free to beneficiaries in their capacity as beneficiaries is a distribution of capital. If the trust is a complying trust, such a distribution will not have any tax consequences (but may be subject to reporting obligations under the Tax Administration Act 1994, see ¶20-030). However, if the trust is a non-complying or foreign trust, such a distribution of capital may be a taxable distribution.

Inland Revenue has provided additional clarification that the determination of a capital gain for the purposes of the definition of "taxable distribution" was modified by the amended s HC 15(5). Accordingly, for these purposes, a capital gain does not include a gain that must be taken into account for the purpose of calculating a person's income. By way of example, s CB 6 provides that an amount that a person derives from disposing of land is income of the person if they acquired the land for a purpose of disposing of it. If s CB 6 did not apply, such an amount might be regarded as a capital amount. However, it is included in the person's income under s CB 6, so cannot give rise to a capital gain for the purposes of the definition of "taxable distribution". See IS 18/01.

¶5-100 Taxable distribution other than a distribution of corpus is valued at current market value

Distributions, other than funds accumulated before 1 April 1988, and corpus will be taxable distributions.

The Income Tax Act does not define a value for taxable distributions, other than distributions of corpus. A prudent approach where value is not self-evident (eg a realised capital gain) would be to use the market value.

¶5-110 Corpus is valued for tax purposes at the time of settlement

Corpus is defined in s HC 4 as follows:

> *Meaning of corpus*
>
> (1) In the trust rules, **corpus** for a trust means the settlement value under subsection (1B) of property settled on the trust that is not excluded by subsection (2).
>
> *Settlement value of settled property*
>
> (1B) For property meeting the requirements of subsection (1), the value under this subsection (the **settlement value**) of the property settled on a trust is–
>
> (a) the market value of the property determined at the time of the settlement of the property, for a single settlement on the trust; or
>
> (b) the total of the amounts determined under paragraph (a) for each settlement of property, if the trustee treats the settlements in the way permitted by section HC 3.

The following from the Commentary on the Taxation (KiwiSaver, Student Loans, and Remedial Matters) Bill clarifies the intent behind the definition of corpus as amended by the Taxation (KiwiSaver, Student Loans, and Remedial Matters) Act 2020:

> "*What is not included in corpus*
>
> The proposed amendment to section HC 4(1) clarifies that if a settlement is not capable of being distributed as income to beneficiaries, it cannot be included in the corpus of the trust, that is, the assets such as property, bank accounts, stocks, etc. For example, the

value of free legal services provided to a trustee for the benefit of the trust is a transfer of value (unless those services are incidental to the operation of the trust). Under current law, the value of those free services:

- the person providing the legal services is a settlor of the trust (the residence of the settlor is important for determining whether a trust is a foreign trust);
- constitute a settlement; and
- is not capable of being distributed.

Consistency with section HC 3 (ITA)

Under trust law, each settlement creates a separate trust. For income tax purposes, this is modified to permit trustees to elect to treat multiple property settlements on the terms of a trust deed as being additions to corpus of the same trust (section HC 3 of the ITA). The value of each settlement is equal to the market value at settlement.

The proposed amendment (new section HC 4(1B)) clarifies that, when a trustee treats multiple property settlements as being on one trust, the total value of corpus is the market value of all those property settlements. This clarification:

- is consistent with practice; and
- ensures that the ordering rules for distributions (section HC 16 of the ITA) can be applied in a manner consistent with the ability of trustees to elect for multiple settlements to be treated as being on one trust for income tax purposes."

The time of valuation is the date of the first settlement onto the trust. However, as different valuation methodologies can be available, the valuation of corpus can be a complex matter: see *Case* Y25 (2008) 23 NZTC 13,270.

Property that would, but for the settlement onto trust, be taxable to a New Zealand resident beneficiary as beneficiary income or a taxable distribution is excluded from corpus for tax purposes: s HC 4(3).

Also excluded from corpus for tax purposes is any settlement in respect of which the settlor is entitled to a deduction or that, but for the fact of the settlement, would be the settlor's income, or would be the settlor's income if the settlor was resident in New Zealand: s HC 4(4), (5).

It is important to note that in respect of income and capital gains, the key test is the realisation of those gains, rather than the accrual of the gains.

Example

The trustee of a foreign trust acquires an asset for $1 million. When the asset is valued at $2 million, the trust becomes a non-complying trust. Eight years later, when the trust is still a non-complying trust, the asset is sold for $4 million. The realised capital gain of $3 million would be a taxable distribution when distributed to a New Zealand resident beneficiary.

¶5-120 Trust's classification for the trust rules can change

A trust is classified for the purposes of the trust rules whenever a distribution is made. However, as a trust's classification can change, good practice requires that the trustee always confirms a trust's classification before making any distribution. This is the case regardless of whether a previous distribution was taxable or exempt.

¶5-130 Ordering rules prevent a trustee from avoiding a taxable distribution

Ordering rules apply to determine the source of distributions from foreign and non-complying trusts. These rules prevent the trustee of a foreign or non-complying trust making tax-free distributions ahead of or instead of taxable distributions: s HC 16.

Any distribution subject to the ordering rules that is made to a beneficiary of a non-complying or foreign trust is deemed, pursuant to the ordering rules, to consist of the following elements in the following order in s HC 16(2):

(aa) first, an amount derived by the trustee that is beneficiary income of the beneficiary in the previous income year:

(a) second, an amount of income that the trustee derives in the income year:

(b) third, an amount of income, other than beneficiary income, that the trustee has derived in an earlier income year:

(c) fourth, an amount that the trustee derives in the income year from the realisation of a capital asset of the trust or another capital gain and that is not income under section HC 15(5B) for the purposes of this section:

(d) fifth, an amount that the trustee has derived in an earlier income year from the realisation of a capital asset of the trust or another capital gain:

(e) last, the corpus of the trust.

Corpus is defined (subject to certain exclusions of property that but for the settlement, would be settlor or beneficiary income or would entitle a settlor to a deduction) as an amount equal to the market value measured as at the date of settlement of property onto a trust: s HC 4.

Example

The Bahamas Island Trust, which was settled on 26 November 1993, is a foreign trust that has $1,000,000 of accumulated income and a realised capital gain of $1,000,000. The trustee has distributed $1,000,000 to a New Zealand resident beneficiary. The ordering rules provide that the distribution will be treated as a taxable distribution of accumulated income for tax purposes rather than a tax free distribution of the capital gain.

¶5-140 Distributions that comprise a supply for less than market value are not subject to the ordering rules

Where a distribution is made from a trust that is not a complying trust by disposing of property at less than market value, or by providing financial assistance or services to a beneficiary at less than market value, the distribution is a taxable distribution and is not subject to the ordering rule in s HC 16: s HC 15(6).

¶5-150 Ordering rules cannot be avoided by inadequate records

Where the records maintained in relation to a trust do not permit the ordering rules to be applied accurately to determine the constituent elements of a distribution, the distribution is treated as a taxable distribution: s HC 15(7).

¶5-160 There are exceptions to the ordering rules

The ordering rules do not apply to distributions from a complying trust, unless there has been an election under s HZ 2 to pay tax on trustee income. Section HZ 2 elections are those made on or before 31 May 1989 in respect of trusts first settled on or before 17 December 1987: s HC 16(6)(a).

The ordering rules do not apply to a foreign trust that becomes a complying trust for which an election is made under s HC 30(2): s HC 16(6)(c).

The ordering rules do not apply to a non-discretionary trust:

- created by will, codicil or a court order varying a will or codicil
- created by an intestacy or partial intestacy
- on which no settlement has been made after 17 December 1987 (s HC 16(6)(b)).

For the purposes of this exception to the ordering rules, a non-discretionary trust is defined as a trust where the trustee has no discretion as to the source, nature and amount of a distribution: s HC 16(8).

¶5-170 Distributions are ignored for classification purposes if the tax treatment of another distribution changes due to that distribution

When determining the constituent elements of a distribution to a beneficiary ("beneficiary A"), distributions to any other beneficiary ("beneficiary B") are treated as not having been made if the effect is that any part of the distribution to beneficiary A is not treated as a taxable distribution. This anti-avoidance rule will not apply if it can be shown that amounts distributed to beneficiary B arose from a genuine transaction carried out in good faith, and that the transaction is not itself a settlement. See s HC 16(5).

¶5-180 Tax losses can be offset against taxable distributions from a non-complying trust

A beneficiary of a non-complying trust may claim a tax loss to which ss IA 2 to IA 10 apply. However, the amount of tax loss cannot be subtracted from the net income for the corresponding tax year for the purposes of s IA 2 (loss balances carried forward): ss HC 22, IA 2(2), IA 3(3).

¶5-190 Appendix

Overview of the taxation of distributions other than beneficiary income:

	Complying Trust	Foreign Trust	Non-complying Trust
Pre-1/4/88 accumulated income or capital gain that s HZ 1 applies to	Exempt income	Exempt income	Exempt income
Corpus	Exempt income	Exempt income	Exempt income
Arm's length capital gain	Exempt income	Exempt income	Taxable distribution taxed at 45% rate
Non-arm's length capital gain	Exempt income	Taxable distribution taxed at beneficiary's marginal rate	Taxable distribution taxed at 45% rate
Accumulated income derived on or after 1/4/88	Exempt income	Taxable distribution taxed at beneficiary's marginal rate	Taxable distribution taxed at 45% rate
Trustee income	Taxed at trustee rate (33%).	Income derived from New Zealand taxed at trustee rate (33%).	Taxed at trustee rate (33%).

¶5-200 Legislation

Income Tax Act 2007

HC 9 CLASSIFYING TRUSTS

A trust is classified at the time it makes a distribution as–

(a) a complying trust under section HC 10:

(b) a foreign trust under section HC 11:

(c) a non-complying trust under section HC 12.

HC 10 COMPLYING TRUSTS

HC 10(1) REQUIREMENTS FOR COMPLYING TRUSTS

A trust is a **complying trust** in relation to a distribution if–

(a) the following requirements are met for the life of the trust up to the time of distribution:

(i) no trustee income derived includes an amount of non-resident passive income, or non-residents' foreign-sourced income, or exempt income under section CW 54 (Foreign-sourced amounts derived by trustees); and

(ii) the tax obligations relating to the trustee's income tax liability have been satisfied for every tax year; or

(ab) the requirements of paragraph (a) are not met and–

(i) a person makes an election meeting the requirements of section HC 30(2) and the requirements of subsection (2) are met; or

(ii) a person makes an election meeting the requirements of section HC 33(1) and for all income years beginning on or after the date on which the election applies to the trust and before the time of distribution, the trustee's tax obligations relating to the trustee's income tax liability for the trustee income, determined consistently with section HC 33(1C), are satisfied; or

(ac) the requirements of paragraph (a) are not met and the distribution meets the requirements of section HC 30(4)(ab); or

(b) it is a superannuation fund.

HC 10(2) FOREIGN TRUST CHOOSING TO BECOME COMPLYING TRUST

A foreign trust may become a complying trust to the extent set out in section HC 30 by–

(a) an election being made under section HC 30(2)–

(i) before the time of distribution; and

(ii) by the election expiry date given by section HC 30(5) for section HC 30(2); and

(b) the requirements of subsection (1)(a) are met for trustee income derived after the election date.

HC 10(3) LIFE OF TRUST

The life of the trust referred to in subsection (1)(a) includes every income year from the start of the income year in which a settlement was first made on the trust up to the time of the distribution.

HC 10(4) COMPLYING TRUSTS: MEETING REQUIREMENTS

For the purposes of subsection (1)(a) and (ab), section HC 29(6) does not apply in determining whether the requirements are met.

HC 11 FOREIGN TRUSTS

A trust is a **foreign trust** at a moment in time if no settlor is resident in New Zealand at any time in the period that–

(a) starts on the later of 17 December 1987 and the date on which a settlement was first made on the trust; and

(b) ends with the moment in time.

HC 12 NON-COMPLYING TRUSTS

A trust is a **non-complying trust** in relation to a distribution if it is neither a complying trust nor a foreign trust.

[...]

HC 15 TAXABLE DISTRIBUTIONS FROM NON-COMPLYING AND FOREIGN TRUSTS

HC 15(1) WHEN SUBSECTION (2) APPLIES

Subsection (2) applies for a trust that is a non-complying trust at the time a distribution to a beneficiary is made.

HC 15(2) TAXABLE DISTRIBUTIONS: NON-COMPLYING TRUSTS

The distribution is a **taxable distribution** to the extent to which it is not a distribution of–

(a) beneficiary income; or

(b) a part of the corpus of the trust; or

(c) a payment or a transaction that represents a distribution of the corpus of the trust.

HC 15(3) WHEN SUBSECTION (4) APPLIES

Subsection (4) applies for a trust that is a foreign trust at the time a distribution to a beneficiary is made.

HC 15(4) TAXABLE DISTRIBUTIONS: FOREIGN TRUSTS

The distribution is a **taxable distribution** to the extent to which it is not a distribution of–

(a) beneficiary income; or

(b) a part of the corpus of the trust; or

(c) a profit from the realisation of a capital asset or another capital gain; or

(cb) a foreign superannuation withdrawal; or

(cc) a pension; or

(d) a payment or a transaction that represents a distribution of either the corpus of the trust referred to in paragraph (b) or a capital gain referred to in paragraph (c).

HC 15(5) DETERMINING AMOUNT OF GAIN

For the purposes of subsection (4)(c),–

(a) the profit or other capital gain does not include a gain that must be taken into account for the purposes of determining an income tax liability:

(ab) if the trustee is not a trustee of a trust referred to in paragraph (ac), the profit or other capital gain does not include an amount of capital gain (the **gain amount**) that is derived by the trustee through a transaction or a series of transactions if–

(i) the transaction or series of transactions is between the trustee and an associated person who is not a natural person or corporate trustee; and

(ii) the gain amount is greater than the capital gain that the trustee would derive from a transaction at market value:

(ac) if the trustee is a trustee of a trust, for which a CFC is a settlor and no person is treated as a settlor under section HC 28(3) or (4), the profit or other capital gain does not include an amount of capital gain that is derived by the trustee through a transaction or a series of transactions between the trustee and an associated person:

(b) the amount of the profit is determined after subtracting any capital loss that the trustee incurs in the income year in which the amount was derived.

HC 15(5B) CERTAIN CAPITAL GAINS FOR TRUSTEE OF FOREIGN TRUST

For a foreign trust, profit described in subsection (5)(ab) or (ac) is income of the trustee for the purposes of section HC 16.

HC 15(5C) SOURCE OF INCOME FROM CAPITAL GAIN

The source of a capital gain that is included in a taxable distribution is determined for the trustee under section YD 4 (Classes of income treated as having New Zealand source) as if the capital gain were an amount of income.

HC 15(5D) SOURCE OF CAPITAL LOSS

The source of a capital loss for the trustee is given by subsection (5C), applied as if the capital loss were a capital gain included in a taxable distribution

HC 15(6) AMOUNTS NOT SUBJECT TO ORDERING RULE

To the extent to which a distribution is made from a trust that is not a complying trust by disposing of property at less than market value or providing financial assistance or services to a beneficiary at less than market value, the distribution is a taxable distribution and is not subject to the ordering rule in section HC 16.

HC 15(7) INADEQUATE RECORDS

If the records of a trust that is not a complying trust do not allow an accurate determination of the elements of a distribution under section HC 16, the distribution is a taxable distribution.

HC 16 ORDERING RULE FOR DISTRIBUTIONS FROM NON-COMPLYING AND FOREIGN TRUSTS

HC 16(1) WHEN THIS SECTION APPLIES

This section applies for the purposes of the trust rules when a trustee of a non-complying trust or a foreign trust makes a distribution in an income year to a beneficiary. Subsections (6) and (7) override this subsection.

HC 16(2) ORDER OF ELEMENTS OF DISTRIBUTION

The distribution is treated as consisting of the following elements in the following order:

(aa) first, an amount derived by the trustee that is beneficiary income of the beneficiary in the previous income year:

(a) second, an amount of income that the trustee derives in the income year:

(b) third, an amount of income, other than beneficiary income, that the trustee has derived in an earlier income year:

(c) fourth, an amount that the trustee derives in the income year from the realisation of a capital asset of the trust or another capital gain and that is not income under section HC 15(5B) for the purposes of this section:

(d) fifth, an amount that the trustee has derived in an earlier income year from the realisation of a capital asset of the trust or another capital gain:

(e) last, the corpus of the trust.

HC 16(3) ORDER AND ELEMENTS

In subsection (2),—

(a) an amount must not be treated as included in the distribution if the amount has been treated under this section as being included in an earlier or contemporaneous distribution from the trust:

(b) the paragraphs are applied in order, and the next paragraph applies only to the extent to which the amount of the distribution is more than the cumulative amounts described in that paragraph and the preceding paragraphs.

HC 16(4) DEDUCTIONS AND CAPITAL LOSSES SUBTRACTED

For the purposes of subsection (2),–

(a) in paragraphs (a) and (b), the amount of income is determined after subtracting the amount of a deduction that is taken into account in the income year in the calculation of net or taxable income for the corresponding tax year:

(b) in paragraphs (c) and (d), the amount is determined after subtracting the amount of a capital loss that the trustee incurs in the income year.

HC 16(5) TRANSACTIONS THAT ARE NOT GENUINE

In the determination of the elements of a distribution to a beneficiary (**beneficiary** A), no amount of income or capital gain derived by the trustee of the trust is treated as distributed to another beneficiary of the trust (**beneficiary** B) if the effect is that some or all of the distribution to beneficiary A would be treated as not being beneficiary income or a taxable distribution, unless the distribution to beneficiary B meets all the following requirements:

(a) it is a genuine transaction entered into and carried out in good faith; and

(b) *(repealed)*

(c) it does not itself constitute a settlement.

HC 16(6) EXCLUSIONS: TERMS OF TRUST

This section does not apply to the following distributions which are instead treated as consisting of the amount that reflects the terms of the trust or the terms of the exercise of the trustee's discretion:

(a) a distribution by the trustee of a complying trust which is treated as exempt income under section CW 53 (Distributions from complying trusts), unless an election to pay income tax on trustee income has been made for the purposes of section HZ 2 (Trusts that may become complying trusts); or

(b) a distribution from a non-discretionary trust–

  (i) created by will or codicil, or by an order of court varying or modifying the provisions of a will or codicil; or

  (ii) created on an intestacy or partial intestacy; or

  (iii) on which no settlement has been made after 17 December 1987; or

(c) a distribution from a trust, other than a non-complying trust, that is settled by a natural person and for which an election is made under section HC 30(2).

HC 16(7) EXCLUSIONS: TAXABLE DISTRIBUTIONS

This section does not apply to a distribution described in section HC 15(6).

HC 16(8) MEANING OF NON-DISCRETIONARY TRUST

In this section, a **non-discretionary trust** is a trust in relation to which the trustee has no discretion as to the source, nature, and amount of distributions to beneficiaries, including but not limited to the classification of trust property as capital or income.

[...]

HC 27 WHO IS A SETTLOR?

HC 27(1) WHEN THIS SECTION APPLIES

(repealed)

HC 27(2) MEANING OF SETTLOR

A **settlor** of a trust is a person who, at any time,–

(a) transfers value–

- (i) to the trust; or
- (ii) for the benefit of the trust; or
- (iii) on terms of the trust:

(ab) provides, for less than market value, services to the trust or for the benefit of the trust that are more than incidental to the operation of the trust:

(b) provides financial assistance to the trust or for the benefit of the trust with an obligation to pay on demand, and the right to demand is not exercised or is deferred:

(bb) is a beneficiary of the trust who is owed money by the trustee and does not meet the requirements of subsection (6):

(c) is treated as a settlor under section HC 28.

HC 27(3) TRUSTS FOR RETIREMENT BENEFITS FOR EMPLOYEES

Despite subsection (2), a person resident in New Zealand who makes a settlement on a trust as an employer for the benefit of 1 or more employees is not a settlor of the trust if the following circumstances apply:

(a) the trust is established or created mainly to provide retirement benefits to natural persons; and

(b) the trust is neither a foreign superannuation scheme nor a superannuation fund.

HC 27(3B) EMPLOYEE SHARE PURCHASE AGREEMENTS

(repealed)

HC 27(3C) CONTRIBUTIONS TO FOREIGN SUPERANNUATION SCHEME

Despite subsection (2), a person who makes a contribution to a trust that is a foreign superannuation scheme is not a settlor of the trust.

HC 27(3D) RESETTLEMENTS

Despite subsection (2), a trustee of a trust (the **head-trust**) who is resident in New Zealand and settles an amount on a second trust (the **sub-trust**), or makes a distribution to, or on terms of, the sub-trust, is not a settlor of the sub-trust if, when the settlement or distribution is made on or to the sub-trust,–

(a) a settlor of the head-trust exists and each settlor of the head-trust is a non-resident; or

(b) no settlor of the head-trust exists and the last surviving settlor of the head-trust was a non-resident when that settlor ceased to exist.

HC 27(4) INDIRECT SETTLEMENT

A person may make a transfer of value, or provision of financial assistance, referred to in subsection (2) directly or indirectly and by 1 transaction or a number of connected transactions.

HC 27(5) NIL VALUE OF BENEFICIARY RELATIONSHIP

The fact that a person is, or will become, a beneficiary of a trust does not constitute the giving or receiving of value.

HC 27(6) BENEFICIARIES OWED MONEY BY TRUSTEE

When a trustee of a trust owes an amount to a beneficiary of the trust, the beneficiary does not become a settlor of the trust under subsection (2) solely as a result of being owed the amount if–

(a) the amount owing at the end of the income year is not more than $25,000:

(b) the amount owing at the end of the income year is more than $25,000 and the trustee pays to the beneficiary, for each income year in which the amount is owing and by the date given for the income year by section HC 6(1B), interest on the amount at a rate equal to the prescribed rate of interest or the market rate.

HC 27(7) DETERMINING AMOUNT OWED TO BENEFICIARY

For the purposes of subsection (6), the amount of money owing to a beneficiary at the end of an income year is the amount of the debt at that time, adjusted to include the effect of transactions that are–

(a) made after the end of the income year and by the date given for the income year by section HC 6(1B); and

(b) included in the financial statements of the trust for the income year.

HC 28 ACTIVITIES TREATED AS THOSE OF SETTLOR

HC 28(1) WHEN THIS SECTION APPLIES

This section applies for the purposes of the trust rules to describe certain activities of a person that result in the person being treated as a settlor.

HC 28(2) AVOIDANCE

A person is treated as a settlor if, in relation to a trust,–

(a) they act, refrain from acting, or enter into a transaction or a series of transactions; and

(b) what is done or not done has the effect of defeating the intent and application of the trust rules.

HC 28(3) SHAREHOLDERS IN CONTROLLED FOREIGN COMPANIES

A person is treated as a settlor of a trust if a controlled foreign company settles an amount on a trust and the person has a control interest of 10% or more in the CFC–

(a) at the time of the settlement:

(b) for the accounting period of the CFC in which the settlement occurs.

HC 28(4) SHAREHOLDERS IN COMPANIES

A person is treated as a settlor of a trust if–

(a) a company settles an amount on the trust; and

(b) the company would have been a CFC at the date of settlement if it had been a foreign company at the time; and

(c) the person would be treated as having a control interest of 10% or more in the company, if the company were a foreign company,–

  (i) at the time of the settlement:

  (ii) under section EX 1(3), for the accounting period of the company in which the settlement occurs.

HC 28(5) SECOND TRUSTS

A person is treated as a settlor of a trust (the **sub-trust**) if–

(a) they are a settlor of a trust (the **head-trust**); and

(b) a trustee of the head-trust settles an amount on the subtrust, or makes a distribution to, or on terms of the subtrust.

HC 28(6) CONTROL OVER TRUSTEE OR SETTLOR

A person is treated as a settlor of a trust if–

(a) they acquire, directly or indirectly, rights or powers in relation to a trustee or a settlor of the trust; and

(b) the acquisition has the purpose or effect of enabling them to require the trustee to treat them, or a nominee, as a beneficiary of the trust.

HC 33 CHOOSING TO SATISFY INCOME TAX LIABILITY OF TRUSTEE

HC 33(1) ELECTION TO SATISFY TAX LIABILITY

A person who is a trustee, settlor, or beneficiary of a trust as described in subsection (2) may choose to satisfy the income tax liability of the trustee of the trust.

HC 33(1B) TRUSTEE TREATED AS MAKING ELECTION

A trustee is treated as making an election under subsection (1), if–

(a) for the period beginning at the start of the income year in which a settlement is first made on the trust and ending before the date on which the trust ceases to be a complying trust as described in paragraph (b), the trust is a complying trust under section HC 10(1)(a); and

(b) the trust ceases to meet the requirement in section HC 10(1)(a)(i) in an income year (the **non-complying year**); and

(c) the trustee meets the tax obligations relating to the income tax liability referred to in subsection (2), for the non-complying year and notifies the Commissioner that the trust is a complying trust for the non-complying year,–

  (i) for a trustee that is required to file a return of income for the non-complying year, in the return of income and by the due date for the return of income:

  (ii) for a trustee that is not required to file a return of income for the non-complying year, by the due date for a return, by a resident foreign trustee, required by section 59D of the Tax Administration Act 1994 for the non-complying year.

HC 33(1C) STATUS OF PERSON MAKING ELECTION AND SETTLOR

From when an election by a person under subsection (1) applies under subsection (3), the tax obligations of the trustee of the trust arising from the trust are determined on the basis that–

(a) the trustee is a New Zealand resident; and

(b) the trust has a settlor who is a New Zealand resident.

HC 33(2) LIABILITY OF PERSON MAKING ELECTION

The person making the election–

(a) must satisfy the tax obligations of the trustee relating to the income tax liability of the trustee; and

(b) is not required to satisfy the income tax liability of the beneficiary that the trustee must satisfy as agent under section HC 32.

HC 33(3) APPLICATION OF ELECTION

The election under subsection (1) applies–

(a) for an election to which section HC 30 applies, on and after the date on which the election is made; or

(b) for an election to which section HC 30 does not apply and that does not meet the requirements of subsection (1B), on and after whichever date (the **effective date**) the person making the election chooses of–

  (i) the date of the election (the **electing date**):

  (ii) the beginning of the income year (the **electing year**) that includes the electing date:

  (iii) the beginning of an income year that is 4 years or less before the beginning of the electing year; or

(c) for an election to which section HC 30 does not apply and that meets the requirements of subsection (1B), on and after the beginning of the non-complying year referred to in subsection (1B)(b).

HC 33(3B) PERIOD OF ELECTION UNDER SUBSECTION (1B)

An election meeting the requirements of subsection (1B) is effective until the beginning of an income year for which the trustee does not–

(a) meet the tax obligations of the trustee relating to the income tax liability of the trustee for the income year:

(b) notify the Commissioner that the trust is a complying trust for the income year in the way that would be required by subsection (1B)(c) for a non-complying year.

HC 33(4) TIME OF PROVIDING ELECTION

If the trustee of a trust is required to file a return of income for an income year, a person making an election under subsection (1) must notify the Commissioner of the election and provide to the Commissioner the information required by section 113F of the Tax Administration Act 1994 within the time allowed for filing a return of income for the income year. If section HC 30 applies, they must give notification by the election expiry date.

HC 33(5) EFFECT ON DISTRIBUTIONS

For a trust (the **distributing trust**) and an election for which the tax treatment of the trust is not given by section HC 30(3),–

(a) a distribution made before the beginning of the electing year has the taxation consequences that it would have in the absence of the election:

(b) a distribution made after the beginning of the electing year from an amount derived by the trustee before the effective date is treated as being a distribution by a trust having the status, of foreign trust or non-complying trust or complying trust, that the distributing trust has when the amount is derived:

(c) a distribution made after the beginning of the electing year from an amount derived on or after the effective date is treated as being made by the trustee as trustee of–

(i) a complying trust, if the requirements of section HC 10(1)(ab) are met for the trustee income derived on or after the effective date:

(ii) a non-complying trust, if subparagraph (i) does not apply:

(d) for the purposes of paragraphs (b) and (c), the amount derived before the effective date by the trustee in an income year that includes, but does not begin with, the effective date is–

(i) the amount derived before the effective date in the income year, if the person making the election does not choose to rely on subparagraph (ii); or

(ii) a proportion of the amount derived in the income year equal to the proportion of the days in the income year that are before the effective date.

HC 33(6) NO LIABILITY FOR PENALTIES FROM INCREASED ASSESSMENTS IN SOME CIRCUMSTANCES

When a person makes an election for a trust under section HC 33(1) with an effective date given by subsection (3)(b)(iii) and the election results in an increase in the assessed income tax liability of the trustee, or in the amount of resident withholding tax payable by the trustee, for an income year before the electing year, the person and the trustee are not liable for a penalty under Part 9 of the Tax Administration Act 1994 arising from the increase if the Commissioner accepts that the trustee's tax position for each income year beginning on or after the effective date and before the electing year is none of–

(a) an unacceptable tax position under section 141B of the Tax Administration Act 1994:

(b) an abusive tax position under section 141D of that Act:

(c) a tax position that causes the trustee to be liable to pay a shortfall penalty for evasion or a similar act under section 141E of that Act.

CHAPTER 6

Beneficiary Distributions

¶6-010 Operating principle

Trustees benefit beneficiaries by making distributions of a trust's income or capital. Distributions other than beneficiary income or taxable distributions can be received as exempt income: ss HC 15, HC 20.

¶6-020 A distribution comprises any payment, transfer or application of trust property

Broadly speaking a distribution from a trust includes, but is not limited to, any payment or transfer or application of trust property (whether income or capital) in favour of a beneficiary.

Where a trust deed provides that beneficiaries have various entitlements to income or capital, the trustees must determine whether any distribution is capital or income before distribution to ensure compliance with the terms of the trust.

For example, making trust property available to a beneficiary for less than market value cannot constitute a distribution of beneficiary income because the distribution is one of capital. A trustee must ensure that any distribution is permissible within the terms of the deed of trust.

The taxation treatment of any distribution is determined independently to any provisions of the deed of trust.

¶6-030 Distributions occur when a transfer of value is made because the recipient is a beneficiary

A trustee makes a distribution for tax purposes when the trustee makes a transfer of value to a person because the person is a beneficiary of the trust: s HC 14(1). The source of the distribution can be income or capital.

The beneficiary receiving a distribution can be the trustee of another trust.

For timing purposes, a distribution is deemed to be made when the property transferred vests absolutely in or is paid to the beneficiary: s HC 14(3).

A distribution can be made directly or indirectly: s HC 14(4).

Example

The trustee of the BEDPMHA Trust resolves to pay a debt of $5,200 owed by a beneficiary of the trust. The beneficiary is a beneficiary as to income and capital. The payment of $5,200 will be recorded as a distribution of capital to the beneficiary, even though the payment was made to a third party.

If a trustee has received a settlement by way of a forgiveness of debt, that amount can be distributed to another trust without derivation of income if the recipient trust was settled mainly to benefit a natural person for whom the original creditor has natural love and affection, or a registered charitable trust: ss EW 50, HC 14(2).

¶6-040 Some distributions have tax consequences

Distributions from complying trusts made out of accumulated trustee income and capital gains will not constitute beneficiary income. However, subject to the ordering rules (see ¶5-130), such distributions may constitute "taxable distributions" when made by foreign and non-complying trusts: see Chapter 5 – *Taxable Distributions*.

Other capital distributions can have tax consequences either because of the status of the trust or because the capital distribution applies to assets that form part of the trustee's tax base.

¶6-050 Distributions from non-complying and foreign trusts can be taxable distributions

A distribution from a non-complying trust that does not comprise beneficiary income or corpus is a taxable distribution for tax purposes: s HC 15(2).

Taxable distributions from non-complying trusts are taxed at the rate of 45%.

A distribution from a foreign trust that does not comprise beneficiary income, a profit from the realisation of a capital asset or another capital gain, a foreign superannuation withdrawal, a pension, corpus, or a payment or transaction that represents corpus is a taxable distribution: s HC 15(4).

Taxable distributions from foreign trusts are taxed at the beneficiary's marginal rate.

It is important that trustees and beneficiaries appreciate the extent of distributions that can comprise distributions from foreign trusts. For example, a distribution from a will trust established overseas is a distribution from a foreign trust. To establish the correct tax treatment it will be necessary to obtain sufficient information to determine what comprises the corpus of the foreign trust, which is exempt income, and what might comprise a taxable distribution of non-arm's length capital gains or accumulate income.

Accordingly, it is important not to presume that any inheritance received from a non-resident testamentary trust will necessarily be received tax-free. The following examples from interpretation statement IS 19/04, "Income tax – distributions from foreign trusts" (see *Tax Information Bulletin* ¶321-112 Vol 32, No 1, February 2020 at 28) are illustrative of the tax treatment of distributions following death.

Example 4: Overseas will trusts

63. David moved to New Zealand from Australia with his mother when he was 12. His parents had separated, and David was their only child. David's father Joe was killed in a mining accident when David was 18. Joe's will left David a specific legacy of a sum of money and a direction that a trust be created with the balance of his residuary estate (mostly comprising commercial properties in Perth) to be held by the trustee, accumulating rents and reinvesting until David turned 21.

64. David has now turned 21, and the trustee has sold the properties and sent everything to David in New Zealand.

65. Assuming the law of administration of estates in Australia not to be materially different to the law in New Zealand, the only tax implications for David when he receives the specific legacy will arise from the fact that the money in question effectively moved from Joe to David at the time of Joe's death (under the "relation back" principle). If Joe invested the money in Australia before sending it to David, income may have been derived that would be taxable to David in New Zealand. If not, it could be argued a bare trust briefly existed with the executors' assent inferred. However, the transfer of the specific legacy will not be recognised as a trust distribution for New Zealand tax purposes.

66. The distribution from the testamentary trust created from the residuary estate, on the other hand, is likely to have tax implications for David under the trust rules. Current year investment income of the trustee distributed to David will be beneficiary income. The trust will be a foreign trust because Joe has never lived in New Zealand and he is the only person who has ever settled anything on the trust. The ordering rules in s HC 16 do not apply, assuming the trust meets the requirements to be a non-discretionary trust. Therefore, the income treatment will be determined by the relevant deed or the trustees' determination. Accumulated rental and investment returns will be a taxable distribution, but the proceeds of sale of the properties will not, being excluded under s HC 15(4) as either corpus or capital gains.

Example 5: Deceased in a civil law country

67. Thomas has lived in Germany for most of his life. His only son Joseph moved to New Zealand in 2005. When his wife died in 2010, Thomas made a will leaving all his property to Joseph.

68. When Thomas passes away in 2016, Joseph travels to Germany and discusses Thomas's estate with the executor, Erich, a professional financial advisor in Berlin. Erich suggests it would be consistent with Thomas's wishes that Joseph does not take the inheritance to New Zealand straight away but keeps it overseas. Erich's advice is to appoint a company in the Cayman Islands to hold the estate on trust for Joseph's family until the trustee determines they need it.

69. Circumstances change and five years later Joseph's family is now short of money. The trust is wound up and everything is distributed to Joseph and his wife.

70. The tax effects of this for Joseph and his wife are very likely to be that they have derived beneficiary income and taxable distributions. Joseph may also not have been

aware that, as a New Zealand resident settlor, he had an obligation to meet the trustee company's New Zealand tax obligations on trustee income (s HC 25) and to disclose under s 59(1) of the TAA the particulars of the trust. Further, amounts distributed that are taxable distributions will not be from a foreign trust, instead they are likely to be from a non-complying trust, meaning a greater tax liability for them. Although Joseph inherited the estate from a deceased person in Germany, a civil law country without trusts and where Joseph directly succeeded to the estate on Thomas's death, Joseph then settled on the Cayman Islands trust assets that had vested in him before the settlement. Joseph is a New Zealand tax resident, so the trust would be a non-complying trust and not a foreign trust (although an election to be a complying trust may be possible ...). The same outcomes could be expected if Joseph had inherited the estate from a deceased person from a common law country.

Example 6: Non-discretionary will trust

71. Cindy moves to New Zealand in 2005 from Canada. Her parents die in a car accident in 2012 leaving wills under which their executors are instructed to establish a non-discretionary trust to hold their estate for their seven children, six of whom have remained living in Canada.

72. In 2018, Cindy receives a substantial payment from the trustees following the sale of some Canadian shares that were part of the estate at the time of her parents' death. The trustees sign a formal resolution to the effect that the proceeds of sale should be distributed to the beneficiaries.

73. Because it is a non-discretionary will trust, the ordering rules in s HC 16 do not apply, and the trustee resolution will determine the tax effect for Cindy. This means there is no taxable distribution to Cindy because the proceeds will be both corpus of the trusts established under the parents' wills and profits from realisation of capital assets (assuming the shares had increased in value since they were settled on the trusts).

Example 7: Discretionary will trust — ordering rules and the importance of records

74. As in Example 6, Cindy's parents die and leave wills, but this time the executors are instructed to establish discretionary trusts.

75. In 2018, Cindy asks the trustees for funds to support her daughter who is about to go to university. The trustees decide to sell some of the Canadian shares and distribute the proceeds to Cindy. They sign a formal resolution to this effect.

76. In this case, the result of the application of the ordering rules in s HC 16(2) may be that Cindy has received a taxable distribution. For this not to be the case, the records of the trust would need to show that there had been no income derived by the trustees in the current or earlier years that had not been distributed to beneficiaries earlier or at the same time. This is despite the distribution by the trustees being intended to be of corpus and capital gains.

77. Further, if Cindy cannot obtain adequate records to be able to determine the elements of the distribution under s HC 16(2), s HC 15(7) will apply to treat the entire distribution to her as a taxable distribution from a foreign trust.

See further at ¶5-080, ¶5-090, ¶5-100, ¶5-110 and ¶5-130.

¶6-060 Making trust property available to a beneficiary is a common form of capital distribution

It is commonplace in New Zealand for a natural person to transfer their interest in a family home to a trust of which that person is a beneficiary, usually but not necessarily, by way of sale at market value, with a debt back to the transferor. The transferor may continue to occupy the family home after the transfer. If the transferor occupies the family home under a lease or occupation licence, the right to occupy is under the terms of the relevant lease or licence and does not represent a distribution.

However, if trust property such as the family home is made available rent-free to a beneficiary in that person's capacity as beneficiary, this will represent a distribution of capital. A distribution of capital to the beneficiary of a complying trust does not give rise to any income tax consequences but may have reporting obligations under s 59BA of the Tax Administration Act 1994. See further at Chapter 20 – *Disclosure and Reporting Obligations*.

If the beneficiary pays rates, insurance and other expenses relating to the property from private funds, it is not clear how the payment of expenses incidental to the occupation of the property should be treated by the trustee who could variously account for these payments as the payment of rent, as payments incidental to occupation that are private to the beneficiary, or an advance to the trustee.

While each case should be determined on its own facts, where in doubt the prudent approach is to treat the payment of such outgoings as an advance to the trustee and the advances should be documented accordingly. See *Peters* v *Peters* [2013] NZHC 1061; (2013) 3 NZTR ¶23-004, which highlights the risks to trustees who presume that an advance is a gift, rather than a loan.

Regardless of the terms on which the beneficiary occupies trust property, the trustee has a duty to ensure that the arrangement is permitted under the terms of the trust and that the appropriate trustee resolutions are made.

There are differing views on whether interest on money borrowed by the trust to acquire the home is an expense incidental to the occupation of the home. Again, the prudent approach, and that usually adopted, is to treat any such payments made by a beneficiary on the trust's behalf as advances to the trust by the beneficiary.

The position is clearer with regard to the payment of principal, and it is widely accepted that payment of principal is not an expense incidental to occupation. If beneficiaries make repayments of principal, absent any other basis such as payment of principal in lieu of rent (that is accounted for by the trustee), this should be treated as an advance to the trust and documented as such.

In the absence of any documentation and/or the appropriate resolutions, Inland Revenue may treat the payment of outgoings by beneficiaries as rental income.

If a beneficiary pays rent to occupy a home owned by a family trust, under general principles, the trust will be taxed on the rental income with a deduction allowed for expenses incurred in deriving that income, for example, interest on money borrowed to acquire the home, repairs and maintenance, depreciation, etc.

If this is the case, there must be a genuine rental arrangement that is permitted under the terms of the trust and the arrangement should be documented accurately.

Inland Revenue's Rental Income publication IR 264 states that in situations where a property is rented out for less than market value (usually to a relative or friend), any loss will generally not be deductible.

However, this is not necessarily the case, and there is authority that rental expenses can be deductible regardless of the existence of a family arrangement. In *Case* E54 (1982) 5 NZTC 59,312, the Commissioner disallowed the rental losses incurred by the taxpayer, contending that the letting of the house to the taxpayer's mother-in-law and later his son were a family arrangement, so the expenses incurred on the house were of a private or domestic nature. However, the Taxation Review Authority (TRA) held that rental losses incurred by a taxpayer were at least in part, deductible. Other costs were considered capital in nature (eg work done to a metre box) and not deductible. The cost of remedial work for damage done during the son's tenancy was disallowed on the basis that such cost was recoverable from the son and in breach of an arm's length letting arrangement). The TRA found that there was a true landlord and tenant relationship that had the necessary nexus for the expenditure to have been incurred in gaining or producing assessable income and not to have been of a private or domestic nature. Since the taxpayer was carrying on a bona fide letting operation, he was entitled to the deductions claimed for rates, lawn mowing and insurance, roof painting, depreciation, interest and the cost of a trip to the house to remedy storm damage.

As each case will turn on its own facts, the availability of deductions should be assessed on a case-by-case basis.

Capital distributions, such as making trust property available to a beneficiary by the trustee of a foreign or non-complying trust, may be taxable distributions that must be accounted for accordingly. See further at Chapter 5 – *Taxable Distributions*.

¶6-063 Deductibility and apportionment of expenditure relating to mixed-use assets

Consideration also needs to be given to the apportionment rules in Subpart DG, which apply where expenditure is incurred on land, boats or aircraft that are used for both business and private purposes. Use of an asset means the active use of the asset for its intended purpose. The rules apply to land from the 2013–14 income year and to boats and aircraft from the 2014–15 income year. See ss DG 1 and DG 3.

One of the most common situations where the "mixed-use asset" rules apply is that of a holiday home that is rented to the public for short-term stays. Inland Revenue has published a fact sheet, "Tax rules of holiday homes" (IR 1021, August 2013), setting out how the rules apply to such a holiday home and providing an example of the calculations required.

The rules apply to relevant mixed-use assets held by sole traders, trusts, partnerships and close companies. Note that the definition of a "close company" is modified for these rules so that a reference to a "natural person" in the definition includes a reference to a "trustee". The usual pre-requisite that requires 5 or fewer natural persons hold 50% or more of the voting interests in a company for it to be a close company is altered for the purposes of the mixed-use asset rules so that the majority of the shares in a company may be held by a trustee and the company will still be treated as a close company. Also see Goods and Services Tax Act 1985, s 20G.

¶6-065 Distributions to beneficiaries on lower tax rates

It is generally acceptable for trustees to exercise their discretion and distribute trust income to beneficiaries on lower tax rates, with tax losses or to a beneficiary to whom the income will be tax exempt. However, there can be circumstances where this could represent tax avoidance. See QB 15/11: "Income tax – scenarios on tax avoidance – 2015". See further at ¶22-080.

¶6-070 The distribution of business assets can have tax consequences even if distributed to the beneficiary of a complying trust

Distribution of capital items that comprise a trust's tax base can have tax consequences independently from those that arise due to a trust's classification.

Capital distributions of business assets used by a trust are treated as a disposal by the trustee and an acquisition by a beneficiary at market value. Therefore, there may be depreciation recovery on any depreciable assets that are distributed to a beneficiary: ss EE 40, FC 1(1)(c), FC 2, YB 6. Apart from the imposition of a deemed market value sale price, the calculation of depreciation recovery income is the same as for a sale to a third party.

For goods and services tax (GST) purposes, the distribution to an associated party (the beneficiary) will be deemed to be a supply at market value. However, this rule does not apply where a beneficiary is GST-registered in respect of the assets transferred: GST Act 1985, s 10(2), (3A). In other words, for GST purposes, the assets do not have to be transferred at the open market value.

¶6-080 Distributions of property are generally treated as an acquisition at market value for tax purposes

Under ss FC 1(1)(c) and FC 2(1), a distribution of property from a trustee to a beneficiary of the trust will be deemed to be a disposal and acquisition at market value. This means that when the trustee of a trust distributes property to a beneficiary that will be utilised within the beneficiary's tax base, the market value of the property transferred is the same value for both the transferor and the transferee. The effective date of the transfer is the date on which the transaction occurs: s FC 2. Note the exceptions in ss FC 3 to FC 6.

The beneficiary can depreciate the assets distributed due to there being a deemed disposition and acquisition at market value. However, certain restrictions will apply in relation to the cost base and the depreciation rate, as this is a transfer of depreciable property between associated persons.

The beneficiary's cost base for depreciation purposes will be limited to the lesser of:

- the cost of the property to the trustee, or
- the cost of the property to the beneficiary (that is the market value on the date of the distribution).

The depreciation rate able to be used by the beneficiary is restricted to:

- where the same depreciation method is used, no more than the rate used by the trust
- where a different depreciation method is used, no more than a rate equivalent to that used by the trust as determined under the rates of equivalence set out in sch 10 (straight-line equivalents of diminishing value rates of depreciation): s EE 40.

The beneficiary will have to use the new depreciation rate for buildings (2% straight-line or 3% diminishing value) if this is less than the rate currently being used by the trustee.

Section FC 1, was amended by the Taxation (Annual Rates for 2015–2016, Research and Development, and Remedial Matters) Act 2016, effective 1 April 2008, to prevent a distribution of property from a trustee to a beneficiary being dealt with under the subpart when the beneficiary pays an amount for the property. Accordingly, s FC 1(1)(c) will only apply if the tax treatment is not determined under another provision.

This was because, in some circumstances, this caused an inappropriate outcome as discussed in the following examples from the commentary to the Taxation (Annual Rates for 2015–2016, Research and Development, and Remedial Matters) Bill at 83.

> "For example, an investor purchases shares for $2,000 and settles those shares on a fixed trust. The shares are distributed to the investor two years later, at which time they are worth $3,000. The cost base of the shares under sections FC 1(1)(c) and FC 2(1) would be $3,000, rather than the $2,000 the investor actually paid for the shares. This means that if the shares are held on revenue account, upon sale of those shares, the investor will be taxable on the difference between the sale price and the higher cost base. So for example, if the shares further increased in value to $4,000 and the investor sold them, they would, under current law, be subject to tax on $1,000 ($4,000 sale proceeds – $3,000 new cost base) but should be subject to tax on $2,000 ($4,000 sale proceeds – $2,000 original cost base).
>
> The reverse is also possible. If the value of the shares falls to $1,000, the shares are distributed (thus setting a $1,000 cost base) and are subsequently sold for $1,250, the investor will derive $250 of assessable income even though they have made a $750 economic loss.
>
> …".

In the example above, the cost of revenue account property provision (s DB 23) would provide an appropriate cost base for the shares.

¶6-090 A lease to a beneficiary for less than market value is a capital distribution

Property leased to a beneficiary for no consideration represents a capital distribution and any consequences are the same as for any other capital distribution.

Where property is leased to a beneficiary for a consideration that is less than market consideration, in addition to considering the position of a capital distribution to the beneficiary, it is also necessary to consider whether the income to the trustee arising from the lease is the rental paid or a deemed market rate.

Section GC 5 provides that where a person leases property to a relative for no rent or rent that is less than that considered adequate by the Commissioner, an adequate rental is deemed to be payable under the lease.

Whether s GC 5 has any application where a beneficiary is leasing trust property for less than market consideration is unclear.

Arguably s GC 5 does not apply because a trust cannot lease property to a relative: a trustee not being able to have a relative in the capacity as trustee (Institute of Chartered Accountants of New Zealand seminar paper "An Anthology on Trusts, Stowing Thrones in Grass Houses", May/July 2002 at 12 and 13). There is tacit support for this view in public binding ruling BR Pub 06/02, "Section GD 10 – Income Tax Act 2004 – Rent deemed to be payable by the lessee", which considers the application of s GD 10 (the equivalent provision from the Income Tax Act 2004 to s GC 5), but does not apply the legislation to trustee lessors.

Some commentators take the view that s GC 5 can apply where a trustee leases property to a beneficiary and have suggested that the section extends to situations in which a trustee leases a property to a relative of a beneficiary (See Tax Education Office seminar "Facts on Tax", March/April 1996, question 14).

An alternative interpretation would be to take the position that to the extent that a capital distribution is permissible within the terms of the deed, the application of s GC 5 (if any) to a distribution from a trustee to a beneficiary would be limited to an arrangement between trustee and beneficiary that could be construed as avoidance.

In any event, s GC 5 will only be an issue if the beneficiary is using the property in the derivation of assessable income. The section has no application if the property is used by the beneficiary for private or domestic purposes.

Example

A farmer wishes to transfer land and buildings to a trust and then lease the land and buildings to a partnership between himself and his son. The partnership would not pay a market rental but the rental would be sufficient to cover the trust's costs.

Will s GC 5 apply?

Section GC 5 may apply. Section GC 5 provides that where property is leased to a relative for inadequate or no rental, Inland Revenue can determine an adequate rent and that amount is deemed to be income to the lessor. Conversely, the lessee (the partnership) will be entitled to

> claim a deduction for the amount of the deemed rental. Section GC 5 applies only in respect of any lease of property that is used by the lessee in the derivation of income.
>
> There are differing views on whether s GC 5 applies to trustees, as a trustee cannot have a relative in the trustee's capacity as a trustee.
>
> A prudent approach would be to ensure that a market rental is paid.

Where a trustee is uncertain regarding the application of s GC 5, the trustee could elect not to claim depreciation or other deductions in respect of property (see Chapter 25 – *Goods and Services Tax* regarding the GST treatment of supplies made by a trustee at less than market rate).

¶6-100 Legislation

Income Tax Act 2007

DG 1 WHAT THIS SUBPART DOES

This subpart sets out the rules for the deductibility and apportionment of expenditure incurred for an income year in relation to an asset when the asset is used partly for income-earning purposes and partly for private purposes, and for a time during the income year, the asset is not in use.

DG 3 MEANING OF ASSET FOR THIS SUBPART

DG 3(1) MEANING OF ASSET

For the purposes of this subpart, an **asset**, for an income year, means an item of property described in subsection (2) held by a person described in subsection (3) to the extent to which the item–

(a) is used by the person in the income year partly to derive income and partly for private use; and

(b) is not in use–

  (i) for at least 62 days in the income year; or

  (ii) when the asset is typically used only on working days, for at least 62 working days in the income year.

DG 3(2) WHAT ITEMS OF PROPERTY?

Subsection (1) applies to an asset that, in the complete form in which the person uses it for income-earning purposes,–

(a) is 1 of the following:

  (i) land, including improvements to land:

  (ii) a ship, boat, or craft used in navigation on or under water, whether or not it has a means of propulsion:

  (iii) an aircraft; and

(b) for an item referred to in paragraph (a)(ii) and (iii), has–

(i) a cost to the person of $50,000 or more; or

(ii) a market value on the date of acquisition of the asset of $50,000 or more, if the asset was not acquired at market value; and

(c) includes any related items, things, or accessories pertaining to the asset.

DG 3(3) WHICH PERSONS?

A person excludes a company other than a close company.

DG 3(4) EXCLUSIONS

Despite subsection (2), an asset is excluded from the operation of the rules in this subpart if–

(a) the use of the asset meets the following criteria:

(i) the private use of the asset is minor; and

(ii) the main use of the asset is use in a business that is not a rental or charter business; and

(iii) for a company or a trustee of a trust, the use of the asset places an obligation on the company or the trustee, as applicable, to pay fringe benefit tax or income tax:

(b) the asset is a residential property and its only income-earning use is as a long-term rental property:

(c) *(repealed)*

DG 3(5) MEANING OF MARKET VALUE

For the purposes of this subpart, other than subsection (2)(b)(ii), **market value** means the price at which the asset is provided for use at a particular time or for a particular season–

(a) in the open market; and

(b) freely offered; and

(c) made on ordinary terms; and

(d) to a member of the public at arm's length.

DG 3(6) PARTNERSHIPS AND LOOK-THROUGH COMPANIES

For the purposes of this section, if the asset is held through a partnership or a look-through company, the value of the interests in the asset held by all the partners in the partnership or all the shareholders in the look-through company, as applicable, is aggregated.

DG 3(7) WHAT CONSTITUTES USE

For the purposes of this subpart, the use of an asset is the active use of the asset for its intended purpose.

[...]

FC 3 PROPERTY TRANSFERRED TO SPOUSE, CIVIL UNION PARTNER, OR DE FACTO PARTNER

FC 3(1) WHEN THIS SECTION APPLIES

This section applies in the circumstances described in section FC 1(1)(a) or (b) when property is transferred on a person's death to the surviving spouse, civil union partner, or de facto partner of the deceased person. However, this section does not apply if–

(a) the property is tax-base property; and

(b) a person who is not a close relative of the deceased person is beneficially entitled under the will or intestacy to other property that is tax-base property.

FC 3(2) DISPOSAL TO SPOUSE OR PARTNER

The transfer of property to the surviving spouse, civil union partner, or de facto partner of the deceased person, including any intervening transfer to an executor or administrator, is treated as a transfer of property under a settlement of relationship property under subpart FB (Transfers of relationship property).

FC 3(3) RELATIONSHIP WITH SUBJECT MATTER

Section FC 9 overrides this section for certain transfers of residential land.

[...]

GC 5 LEASES FOR INADEQUATE RENT

GC 5(1) WHEN THIS SECTION APPLIES

This section applies in relation to leases of real and personal property if and to the extent to which–

(a) a property is leased; and

(b) the lease is 1 of the types referred to in subsection (2); and

(c) the lessee uses the property in deriving income; and

(d) no rent is payable, or the Commissioner considers that the rent is less than adequate.

GC 5(1B) WHEN THIS SECTION DOES NOT APPLY

This section does not apply when the property is an asset to which subpart DG (Expenditure related to use of certain assets) applies.

GC 5(2) TYPES OF LEASES

The following types of leases are subject to this section:

(a) a lease by a company:

(b) a lease by a person to a relative or a related company:

(c) a lease by 2 or more persons to a relative or a related company of any of those persons:

(d) a lease by a partnership to a relative of a partner or a related company of the partnership.

GC 5(3) LEASE TREATED AS HAVING ADEQUATE RENT

The lessee is treated as paying, and the lessor is treated as deriving as income, an adequate rent determined by the Commissioner.

GC 5(4) TIMING

The adequate rent is treated as–

(a) paid on the rent payment dates set out in the lease, if any; and

(b) paid on a daily basis on each day of the lease term, if there are no rent payment dates; and

(c) income derived by the lessor on the date on which it is treated as being paid; and

(d) accruing on a daily basis.

GC 5(5) SOME DEFINITIONS

In this section,–

lease means a tenancy of any duration, including a sublease or bailment

related company means a company that is associated with–

(a) in the case of a single lessor, the lessor, 1 or more relatives of the lessor, or a combination of them:

(b) in the case of multiple lessors, including a partnership, any of the lessors, 1 or more relatives of any of the lessors, or a combination of them

rent includes a premium or other consideration for the lease.

HC 14 DISTRIBUTIONS FROM TRUSTS

HC 14(1) TRANSFERS OF VALUE

A trustee makes a **distribution** when the trustee transfers value to a person because the person is a beneficiary of the trust.

HC 14(2) TRANSFERS TO OTHER TRUSTS INCLUDED

Despite subsection (1), a settlement for the benefit of a beneficiary is treated as a transfer of value only—

(a) if the amount or the property being settled would have been beneficiary income of, or a taxable distribution to, a beneficiary, had it been distributed at the time to a beneficiary resident in New Zealand; or

(b) when sections EW 50 or EZ 39 (which relate to forgiveness of debt) applies, if the property being settled is an amount forgiven and treated as paid as described in section EW 44(1) or (2) (Consideration when debt forgiven for natural love and affection) or EZ 39(1).

HC 14(2B) PAYMENT OF INTEREST AT RATE ABOVE MARKET RATE NOT DISTRIBUTION

If a trustee pays to a beneficiary interest on an amount owed to the beneficiary, the payment is not a distribution by the trustee except to the extent to which the interest exceeds the amount given by the rate that is the greater of the market rate and the prescribed rate of interest.

HC 14(3) WHEN DISTRIBUTION MADE

A distribution is made when what is transferred—

(a) vests absolutely in interest in the person; or

(b) is paid to the person.

HC 14(4) MANNER OF DISTRIBUTION

A distribution may be made directly or indirectly, or by 1 transaction or a number of transactions, whether related, connected, or otherwise.

HC 14(5) NIL VALUE OF BENEFICIARY RELATIONSHIP

The fact that a person is, or will become, a beneficiary of a trust does not constitute the giving or receiving of value.

CHAPTER 7

Taxation of Trustee Investment Income

¶7-010 Operating principle

With some exceptions relating to method and thresholds, a trustee accounts for investment income on the same basis as any other person. However, as the trustee-specific provisions do not apply to all trusts, care is required to correctly identify how to calculate investment income and, where applicable, how to determine the most appropriate tax rate.

¶7-020 The taxation rules applicable to investment income depend on the nature of the investment

At the simplest level of investment, such as a direct investment in a term deposit with a bank, a trustee is taxed in the same way as that which applies to any other investor. For example, in the case of investment in an interest-bearing deposit, a trustee earns interest income and, unless a certificate of exemption is held, resident withholding tax (RWT) is deducted when interest is paid.

However, investments such as offshore or portfolio investments are subject to specific tax regimes that have provisions and exemptions that may apply to trustees.

This chapter concerns the regimes that apply to trustee investment in foreign investment funds (FIFs), in controlled foreign companies (CFCs) and in portfolio investments.

Such is the broad range of investment structures, as well as the differing circumstances where beneficiaries have different marginal tax rates, that it is recommended readers should regard the contents of this chapter as indicative only and should take advice with respect to specific investment proposals.

¶7-030 Not all foreign investment gains are taxable

Subparts CQ and EX of the Income Tax Act 2007 comprise rules that tax New Zealand residents' investments in FIFs and CFCs (foreign companies controlled by 5 or fewer New Zealand residents) respectively.

In very broad terms, attributable income in relation to a CFC comprises passive income, such as rent, royalties, certain dividends and interest. While this income is still taxed on an accrual basis, non-attributing active CFCs and non-attributing Australian CFCs are exempt from the requirement to attribute income: ss EX 21B, EX 22.

A CFC is classified as a non-attributing active CFC if less than 5% of its total income is attributable income: ss EX 21C–EX 21E. Where this is the case, neither its income nor its losses are attributable. As a general proposition, if a CFC is resident and subject to tax in Australia, it is a non-attributing Australian CFC and is exempt from attribution: s EX 22.

See *Tax Information Bulletin* ¶218-119 Vol 21, No 8, October/November 2009, Part II at 1.

¶7-040 An exemption for FIF interests of less than $50,000 will not apply to most family trusts

The FIF rules do not apply to natural persons and certain trusts if the total cost of FIF interests is $50,000 or less at all times in an income year.

However, as the exemption for trusts is limited to deceased estates within 5 years of the deceased person's death, trusts settled by the Accident Compensation Corporation and trusts where the settlor is required to pay damages under a court order, the exemption has only limited application: s CQ 5(1), (5).

Where the exemption applies, income from the FIF interests is returned in accordance with ordinary rules.

Example

The DF Trust is a discretionary trust settled by Anika. The beneficiaries include Anika and her 2 children. The DF Trust invested NZ$45,000 in Australian securities that are not exempt from being an attributing interest in a FIF (s CQ 5(1)(c)). The DF Trust typically makes capital distributions to Anika and her 2 children each year. Does the $50,000 exclusion apply?

No. The FIF regime will apply. The $50,000 FIF exclusion only applies to natural persons, deceased estates, trusts settled by the Accident Compensation Corporation and trusts where the settlor is required to pay damages under a court order.

¶7-050 Methods available to calculate FIF income

A person, including a trustee, has FIF income if at any time in an income year the person has an interest in a FIF, and if none of the FIF exemptions apply.

A FIF is defined to include a foreign company, a foreign superannuation scheme, an insurer under a life policy offered or entered into outside of New Zealand, and any other entities treated as FIFs: s EX 28.

Where a person has FIF income (s CQ 5) or a FIF loss (s DN 6), unless an exclusion applies, the income or loss is calculated in accordance with one of 5 methods:

- attributable FIF income
- comparative value (CV)
- deemed rate of return
- fair dividend rate (FDR), or
- cost: s EX 44.

Restrictions apply that limit the adoption of some of the calculation methods. These are referred to below, as part of the outline of each calculation method.

This chapter pays particular attention to the FDR and CV methods, which have trustee-specific provisions. However, for a more comprehensive review of all the calculation methods, see the CCH, *New Zealand Master Tax Guide 2020* at Chapter 26 and subsequent versions.

¶7-060 The FDR method deems FIF income to be 5% of the opening market value

Under the FDR method, FIF income is 5% of the market value of the FIF interest at the start of an income year, regardless of the actual return. The FDR method is available in respect of offshore share investments in foreign companies where those shares are not guaranteed return type shares and the shares have a verifiable market value.

If the FDR method is applied, dividend income is exempt income unless the FIF:

- is resident and taxable in Australia and does not enjoy an exemption from tax for ex-Australian income or offshore banking units, and
- interest was 10% or more at the beginning of the income year.

Since the FDR method applies to FIF interests held on 1 April, it does not create FIF income for FIF interests purchased during the income year (unless the purchase becomes a "quick sale" FIF, as below).

When FIF interests are purchased and sold within the income year, the FDR method recognises the "quick sale" FIF income as the lesser of 5% of the cost of the quick sale FIF interest or the gain realised from the purchase and sale: s EX 52.

¶7-070 Some trustees can change between the FDR and CV methods after the end of each income year

A method used for one period must generally be used in the next period. However, an exception that applies to most testamentary and family trusts allows a trustee to change an unlimited number of times between the FDR and CV methods: s EX 62(8).

For the exception to apply, the trustee must be a trustee of a trust that:

- has no gifting settlor who is not a natural person or a deceased person, and
- is mainly for the benefit of a:
  - natural person for whom the gifting settlor or settlors of the trust have (or if deceased had) natural love and affection, or
  - registered tax charity.
- is not a superannuation scheme.

The minimum period a method must be used is a single income year.

¶7-080 Same method must be applied to entire portfolio

If a trust meets the requirements to change between methods, all FIF income must be calculated in accordance with the same method. It is not permissible to have some FIF income calculated under the FDR method and the balance calculated under the CV method.

Where it is possible to switch between methods, it will generally be the case that trustees will use the FDR method for their FIF interests in a year when the actual return on their portfolio (including unrealised gains and losses) is more than 5%, and the trustees will use the CV method when it is less than 5% (recognising that the trustee will not be able to claim a deduction for any net loss under the CV method).

¶7-090 The trustee is taxed on net gain if the CV method is used

Some investors, including trustees of some complying trusts, may elect to use the CV method as an alternative to the FDR method.

If used, the CV method provides that the investor's taxable FIF income is the net gain in value for the year together with dividends and net sale proceeds.

The CV method is preferable to the FDR method where the actual and unrealised gain is less than 5%. However, as discussed above, if a trustee uses the CV method as an alternative to the FDR method, the trustee must apply the CV method to the trust's entire portfolio of FIF interests.

¶7-100 Only trustees of certain complying trusts can use the CV method

The CV method is available to a trustee of a complying trust if the trust (s EX 46(6)):

- has no gifting settlor who is not a natural person or a deceased person, and
- is established mainly for the benefit of:
    - a natural person for whom the gifting settlor, or settlors, has natural love and affection (or had natural love and affection while alive), or
    - a tax charity
- is not a superannuation scheme.

Note that the natural love and affection requirement must be met at all times, not just when the trust was settled. See *Tax Information Bulletin* ¶203-132 Vol 20, No 3, April 2008 at 114.

Example

Jeff, a serious wine enthusiast, settled Jeff's Trust. The sole beneficiary of Jeff's Trust is the Wine-buffs Charitable Trust, which is not a tax charity. Jeff's Trust has A$55,000 invested in a FIF. Can the trustee use the CV method to calculate the FIF income?

No. Jeff's Trust was established mainly for the benefit of a charity. Jeff cannot have natural love and affection for the charity (regardless of how enthusiastic he is about wine). As the natural love and affection condition is not met, and the charity is not a taxable charity, the CV method cannot be applied.

¶7-110 Gifting settlor defined to include any person who has made a settlement onto a trust

A gifting settlor is a natural person, including a deceased person, who has made a settlement onto a trust and includes persons that would not be recognised as a settlor for trust law purposes.

Where a trust receives property by way of a resettlement, the gifting settlor is not the trustee of the resettling trust, but the settlor of the trust making the resettlement. This is the case whether the resettlement is directly from one trust to another, or through the trustee of other trusts. See s EX 46(12)(a).

¶7-120 A trust is not ineligible to apply the CV method only because a resettling trust has a corporate trustee

The definition of gifting settlor excludes the trustee of a trust: s EX 46(12)(b). If a trust receives property by way of resettlement from a trust with a corporate trustee, the gifting settlor is not the corporate trustee but the settlor (directly or indirectly) of the resettling trust. A trust is not ineligible to apply the CV method only because a resettling trust has a corporate trustee.

¶7-130 A trust that has received a settlement from a non-natural person is not eligible to apply the CV method

If any settlement is made onto a trust by a company or another trust that does not meet the requirements to apply the CV method, the trustee will not be able to use the CV method. Given the broad definitions of settlor and settlement, which includes any transfer of value, vigilance is required to ensure that the requirements of the CV method are met from year to year.

An example of a trust that is ineligible to use the CV method is one that has received a settlement from a related company. In this regard, care must be taken to identify all settlements, as these are not always obvious.

Settlements that will make a trust ineligible to use the CV method include where a company makes assets available to a trust:

- at below market value
- for a debt back at below market rates.

¶7-140 Losses cannot be offset using the CV method unless the FDR method is not available

Unless the CV method is used because the FDR method cannot be used (as is the case with guaranteed return type investments), no deduction is available if the FIF investment declines in value.

If a FIF interest loses all value in a year so that the closing value is less than the opening value, the resulting loss cannot be offset against income: s EX 51(8).

However, FIF losses can be offset against FIF income if the CV method is used.

Example

Trust A holds shares in 2 foreign companies. Applying the CV method gives FIF income of $10,000 in respect of the shares in one company and a loss of $6,000 in respect of shares in the other. Trust A will be entitled to offset the loss from one FIF interest against the income from the other FIF interest and will, therefore, have overall FIF income of $4,000.

Trust B holds shares in 2 foreign companies. Applying the CV method gives FIF income of $10,000 in respect of the shares in one company and a loss of $16,000 in respect of shares in the other. Although Trust B has suffered an overall loss of $6,000, that loss will be reduced to zero. Accordingly, Trust B will have no overall FIF income in respect of the 2 investments, but no FIF loss either.

¶7-150 FIF loss cannot be distributed as beneficiary income

Where an FIF loss is allowed, these losses, as with losses calculated under other income tax provisions, cannot be allocated to beneficiaries. This means that where a trustee has net income that has been reduced by the application of a FIF loss, care must be taken in determining the amount of income that can be distributed as beneficiary income from both a trust and tax law perspective. See further at Chapter 3 – *Beneficiary Income.*

¶7-160 FIF income is 5% of the cost of the FIF interest if the cost method is applied

The cost method may be adopted in circumstances where the FDR method is available but the market value of the FIF interest is not readily verifiable (s EX 46(9)).

If the cost method is applied, FIF income is 5% of the cost of the FIF interest: s EX 56. The cost method does not recognise income for the year of acquisition of the FIF. This is because there is no acquisition cost at the start of that year. Under the cost method, FIF income also includes 5% of the cost of any FIF interest purchased or sold during the income year. The cost of the FIF interest may be reset every 5 years by an independent valuation.

¶7-170 The deemed rate of return method applies a rate of return specified by regulation

The deemed rate of return method may be adopted for a FIF shareholding where the attributing interest is a non-ordinary share and it is not practical to use the CV method because the market value of the interest cannot be determined at the end of the income year (ss EX 46(5), EX 47).

Under the deemed rate of return method, FIF income is the book value of the FIF interest multiplied by a rate of return prescribed by regulation: s EX 55.

New orders specifying the rate to apply to a tax year are set after the end of the tax year to which they apply. The latest deemed rate of return at the time of publication was that for the 2019–20 year, a rate of 5.05%.

¶7-180 Receiving FIF income does not make a complying trust a non-complying trust

Regardless of the method used to calculate FIF income, a complying trust will not become a non-complying trust only because the trustee is in receipt of FIF income.

A foreign-sourced amount will not be exempt income under s CW 54 if the requirements of a complying trust are not met (s HC 10) if the trust has a New Zealand resident settlor or if the settlor died in New Zealand: s HC 26.

¶7-190 The FIF rules apply to the legal rather than the beneficial owner of an FIF interest

The FIF rules apply to the legal owner of the investment. This means that the FIF rules do not apply directly to a beneficiary receiving a trust distribution derived from a foreign investment.

Example

Amy is a beneficiary of a New Zealand complying trust that holds some shares in a United Kingdom company. For the purposes of applying the FIF rules, it is the trust that is treated as holding the FIF investment, not Amy. Therefore, the FIF rules do not apply to Amy in respect of the United Kingdom shares.

¶7-200 The CFC regime applies to trustee investors

The CFC regime applies to trustee investors in the same way as it applies to other taxpayers.

However, there is a specific provision (s EX 19) that addresses the situation where a CFC derives a taxable distribution from a non-complying trust and an investor has or would have had attributed CFC income if the taxable distribution was included in the CFC's net attributable CFC income.

Where that is the case, a pro-rated amount of additional CFC income is attributed to the investor. The tax rate on this income is the 45% rate that applies to taxable distributions.

¶7-210 CFC income is not attributable while transitional resident rules apply

A transitional resident, in the process of migrating to New Zealand, is exempt from New Zealand tax from foreign-sourced amounts, including FIF and CFC income.

Example

X and Y are transitional residents. Together with their children, X and Y are beneficiaries of the Li Trust. X is the sole settlor of the Li Trust, which was settled by X before his arrival in New Zealand. The Li Trust owns 98% of the shares in USCO Ltd, a company incorporated in the United States. USCO Ltd is a share trader and pays tax on its profits in the United States. USCO Ltd pays regular dividends to the Li Trust.

Is any CFC income attributable to the Li Trust during the 4-year transitional period?

No. CFC income is not attributable to the Li Trust as long as the transitional resident rules apply.

¶7-220 Trustees have disclosure obligations in respect of FIF and CFC interests

A trustee with an attributing interest in a FIF or an income or control interest in a foreign company must disclose the existence and nature of the interest to the Commissioner together with any other information required: Tax Administration Act, s 61, and see *Tax Information Bulletin* ¶182-110 Vol 18, No 2, March 2006 at 28.

There are exemptions from disclosure. See s 61(2) of the Tax Administration Act.

¶7-230 PIE regime allows the investor to choose a tax rate that aligns with the underlying investor's tax rate

An extensive analysis of the PIE regime, which came into effect in October 2007, is beyond the scope of this book. However, as trustee investors in PIEs will need to decide what tax rate to elect, a basic understanding is helpful.

The PIE regime (contained largely in Subparts HM and LS of the Income Tax Act) was introduced to align the tax treatment of individual investors who invest directly in shares with those who invest using financial intermediaries (such as managed funds). These parts of the Income Tax Act provide that certain financial intermediaries (called portfolio investment entities or PIEs) have a tax treatment that is more closely aligned with the tax treatment of their underlying investors.

There are 5 types of PIEs:

- *a multi-rate PIE*, which is an unlisted entity that calculates and pays tax on the basis of the portfolio investor rate notified by its investors and which may maintain more than one portfolio investor class
- *a listed PIE*, which is a company listed on a recognised exchange in New Zealand which has only one portfolio investor class and which is subject to the company rate of income tax
- *a benefit fund PIE*, which is a registered superannuation scheme operating on the principle of unallocated funding which does not attribute income to investors
- *a life fund PIE*, which is a discrete investment fund maintained by a life insurer with investment returns directly linked to benefits payable under life insurance policies associated with the fund
- *a foreign investment PIE*, which is further classified into a zero rate and variable-rate foreign investment PIE. See s HM 2(2).

The regime provides that the income of a PIE is taxed using a tax rate based on the tax rates of the underlying investors. Gains realised on New Zealand equities (and certain Australian equities) held by a PIE will not be taxed. This treatment aligns the tax treatment for an investor through a PIE with the tax treatment of an individual direct investor. However, limitations in the tax rates available to trustees mean that there is limited ability to align the applicable tax rate with the marginal rate that applies to the trust's beneficiaries.

¶7-240 Multi-rate PIEs are the most common type of PIE

A multi-rate PIE is a company, superannuation fund or a group investment fund that:

- meets the requirements of s HM 7
- has made a valid election choosing to be a multi-rate PIE
- has not chosen to cancel its PIE status, and
- is not a benefit fund PIE.

A multi-rate PIE must generally have at least 90% (by value of its assets) invested in:

- land
- financial arrangements
- excepted financial arrangements, and/or
- rights or options in any of the 3 categories above.

In very general terms, the investment income of a multi-rate PIE is notionally attributed to its respective investors on the basis of their investment in the multi-rate PIE, and income tax is paid by the multi-rate PIE on behalf of those investors based on their individual income attributions and at a tax rate notified to the PIE by each investor (the notified investor rate). This resembles the liability that would arise if the investors had made the investments separately.

A multi-rate PIE must distribute income to investors after deducting the appropriate tax liability. A multi-rate PIE can choose how frequently it attributes PIE income, expenses, losses and credits to its investors. Attributions are made for an investor as a member of an investor class. The attribution period selected by a multi-rate PIE determines the period and frequency at which attributed PIE income and losses are attributed to investors. The attribution period can be daily, monthly, quarterly or annually, and on investor exit. A multi-rate PIE cannot elect an attribution period that is longer than its calculation period. If a multi-rate PIE makes no election, its attribution period is daily.

A multi-rate PIE can also choose how often it calculates its investors' income tax liability during an income year. A calculation period may cover a number of attribution periods. A multi-rate PIE can elect to calculate its investors' income tax liability quarterly, as a provisional taxpayer, or annually and on investor exit. In that case, the entity either pays tax when the investors exit the entity, under s HM 42, or, for investors who remain in the entity, within one month of the end of the tax year. The tax liability would be the PIE tax liability for all calculation periods of the tax year. If no election is made, a multi-rate PIE is required to calculate its investors' income tax liability quarterly.

The multi-rate PIE may receive a tax credit for an investor's attributed PIE loss. This is provided the investor is not a zero-rated investor (or an exiting investor who is treated as a zero-rated investor: see s HM 61).

¶7-250 Trustee investors in multi-rate PIEs must choose a prescribed investor rate

The prescribed investor rate applied by a multi-rate PIE varies from investor to investor.

From 1 October 2010 the prescribed investor rates available to trustees are (see sch 6):

- 0% if the trust is:
    - a charity that is registered under the Charities Act 2005, or
    - if the trustee has not chosen a 17.5% or 28% rate

  (these investors are termed "zero-rated investors")
- 10.5% for the trustees of certain testamentary trusts
- 17.5%, or
- 28%.

The appropriate prescribed investor rate for a trustee investor in a multi-rate PIE will depend on the circumstances of the trust and its beneficiaries.

¶7-260 Zero-rated investors are taxable on their attributed PIE income under the usual tax rules applying to trusts

Where a trustee has PIE income, this income will not be excluded income of the trust where the 0% or 17.5% prescribed investor rate is chosen. If the trustee elects 0%, no tax will be paid by the PIE in respect of the income attributed to the trust, and the trust will have to pay tax on the income (after taking into account tax credits such as RWT, imputation credits and foreign tax credits which are attributed to the trust).

Where there are PIE losses, the trustee will only get a deduction for the losses if it has elected a 0% rate. That said, although the trustee cannot claim a deduction for losses if it elects the 17.5% rate, it will still benefit from the losses. This is normally done by adjusting the trustee's interest in the PIE.

As the trustee will derive the benefit of the losses whether it elects a 0% or 17.5% prescribed investor rate, the choice of which option is more beneficial may be based on whether the trustee has other income that the deduction will offset. If the trustee does not have other income, it may prefer to obtain the benefit of the losses by way of increasing the number of units in the PIE. The trustee may also prefer to take the option that ensures the tax position is dealt with by the PIE, so the trust does not have to deal with the compliance issues of including the deduction for PIE income in its tax return.

¶7-265 Electing a 17.5% prescribed investor rate

If the trustee elects 17.5%, the PIE will pay tax in relation to the trustee's attributed income at 17.5%. The trustee will include the income in its tax return and get a tax credit in respect of the tax paid by the PIE on that income.

¶7-270 Charitable trusts can only elect a 0% rate

The trustee of a charity that is registered under the Charities Act 2005 (a tax charity) is only permitted to use the prescribed investor rate of 0%. See s HM 57.

¶7-275 Certain testamentary trusts are entitled to elect a rate of 10.5%

A trustee of a testamentary trust can elect a prescribed investor rate of 10.5% if the trust is a trust to which s HC 37 applies. That is, a trust that is not subject to the minor beneficiary rule. See ¶10-150. This provision means that the trustee may be able to ensure a more appropriate tax rate for minor beneficiaries. See sch 6 (table 1 row 7).

¶7-280 The 28% PIE rate may not be a final tax if no election is made

While it is correct that the PIE tax is meant to be a final tax, this is only the case for a trust where the trust has actively elected a 28% prescribed investor rate. If no election has been made, the PIE tax is not final. The default rate of 28% will apply and the income must be included in the trust's tax return. This can potentially lead to a top up tax of 5% being paid on the income or treated as beneficiary income and taxed at the beneficiaries' marginal rates.

If the 28% rate is elected and this subsequently proves to be too high, there is no tax credit available in respect of any overpaid tax.

As with FIF income, income earned by a PIE that is attributable to a New Zealand investor who is not a natural person is taxable to the investor at the time the income is earned, regardless of whether the income is realised by the investor.

¶7-285 Care is required to elect the most appropriate rate where a trust has multiple beneficiaries on different marginal tax rates

If a trust has beneficiaries on marginal rates that are both above and below 28%, this makes the choice of the prescribed investor rate difficult. If the 0% rate is elected and the income allocated by the PIE is treated as beneficiary income, this is advantageous where the beneficiaries are on lower marginal tax rates, as the income may be able to be taxed at the lower rate. However, beneficiaries taxed at the higher rate will be disadvantaged as they lose the benefit of the effective cap of 28%. Accordingly, beneficiaries on higher marginal rates would prefer the trustees to elect a 28% portfolio investor rate.

Where this is the case, the trustee needs to consider the election of the portfolio investor rate carefully.

Example

Hugh has settled a trust for his 2 children. His autistic son, Karl, has no personal income. His daughter, Elizabeth, a well-regarded psychiatrist, is in paid employment and is taxed at the highest marginal rate. What is most appropriate portfolio investor rate for the trust's PIE investment?

As a general rule the 28% rate should be elected where taxable income would otherwise be taxed at the trustee rate of 33%, or would be taxable in the hands of beneficiaries whose marginal tax rate is also 33%. The 0% rate should be elected where trust income is to be distributed to beneficiaries on the lower marginal rates.

An alternative option would be for the trustee to consider investing in 2 different PIEs. This would allow the trustee to elect prescribed investor rates that are suitable for both Karl and Elizabeth.

Income under the PIE rules can include notional income that has not been received by the trust (eg FIF income calculated under the FDR method). As discussed previously, that income may not be able to be paid to or vested in a beneficiary, and so as a matter of prudence should be taxed as trustee income.

¶7-290 The choice of prescribed investor rate will determine whether the trustee can offset other losses

If a trustee has elected a prescribed investor rate of 0% for PIE income, losses from other sources can be offset against the PIE income. However, if a 28% rate is elected, the PIE income will be exempt income and so, in the absence of other income, there will be no assessable income against which the loss can be offset.

Example

Julie's family trust owns 4 rental properties in Wanaka. The trust also has a large cash deposit with a New Zealand financial institution that is a registered PIE. None of the rental properties are profitable. Can the rental losses be offset against the PIE income?

The answer depends on the trust's prescribed investor rate. If the trustee has elected a prescribed investor rate of 0%, the PIE income will flow through to the trust and can be offset against the rental losses. However, if the trustee has elected a prescribed investor rate of 28%, the income earned from the cash deposit is excluded income, and there will be no assessable income to offset the losses against.

¶7-300 Trustee investors in a PIE may need to comply with the provisional tax regime

The prescribed investor rate chosen by the trustee will have an impact on whether income from the PIE must be accounted for by the trust as trustee income (or by the beneficiaries if the income is distributed as beneficiary income). If insufficient tax is paid at the PIE level, it may expose the trustee to an additional income tax liability. This means that trustee investors may be required to comply with the provisional tax regime.

Therefore, trustee investors will have to consider how best to meet the trust's taxation obligations, particularly if the trust has no other cash assets.

¶7-310 Listed PIEs pay tax at a flat rate of 28%

A listed PIE is a company that is listed on a recognised exchange in New Zealand or an unlisted company that satisfies the requirements of s HM 18. It does not include a life fund PIE. Section HM 18 allows unlisted companies to be treated as listed PIEs if they meet a number of criteria. The company must have at least 100 shareholders and unless it has qualified for an extension must be listed on a recognised exchange within 2 years of it electing to be a listed PIE in order to retain that status.

A listed PIE is generally subject to tax in the same manner as a conventional company, although subject to the rules for portfolio investment entities (PIEs) generally – such as the treatment as excluded income of gains from the sale of New Zealand shares and Australian ASX listed shares.

A listed PIE must attach full imputation credits (to the extent available) to distributions.

A dividend or distribution derived by an investor in a listed PIE may be excluded income if the investor is a natural person or trustee investor resident in New Zealand who does not include the receipt in a return of income. A natural person or a trustee may elect to treat the distribution as a taxable amount and use any excess imputation credits as a credit against tax on other taxable income. See *Tax Information Bulletin* ¶193-114 Vol 19, No 3, April 2007 at 50. A deliberate feature of the taxation of investors in a listed PIE is to allow the returns of a New Zealand resident trustee to be subject to the company rate of income tax rather than the trustee rate (see *Tax Information Bulletin* ¶203-133 Vol 20, No 3, April 2008 at 117).

Example

A trust has shares in a listed PIE. The trustee distributes the trust's income to the beneficiaries who are on the lowest marginal tax rate. The dividend advice shows an "excluded distribution" of $120. No imputation credits are attached.

Can the distribution be treated as assessable income and distributed as beneficiary income?

No. Although a New Zealand resident trustee investor can elect to include a distribution from a listed PIE as assessable income, this only applies to the extent that the distribution is fully imputed. This is to ensure that income that has not been taxed at the listed PIE level (eg capital gains from the sale of shares in a New Zealand company) can be distributed to investors, without the investors paying tax on that income. A listed PIE must attach full imputation credits (to the extent available) to distributions.

In this case, the distribution is excluded income, because the distribution is not fully imputed. Therefore, the trust cannot include the distribution as assessable income or distribute the excluded distribution as beneficiary income.

¶7-320 A benefit fund PIE does not allocate income

A benefit fund PIE is a superannuation scheme or workplace savings scheme (within the meaning of s 6(1) of the Financial Markets Conduct Act 2013) that operates on the principle of unallocated funding.

Unlike a multi-rate PIE, a benefit fund PIE does not allocate income to investors and its tax liability is not determined by reference to investors' tax rates. Instead, a benefit fund PIE is subject to tax on its taxable income at the 28% flat rate applicable to "widely-held superannuation funds". In respect of distributions from a benefit fund PIE, they should generally not be taxable to the investor.

¶7-330 Legislation

Income Tax Act 2007

CP 1 ATTRIBUTED INCOME OF INVESTORS IN MULTI-RATE PIES

CP 1(1) WHEN THIS SECTION APPLIES

This section applies when a multi-rate PIE attributes an amount of income for an income year calculated under sections HM 35, HM 35C, and HM 36 (which relate to the attribution of amounts to investors) to a person who is an investor in the PIE.

CP 1(2) INCOME

The amount is income of the person in the income year of the person in which the PIE's income year ends.

[...]

CQ 5 WHEN FIF INCOME ARISES

CQ 5(1) GENERAL RULE

A person has **FIF income** in an income year if–

(a) at any time in the year, the person has–

  (i) rights in a foreign company, or a foreign superannuation scheme, or an entity listed in schedule 25, part A (Foreign investment funds); or

  (ii) rights under a life insurance policy issued by a non-resident; and

(b) at that time, the rights are an attributing interest in a FIF under section EX 29 (Attributing interests in FIFs); and

(c) at that time, the rights are not exempt from being an attributing interest in a FIF under any of–

  (i) the exemption for ASX-listed Australian companies in section EX 31 (Exemption for ASX-listed Australian companies):

  [...]

  (xiv) the annuity or pension exemption in section EX 43 (Non-resident's pension or annuity exception):

  [...]

(d) if the person is a natural person,–

  (i) the total cost, calculated under section EX 68 (Measurement of cost), of attributing interests in FIFs that the person holds at any time in the year when the person is a New Zealand resident is more than $50,000:

  (ii) the person includes, in a return for the year, FIF income or loss from an attributing interest in a FIF:

(iii) the person has, in the return for 1 of the preceding 4 income years (the **earlier year**), included FIF income or loss from attributing interests in FIFs with a total cost of $50,000 or less, calculated under section EX 68, at all times in the earlier year when the person is a New Zealand resident; and

(e) if the person is acting as trustee of a trust that meets the requirements of subsection (5),–

(i) the total cost, calculated under section EX 68, of attributing interests in FIFs that the person holds at any time in the year is more than $50,000:

(ii) the person includes, in a return for the year, FIF income or loss from an attributing interest in a FIF:

(iii) the person has, in the return for 1 of the preceding 4 income years (the **earlier year**), included FIF income or loss from attributing interests in FIFs with a total cost of $50,000 or less, calculated under section EX 68, at all times in the earlier year; and

(f) at any time in the year, the person is a New Zealand resident who is not a transitional resident and holds the attributing interest; and

(g) under the relevant calculation method chosen by the person, an income amount is calculated for the year under sections EX 44 to EX 56 (which relate to the calculation of FIF income or loss), EX 60 or EX 61 (which relate to top-up FIF income).

[...]

CQ 5(5) REQUIREMENTS FOR TRUSTEES

Subsection (1)(e) applies to the trustee of a trust for an income year if–

(a) the trust is of the estate of a deceased person and the income year begins on or before the day that is 5 years after the person's death:

(b) the settlor of the trust–

(i) is a relative or legal guardian of a beneficiary of the trust, or a person associated with a relative or legal guardian of a beneficiary of the trust; and

(ii) is required by a court order to pay damages or compensation to the beneficiary:

(c) the settlor of the trust–

(i) is the estate of a deceased person; and

(ii) is required by a court order to settle on the trust the proceeds of damages or compensation for the beneficiaries of the trust:

(d) the settlor of the trust is the Accident Compensation Corporation.

[...]

CX 56 ATTRIBUTED INCOME OF CERTAIN INVESTORS IN MULTI-RATE PIES

CX 56(1) WHEN THIS SECTION APPLIES

This section applies when an investor in a multi-rate PIE derives income attributed under section CP 1 (Attributed income of investors in multi-rate PIEs) in an income year, and—

(a) the prescribed investor rate for the investor in the relevant calculation period is more than zero; and

(b) that rate is not more than the notified investor rate in relation to the investor when the PIE calculates—

  (i) its income tax liability under section HM 47 (Calculation of tax liability or tax credit of multi-rate PIEs) in relation to the income; or

  (ii) a voluntary payment under section HM 45 (Voluntary payments) that is intended to be a final payment of its income tax liability in relation to the income.

CX 56(1B) WHEN THIS SECTION ALSO APPLIES

This section also applies when a foreign investment PIE attributes income to an investor who is, for the calculation period in which the amount is attributed,—

(a) a notified foreign investor other than a person referred to in section HM 55D(6):

(b) a transitional resident who has chosen a prescribed investor rate referred to in schedule 6, table 1, row 10 (Prescribed rates: PIE investments and retirement scheme contributions):

(c) a transitional resident when the calculation period falls in the tax year in which the person becomes or ceases to be a transitional resident:

(d) an investor in the PIE when the calculation period falls in the tax year in which the person either becomes or ceases to be resident in New Zealand.

CX 56(1C) WHEN THIS SECTION ALSO APPLIES

When a trustee of a trust is an investor in a multi-rate PIE and an election is made in an income year (the election year) for the trust under section HC 33 (Choosing to satisfy income tax liability of trustee), this section also applies to the trustee for the income years that end before the election year and for which the election applies.

CX 56(2) WHEN THIS SECTION DOES NOT APPLY

This section does not apply when—

(a) the PIE calculates its income tax liability using the quarterly calculation option under section HM 43 (Quarterly calculation option) and the amount is attributed to an investor who is treated under section HM 61 (Certain exiting investors zero-rated) as zero-rated:

(b) an amount of attributed PIE income is derived by a trustee who has chosen a prescribed investor rate referred to in schedule 6, table 1, row 5 or 7, as applicable:

[...]

CX 56(3) EXCLUDED INCOME

The amount is excluded income of the investor.

[...]

EX 19 TAXABLE DISTRIBUTION FROM NON-COMPLYING TRUST

EX 19(1) APPLICATION OF THIS SECTION

This section applies when–

(a) a CFC derives a taxable distribution from a non-complying trust in an accounting period; and

(b) a person has attributed CFC income or loss from the CFC for the period, or would have if the taxable distribution were included in the CFC's net attributable CFC income.

EX 19(2) ADDITIONAL ATTRIBUTED CFC INCOME

The taxable distribution is excluded under section EX 21(32) when calculating the CFC's net attributable CFC income or loss, and instead the person has additional attributed CFC income.

EX 19(3) CALCULATION OF ADDITIONAL ATTRIBUTED CFC INCOME

The amount of the additional attributed CFC income is calculated using the formula–

$$\text{person's income interest in CFC for accounting period} \times \text{taxable distribution.}$$

EX 19(4) NON-COMPLYING TRUST TAX RATE

The person is liable for income tax on the additional attributed CFC income at the rate in schedule 1 (Basic tax rates: income tax, ESCT, RSCT, RWT, and attributed fringe benefits) that applies to amounts under section HC 19 (Taxable distributions from non-complying trusts).

EX 19(5) DISCLOSURE RESTRICTIONS ON GREY LIST CFCS

(repealed)

[...]

EX 44 FIVE CALCULATION METHODS

EX 44(1) USE OF 1 METHOD

If the tests in section CQ 5 (When FIF income arises) or DN 6 (When FIF loss arises) are met, the amount of a person's FIF income or loss from an attributing interest is calculated under–

(a) *(repealed)*

(b) the attributable FIF income method; or

(c) the comparative value method; or

(d) the deemed rate of return method; or

(e) the fair dividend rate method; or

(f) the cost method.

EX 44(2) CHOOSING METHOD

The person must choose which calculation method applies by completing their return of income accordingly, but the choice is limited by sections EX 46, EX 47, EX 47B, EX 48, and EX 62.

[...]

EX 46 LIMITS ON CHOICE OF CALCULATION METHODS

EX 46(1) SAME METHOD FOR SAME FIF

If a person has 2 or more attributing interests in the same FIF for the same period, the person must use the same calculation method for calculating FIF income or loss from each interest in that period, except to the extent to which–

(a) the interests are of different classes; and

(b) the choice of method for a class is limited by this section or section EX 47, EX 48, or EX 62.

EX 46(2) ACCOUNTING PROFITS METHOD

(repealed)

EX 46(3) ATTRIBUTABLE FIF INCOME METHOD

A person may use the attributable FIF income method to calculate FIF income or loss from an attributing interest in a FIF for an accounting period only if the person can provide to the Commissioner, if requested, sufficient information to enable the Commissioner to check the calculations required by section EX 50 and,–

(a) at all times in the accounting period,–

  (i) the FIF is a company; and

  (ii) the item "income interest" given by section EX 50(4) for the person and the FIF is 10% or more; and

  (iii) the person is not a portfolio investment entity:

(b) the FIF is a CFC and the person cannot determine the market value of the attributing interest at the beginning of the accounting period except by independent valuation and neither the person nor a person who has a direct income interest of 10% or more in the FIF is–

(i) a listed company:

(ii) a group investment fund:

(iii) a portfolio investment entity:

(iv) a superannuation scheme:

(v) a unit trust:

(vi) a trustee of a trust with a beneficiary described in 1 or more of subparagraphs (i) to (iv).

EX 46(4) DEEMED RATE OF RETURN METHOD: GENERAL RULE

(repealed)

EX 46(5) DEEMED RATE OF RETURN METHOD

A person may use the deemed rate of return method to calculate FIF income or loss from an attributing interest in a FIF only if the person is required by section EX 47 to use the deemed rate of return method for the interest.

EX 46(6) COMPARATIVE VALUE METHOD: SHARES IN FOREIGN COMPANIES

A person may use the comparative value method to calculate FIF income or loss from an attributing interest in a FIF that is a share in a foreign company for an income year only if–

(a) the person is a natural person:

(b) the person is the trustee of a trust that–

(i) has no gifting settlor who is not a natural person or deceased person; and

(ii) at all times in the income year, is a complying trust for a distribution made at the time; and

(iii) is, at all times in the income year, mainly for the benefit of a natural person for whom the gifting settlors of the trust have natural love and affection (or had natural love and affection when alive) or is mainly for the benefit of an organisation or trust with income that is exempt income under section CW 41 or CW 42 (which relate to the income of charities); and

(iv) is not a superannuation scheme:

(c) *(repealed)*

(d) the share is a non-ordinary share described in subsection (10):

[...]

EX 46(12) MEANING OF GIFTING SETTLOR

A **gifting settlor**, for a trust (the **relevant trust**), means a person who–

(a) makes a transfer of value, by disposing of property, to the trustee of–

  (i) the relevant trust:

  (ii) a trust with a trustee who settles property on the relevant trust, directly or through the trustees of other trusts; and

(b) is not the trustee of a trust.

[...]

EX 62 LIMITS ON CHANGES OF METHOD

[...]

EX 62(8) REPEATED CHANGES BETWEEN FAIR DIVIDEND RATE METHOD AND COMPARATIVE VALUE METHOD

A person may change more than once from the fair dividend rate method to the comparative value method and from the comparative value method to the fair dividend rate method if the person is a natural person or the trustee of a trust that–

(a) has no gifting settlor who is not a natural person or deceased person; and

(b) at all times in the income year, is a complying trust for a distribution made at the time; and

(c) is–

  (i) at all times in the income year, mainly for the benefit of a natural person for whom the gifting settlors of the trust have natural love and affection, or had natural love and affection when alive:

  (ii) mainly for the benefit of an organisation or trust with income that is exempt income under section CW 41 or CW 42 (which relate to the income of charities); and

(d) is not a superannuation scheme.

[...]

HM 57 PRESCRIBED INVESTOR RATES FOR CERTAIN INVESTORS: 0%

An investor (a **zero-rated investor**) in a multi-rate PIE has a prescribed investor rate of 0% if they are resident in New Zealand and are–

[...]

(f) a person who derives income as a trustee and does not choose a rate under schedule 6, table 1, row 3, 5, or 7.

[...]

Table 1

SCHEDULE 6 PRESCRIBED RATES: PIE INVESTMENTS AND RETIREMENT SCHEME CONTRIBUTIONS

The prescribed investor rate for a person who is an investor in a multi-rate PIE is set out in table 1.

Row	Conditions	Prescribed rate
[...]		
3	For a person who– (a) is resident in New Zealand and who derives income for the relevant tax year as a trustee of a trust other than a trust with income that is exempt income under section CW 41 or CW 42; and (b) notifies this rate for the relevant tax year.	0.280
[...]		
5	For a person who– (a) is resident in New Zealand and derives income for the relevant tax year as a trustee of a trust other than a trust with income that is exempt income under section CW 41 or CW 42; and (b) notifies this rate for the relevant tax year.	0.175
[...]		
7	For a person who– (a) is resident in New Zealand and derives income for the relevant tax year as a trustee of a testamentary trust to which section HC 37 applies other than a trust with income that is exempt income under section CW 41 or CW 42; and (b) notifies this rate for the relevant tax year.	0.105
[...]		
8	For a person who is a zero-rated investor or an investor treated under section HM 61 as zero-rated.	0.000

How to use this table

Find the applicable condition, in the second column, in order to find the relevant rate to apply, in the third column.

CHAPTER 8

Migration of Settlors, Trustees and Beneficiaries

¶8-010 Operating principle

There is no universal test of residence for trusts (other than unit trusts), trusts not being entities that can exist independently of the trust's trustees and beneficiaries: *North* v *C of IR* (1985) 7 NZTC 5,192 at 5,193.

For this reason, trusts as such cannot migrate. However, through the application of tax treatments that are dependent on the residence of persons connected with a trust, trusts can, in effect, migrate from one tax jurisdiction to another.

In certain circumstances, income or distributions from a trust can become subject to taxation in multiple jurisdictions, as the taxation treatment of trusts differs in different jurisdictions.

¶8-020 Trustee's residence does not determine tax liability

The policy behind the taxation of trusts in New Zealand is that the residence of a trustee does not determine tax liability. Instead the liability for taxation turns in most part on the residence of the settlor, as the trust's economic agent, or the beneficiary in receipt of beneficiary income. See interpretation statement IS 18/01, "Taxation of trusts – income tax" at 1.32, which provides that:

> "1.32 The settlor-based taxation approach is a change from the rules that applied before 1 April 1988. Previously, foreign-sourced amounts derived by the trustees of a trust with New Zealand resident settlors were not subject to tax in New Zealand where the trustees were non-resident. The settlor-based taxation regime was chosen because it was considered too easy to avoid tax on foreign-sourced amounts under the old regime by appointing non-resident trustees. It was also considered that, in economic terms, the residence of the settlor provides a more appropriate basis for taxing foreign-sourced amounts derived by a trustee."

Accordingly, income sourced in New Zealand is taxable regardless of where the recipient of that income is resident and regardless of whether the recipient derives the income in the capacity of beneficiary or trustee.

Where the income has a foreign source, the liability to taxation generally turns on the recipient's residence.

The rules that determine residence for a person are not modified to reflect a person's capacity as a beneficiary, trustee or settlor.

¶8-030 Taxation of beneficiary income is subject to residence

The taxation of beneficiary income depends on the residence of the beneficiary and the source of the income. This is the case regardless of where the trustee and settlor are resident: *FC of T* v *Belford* (1952) 10 ATD 105; 88 CLR 589.

Foreign-sourced beneficiary income is taxable in New Zealand if the beneficiary is resident in New Zealand.

However, foreign-sourced income derived by a non-resident beneficiary is not taxable in New Zealand.

Beneficiary income sourced in New Zealand will be taxable whether the beneficiary is resident in New Zealand. If a beneficiary is non-resident, any income paid to that beneficiary will either be taxed at the beneficiary's marginal rate or subject to non-resident withholding tax (NRWT). NRWT is imposed on non-resident passive income (broadly, dividends, interest and royalties) derived from New Zealand by a person who is not resident in New Zealand for tax purposes. When NRWT applies, it is usually the only New Zealand tax to which the income is subject: Subpart RF.

¶8-040 Taxation of trustee income is subject to settlor's residence

Trustee income sourced in New Zealand is taxable regardless of whether the trust has a New Zealand resident settlor.

However, the rules that determine when beneficiary income is taxable do not apply in the same way to trustees. Instead, a trustee's liability to income tax on foreign income will generally turn on the residence of the trust's settlor during the income year in question.

With some exceptions (discussed below), foreign-sourced trustee income derived by a non-resident trustee is assessable for income tax in New Zealand if, at any time in an income year, a settlor of the trust who is not a transitional resident, is resident in New Zealand: s HC 25. This is the case even if there are one or more other settlors who are non-resident. A settlor for these purposes is a "settlor" as defined for taxation purposes (s HC 27(2)), which can include a person who is not named as a settlor in the deed of trust.

Foreign-sourced trustee income is also assessable to the trustee if the trustee is resident in New Zealand and a settlor of a trust dies resident in New Zealand: s HC 25(2)(c). This is still the case if the deceased settlor is survived by another settlor or person who has made a settlement onto the trust.

¶8-050 Taxation of trusts settled on or before 17 December 1987

Foreign-sourced amounts derived by a non-resident trustee are not assessable in New Zealand if no settlement has been made after 17 December 1987. This exception will still apply, even if an election was made that the trust be treated as a complying trust (s HZ 2) provided that the trustee did not make any election: s HC 25(3).

Foreign-sourced amounts derived by a non-resident trustee are not assessable in New Zealand if the trustee was not resident in New Zealand at any time between 17 December 1987 and the date of settlement: s HC 25(4).

¶8-060 Settlor's liability to income tax as trustee's agent

A resident settlor has a residual liability to income tax if there is no resident trustee. A settlor liable for income tax is liable, subject to a number of exceptions, as the trustee's agent. Where there is more than one settlor, liability is joint and several: s HC 29.

A settlor will not be liable for income tax in respect of settlements made on or before 17 December 1987.

Unless an election is made under s HC 33, a settlor will not be liable for income tax if the settlor is not resident in New Zealand at any time a settlement is made onto the trust in question.

A settlor is not liable for tax:

- on any beneficiary income that must be satisfied by the trustee as agent for the beneficiary: s HC 29(2), or
- to the extent that the settlor can demonstrate that it is more appropriate for another person who has settled property on the trust to be liable: s HC 29(6).

¶8-070 Tax residence in New Zealand is determined by reference to personal presence and an overriding permanent place of abode in New Zealand

A natural person, whether the person is a beneficiary, trustee or settlor, is resident in New Zealand if the person has a permanent place of abode in New Zealand: s YD 1(2). This is the case even if the person also has a permanent place of abode outside New Zealand: *Case* Q55 (1993) 15 NZTC 5,313. However, as the term "permanent place of abode" is not defined for the purposes of the Income Tax Act, each case is determined on its own facts.

Guidance as to what comprises tax residence in New Zealand is provided by interpretation statement IS 16/03, "Tax residence" (*Tax Information Bulletin* ¶2810-102 Vol 28, No 12, November 2016). This interpretation statement updates for the amended "permanent place of abode test" following the Court of Appeal decision in *C of IR* v *Diamond* [2015] NZCA 613; (2015) 27 NZTC ¶22-035 and replaces IS 14/01, "Tax residence" (*Tax Information Bulletin* ¶263-103 Vol 26, No 3, April 2014).

The permanent place of abode test is the overriding test of residence for individuals. As noted in *C of IR* v *Diamond* (supra), abode means a "habitual residence, house or home or place in which the person stays, remains or dwells". However, simply having a dwelling available is not sufficient, the dwelling must also be a person's permanent place of abode.

The following non-exhaustive factors from *C of IR* v *Diamond* (supra) at [59] provide guidance in determining whether there is a permanent place of abode in New Zealand include:

"(a) The continuity or otherwise of the taxpayer's presence in New Zealand and in the dwelling;

(b) The duration of that presence;

(c) The durability of the taxpayer's association with the particular place;

(d) The closeness or otherwise of the taxpayer's connection with the dwelling – the situation before and after a period or periods of absence from New Zealand should be considered.

(e) The requirement for permanency is to distinguish merely transient or temporary places of abode. Permanency refers to the continuing availability of a place on an indefinite (but not necessarily everlasting) basis.

(f) The existence of another permanent place of abode outside New Zealand does not preclude a finding that the taxpayer has a permanent place of abode in New Zealand".

Note that it does not matter how strong a person's ties to New Zealand are if those ties do not link to a permanent place of abode. See interpretation statement IS 16/03 at [28]. See also s YD 1 (as amended).

To determine whether a person has a permanent place of abode, all of the factors are examined with no single factor being determinative. Inland Revenue's IR 886 (New Zealand tax residence questionnaire) is also helpful to determine a person's tax residency if the person is leaving or has left New Zealand.

Regardless of whether a person has a permanent place of abode in New Zealand, a person will be resident for tax purposes if the person is personally present in New Zealand for more than 183 days in any 12-month period. A day includes any part of a day and a person who is present in New Zealand for part of a day is treated as present in New Zealand for the whole day and not absent from New Zealand for any part of the day (s YD 1(8)) in any 12-month period. The 183 days are the total of all days present and need not be a continuous period of 183 days. Once personal presence exceeds

183 days, that person is deemed to be resident from the first day within the 12-month period in which he or she was personally present in New Zealand.

The "days" test does not relate to either a calendar or tax year but instead apply on a continuous rolling basis. This means that a person concerned about avoiding resident status must be careful to ensure not only that they spend half of each year outside of New Zealand, but also to ensure that the time is evenly spread so as to avoid more than 183 days presence in New Zealand.

The decision in *Van Uden* v *C of IR* [2017] NZHC 2554; (2017) 28 NZTC ¶23-037 highlights the importance of recognising when a property owned by a trust can comprise a permanent place of abode and the challenges that confront global travellers. Mr Van Uden is a marine master, who spends 8 months a year working at sea. The question for the High Court was whether the house owned by trustees of a trust settled by Mr Van Uden's wife comprised a permanent place of abode for him in New Zealand between 31 March 2005 and 31 March 2009.

The Taxation Review Authority had found that Mr Van Uden had regularly stayed at the property over a period of 12 years and, while Mr Van Uden was not a beneficial owner of the property, he was a trustee and discretionary beneficiary of the Trust that owned it, and the property was available to him for use as evidenced by his long-standing use of it when he was in New Zealand.

The relevant definition is in s OE 1(1) Income Tax Act 1994 (the Income Tax Act that applied at the time):

> "OE 1 Determination of residence of person other than a company
>
> (1) Notwithstanding any other provision of this section, a person, other than a company, is resident in New Zealand within the meaning of this Act if that person has a permanent place of abode in New Zealand, whether or not that person also has a permanent place of abode outside New Zealand.
>
> [...]".

As confirmed in *C of IR v Diamond* (supra), the relevant consideration is that the words of the legislation are given their ordinary meaning. Simply put, where is the taxpayer's home? The factors to take into consideration, on a non-exhaustive basis, are listed at [39] in *Van Uden* as:

> "(a) The continuity or otherwise of the taxpayer's presence in New Zealand and in the dwelling;
>
> (b) The duration of that presence;
>
> (c) The durability of the taxpayer's association with the particular place;
>
> (d) The closeness or otherwise of the taxpayer's connection with the dwelling – the situation before and after a period or periods of absence from New Zealand should be considered.
>
> (e) The requirement for permanency is to distinguish merely transient or temporary places of abode. Permanency refers to the continuing availability of a place on an indefinite (but not necessarily everlasting) basis.

(f) The existence of another permanent place of abode outside New Zealand does not preclude a finding that the taxpayer has a permanent place of abode in New Zealand."

The inquiries are very case dependent. As noted in *Van Uden* at [60] and [61]:

> "[60] In assessing a particular case the factual inquiry will be on the tax years in question. However, we consider evidence of the relevant circumstances both before and after those tax years may be taken into account to the extent they bear upon the question whether the taxpayer had a permanent place of abode in New Zealand in the tax years in question.
>
> [61] Importantly the focus is on whether the taxpayer, not members of the taxpayer's family, have a permanent place of abode in New Zealand. Accordingly the fact that a taxpayer may provide a home for his family in circumstances where the taxpayer lives elsewhere would not necessarily be sufficient to establish that the taxpayer had a permanent place of abode in New Zealand."

Some useful observations from *Van Uden* are that the enquiry is not as to motive but rather practical reality. In *Van Uden*, the taxpayer did not intend to settle long-term in New Zealand, rather it was convenient for him to spend his shore leave with his wife. However, this did not mean that the Trust property was not his permanent place of abode. Where a person returns regularly to a country, the habitual nature of that may be determinative:

> "[47] As a seaman the appellant spent an average of at least eight months a year at sea. The reasons for returning to New Zealand and his connections with New Zealand may have changed over time but the consistent pattern when he was not on the ship and not holidaying or travelling was that he would return to New Zealand and spend time in New Zealand. When he did return to New Zealand over the relevant time period he lived at 27 Evelyn Road. As a seaman spending eight months of the year at sea he was never going to be spending time continuously in New Zealand. What is important is that when not at sea and not otherwise holidaying or travelling he returned to New Zealand and based himself at 27 Evelyn Road.
>
> [48] The appellant was born in New Zealand in 1957. Apart from the extended holiday with his family in The Netherlands followed by the period of approximately 18 months when his parents returned to The Netherlands and attempted to settle there and then later a period in the 1980's where he based himself in the Philippines and met his first wife, he has had a continuous presence in New Zealand."

Between 2004 and 2009, Mr Van Uden spent between 6 weeks and 5 months a year in New Zealand. From 1998 onwards, there was a home available to Mr Van Uden notwithstanding that it was owned by a trust. In later years, he was appointed a trustee and a beneficiary. Arguments that the fact that the property was owned by a trust were not successful to deflect the proposition that the property was a permanent place of abode for Mr Van Uden. While it was Mrs Van Uden that had the power of appointment of trustees (and could have him removed as a trustee and then as a beneficiary), arguments as to the transience of his rights of occupation were mitigated by the fact that Mr Van Uden had transferred his rental properties to a partnership of himself and Mrs Van Uden and then from that partnership to the Trust.

Mr Van Uden was also shown through credit card receipts to have made ongoing contributions to maintenance costs. This address was used to register cars and to receive mail and he was registered on the electoral roll at this address. The existence of a Sky account was also considered a further indication of permanence.

Leave to appeal the decision was dismissed in a judgment of the Court of Appeal dated 19 March 2019: *Van Uden* v *C of IR* [2018] NZCA 487; (2018) 28 NZTC ¶23-081.

¶8-080 A company is tax resident in New Zealand if the company is incorporated or managed in New Zealand

A company, whether the company is a settlor, trustee or beneficiary, is resident in New Zealand if it is incorporated in New Zealand, its head office is in New Zealand, its centre of management is in New Zealand or the directors, acting in their capacity as directors, exercise control in New Zealand, even if there is some decision-making outside New Zealand: s YD 2(1).

For a company to retain registration as a company in New Zealand, at least one director must meet the Residency Requirements for the purposes of the Companies Act 1993. That is, one director must live in New Zealand or must live in an "enforcement country" (as at the time of writing Australia is the only enforcement country) and be a director of a company registered in that country that is not the equivalent of an overseas country. See Companies Act 1993, s 10.

A director is considered to "live in" New Zealand if the director is physically present in New Zealand for at least 183 days in any particular year. However, a director can still be treated as "living in" in New Zealand if absent from New Zealand for more than 183 days a year if an assessment of the following relevant considerations resulted in an assessment that a director does live in New Zealand:

- The amount of time the director spends in New Zealand
- The director's connection with New Zealand
- The other ties the director has to New Zealand, and
- How the director lives when in New Zealand.

See *Re Carr* [2016] NZHC 1536, where a director who spent on average a third of each year in New Zealand over the previous 6 years (and in one year only 69 days) was found to live in New Zealand. Factors taken into account included the fact that Mr Carr is a New Zealander who owns 2 residences in New Zealand. His partner lives most of the year in one of them (rather than travel extensively with him). He has several New Zealand companies which employ staff and require his supervision. He owns several parcels of land in New Zealand. He otherwise enjoys or possesses many of the trappings of a New Zealand resident – driver's licence, firearms licence, Tax Agent status, New Zealand voter, New Zealand bank accounts and credit cards, membership of organisations, and long-term telephone numbers. His primary care physician is a New Zealand general practitioner.

¶8-090 There is no test of residence for a trust

There is no test of residence for a trust (other than a unit trust). The liability for tax from income or distributions from a trust generally turning for taxation purposes on the residence of the settlor or beneficiary (as relevant).

As a general rule, it is the residence of the settlor not the trustee that is relevant in determining the treatment of foreign-sourced trustee income. This means that if the tax residence of a settlor of a trust changes, there may be tax implications in relation to the treatment of trustee income. Beneficiary income is taxed according to the normal rules about residence and source, though there is a rule that characterises income paid to beneficiaries who cease to be resident in New Zealand and become resident again within 5 years. See ¶8-210.

The following table from IS 16/03 shows how trust income is taxed, depending on whether it is beneficiary income or trustee income, and on the residence of the persons connected with the trust.

How trust income is taxed

<table>
<tr><td colspan="5">Beneficiary income
[See [420] as to when amounts will be beneficiary income]</td></tr>
<tr><td colspan="2">*NB Trustees are liable as agent for the income tax liability of a beneficiary for their beneficiary income and taxable distributions derived*</td><td colspan="2">Beneficiary resident in NZ
• All beneficiary income is included as assessable income</td><td>Beneficiary not resident in NZ
• Only NZ-sourced beneficiary income is included as assessable income</td></tr>
<tr><td colspan="5">*NB There is a special rule in relation to beneficiaries who cease to be resident in NZ and become resident again within five years – see [436]*</td></tr>
<tr><td colspan="5">Trustee income
[See [419] as to when amounts will be trustee income]</td></tr>
<tr><td colspan="3">A settlor of the trust was resident (and not a transitional resident) in NZ at some point during the income year</td><td colspan="2">No settlor of the trust was resident (and not a transitional resident) in NZ at any point during the income year[1]</td></tr>
<tr><td colspan="3">• NZ-sourced income is included as assessable income</td><td colspan="2">• NZ-sourced income is included as assessable income</td></tr>
<tr><td colspan="3">• Foreign-sourced income is included as assessable income[2]</td><td>A trustee resident in NZ</td><td>• Foreign-sourced income is exempt[3]</td></tr>
<tr><td></td><td colspan="2"></td><td>No trustee resident in NZ</td><td>• Foreign-sourced income is not included as assessable income</td></tr>
</table>

[1] And the trust was not, at any time in the income year, a superannuation fund, or a testamentary trust or an inter vivos trust of which any senior was resident in NZ when they died.

[2] With the exceptions noted at [426].

[3] With the exception noted at [424].

Note: The references in the table are all to text in IS 16/03.

¶8-100 Planning opportunities can exist when acquiring or losing New Zealand tax residence

As a result of New Zealand policy, which provides that tax liability turns on the residence of the beneficiary or settlor, there are certain tax-planning opportunities and pitfalls to consider when acquiring or losing New Zealand tax residence.

However, as all jurisdictions do not tax trusts on the same basis, particular care must be taken whenever settlors or trustees migrate from New Zealand, even if there will still be New Zealand resident trustees. This is because the treatment of trusts in different jurisdictions can depend on factors that are different to those applied in New Zealand. For example, a trust could be a complying trust in New Zealand because of the presence of New Zealand resident settlors; but also subject to taxation in a foreign jurisdiction due to the presence of offshore resident trustees.

¶8-110 There can be tax consequences for a trust when a settlor migrates from New Zealand

The legislation does not differentiate between single and joint settlors. This means that where there is more than one settlor, the consequences of the settlors' migration only apply when all the settlors have migrated: s HC 26(1). It is important to note that, in this regard, the definition of settlor is not limited to the person or persons named as settlor in the deed of trust, but refers to a settlor as defined for the purposes of the Income Tax Act, which essentially means any person who has provided value to the trust for less than market consideration.

If all of a trust's settlors cease to be tax resident in New Zealand, the trust does not automatically cease to be a complying trust; nor does it become a foreign trust. A complying trust is defined by reference to a distribution from a trust. Therefore, regardless of the settlor's residence, the status of the trust will not change until a distribution is made. At the time of a distribution, presuming all the trustee's tax obligations have been satisfied, the trust will lose its complying status only if the trustee has received any foreign-sourced income while there has been no New Zealand resident settlor who is not a transitional resident. See further at ¶5-060 regarding a trustee being treated as making an election to satisfy the trust's income tax liability if the trustee meets all of the trust's income tax liabilities regarding the trust's worldwide income and the trustee indicates its intention that the trust remain a complying trust.

A transitional resident is a natural person who has not previously been a transitional resident who is resident in New Zealand after having been non-resident for at least 10 continuous years: s HR 8.

Transitional residents are exempt from income tax in respect of foreign-sourced amounts, excluding income from employment and personal services. The exemption, which can only be claimed once, lasts for 4 years. However, a person who would otherwise be a transitional resident can make an irrevocable election not to be a transitional resident (this will also occur by default if the person applies for any family tax credits). The transitional resident exemption arose from the Government's wish to assist New Zealand businesses to attract skilled and knowledgeable individuals from offshore: ss CW 27, HR 8.

Where complying trust status is lost, the trust will be a non-complying trust and, subject to the ordering rules, distributions may be taxable distributions that are taxed at the rate of 45%.

The loss of complying trust status can be a significant disadvantage; however, the corollary position is that any foreign-sourced income is exempt income once there is no New Zealand resident settlor. These outcomes are the case regardless of the trustee's residence.

It is possible for an election to be made so that a foreign trust can be treated as a complying trust in respect of income derived by the trustee from the date of the election: s HC 33.

At a general level, it can be stated that:

- a complying trust will not lose complying status, presuming the trustee continues to meet all tax obligations, if the trustee does not earn any foreign-sourced income. This is in effect a management issue and where it is desirable to retain a New Zealand trust but also for there to be foreign-sourced income, a new trust could be settled in the settlor's new jurisdiction so that there are separate ownership vehicles for onshore and offshore investments
- the loss of complying status may be outweighed by the benefit of the foreign-sourced income being tax exempt in New Zealand. To a large extent, this will depend on the tax regime that is otherwise applicable
- there are creditor and other risks associated with assets being distributed from a trust and, in certain circumstances, the increased tax rate for taxable distributions will outweigh the risk of distributing assets from a trust and the administrative costs to settle a new trust
- it is possible to elect to retain complying trust status.

Specific advice should be sought whenever it is possible that all the settlors will emigrate.

Example

Tim, the sole New Zealand resident settlor of a complying trust (the TT2 Trust), has emigrated from New Zealand.

Does the TT2 Trust become a foreign trust because its settlor is no longer resident in New Zealand?

The trust will not become a foreign trust.

However, once the TT2 Trust ceases to have a New Zealand resident settlor, it will become a non-complying trust if the trustees derive foreign-sourced income. When this is the case, the trustees of the trust, whether tax-resident in New Zealand or not, will no longer be liable for New Zealand tax on their foreign-sourced income.

However, distributions from non-complying trusts that are not beneficiary income or corpus are taxed at the penal rate of 45%.

Where it is desirable to remain a complying trust, in which case the trustee remains liable for tax in New Zealand on the trust's worldwide income, it may be possible to either elect to continue to be taxed as a complying trust; or to ensure the trust retains a New Zealand settlor.

Settlors must also consider the tax consequences that might arise in any new jurisdiction the settlor becomes resident in. Specialist advice should be sought by any settlor who emigrates from New Zealand.

¶8-120 Foreign trusts are defined by reference to the settlor's residence

A trust settled before a settlor acquiring a New Zealand tax residence is a foreign trust. This is the case regardless of the residence of the trust's trustees and beneficiaries.

Foreign trusts are only taxed in respect of income sourced in New Zealand.

Non-resident beneficiaries of foreign trusts are only subject to income tax on distributions of beneficiary income that is sourced in New Zealand.

Trustees of foreign trusts are only taxed on income from the trust that has a New Zealand source. This is the case regardless of where the trustee is resident.

The definition of a foreign trust is determined by reference to there being no New Zealand resident settlor from the later of the first settlement onto the trust, or 17 December 1987, until a distribution is made: s HC 11. This means that, if a single settlor (where there are multiple settlors) acquires a New Zealand tax residence, distributions from that trust can become subject to the New Zealand tax regime. It is important in this respect to keep in mind the fact that the definition of settlor for tax purposes includes any person who has made a settlement onto or provided value to the trust, which can be a far broader category than the person or persons named as settlor in the deed of trust.

This outcome is not altered by the existence of any double tax agreements (DTA) because any income subject to taxation in New Zealand as a result of coming under the New Zealand tax regime is not the settlor's income but is beneficiary or trustee income.

Once a settlor of a foreign trust acquires New Zealand tax residency, the trust can only remain a foreign trust on the anniversary of the date on which the settlor acquires New Zealand tax residency and ceases to be a transitional resident.

¶8-130 A foreign trust can become a complying trust

If a settlor becomes resident in New Zealand and is not or ceases to be a transitional resident, an election can be made to satisfy the trust's income tax liability. See ¶5-045.

An election to become a complying trust requires that a settlor, trustee or beneficiary assumes liability for the trust's income tax liability.

If an election is made, the trust is still treated as a foreign trust to the extent to which any distribution comprises trustee income derived before the date of the election: s HC 30(3). Where an election is made during an income year, the amount applicable to the period before the election is, at the option of the person making the election, the amount of trustee income actually derived or a pro-rated amount calculated in accordance with the formula in s HC 30(6).

¶8-140 A foreign trust will become a non-complying trust if no election is made within the relevant time frame

There is no ability to elect for a foreign trust to remain a foreign trust. At the end of the applicable period, if no election is made, the trust will be a non-complying trust in respect of taxable distributions.

The tax regime that applies to a non-complying trust provides that all distributions of beneficiary income are taxable in New Zealand at the beneficiary's marginal rate; and distributions of accumulated income and capital gains are subject to tax at the rate of 45%: s HC 34.

However, the trustee of a foreign trust will not be subject to an income tax liability only because that trustee has become tax resident in New Zealand.

¶8-150 Valuation of property, trading stock and financial arrangements when trusts come into the New Zealand tax base

Where a trustee derives income that is taxable in New Zealand, but that previously would not have been, for example, because a settlor becomes resident in New Zealand, the person liable to satisfy the trustee's income tax liability can elect on how the trust property is to be valued.

The cost of trust property, including any premises, plant, equipment and trading stock is valued at:

- the historical cost of the property less depreciation, or
- a value that is no higher than market value that the trustee used for income tax purposes before the trustee income becoming assessable for income tax in New Zealand. To use this method, the trustee must have been liable to income tax in another jurisdiction and the property must have had a tax book value for the purposes of calculating income tax, or
- the value under the Income Tax Act, as if the trustee's income had always been assessable for income tax in New Zealand: s HC 31(3)(a).

The consideration for financial arrangements is either the:

- market value of the financial arrangement on the day on which the trustee income becomes assessable for income tax in New Zealand, or

- consideration paid before the day on which the trustee income becomes assessable in New Zealand, plus expenditure that would have been incurred under the financial arrangement rules before that date, less consideration paid before that date, less income that would have been derived before that date under the financial arrangements rules: s HC 31(4), (5).

¶8-160 Planning opportunities can exist when moving between tax jurisdictions

A comprehensive analysis of tax-planning opportunities available in respect of trusts settled before the settlor acquiring tax residence in New Zealand (pre-migration trusts) is beyond the scope of this book. However, the following general propositions can be stated:

- A foreign trust can become a complying trust by election: s HC 30. Such an election can be made by a beneficiary, trustee or settlor at any time in the 12-month period from the date on which a settlor becomes tax resident in New Zealand and ceases to be a transitional resident. See Chapter 20 – *Disclosure Obligations*.
- If no election is made, a foreign trust will become non-complying trust 12 months from the date on which a settlor of the trust becomes tax resident in New Zealand and ceases to be a transitional resident.
- If a foreign trust becomes a non-complying trust, no tax liabilities will arise unless or until any distribution is made to a New Zealand resident beneficiary. If capital funds can be left offshore and recourse to those assets is not required, a non-complying trust may still prove suitable. Consideration may need to be given to disclosure obligations. See Chapter 20 – *Disclosure Obligations*.
- Distributions of arm's length capital gains are tax-free from a foreign trust.
- Distributions of capital gains are taxable from a non-complying trust. For this reason, care should be taken to assess whether capital gains should be distributed before a foreign trust acquiring non-complying status.

Each situation needs to be assessed on individual merits and the appropriate structure will depend on, amongst other things, the nature of trust assets, the duration of a New Zealand tax residence and the tax treatment of the alternate jurisdiction(s). For example, even if a person is no longer domiciled in the United Kingdom under general law, a person can be deemed to be domiciled in the United Kingdom for inheritance tax purposes: see Inheritance Tax Act 1984 (United Kingdom), s 267.

¶8-170 There is no legislative standard that determines the adoption of a new domicile

A person's domicile is determined in accordance with the Domicile Act 1976. This Act adopts and modifies the common law principles of domicile. The principles of domicile are:

- every person has a domicile
- a person's first domicile is that acquired at birth
- a person is capable of having an independent domicile at the earlier of marrying or of obtaining age 16
- a child has his or her father's domicile if the child's parents live together
- if a child's parents are separated, the child retains the father's domicile, unless the child lives with his or her mother, in which case, the mother's domicile is adopted
- an adult may abandon a domicile by taking up new permanent residence
- a domicile of choice is not lost by moving to another country
- it is not possible to have more than one domicile, unless domiciled in a country that forms part of a union.

Care must be taken when determining domicile as, unlike the days test for determining tax residence, which is singularly determinative, there are a number of factors to take into account when determining domicile. Such factors include the person's citizenship; the country or countries where a home is available; where income is sourced and investments located; cultural ties; whether the person speaks the language of the country of current residence; the location of family members, both close and extended; social integration; and the location of personal effects.

Principles derived from case law include:

- regardless of how long a person lives in a country that is not the country of domicile, adoption of a new domicile requires a fixed and settled intention of abandoning the former domicile: *Bosworth* v *C of IR* (1973) 1 NZTC 60,996, *Winans* v *A-G* [1904] AC 287 (HL)
- the adoption of a new home is not necessarily the adoption of a new domicile: *Geothermal Energy New Zealand Ltd* v *C of IR* (1979) 4 NZTC 61,478
- the character of domicile of origin is more enduring than that of a domicile of choice: *Winans* v *A-G* (supra) at 290
- it is more difficult to prove the abandonment of a domicile of origin than the abandonment of a domicile of choice: *Humphries* v *Humphries* (1991) 7 FRNZ 655
- the standard of proof required to evidence a new domicile is the civil standard of balance of probabilities: *In the Estate of Fuld (dec'd) (No 3)* [1965] 3 All ER 776
- applying for citizenship will not necessarily prove the abandonment of domicile: *In re Dix (dec'd), Public Trustee* v *Plotkin* [1951] NZLR 642
- the onus of proof lies upon the party who asserts that a domicile has been lost.

Domicile is becoming supplanted by the concept of "habitual residence" to determine which law has application to a person. The concept of habitual residence is used in a number of international conventions, beginning with the first Hague Convention on Civil Procedure of 14 November 1896. Habitual residence, domicile and residence (as variously determined) may have relevance to settlors and beneficiaries of trusts who retain ties with European Union countries that have adopted The European Succession Regulation, 4 July 2012, No 650/2012. With effect from 17 August 2015, EU Member States will now look primarily at habitual residence, although residents (however determined) may have the option to elect the law of which state will have application. This has relevance with respect to disposition of property by will or trust and requires a clear understanding of all jurisdictions that might have rights to determine how property is distributed, and consequently what taxation regime(s) might have application.

¶8-180 Trustee migration can have tax consequences

The emigration of a single trustee can have tax consequences for a trust if the trustee moves to a jurisdiction where a trust is taxed based on the trustee's residence. This can be the case regardless of the fact that the trust's settlor remains in the jurisdiction where the trust was settled, or if other trustees do not migrate.

The different tests of residence are of particular relevance to New Zealand residents due to the relative ease with which New Zealanders can migrate to Australia, where, as is the case with most international jurisdictions, trusts are taxed in terms of residence or control. For Australian tax purposes, a trust will be regarded as resident in Australia for tax purposes if a single trustee is resident at any time during an income year or if the central management and control of the trust was in Australia at any time during an income year: s 95(2) of the Australian Income Tax Assessment Act 1936. Central management and control is not defined in the Australian Act. Although the tests of central management and control, such as identifying where decisions are made or who has the right to control the decision makers, may assist (see, for example, *Wood* v *Holden (HMIT)* [2005] BTC 253, *Duha Printers (Western) Ltd* v *The Queen* 98 DTC 6334), care must be taken to ensure that these factors are not treated as necessarily being of equal application to a trust.

Even where a trust has no income, tax residence in another jurisdiction can still result in liability for tax on capital gains.

Therefore, any trustee who is migrating from New Zealand, should seek tax advice regarding the effect the trustee's migration will have on the trust.

For the same reason, the settlor or remaining trustee of any trust where a trustee has migrated should also seek advice to ensure that the trustee does not have a previously unrecognised offshore tax liability.

¶8-190 Disclosure obligations can apply to settlements onto a trust

Certain settlements onto a trust must be disclosed to the Commissioner: Tax Administration Act 1994, s 59. A settlor must disclose the existence of a trust settled after 17 December 1987, together with the details of the trust's trustees and beneficiaries if:

- the settlor is resident but there is no resident trustee at the time of the settlement
- the settlor is resident but at any time after the trust is settled, there is no resident trustee
- a settlement is made by a New Zealand resident nominee, and there is no resident trustee.

Disclosure is made on IR 462 "Settlors of trusts disclosure". Also see ¶20-090.

During 2021, the Taxation (Annual Rates for 2020–21, Feasibility Expenditure, and Remedial Matters) Act 2021 came into effect amending s 59BA of the Tax Administration Act to add requirements for increased record-keeping and information disclosure, especially concerning settlements onto trust and distributions made from a trust, as part of a suite of reforms in conjunction with changes to personal marginal tax rates. The amendments to s 59BA are highly prescriptive as to the information to be disclosed, affecting most trusts deriving assessable income in New Zealand. Under s 59BA(4), if the trustee of a trust is non-resident, a New Zealand-resident settlor of the trust is responsible for ensuring compliance with the disclosure obligations. Also see Chapter 20 – *Disclosure Obligations*.

¶8-200 A trust is not liable for tax in New Zealand only because a trustee migrates to New Zealand

A trust will not be liable to taxation in New Zealand only because a trustee has become tax resident in New Zealand. This will be the case if a trustee is resident in New Zealand, but no settlors or beneficiaries are resident in New Zealand and no income is sourced in New Zealand.

However, New Zealand resident trustees of foreign trusts must disclose the existence of the trust together with trust particulars including whether the trust has an Australian resident settlor: Tax Administration Act, s 59B. Disclosure is made on IR 607 "Foreign trust disclosure".

Note that proposed new disclosure obligations will apply to foreign trusts. See ¶20-070.

¶8-210 New Zealand resident beneficiaries are taxed on income and taxable distributions from any trusts

A New Zealand resident beneficiary is taxed on all beneficiary income and taxable distributions whether comprised of amounts derived from New Zealand or from offshore.

In the event that a person ceases to be a New Zealand resident and later, but within a period of 5 years, the person becomes resident in New Zealand again, any beneficiary income derived from a foreign or non-complying trust or any taxable distribution derived during the beneficiary's absence, commencing with the day on which the person ceased to be resident in New Zealand and ending when that person again became resident in New Zealand, is taxed in the year the beneficiary again becomes resident: s HC 23. This rule is designed to prevent a beneficiary changing residence to defeat the trust rules.

A tax credit may be available for foreign tax or NRWT paid in respect of beneficiary income derived while non-resident.

However, there is no provision for the payment of a credit in relation to any foreign income tax paid in respect of any foreign tax paid on taxable distributions. This is because Subpart LJ of the Income Tax Act only provides a tax credit for tax that is substantially the same as NRWT: s LJ 6(2). Ordinary tax paid would not qualify for a tax credit: s LJ 6(2).

¶8-220 Double Tax Agreements do not generally apply to trusts

The New Zealand Government has entered into a number of treaties with the governments of other countries for the purpose of avoiding double taxation. These treaties, referred to as Double Tax Agreements (DTA)s, provide for the situation in which a resident of one country derives income that has a source either wholly or partly in another country. Generally, income tax would be payable in both countries on the same income – in the taxpayer's home country, because the taxpayer is a resident there, and in the other country, because that is the source from where the income is wholly or partly derived. Where a DTA applies, it is intended that income will be attributed, under the agreement, to one country or the other. The agreement allocates taxing jurisdiction between the respective governments.

A DTA is paramount over the domestic tax law that has been enacted in New Zealand: s BH 1(4). This means that income is taxed under the treaty and irrespective of the treatment required by the domestic law.

DTAs also set maximum tax rates on dividends, interest and royalties.

Example

The Income Tax Act imposes tax on certain non-imputed dividends at a rate of 30% of the gross amount of the dividend payment: s RF 8. However, most DTAs to which New Zealand is a party limit the maximum tax New Zealand may impose on dividends paid to residents of the other treaty country to 15%. This means that dividends paid to residents of treaty countries are taxed at a 15% rate and dividends paid to residents of other countries are taxed at a 30% rate.

As a general proposition, New Zealand's DTAs are silent regarding trusts. This presents no problems in determining a question of residence, as the trustee, whether a natural person or a body corporate, qualifies as a person under a treaty. However, as it is necessary to show the receipt of income before a DTA will apply, this can be problematical where a trustee derives income in a contracting country only in a personal capacity and all the income derived in a trustee capacity is sourced from another contracting state.

If a trust has no New Zealand resident settlor, but a trustee is resident in New Zealand, and the trust's only income is exempt because the income is derived offshore and there is no resident settlor, the question to address is whether such a trustee is resident in New Zealand for treaty purposes given that the only liability to tax in New Zealand is the potential liability for New Zealand-sourced income.

The significance of this arises, for example, when a trust with no New Zealand resident settlor but with a New Zealand resident trustee seeks to apply a DTA so as to obtain a more favourable tax treatment.

This is a specialised topic, the consideration of which is largely beyond the scope of this text. However, at a general level, the following points can be made about DTAs in the context of trusts:

- The Australian Tax Office has ruled that the New Zealand-Australia DTA does not have any application to determine Australia's taxing rights in respect of Australian-sourced income accumulated by a trustee of a New Zealand resident trust. The explanation in support for this position being that a person (a trustee) is not a resident of a Contracting State for the purposes of a DTA if the trustee is only liable for tax in respect of income sourced in that Contracting State. This argument recognises the dual capacity of trustees and, if the trustee would not be resident in the trustee's personal capacity, then the residence criteria is not satisfied if the trustee is only resident in a trustee capacity: TR2005/14 Income tax: application of the Australia/New Zealand Double Tax Agreement to New Zealand Resident Trustees of New Zealand Foreign Trusts.
- The contrary view is that if a resident is liable for tax on any income, regardless of the capacity in which that income is received, the tests of residence and income are met and the majority of DTAs will apply: see, for example, J Prebble, Accumulation Trusts and Double Tax Conventions [2001] British Tax Review 69, at 70–75.
- It is possible to arrange a trust's affairs to take advantage of certain DTAs. However, trustees who do so should be mindful to consider the application of the anti-avoidance provisions in the legislation: see D Martin, Developments in Double Treaty Law of Relevance to New Zealand Tax Practice Paper delivered to the New Zealand Institute of Chartered Accountants 7 and 8 October 2005, Rotorua.

Although no definitive position can be given on the above points unless, or until, either there is a case on the point or Inland Revenue releases a statement confirming its position, care must be taken when applying a DTA to a trustee, particularly where the DTA only has initial application by reference to the person's personal rather than trustee capacity.

See further CCH, *New Zealand Double Tax Agreements Law and Practice.*

¶8-230 Legislation

Income Tax Act 2007

CV 15 AMOUNTS DERIVED FROM TRUSTS WHILE PERSON ABSENT FROM NEW ZEALAND

To the extent to which section HC 23 (Temporary absences of beneficiaries) applies to an amount of beneficiary income or taxable distribution, the amount is income of the person derived on the day on which the person becomes resident in New Zealand again.

[...]

HC 23 TEMPORARY ABSENCES OF BENEFICIARIES

HC 23(1) WHEN THIS SECTION APPLIES

This section applies when–

(a) a person who is a beneficiary of a trust and who is resident in New Zealand stops being resident; and

(b) within a period of 5 years from the date of the end of their residence, they become resident in New Zealand again.

HC 23(2) INCOME DERIVED DURING THE PERIOD

The person is treated as deriving income under section CV 15 (Amounts derived from trusts while person absent from New Zealand) to the extent to which they would have been treated as deriving an amount of beneficiary income or a taxable distribution from a foreign trust or a non-complying trust if they had remained in New Zealand for the period of their absence.

[...]

HC 30 TREATMENT OF FOREIGN TRUSTS WHEN SETTLOR BECOMES RESIDENT

HC 30(1) WHAT THIS SECTION APPLIES TO

This section applies for the purposes of section HC 15 and the definition of **taxable distribution** when–

(a) a settlor of a trust is a natural person who on a day (the **transition date**)–

  (i) becomes resident in New Zealand and is not a transitional resident:

  (ii) stops being a transitional resident and continues to be a New Zealand resident; and

(b) the trust would be a foreign trust in relation to a distribution if a distribution were made immediately before the settlor became resident.

HC 30(2) CHOOSING TO SATISFY TAX LIABILITY

A settlor, trustee, or beneficiary of the trust may choose to satisfy the income tax liability of the trustee under section HC 33. They must make the election by the election expiry date.

HC 30(3) TAX CONSEQUENCES OF MAKING ELECTION

If an election under subsection (2) is made, the trust is treated as follows:

(a) as a foreign trust to the extent to which the distribution consists of an amount derived by the trustee before the date of the election and which does not give rise after the transition date to an income tax liability that is paid before the distribution is made:

(b) as a complying trust to the extent to which the distribution consists of an amount that is derived by the trustee–

 (i) before the date of the election and gives rise on or after the transition date to an income tax liability that is paid before the distribution is made; or

 (ii) on or after the date of the election, if the requirements of section HC 10(1)(a) are met for the trustee income derived on or after the date of the election:

(c) as a non-complying trust to the extent to which the distribution consists of an amount that would not be included in a distribution described in paragraphs (a) and (b).

HC 30(4) TAX CONSEQUENCES WHEN NO ELECTION MADE

If an election under subsection (2) is not made, the trust is treated as follows:

(a) as a foreign trust to the extent to which the distribution consists of an amount that is derived by the trustee before the election expiry date and does not give rise on or after the transition date to an income tax liability:

(ab) as a complying trust to the extent to which the distribution consists of an amount derived by the trustee that gives rise on or after the transition date to an income tax liability meeting the requirements of subsection (4B) or section HC 10(1)(ab):

(b) as a non-complying trust to the extent to which the distribution consists of an amount derived by the trustee that gives rise on or after the transition date to an income tax liability that is not satisfied before the distribution is made.

HC 30(4B) TAX SHORTFALL VOLUNTARILY DISCLOSED

An income tax liability meets the requirements of this subsection if–

(a) the income tax liability is satisfied before the distribution is made, other than for the trust as a complying trust under an election under section HC 33; and

(b) the income tax liability gives rise to a tax shortfall for the trustee for an income year ending before the distribution is made; and

(c) where a shortfall penalty arises for the tax shortfall, the shortfall penalty is satisfied before the distribution is made.

HC 30(5) ELECTION EXPIRY DATE

In this section, the **election expiry date** is the day that is the first anniversary of the transition date.

HC 30(6) CALCULATING INCOME DERIVED BEFORE ELECTION OR ELECTION EXPIRY DATE

For the purposes of subsections (3) and (4), the amount derived in the part of the income year before the person makes the election, or before the election expiry date, as applicable, is at the option of the person either–

(a) the amount actually derived in the part year; or

(b) an amount calculated using the formula–

$$\text{amount derived in income year of election} \times \frac{\text{days before election date or election expiry date}}{365}.$$

[...]

LJ 1 WHAT THIS SUBPART DOES

LJ 1(1) WHEN TAX CREDITS ALLOWED

This subpart provides the rules for dividing assessable income from foreign-sourced amounts into segments and allows a tax credit for foreign income tax paid in relation to a segment of that income.

LJ 1(2) LIMITED APPLICATION OF RULES

The rules in this subpart apply only when–

(a) a person resident in New Zealand derives assessable income that is sourced from outside New Zealand; and

(b) foreign income tax is not paid in a country or territory listed in schedule 27 (Countries and types of income with unrecognised tax) to the extent to which the foreign income tax is paid on the types of income listed in the schedule.

LJ 1(3) WHEN TREATED AS ASSESSABLE INCOME

(repealed)

LJ 1(4) SOURCE OF DIVIDENDS

If a company is not resident in New Zealand, and is resident in another territory or is resident in another territory for the purposes of a double tax agreement between New Zealand and the territory, and foreign income tax is imposed by the territory on a dividend paid by the company, a dividend paid by the company has a source in the territory.

LJ 1(5) DOUBLE TAX AGREEMENTS

(repealed)

LJ 1(6) RELATIONSHIP WITH SECTION YD 5

Section YD 5 (Apportionment of income derived partly in New Zealand) applies to determine how an amount is apportioned to sources outside New Zealand.

LJ 2 TAX CREDITS FOR FOREIGN INCOME TAX

LJ 2(1) AMOUNT OF CREDIT

A person described in section LJ 1(2)(a) has a tax credit for a tax year for an amount of foreign income tax paid on a segment of foreign-sourced income, determined as if the segment were the net income of the person for the tax year. The amount of the New Zealand tax payable is calculated under section LJ 5.

LJ 2(2) LIMITATION ON AMOUNT OF CREDIT

The amount of the person's credit in subsection (1) must not be more than the amount of New Zealand tax payable by the person in relation to the segment calculated under section LJ 5(2), modified as necessary under section LJ 5(4).

LJ 2(3) AMOUNT ADJUSTED

The amount of the person's credit in subsection (1) may be reduced or increased if either section LJ 6 or LJ 7 applies.

LJ 2(4) WHEN PERSON BOTH RESIDENT IN NEW ZEALAND AND ANOTHER COUNTRY

A person described in section LJ 1(2)(a) who has, because they are a citizen or resident of, or are domiciled in, a foreign country, paid foreign income tax on their assessable income, has a credit under subsection (1). However, the amount of the credit is limited to the amount of foreign income tax that would have been paid in the foreign country if the person were treated as not a citizen or resident of, or domiciled in, that foreign country.

[...]

LJ 4 MEANING OF SEGMENT OF FOREIGN-SOURCED INCOME

For the purposes of this Part, a person has a **segment of foreign-sourced income** equal to an amount of assessable income derived from 1 foreign country that comes from 1 source or is of 1 nature.

LJ 5 CALCULATION OF NEW ZEALAND TAX

LJ 5(1) WHAT THIS SECTION DOES

This section provides the rules that a person must use to calculate the amount of New Zealand tax for an income year in relation to each segment of foreign-sourced income of the person that is allocated to the income year.

[...]

LJ 5(5) PERSON'S NOTIONAL INCOME TAX LIABILITY

For the purposes of this section, a person's notional income tax liability for a tax year is calculated using the formula–

(person's net income – losses) × tax rate.

LJ 5(6) DEFINITION OF ITEMS IN FORMULA

In the formula in subsection (5),–

(a) **person's net income** is the person's net income for the tax year:

(b) **losses**–

  (i) is the amount of the loss balance carried forward to the tax year that the person must subtract from their net income under section IA 4(1)(a) (Using loss balances carried forward to tax year):

  (ii) must be no more than the amount of the person's net income:

(c) **tax rate** is the basic rate of income tax set out in schedule 1, part A (Basic tax rates: income tax, ESCT, RSCT, RWT, and attributed fringe benefits).

[...]

YD 1 RESIDENCE OF NATURAL PERSONS

YD 1(1) WHAT THIS SECTION DOES

This section contains the rules for determining when a natural person is a New Zealand resident for the purposes of this Act.

YD 1(2) PERMANENT PLACE OF ABODE IN NEW ZEALAND

Despite anything else in this section, a natural person is a New Zealand resident if they have a permanent place of abode in New Zealand, even if they also have a permanent place of abode elsewhere.

YD 1(3) 183 DAYS IN NEW ZEALAND

A natural person is a New Zealand resident if they are personally present in New Zealand for more than 183 days in total in a 12-month period.

YD 1(4) PERSON TREATED AS RESIDENT FROM FIRST OF 183 DAYS

If subsection (3) applies, the natural person is treated as resident from the first of the 183 days until the natural person is treated under subsection (5) as ceasing to be a New Zealand resident.

YD 1(5) ENDING RESIDENCE: 325 DAYS OUTSIDE NEW ZEALAND

A natural person treated as a New Zealand resident only under subsection (3) stops being a New Zealand resident if they are personally absent from New Zealand for more than 325 days in total in a 12-month period.

YD 1(6) PERSON TREATED AS NON-RESIDENT FROM FIRST OF 325 DAYS

The natural person is treated as not resident from the first of the 325 days until they are treated again as resident under this section.

[...]

YD 2 RESIDENCE OF COMPANIES

YD 2(1) FOUR BASES FOR RESIDENCE

A company is a New Zealand resident for the purposes of this Act if–

(a) it is incorporated in New Zealand:

(b) its head office is in New Zealand:

(c) its centre of management is in New Zealand:

(d) its directors, in their capacity as directors, exercise control of the company in New Zealand, even if the directors' decision-making also occurs outside New Zealand.

YD 2(1B) TREATMENT OF TRUSTEES

In this section, a company includes a company that is acting in the capacity of trustee.

[...]

Income Tax Assessment Act 1936 (Commonwealth of Australia)

[...]

95(2) For the purposes of this Division, a trust estate shall be taken to be a resident trust estate in relation to a year of income if:

(a) a trustee of the trust estate was a resident at any time during the year of income; or

(b) the central management and control of the trust estate was in Australia at any time during the year of income.

[...]

CHAPTER 9

Trading Trusts

¶9-010 Operating principle

A trading trust is a trust that carries on a business. If the trustee of the trading trust is a corporate trustee, the trustee must comply with company law obligations as well as tax and trust law obligations.

¶9-020 A trading trust can provide a flexible business structure

Trading trusts are not used as frequently as other business structures. However, trading trusts are more often employed as a means of operating or owning a business where it is desirable to insulate ownership and management of business assets from the persons who will receive the benefit of the income or capital gain in the business, whether directly or indirectly.

Trading trusts also provide a flexible means of transferring business profits that does not require pre-determination of who will benefit and to what extent (as is the case with respect to companies and partnerships).

Whether a trading trust is the most appropriate structure for operating a business will depend on a number of considerations, the discussion of which is outside the scope of this text. However, the Appendix to this chapter at ¶9-260 provides a useful overview of factors to take into account.

¶9-030 Some trading trust structures can amount to a tax avoidance arrangement

Before settling a trading trust, careful consideration must be given to whether the arrangement could be construed as a tax avoidance arrangement.

As a general proposition, this is less likely to be the case where a new business is being established rather than where there is a reorganisation of an existing structure. The Privy Council decision in *Europa Oil (NZ) Ltd* v *C of IR (No 2)* (1976) 2 NZTC 61,066 remains the leading authority in support of the proposition that a person starting a business is entitled to adopt any business structure, regardless of the fact that one will be more tax effective than another (also see *Mangin* v *C of IR* 70 ATC 6001; [1971] NZLR 591, *Rippon* v *FC of T* 92 ATC 4186 and *Ben Nevis Forestry Ventures Ltd* v *C of*

IR; *Accent Management Ltd* v *C of IR* [2008] NZSC 115; (2009) 24 NZTC 23,188). Also see *Full-Circle Staffing, LLC, Watchman Investment Trust, Financial & Tax Services, Inc, Trustee, Tax Matters Partner, et al v Commissioner of Internal Revenue* Docket Nos 12883-15, 17279-15, 17280-15, 17281-15, 17282-15, 21187-15, 5053-16. Filed May 17, 2018 (Full Circle).

Although it is possible to restructure an existing business so that it is carried on by the trustee of a trading trust, care must be taken to ensure that the arrangement does not amount to tax avoidance: *Case* V20 (2002) 20 NZTC 10,233, *Case* W33 (2004) 21 NZTC 11,321, *C of IR* v *Penny and Hooper* [2010] NZCA 231; (2010) 24 NZTC 24,287 (upheld by the Supreme Court in *Penny and Hooper* v *C of IR* [2011] NZSC 95; (2011) 25 NZTC ¶20-073). As a general principle, a restructure is less likely to amount to tax avoidance where strong commercial reasons are present, and any tax advantage is demonstrably incidental. See further at Chapter 21 – *Trustee's Liability for Tax* and Chapter 24 – *Asset Planning*. Also see Chapter 23 – *Attribution*.

¶9-035 Trustees need to recognise when trust activities comprise trade

Trustees who carry on activities that may not overtly suggest a trading activity also need to be aware of tax liabilities that can arise from the activity. If a property is purchased with the intention of resale, the proceeds of sale can be income for income tax purposes. Where there are regular sales and purchases, the question of whether a taxable activity is being carried on for income tax purposes must also be considered.

In the case of the *Case* 5/2013 [2013] NZTRA 05; (2013) 26 NZTC ¶2-004, the Taxation Review Authority (TRA) held that the proceeds of sale derived by trustees of a trust (the Trust) that bought and sold 11 properties over 12 years was income, the TRA finding that the properties were acquired for the purpose of intention of sale. The TRA also held that the Trust was in the business of erecting buildings and that the residential land exemption did not apply. The TRA found that the Trust was deemed to be registered for GST and accordingly the Trust was also liable for GST.

In addition, penalties were applied on the basis of the Trust's gross carelessness for failing to correctly identify the Trust's tax position. See further at ¶21-035.

¶9-040 The deed of a trading trust must provide sufficient powers to operate a business

The deed for a trading trust can be in the same format as a standard deed for a discretionary trust used in an asset and estate planning context. However, if a trustee is to carry on a business, the deed of trust must confer sufficient powers to do so.

Where trading is intended, at a minimum, the deed of trust should provide for trustee powers including:

- wide powers and the discretion to carry on a business
- the power to invest, including holding non-diversified, high-risk investments

- wide borrowing and lending powers, and
- the power to guarantee and mortgage.

The deed of trust should also provide that the default duty to invest prudently under s 30 of the Trusts Act 2019 is expressly excluded. Consideration also needs to be given as to whether s 34 (duty to avoid conflict of interest) also needs to be amended or modified.

¶9-050 A trading trust can, but need not, have a corporate trustee

It is common but not necessary for the deed of a trading trust to make provision for a corporate trustee (rather than a natural person trustee). A company's ability to act as a trustee, unless its power to do so is limited by its constitution, was confirmed in the case of *In re Levin & Co Ltd* [1936] NZLR 558 (CA); see also Companies Act 1993, s 16.

In practice most trading trusts that operate business undertakings tend to use corporate trustees for practical purposes, including contracts, finance and credit arrangements. An example of a case where the trustees acted personally but found they needed a company to transact with a supplier, resulting in later problems, is *Owens* v *Shaw* [2016] NZHC 1400. See further at ¶9-070.

The use of a corporate trustee has obvious continuity advantages in certain circumstances, such as the death of a director (as opposed to the death of a trustee), bankruptcy of one director (unrelated to the trading of the trust) or in the event of a relationship breakup.

¶9-060 Limitation of liability means that the shareholders are not generally liable for a company's costs

Where a trust has a corporate trustee, it is important to appreciate that a company's limitation of liability generally protects the corporate trustee's shareholders rather than the directors. Directors of limited liability companies have obligations to the company as well as to third parties, which, if not met, can still leave the director personally liable.

¶9-070 A trustee is personally liable for actions carried out in the capacity as trustee

Trustees act personally. This means that a trustee is personally liable for any debt incurred when acting as a trustee, regardless of whether the trustee can benefit personally from the trust. There is no special status at law that attaches to acting as a trustee such that personal liability can be avoided. This is particularly relevant in respect of liabilities for tax, where, for example, the trustee of an insolvent trust could incur a personal tax liability regardless of any independent status. See further at Chapter 21 – *Trustee's Liability for Tax*.

The position is no different for a corporate trustee. This means that unless there is express agreement to the contrary, the corporate trustee of a trading trust is liable for debts incurred in the execution of the trust: *Vacuum Oil Co Pty Ltd* v *Wiltshire* (1945) 72 CLR 319.

In this regard it is important to appreciate that any limitation of liability in a deed of trust, such as a clause limiting the trustee's liability to the assets of the trust, only applies between the trustee and the beneficiaries, not between the trustee and the world at large: *Sovereign Homes Ltd* v *Meurant* [2007] NZHC 1732; (2007) 2 NZTR ¶17-016. This means that if a trustee contracts with a third party, the trustee must ensure that the terms of that contract expressly limit the trustee's liability as the limitation of liability in the deed of trust is not binding on third parties, such as the trust's bankers or Inland Revenue. See *Williamson* v *Bennett* [2009] NZHC 155; (2009) 2 NZTR ¶19-002 and *AMP General Insurance Ltd* v *Macalister Todd Phillips Bodkins* [2005] NZCA 416; (2006) 22 NZTC 19,740; (2005) 1 NZTR ¶15-015. See further at Chapter 29 – *Unit Trusts.*

A common response to the issue of liability is for a person to act as the director of a trustee company (a corporate trustee), rather than as a trustee in a personal capacity. The trustee company in question may limit the ability to have recourse to the trust's assets and will likely have no assets of its own to settle any claim against the trustee.

However, it is important to appreciate that a director, regardless of whether a company is a trustee company, must (under the provisions of the Companies Act):

- act in the best interests of the company: Companies Act, s 131
- exercise any power for a proper purpose: Companies Act, s 133
- not act, or agree to the company acting, in contravention of the Companies Act or constitution: Companies Act, s 134
- not trade recklessly such that there is substantial risk to the company's creditors: Companies Act, s 135
- not incur an obligation unless the director believes on reasonable grounds at the time that the company will be able to perform the obligation when required: Companies Act, s 136
- exercise the care, diligence, and skill that a reasonable director would exercise in the same circumstances taking into account the nature of the company: Companies Act, s 137.

The extent of the duties incumbent on a director mean that the unconsidered interpolation of a trustee company can leave the director of the trustee company liable to suit for failure to act in accordance with the Companies Act.

In *Owens* v *Shaw* [2016] NZHC 1400, the 2 trustees of a trading trust were also directors of a company which, although not a trustee company, was interposed for certain trust transactions. When the trust ceased to support the company, rendering it insolvent, the High Court found that although the trustees were not liable in their capacity as trustees, they were liable as directors for breach of provisions of the Companies Act. So, for example, where a corporate trustee allows a trust business to trade recklessly, its directors may be similarly liable.

When a corporate trustee is appointed, while the company acts as a trustee and as such has all the powers and discretions of a natural person trustee, the director of the corporate trustee is responsible to the company, not the trust, when it comes to matters such as reckless trading and failure to act in the company's best interests.

Such risks are more likely to arise where the corporate trustee has limited or no capital. This is because any transaction entered into by a corporate trustee must be assessed not just from the trustee perspective but also from the perspective of any risk that can flow to the corporate trustee in its own capacity. If a corporate trustee has a low level of capitalisation, as is often the case, the director must be vigilant to the possibility of breaching the prohibition against reckless trading, particularly if the deed of trust or the company's constitution negates the corporate trustee's right of indemnity from the trust's assets. This risk is magnified should a corporate trustee act as trustee for multiple trading trusts (see ¶9-170 below).

The appointment of assetless trustee companies as corporate trustees has come under some criticism regarding, in particular, risk to the creditors of the trading business and protection of beneficiaries' interests. See, for example, HAJ Ford, *Trading Trusts and Creditors' Rights* (1981) 13 Melbourne University Law Review 1 where Professor Ford describes "[t]he fruit of this union of the law of limited liability companies [as] a commercial monstrosity". Also see *C of IR* v *Chester Trustee Services Ltd* [2002] NZCA 258; (2002) 20 NZTC 17,925 at [63], *Re OPC Managed Rehab Ltd (in liq)*; *Levin* v *Ikiua* [2009] NZHC 879; (2009) 2 NZTR ¶19-022.

¶9-080 The directors risk personal liability if a corporate trustee has no right of indemnity

In *Levin* v *Ikiua* [2009] NZHC 879; (2009) 2 NZTR ¶19-022; [2010] 1 NZLR 400, Heath J drew a distinction between the bankruptcy of an individual trustee and the liquidation of a corporate trustee. His Honour held that the assets of the company do not vest in a liquidator. Therefore, any property held in trust will be excluded from property available for distribution to company creditors. Accordingly, if a trustee company fails, the only assets available to the creditors of the company in liquidation will be the trustee's right to indemnity out of such assets of the trust as may still be available. The constitution or deed of trust can provide that there is no right of indemnity. However, it is not clear whether this is a right that can be excluded, as the right of indemnity out of trust property is an ordinary and integral incident arising from the office of a trustee.

In addition to rights of indemnity at equity, trustees also have a statutory right of indemnity: Trustee Act, s 38. Whether or not this indemnity can be excluded has yet to be comprehensively determined.

For further consideration of common law views regarding indemnity, see *Exhall Coal Co Ltd*; *In re Bleckley* (1866) 35 Beav 449; 55 ER 970, *Kemtron Industries Pty Ltd* v *Commissioner of Stamp Duties (QLD)* 84 ATC 4380; (1984) 15 ATR 627, *RWG Management Ltd* v *Commissioner for Corporate Affairs* (1984) 9 ACLR 739; [1985] VR 385.

Even if it is possible to contract out of all rights of indemnity to protect the trust's assets, there is a risk that the directors who act where there is no indemnity could become personally liable for breach of the duty not to trade recklessly.

This is because, at company law, a director cannot incur an obligation unless the director believes on reasonable grounds that the company can perform the obligation. Where a trustee company has no assets of its own, particular care must be taken to establish that the director is not trading recklessly and that the company has the ability to perform obligations. Also see *Owens* v *Shaw* [2016] NZHC 1400.

Directors of corporate trustees as well as trustees who act personally need to consider any potential liability under the Health and Safety at Work Act 2015. Where a trust owns or operates premises or employs staff, the trustees will be "Persons in Control of a Business or Undertaking" (PCBU). PCBU status brings a primary duty of care to ensure so far as is reasonably practicable that employees (wherever they may be working) and others on trust-owned premises are not put at risk. Failure to observe the duty of care, resulting in harm to employees or to others working or visiting at trust premises, may result in significant liabilities, including fines. It is not possible to insure against liability under the Health and Safety at Work Act.

¶9-085 Trading trust structures can cause unexpected associations for GST purposes

While the GST Act does not have any specific provisions relating to shares held on trust, it is possible through the interpolation of closely controlled corporate trustees, to create an unintended association for GST purposes. See *Concepts 124 Ltd* v *C of IR* [2014] NZHC 2140.

See further at ¶25-065.

¶9-090 A director can also be liable when a trustee company fails to fulfil its trustee obligations

A director's failure to act in the best interests of the company can result in the company failing to meet its trustee obligations.

Vance v *Lamb* [2008] NZHC 1902; (2008) 2 NZTR ¶18-024 demonstrates the risk that can arise to a director in such a situation. In that case, a corporate trustee was appointed in circumstances where the natural person trustee was concerned to avoid risk from a sale that would provide inadequate funds to meet all related costs. The director was held to have failed to act in the best interests of the company by failing to ensure that the company fulfilled its duty as trustee to obtain the best possible price for the sale of a trust asset. The breach of duty did not occur because of the resultant loss, but because of the trustee's failure to test the market.

Regardless of whether any beneficiaries bring an action against the trustee for the trustee's failure to obtain the best price, where the director is in breach of the director's obligations, the director is personally liable to third party creditors for the director's failure to act in the company's best interests.

Where a transaction leaves the corporate trustee unable to meet liabilities, regardless of whether those liabilities were incurred as a trustee, the director is responsible for the harm done to the company. It is no defence that the action was carried out by the company acting as a trustee.

¶9-100 The director of a trustee company has no right to indemnification from trust assets

The director of a trustee company does not owe a fiduciary obligation to the beneficiaries of the trust: *Wilson* v *Lord Bury* (1880) 5 QBD 518, *Bath* v *Standard Land Co Ltd* [1911] 1 Ch 618.

This means that a director in breach of a duty owed to the trustee company cannot generally (see below) be liable to the beneficiaries of the trust.

> "Directors stand in a fiduciary relationship to the company, but not to a stranger with whom the company is dealing. It is of course true that a company acts through its directors. But that does not involve the proposition that if a breach of trust is committed by a company acting through its board, a beneficiary can maintain any action against the directors in respect of such breach of trust. Of course I expect the case where trust property can be followed into the hands of a director or any stranger with notice."

Gregson v *HAE Trustees Ltd* [2009] 1 All ER (Comm) 457 Ch at [27]

However, the corollary position is that a director of a trustee company, unlike the trustee company itself, has no right to indemnification from the trust's assets.

This means that the director cannot have recourse to the trust's assets to meet any liability that flows from the appointment as a director.

With this in mind it is important for the director of a trustee company to establish what actions relate to the office of director and what relate to the actions carried out as a trustee. The significance of this dichotomy is that liability accruing to the director is personal and any costs that flow from that liability cannot be recovered from the trust as a matter of right.

Regardless of the lack of a direct duty of care from director to beneficiary, there is limited potential for beneficiaries to bring suit, referred to as a dog-leg claim, against directors. The basis for such a claim is the fact that the director of a corporate trustee owes a duty of care to the company and that where the director breaches that duty resulting in loss, that loss is a chose in action. The existence of that chose, which is property of the trust, can enable a beneficiary of the trust to bring suit against a director where the corporate trustee cannot or will not do so itself. See *Royal Brunei Airlines Sdn Bhd* v *Tan Kok Ming* [1995] 2 AC 378, *HR* v *JAPT* [1997] PLR 99.

¶9-110 The director of a trustee company can also be liable in tort

Although the director will owe no duty to the beneficiaries, the director can still be liable to other third parties in tort through negligence arising, for example, from trading activities. This can be the case irrespective of any contractual obligations or waivers. Take, for example, the case of a trust that owns a dental practice. A director acting negligently could face liability in tort to a patient in the same way as a negligent employee.

As with any other loss, the director, absent any indemnity, will be unable to cover the loss as of right from the trust.

¶9-120 A corporate trustee must comply with company law and trust law

Corporate trustees are not subject to regulations regarding matters such as minimum levels of capitalisation or indemnity insurance.

The Companies Act does not differentiate between transactions carried out on the company's behalf or in its capacity as a trustee.

Accordingly, a corporate trustee will have to file an annual return and meet its filing obligations under the Companies Act as is the case with any other company.

A share register must be maintained: Companies Act, s 87.

The corporate trustee does not require a constitution, as where a constitution is not adopted a constitution will be implied under ss 26 and 28 of the Companies Act. However, as an implied constitution will generally be unsuitable for a corporate trustee, it is appropriate for constitution to be adopted that includes (as a minimum) provisions that:

- provide for the distribution of assets held on trust on liquidation; that is, it is clarified that these assets are not held for the company's shareholders
- address pre-emptive rights
- specify the process for the appointment and removal of directors, and
- require unanimity between directors.

In addition to resolutions made in the capacity as a trustee, the director and shareholders must maintain resolutions required in accordance with the Companies Act. For example, where appropriate, a resolution not to appoint an auditor.

The shareholder(s) of a corporate trustee must also approve any major transactions made by the trustee.

¶9-130 The use of a dedicated corporate trustee can enable cost-effective transfer of assets

Irrespective of any risk avoidance potential, there are practical advantages that apply to the use of a corporate trustee. For example, where a trust's assets are owned by a dedicated trustee company, changes in the company's directors will not require the transfer of the trust's assets, as is the case when there is the retirement or appointment of natural person trustees. As a general observation, the larger or more complex the business of a trading trust, the less suitable individual trustees will be and the more likely that a corporate trustee will be the only practicable working solution because of the constraints.

¶9-140 It can be convenient not to promote a trust publicly

As the corporate trustee of a trading trust represents the "public face" of the trust, for most purposes, parties dealing with the trust will not know, nor have reason to enquire, as to the fact that the company is a corporate trustee.

While it may be convenient not to overtly state that the company is a trustee, care must be taken to ensure that there is no breach of the Fair Trading Act 1986.

Example

If a trustee company has no right of indemnity from trust assets, creditors unaware of this fact could claim a breach under s 9 of the Fair Trading Act, which prohibits misleading or deceptive conduct.

A corporate trustee can also be used to minimise certain audit requirements. For example, offshore businesses trading in New Zealand may not want their financial records being a matter of public record. However, if that business wishes to operate as a company in New Zealand, it may have statutory audit and filing obligations under Pt 11 of the Companies Act 1993. Even so, the publicly available financial statements of a corporate trustee, if required to be filed, will not reflect assets or liabilities held on the trust; only the income, assets and liabilities of the trustee company itself.

By contrast, currently a New Zealand settled trading trust with foreign beneficiaries does not have any statutory audit and filing obligations. By contrast, if the trust had a foreign incorporated corporate trustee and is large enough, that company would have to disclose its financial statements in accordance with the requirements of the Companies Act.

As the shareholding of a corporate trustee need not reflect the beneficial ownership of the trust's assets, a foreign business could incorporate a New Zealand resident company to act as trustee and the company would not be subject to the audit and filing obligations of a foreign company.

The trustee's disclosure obligations under the Tax Administration Act would remain regardless of the trustee company's shareholding.

¶9-150 Income tax is returned on the trust's tax return

A trust with a corporate trustee is generally subject to tax on the same basis as any other trust.

This is because income is trustee income, and taxed accordingly, at the current trustee rate of 33% rather than the current corporate rate of 28%, due to that income being derived by a trustee in its capacity as trustee, regardless of whether that trustee is a body corporate or a natural person.

Where the trustee is a company, both the trustee company and the trust require an IRD number.

From an income tax point of view, the taxpayer is the trust itself and the tax return should show the name of the trust.

Of course, if the trustee company earns any income on its own behalf, including any fees or cost reimbursement for acting as trustee, this income must be accounted for on the company's behalf.

¶9-160 Tax invoices should generally be issued in the name of the trust

A trustee is not automatically deemed to be an agent for the trust: GST Act, s 57; Tax Administration Act; *Case* P20 (1992) 14 NZTC 4,136; A McKenzie *GST – A Practical Guide* (Edition 8, CCH, 2008) at 501, 602.

The trustee company could register for GST and indeed should do so if it is carrying on a taxable activity in its own right. However, it is generally accepted that the GST registration should be in the name of the trust, as is the case when natural person trustees register for GST.

Example

A company is the trustee of a trading trust. The trading trust carries on a business. Invoices are sent out under the company name and the business cards only have the company name on them. Is this correct?

It is a common practice with trading trusts to show the name of the corporate trustee without mentioning the name of the trust.

As a consequence, any party that enters into any contract with the trustee may believe the party is contracting with the company and not the trust.

A simple solution to this matter would be to issue invoices in the name of the trustee company as trustee for the trust.

¶9-170 It can be unwise to appoint a corporate trustee with no or minimal value to act as the trustee for multiple trusts

If a corporate trustee becomes insolvent and is liquidated, it may be necessary for a new trustee to be appointed. This can be the case regardless of whether the company has more than one appointment as trustee: *C of IR* v *Chester Trustee Services Ltd* [2002] NZCA 258; (2002) 20 NZTC 17,925.

This will leave each trust with the costs of retiring the existing trustee and appointing another trustee together with any conveyancing costs or any other costs associated with the transfer of assets.

The Court of Appeal applied its decision in Chester Trustee Services in *C of IR* v *Newmarket Trustees Ltd* [2012] NZCA 351; (2012) 25 NZTC ¶20-139. Newmarket Trustees Ltd was the trustee of over 100 trusts. The co-trustee in one trust entered into transactions that resulted in an assessment by the Commissioner for GST and income tax. The co-trustee failed to notify Newmarket Trustees of the correspondence with Inland Revenue or of the assessments. He was later adjudicated bankrupt. The Commissioner served a statutory demand on Newmarket Trustees as co-trustee on the grounds it was jointly and severally liable for the debts of the trust. As it had no other assets, it was clearly insolvent.

In the High Court, Associate Judge Bell declined to make a liquidation order in respect of the insolvent trustee company on the grounds that, notwithstanding its insolvency, the impact on other trusts would be such that it would be impractical and inappropriate to use the remedy of liquidation (*C of IR* v *Newmarket Trustees Ltd* (2011) 25 NZTC ¶20-030).

The Court of Appeal found, however, that the High Court had exercised its discretion not to order liquidation on an erroneous basis, even though Newmarket Trustees had no assets available to satisfy its creditors. Instead there were good reasons why an insolvent trustee company should be placed in liquidation, including: the Court's overriding duty to ensure that trusts are administered properly; recognition that an insolvent trustee should be considered unfit to be a trustee; protection of the assets and the beneficiary interests of other trusts of which the company was trustee; and, reflecting the then s 51(2) of the Trustee Act 1956 (now see ss 112–114 of the Trusts Act), to power of the Court to remove undesirable trustees. Also see *Black* v *Giltech Precision Castings (2004) Ltd* [2012] NZHC 2117; (2012) 3 NZTR ¶22-021.

¶9-180 A trading trust that is a unit trust is taxed as a company

Care should be taken to ensure that a trading trust does not inadvertently fall within the definition of a unit trust. If it does, the trust will be taxed as a company. That is, the unit holder is deemed to be a shareholder, the units are deemed to be shares, and distributions are deemed to be dividends. See Chapter 29 – *Unit Trusts.*

¶9-190 A trust that employs staff must pay ACC levies

The trustee of a trading trust must pay Accident Compensation Corporation (ACC) levies as is the case with any other employer. This is the case whether the employee is a beneficiary. Accordingly, if the trustee employs a beneficiary, ACC levies will be payable by the trustee (and by the beneficiary-employee) in relation to liable earnings (salary and wages) paid to the beneficiary-employee.

¶9-200 Distributions to beneficiaries are not liable for ACC levy

A distribution to a beneficiary that does not comprise salary or wages is not subject to ACC levies. However, care must be taken when making distributions to a beneficiary who is also an employee to ensure that the distribution is not being made in lieu of the payment of wages or salary.

Distributions to beneficiaries in their capacity as beneficiaries should be recorded accurately so that it is clear whether any payment represents a trustee distribution or liable earnings.

Salary and wages paid under the guise of a distribution to a beneficiary are unlikely to withstand scrutiny. Where an employee is not paid a market salary for services provided in the capacity as an employee, avoidance risks can arise.

Example

Beneficiaries of a trading trust (carrying on the business of farming) receive allocations of beneficiary income at the end of the financial year for services provided to the trust. How is the ACC levy calculated?

The ACC levy is calculated by reference to earnings and so, unless the "income" distributed is treated as salary or wages, no ACC levy will be payable.

¶9-210 Distributions made in lieu of income could be subject to ACC levies and anti-avoidance

Where a beneficiary is providing services to the trust for no or below market remuneration, there is a risk that Inland Revenue could invoke the anti-avoidance provisions and deem the beneficiary to have avoided ACC levies in respect of the personal services provided: ss BG 1, GA 1.

In addition to the risk of anti-avoidance provisions being applied, it is also important to consider what will happen if a beneficiary has an accident. If the beneficiary has not been adequately remunerated for the services performed, in the event of an accident, the beneficiary may not have a sufficient entitlement to earnings-related compensation.

The risk that general anti-avoidance provisions will apply to a trust that makes distributions of beneficiary income to a beneficiary in lieu of salary or wages is substantially increased where an existing business is transferred to a trust, and the business income is primarily generated through the personal exertion of the previous owner of the business: see Revenue Alert 08/01.

¶9-220 FBT regime applies to a trustee that employs staff

A benefit provided to an employee will be brought within the fringe benefit tax (FBT) regime if the benefit is received in relation to, in the course of, or by virtue of, employment: s CX 2. This is the case whether any employee is also a beneficiary. The corollary position being that benefits not connected with the employment relationship should not be subject to FBT.

A benefit is provided "in connection with" the employment relationship if the employment relationship is the reason for, or at least a substantial reason for, the provision of the benefit.

Whether a benefit for which market value is paid by an employee is "in connection with" an employment relationship depends on the facts in each case.

Example

Making a house owned by the trustee available to a beneficiary in his or her capacity as a beneficiary should not be subject to FBT solely by virtue of the fact that the beneficiary is also an employee of the trust. To support an argument that the benefit is provided to a beneficiary in his or her capacity as a beneficiary, the trustee should document the provision of the benefit clearly in a trustee resolution stating that the beneficiary enjoys the benefit in his or her capacity as a beneficiary.

If the employer's business does not include the provision of goods or services of the type provided to the employee, it is unlikely that the goods or services would have been provided to the employee if not for the employment relationship.

However, if the goods or services provided to an employee are of a type that the employer customarily makes available to the general public, and the goods and services are provided at the same price and on the same terms as the price and terms available to a member of the general public, it is likely that the goods or services would be provided because the employee has paid for such goods or services, rather than because of the employment relationship.

If a beneficiary is also an employee of the trust, no FBT liability arises in respect of benefits, provided the beneficiary-employee enjoys the benefit in his or her capacity as a beneficiary, not as an employee. The trustee should document the provision of the benefit clearly stating that the beneficiary-employee enjoys the benefit in his or her capacity as a beneficiary.

If benefits are provided to a beneficiary who is not an employee of the trust or a person associated with an employee, FBT should not apply because the beneficiary is not receiving the benefit as an employee. No deduction is available to the trust for any expenses incurred in providing the benefit.

If a beneficiary works for a trust, and the remuneration for the services provided is beneficiary income rather than salary or wages, arguably any benefits provided will not be subject to the FBT regime.

The contrary, and safer, view is that if a beneficiary provides services to a trust for which the beneficiary is not formally remunerated, or if the beneficiary receives a benefit that would otherwise be subject to FBT, the provision of such services or benefit is still sufficient to provide that the beneficiary is an employee for the purposes of the FBT rules.

If benefits are provided to a beneficiary who is not an employee of the trust or a person associated with an employee, FBT should not apply because the beneficiary is not receiving the benefit as an employee. The corollary of this is that no deduction is available to the trust for any expenses incurred in providing the benefit.

The solution is to ensure that care is taken where a beneficiary is also an employee of the trading trust so that it is clear whether any benefits received by the beneficiary of the trust arise out of the beneficiary's employment by the trust (whether this is remunerated), or by virtue of the employee's capacity as a beneficiary.

For a comprehensive consideration of the FBT regime, see B Ashwell, M Baker *Fringe Benefits – A Practical Guide to Managing Your Tax Costs* (3rd ed, CCH, Auckland, 2007).

¶9-230 Fringe benefits provided by charities are generally exempt from FBT

An exemption to the FBT rules excludes benefits provided by a charitable organisation (including a charitable trust) to its employees from the FBT regime: s CX 25. However, this exemption is limited to employment in relation to the charity's charitable purposes.

A further limitation provides that the exclusion does not apply to a benefit that comprises a short-term charge facility (s CX 25(2), (3)), if the value of the benefit for a tax year is more than the lesser of 5% of the employee's salary or wages, or $1200.

It is important to note that for the purposes of the exemption from FBT, a charity (s YA 1 "charitable organisation") is defined by reference to recipients of charitable or public benefit gifts, previously referred to as donee organisations (s LD 3) and charitable organisations listed in sch 32; not by whether the charity is registered on the Charities Register. Universities and local and public authorities are expressly excluded from the definition.

¶9-240 Non-cash benefits paid to non-employee shareholders are dealt with under the dividend rules

In private company situations, it is reasonably common for salaries or dividends to be paid at year-end to clear shareholder's overdrawn loan accounts. Unless interest is charged, an overdrawn loan account will give rise to a fringe benefit or deemed dividend depending on whether the loan is provided due to an employment or shareholding relationship.

Although the FBT rules apply to non-cash benefits provided to shareholder-employees, benefits to shareholders who are not employees, such as trustee shareholders, are generally dealt with under the dividend rules.

¶9-250 The use of trading trusts is evolving and is subject to regular review

For a more detailed discussion of some of the commercial and tax issues associated with trading trusts, see “Trading trusts and tax avoidance” by Stephen Tomlinson in CCH, *New Zealand Tax Updater*, No 4 – May 2003; *Trading Trusts, The Corporate Trustee – Risks and Responsibilities*, Alison Gilbert presented at the Auckland District Law Society Conference 10 August 2006; *Everything You Need to Know about Trading Trusts: Legal, Tax and Accounting Issues*, a presentation by John Hart, Anderson Legal and Des Trigg and Ian Masson, Spicer and Oppenheim.

¶9-260 Appendix

	Sole Trader	General Partnership	Limited Partnership	Company	Contractual Joint Venture	Trading Trust
Overview	▪ Individual conducting business ▪ Limited to life of owner ▪ Unlimited liability	▪ Relationship between persons carrying on business with a view to profit ▪ Not separate legal entity ▪ Combines resources and expertise of partners ▪ Unlimited liability	▪ Separate legal entity created by statute ▪ No natural life span ▪ Limited liability for Limited Partners provided that Limited Partners do not participate in management of the Limited Partnership	▪ Separate legal entity created by statute ▪ No natural life span ▪ Limited liability for owners and directors have statutory duties	▪ Contractual arrangement between parties wishing to carry on a venture with a view to profit ▪ Limited to life of venture ▪ Not a separate legal entity ▪ Liability depends on joint venture agreement and contracts entered into by parties	▪ Trust conducting business with a view to profit ▪ Trustee can be a company to limit liability
Governing law/ constituent document	▪ N/A	▪ Partnership Law Act 2019 ▪ Partnership deed	▪ Limited Partnership Act 2008	▪ Companies Act 1993 ▪ Constitution ▪ May be a shareholders' agreement	▪ Contract Law ▪ Joint Venture agreement ▪ Equity (fiduciary relationship)	▪ Equity ▪ Trusts Act 2019 ▪ Trust deed
Establishment	▪ N/A (formalities for starting business are that of an ordinary individual)	▪ Entry into partnership deed ▪ No limit on number of partners ▪ Some occupations governed by licensing/rules	▪ Entry into Partnership Agreement ▪ Registration on the Limited Partnerships Register	▪ Registration on the Companies Register	▪ Entry into written joint venture agreement	▪ Written trust deed executed by settlor

	Sole Trader	General Partnership	Limited Partnership	Company	Contractual Joint Venture	Trading Trust
Owner Liability	▪ Unlimited liability for all debts	▪ Unlimited joint and several liability for all debts	▪ Liability of Limited Partners limited to the amount subscribed	▪ Limited to amount payable on shares Liability under any personal guarantees ▪ made by shareholders Director duties and potential criminal liability under Companies Act ▪	▪ Liability depends on joint venture agreement terms and contracts entered into by parties	▪ Trustee is personally liable if the trustee acts personally; ▪ Directors of a corporate trustee are not generally liable for any breach of trust by the trustee but can have liability for actions as a director; ▪ Trustee indemnity from assets of trust and possibly beneficiaries of trust ▪ Trustee liability unlimited if breach of trust.
Control	▪ Complete	▪ Depends on partnership deed. ▪ May be need for majority or unanimous decisions	▪ General Partner responsible for management and direction of ▪ company Limited Partners approval of major transactions	▪ Directors responsible for management and direction of company ▪ Shareholders approval of major transactions Shareholders may ▪ have rights under shareholders agreement but not deemed director rules	▪ Depends on terms of joint venture agreement. ▪ Votes usually depend on capital contribution ▪ May be management committee	▪ By trustees but subject to fiduciary obligations and terms of trust deed.

	Sole Trader	General Partnership	Limited Partnership	Company	Contractual Joint Venture	Trading Trust
Continuity	▪ Ceases on death of individual	▪ Ceases on death, retirement or bankruptcy of partner	▪ Perpetual existence until removed from the Limited Partnerships Register	▪ Perpetual existence until removed from the Companies Register	▪ Ceases on termination by the parties or end of venture	▪ Until trust wound up ▪ Perpetuities Act 1964 – maximum 80 years
Admission of new investor	▪ N/A	▪ Subject to partnership deed and agreement of partners	▪ Governed by Partnership Agreement ▪ Investor becomes Limited Partner on entry onto the Limited Partnerships Register	▪ Governed by constitution ▪ Usually preemptive rights for shareholders	▪ Governed by joint venture agreement	▪ Usually restricted by terms of trust deed
Ease of transfer	▪ Relatively complex – all assets have to be transferred	▪ Relatively complex – all assets (or an interest in them) have to be transferred. ▪ A new partnership is created with the change in partners or partners interests	▪ Transfer of partnership units (simple) ▪ Sale of assets, followed by liquidation (more complex)	▪ Sale of shares (simple) Sale of assets, ▪ followed by liquidation (more complex)	▪ Relatively complex – assets of joint venture parties would have to be transferred Joint venture ▪ agreement likely to regulate transfers	▪ This can be complex ▪ The assets will generally be in the name of the corporate trustee but beneficially owned by the trust ▪ Therefore all assets have to be transferred (with tax implications to be considered)

	Sole Trader	General Partnership	Limited Partnership	Company	Contractual Joint Venture	Trading Trust
Winding up	▪ By proprietor (or creditor)	▪ On death, bankruptcy or retirement of partner or by agreement	▪ Appointment of liquidator by (among others): ▪ Limited Partners ▪ The General Partner on occurrence of event listed in Partnership Agreement ▪ The court on application by a creditor	▪ Appointment of liquidator by (among others): ▪ Shareholders ▪ Directors on occurrence of event listed in constitution The court on ▪ application by a creditor	▪ In accordance with the joint venture agreement or agreement of the parties	▪ According to trust deed
Impact of death of owner	▪ Potential issues with creation of estate	▪ Death of a partner creates a new partnership	▪ Limited Partner's interest becomes property of the estate of the Limited Partner	▪ Shares become the property of the estate of the shareholder Constitution may ▪ contain provisions dealing with death of shareholder	▪ Depends on terms of joint venture agreement and nature of entity (if any) through which owner invests	▪ The death of a beneficiary has no effect, nor does the death of a trustee
Tax Rate	▪ Individual marginal tax rates: ▪ Up to $14,000 – 10.5% $ 14,001– ▪ $48,000 – 17.5% $48,001– ▪ $70,000 – 30% $70,000– ▪ $180,000 – 33% Over ▪ $180,000 – 39%.	▪ Income/ expenditure attributed to each partner ▪ Partner taxed at partner's tax rate	▪ Income/ expenditure attributed to each limited partner ▪ Limited Partner taxed at limited partner's tax rate	▪ Company tax rate 28%	▪ Income/ expenditure attributed to each JV party ▪ JV party taxed at JV party's tax rate	▪ Complying trust – trustee income taxed at 33%, beneficiary income generally taxed at beneficiary's tax rate ▪ Special rules in relation to minor beneficiaries

	Sole Trader	General Partnership	Limited Partnership	Company	Contractual Joint Venture	Trading Trust
Tax on Distributions	▪ None	▪ None	▪ [None]	▪ Generally taxed in hands of investor at investor's rate, with credits (imputation credits) for company tax paid Special rules for QCs/ ▪ LAQCs	▪ None	▪ Complying trust – capital distributions are not taxable. ▪ Capital distributions from non-complying and foreign trusts can be taxable.
Taxation on sale of business	▪ Tax on profit from sale of trading stock, other revenue assets, and depreciation recapture	▪ Tax on profit from sale of trading stock, other revenue assets, and depreciation recapture	▪ Tax on profit from sale of trading stock, other revenue assets, and depreciation recapture ▪ Sale of shares not usually taxable	▪ Sale of shares not usually taxable ▪ Sale of certain company assets taxable ▪ Tax on distribution of gains unless QC/LAQC or exclusions apply (e.g capital gains upon liquidation)	▪ Tax on profit from sale of trading stock, other revenue assets, and depreciation recapture	▪ Tax on profit from sale of trading stock, other revenue assets, and depreciation recapture
Tax Losses	▪ Unlimited ability to carry forward losses	▪ Income/ expenditure attributed to each partner	▪ Income/ expenditure attributed to each limited partner	▪ Losses trapped at company level, unless LAQC ▪ Carry forward dependent upon shareholder continuity	▪ Income/ expenditure attributed to each JV party	▪ Losses trapped at trustee level

¶9-270 Legislation

Companies Act 1993

16 CAPACITY AND POWERS

16(1) [Full capacity]

Subject to this Act, any other enactment, and the general law, a company has, both within and outside New Zealand,–

(a) full capacity to carry on or undertake any business or activity, do any act, or enter into any transaction; and

(b) for the purposes of paragraph (a), full rights, powers, and privileges.

16(2) [Constitution may only restrict]

The constitution of a company may contain a provision relating to the capacity, rights, powers, or privileges of the company only if the provision restricts the capacity of the company or those rights, powers, and privileges.

[...]

87 COMPANY TO MAINTAIN SHARE REGISTER

87(1) [Duty to maintain register]

A company must maintain a share register that records the shares issued by the company and states–

(a) whether, under the constitution of the company or the terms of issue of the shares, there are any restrictions or limitations on their transfer; and

(b) where any document that contains the restrictions or limitations may be inspected.

87(2) [Required information]

The share register must state, with respect to each class of shares,–

(a) the names, alphabetically arranged, and the latest known address of each person who is, or has within the last 10 years been, a shareholder; and

(b) the number of shares of that class held by each shareholder within the last 10 years; and

(c) the date of any–

 (i) issue of shares to; or

 (ii) repurchase or redemption of shares from; or

 (iii) transfer of shares by or to–

each shareholder within the last 10 years, and in relation to the transfer, the name of the person to or from whom the shares were transferred.

[...]

131 DUTY OF DIRECTORS TO ACT IN GOOD FAITH AND IN BEST INTERESTS OF COMPANY

131(1) [Duty]

Subject to this section, a director of a company, when exercising powers or performing duties, must act in good faith and in what the director believes to be the best interests of the company.

131(2) [Wholly-owned subsidiaries]

A director of a company that is a wholly-owned subsidiary may, when exercising powers or performing duties as a director, if expressly permitted to do so by the constitution of the company, act in a manner which he or she believes is in the best interests of that company's holding company even though it may not be in the best interests of the company.

131(3) [Subsidiaries not wholly owned]

A director of a company that is a subsidiary (but not a wholly-owned subsidiary) may, when exercising powers or performing duties as a director, if expressly permitted to do so by the constitution of the company and with the prior agreement of the shareholders (other than its holding company), act in a manner which he or she believes is in the best interests of that company's holding company even though it may not be in the best interests of the company.

131(4) [Joint venture companies]

A director of a company that is carrying out a joint venture between the shareholders may, when exercising powers or performing duties as a director in connection with the carrying out of the joint venture, if expressly permitted to do so by the constitution of the company, act in a manner which he or she believes is in the best interests of a shareholder or shareholders, even though it may not be in the best interests of the company.

[...]

133 POWERS TO BE EXERCISED FOR PROPER PURPOSE

A director must exercise a power for a proper purpose.

134 DIRECTORS TO COMPLY WITH ACT AND CONSTITUTION

A director of a company must not act, or agree to the company acting, in a manner that contravenes this Act or the constitution of the company.

135 RECKLESS TRADING

A director of a company must not–

(a) agree to the business of the company being carried on in a manner likely to create a substantial risk of serious loss to the company's creditors; or

(b) cause or allow the business of the company to be carried on in a manner likely to create a substantial risk of serious loss to the company's creditors.

136 DUTY IN RELATION TO OBLIGATIONS

A director of a company must not agree to the company incurring an obligation unless the director believes at that time on reasonable grounds that the company will be able to perform the obligation when it is required to do so.

137 DIRECTOR'S DUTY OF CARE

A director of a company, when exercising powers or performing duties as a director, must exercise the care, diligence, and skill that a reasonable director would exercise in the same circumstances taking into account, but without limitation,–

(a) the nature of the company; and

(b) the nature of the decision; and

(c) the position of the director and the nature of the responsibilities undertaken by him or her.

Goods and Services Tax Act 1985

57 UNINCORPORATED BODIES

[...]

57(2) [Members of an unincorporated body]

Where an unincorporated body that carries on any taxable activity is registered pursuant to this Act,–

[...]

(d) that registration shall be in the name of the body, or where that body is the trustees of a trust, in the name of the trust; and

[...]

Income Tax Act 2007

CX 2 MEANING OF FRINGE BENEFIT

CX 2(1) MEANING

A **fringe benefit** is a benefit that–

(a) is provided by an employer to an employee in connection with their employment; and

(b) either–

  (i) arises in a way described in any of sections CX 6, CX 9, CX 10, or CX 12 to CX 16; or

  (ii) is an unclassified benefit; and

(c) is not a benefit excluded from being a fringe benefit by any provision of this subpart.

[...]

CX 25 BENEFITS PROVIDED BY CHARITABLE ORGANISATIONS

CX 25(1) WHEN NOT FRINGE BENEFIT

A charitable organisation that provides a benefit to an employee does not provide a fringe benefit except to the extent to which–

(a) the employee receives the benefit mainly in connection with their employment; and

(b) the employment consists of the carrying on by the organisation of a business whose activity is outside its benevolent, charitable, cultural, or philanthropic purposes.

CX 25(2) WHEN EMPLOYER PROVIDES CHARGE FACILITIES

Subsection (1) does not apply, and the benefit provided is a fringe benefit, if a charitable organisation provides a benefit to an employee by way of short-term charge facilities and the value of the benefit from the short-term charge facilities for the employee in a tax year is more than the lesser for the tax year of–

(a) 5% of the employee's salary or wages:

(b) $1,200.

[...]

HC 7 TRUSTEE INCOME

HC 7(1) MEANING

To the extent to which it is not beneficiary income, an amount of income derived by a trustee of a trust is **trustee income**.

[...]

HC 24 TRUSTEES' OBLIGATIONS

HC 24(1) LIABILITY AS INDIVIDUAL FOR TRUSTEE INCOME

A trustee must satisfy the income tax liability for their taxable income as if they were an individual beneficially entitled to the trustee income.

[...]

Accident Compensation Act 2001

168 EMPLOYERS TO PAY LEVIES

168(1) [Employers' levies]

An employer must pay, in accordance with this Act and regulations made under this Act, levies to fund the Work Account.

168(2) [Prescribed period]

A levy must relate to a prescribed period.

168(3) [Date of payments]

An employer must pay the levy by the date specified for payment, whether in an invoice or other appropriate document given to the employer by the Corporation or an agent of the Corporation, being a date not less than 30 days after the date of the invoice or other appropriate document.

Trusts Act 2019

81 TRUSTEE'S LIABILITY FOR EXPENSES AND LIABILITIES INCURRED, AND TRUSTEE'S RIGHT TO INDEMNITY

81(1) [Personal liability of trustees]

A trustee is personally liable for an expense or a liability incurred by the trustee when acting as a trustee.

81(2) [Trustee indemnity from trust fund for reasonably incurred expenses]

However, a trustee who incurs an expense or a liability when acting reasonably on behalf of the trust is entitled,–

(a) if the trustee has paid the expense or discharged the liability out of the trustee's own funds, to reimbursement from the trust property; or

(b) in any other case, to pay the expense or discharge the liability directly from the trust property (or to have it paid or discharged by a remaining trustee).

81(3) [Indemnity governed by common law and equity rules]

The operation and enforcement of the indemnity in this section is governed by the rules of the common law and equity relating to trusts.

81(4) [Indemnities at common law or equity not limited]

This section does not limit any indemnity available at common law or in equity.

[...]

CHAPTER 10

Minor Beneficiary Income

¶10-010 Operating principle

Subject to certain exceptions, beneficiary income derived by a minor is taxed as trustee income at the trustee rate of 33%, irrespective of the beneficiary's marginal rate.

The rules that apply to the taxation of a minor beneficiary are referred to as the minor beneficiary rule.

However, as the minor beneficiary rule relates to the nature of settlements, rather than the fact of a distribution to a minor, it can be possible to avoid the application of the rule by ensuring settlements are made onto trusts that are not subject to the rule.

¶10-020 The minor beneficiary rule is an anti-avoidance measure introduced to prevent income streaming

The minor beneficiary rule (contained in ss HC 35–HC 37) was introduced to prevent "income streaming" whereby income is attributed to minors with more favourable tax rates, rather than to (usually) parents.

In commenting on the policy underlying the minor beneficiary rule, the Policy Advice Division of Inland Revenue stated:

> "The purpose of the proposed minor beneficiary rule is to limit the ability of some families to gain a tax advantage by meeting expenses of the children through the use of a trust. Parents generally meet the expenses of their children from their after-tax income. However, by settling income-earning assets on a trust and distributing the income to the children, these expenses can be met from income taxed at the marginal tax rates of the children. Thus, where the parents' marginal tax rate is 33% or 39% and that of the children is 19.5%, income that would otherwise be taxable to the parents at the higher rate becomes taxable to the children at the lower rate. Whilst this income is legally that of the child, it is unlikely in these cases that the children are actually determining how the funds are spent. In fact, the income distribution is likely to take the form of payment of school fees or expenses, rather than a cash distribution. The limitation of the rule to minors under 16 years recognises that above that age it is increasingly likely that beneficiary income is not, in fact, used to meet family expenses.
>
> For example, Inland Revenue records show that in the 1999 income year, about 3000 children under the age of six received beneficiary income exceeding $21 million in total.

> This is an average of $7,000 income for each child under the age of six and excludes interest and dividend income distributed by trusts".

See Taxation (Beneficiary Income of Minors, Services-related Payments and Remedial Matters) Bill: Officials' Report to the Finance and Expenditure Committee on Submissions on the Bill, 19 February 2001, at 5.

However, given the limited exceptions to the minor beneficiary rule, and the inherent presumption that any parent of a minor beneficiary is taxed at the higher marginal rates, "genuine" distributions of income to minors are also caught.

Additionally, although it is possible to avoid the application of the rule by not making settlements onto trusts to which the rule applies, it is not always practicable to ensure settlement onto an alternative trust.

The applications of exemptions are fact specific and require a trustee to have comprehensive knowledge of the nature of settlements onto a trust.

A general overview of the regime is provided by the flow chart at ¶10-270.

¶10-030 Beneficiary income is taxed as trustee income if the minor beneficiary rule applies

Income subject to the minor beneficiary rule is excluded income of the minor (s CX 58) and is taxed as trustee income. This means that when the minor beneficiary rule applies, irrespective of the beneficiary's marginal tax rate, the trustee must pay income tax on the minor beneficiary's income at the trustee rate of 33%.

For the purpose of debiting and crediting the minor beneficiary's trust account, income tax paid by a trustee on beneficiary income is paid for the beneficiary as the beneficiary's agent: s HD 12(1).

Accordingly, income distributed to minor beneficiaries should be included in the trust tax return as trustee income and not as beneficiary income on the IR 6B ("Estate or trust beneficiary details") or in any return of the minors. See Inland Revenue newsletter, *Agents Answers*, Issue 46, June 2003.

¶10-040 Who is a minor?

A minor is defined for the purposes of the minor beneficiary rule as a natural person:

- who is a New Zealand resident, and
- who is under 16 years old on the balance date of the trust making the distribution of beneficiary income: s HC 35(3).

The balance date for the purposes of s HC 35(3) is the balance date for the income year in which the trust derives the income from which the distribution of beneficiary income is made.

Example

The trustee of a trust wishes to make a distribution to a minor beneficiary. The child was 15 years old at balance date, being 31 March, but will be 16 years old on 27 May following the balance date, when the trustees propose to make the distribution. Will the minor beneficiary rule apply?

Yes. The minor beneficiary rule will apply to any distribution of beneficiary income made from income derived by the trustees in the year ended 31 March, because the test is referenced to the minor's age on the trust's balance date, not the time of distribution.

¶10-050 Application of the minor beneficiary rule

Unless an exception applies (see ¶10-060 and ¶10-070), the minor beneficiary rule can apply to beneficiary income regardless of whether the distribution is from a complying, non-complying or foreign trust.

¶10-060 The minor beneficiary rule does not apply to small distributions

There is an exemption for small distributions of beneficiary income.

If a minor derives beneficiary income of $1,000 or less in an income year, the minor beneficiary rule does not apply: s HC 35(4)(a). Where the rule does not apply, the beneficiary income is included in the beneficiary's income and taxed at the beneficiary's marginal rate of tax.

If this exemption does not apply, all of the beneficiary income received by the beneficiary will be subject to the minor beneficiary rule: *Tax Information Bulletin* ¶135-112 Vol 13, No 5, May 2001.

The exemption for small distributions applies to each trust that a minor receives beneficiary income from in an income year (QB 07/02: Whether the minor beneficiary rule exemption in section HH 3B (now HC 35(4)(a)) applies on a $1,000 "per beneficiary" or on a $1,000 "per beneficiary per trust" basis: *Tax Information Bulletin* ¶194-103 Vol 19, No 4, May 2007.

However, where multiple small distributions are made to the same beneficiary from different trusts, it would be prudent to consider whether the anti-avoidance provisions could apply.

In calculating whether the exemption for small distributions applies, income from other sources is disregarded.

Example

In addition to $1,040 wages per annum, 15-year-old Scott receives $990 beneficiary income from a trust settled by his father. As Scott has derived total income in excess of the small distribution threshold, will the minor beneficiary rule apply?

No. In calculating whether the small distribution threshold has been exceeded, income derived from sources other than distributions from a trust or trusts are disregarded.

As the distribution of beneficiary income is $1,000 or less, the small distribution exemption will apply and both the $1,040 wages and the distribution of beneficiary income will be subject to income tax at the Scott's marginal tax rate (subject to any rebates allowed).

The $1,000 small distribution limit is not affected by the tax position of the minor beneficiary. This means that if a minor beneficiary has tax losses to carry forward, it is not possible to increase the exemption limit by taking the tax losses into account.

Example

A minor beneficiary has accumulated tax losses of $2,000. Beneficiary income of $2,500 is distributed to the beneficiary. Will the $2,000 tax loss be offset against the distribution of $2,500 so that the net income of $500 distributed to the beneficiary will not be subject to the minor beneficiary rule?

No. The small distribution exemption applies to the gross amount distributed without allowance for any tax losses that would otherwise be offset against the income. As the $1,000 small distribution limit has been exceeded, the minor beneficiary rule will apply.

The income will be taxed as trustee income and the tax losses carried forward by the minor beneficiary personally.

¶10-070 Settlements from certain trusts are excluded from the minor beneficiary rule

The minor beneficiary rule will not apply to beneficiary income derived by a minor if all the settlements onto the trust were made by a person who is neither a relative nor a guardian of the minor beneficiary, nor associated with a relative or guardian: s HC 36(1)(a). This exception reflects the policy basis of the minor beneficiary rule that the rule's primary application is to prevent income splitting within family groups.

Any settlement is defined by reference to a settlor: s YA 1 "settlement".

The definition of settlor is modified for the purposes of the minor beneficiary rule and means a person who transfers value to a trust, provides financial assistance or is treated as a settlor under s HC 28. However, if the transfer of value is the provision of a low interest loan existing on or after 1 April 2002, to comply with the definition, the interest rate must be less than the fringe benefit tax prescribed interest rate on 31 March of the previous tax year.

Also excluded from the definition is any transfer of value that includes:

- the provision of financial assistance by way of a guarantee that was not called on or the provision of security that was not called on, and
- services that are incidental to the operation of the trust, such as bookkeeping or accounting services or those provided in being a trustee: ss HC 27, YA 1 "settlor".

¶10-080 Relative

A "relative" for the purposes of the minor beneficiary rule is defined by reference to the definition of relative in s YA 1, extended to include being in a marriage, civil union or de facto relationship with a person connected to the other through adoption (as described in paragraph (a)(iv) of the definition of relative), or guardianship.

"Relative" is defined in s YA 1 as a person connected with another person by:

- being within the second degree of blood relationship: see para (a)(i)
- being the other person's spouse, civil union or de facto partner: see para (a)(ii)
- being in a marriage, civil union or de facto partnership with a person who is within the second degree of blood relationship to the other person: see para (a)(iii)
- being adopted as a child, or as a child of a person who is within the first degree of relationship to the other person: see para (a)(iv) and s HC 36(5) ("relative")
- the trustee of a trust under which a relative of the person has benefited or is eligible to benefit: see para (a)(v).

¶10-090 Calculating degrees of relationship for purposes of the definition of relative

Degrees of relationship are ascertained by counting the relationship steps between people by reference to common parents.

For example, Dulcie and Jordan are grandmother and grandson. There is one degree of relationship between Jordan and his mother Tracey. There is one degree of relationship between Tracey and her mother Dulcie. Accordingly, there are 2 degrees of relationship between Jordan and his grandmother Dulcie (Tracey's mother).

¶10-100 Eligible to benefit for the purposes of the definition of relative

To be eligible to benefit from a trust, a person must be either named as a beneficiary or a member of a class of beneficiaries, for example, "the settlor's children". A person is not eligible to benefit only if the person is someone who could be appointed as a beneficiary, for example, under a power of appointment of beneficiary.

¶10-110 Guardian for the purposes of the minor beneficiary rule

For the purposes of the minor beneficiary rule, guardian is defined by reference to the meaning of the term "guardianship" in s 15 of the Care of Children Act 2004, subject to specified exclusions: s HC 36(5).

Guardianship means having all the duties, powers, rights and responsibilities of a parent. It does not mean custody but includes the right (subject to any order of the court) to decide who has the day-to-day care of a child.

Excluded from the definition are guardians appointed under:

- s 110(1)(a)–(d) of the Oranga Tamariki Act 1989 (when a child or young person who has been declared by a court to be in need of care or protection, these sections allow the appointment as guardian any of the chief executive of the Department administering the Children, Young Persons and their Families Act, an iwi social service, a cultural social service, the director of a child and family support service or any other person)
- s 31 of the Care of Children Act 2004 (this provision allows the Family Court or the High Court to place an unmarried child under the guardianship of the court)
- s 53 of the Public Trust Office Act 1957
- s 7(4) of the Adoption Act 1955 (pending an adoption order, a parent may appoint the chief executive of the Department administering the Children, Young Persons and Their Families Act 1989 as a temporary guardian of a child).

¶10-120 Settlements from unrelated parties are not subject to the minor beneficiary rule

The minor beneficiary rule does not apply if all settlements onto the trust were made by a settlor who is a relative, guardian or a person associated with a relative or guardian; and that settlor is acting as the minor beneficiary's agent and has received the property from an unrelated person: s HC 36(1)(b)(i).

The associated person test for the purposes of the minor beneficiary rule is that contained in subpart YB, but does not include a person associated only because a relative is treated as an associated person under ss YB 4 and YB 5: s HC 36(5).

¶10-130 Settlements made under a court order may not be subject to the minor beneficiary rule

The minor beneficiary rule does not apply if all settlements onto the trust are made in accordance with a court order that requires a settlor (who is a relative, guardian or a person associated with a relative or guardian) to pay damages or compensation to the minor: s HC 36(1)(b)(ii).

There is little commentary on the exemption for such settlements and as to what kinds of court-ordered damages or compensation it is intended should qualify for the exemption. However, it is clear that the exception does not apply to court orders made in accordance with the Property (Relationships) Act 1976, which provide for the settlement of property upon a trust whether on the breakdown of a family or otherwise (see the report to the Finance and Expenditure Committee on the Taxation (Beneficiary Income of Minors, Services-related Payments and Remedial Matters) Bill prepared by the Policy Advice Division of Inland Revenue and Treasury (19 February 2001, at 25)).

Example

A husband and wife formed a trust for their children after a lengthy relationship property battle that proceeded through the court. The court appointed a mediator who mediated an agreement for a trust of $1 million to be created for the children.

After mediation, the agreement was ratified by the court and put in place. The trustees now wish to distribute $40,000 income to the minor children.

The exemption from the minor beneficiary rule that applies where all settlements upon a trust are made by a relative, legal guardian or associated person and the settlor is required by court order to pay damages or compensation to the minor will not apply. The minor beneficiary rule will apply and the distributions will be taxed as trustee income.

Some assistance may also be provided by reference to the comparable provision in the Australian Income Tax legislation (see Division 6AA of the ITA Act 1936), which includes exceptions contained in ss HC 36 and HC 37. The Australian exclusions concern situations where the potential for income splitting is limited. The New Zealand exceptions are similar to those in place in Australia, as modified during the consultation process to suit circumstances in New Zealand.

¶10-140 Settlements made in relation to a protection order are not subject to the minor beneficiary rule

The minor beneficiary rule does not apply if all settlements onto the trust were made by a settlor (who is a relative, guardian or a person associated with a relative or guardian) if the minor is a "protected person" (as defined in s 8 of the Family Violence Act 2018) in relation to a protection order and if the settlement occurs before the protection order is made or when the order is in force: s HC 36(1)(b)(iii).

¶10-150 Settlements onto qualifying testamentary trusts are not subject to the minor beneficiary rule

The minor beneficiary rule does not apply to beneficiary income derived by a minor if all the settlements onto the trust were made under a will, codicil, intestacy or court variation; and:

- the minor is alive within 12 months of the settlor's death, or
- the minor has a sibling or half-sibling alive within 12 months of the date of the settlor's death: s HC 37(1).

This exception will not apply if a will is varied by a deed of family arrangement, otherwise than due to a court order.

¶10-160 Beneficiary income derived from a Māori authority is not subject to the minor beneficiary rule

The minor beneficiary rule does not apply to beneficiary income derived by a minor from a Māori authority: s HC 35(4)(b)(iii). Trusts eligible to elect to become Māori authorities include trusts established by orders under or else owning land subject to the Te Ture Whenua Maori Act 1993, trusts that are mandated iwi organisations under the Maori Fisheries Act 2004 or trusts mandated to receive assets transferred by the Crown as part of the settlement of claims under the Treaty of Waitangi.

¶10-170 Beneficiary income derived from a group investment fund is not subject to the minor beneficiary rule

The minor beneficiary rule does not apply to beneficiary income derived directly by a minor from a group investment fund: s HC 35(4)(b)(iv).

¶10-180 Beneficiary income derived by a minor who receives a child disability allowance is not subject to the minor beneficiary rule

The minor beneficiary rule does not apply to beneficiary income derived by a minor in receipt of a child disability allowance paid under the Social Security Act 2018.

This exception applies regardless of the amount of beneficiary income derived by a minor.

¶10-190 Exemption for small additional settlements

The minor beneficiary rule does not apply if the only settlements that do not come under an exclusion to the rule are settlements comprising:

- dispositions of property that do not exceed $5,000 in total value at the end of the trust's income year (each settlement being valued at the date of settlement: s HC 36(3)(a), or
- the provision of financial assistance for less than market value that has a total value not exceeding $1,000 on any day in the trust's income year: s HC 36(3)(b).

Financial assistance is defined broadly and includes the provision of a loan, guarantee, security, or other assistance. For the avoidance of doubts, an amount payable on demand where demand is not exercised or is deferred is the provision of a loan for less than market value: s HC 36(5) "financial assistance".

Trusts that have received such settlements are sometimes referred to as mixed trusts for the purposes of the minor beneficiary rule. Care must be taken before making any further settlement onto a mixed trust to ensure that the thresholds are not exceeded. As a matter of pragmatism, rather than relying on the small additional settlements exclusion, a trustee of a trust that is otherwise untainted may wish to consider refusing settlements that will taint a trust, where possible directing these settlements to separate trusts. The term "tainted" is used in the context of the minor beneficiary rule to reflect a trust to which the rule will apply.

It would also be wise to canvas the possibility of avoidance in situations in which a trustee wishes to avoid a settlement that will taint a trust. However, as the matter has already been flagged as a transitional issue (see statement below), any avoidance risk should be limited to extreme situations.

The Official's report to the Finance and Expenditure Committee on the Taxation (Beneficiary Income of Minors, Services-Related Payments and Remedial Matters) Bill suggests that the issue of mixed trusts is a transitional one. It notes in relation to the s HH 3C (now s HC 36(3)) exemption that:

> "... it sets a clear rule for the future. Untainted settlements can be settled in a separate trust from property that is subject to the rule to ensure that the 33% rate will not apply to all beneficiary income".

Taxation (Beneficiary Income of Minors, Services-related Payments and Remedial Matters) Bill: Officials' Report to the Finance and Expenditure Committee on Submissions on the Bill, 19 February 2001, at 10.

The exception for small additional settlements does not apply if services are supplied to a trust by a relative, guardian or associated person. However, for this purpose, the term "services" does not include services incidental to the operation of the trust, such as bookkeeping or accounting services, or services as a trustee. This rule is intended to ensure that income distributed to minor beneficiaries from trading trusts is not exempted from the minor beneficiary rule: s HC 36(4).

Example

A sum of $6,000 is advanced to a trust interest-free and repayable on demand. The beneficiaries of the trust include the minor children of the settlor who made the advance. No other settlements have been made onto the trust.

The interest-free advance gives rise to a settlement onto the trust because the value of the loan exceeds the $1,000 financial assistance threshold.

Any further settlements onto the trust will be tainted settlements and the minor beneficiary rule will apply to distributions of beneficiary income to minor beneficiaries, unless one of the other exemptions applies, for example, distributions of less than $1,000 to a minor beneficiary.

If the advance was forgiven on the settlor's death, the trust would become a mixed trust, assuming that the settlor's minor children are alive at the date of the settlor's death, because the "tainted" settlement, by way of forgiveness of debt of $6,000, is greater than $5,000, and the loan had a value greater than $1,000.

If no exception applies, all beneficiary income derived by a minor beneficiary from the trust will be subject to the minor beneficiary rule.

¶10-200 Tracing is not available

Where a trust contains settlements from tainted and untainted settlements, it is not possible to trace distributions so that the rule can be avoided by limiting a distribution to untainted settlements. Where an earlier settlement has "tainted a trust", the only way to avoid this effect would be for a subsequent "untainted settlement" to be onto a new or different trust that was subject to an exclusion from the minor beneficiary rule. The veracity of doing so will likely depend in the most part on the value of such an untainted settlement and the cost of the application of the rule, presuming it is still desirable or necessary to make distributions of beneficiary income to a minor, who would otherwise be subject to the rule.

¶10-210 Losses incurred by the minor cannot be offset against minor beneficiary income

Income subject to the minor beneficiary rule is the minor's excluded income for tax purposes. This means that losses incurred by a minor cannot be offset against any minor beneficiary income.

Example

A minor beneficiary receives $5,000 as beneficiary income from a trust settled by the minor's parents. The minor beneficiary has a tax loss carried forward from the previous income year.

Can the loss be offset against the minor beneficiary income?

No. Due to the application of the minor beneficiary rule, the $5,000 is not income of the minor and is taxed as if it were trustee income. No adjustment is made to the minor beneficiary's loss carried forward. Unless the minor beneficiary derives other income in his or her own name, the loss will continue to be carried forward.

¶10-220 A minor's correct tax rate is determined without reference to any minor beneficiary income

Income subject to the minor beneficiary rule is not taken into account when calculating income tax on income earned by the minor beneficiary in that beneficiary's personal capacity.

Example

A trust carrying on a farming business employs a 14-year-old beneficiary. PAYE is deducted from his wages. As a beneficiary, the 14-year-old receives a distribution of $70,000 as beneficiary income (to which the minor beneficiary rule applies) in the current tax year. The minor beneficiary's gross wages are $16,000 for the year.

As the minor's total income is in excess of $70,000, will the minor pay income tax at the top marginal rate on his wages?

No. The $70,000 beneficiary income is treated as trustee income. Tax paid by the trustee on the $70,000 is capped at 33%. The $16,000 wages will be included in the minor beneficiary's gross income and taxed at the applicable marginal rate.

¶10-230 The trustee is liable for any provisional tax in respect of minor beneficiary income

Trustees are liable to pay any provisional tax due in respect of income paid to a minor beneficiary. Use of money interest will apply if provisional tax is underpaid by the trustee. The safe harbour provisions do not apply to trustees.

¶10-240 The minor beneficiary rule can apply to children's bank accounts

Care needs to be taken when establishing children's bank accounts to ensure that the account is not a trust to which the minor beneficiary rule might apply.

The Commissioner of Inland Revenue's view is that a child's bank account will be a trust to which the minor beneficiary rule applies if:

- a parent opens a bank account in the parent's own name using funds that are the property of the child, and
- the parent has signing authority over that account, and either deposits additional funds from time to time and/or withdraws amounts periodically for the benefit of the child: *Tax Information Bulletin* ¶135-112 Vol 13, No 5, May 2001.

There is a trust because of the separation of legal and beneficial ownership – the parent holding legal title and the child holding the beneficial interest.

There may not be a trust if the parent was acting as bare trustee or nominee for the child. That is, the parent operates the account on the instructions of the child. In practice this is unlikely to be the case. However, it does demonstrate the need to carefully consider all of the background facts (not just the name of, and the signatories to, the account). If no trust is intended, the account should be opened in the name of the child alone to avoid any suggestion that there is a trust in terms of the Commissioner's stated policy.

For the same reasons, no trust would exist if:

- an account is opened or operated in the name of the child, but the parent possesses signing authority either alone or together with the child, or
- an account is opened or operated in the child's name – only the child has signing authority and the child makes withdrawals from the account.

A trust in respect of a child's bank account will only be of significance for the purposes of the minor beneficiary rule if the interest on the account is more than $1,000 in any tax year.

¶10-250 Correct identification of distributions is prudent

Care should be taken to carefully consider the wisdom of treating distributions to minor beneficiaries as loans that are repaid when the beneficiary ceases to be a minor.

From a trust perspective treating beneficiary distributions as loans so that a minor beneficiary's beneficiary account is overdrawn raises questions as to whether a loan to a minor is an appropriate exercise of the trustee's discretion, given the unenforceability of the loan against a minor. See the Contract and Commercial Law Act 2017, Pt 2, Subpart 6. Also see ¶22-110.

Further, if distributions to a minor beneficiary are accumulated in an overdrawn current account and later offset by a distribution of beneficiary income (when the beneficiary is no longer a minor for the purposes of the minor beneficiary rule), consideration should be given as to whether this could amount to tax avoidance. See ¶22-110.

¶10-260 Capital distributions

The minor beneficiary rule only applies to distributions of income. Distributions of capital are not subject to the rule.

Example

All the current year income of a complying trust has been distributed to an adult beneficiary. A distribution of capital is made to the minor beneficiary.

The capital distribution will not be subject to the minor beneficiary rule. Distributions (not being beneficiary income) derived by a beneficiary of a qualifying trust are not taxable to the beneficiary. Even if the capital distribution were taxable to the beneficiary, for example, if the distribution were made from a foreign or non-qualifying trust, the minor beneficiary rule only applies in relation to distributions of beneficiary income. Note that in the case of a foreign or non-complying trust, the ordering rules would need to be applied to determine the nature of the distribution, for example, whether it consisted of beneficiary income or a capital distribution or other amount.

¶10-270 Flow chart demonstrating the application of the minor beneficiary rule

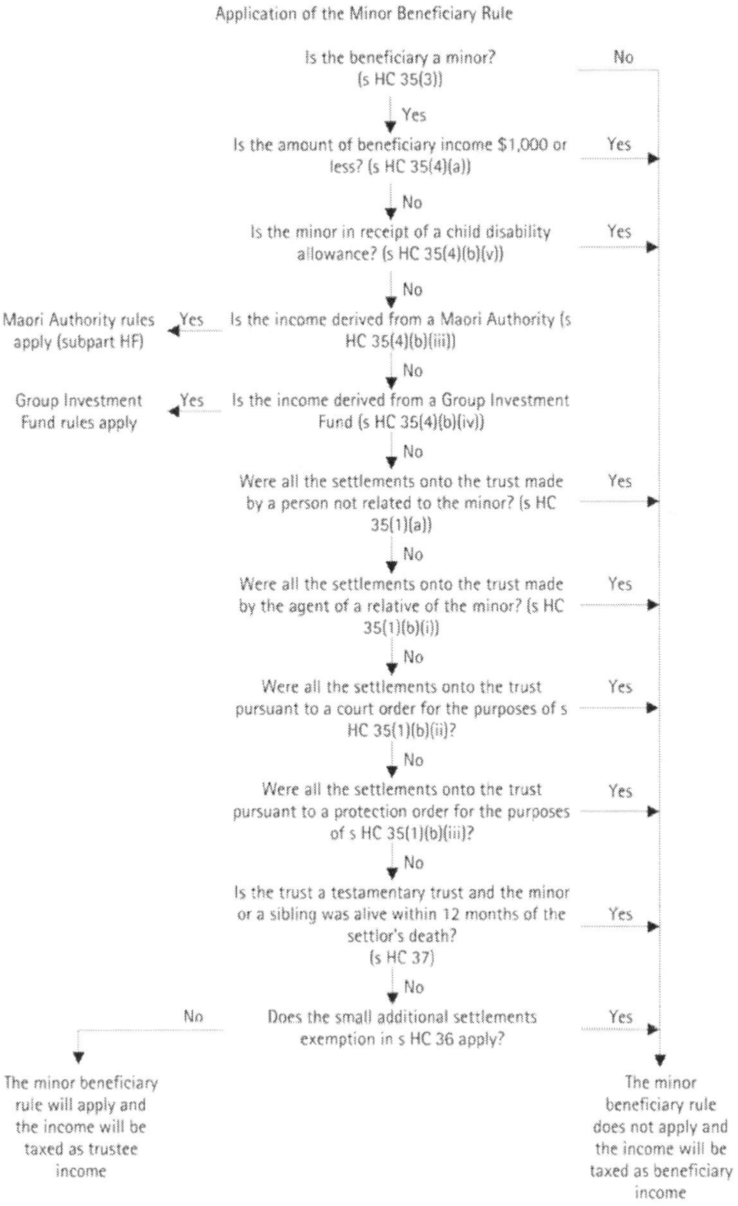

¶10-280 Legislation

Income Tax Act 2007

HC 35 BENEFICIARY INCOME OF MINORS

HC 35(1) WHEN THIS SECTION APPLIES

This section applies when a person who is a minor derives an amount of beneficiary income from a trust in an income year. Subsection (4) and sections HC 36 and HC 37 override this subsection.

HC 35(2) TREATMENT OF AMOUNT DERIVED

The amount is–

(a) excluded income of the minor under section CX 58 (Amounts derived by minors from trusts):

(b) treated as trustee income for the purposes of determining the rate of tax that applies, who pays the relevant tax, and who provides the return of income.

HC 35(3) MEANING OF MINOR

For the purposes of this section, and sections HC 36, HC 37, LE 4, and LF 2 (which relate to the treatment of tax credits of beneficiary minors), a **minor** is a natural person resident in New Zealand who is under 16 years of age on the trust's balance date for the income year.

HC 35(4) EXCLUSIONS

This section does not apply–

(a) if the total amount of beneficiary income that the minor derives from the trust in the income year is $1,000 or less; or

(b) to beneficiary income derived–

  (i) from a trust settled in the way described in section HC 36:

  (ii) from a testamentary trust described in section HC 37:

  (iii) from a Maori authority:

  (iv) directly from a group investment fund:

  (v) by a person for whom a child disability allowance is paid under the Social Security Act 2018.

HC 35(5) RELATIONSHIP WITH OTHER PROVISIONS

This section overrides sections HC 5, HC 18 to HC 20, HC 22, HC 23, and HC 32.

HC 36 TRUSTS AND MINOR BENEFICIARY RULE

HC 36(1) TRUSTS EXCLUDED FROM APPLICATION OF MINOR BENEFICIARY RULE

Section HC 35(2) does not apply to an amount of beneficiary income derived by a minor if all settlements on the trust meet the requirements of section HC 37(1) or were made by–

(a) a person who is neither a relative or a guardian of the minor, nor a person associated with a relative or a guardian; or

(b) a person who is a relative, guardian, or a person associated with a relative or guardian, if–

  (i) the settlor is acting as agent of the minor and has received the property from a person other than a relative, guardian, or their associate:

  (ii) the settlor is required by a court order to pay damages or compensation to the minor:

  (iii) the minor is a protected person, as defined in section 8 of the Family Violence Act 2018, in relation to a protection order, and the settlement, whether made jointly with another person or not, is made before the protection order is made or during the time the order is in force.

HC 36(2) WHEN SOME SETTLEMENTS DO NOT MEET REQUIREMENTS

Subsection (3) applies when more than 1 settlement is made on a trust, and 1 or more but not all settlements meet the requirements of subsection (1) or section HC 37(1).

HC 36(3) SMALL ADDITIONAL SETTLEMENTS PERMITTED

Section HC 35(2) does not apply to an amount of beneficiary income derived by a minor if the only settlements that do not meet the requirements are made through–

(a) the disposal for less than market value of property whose total value is no more than $5,000 at the end of the trust's income year, valuing each settlement at the date of settlement; or

(b) providing financial assistance for less than market value in the form of a loan whose total value is no more than $1,000 on any day in the trust's income year.

HC 36(4) EXCLUSION IF SIGNIFICANT SERVICES PROVIDED TO TRUST

Subsection (3) does not apply if services are provided to the trust by a relative, guardian, or associated person, unless those services are incidental to the operation of the trust. Examples of incidental services are bookkeeping, accounting, or trustee services.

HC 36(5) SOME DEFINITIONS

In this section,–

associated person or **person associated** does not include a person associated only under sections YB 4 and YB 5 (which relate to relatives who are treated as associated persons)

guardian has the meaning set out in section 15 of the Care of Children Act 2004, and persons are connected by guardianship if 1 is the guardian of the other, but guardian does not include a guardian appointed under–

(a) section 110(1)(a) to (d) of the Oranga Tamariki Act 1989; or

(b) section 31 of the Care of Children Act 2004; or

(c) section 53 of the Public Trust Office Act 1957 by a court order; or

(d) section 7(4) of the Adoption Act 1955

relative means a person referred to in paragraph (a) of the definition of **relative** in section YA 1 (Definitions) extended to include being in a marriage, civil union, or de facto relationship with a person connected to the other through adoption, as described in paragraph (a)(iv), or guardianship.

HC 37 TESTAMENTARY TRUSTS AND MINOR BENEFICIARY RULE

HC 37(1) TESTAMENTARY TRUSTS NOT SUBJECT TO MINOR BENEFICIARY RULE

Section HC 35(2) does not apply to an amount of beneficiary income derived by a minor if all the settlements on the trust meet the requirements of section HC 36(1) or were made under a will, codicil, intestacy, or court variation and–

(a) the minor is alive within 12 months of the date of the settlor's death; or

(b) the minor has a brother, sister, half-brother, or half-sister alive within 12 months of the date of the settlor's death.

HC 37(2) SMALL ADDITIONAL SETTLEMENTS PERMITTED

Section HC 36(3) may apply to extend the application of this exemption.

[...]

YA 1 DEFINITIONS

[...]

relative,–

(a) for the purposes of only this Act, other than in section HC 36 (Trusts and minor beneficiary rule) and the definition of **look-through company**, means a person connected with another person by–

(i) being within the second degree of blood relationship to the other:

(ii) being in a marriage, civil union, or de facto relationship with the other:

(iii) being in a marriage, civil union, or de facto relationship with a person who is within the second degree of blood relationship to the other:

(iv) being adopted as a child of the other or as a child of a person who is within the first degree of relationship to the other:

(v) being the trustee of a trust under which a relative has benefited or is eligible to benefit:

(b) is defined in section HC 36(5) for the purposes of only that section:

[...]

CHAPTER 11

Losses

¶11-010 Operating principle

Losses incurred by a trustee can be carried forward to offset against future income, but cannot be distributed to any beneficiary of the trust.

¶11-020 The principles of deductions apply to a trustee in the same way as to any other taxpayer

The general permission provides that a person, including a trustee, is allowed a deduction for any loss, including a depreciation loss incurred deriving income or in the course of carrying on a business: s DA 1.

This means that a trustee that owns a family home that is not used to derive any income cannot claim a deduction for any expenses incurred in respect of that home. However, if the same trustee owns a rental property, the expenses incurred from the rental of the property, including any allowable depreciation, can be deducted from the rental business income.

¶11-030 Net losses incurred by a trustee cannot be attributed to a beneficiary but can be carried forward

If a trustee is carrying on a business, any loss arising from that business is a loss to the trustee, not to the beneficiaries. Although a net loss can be carried forward, it cannot be distributed or otherwise attributed to any beneficiaries.

A beneficiary who receives beneficiary income cannot claim a deduction for any expenditure or loss incurred by the trustee in deriving that income: s DV 9(1).

This is the case regardless of the terms of the trust.

However, for the purpose of determining whether a trustee is entitled to a deduction for any loss or expenditure, any income distributed to beneficiaries as beneficiary income is treated as trustee income: s DV 9(2).

Example

The Macaroon Trust borrows $1 million to purchase shares in Bakers Limited (the Company). During the income year, the Macaroon Trust receives a gross dividend of $100,000 (with $28,000 of imputation credits attached from the Company) and pays $85,000 interest on the loan.

Can the trustee of the Macaroon Trust distribute the net income of $15,000 (being the gross dividend less the interest on the loan) to an adult beneficiary, along with the $28,000 imputation credits attached to the dividend?

The trustee of the Macaroon Trust cannot distribute the interest deduction to the beneficiary. A beneficiary who receives beneficiary income cannot claim a deduction for any expenditure or loss incurred by the trustee in deriving that income.

However, the trustee of the Macaroon Trust could distribute the $100,000 dividend and claim a deduction for the $85,000 interest on the loan. This is because, when determining a trust's entitlement to a deduction, income distributed as beneficiary income is treated as trustee income.

The rules regarding losses also apply to the trustee of a testamentary trust: *Tax Information Bulletin* ¶72-114 Vol 7, No 2, July 1995 at 19.

Example

Trustees were permitted to deduct the loss from one income year against the profits of the subsequent income year. This was although the testator's will provided that any losses should be recouped out of capital, not profit: *Rutherford* v *C of IR* (1964) 14 ATD 32.

However, if a trustee has the power to recoup losses from future beneficiary income, on the exercise of that power, the beneficiary is taxed on net income with a deduction allowed for loss recouped by the trustee.

¶11-035 Tax losses can be offset against taxable distributions from a non-complying trust

A beneficiary of a non-complying trust may claim a tax loss to which ss IA 2 to IA 10 apply. However, the amount of tax loss cannot be subtracted from the net income for the corresponding tax year for the purposes of s IA 2 (loss balances carried forward): ss HC 22, IA 2(2), IA 3(3). See further in Chapter 5 – *Taxable Distributions*.

¶11-040 Losses cannot pass on death to a testamentary trust

Net losses are generally available to be carried forward to offset against subsequent income: s IA 2. However, net losses are lost at death and cannot be carried forward to the deceased person's estate, which is a different person for tax purposes: *Tax Information Bulletin* ¶72-124 Vol 7, No 2, July 1995 at 31.

¶11-050 A loss incurred in respect of a vested interest can be offset against beneficiary income

If a beneficiary has a vested share in trust property in the year in which a loss is incurred, that loss can be carried forward and set off against beneficiary income.

¶11-060 A loss incurred by a bare trustee can be offset against beneficiary income

Bare trusts are generally disregarded for income tax purposes. See s YB 21, which provides that, unless the context provides otherwise, where a person holds something or does something as a nominee, the nominee is ignored. However, a trustee is a nominee only if the trustee is a bare trustee. The principles developed through the courts on what amounts to a "bare trust" are summarised in interpretation statement IS 12/01, "Income tax: timing of share transfers for the purposes of the continuity provisions" *Tax Information Bulletin* ¶247-103 Vol 24, No 7, August 2012 at [112]. Three principles can be distilled from these authorities:

- A "bare trustee" is a person who holds property on trust for the absolute benefit of other persons and has no beneficial interest in the property.
- A "bare trustee" does not have any duties to perform in regard to the property, except to convey or transfer it to a person entitled to hold it when required to do so.
- For a bare trust relationship to exist, the three certainties of a trust must be satisfied.

If a trustee carries on business as a bare trustee, any loss incurred can be carried forward and offset against income of those persons absolutely entitled to the income. An example of such a situation is where a trustee has no authority under a will, but acts with the agreement of beneficiaries with an absolute interest. See ¶25-035 regarding GST considerations and bare trusts and also ¶24-070 regarding bare trust structures.

¶11-070 Losses carried forward must be offset in the immediately succeeding year

Losses must be offset in the next tax year where there is income to offset the losses against: s IA 3.

Income can only be determined by subtracting any available net losses that the person has from their net income: s BC 4(3). This means that, if there are losses to be offset against current year trustee income, that income cannot be paid out as beneficiary income and the loss is carried forward to a future year or years.

See *Tax Information Bulletin* ¶15-117 Vol 1, No 5, November 1989, which provides at Appendix [8.41] that:

> "Where losses are able to be carried forward for offset against future income they are deducted from the income derived by the trustee in the succeeding income year. If after the deduction of such losses in the succeeding income year there is income remaining this income will be beneficiary income or trustee income, depending upon whether the income is vested in or paid or applied to or for the benefit of the beneficiary. Thus, the loss is not carried forward and deducted against beneficiary income or trustee income: rather, it is carried forward and deducted from income derived by the trustee in the succeeding income year in determining whether there is any income in that year which may be classified as beneficiary income or trustee income".

However, as beneficiary income is defined in gross income terms, it is arguable that amounts distributed as beneficiary income can exceed the accounting surplus and/or taxable income of the trust, as that is defined for tax purposes. For example, this situation could arise if the distributions made by the trustees simply exceeded the accounting surplus or taxable income of the trust. In this regard, there would appear to be no tax requirement for the trustees to first apply the gross income of the trust in meeting its expenses. In appropriate circumstances, the trustees could choose to meet these expenses out of trust capital or corpus.

That said, the trustee would need to confirm whether the deed of trust permitted the trustee to make a distribution that exceeds the trustee's taxable income and to resort to the trust capital. If there is no permission, the trustee would be in breach of trust and vulnerable to a claim from the capital beneficiary/beneficiaries.

¶11-080 A trustee cannot create a tax loss by making distributions in excess of current year profit

If distributions to beneficiaries exceed current year taxable income, for example, if there are distributions of income and capital, a trustee has not created a tax loss in the current year that can be carried forward.

In terms of the tax legislation, an allocation to a beneficiary is either beneficiary income, which is taxable in the beneficiary's hands, or a distribution that is outside the definition of beneficiary income.

Any distribution in excess of the current year's taxable income will not create a tax loss for the trust.

Example

The trustee of the Peggy Black Trust, a complying trust, has $24,000 of taxable income. The trustee pays $50,000 to Alice, who is a beneficiary as to income and capital.

The distribution to Alice is taxable to her as beneficiary income as to $24,000. The balance is a (tax-free) distribution of capital. Had the trustee retained the $24,000 and made a distribution of $24,000 capital to Alice, the $24,000 retained by the trustee would still be taxable as trustee income as the payment of capital could not be offset against the trustee income.

¶11-090 Losses can prevent the allocation of accounting income

Where a trustee has both losses and accounting profits, it can be difficult to reconcile the allocation of trustee income and beneficiary income.

Example

A trustee has tax losses and current year accounting profit. If the losses are offset against the current year income, despite the accounting profit, there is no income to distribute to beneficiaries. Where this situation arises, the deed of trust should be referred to for any guidance on how losses are to be allocated between income and capital.

If any income has been paid to a beneficiary, for the purposes of the Income Tax Act, only the balance of any income retained by the trustee would be trustee income against which losses can be offset.

¶11-100 Any losses are lost when a trust is wound up

If a trust is wound up, any losses will be extinguished. See Chapter 34 – *Winding Up*.

¶11-110 Legislation

Income Tax Act 2007

BC 4 NET INCOME AND NET LOSS

[...]

BC 4(3) DEDUCTIONS MORE THAN INCOME

If, for a tax year, a person's annual total deduction is more than their annual gross income, the difference is their net loss for the year, and their net income for the year is zero.

[...]

DV 9 TRUSTS

DV 9(1) NO DEDUCTION

A person who derives beneficiary income is denied a deduction for expenditure or loss that a trustee incurs in deriving the income.

DV 9(2) TRUSTEE INCOME

For the purpose of determining the deductions that a trustee is allowed in an income year, beneficiary income of beneficiaries of the trust in the income year is treated as trustee income.

DV 9(3) LINK WITH SUBPART DA

The link between this section and subpart DA (General rules) is as follows:

(a) subsection (1) overrides the general permission:

(b) subsection (2) supplements the general permission; the general limitations still apply.

[...]

IA 2 TAX LOSSES

IA 2(1) WHAT IS A TAX LOSS?

A person's tax loss for a tax year is found by adding together the amounts referred to in subsections (2) to (4).

IA 2(2) LOSS BALANCES CARRIED FORWARD

If the person has a loss balance carried forward under section IA 3(4) to the tax year, the amount is included in their tax loss for the tax year to the extent to which it is not subtracted under section IA 4(1)(a) from their net income for the tax year.

IA 2(3) NET LOSSES

If the person has a net loss under section BC 4 (Net income and net loss) for the tax year, the amount is a tax loss component included in their tax loss for the tax year.

[...]

IA 3 USING TAX LOSSES IN TAX YEAR

[...]

IA 3(3) TAXABLE DISTRIBUTIONS

The amount of a tax loss for a tax year of a beneficiary of a non-complying trust may be used under section HC 22 (Use of tax losses to reduce taxable distributions from non-complying trusts) to adjust the amount of a taxable distribution derived in the corresponding income year.

IA 3(4) REMAINING LOSS BALANCES CARRIED FORWARD

If a person has a balance of tax loss remaining for a tax year after the uses described in this section, the balance is carried forward to the next tax year as a loss balance.

IA 3(5) RELATIONSHIP WITH OTHER PROVISIONS IN THIS SUBPART

Sections IA 3B, IA 5, IA 8, and IA 10 override this section.

[...]

Part III

LIFE LEASES AND DEBT FORGIVENESS

CHAPTER 12

Life Leases

¶12-010 Operating principle

Granting a lease in respect of a property before its transfer to a trust can ensure occupation rights as well as a reduction in the value of the property.

However, care must be taken as seemingly minor differences in arrangements can result in unanticipated income tax implications.

¶12-020 Reservation of rights

Historically, it has been common for the owner of property to grant a lease for life or a term of years before the sale to a trustee. The grant of a lease before sale is a variation on the "conventional" approach of selling assets to a trust, followed by a gifting program.

The owner of the property grants a lease back to the owner before transfer. The value of the lease is deducted from the value of the property. This means that the value of assets available to creditors, or that can be taken into account when assessing any entitlement to any long-term residential care subsidy is limited to the value of the lease.

Importantly, the lease also provides that the lessee has the right of exclusive possession for the term of the lease, which can address concerns a person might have about transferring a property that was a family home to trustees.

There are 2 steps to the lease process in the context of a transfer to a trust. The first step involves the creation of the lease. The second step is to transfer the residual interest in the property. Life interest leases or leases for a period of time can also be used in other asset and estate planning scenarios and are not limited to circumstances in which this is a sale to trustees.

The valuation and timing of the grant of the lease is crucial, and the lease must be granted before a transfer of property to avoid income tax consequences that can arise where a lease is granted for consideration.

¶12-030 A life lease must be recorded in writing

It is possible to grant a lease to oneself because the right to do so is provided for at law. Such a lease can be to the owner or to the owner jointly with another person: Property Law Act 2007, s 56.

A lease can be for the lessee's lifetime or some shorter period of time. However, to be effective, the lease must be recorded in writing and the term of the lease must be certain or capable of certainty: Land Transfer Act 2017, s 91. The lease must also include the terms of the lease as agreed between the parties.

Appropriate terms could include:

- the amount of any rent to be paid to the lessor; however, where rent is paid, it must be accounted for by the lessor
- a prohibition against the lessee subleasing or assigning the lease without the lessor's consent, and
- provision for a replacement property if the property subject to the lease is sold.

Where there is no prohibition against assigning or subletting, the lease will be an asset to the lessee that can have value to creditors or other interested parties.

If the property to be leased is subject to a mortgage, the consent of the mortgagee must be obtained.

Leases for a period not exceeding 35 years can be registered on a property's title. See the Resource Management Act 1991, s 218. However, the failure to register the life lease will not render the lease void. Where registration is not permissible, consideration should be given to lodging a caveat so that the lease cannot be overlooked.

If a property subject to a life lease or a lease for a term of years is sold and the lease is not terminated, the purchaser takes the property subject to that lease.

¶12-040 A life lease protects the transferor's right to live in the property

Life leases and leases for a term of years are common in the context of the sale of property to trustees in an asset and estate planning context. The lease protects the transferor's right to live in the property for a stated period and reduces the cost of the property to the trustees.

The reduction in the cost of the property reflects the fact that the trustee-owner does not have the use of the property for the duration of the lease.

¶12-050 A life lease is valued by reference to life expectancy

A life lease is usually valued by reference to the property owner's life expectancy. The value of the lease relates to the time the purchaser of the property, in this context, the trustee, does not have possession of the property. If all lessees have a right of occupation until their respective deaths, the discount of the property's value relates to the longest expected occupation of any of the lessees. This is usually by reference to the lifetime of the youngest owner.

Although an actuary or valuer can determine the value of the lease, it is more common for a lease to be valued by reference to the annuity tables in sch 2 of the

Estate and Gift Duties Act 1968 (EGD Act), despite these tables being extremely dated (because life expectancies have increased materially since). Valuations in accordance with sch 2 are usually acceptable to the Commissioner of Inland Revenue.

The annuity tables provide the life expectancy of a person and prescribe, amongst other things, a present value for income on capital for life.

Table A in sch 2 of the EGD Act provides the present value of an annuity or other interest for males. Table B provides for the present value of an annuity or other interest for females.

Where there are 2 or more registered proprietors, the age used is normally that of the youngest proprietor.

Example

The freehold value of a property is $400,000. Chintel, a 50-year-old woman, wishes to grant a lease to herself for life.

The figure to use to determine the value of the lease is the figure that corresponds to the present value of income on capital of $1 for life for a person who is 50 years old, which is 0.72787.

Table B – Present value of annuity or other interest for life of female or expectant on death of female

Years of age	Expectation of life of female	Present value of $1 per annum for life	Present value of $1 payable on death	Present value of income on capital of $1 for life
	Years	$	$	$
0	72.43	19.41600	0.02920	0.97080
1	72.90	19.42934	0.02853	0.97147
...				
49	27.54	14.78078	0.26096	0.73904
50	26.68	14.55732	0.27213	**0.72787**
51	25.82	14.32456	0.28377	0.71623
...				
99	1.19	1.12472	0.94376	0.05624
100	1.07	1.01587	0.94921	0.05079

Therefore, the lease has a value of $291,148 ($400,000 × 0.72787). The remainder interest in the property has a value of $108,852.

¶12-060 Lease for a term of years

If instead of a life lease, a lease for a period of years is required, the calculation is worked under Table D in sch 2 of the EGD Act.

Example

The market value of the property is $400,000. A 10-year lease is required.

The figure to use to determine the value of the lease is the figure that corresponds to the present value after a period, which for a period of 10 years is 0.61391.

The market value of the remainder interest in the property has a value of $247,720 ($400,000 × the multiplier for the preset value after a period of 10 years).

Table D – Present value of annuity or other interest for period other than life or expectant on event other than death

	Present value of $1 per annum for period	Present value of $1 per annum after period	Present value of income on capital of $1 for period
Years	$	$	$
1	0.95238	0.95238	0.04762
...			
9	7.10782	0.64461	0.35539
10	7.72173	**0.61391**	0.38609
11	8.30641	0.58468	0.41532
...			
100	19.84791	0.00760	0.99240

Accordingly, the lease has a value of $152,280 (the value of the property less the remainder interest).

¶12-070 There are circumstances in which it is inappropriate to value a life lease by reference to life expectancy

In some circumstances it can be inappropriate to value a life lease by reference to life expectancy. For example, if a person is suffering from a terminal illness. Where this is the case, Table D of sch 2 of the EGD Act can be used with the term of years being by reference to the estimated life expectancy. Also see *Johnson* v *Simpson* [2013] NZHC 2285.

¶12-080 Life interests must be accounted for on the sale of a property

If a property subject to a lease is to be sold, the property can either be sold subject to the lease or the lease can be surrendered.

If the property is sold subject to the lease, the sale proceeds must be apportioned between the 2 interests.

However, if the lease is surrendered, the value of the lease must be calculated as at the date of surrender and this must be accounted for by the owner of the property.

If the value of the property has appreciated, it can be possible for the value of the lease at the time of surrender to be worth more than when originally granted, thus defeating in part the purpose of the original transaction.

¶12-090 Income tax implications can arise from transactions involving leases

Tax implications can result from some transactions involving leases if there is any income attributable to the lease: s CC 1.

It is possible to structure a transfer of property subject to a lease so that there are no tax consequences.

However, care must be taken as the tax treatment of life leases and the variants on this theme are very fact specific. For any lease or other interest, it is necessary to consider the legal nature of the interest granted, whether any income arises from the interest.

The tax outcome for a transaction where property is transferred subject to a lease generally turns on the nature of the interest reserved to the original owner of the property.

¶12-100 No income is derived if a lease for life or a term of years is granted before the transfer of the reversionary interest

If a property is transferred subject to a lease, none of the consideration paid for the property is attributable to the lease. Accordingly, no income is derived by either the transferor or the transferee for the purposes of s CC 1 of the Income Tax Act.

Again, this is the case whether the grant of the lease occurs before or simultaneously with the transfer of the reversionary interest.

¶12-110 The income tax outcome is different for an occupation licence

A life lease or a lease for a term of years is sometimes referred to as a "licence to occupy". However, this can be misleading. A lease that is called a licence will be effective regardless of the name given.

¶12-120 An occupation licence, unlike a lease, is not binding on third parties

An occupation licence provides that the licensee is permitted to enter a property. However, an occupation licence, unlike a life lease, does not create a proprietary right that is binding on third parties.

Although a licence gives certain rights, it is not possible to grant a licence to oneself. A lease can be granted to oneself because it is a registrable interest in land. However, at law, a licence (and the attendant rights), can only be granted to a third party. See Hinde, McMorland & Sim *Land Law in New Zealand* (Butterworths, Wellington, 1997) at [5.008]. This is because there are no provisions comparable to those in ss 56 and 278 of the Property Law Act applying to licences. Therefore, a landowner cannot licence himself or herself to be a licensee.

¶12-130 A licence to occupy granted before transfer is not a reservation

A transferor can purport to grant himself or herself a licence to occupy and transfer the balance of the property to another person.

However, as a transferor cannot legally grant himself or herself a licence to occupy, the full property interest will be transferred to the transferee.

The ineffective grant of the licence will not give rise to income to the transferor or the transferee under s CC 1(1) of the Income Tax Act as there is no licence that any income can be attributed to.

The outcome is the same if the purported licence is granted simultaneously with the transfer.

For this treatment to apply, it must be clear from the documents that the transferor was to retain the benefit of the licence.

¶12-140 The most commonly made mistake in the context of leases or licences is for the lease or licence to be granted following the transfer of property

The standard arrangement regarding a life lease in an asset and estate planning context is for a lease to be granted before transfer. The value of the lease is taken into consideration when the property is sold, and the market value reduced accordingly.

If instead the property is sold with an agreement that a lease or licence will be granted after the transfer, there is a reservation of interest rather than a transfer.

Any reduction in the debt or the payment that is attributable to the lease is income to the trustee-transferee: s CC 1(1).

When determining the application of s CC 1, it is necessary to establish that:

- income is derived that comprises a rent, a fine, a premium, or other revenues
- the income is derived by the land owner, and
- the income is derived from a lease or a licence.

Income is defined broadly for the purpose of s CC 1. In addition to amounts normally associated with a lease, such as rent, the definition also includes other revenues, which the Commissioner of Inland Revenue considers includes any other amount derived under an arrangement relating to the transfer of interests in land.

Derived in the context of deriving income is defined broadly and does not require payment. Income will be derived when an amount is credited to an account or otherwise dealt with for the person's interest or benefit.

Example

Income can be derived by the recipient transferee of property if:

- the price of the property is reduced, or
- a debt owing by the transferee is reduced.

In this context, the income is derived by the trustee-landowner.

However, for any income to be derived from a lease or licence, there must also be a grant of a lease or licence and an amount attributable to that lease or licence.

¶12-150 Leases can be cancelled

If a lease is to be cancelled, for example, because the property is to be sold, the value of the lease at that time is calculated based on the current market value of the property subject to the lease.

¶12-160 Payments on account of a valid lease can be liable to income tax

If a lease or licence is granted at any time independently of any arrangement, any payment on account of the lease or licence will comprise income to the trustee-owner: s CC 1(1).

This is the case whether the trustees could have resolved that the licensee or lessee could have occupied the property as a beneficiary at no cost to the beneficiary.

A situation in which this could occur is where the trustee borrows the purchase price from a third party, for example, a bank, and then grants a lease or licence to the beneficiary occupants, the consideration for which is, or includes, meeting the trustee's repayment obligations.

If an income-producing arrangement was what the parties intended, nothing turns on such an arrangement. However, if the parties' intention was really that the beneficiary occupants would make advances to the trustee on account of the trustee's repayment obligations, then a licence such as that discussed above would not be appropriate and could have unintended tax consequences.

¶12-170 It is acceptable to include a clause that will increase a price if the price used is found to be too low

It is common to include a "sliding value" value clause so that the price at which property is transferred to a trustee can be increased if necessary to reflect market value.

¶12-180 Legislation

Income Tax Act 2007

CC 1 LAND

CC 1(1) INCOME

An amount described in subsection (2) is income of the owner of land if they derive the amount from–

(a) a lease, licence, or easement affecting the land; or

(b) the grant of a right to take the profits of the land.

CC 1(2) AMOUNTS

The amounts are–

(a) rent:

(b) a fine:

(c) a premium:

(d) a payment for the goodwill of a business:

(e) a payment for the benefit of a statutory licence:

(f) a payment for the benefit of a statutory privilege:

(g) other revenues.

[...]

CC 1(2B) AMOUNTS DERIVED FROM CERTAIN ASSETS

Despite subsections (1) and (2), an amount referred to in section CW 8B (Certain amounts derived from use of assets) is not a payment of rent or another amount for the purposes of this section.

CHAPTER 13

Gift Duty

¶13-010 Operating principle

Gift duty has been abolished in respect of gifts made on or after 1 October 2011. See Taxation (Tax Administration and Remedial Matters) Act 2011. For the position before the abolition of gift duty, see Vicki Ammundsen *Taxation of Trusts* (Ed 2, CCH, Auckland, 2011).

¶13-020 Gift duty still has historic application

While gift duty has been abolished, the abolition of gift duty does not abolish any historic gift liabilities; and care is still required when assessing any historic gift duty liability trustees might have.

It is also important to appreciate that the abolition of gift duty does not mean that outstanding debts are automatically forgiven. See Chapter 14 – *Forgiveness of Debt* and Chapter 24 – *Asset Planning.*

¶13-030 The abolition of gift duty does not amend the gifting rules that apply to long-term residential care subsidies

Another consideration that is commonly overlooked following the abolition of gift duty is that the permissible gifting limits for long-term residential care subsidy (RCS) purposes were not contemporaneously amended. The position here remains that 5 years before an application for a RCS (the gifting period), the gifting limit is $30,000 over the 5-year period ("the gifting period").

Outside the gifting period, the limit is $27,000 per year. Another aspect of permissible gifting with respect to the RCS regime that also requires consideration is whose gifting is assessed. As a general proposition is that gifts made by the applicant and the applicant's spouse or partner are taken into consideration. The treatment of gifts by spouses or partners was confirmed in *Bridgford* v *Chief Executive of the Ministry of Social Development* [2013] NZCA 410 by the Court of Appeal, which noted that:

- "The position in relation to the assets of spouses or partners and any gifting by them is therefore clearly stated. When individuals in relationships are seeking entitlement to means tested state assistance, they are to have their resources considered together as a couple ..., rather than as individual persons." [17]

- Section 147A of the Social Security Act (since repealed. See Residential Care and Disability Support Services Act 2018, ss 39 and 40) is "is not concerned with any exemption for gifts, but rather the proposition that direct or indirect actions depriving a party of assets *may be disregarded* by the Chief Executive for the purposes of calculating means". [19]

CHAPTER 14

Forgiveness of Debt

¶14-010 Operating principle

Debts owing by a trustee can be forgiven immediately or progressively. However, care must be taken to ensure that the terms of the acknowledgment of debt do not comprise inadvertent income. Whether trustees can forgive debts will depend on the terms of the Trust, the trustees' duties in accordance with the Trusts Act and the trustees' fiduciary obligations as trustees and the relevant income tax considerations.

¶14-020 Forgiveness of debt can have income tax consequences

A common asset and estate planning scenario provides that a settlor or other person who wishes to transfer assets to a trust sells the assets at market value to the trustee. The purchase price is met by way of a debt back. This debt, which can be progressively forgiven, is commonly interest-free and repayable on demand.

Income tax consequences can arise from the terms of the debt and upon any forgiveness of debt. Also see ¶4-110 regarding forgiveness of debts owing by a charitable trust.

¶14-030 An interest-free debt repayable on demand is an excepted financial arrangement

A debt is a financial arrangement. Accordingly, the consequences of any debt must be considered in the context of both the lender and the borrower.

A debt that is interest-free and repayable on demand is an excepted financial arrangement to the lender: s EW 5(10). This means that no income accrues to the lender from the arrangement.

Where the terms of the debt provide for the payment of interest or for an agreed term, the debt will not be an excepted financial arrangement and any interest income must be accounted for by the lender.

From the borrower's perspective, the loan is subject to the financial arrangements rules. Where a debt is forgiven, the rules that apply to financial arrangements provide that income can accrue to the trustee borrower. However, these rules do not apply where the debt is forgiven in consideration of natural love and affection: s EW 50. See ¶4-110.

Natural love and affection is not defined for the purposes of the Income Tax Act. Public binding ruling BR Pub 99/7 "Debt forgiveness in consideration of natural love and affection" (since expired) considered that the phrase "natural love and affection" is used to describe an action by a person where the motive is induced, not by a promise of something in return, but by the natural love and affection that the person has for another. An action undertaken in consideration of natural love and affection does not entice reciprocation, so that there is nothing in turn expected from the debtor. Natural love and affection is generally considered to subsist between relatives. The Commissioner has also accepted that natural love and affection can be present outside family relationships. See *Tax Information Bulletin* ¶119-133 Vol 11, No 9, October 1999 at 34.

An exception to s EW 50 provides that distributions to another trust with beneficiaries who are persons for whom the creditor has natural love and affection do not result in trustee income. This exclusion envisages a resettlement of trust assets onto a trust that will benefit a beneficiary or beneficiaries of the resettling trust: s EW 50(2). See Chapter 32 – *Variation*.

Where the debtor is a trustee, natural persons are able to forgive debts owed to them by the trustee without income tax consequences if the trust was established mainly to benefit "a natural person for whom the creditor has natural love and affection" and/or a registered charity: s EW 50.

However, where trustee debts have been forgiven, and the trustees of the trust subsequently make distributions to persons other than those for whom the creditor has natural love and affection or registered charities, such distributions will be income to the trustees in the year in which the distribution is made to the extent that the distributions do not exceed the amounts of the debts forgiven: s EW 50.

Where a debt is forgiven in consideration of natural love and affection, the debt is treated as having been paid and no income is derived by the trustee: s EW 44.

The trustee is required to keep a record of releases of debt and distributions to beneficiaries over the life of the trust: Tax Administration Act, s 22B. Records of debt forgiveness and distributions also come within the definition of core documents that trustees must retain under s 45 of the Trusts Act 2019.

Where a debt is progressively forgiven, a balance should be kept of total debt forgiven less any distributions that have given rise to trustee income.

The trustee should reconcile any advances or capital distributions to a settlor beneficiary where there is an outstanding debt owing by the trustee, and clearly record the nature of any payment.

A trustee is not obliged to accept a gift. If a trustee plans on or considers the possibility of making distributions to unregistered charities or beneficiaries for whom a creditor cannot have natural love and affection, the trustee should consider whether the trustee wishes to accept the gift. In this way, a trustee could eliminate or reduce the exposure to income due to the forgiveness of debt.

¶14-040 Gifting also requires management for "non-tax" reasons

Following the abolition of gift duty, the impetus that formerly existed to gift in the form of an annual permissible gifting limit no longer exists.

As a consequence, creditor protection that a trust can otherwise provide can be compromised where gifting programs are not maintained. See, for example, *Official Assignee* v *Wheeler* [2015] NZHC 1644.

In this case, a trust's settlor sold over $2.4 million of assets that he owned to the trust in 2004. The trustees were the settlor, Mr Wheeler, and his accountant. The purchase price for the assets sold to trust was left as a debt owing to Mr Wheeler. Between 2004 and 2010, 5 gifts of $27,000 were made, leaving a debt owing to Mr Wheeler of $2.279 million.

One of the trust's assets was an investment of over $1.4 million in Transbank Capital Corporation (Transcap), which it transpired was essentially a Ponzi scheme. However, Mr Wheeler was not aware of this and funds were borrowed from AMP to assist in property development through a separate trust and for further investment in Transcap. Ultimately, Mr Wheeler and the trust lost all the capital invested in Transcap. Mr Wheeler also fell into arrears with AMP and was ultimately bankrupted with debts owing of $775,843.

The Official Assignee discovered the existence of the trust and successfully made demand on account of the debt still owing between the trustees and Mr Wheeler.

¶14-050 Legislation

Income Tax Act 2007

EW 5 WHAT IS AN EXCEPTED FINANCIAL ARRANGEMENT?

[...]

EW 5(10) LOAN IN NEW ZEALAND CURRENCY

A loan to which all the following apply is an excepted financial arrangement for the lender:

(a) the loan is in New Zealand currency; and

(b) the loan is interest-free; and

(c) the loan is repayable on demand.

[...]

EW 44 CONSIDERATION WHEN DEBT FORGIVEN FOR NATURAL LOVE AND AFFECTION

EW 44(1) WHEN THIS SECTION APPLIES: FIRST CASE

This section applies when–

(a) a person is a debtor; and

(b) the creditor is a natural person; and

(c) the creditor forgives the debtor's debt because of the natural love and affection the creditor has for the debtor.

EW 44(2) WHEN THIS SECTION APPLIES: SECOND CASE

This section also applies when–

(a) a trust is a debtor; and

(b) the trust was established mainly to benefit 1 or both of the following:

   (i) a natural person for whom the creditor has natural love and affection:

   (ii) an organisation or a trust whose income is exempt under section CW 41 (Charities: non-business income) or CW 42 (Charities: business income); and

(c) the creditor is a natural person; and

(d) the creditor forgives the debtor's debt.

EW 44(3) TWO POINTS ABOUT SUBSECTIONS (1) AND (2)

For the purposes of subsections (1) and (2),–

(a) the debtor's debt includes an amount accrued and unpaid at the time of the forgiveness; and

(b) the means by which the debt is forgiven, whether in a will or otherwise, is immaterial.

EW 44(4) CONSIDERATION

The debtor is treated as having paid the debt on the date on which the creditor forgives it.

[...]

EW 50 INCOME WHEN DEBT FORGIVEN TO TRUSTEE

EW 50(1) WHEN THIS SECTION APPLIES

This section applies when–

(a) a trust is a debtor; and

(b) the trust was established mainly to benefit 1 or both of the following:

  (i) a natural person for whom the creditor has natural love and affection; or

  (ii) an organisation or a trust whose income is exempt under section CW 41 (Charities: non-business income) or CW 42 (Charities: business income); and

(c) the creditor is a natural person; and

(d) the creditor forgives the debtor's debt; and

(e) a trustee of the trust makes a distribution, including a distribution of beneficiary income, to a beneficiary; and

(f) the beneficiary is–

  (i) not a natural person for whom the creditor has natural love and affection; and

  (ii) not an organisation or a trust whose income is exempt under section CW 41 or CW 42; and

(g) the distribution is made on or after 20 May 1999.

EW 50(2) EXCLUSION

This section does not apply when–

(a) a trust (**trust** A) is a debtor; and

(b) trust A was established mainly to benefit 1 or both of the following:

  (i) a natural person for whom the creditor has natural love and affection; or

  (ii) an organisation or a trust whose income is exempt under section CW 41 or CW 42; and

(c) the creditor is a natural person; and

(d) the creditor forgives the debtor's debt; and

(e) a trustee of the trust makes a distribution to another trust (**trust** B); and

(f) at the time the distribution is made, trust B is also established mainly to benefit 1 or both of the following:

  (i) a natural person for whom the creditor has natural love and affection; or

  (ii) an organisation or a trust whose income is exempt under section CW 41 or CW 42.

EW 50(3) TWO POINTS ABOUT SUBSECTIONS (1) AND (2)

For the purposes of subsections (1) and (2),–

(a) the debtor's debt includes an amount accrued and unpaid at the time of the forgiveness; and

(b) the means by which the debt is forgiven, whether in a will or otherwise, is immaterial.

EW 50(4) DISTRIBUTION IS INCOME OF TRUSTEE

The distribution is income of the trustee, under section CC 3(2) (Financial arrangements), to the extent to which it is less than or equal to the total amount of the debts of the trust forgiven to it by the creditor.

EW 50(5) DISTRIBUTION SUBTRACTED FROM TOTAL AMOUNT FORGIVEN

The distribution is subtracted from the total amount of the debts of the trust forgiven to it by the creditor as the total amount stands at the time of the distribution.

EW 50(6) TIMING

The income is derived by the trustee in the income year in which the distribution is made.

EW 50(7) APPLICATION OF TAX ADMINISTRATION ACT 1994

Section 22B of the Tax Administration Act 1994 applies to a trustee to whom this section applies.

Part IV

SPECIAL RULES

CHAPTER 15

Imputation

¶15-010 Operating principle

Imputation credits distributed to beneficiaries are allocated according to the proportion of total distributions made to each beneficiary from the trust in that year. This allocation prevents streaming of imputation credits to beneficiaries most able to utilise the credits.

¶15-020 The imputation regime prevents the same dividend income from being taxed twice

The imputation regime contained in Subpart LE of the Income Tax Act 2007 provides that a company may attach imputation credits to cash and non-cash dividends, and taxable bonus issues, collectively referred to as dividends for convenience, which are distributed to shareholders.

Dividend income retains its character as a dividend whether it is retained by the trustee-shareholder or distributed to a beneficiary. However, imputation streaming rules can reduce the imputation credits available to beneficiary recipients.

¶15-030 Imputation credits cannot be streamed to beneficiaries best able to utilise the credit

A trustee is not permitted to stream imputation credits (s LE 5) to the beneficiaries best placed to use them.

Beneficiaries receiving dividend income with imputation credits attached are subject to tax on the dividend including the amount of the credit. However, when a dividend is beneficiary income, a limit is placed on the amount of the credit that is recognised as being attached to the dividend. This limit allocates credits to beneficiaries based on a formula that can be restated for practical purpose as follows:

$$\frac{\text{distributions to individual beneficiary}}{\text{total distributions}} \times \begin{array}{l}\text{total credits – any supplementary}\\ \text{dividends paid to an individual beneficiary}\end{array}$$

The application of this formula prevents trustees from streaming credits to beneficiaries who are able to use them in preference to those beneficiaries who are not in a position to use them, such as beneficiaries who are taxed at a lower marginal rate than other beneficiaries, or who are non-resident or tax exempt.

When applying the formula, all distributions, including those of a capital or non-taxable nature, are taken into account. In other words, the formula does not apply only in relation to distributions that are beneficiary income. The formula will apply to reduce the amount of credits included with beneficiary income even if the terms of the trust may require a distribution that results in a reduction of credits.

The same formula applies whether the trustee has any discretion regarding differentiating between different beneficiaries; for example, if there are capital beneficiaries and income beneficiaries, the formula applies without modification if a capital beneficiary has no entitlement to any distribution of dividend income.

Example

A trust has 3 beneficiaries A, B and C. None of the beneficiaries are "minor beneficiaries". The trust earns income of $30,000 comprising:

- Interest $20,000
- Dividends $10,000 ($2000 of imputation credits attached)

The income is distributed equally between beneficiary A and beneficiary B. The trustee also makes a distribution of $20,000 out of trust capital to beneficiary C, who is a beneficiary as to capital only.

The allocation of credits in accordance with the formula in s LE 5(2) is as follows:

Beneficiary	Total Distribution	Imputation Credits
A	$15,000.00	$15,000/$50,000 (30%) × 2000 = 600
B	$15,000.00	30% × 2000 = 600
C	$20,000.00	nil
Totals	$50,000.00	1,200

Beneficiary C is not entitled to an allocation of imputation credits, as Beneficiary C has no entitlement to the dividend, being a capital beneficiary only. Accordingly, imputation credits of $1,200 have been allocated to beneficiaries out of a total pool of $2,000. The remaining $800 of imputation credits are lost.

If there was no capital distribution to C, and all other facts remained as above, the application of the formula would provide that A and B would each receive 50% of the imputation credits and no imputation credits would be lost.

¶15-040 Imputation credits are allocated in the same proportion as the dividend payment

When imputed dividend income is divided between the trustee and the beneficiaries, the credits are allocated in the same proportion as the dividend allocation.

Example

The trustee of the Seaside Trust receives $1,000 dividend income with $280 of imputation credits attached.

$600 (60% of the dividend income) is distributed as beneficiary income to a single beneficiary. $400 (40% of the dividend income) is retained as trustee income. No capital distributions are made.

$168 (60%) of the imputation credits are attached to the dividend income distributed to the beneficiary and $112 (40%) of the attached imputation credits are retained by the trustee.

¶15-050 Dividend streaming rules do not apply if all dividend income is retained by the trustee

The application of the formula to allocate credits only applies when dividends are paid to one or more beneficiaries.

If all the dividend income is retained by the trustee, the trustee retains all the credits attached.

This is the case whether other income is distributed to beneficiaries, as it is the payment of any dividend income to a beneficiary that triggers the application of the anti-streaming provisions.

Example

The trustees of a trust have received the following income:

Rental	$20,000
Interest	$500
Dividend	$220,000 with imputation credits attached of $61,600

The rental and interest income of $20,500 is distributed as beneficiary income. The dividend income is all retained by the trustee.

The rules preventing streaming of imputation credits do not apply as no dividends are paid out as beneficiary income. Accordingly, no imputation credits are distributed to beneficiaries.

¶15-060 Excess imputation credits paid to a trustee are converted to a loss

When an imputed dividend is paid, both the dividend and the credit is included in the shareholder's assessable income. The credit allowed against the shareholder's income tax liability is an amount equal to the attached credits. Where this credit exceeds the shareholder's income, the tax credit can be carried forward.

When a dividend that is received by a trustee and retained as trustee income has a credit attached, the trustee is subject to tax on that dividend, including the amount of the credit, in the same way as an individual shareholder. The tax credit can be set off against the trustee's current year tax liability: s LE 1.

However, a trustee is not able to obtain a refund for or carry forward excess imputation credits. Instead, excess credits are converted to a net loss, which can be offset against the net income of succeeding tax years.

The amount of net loss to be carried forward is the amount of the unused credit, divided by the basic rate of income tax for trustees: s LE 2.

Unused credits converted to net losses and not used are lost if a trust is wound up.

¶15-070 Excess imputation credits derived by a beneficiary are carried forward

Imputation credits paid to a beneficiary are set off against the beneficiary's current year tax liability: s LE 1. Any excess credits that cannot be utilised are carried forward: s LE 3.

¶15-080 Distribution of excess imputation credits due to a lower marginal tax rate will not breach the anti-streaming provisions

There may be excess credits, after allowing for the payment of tax, if all dividend income has been distributed to a beneficiary with a marginal tax rate that is lower than the company tax rate.

Where this is the case, the excess credits can be distributed to the beneficiary who received the dividend income if this does not breach the anti-streaming provisions.

¶15-090 RWT credits can be allocated at the trustee's discretion, subject to certain controls

Trustees can allocate RWT credits in respect of beneficiaries' and trustees' income at the trustee's discretion by way of a substitution payment mechanism.

Although trustees may make RWT substitution payments in substitution for RWT credits, this option only applies to the extent that the substitution payment is equal to or less than the amount of RWT withheld from the amount treated as beneficiary income.

RWT substitution payments work as follows:

The trustee of a Trust resolves to distribute $100.00 interest income ($67.00 cash and $33.00 RWT credit) to a beneficiary with a marginal tax rate of 17.5%.

Example

The beneficiary's tax liability on $100 interest income is $17.50.

If the full $33 RWT credits in relation to that income are allocated to the beneficiary, the beneficiary will have excess RWT credits of $15.50. Instead of allocating $33 of RWT credits to the beneficiary, the trustee can:

- pay interest income of $67
- make a substitution payment (cash payment) of $15.50
- allocate RWT credits of $17.50 (the balance of the $33 RWT credits)
- the trustee offsets the substitution payment of $15.50 with the balance of the RWT credit of $15.50 and is in a revenue neutral position.

The beneficiary is treated as deriving interest income of $100. The tax on $100.00 for this beneficiary is $17.50, so the beneficiary receives cash of $82.50 and the $17.50 RWT.

A trustee who pays an RWT substitution payment has a tax credit equal to the payment. See LB 3(5).

The trustees cannot allocate the entire amount of RWT to the beneficiaries when only part of the interest is distributed to them. If 70% of the interest income is distributed to the beneficiaries, a maximum of 70% of the RWT credits can be allocated to the beneficiaries: ss LB 3, RE 2. Also see ¶3-210.

¶15-100 Any imputation credits are allocated to the trustee when dividend income is paid to a minor beneficiary

Special provision is made when dividend income with credits attached is paid to a minor beneficiary. See Chapter 10 – *Minor Beneficiary Income.*

When dividend income is distributed to a minor beneficiary, any imputation credits are allocated to the trustee, rather than the minor beneficiary: ss LE 4, LF 2. The amount of credit that may be attached to the dividend is calculated as if the minor beneficiary rule did not apply: s LE 5.

This means that the credits are included in the trustee's income and do not form part of the minor beneficiary's gross income.

Credits allocated to other beneficiaries are unaffected.

The minor beneficiary's share of credits in respect of dividend income distributed to that beneficiary is available to the trustee as a credit against any tax payable by the trustee on minor beneficiary income.

¶15-110 A non-resident beneficiary is only taxed on dividend income derived in New Zealand

Non-resident shareholders, including the non-resident beneficiaries of trustee-shareholders, can be taxed twice on income distributed from New Zealand companies: once by way of tax paid at the company level and again by way of NRWT deducted on distribution of the income. Under the imputation rules, credits attached to dividends paid to non-residents cannot be offset against NRWT liabilities.

Tax relief where this occurs can be achieved by the payment of an additional "supplementary dividend" to foreign investors. The supplementary dividend is equal to the amount of NRWT imposed on the dividend. A credit against income tax liability based on the dividend imputation credit and equal to the supplementary dividend is allowed to the New Zealand resident company that pays an imputed dividend and a supplementary dividend to the same foreign investor. While NRWT remains payable, it is counteracted by the supplementary dividend.

The anti-streaming rules are modified to take into account the effect of any supplementary dividend by including all supplementary dividends in the calculation of the credit available for allocation.

Trustee-shareholders are required to advise New Zealand resident companies in which they hold shares if they have non-resident beneficiaries that will derive dividends as beneficiary income, so that non-resident beneficiaries receiving dividend income are able to participate in the supplementary dividend tax credit regime.

However, while the trustees may believe at the time they notify the New Zealand resident company that the dividend will be paid out as beneficiary income, subsequent events, such as the trust making an overall loss for the year, may mean that this does not happen: See *Tax Education Office* "Facts on Tax" seminar, March/April 1996 and *Tax Information Bulletin* ¶711-104 Vol 7, No 11, March 1996.

If the terms of the trust require that dividend income must be distributed to a beneficiary, the distribution of a supplementary dividend to the same beneficiary will not be a breach of trust (s LP 6), which could otherwise be the case. See *Tax Information Bulletin* ¶711-104 Vol 7, No 11, March 1996 at 28. However, this provision is drafted in terms of a fixed trust and has yet to be tested in terms of a discretionary trust. If in doubt, the trustee of a discretionary trust could declare that the relevant part of dividend income is vested in possession in a beneficiary before distributing such income.

¶15-120 Anti-avoidance provision

A specific anti-avoidance provision applies to arrangements that have the effect of defeating the anti-streaming provisions: ss GB 34–GB 38.

¶15-130 Legislation

Income Tax Act 2007

LB 3 TAX CREDITS FOR RESIDENT WITHHOLDING TAX

LB 3(1) TAX CREDIT

A person has a tax credit for a tax year equal to the amount of tax withheld and paid in relation to their resident passive income for the tax year if the evidential requirements of section 78D of the Tax Administration Act 1994 are met. The amount of tax includes a payment of RWT for a non-cash dividend.

LB 3(2) EXCLUSION

No credit exists under subsection (1) for an amount of tax for resident passive income that is a replacement payment.

LB 3(3) MULTI-RATE PIES AND THEIR INVESTORS

For a multi-rate PIE and an investor in a multi-rate PIE, the amount of a tax credit is limited to the extent allowed under subpart HM (Portfolio investment entities).

LB 3(4) DETACHED TAX CREDITS

A trustee of a trust may detach some or all of a tax credit referred to in subsection (1) for resident passive income–

(a) that is derived by the trustee in an income year; and

(b) that is distributed to a person (**person A**) who is a beneficiary of the trust in–

  (i) the income year referred to in paragraph (a); or

  (ii) the extended period referred to in section HC 6(1)(b) (Beneficiary income); and

(c) in relation to which the trustee makes an RWT substitution payment under section RE 2(7).

LB 3(5) ALLOCATION AND TAX CREDITS

The trustee may, in a return of income for the income year referred to in subsection (4)(a), choose to allocate, for that year, an amount to a beneficiary of the trust that is equal to some or all of the amount of the detached tax credit referred to in subsection (4). The trustee has a tax credit equal to the amount that is not allocated to a beneficiary, and a beneficiary has a tax credit for the amount that is allocated to them.

LB 3(6) TREATMENT OF AMOUNTS

Despite subsection (1), an amount of a tax credit that person A would have under this section in the absence of subsections (4) and (5) must be reduced by an amount equal to the RWT substitution payment received by person A.

LB 3(7) EVIDENTIAL REQUIREMENTS

Subsection (5) does not apply in the circumstances set out in section HD 4(b) (Treatment of principals).

LB 3(8) MEANING OF DETACHED TAX CREDIT

A **detached tax credit**, for a beneficiary and an income year, means an amount equal to the amount of an RWT substitution payment referred to in subsection (4)(c) that meets the requirements of subsection (4)(a) and (b).

LE 1 TAX CREDITS FOR IMPUTATION CREDITS

LE 1(1) AMOUNT OF CREDIT

A person whose assessable income for an income year includes an imputation credit has a tax credit for the tax year corresponding to the income year of an amount equal to the sum of the amount of the imputation credit and any credit carried forward from an earlier tax year. Section OZ 11 (Tax credits for imputation credits) may apply to modify this section.

[...]

LE 2 USE OF REMAINING CREDITS BY COMPANIES AND TRUSTEES

LE 2(1) WHEN THIS SECTION APPLIES

This section applies when–

(a) a person described in subsection (2) has an amount of tax credit remaining for a tax year under section LA 5(4) (Treatment of remaining credits):

[...]

LE 2(2) CERTAIN PERSONS ONLY

The person referred to in subsection (1)(a) must be–

(a) a company that is not a life insurer; or

(b) a trustee (other than the Maori trustee); or

(c) a Maori authority.

LE 2(3) CALCULATING AMOUNT OF TAX LOSS COMPONENT

The person or the life insurer, as applicable, has a tax loss component for the corresponding income year equal to an amount calculated using the formula–

$$\frac{\text{person's remaining credit}}{\text{tax rate}}.$$

LE 2(4) DEFINITION OF ITEMS IN FORMULA

In the formula,–

(a) **person's remaining credit** is the amount of the tax credit remaining for the tax year under section LA 5(4), but, for a life insurer, only to the extent to which the amount is for their shareholder base:

(b) **tax rate** is the basic rate of income tax set out in schedule 1, part A (Basic tax rates: income tax, ESCT, RSCT, RWT, and attributed fringe benefits).

[...]

LE 3 USE OF REMAINING CREDITS BY OTHERS

LE 3(1) WHEN THIS SECTION APPLIES

This section applies when a person other than a person referred to in section LE 2(2) or a life insurer has an amount of tax credit remaining for a tax year under section LA 5(4) (Treatment of remaining credits).

LE 3(2) AMOUNT CARRIED FORWARD

The amount may be carried forward to the next tax year as a credit carried forward.

[...]

LE 4 TRUSTEES FOR MINOR BENEFICIARIES

LE 4(1) WHEN THIS SECTION APPLIES

This section applies when a person who has a tax credit under section LE 1 is the trustee of a trust for a minor who derives beneficiary income from the trust.

LE 4(2) TRUSTEE TREATED AS BENEFICIARY

To the extent to which section HC 7(2) (Trustee income) applies, the person is treated as deriving the minor's beneficiary income as a beneficiary.

LE 5 BENEFICIARIES OF TRUSTS

LE 5(1) WHEN THIS SECTION APPLIES

This section applies when a person who has a tax credit under section LE 1 is the beneficiary of a trust and, in that capacity, derives a dividend with an imputation credit attached.

LE 5(2) LIMITATION ON AMOUNT OF CREDIT

The person's credit is limited to an amount calculated using the formula–

$$\frac{\text{person's distributions}}{\text{trust distributions}} \times \text{total beneficiary credits} - \text{person's supplementary dividend}$$

LE 5(3) DEFINITION OF ITEMS IN FORMULA

In the formula,–

(a) **person's distributions** is the total distributions for the tax year made to the person in their capacity as beneficiary of the trust:

(b) **trust distributions** is the total distributions for the tax year made to all beneficiaries of the trust in their capacity as beneficiaries and includes all supplementary dividends paid to them:

(c) **total beneficiary credits** is the total imputation credits attached to dividends and total supplementary dividends for the tax year paid to all beneficiaries of the trust in their capacity as beneficiaries:

(d) **person's supplementary dividend** is the total supplementary dividends for the tax year paid to the person in their capacity as beneficiary of the trust.

[...]

LP 6 DERIVING SUPPLEMENTARY DIVIDEND AND BREACH OF TERMS OF TRUST

[...]

LP 6(2) TRUSTS

If a trustee derives a dividend and is required under the terms of a trust to distribute it as beneficiary income to a beneficiary, the trustee's distribution of a supplementary dividend does not breach the terms of the trust.

[...]

RE 2 RESIDENT PASSIVE INCOME

RE 2(1) INTEREST, DIVIDENDS, AND CERTAIN DISTRIBUTIONS

Resident passive income means an amount paid to a person to the extent to which it consists of–

(a) interest:

(b) a dividend:

(c) a taxable Maori authority distribution other than a retirement scheme contribution:

(d) a replacement payment paid to a person under a share-lending arrangement.

[...]

RE 2(6) BENEFICIARY INCOME

If a person derives an amount described in this section in their capacity as trustee and the amount is beneficiary income, the amount is treated as not derived by the trustee.

RE 2(7) TRUSTEES' RWT SUBSTITUTION PAYMENT

A trustee may pay an amount of money (the **RWT substitution payment**) to the relevant beneficiary that is equal to or less than the amount of RWT withheld for an amount to which subsection (6) applies (the **RPI beneficiary income**).

RE 2(8) EFFECT OF RWT SUBSTITUTION PAYMENT

The RWT substitution payment is treated as an amount of resident passive income that is beneficiary income, with the same nature as the RPI beneficiary income. There is no liability or obligation to withhold RWT in relation to the RWT substitution payment.

CHAPTER 16

Closely Held Companies

¶16-010 Operating principle

The term "closely held companies" in New Zealand is applied for tax purposes to look-through companies (LTCs) and qualifying companies. The rules that apply to the respective closely held company regimes are modified for trustee-shareholders.

With effect from 1 April 2011, it is no longer possible to enter into the qualifying company regime. However, existing qualifying companies had the option to transition into LTCs, partnerships, sole trader or remain as qualifying companies (with no ability to attribute losses to shareholders in the case of loss-attributing qualifying companies (LAQCs)).

¶16-020 Background to the look-through regime

The tax rules that applied to qualifying companies and LAQCs were changed to address concerns that the old rules were undermining the integrity of the tax system. Following consultation, rules providing for an elective look-through treatment for closely held companies were introduced with application from 1 April 2011.

For more information on the background or application of the LTC rules, see *Tax Information Bulletin* ¶231-111 Vol 23, No 1, Feb 2011.

¶16-030 LTCs are transparent for income tax purposes

The LTC regime is an elective regime. Companies that elect to be LTCs are transparent for income tax purposes. An LTC's income, expenses, tax credits, rebates, gains and losses are allocated to the company's owners in proportion to each ownership interest. See Subpart HB. Practically, this means that the income and expenditure of the LTC is returned (and assessed) in each owner's tax return according to their interest in the LTC. Losses can, therefore, be offset against the owner's other income subject to a loss limitation rule (see ¶16-090). A return at the LTC level (IR 7: Partnerships and look-through companies (LTCs) income tax return) is still required outlining how the income, expenditure and other items are allocated to each owner.

A company that has elected into the LTC regime is excluded from the definition of company for the purposes of the Income Tax Act but is treated as a company for all other purposes. This means that LTCs do not keep memorandum accounts and the rules that apply to the payment of dividends do not apply to LTCs. Therefore, LTCs do not need to maintain imputation credit accounts; and shareholders are not required to account for tax on dividends received from the company.

However, LTCs are treated as a company for the purposes of the PAYE, FBT, RWT, NRWT, ESCT and RSCT rules. LTCs are also treated as a company for the purposes of the rules that apply to the amalgamation of companies: Subpart FO. This means that the company itself will continue to be liable to file returns such as the employer monthly schedule and FBT returns.

¶16-040 Requirements to elect to be an LTC

To enter into the LTC regime, a company must:

- be a New Zealand resident company (see s YD 2), and
- not be treated as a non-resident company under a double tax agreement, and
- not be a flat-owning company, and
- have a single class of shares with the same voting rights with regard to company distributions, the company's constitution, capital, director appointments, and distributions of profits and assets – this requirement prevents streaming of income or deductions under the LTC rules.

Shareholders in an LTC must:

- all be natural persons
- all be trustees, or
- be another LTC.

See s YA 1 ("look-through interest"). See also ¶16-130 regarding proposed amendments to the LTC rules affecting eligibility criteria.

¶16-050 An LTC cannot have more than 5 look-through counted owners

LTCs must have 5 or fewer look-through counted owners. The term "look-through counted owner" only applies for the purposes of the count test. Although an owner for the purposes of this test will usually also be a shareholder, this will not always be the case.

A person is a look-through counted owner if the person is a natural person that is not a trustee and has a look-through interest for the entity.

A person is also a look-through counted owner if the person:

- is a natural person who has derived, as beneficiary income of a trust, income that arose from a direct or indirect beneficial interest in a look-through interest for the entity for the current income year or one of the last 3 income years, or

- is a natural person that has a voting interest or a market value interest in relation to a company that has derived, as beneficiary income from a trust, income that arose from a direct or indirect beneficial interest in a look-through interest for the entity for the current income year or one of the last 3 income years.

A trustee is a look-through counted owner if the trustee:

- has a look-through interest for the entity or has a direct or indirect beneficial interest in a look-through interest for the entity, treating co-trustees as one person, and
- has not distributed, as beneficiary income, all income that arose from a direct or indirect beneficial interest in a look-through interest for the entity for the current income year and all of the last 3 income years.

Broadly, for the purposes of counting owners, shareholders related by blood relationship (to the second degree), by marriage, civil union or de facto relationship, or by adoption are counted as a single owner.

Example 2: Trustee shareholder

All the shares in Mountain Design Ltd, an LTC, are held by Walton Trust.

Walton Trust is managed by a corporate trustee. It distributes all of the income from Mountain Design Ltd to the following beneficiaries:

20X1, 20X2 and 20X3	Cora and Emily
20X4	Elizabeth, Emily and Mamie (Emily's sister)
20X5	Rosemary, Erin and Aimee (Cora's daughter)

In 20X1, 20X2 and 20X3 there are 2 look through counted owners as between them Cora and Emily derived all of the LTC's income as beneficiary income.

In 20X4 there are 3 look-through counted owners, Cora, Elizabeth and Emily/Mamie. Because Mamie is Emily's sister (a 2-degree blood relative) they are counted as one owner.

In 20X5 there are 5 look-through counted owners, because the test considers who received beneficiary income in the current income year (20X5), and any of the 3 preceding income years (20X2, 20X3 and 20X4). The look-through counted owners are:

- Cora/Aimee (counted as one)
- Elizabeth
- Mamie/Emily (counted as one)
- Rosemary
- Erin.

Tax Information Bulletin ¶231-111 Vol 23, No 1, February 2011, at 49, Example 2.

As LTCs can only have 5 or fewer look-through counted owners, care needs to be taken when a trust holds shares in the LTC. This is because the distribution of beneficiary income can have an impact on the number of owners and, therefore, whether LTC status is maintained.

See also ¶16-130 regarding proposed amendments to the LTC rules affecting criteria for assessing look-through counted owners.

¶16-060 All owners must elect for a company to become an LTC

To elect into the LTC regime, a director or an authorised person must sign the LTC election together with all of the owners of look-through interests. Where a trustee is an owner of a look-through interest in an LTC, the trustee makes the election. Where there are multiple trustees, only one trustee signs the election. The form used for making an LTC election is IR 862 (Look-through company election). See www.ird.govt.nz.

¶16-070 Eligibility to be an LTC must be maintained at all times

LTCs must continue to meet the eligibility criteria at all times during an income year. If an LTC breaches the eligibility criteria at any time during an income year, LTC status is lost from the first day of the income year in which the eligibility criteria was breached.

If a company breaches the LTC eligibility criteria, the company cannot apply the LTC rules for the year of breach or the 2 subsequent income years.

¶16-080 A change of trustee is not a deemed revocation for the LTC rules

Unlike a qualifying company, LTCs are not subject to deemed revocation by event. A change of trustee will not cause a breach in eligibility criteria for the LTC in the same way that a change in trustee is a deemed revocation for the purposes of the qualifying company rules. See ¶16-290. Look-through company status is only lost if the LTC breaches eligibility criteria or the LTC election is revoked in writing. See the "Revocation of look-through company election" form (IR 896).

¶16-090 A loss limitation rule applies to LTCs

Owners' deductions are restricted if the amount of the deduction exceeds the adjusted tax book value of the owner's investment in the LTC. This is an anti-avoidance provision that applies to limit losses that can be claimed to reflect true economic loss. See ss HB 11, HB 12.

See also ¶16-130 regarding proposed amendments to the LTC rules that would restrict the loss limitation rules to only those LTCs in partnership and joint ventures. This means that once the amendment becomes law, most LTCs will not be bound by the loss limitation rule.

¶16-100 Electing out of the LTC regime is done on a prospective basis

A company will cease to be an LTC if the owners no longer meet the eligibility criteria. When an LTC fails to meet the eligibility criteria, it ceases to be an LTC from the first day of the income year in which it failed to meet the requirements.

However, if the owners revoke the LTC election, the revocation generally takes effect from the start of the following income year. See s HB 1(2), (3).

If LTC status is revoked, the company is treated as an ordinary company for tax purposes and the shareholders are treated as disposing of the LTC's underlying property at market value.

¶16-110 The sale of shares in an LTC is treated as a disposal of the underlying property

The owners of an LTC are treated, for tax purposes, as holding the company's property directly (in proportion to their effective look-through interests). It follows that when a shareholder of an LTC disposes of a shareholding in an LTC, the owner is treated as disposing of their share of the underlying assets. This deemed disposal of the underlying assets can give rise to tax consequences if minimum thresholds are exceeded. Briefly, an exiting owner will not be required to account for tax if the difference between any sale proceeds and the net tax book value of the owner's interest in the company does not exceed $50,000. See also ¶26-202–¶26-209.

¶16-120 There is no limitation of liability for trustee owners of LTC interests

The liability of independent trustee-shareholders in qualifying companies is limited to the relevant trust's assets. See ¶16-250. However, there is no corollary provision for the purposes of the LTC regime.

¶16-130 Later changes to the LTC regime

Amendments made to the Income Tax Act 2007 from 1 April 2017 reflected concerns from when the LTC regime came into effect that the rules were not working as intended for small businesses, and indeed that they may have deterred companies from becoming LTCs. Moreover, concerns were expressed regarding compliance costs imposed on small businesses electing to become LTCs.

The major changes were as follows:

Entry and eligibility criteria

Although direct ownership of shares in an LTC by companies (other than LTCs) is prohibited, a trust that owns an LTC interest can have a corporate beneficiary. It was realised that this could unintentionally provide widely held non-LTC corporates with a way to circumvent the prohibition on direct ownership. Accordingly, amendments were made so that trusts that own LTCs are expressly precluded from making distributions to corporate beneficiaries.

Trustees of a trust are not counted owners if all LTC income is distributed as beneficiary income for the current income year and all of the last 3 income years. If the income from an LTC is retained by a trust and is not paid out as beneficiary income during those income years, the trustees will be counted as one look-through counted owner.

Charities and Māori Authorities

The definition of "look-through company" looks through to the ultimate beneficiaries to LTCs owned by tax charities and Māori authorities.

To avoid additional compliance costs for Māori authorities a definition of a "grandparented Māori authority" includes not only direct ownership interests, but also a Māori authority beneficiary of a trust that is an owner in an LTC and a Māori authority that has entered into an arrangement to become an LTC owner before 3 May 2016, the date of introduction of the Taxation (Annual Rates for 2016–17, Closely Held Companies, and Remedial Matters) Bill.

Foreign income

As an LTC is not intended as a conduit vehicle, the Act now also contains proposals to restrict an LTC's foreign income to the greater of $10,000 and 20% of its gross income when more than 50% of the LTC's shares are held by foreign LTC holders. A "foreign LTC holder" will be a non-resident, and will include a trustee of a trust if the trust has a non-resident settlor or a person that is non-resident has power to appoint or remove a trustee of the trust.

Share classes

The amended Act proposes an amendment from 1 April 2017 to allow more than one class of share, provided all shares have uniform entitlements to all distributions. This will enable LTCs to have shares carrying different voting rights.

Tax book value clarification

The Act was amended to clarify, for the avoidance of doubt, that a company that elects to become an LTC effectively steps into the shoes of the superseded company and must use the tax book values of the company at the time of entry for all purposes under the LTC rules.

Partnership and JV Deduction limitation rule

The restriction that limits an owner's LTC deductions to the amount they have at risk will be confined to LTCs in partnership or joint venture. Deductions that have had to be carried forward will be able to be used as an immediate deduction against the shareholders' other income from the 2017–18 income year. To ensure LTC owners do not claim excessive deductions, the existing anti-avoidance rule in s GB 50 (which treats transactions between partners and their partnerships entered into for a consideration greater or less than market value for an avoidance purpose as taking place at market value) was extended to LTCs and their owners.

Remission income

Debt remission, the extinguishing of a debtor's liability either by operation of law or through forgiveness by the creditor, gives rise to debt remission income to the debtor under the financial arrangement rules. Under current tax law, debt remission produces taxable income to the debtor. Problems arise from the interaction of the LTC (and partnership) rules with the financial arrangement rules that produce remission income in circumstances when, due to the transparency of the LTC or partnership, the debt is effectively self-remitted. When one owner of an LTC remits debt owed to them by the LTC, as a consequence all of the LTC owners derive debt remission income because of the look-through nature of an LTC. This includes the owner that remitted the debt who is required to pay tax on their share of the remission income – despite making an economic loss (to the extent of the portion that is attributed to the other shareholders). Generally, they are unable to claim a deduction for the remitted bad debt. This results in over-taxation of the owner who remitted the debt.

There is no remission income for an LTC owner when an amount owed to them by the LTC is remitted.

In respect of a debt owed by an LTC to a third party, it was clarified that the market value of the debtor's interest in the debt is adjusted for any credit impairment.

The 2017 amendments mean that remission income does not arise to an LTC owner who remits a debt owed to them by the LTC (referred to in the proposed amendment as "self-remission").

Another 2017 amendment clarified that in respect of a debt owed by an LTC to a third party, the market value of the debtor's interest in the debt is adjusted for any credit impairment. It was stated that this was always the intention, but interpretations to the contrary have been taken. The amendment ensures the debt remission rules apply as intended, so that debt remission income arises when an LTC is either liquidated or elects out of the LTC rules. This is important given the proposed limiting of the scope of the deduction limitation rules, as the debt remission rules are one of the backstops in the Income Tax Act that help to preclude excessive deductions.

Entry matters

The income adjustment done at the time of entering into the LTC regime (the untaxed reserves formula) was changed to ensure that the taxable income that arises to LTC owners is taxed at shareholders' marginal tax rates rather than the company rate of 28%. A technical change clarified the values at which an LTC's assets and liabilities are deemed to be held by LTC owners on the company entering the regime.

¶16-140 The qualifying company regime allows companies to be treated as a partnership for tax purposes

The qualifying company rules treat small, closely held companies in a similar way to partnerships for tax purposes. Capital gains in a qualifying company are distributed tax-free. If a shareholder in a qualifying company is a trustee of a trust, all dividends must ordinarily be paid out to natural person beneficiaries.

The qualifying company regime, which is an elective regime, is provided for in Subpart HA of the Income Tax Act.

¶16-150 The qualifying company regime is not recognised for company law purposes

A qualifying company and its shareholders are deemed to be one entity for tax purposes.

The qualifying company regime is a taxation concept that is not recognised for company law purposes. Nevertheless, all the benefits of corporate ownership, in particular limited liability, remain.

A qualifying company is assessed for income tax in the same way as any other company. Qualifying companies are subject to the imputation regime and are required to maintain an imputation credit account.

Payments of dividends to shareholders of qualifying companies are made in exactly the same way as those to non-qualifying company shareholders, except to the extent that the retained earnings are unimputed, in which case, the dividend is paid tax-free.

There is no change in the status of a qualifying company for the purposes of the Companies Act.

Dividend statements and company resolutions are still required.

¶16-160 Capital gains from qualifying companies are distributed tax-free

A qualifying company pays tax on its profits in the same way as other companies. However, only fully imputed dividends are taxable to the shareholders of a qualifying company. Capital gains are distributed to shareholders as tax-free exempt dividends.

Fully imputed (taxable) dividends are paid to the extent of the imputation credits available to the company.

Once any imputation credits have been exhausted, any further dividends paid are exempt income and are distributed to shareholders free of tax: ss HA 13–HA 18. This means that capital gains can be distributed to shareholders tax-free without the necessity of liquidating the company.

The exemption remains where dividend income received by a trustee-shareholder is then distributed as beneficiary income. In other words, a New Zealand resident beneficiary receives such dividends as exempt income as if the beneficiary was the shareholder: ss CW 15, HA 14.

Any dividends paid to non-resident shareholders constitute non-resident passive income and are subject to NRWT. The ability to pay capital gains as tax-free dividends avoids the need to liquidate a company to realise tax-free capital gain.

A dividend paid to a trustee-shareholder that is, or becomes, beneficiary income of a New Zealand resident trust is exempt income as if it had been paid directly to the beneficiary and the beneficiary was the shareholder: s HA 16(2).

¶16-170 Concessions available to companies do not apply to qualifying companies

Qualifying companies are not entitled to an automatic interest deduction and instead must meet the general permission: ss DA 1, DB 7.

In addition to this, the income tax exemption for dividends received from a wholly owned subsidiary does not apply to a qualifying company. Instead, although the qualifying company may claim any imputation credits attached, dividends received are taxable.

Any losses are forfeited when a qualifying company election is made.

¶16-180 Companies can no longer elect to enter into the qualifying company regime

With effect from 1 April 2011, companies can no longer enter into the qualifying company regime. Existing qualifying companies were able to transition into the LTC rules or change to another entity such as a partnership without tax cost during a transitional period that ended on 31 March 2013. Companies that did not transition to LTC rules could remain as qualifying companies with the exception that LAQCs could no longer attribute losses to its shareholders.

See ¶16-010 et seq for commentary on LTCs. Also see *Tax Information Bulletin* Vol 23, No 2, February 2011.

For a company to become or remain a qualifying company, the company must:

- have 5 or fewer eligible shareholders: s HA 6(1)(a), or
- be a flat-owning company: s HA 6(1)(b).

A flat-owning company is a company through which shareholders obtain use of residential property: ss CD 31(2), YA 1 ("flat-owning company").

¶16-190 Not all shareholders are eligible shareholders

To be eligible as a shareholder of a qualifying company, each shareholder must be:

- a natural person: s HA 7(1)(a)
- the trustee of a trust from which all cash dividends other than taxable bonus issues are distributed to beneficiaries and the beneficiaries are not trustees or companies other than qualifying companies: s HA 7(1)(b), (2), or
- another qualifying company: s HA 7(1)(c).

¶16-200 A qualifying company must have no more than 5 shareholders

A qualifying company cannot have more than 5 eligible shareholders – s HA 6(1)(a). However, there are special rules for calculating shareholder numbers, and some groups of shareholders will count as a single shareholder for the purposes of the 5 or fewer shareholding test.

First-degree relationships count as a single person: s HA 7(3)(a). To ascertain a relationship within the "first degree", Inland Revenue follows the procedure of counting the steps back to a common ancestor and then counting the steps forward to the other person. A parent and child, whether natural or adopted, count as a single person. The same applies to a married, de facto or civil union couple.

On this basis, a parent and child or a husband and wife each count as a single shareholder.

However, parties to relationships outside the first degree will each count as a single shareholder. For example, a brother and sister would be within the second degree of relationship and so would count as 2 shareholders. This is because there is one degree between one child and the mutual parent and a second degree between that parent and the child's sibling.

A person who is counted as a shareholder in multiple capacities, for example, as a shareholder and as a beneficiary of a trust, is only counted as one shareholder.

Shares held by another company are counted as being held by the shareholders of the interposed company: s HA 7(3)(b).

Nominee-shareholders are looked through to beneficial owners: s YB 21.

If a shareholder is a trustee or a group of trustees, the trustee or trustees are disregarded, and the shareholders are counted as the larger of:

- the beneficiaries receiving dividends from any qualifying company from the first day of the 1991–92 income year onwards, or
- the persons who signed the shareholder election.

Groups that count as one when the company became a qualifying company continue to do so despite subsequent death or the end of a marriage, civil union or de facto relationship: s HA 7(3)(a).

More than one rule for counting can apply to a particular situation.

Example

A company has 3 shareholders, Arnold, Betty, and the Pigeon Family Trust (the Trust). Arnold and Betty, who are de facto partners, are the Trust's settlors. Tom is the trustee. The beneficiaries are Arnold, Betty, their 6-year-old twin daughters, 8-year-old triplets and their 15-year-old adopted son. The children's cousins are also discretionary beneficiaries.

Does the company meet the shareholder count test for the purposes of the qualifying company regime if all dividend income derived by the Trust is paid to Arnold, Betty and their children?

The shareholder count in this case will be one because all the relationships are within one degree. Accordingly, the shareholder count test is satisfied. However, if the children's cousins receive beneficiary income that comprises dividends from the qualifying company, the shareholder count will increase.

Example

Flintlock Limited is a company with 3 shareholders: Mr A, Mr B and the Ramrod Trust (the Trust). The beneficiary of the Trust is another company, Minuteman Limited, a qualifying company with 5 individual shareholders (taking into account family relationships). Neither Mr A nor Mr B is related to the shareholders in Minuteman Limited.

For the trustee of the Trust to be a shareholder of Flintlock Limited, for the purposes of the qualifying company regime, all cash dividends must be distributed either to persons who are not trustees or to other qualifying companies. If the trustee is a shareholder and a shareholder election has been made, the trustee substitution rule applies for the purposes of determining whether there are 5 or fewer qualifying company shareholders. Each beneficiary to whom the dividends were paid is treated as the shareholder, assuming the group of persons who made the election are not greater in number. The result is that Minuteman Limited, rather than the Ramrod Trust, is deemed to be a shareholder in Flintlock Limited.

For the purposes of counting, the individual shareholders in Minuteman Limited are treated as shareholders in Flintlock Limited. Therefore, there are 7 shareholders in Flintlock Limited, being Mr A, Mr B and the 5 individuals who are shareholders in Minuteman Limited.

This being the case, Flintlock Limited does not pass the test of 5 or fewer shareholders and it cannot be a qualifying company.

¶16-210 All beneficiaries must be natural persons or a qualifying company if a trustee is a shareholder in a qualifying company

Where a trustee is a shareholder in a qualifying company, the beneficiaries of the trust cannot be trustees or non-qualifying companies. However, a trustee can be a shareholder in a qualifying company even when the trust's beneficiaries include trustees of another trust, provided that no beneficiary, in his or her capacity as trustee of another trust, receives beneficiary income in the form of dividends derived from a qualifying company by the shareholder-trustee. Non-cash dividends are not included for this purpose: s HA 7(1), (2).

The beneficiary limitation prevents the trustee distributing income from a qualifying company to persons who are neither natural persons nor another qualifying company. This is consistent with the legislative intent of the qualifying company rules that ultimate control of a qualifying company should rest with natural persons. Since any other qualifying company is controlled by a limited number of natural persons, it is acceptable for the purposes of the qualifying company regime for a beneficiary to be a qualifying company: see *Tax Information Bulletin* ¶710-112 Vol 7, No 10, March 1996 at 20.

When a qualifying shareholder dies, situations can arise that provide that there is no qualifying beneficiary, for example, where shares have been bequeathed as a non-specific legacy and the company pays dividends during the period of executorship. As there is no defined beneficiary to pay the dividends to (income derived from assets that form part of a residuary gift may not be treated as beneficiary income), the beneficiary limitation is not met.

¶16-220 Trustees who are also beneficiaries can receive beneficiary income

The beneficiary limitation is not breached if a trustee-shareholder is a beneficiary of the trust of which the beneficiary is also a trustee, provided that beneficiary income is received in the capacity of a beneficiary and not as trustee.

"**Example**

P is a shareholder in QC Ltd, a QC, and holds the shares as trustee for the X Family Trust. The beneficiaries of the X Family Trust are P, M, and Company Ltd. Company Ltd is a beneficiary only in its capacity as the trustee of the Y Family Trust. In the relevant income year, P, as trustee of the X Family Trust derives dividends from QC Ltd.

QC Ltd will lose its QC status if:

P distributes any cash dividends or taxable bonus issues from QC Ltd to Company Ltd. (It is not relevant whether or not Company Ltd is a QC: it is its status as a trustee that is relevant).

QC Ltd may retain its QC status if:

P distributes all the dividends from QC Ltd as beneficiary income to M or himself; but not Company Ltd. The fact that P also happens to be a trustee as well as a beneficiary is acceptable, as he is receiving the beneficiary income in his capacity as a beneficiary.

Subject to the powers in the trust deed, P may also distribute non-cash dividends in accordance with the trust document from QC Ltd (none of which are taxable bonus issues) to Company Ltd."

See *Tax Information Bulletin* ¶710-112 Vol 7, No 10, March 1996 at 21.

¶16-230 A qualifying company has to meet the shareholder count test at all times

A company will not qualify for the qualifying company regime if the shareholder count increases beyond 5.

For this reason, trustees must ensure continued compliance with the shareholder count when making distributions to beneficiaries. If the number of beneficiaries who have received income increases over time, a company may find that it inadvertently falls out of the qualifying company regime.

Example

In the example above at ¶16-200 involving the Pigeon Family Trust (the Trust), the trustee distributes the dividend income to Arnold and Betty and 6 of Arnold's and Betty's nieces and nephews (the children's cousins), who are also discretionary beneficiaries.

The number of beneficiaries receiving dividend income has not changed. However, the company will no longer meet the shareholder count test.

This is because, although Arnold and Betty still count as a single shareholder, the 6 cousins are not within the first degree of relationship and so each count individually; accordingly, for the purposes of the shareholder count test, there are 7 shareholders and the company no longer meets the criteria for the qualifying company regime.

If no deferral is available, a qualifying company that falls out of the qualifying company regime will do so effective from the first day of the tax year in which the company fails to meet the requirements of a qualifying company: s HA 11. See further at ¶16-210.

If a qualifying company ceases to comply with the requirements for the qualifying company regime, the benefits of the regime cease to apply from the last day of the year in which the company met the requirements of the regime.

¶16-240 All dividends derived by a trustee-shareholder must be distributed as beneficiary income

All dividend income derived by a trustee from a qualifying company during an income year must be distributed to beneficiaries (s HA 7(2)) by no later than 30 September, assuming the trust has a standard 31 March balance date. Note that under s HC 6 the requirement to allocate income is the later of the end of the 6-month period ending 30 September for a trust with a standard balance date, or the period within which the trustee files, or is required to file, a return. This change reflects a relaxation of the rules where a tax agent is appointed.

However, a company will not lose its qualifying company status by reason only of its failure to comply with the dividend income requirement provided that (s HA 11(5)):

- as much of the dividend as is available to be distributed under general trust law is beneficiary income of beneficiaries who are neither trustees or companies that are not qualifying companies, and
- at least some dividends must have been paid or vested as beneficiary income since the company became a qualifying company.

This exception recognises that there is not always perfect symmetry between tax and trust law, and that there will be situations in which not all of a qualifying company's dividends can be paid out as beneficiary income.

Non-cash dividends, other than taxable bonus issues, derived by the trustee, for example, those arising from an interest-free loan, do not have to be passed out to the beneficiaries and are exempt income to the trust.

Example

You understand all dividends for a qualifying company must be distributed to the beneficiaries.

Is there a system for deciding which beneficiary should receive such dividends, and whether taxable/non-taxable income must be distributed in any set manner?

There are no tax rules that specify to whom the dividends should be allocated. However, the dividends should be allocated in accordance with the terms of the deed of trust.

¶16-250 The liability of independent trustee-shareholders is limited to the trust's assets for income tax only

In addition to electing to enter the qualifying company regime, shareholders must also elect to be personally liable for the company's income tax.

The liability for income tax is proportionate to each shareholder's shareholding. This rule is modified for trustee-shareholders who are not beneficiaries, so that liability for those shareholders is limited to the assets of the trust: ss HA 5, HA 8, HA 28.

The tax liability is limited to income tax and does not extend to liability for PAYE or GST.

A director of a qualifying company is not liable for a qualifying company's unpaid tax unless the director is also a shareholder who has elected to be liable.

¶16-260 No income limits apply to prevent entry to the qualifying company regime

There are no income threshold limits that apply to qualifying companies. This means that if a company meets all the criteria, irrespective of the company's turnover, the company can remain a qualifying company.

¶16-270 Shareholder elections can be revoked by notice or event

A shareholder election can be revoked voluntarily or due to a relevant event.

A shareholder can revoke an election voluntarily by giving notice in writing to both the Commissioner and the company. See s HA 32.

A shareholder election will be deemed to be revoked with a consequential loss of qualifying company status, unless new elections are made within periods of grace, if certain events happen. See s HA 33.

Events that trigger a deemed revocation include the death of a shareholder or a beneficiary attaining legal capacity.

Where there is a deemed revocation because a beneficiary attains legal capacity, the company will not lose its qualifying company status if a fresh election is made by the beneficiary. To be effective, the election must be made within 63 days or such extended period allowed by the Commissioner of Inland Revenue: ss HA 33, HA 35.

The death of a director does not cause a company to lose its status as a qualifying company. However, if a director is also a shareholder, the death of that director-shareholder will cause a deemed revocation.

¶16-280 Revocation of qualifying status applies from the beginning of the income year unless a grace period applies

The loss of qualifying company status due to an event will generally apply from the beginning of the income year in which the event occurred. This will occur regardless of whether it was known, or whether it was possible to ascertain at that time, that the company had ceased to comply. However, a company can apply to the Commissioner to defer the cessation of qualifying company status until the first day of a later income year. This application can be made where, at the particular time, the company did not know, and could not reasonably be expected to know, that it would cease to be a qualifying company because of a reasonable expectation that a new election would be made within the period of grace.

An application can also be made where the company did not know, and could not reasonably be expected to know, that it would cease to be a qualifying company because it had a reasonable expectation that the company's foreign non-dividend income would not exceed the $10,000 limit or a reasonable belief that qualifying company dividend income derived by a trustee-shareholder would be distributed as beneficiary income. In exercising her discretion, the Commissioner must be satisfied that – with regard to the period of time elapsing between the beginning of the income year, the date of failing to comply with the qualifying company status and the date on which the failure to comply became known, and with regard to any other transactions of the company and any other circumstances – it would be unduly harsh, or inappropriate, to treat the company as having ceased, for the purposes of the Income Tax Act, to be a qualifying company: ss HA 4, HA 11.

¶16-290 Change of trustee is a deemed revocation

The transfer of shares held by a trustee to a new trustee constitutes a disposal of the shares and will trigger a deemed revocation requiring a new election if qualifying company status is to be retained: *Tax Information Bulletin* ¶65-106 Vol 6, No 5, November 1994 at 6.

Example

Morse wishes to resign from his position as trustee of the Dexter Family Trust and has arranged for the Dexter family's lawyer to become the new trustee. Morse, in his capacity as the trustee of the Dexter Family Trust, is a shareholder in Oxford Limited, a qualifying company.

The transfer of shares from Morse to the new trustee will be a "disposal" of shares that will trigger a deemed revocation of Morse's trustee election. The company's qualifying company status will be lost unless the new trustee makes a fresh election, within 63 days, that Oxford Limited becomes a qualifying company and accepts liability, to the extent of the trust's net assets, for income tax payable by Oxford Limited.

¶16-300 Deemed revocations are effective from beginning of the income year unless a period of grace applies

Subject to any period of grace, a deemed revocation takes effect from the beginning of the income year in which the event giving rise to the deemed revocation occurs.

Where an election has been revoked, if a new election is made within specified periods, referred to as a "period of grace", the company will not lose its qualifying company status by reason only of the revocation.

The period of grace is 12 months where an election is revoked due to the death of a shareholder: s HA 34. In all other cases, the period of grace is 63 days. The period of grace may be extended at the discretion of the Commissioner on application of the company or a person who is entitled to make an election in respect of the relevant shareholding. For instance, it may be necessary to apply to the Commissioner for an extension of the period of grace where a deceased shareholder's estate is extensive and the executors of the estate take longer than a year to finalise matters.

Example

Shares in a qualifying company are acquired by the trustees of a family trust, the trustees of that trust plus any one or more of the natural person beneficiaries with legal capacity must make a shareholder election within 63 days of acquiring the shareholding in the qualifying company to retain qualifying company status.

¶16-310 Dividends from qualifying companies are exempt income to beneficiaries

Income retains its character. This means that, if a dividend that is exempt income to the trustee is distributed as beneficiary income, the income is exempt income to the beneficiary: s CW 15.

¶16-320 Overdrawn current accounts can be written off

If the shareholder of a qualifying company has an overdrawn current account, the current account can be written off without tax consequences. This is because any deemed dividend, which would occur if the company was not a qualifying company, would be exempt to the shareholder.

¶16-330 Changes to the qualifying company regime

On 1 April 2017, amendments to the qualifying company regime came into effect so that remaining qualifying companies lose their status as a qualifying company if there is a change in control of the company – s HA 6(3).

The change in control is measured using a continuity test and requires a "minimum continuity interest" (being the lowest voting or market value interest during the continuity period) of at least 50% for the qualifying company continuity period.

¶16-340 Legislation

Income Tax Act 2007

CW 15 DIVIDENDS PAID BY QUALIFYING COMPANIES

CW 15(1) EXEMPT INCOME OF SHAREHOLDER

To the extent to which the amount of a dividend that a qualifying company pays to a person resident in New Zealand is more than a fully imputed distribution, the amount is exempt income of the person.

CW 15(2) EXEMPT INCOME OF BENEFICIARY

If a dividend paid by a qualifying company to a trustee shareholder is, or becomes, beneficiary income of a beneficiary resident in New Zealand, the dividend is exempt income of the beneficiary.

[...]

HA 1 WHAT THIS SUBPART DOES

HA 1(1) DISTRIBUTING PROFITS AND ATTRIBUTING TAX LOSSES

The rules in this subpart allow a company to choose, for taxation purposes,—

(a) to have a distribution of profits to shareholders imputed or, to the extent not imputed, distributed as exempt income; and

(b) *(repealed)*

[...]

HA 1(5) ELECTIONS REQUIRED

For a company to be a qualifying company, all the directors of the company, and every shareholder in the company with legal capacity, must sign an election referred to in section HA 5. An exception applies for a minority shareholder in the situation described in section HA 29.

HA 1(6) SHAREHOLDER'S PERSONAL LIABILITY

A shareholder who makes an election referred to in subsection (5) must agree to take personal liability to the extent described in section HA 8.

[...]

HA 5 ELECTIONS TO BECOME QUALIFYING COMPANY

HA 5(1) MAKING ELECTIONS

A company that meets the requirements of sections HA 6 to HA 9 may be a qualifying company only if all the directors of the company and every shareholder in the company with legal capacity, choose, before the start of the grandparenting income year, that the company is to become a qualifying company. Every director and every shareholder with legal capacity must sign a notice of election and give it to the Commissioner.

[...]

HA 6 CORPORATE REQUIREMENTS

HA 6(1) REQUIREMENTS

A qualifying company must, in an income year,–

(a) have 5 or fewer shareholders who meet the requirements of section HA 7; or

(b) be a flat-owning company.

HA 6(2) EXCLUSIONS

A company is not eligible to be a qualifying company if, at any time in an income year, it is–

(a) a company that is not resident in New Zealand; or

(b) a company that is resident in New Zealand but is treated under and for the purposes of a double tax agreement, as not resident in New Zealand; or

(c) *(repealed)*

HA 7 SHAREHOLDING REQUIREMENTS

HA 7(1) NATURAL PERSONS, CERTAIN TRUSTEES, AND QUALIFYING COMPANIES

A shareholder in a qualifying company must be 1 of the following:

(a) a natural person; or

(b) a trustee of a trust, but only if subsection (2) applies in relation to dividends derived by the trustee; or

(c) another qualifying company.

HA 7(2) DIVIDENDS DERIVED BY TRUSTEES

For the purposes of subsection (1)(b), all dividends that the trustee of a trust derives from a qualifying company in an income year must be beneficiary income of 1 or more persons who are not trustees or companies other than qualifying companies. However, this subsection does not apply to non-cash dividends other than taxable bonus issues.

HA 7(3) SPECIAL SHAREHOLDING RULES

When the shares in a qualifying company that has 5 or fewer shareholders are held by relatives, other companies, and trustees, the following special rules apply:

(a) if a shareholder in a qualifying company is connected within the first degree of relationship to another shareholder in the company by either blood relationship, marriage, civil union or de facto relationship, or adoption, they are treated as a single shareholder, and this treatment continues while they remain a shareholder in the company despite any later death or dissolution:

(b) shares in a qualifying company that are held by another company are treated as held by the shareholders in that other company:

(c) if a shareholder in a qualifying company is a trustee, the shareholders are counted, without the trustee, as the larger of the following:

    (i) the group who signed the election as shareholder; or

    (ii) the group who derived beneficiary income from dividends from the qualifying company in the period between the first day of the 1991-92 income year and the time of counting.

[...]

HA 8 SHAREHOLDERS' PERSONAL LIABILITY

HA 8(1) AGREEMENT REQUIRED FOR ELECTION

A person making an election as shareholder as described in section HA 5 must agree for each income year in which the election is in effect, to take personal liability on the basis of their effective interest in the company–

(a) for their share of the company's income tax liability for the income year; and

(b) if the company has made an election as shareholder in another company, for any income tax payable in relation to that other company for the income year.

HA 8(2) TRUSTEE SHAREHOLDERS

A person making an election as trustee under section HA 28 must agree to take personal liability under subsection (1), modified as follows:

(a) the trustee together with 1 or more beneficiaries who have legal capacity must make the election; and

(b) the personal liability as trustee is limited to the extent of the net assets of the trust; and

(c) if the election is made for a majority shareholding under section HA 29, the personal liability includes the effective interests of the minority shareholding.

[...]

HA 8(4) BENEFICIARIES

In subsection (1), the person includes a beneficiary who makes an election under section HA 28 or a person who assumes liability on their behalf.

HA 8(5) NATURE OF LIABILITY

In sections HA 13 to HA 27, when more than 1 person agrees to take personal liability as described in subsection (3) for a percentage of an income tax liability or for income tax payable in an income year, the liability is joint and several.

[...]

HA 11 WHEN REQUIREMENTS NO LONGER MET: QUALIFYING COMPANIES

HA 11(1) WHEN THIS SECTION APPLIES

This section applies when, through changed circumstances, a qualifying company no longer meets the requirements of sections HA 5 to HA 9.

[...]

HA 11(5) DISTRIBUTION OF DIVIDENDS

Despite subsection (1), a company's status as a qualifying company is not ended merely because it does not comply with section HA 7(2) when–

(a) all dividends that can, under general law, be distributed by the trustee are beneficiary income of a beneficiary other than–

  (i) a trustee beneficiary; or

  (ii) a beneficiary that is a company other than a qualifying company; and

(b) some of the dividends derived by the trustee from the qualifying company have vested or have been distributed as beneficiary income of a beneficiary other than–

  (i) a trustee beneficiary; or

  (ii) a beneficiary that is a company other than a qualifying company.

HA 11(6) DEFERRING DATE

On an application by a qualifying company, the Commissioner may defer the date on which the company's status ends to the start of a later income year if–

(a) the company did not know, and could not reasonably be expected to have known, at the time the circumstances arose that it no longer met the requirements; and

(b) in the circumstances, it would be an unduly harsh or inappropriate outcome.

HA 11(7) EXAMPLES FOR SUBSECTION (6)(a)

Examples of the circumstances that may apply for the purposes of subsection (6)(a) are a reasonable expectation or belief that–

[...]

(c) the dividends referred to in section HA 7(2) would be distributed as beneficiary income.

[...]

HA 14 DIVIDENDS PAID BY QUALIFYING COMPANIES

HA 14(1) WHEN THIS SECTION APPLIES

This section applies when a qualifying company pays a dividend to a person resident in New Zealand.

HA 14(2) GENERAL TREATMENT

The dividend is exempt income of the person under section CW 15 (Dividends paid by qualifying companies) to the extent to which it is more than a fully imputed distribution.

[...]

HA 15 FULLY IMPUTED DISTRIBUTIONS

HA 15(1) WHEN THIS SECTION APPLIES

This section applies when a qualifying company with an imputation credit account pays a dividend. However, this section does not apply to a non-cash dividend other than a taxable bonus issue.

HA 15(2) CALCULATING AMOUNT OF FULLY IMPUTED DISTRIBUTION

The amount of a fully imputed distribution is calculated using the formula–

$$\text{attached imputation credit} \div \text{tax rate}.$$

HA 15(3) DEFINITION OF ITEMS IN FORMULA

In the formula in subsection (2),–

(a) **attached imputation credit** is the amount determined under subsection (4), and the amount is zero if no imputation credit is attached:

(b) *(repealed)*

(c) **tax rate** is the basic rate of income tax set out in schedule 1, part A, clause 2 (Basic tax rates: income tax, ESCT, RSCT, RWT, and attributed fringe benefits) at the time the shareholder derives the dividend, modified as applicable by section OZ 14 (Dividends from qualifying companies).

HA 15(4) ICA COMPANIES

A qualifying company that is an imputation credit account (ICA) company is treated as having attached an imputation credit to the dividend. The amount of the imputation credit is the lesser of–

(a) the maximum imputation credit that may be attached to the dividend under section OA 18 (Calculation of maximum permitted ratios) modified as applicable by section OZ 14; and

(b) an amount calculated using the formula in subsection (6).

HA 15(5) FDPA COMPANIES

(repealed)

HA 15(6) FORMULA

The formula referred to in subsection (4) is–

attached credits × amount of dividend ÷ amount paid before credits attached.

HA 15(7) DEFINITION OF ITEMS IN FORMULA

In the formula in subsection (6),–

(a) **attached credits** is the balance in the company's imputation credit account on the last day of the tax year in which the dividend is paid before a debit is made for any imputation credits that are attached:

(b) **amount of the dividend** is the amount before any imputation credits are attached:

(c) **amount paid before credits attached** is the total amount of dividends, excluding non-cash dividends other than taxable bonus issues, paid by the company during the tax year before any imputation credits are attached.

HA 15(8) RELATIONSHIP WITH IMPUTATION RULES

An imputation credit may not be attached to a dividend by a qualifying company except under this section.

HA 15(9) RELATIONSHIP WITH SECTIONS HA 14 AND HA 16

If part of the dividend is exempt income under sections HA 14 and HA 16, an imputation credit is treated as attached to the part that is not exempt income.

HA 16 DIVIDENDS PAID BY QUALIFYING COMPANIES TO TRUSTEE SHAREHOLDERS

HA 16(1) WHEN THIS SECTION APPLIES

This section applies when a dividend referred to in section HA 14(2) is derived by a trustee to the extent to which the dividend is exempt income of the trustee under section CW 15(1) (Dividends paid by qualifying companies).

HA 16(2) EXEMPT INCOME

To the extent to which the dividend is also beneficiary income of a beneficiary resident in New Zealand, the dividend is exempt income of the beneficiary under section CW 15(2).

[...]

HA 28 ELECTIONS BY TRUSTEE SHAREHOLDERS

If a shareholder referred to in section HA 5 is acting as trustee, they must make an election together with–

(a) 1 or more beneficiaries of the trust who are natural persons with legal capacity; or

(b) if no beneficiary has legal capacity, a natural person, who may also be the trustee, who assumes liability on behalf of beneficiaries.

HA 29 ELECTIONS BY MAJORITY SHAREHOLDERS

HA 29(1) WHEN THIS SECTION APPLIES

This section applies when 1 or more shareholders (the **majority**) in a company have, at the time of making an election, effective interests in the company of 50% or more, and the effective interest of 1 or more other shareholders (the **minority**) is less than 50%.

[...]

HA 33 REVOCATION OF SHAREHOLDERS' ELECTIONS: BY EVENT

HA 33(1) EVENT

An election by a person as shareholder under section HA 5 is revoked if an event described in the following paragraphs occurs:

[...]

(c) if section HA 28(b) applies, or section HA 29 applies and the election is made in accordance with section HA 28(b), a beneficiary acquires legal capacity:

[...]

HB 1 LOOK-THROUGH COMPANIES ARE TRANSPARENT

HB 1(1) WHEN THIS SECTION APPLIES

This section applies for the purposes of this Act, other than the PAYE rules, the FBT rules, the NRWT rules, the RWT rules, the ESCT rules, and the RSCT rules, for a person in their capacity of owner of an effective look-through interest for a look-through company (the LTC), for an income year, if–

(a) for the LTC, an LTC election described in section HB 13(1) and (2) has been received by the Commissioner under section HB 13(3) and (4) for the income year; and

(b) the LTC meets the requirements in the definition of **look-through company** at all times in the income year; and

(c) the election has not been revoked for the income year by an owner of a look-through interest for the LTC by notice received by the Commissioner before the start of the income year.

HB 1(2) WHEN THIS SECTION APPLIES: COMMISSIONER'S DISCRETION AS TO REVOCATION

A revocation notice that is received by the Commissioner after the start of the income year is treated as received before the start of the income year if the Commissioner decides that exceptional circumstances are the sole cause of the lateness.

HB 1(3) WHEN THIS SECTION APPLIES: REVOCATION IGNORED

An owner's revocation notice for the income year is ignored for the purposes of this section and section HB 13(4)(a) if the owner stops having a look-through interest in the LTC and the new owner reverses the revocation notice before the start of the income year by notice to the Commissioner.

HB 1(4) LOOK-THROUGH FOR EFFECTIVE LOOK-THROUGH INTEREST

For a person, unless the context requires otherwise,–

(a) the person is treated as carrying on an activity carried on by the LTC, and having a status, intention, and purpose of the LTC, and the LTC is treated as not carrying on the activity or having the status, intention, or purpose:

(b) the person is treated as holding property that the LTC holds, in proportion to the person's effective look-through interest, and the LTC is treated as not holding the property:

(c) the person is treated as being party to an arrangement to which the LTC is a party, in proportion to the person's effective look-through interest, and the LTC is treated as not being a party to the arrangement:

(d) the person is treated as doing a thing and being entitled to a thing that the LTC does or is entitled to, in proportion to the person's effective look-through interest, and the LTC is treated as not doing the thing or being entitled to the thing.

HB 1(5) EFFECTIVE LOOK-THROUGH INTEREST

For the purposes of this section, **effective look-through interest** means for a person and an LTC, treating the LTC as a company for the purposes of this subsection,–

(a) a person's average daily look-through interest for the company for the income year, if there is no market value circumstance for the LTC and paragraph (b) does not apply:

(b) a person's look-through interest for the relevant time of look-through under subsection (4), if there is no market value circumstance for the LTC, and–

(i) the assessable income of the LTC, ignoring this subpart, is or will be $3,000,000 or more in a 12-month period including the relevant time of look-through, and the Commissioner has notified the LTC that look-through interests for the relevant time of look-through under subsection (4) must be used under this section:

(ii) all persons with look-through interests have agreed to use their look-through interests for the relevant time of look-through:

(c) if there is a market value circumstance for the LTC and paragraph (d) does not apply, the average of the following 2 amounts:

(i) a person's average daily look-through interest for the income year:

(ii) a person's average daily market value interest for the income year:

(d) if there is a market value circumstance for the LTC, and the assessable income and notification requirements described in paragraph (b)(i) are met, the average of the following 2 amounts:

(i) a person's look-through interest for the time of look-through under subsection (4):

(ii) a person's market value interest for the time of look-through under subsection (4).

[...]

HB 13 LTC ELECTIONS

HB 13(1) LTC ELECTIONS

For the purposes of section HB 1, an LTC election (the **election**) is a notice that–

(a) is signed and dated by a director of the company that becomes a look-through company (the **LTC**) or other agent with appropriate authority; and

(b) is in the form prescribed by the Commissioner; and

(c) specifies an income year beginning on or after 1 April 2011 for which it may first operate; and

(d) has attached to it notices–

(i) signed and dated by all persons who, on the date of signing the election, own look-through interests in the LTC; and

(ii) evidence unanimous agreement of the owners in choosing to apply section HB 1.

HB 13(2) LEGAL INCAPACITIES

If a person owns a look-through interest in the LTC, and either they are under 18 years old with a guardian or a contract they enter into could be unenforceable, cancelled, void, or voidable due to any legal incapacity other than age, the notice requirement in subsection (1)(d) is modified so as to require a guardian, person with power of attorney, or other legal representative to sign and date the notice, instead of the person.

[...]

YA 1 DEFINITIONS

look-through company means an entity—

(a) that is described in paragraph (a) of the definition of **company**; and

(b) that, treating the entity as a company for the purposes of this definition, is resident in New Zealand under section YD 2 (Residence of companies); and

(c) that is not treated under, or for the purposes of, a double tax agreement as not resident in New Zealand; and

(d) for which there are 5 or fewer look-through counted owners, treating look-through counted owners who are relatives, ignoring any later death or dissolution of marriage, union, or relationship, as 1 person; and

(e) for which all owners have only look-through interests; and

(eb) for which an owner that is a trustee of a trust does not make a distribution to a company that is directly or indirectly a beneficiary of the trust, unless the company is—

(i) a grandparented Maori authority for the entity:

(ii) a tax charity that has no control or influence in relation to the operation of the entity and no control or influence in relation to the distributions of the trust; and

(ec) for which no owner is a tax charity, unless the tax charity is a grandparented charity for the entity; and

(ed) for which an owner that is a trustee of a trust does not make a distribution of income to a tax charity that is a beneficiary of the trust, unless the tax charity has no control or influence in relation to the operation of the entity and no control or influence in relation to the distributions of the trust; and

(ee) for which no owner is a Maori authority, unless the Maori authority is a grandparented Maori authority for the entity; and

(ef) for which an owner that is a trustee of a trust does not make a distribution to a Maori authority that is directly or indirectly a beneficiary of the trust, unless the Maori authority is a grandparented Maori authority for the entity; and

(eg) that, treating the entity as a company for the purposes of this definition, in the case where more than 50% of the total ownership interests in the entity are held by foreign LTC holders, the entity has a foreign-sourced amount for the income year that is not more than—

(i) $10,000; or

(ii) if 20% of the entity's gross income for the year (the 20% gross amount) is greater than $10,000, the 20% gross amount; and

(f) that is not a flat-owning company; and

(g) for which an election under section HB 13 (Valid elections) has been received by the Commissioner

look-through counted owner means, for an entity, a person who–

[...]

(c) is a trustee of a trust that–

(i) has a look-through interest for the entity or has a direct or indirect beneficial interest in a look-through interest for the entity, treating co-trustees as 1 person; and

(ii) has no beneficiary that is a look-through counted owner:

[...]

look-through interest means a person's shares in an entity, or in a look-through company (LTC) treating the look-through company as a company for the purposes of this definition, if–

(a) *(repealed)*

(b) every other shareholder has the same rights, proportionally, as the person in relation to a distribution by the entity or LTC; and

(c) the entity or LTC has only shareholders that are natural persons, or trustees.

CHAPTER 17

Continuity

¶17-010 Operating principle

A company cannot carry forward imputation credits unless a continuity of shareholding test is satisfied. This test limits the carry-forward of imputation credits for subsequent utilisation to situations in which at least 66% of those shareholders who will benefit from the credits bore the tax liability that gave rise to the credit.

These rules are modified in relation to trustees so that a change of trustee will not result in a loss of continuity. However, the rules can apply to transactions even where there is no change in beneficial ownership.

There are no corresponding modifications to the rules that require a 49% continuity to retain tax losses.

¶17-020 Imputation credits are lost if less than 66% continuity is maintained

A company cannot carry forward imputation credits unless a continuity of shareholding test is satisfied: s OA 8. The continuity of shareholding test requires that there is a group of persons the aggregate of whose minimum voting interests in the company (or market value interests if the company has a market value circumstance) is equal to or greater than 66% for the entire period from the date on which a particular credit arose until the time that it is otherwise cancelled out by a debit to the imputation credit account (eg by a dividend distribution to which imputation credits are attached). Sections YC 7–YC 16 of the Income Tax Act set out detailed rules for measuring these interests. The rules are modified for the purpose of the continuity provisions in the case of trustee-shareholders.

The continuity rules mean that the transfer of more than 34% of the shares in a company will result in a loss of continuity and that any imputation credits that cannot be cancelled out by the payment of a dividend before transfer will be lost.

¶17-030 Continuity rules do not apply to qualifying companies

The shareholder continuity rules for maintaining imputation credit accounts do not apply to qualifying companies: s OA 8(3B).

While a company is a qualifying company, the imputation shareholder continuity requirement of 66% for maintaining an imputation credit account balance will not apply. During this time, debits arise only from attachments to dividends and refunds of income tax.

When a company ceases to be a qualifying company, there is a debit to the imputation credit account that is equal to the lesser of the balance at that time (after attaching the maximum possible imputation credits to the dividends paid during the imputation year) and the greatest previous balance in the ICA at that date of any previous breach of the 66% continuity rule.

Look-through companies do not keep imputation accounts and so continuity rules for maintaining imputation credit accounts do not apply.

See further on qualifying companies at Chapter 16 – *Closely Held Companies*.

¶17-040 A change in trustee will not breach continuity

Shares or options held by the trustees of a trust are deemed to be held by the same single person at all times notwithstanding any change in the trustees: s YC 9(1). This means that a change in trustee should not breach continuity.

However, this concession is subject to the anti-avoidance provisions and only applies if the establishment or termination of a trust, or any change in trustees, does not have a purpose or effect of defeating the intent and application of any of the continuity provisions: s GB 5.

¶17-050 Shares held by a corporate trustee are not attributed to the trustee's shareholder for continuity purposes

Where a trustee is a corporate trustee, with the exception of the Public Trust, any company in which the Public Trust holds all voting and market value interests, or a statutory trustee company, any change in the corporate trustee's shareholding will cause a loss of continuity in respect of shares held by it unless the disposal of the shares has:

- no effect on the beneficial interest in the shares, and
- no purpose or effect of defeating the continuity rules: s YC 9(3).

This means that shares held by a corporate trustee are not attributed to the corporate trustee's shareholders. This treatment of a corporate trustee recognises that shares held by a corporate trustee are in substance held not so much by a "company", which should normally be looked through to the shareholder, but rather are held by a trustee, which happens to be a company. Therefore, a change in the shareholding of a corporate trustee will not breach continuity of any company of which the corporate trustee is a shareholder to the extent that the change in shareholding does not reflect a change of beneficial ownership of the assets of the trust.

¶17-060 The death of a shareholder will not breach continuity

Where a trustee acquires shares on the death of any other person, the shares are deemed to have been acquired on the date the deceased acquired them and to have been held by the trustee at all times since. This treatment applies to both a trustee under the will or intestacy of the deceased person and to any beneficiary of the estate: s YC 8.

Example

A company, 100% owned by Richard, has significant imputation credits. If Richard leaves the shares to a discretionary trust in his will, are any imputation credits lost?

No. The trustee of the estate will be deemed to have acquired the shares on the same date on which Richard acquired the shares and to have held them at all times since then.

Example

Eli's will provides for a life interest in shares: the shares are to be held in trust with income to his wife, Janet, during her lifetime and for the shares to pass to their children on Janet's death. Is continuity breached?

No. The shares are acquired by the children as beneficiaries of a testamentary trust and are deemed, for continuity purposes, to have been acquired by them on the date their father acquired them.

¶17-070 A breach of continuity can occur where there is no change in shareholding but the capacity in which the shareholder owns the shares changes

A loss of continuity cannot be avoided where there is a sale from a person owning the shares in one capacity to the same person in a different capacity. For example, where a person sells shares owned personally to themselves in the capacity as a trustee.

Example

Sara owns all the shares in Sara's Fine Foods Limited, which is not a qualifying company. Sara sells her shares in the company to the S & G Elliot Family Trust, of which Sara is the sole trustee.

The trust is a different shareholder for shareholder continuity purposes. Shares held by discretionary trustees are not covered by the nominee provisions. No look-through rule operates in respect of discretionary trustees.

Accordingly, a breach of shareholder continuity occurs, and any imputation credits are lost once Sara transfers the shares from herself personally to herself as a trustee.

This will be the case regardless of whether there is any change of beneficial ownership.

Example

Kirsty owns all the shares in Brook's Excellent Sign-Writing Company. Kirsty sells all her shares in the company to Andrew and Andrea, the trustees of the Cole Trust, of which Kirsty is the sole beneficiary.

The trustees are a different shareholder for shareholder continuity purposes. Accordingly, a breach of shareholder continuity occurs, and imputation credits are lost once Kirsty ceases to be the legal owner of the shares, regardless of the fact that she remains the beneficial owner.

A trustee's shareholding in respect of a particular trust is not aggregated with any shares that the trustee holds in a capacity other than as trustee of that trust. For example, a trustee's shareholdings are not aggregated with shares held in the trustee's personal capacity or in that trustee's capacity as a trustee under a different trust. See *Case* L72 (1989) 11 NZTC 1,419.

¶17-080 Specific anti-avoidance provisions apply to beneficiary changes

The general rule is that changes in a trust's beneficiaries will not affect the continuity tests, as voting or market value interests are not required to be traced through the trustee to the beneficiaries.

However, a specific anti-avoidance provision provides that where there is a change in the beneficiaries of a trust under an arrangement that has a purpose or effect of defeating the intent and application of any of the continuity provisions, there is a deemed disposition by the trustee of the shares to an unrelated third party and an immediate reacquisition: ss GB 5, YC 9(5).

The effect of the deemed sale and re-acquisition is that, where the trustee holds in excess of 34% of the shares in a company, there will be a breach of continuity in respect of that company for imputation purposes.

There is little guidance on what change of beneficiary will amount to avoidance. However, a starting point would be an assessment as to whether the change of beneficiaries is such that it cannot be said that the same persons who will enjoy the benefit of the imputation credits bore the tax liability giving rise to the credits.

Inland Revenue has stated that where a settlor is made a beneficiary under a discretionary trust, there generally will be an issue as to whether such an arrangement exists: *Tax Information Bulletin* ¶37-122 Vol 3, No 7, April 1992 at 23. The basis for this position is not clear. However, guidance as to whether changes to a trust, including a change of trustee and changes to the class of beneficiaries, resulted in the creation of a new trust in the context of continuity for the purpose of carrying forward losses was considered by the High Court of Australia in *FC of T* v *Commercial Nominees of Australia Ltd* 2001 ATC 4336.

In *FC of T* v *Commercial Nominees of Australia Ltd*, it was alleged that the changes to the fund had either extinguished or effected a resettlement of the original trust, destroying the necessary continuity the "taxpayer" required in order to carry forward and offset the losses against future income.

Although the case could be limited in applicability to superannuation funds, it does provide guidance as to the indicia of continuity in respect of a trust, which are:

- the constitution of the trusts under which the fund operated
- the trust property, and
- membership.

The High Court of Australia found that to destroy the necessary continuity, changes in one or more of these indicia must be such as to terminate the existence of the eligible entity, or to produce the result that it did not derive the income against which the losses were sought to be offset. In the case at hand, the court found that the property that was the subject of the trusts did not alter at the time the deed was amended. Persons who were members of the fund before the amendments remained members of the fund after the amendments. In the result, the High Court of Australia found that the superannuation fund did not come to an end at the time of the amendment.

¶17-090 General anti-avoidance provisions can also apply

In addition to the specific anti-avoidance provision in s GB 5, the general anti-avoidance provisions in relation to imputation credits can also have application to a restructuring or an arrangement involving shares held by trustees: ss GB 5, GB 36.

These anti-avoidance provisions apply to arrangements to obtain a tax advantage in relation to imputation credits or FDP credits. For the purposes of this section, a "tax advantage" includes obtaining of a credit of tax. There will be an arrangement to obtain a tax advantage where there is a disposal or issue of shares in circumstances where it may be reasonably contemplated that there would be a payment of a dividend with credits attached. It must be a purpose, and not merely an incidental purpose, of such an arrangement that there will be a tax advantage. There will also be an arrangement to obtain a tax advantage where a company streams the payment of dividends, or makes bonus issues, in such a way as to prefer some shareholders over others in respect of credits.

Where there is found to be an arrangement to obtain a tax advantage, the Commissioner has wide powers to counteract any advantage associated with the arrangement.

Example

There are 10,000 shares in Cochrane Limited, which has accumulated imputation credits. The shares are owned by Bethany and Rose equally.

Bethany and Rose propose to transfer 9,800 of their shares to a trust. Before transfer, it is proposed that these shares will be converted to non-voting shares that carry the right to receive dividends. Bethany and Rose intend to retain the 200 voting shares. Will the imputation credits be retained or lost on the transfer of shares to the trust?

While on the face of it control (100% of the voting interest in the company) is still with Bethany and Rose, there is a risk that there would be a "market value circumstance" and that the value of all shares (voting and non-voting) would have to be taken into account in determining the shareholders' interests in Cochrane Limited for continuity purposes. If the value of all shares were taken into account in determining the shareholders' interests in the company for continuity purposes, there is likely to be a breach in continuity and imputation credits would be lost.

In addition, as rights attaching to the shares in Cochrane Limited have been extinguished or altered for the purpose of enabling the company to meet the imputation continuity requirements the anti-avoidance provisions will likely apply.

¶17-100 Liquidation of a corporate trustee should not breach continuity

There are no specific provisions that apply to the liquidation of a corporate trustee. However, as a practical matter, the liquidation of a corporate trustee, which will necessarily result in the appointment of a new trustee, should be treated in the same way as a change of trustee. That is, there should be no loss of continuity subject to any intention to defeat the continuity rules.

¶17-110 A resettlement will result in a loss of continuity

The resettlement of a trust onto a new trust is a transaction between 2 different trusts that will necessarily give rise to a breach in continuity for imputation purposes, for example, where the trustees of the old trust hold 34% or more of the shares in a company (other than a qualifying company).

However, if the company is in a position to declare an imputed dividend, some or all of the credits may be utilised before the resettlement.

See further on resettlement at Chapter 33 – *Resettlement*.

Example

Trust A owns 98% of the shares in a qualifying company (QC). Two individuals, who are also the trustees and beneficiaries of Trust A, own the remaining 2%. The 2 individuals are also trustees and beneficiaries of Trust B. The company currently has imputation credits.

The trustees wish to resettle Trust A's shares in the company to Trust B. Does the company need to declare a dividend to use its imputation credits before Trust A resettles the shares to Trust B or can the resettlement be effected without forfeiting the imputation credits because the trustees of the 2 trusts are the same individuals?

The resettlement constitutes a change of more than 34% ownership of the company. While the company remains a QC, it is not required to comply with the 66% shareholder continuity requirement to carry forward a credit balance in its imputation credit account (ICA).

For the company to maintain its QC status after the change in shareholding, the trustees of Trust B must file an election to remain a QC within 63 days of the shareholding change. If they do not file an election, the company ceases to be a QC from the first day of the income year in which the shareholding change occurred.

If the company ceases to be a QC and there has been a breach (or breaches) in shareholder continuity while it was a QC, there will be a debit to the ICA equal to the lesser of:

- the balance of the ICA at the time the company ceases to be a QC, and
- the largest debit to the ICA that would have arisen for a breach of shareholder continuity had the company not been a QC.

Therefore, provided that the trustees of Trust B elect for the company to remain a QC, Trust A can resettle its 98% shareholding in the company to Trust B without the company forfeiting its imputation credits.

If the company was not a QC, the transfer of 98% of the shares by the Trust A trustees to the trustees of Trust B would breach shareholder continuity. While the trustees of both trusts are the same individuals, they are acting in different capacities as trustees of Trust A and as trustees of Trust B (ie the 2 trusts are different taxpayers). All the trustees of a trust holding a share in a company under the trust are treated as the same notional single person that is separate and distinct from the trustees in their capacities other than as trustees of the trust.

¶17-120 Bare trustees

The continuity provisions applicable to trustees do not apply to bare trustees.

Bare trustees are treated differently from other trustees. Any voting or market value interest held by a bare trustee for a person is deemed to be held by that person and not by the bare trustee: s YB 21(2).

¶17-130 Continuity provisions for determining whether a loss can be carried forward are not modified in respect of trustee-shareholders

Subject to limited exceptions (s IA 7), a company, other than a look-through company, can only carry forward a tax loss component of a loss balance if at all times during the period from the beginning of the year of loss to the end of the year of carry-forward (the continuity period), a group of persons holds an aggregate of at least 49% of the minimum voting interest in a company: s IA 5. A person's voting interest in a company is measured on the basis of the percentage of shareholder decision-making rights that the person holds in the company. Those rights are ascertained from the rights carried by shares, or options over shares, held by the person in the company: ss YA 1 ("shareholder decision-making right"), YC 2.

The continuity rules for determining whether a tax loss can be carried forward are not modified in respect of trustee-shareholders.

The Taxation (Annual Rates for 2016–17, Closely Held Companies, and Remedial Matters) Bill (130-1) introduced a number of reforms including changes to the look-through company eligibility requirements and other measures relating to closely held companies. See Chapter 16 – *Closely Held Companies.*

¶17-140 Legislation

Income Tax Act 2007

GB 5 ARRANGEMENTS INVOLVING TRUST BENEFICIARIES

GB 5(1) WHEN THIS SECTION APPLIES

This section applies when–

(a) a share in a company or option over a share in a company is held by a trustee; and

(b) a change occurs in the beneficiaries of the trust; and

(c) a purpose or effect of the change is to defeat the intent and application of a continuity provision.

GB 5(2) TRUSTEE TREATED AS DISPOSING OF SHARE OR OPTION

The trustee is treated as having disposed of the share or option to an unrelated person at the time of the change in beneficiaries, and as having reacquired it immediately afterwards.

GB 5(3) LIMITED APPLICATION OF SUBSECTION (2)

Subsection (2) applies only for the purposes of the application of the rules in sections YC 2 (Voting interests) and YC 3 (Market value interests) in the case of the continuity provisions.

[...]

YC 8 DEATH OF SHARE OR OPTION HOLDER

If a person acquires a share or option over a share on the death of a person (the deceased person), as a beneficiary or trustee under the will or intestacy, the person is treated as–

(a) having acquired the share or option on the date the deceased person acquired it; and

(b) having held it until the person in fact acquired it.

YC 9 SHARES OR OPTIONS HELD BY TRUSTEES

YC 9(1) TRUSTEES TREATED AS NOTIONAL SINGLE PERSON

All the trustees of a trust holding a share or an option over a share in a company under the trust are treated as the same notional single person that is–

(a) not a company; and

(b) separate and distinct from the trustees in their capacities other than as trustees of the trust.

YC 9(2) EXCEPTION TO SUBSECTION (1)

Subsection (1) does not apply if any of the following has a purpose or effect of defeating the intent and application of a continuity provision:

(a) the establishment of the trust:

(b) the termination of the trust:

(c) a change in the trustees of the trust.

YC 9(3) CHANGE IN OWNERSHIP OF CORPORATE TRUSTEE

Subsection (4) applies if–

(a) any share in a company (the **first company**) or option over a share in the first company is held by a trustee; and

(b) the trustee is a company other than–

  (i) Public Trust:

  (ii) any company in which Public Trust holds all voting and market value interests:

  (iii) a statutory trustee company; and

(c) any share in the trustee or option over a share in the trustee is disposed of, issued, or granted; and

(d) to the extent to which the disposal, issue, or grant changes the beneficial ownership of the share or option over a share in the first company, unless it can be shown not to have a purpose or effect of defeating the intent and application of any of the continuity provisions.

YC 9(3B) COMPANY ACTING AS TRUSTEE

A reference to company in subsection (3)(b) includes a company that is acting in the capacity of trustee.

YC 9(4) TRUSTEE TREATED AS DISPOSING OF SHARE OR OPTION

The trustee is treated as having disposed of the share or option in the first company, at the time of the disposal, issue, or grant, to an unrelated person and having immediately reacquired the share or option.

YC 9(5) AVOIDANCE

Section GB 5 (Arrangements involving trust beneficiaries) may apply to treat a share or option held by a trustee as being disposed of at the time of a change in trust beneficiaries.

CHAPTER 18

Associated Persons

¶18-010 Operating principle

The associated persons provisions have the effect of anti-avoidance provisions that prevent parties from structuring their affairs to avoid the incidence of tax. However, the provisions apply regardless of whether any tax avoidance was contemplated or would occur.

¶18-020 Associations between parties can alter the incidence of taxation due to different relationships

The policy behind the associated persons provisions is legislative determination that while certain associated persons are legally separate persons or entities, these persons are not necessarily economically independent. From a policy perspective, certain associated persons are regarded as single economic entities because of this community of economic interests. Whether this is in fact the case does not alter the application of the rules.

¶18-030 Rules of association

The rules of association were substantively altered with general effect from the 2010–11 income year but from 6 October 2009 for the purposes of the land provisions. See ¶18-080. The rules of association, which are contained in subpart YB of the Income Tax Act 2007, apply to persons, companies, trusts and partnerships.

Before the application of the current rules, it was common for affairs to be structured with the use of an interposed trust so as to avoid what is commonly referred to as "tainting" by association. However, the scope of the rules of association is such that it is now very difficult to structure affairs so as to avoid an undesirable association. Further, where a structure does avoid association, given the breadth of the new rules of association, it would be appropriate to assess whether any structure where an association is avoided would amount to tax avoidance. See Chapter 22 – *Avoidance*.

¶18-040 The most significant application of the rules is in the context of land transactions

Parliament's stated intention is that land dealers, developers and builders should, as a general proposition, be taxed on all gains of property sold within 10 years of acquisition.

This means that dealers, developers and builders cannot hold non-taxable investment portfolios. The application of the associated persons rules in connection with dealing in land, developing land and building activity prevents dealers, developers and builders from circumventing the rules by having a related party make an acquisition that would otherwise be taxable.

Accordingly, unless any exception applies, where there is a disposal of land, and either the person disposing of the land or an associated person carries on a land dealing or developing activity or is a builder when the land being disposed of was acquired, income will arise under the provisions that relate to land:

- acquired for the purposes of dealing, developing or building: s CB 7
- sold within 10 years of acquisition (ss CB 9, CB 10) or in the case of a builder's improvements, within 10 years of completing the improvements (s CB 11).

Land that is transferred between associated persons, and later sold by the transferee, gives rise to income in the hands of the transferee where:

- the transferee derives a gain when land is on sold, and
- disposal of the land by the transferor would have given rise to income in the hands of the transferor if the land had been sold to a third party and not the associated transferee: s CB 15.

Provisions that allow an election for land acquired for a landfill to be on revenue account, so that any losses on sale can be claimed, do not apply where the land is acquired from an associated party: s CB 8.

There are residential, business, farm land and investment exclusions from the land provisions: s CB 16–CB 23. However, care must be taken when assessing the application of those exclusions by a trustee, as only the residential exclusion in s CB 16 specifically provides that it applies to the trustee of a trust.

There is also a main home exclusion to s CB 6A in s CB 16A, which provides for an exclusion from the bright-line test for beneficiaries of a trust if the principal settlor does not have a main home or the home being disposed of is the main home. See further at ¶19-080 regarding the "bright-line" test.

An associated transferee is treated as having acquired the land on the date on which the land was first acquired by the transferor. That treatment applies for the purposes of the land disposal provisions relating to the other land of a dealer, developer or builder, a development or division begun within 10 years and rezoning gains: s CB 15(2).

Although, in most instances, the rules of association serve to tax income that would otherwise be on capital account, adoption of the associated transferor's acquisition date can have a favourable outcome in limited circumstances. For example, the land disposal provisions relating to a development or division commenced within 10 years of acquisition do not apply where the land was acquired from a majority shareholder, an associated person, who had acquired it more than 10 years before commencement of development of the land by the company. See *Paul Stephens Construction Ltd* v *C of IR* (1990) 12 NZTC 7,192 (HC).

¶18-050 Land provisions are not the only provisions with associated persons provisions

Although the land provisions generally represent the most significant effect from the rules of association, the rules have other applications. Accordingly, it is important that a trustee is well aware of all associations that could have tax implications.

This requires a trustee to appreciate the application of taxing provisions that are altered by association as well as having knowledge of the identity and circumstances of parties related by association.

The approved issuer levy (AIL) is not available if the lender and borrower are associated parties. Non-resident withholding tax (NRWT) must be deducted from interest payments to non-residents unless an AIL of 2% can be paid. Where AIL is paid, no NRWT is required to be deducted from the interest payments. However, the option of paying AIL is not available if the lender and borrower are associated persons.

Example

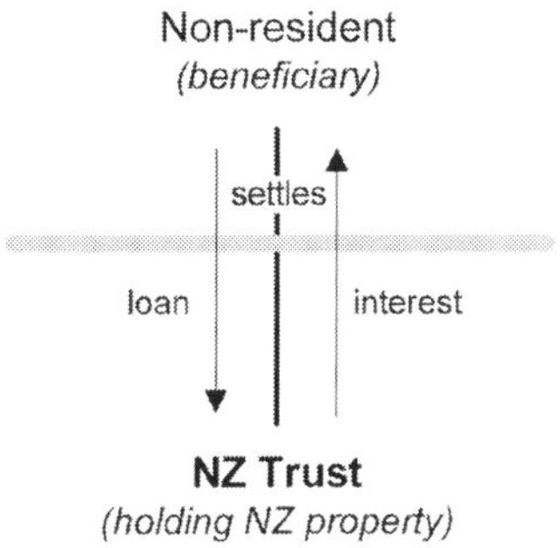

In this example, a non-resident settles a New Zealand trust (with a New Zealand-incorporated company as trustee) which owns New Zealand land and buildings. This investment by the trustee is funded by a loan from the non-resident settlor. If the non-resident settlor is not associated with the New Zealand trustee, then the interest paid on this loan qualifies for the approved issuer levy (AIL) of 2% instead of being subject to the higher non-resident withholding tax (NRWT) rate.

The previous associated persons definition used in the AIL rules was generally deficient in relation to arrangements involving trusts. In this example, in particular, without a trustee and settlor test of association, the interest would qualify for AIL treatment despite the in-substance association between the two parties.

The new trustee and settlor test in section YB 8 would associate the non-resident settlor with the New Zealand trustee. Accordingly, the interest derived by the non-resident settlor from New Zealand would be subject to a higher rate of NRWT instead of AIL at 2%, which is the appropriate treatment.

A special report from the Policy Advice Division of Inland Revenue, 15 October 2009: New definitions of "associated persons" at 20.

A trustee's depreciation deduction may be limited if the trustee is associated with the vendor. The purchaser of an asset from an associated person may be restricted to the deduction for depreciation losses that the vendor would have been allowed. This is because the depreciable cost for the purchaser may be the cost of the asset for the vendor and not the purchaser's actual cost. In addition, the purchaser may be unable to adopt a depreciation rate exceeding the rate applied by the vendor: s EE 40.

The restriction potentially applies to a purchaser who acquires an item of depreciable property from an associated person. The restriction extends to an asset that the vendor elected not to be treated as depreciable property.

The Commissioner has the discretion to decide whether the use of the purchaser's cost is appropriate. See standard practice statement SPS 07/05, "Transfer of depreciable property between associated persons – section EE 33 of the Income Tax Act 2004" published in *Tax Information Bulletin* ¶199-105 Vol 19, No 9, October 2007 at 16, which sets out the factors that the Commissioner will consider when deciding whether to allow a purchaser acquiring an asset from an associated person to depreciate the asset based on the purchaser's cost. Factors taken into account by the Commissioner include:

- whether the transfer is genuine
- whether the transfer is made at no more than market value
- whether there is a permanent transfer of legal ownership of the property
- whether the associated vendor (or its controllers) continues to retain virtual ownership of, or a beneficial interest in, the transferred property through:
  - power over or control of the associated purchaser
  - a leaseback agreement, or
  - continued actual use of the property for income-producing purposes, and
- the commercial or non-tax reasons for transfer of the asset.

These restrictions do not apply when the disposal is a bequest of property and the disposal takes place at market value under Subpart FC of the Income Tax Act 2007. See Chapter 26 – *Deceased Estates* at ¶26-202.

Associated persons provisions can apply to debt parking. The debtor under a financial arrangement is required to calculate a base price adjustment if the creditor sells the debt to an associate of the debtor for 80% or less of the market value of the debt: ss EW 43, EW 49. This anti-avoidance provision prevents the assignment of debt to circumvent debt remission rules.

Deductions for the disposal of timber are limited to the proceeds of sale when the purchaser is associated with the vendor. Where timber or the right to take timber or standing timber is disposed of to an associated person, the deduction for the cost of timber is limited to the proceeds of sale, which are included in income. Where the proceeds of a sale to an associated person are exceeded by the deductible cost of the timber, the excess is transferred to the purchaser. The cost of the timber to the associate is the total of the cost of timber to that person and any amount that the seller of the timber has not been able to deduct, because it exceeded the amount of the sale proceeds: s DP 10(3), (4), (5). See J Aubrey, C Brenton-Rule, T Marshall, C Rau, G Roan, R Saheed, L Treadaway *Tax Guide to Farming, Forestry and Fishing* (Edition 2, CCH, Auckland, 2014) at [9.2.3].

The business income exemption is not available to a charitable trust if a person associated with the charity can benefit from the charity. However, the person does not need to actually receive the benefit. If the trust fails to satisfy this condition of the business income exemption, the whole of the trust's business income is taxable income to the trustee: s CW 42. See ¶30-250.

Certain payments to associated persons are treated as a dividend. The dividend rules in ss CD 3 to CD 5 treat any payment of money (or money's worth) made by a company to an associated person of a shareholder of the company as a dividend if that payment would have been a dividend if it had been made to the shareholder: s CD 6(1)(a)(ii).

Example

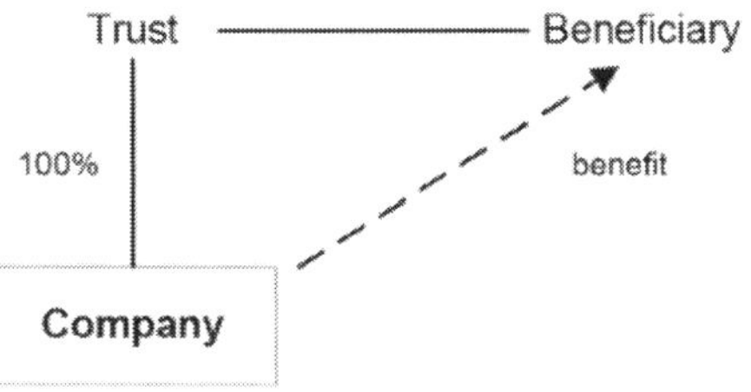

In this example, the company provides a benefit to a beneficiary of its trustee shareholder. The company provides the benefit because the trustee is its sole shareholder. Section CD 6(1)(a)(ii) in the dividend rules treats payments to associated persons of shareholders as dividends. However, without a trustee and beneficiary test, this simple arrangement would avoid the dividend rules.

Under the new trustee and beneficiary test, because the company is providing a benefit to an associated person (Beneficiary) of a shareholder in the company (Trust), the company has made a dividend to the beneficiary under section CD 6(1)(a)(ii).

A special report from the Policy Advice Division of Inland Revenue, 15 October 2009: New definitions of "associated persons" at 16.

¶18-060 The rules of association have a very broad application

The rules of association were amended in 2009 to address concerns that the rules were too easy to circumvent, particularly in the context of land transactions.

The rules of association do contain some exceptions that only apply in respect of land provisions for some trust relationships. However, even with these exceptions, the current rules are extremely far reaching and will provide that a vastly increased number of land transactions are subject to income tax due to trust relationships.

Under the associated persons rules:

- the trustee of a trust is associated with the settlor and any person with the power to appoint or remove trustees (unless the appointor is a professional who is subject to the professional code of conduct and disciplinary processes of an approved organisation)
- 2 trusts are associated if they have a common settlor
- a settlor is associated with a beneficiary
- a trustee is associated with a beneficiary
- a person is associated with a relative's trustee, and
- a trustee can be associated with a company.

In addition, a tripartite test means that any 2 persons associated with the same third person are also associated: s YB 14.

See ¶18-110 for a discussion of the relative test.

¶18-070 There are limited exceptions to the application of the rules of association

The rules of association apply unless an exception applies: s YB 1(4).

The main exceptions to the associated persons rules in the land provisions (as defined in s YA 1) provide that the following associated persons rules will not apply for the land provisions:

- the person and trustee for a relative test: s YB 5
- the trustee and beneficiary test: s YB 6
- the settlor and beneficiary test: s YB 9.

The trustee and settlor test does not apply to charitable trusts: s YB 8. See ¶18-200.

The following excerpt from page 22 of A "special report" from the Policy Advice Division of Inland Revenue, 15 October 2009: New definitions of "associated persons" provides useful guidance of the definition of settlor in the context of the taxation rules in the Income Tax Act:

> "The definition of 'settlor', in conjunction with the nominee look-through rule in section YB 21, does not include professional advisers acting on behalf of clients and other persons such as friends and family members who simply allow their name to be listed as the settlor on a trust deed. The definition of 'settlor' that is being used is essentially the same as that originally enacted in 1988 as part of a reform of the trust rules (with the exception that the provision of services at less than market value are excluded). The main focus of this definition is on persons who provide the trust property, and therefore does not include persons who merely allow their name to go on the trust deed as the named settlor.
>
> It is therefore the client of the professional adviser, or the person that the friend or family member is acting for, who is treated as the settlor under the settlor-based tests in s YB 7 to YB 9.

This position is consistent with the Inland Revenue's long-standing policy. *Tax Information Bulletin* of November 1989 on the trust rules at paragraph 6.93 states:

> 'Often professional advisers or relatives will assist in establishing a trust by settling a nominal sum on trust on behalf of another person. In these circumstances it is not appropriate to expose the professional adviser or relative to a potential tax liability. The professional adviser or relative is not the real settlor of the trust but is in effect only an intermediary or facilitator. The real settlor is the person on whose behalf the professional adviser or relative acted in making the settlement. Thus, s.226(3) [now section YB 21 of the Income Tax Act 2007] treats the person for whom the nominee or the nominal settlor acted as the settlor rather than the nominee or nominal settlor'."

¶18-080 The general application date for the rules of association is the 2010–11 income year

With the exception of the provisions relating to land transactions, the rules of association apply from the 2010–11 income year.

For land transactions, other than the disposal of land within 10 years of completing improvements (s CB 11), the current rules apply to land acquired on or after 6 October 2009. For any land acquired before 6 October 2009, the former associated persons provisions will still apply.

For the purposes of s CB 11, the current rules apply to land where the improvements commenced on or after 6 October 2009. As with other land transactions, where improvements commenced before 6 October 2009, the former provisions will apply.

The commencement date applies regardless of the land owner's balance date.

Identifying the date of acquisition will become of critical importance as this will determine which rules, if any, apply. The taxation consequences of association only apply where there is an association with a dealer, developer or builder at the time the land is acquired (or, in the case of building work, at the time the improvements began).

Property is acquired when the agreement for sale and purchase becomes unconditional. Where land is occupied under a lease with an option to purchase, and the option is exercised, the date of acquisition is the date on which the option is exercised and not the date of settlement: *Beetham* v *C of IR* 72 ATC 6042.

¶18-090 Two companies can be associated

Two companies are associated if (s YB 2):

- there is a group of persons whose total voting interest is 50% or more
- a market value circumstance exists for either company and there is a group of persons whose total market value interests in each company are 50% or more. A "market value circumstance" is defined in s YA 1, and a "market value interest" is defined in Subpart YC
- there is a group of persons who control both companies by any other means.

The rules associating companies are extended by an aggregation rule. The aggregation rule, which is modified for the land provisions (see below), provides that a person is treated as holding anything held by any persons associated with that person under ss YB 4–YB 14.

The aggregation rule prevents the test being circumvented by the fragmentation of interests among associated persons.

Example

Application of general aggregation rule in two companies test

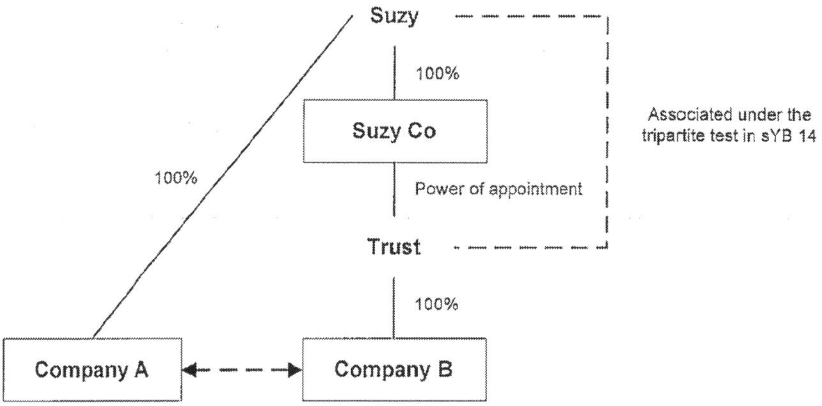

In this example the aggregation rule, in conjunction with the tripartite test, can be applied to treat Suzy as holding Trust's shares in Company B. Specifically, Suzy is associated with Suzy Co under the company and person other than a company test in section YB 3, and Suzy Co (with power of appointment of the trustees of Trust) is associated with Trust under section YB 11. Therefore, Suzy and Trust are associated under the tripartite test, and the aggregation rule in section YB 2(4) treats Suzy as holding Trust's shares in Company B. Taking into account the shares Suzy holds directly in Company A, Company A and Company B are associated under the two companies test in section YB 2.

A special report from the Policy Advice Division of Inland Revenue, 15 October 2009: New definitions of "associated persons" at 7.

The aggregation rule as modified for the land provisions effectively provides that the beneficiary-related trust tests in ss YB 5 and YB 9, and the relatives test in s YB 4, insofar as it affects land provisions, will not arise under the aggregation rule to be applied as part of the test of association for a company and a person: s YB 3(4).

That said, the modified aggregation rule, with the amended rules of association mean that there will be associations involving trusts that would have been avoided under the former rules.

Example

Application of aggregation rule in two companies test in the context of the land provisions

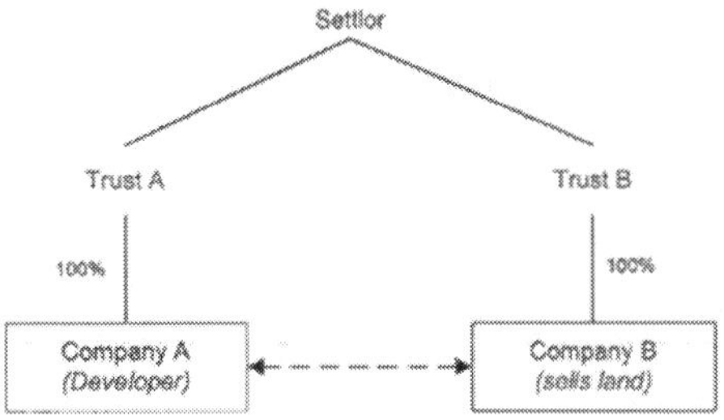

In this example, Trust A and Trust B are associated under the two trustees with common settlor test in section YB 7. Trust A owns 100% of the voting interests in Company A, which is a property developer, and Trust B owns 100% of the voting interests in Company B, which sells some land within 10 years of acquisition.

The two companies are associated under the two companies test through the use of the aggregation rule contained in that test. Applying the aggregation rule to this example, Trust A is treated as holding anything held by persons associated with it. In this case, Trust A and Trust B are associated under the two trustees with common settlor test in section YB 7. Accordingly, taking into account Trust A's direct shareholding in Company A, Trust A is treated as holding all the voting interests in Company A and Company B, meaning these two companies are associated.

The aggregation rule can also be applied to treat the common settlor as holding all the voting interests in Company A and Company B because the settlor is associated with Trust A and Trust B under the trustee-settlor test in section YB 8. This also means the two companies are associated.

A result of Company A and Company B being associated is that Company B is liable to tax on the sale of land. Without the aggregation rule, Company A and Company B would not be associated despite their close community of interests.

A special report from the Policy Advice Division of Inland Revenue, 15 October 2009: New definitions of "associated persons" at 9.

¶18-100 A company is associated with a trustee under the company-person test if the trustee has a 25% voting interest

A company and a person, including a trustee, are associated if the person has a voting interest in the company of 25% or more: s YB 3(1). Voting interests are defined in Subpart YC.

A company and a person will also be associated if a market value circumstance exists for the company and the person has a market value interest in the company of 25% or more: s YB 3(2).

A corporate trustee is treated as a person for the purposes of s YB 3. This means that the company look through rules in Subpart YC applying to voting and market value interests do not apply to a corporate trustee. Consequently, the voting interests or market value interests held by a corporate trustee are not traced through to the shareholders of that corporate trustee. See *Tax Information Bulletin* ¶37-122 Vol 3, No 7, April 1992 at 23. Accordingly, the relevant test for determining association between a corporate trustee and a company is the company person test and not the two companies test.

The aggregation rules discussed above also apply for the purposes of the company person test.

Example

Application of the general aggregation rule in the company and person other than a company test

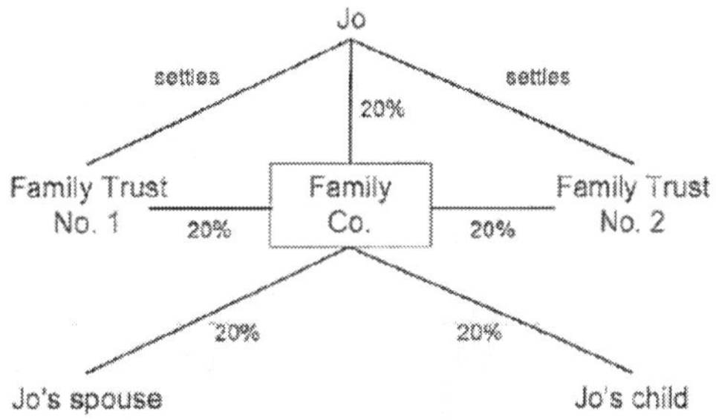

Jo settles Family Trusts No. 1 and No. 2 and arranges for each of them to hold 20% of the shares in Family Co. Jo also arranges for his spouse and child to hold 20% each in Family Co. Jo directly holds only 20%. Under the aggregation rule in section YB 3(3), Jo is treated as holding the shares in Family Co held by the family trusts and relatives because they are his associates. Accordingly, Jo is associated with Family Co. Without the rule aggregating the interests held by associated persons Jo would not be associated with Family Co despite the close community of interests.

Example

Application of aggregation rule in the company and person other than a company test in the context of the land provisions

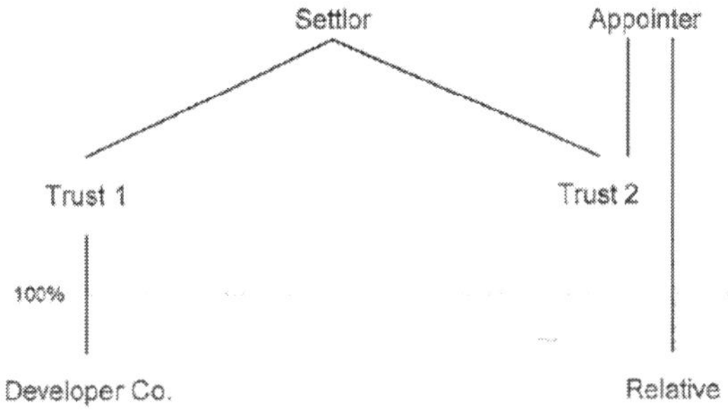

> The question in this case is whether the appointer of the trustee in Trust 2 is associated with Developer Co under the test in section YB 3 associating a company and a person other than a company. The appointer is associated with Developer Co under this test because of the application of the aggregation rule for land provisions in section YB 3(4) which treats a person as holding anything held by their associates. The appointer is associated with Trust 1 under the tripartite test in section YB 14. Specifically, the appointer is associated with Trust 2 under the test in section YB 11 associating a trustee and their appointer, and Trust 2 is associated with Trust 1 under the test in section YB 7 associating two trustees with a common settlor. Therefore, under the aggregation rule for land provisions in section YB 3(4) the appointer is treated as holding Trust 1's shares in Developer Co. Accordingly, the appointer and Developer Co are associated under section YB 3.
>
> Note, however, that the relative of the appointer would not be associated with Developer Co. In particular, the tripartite test does not associate Trust 1 and the relative and therefore the relative is not treated as holding Trust 1's shares in Developer Co. The aggregation rule is applied afresh to the relative, and not to the appointer, for the purposes of determining whether the relative is associated with Developer Co. Therefore, the fact that the appointer is treated under the aggregation rule as holding Trust 1's shares when testing for association between the appointer and Developer Co is disregarded when testing for association between the relative and Developer Co.

A special report from the Policy Advice Division of Inland Revenue, 15 October 2009: New definitions of "associated persons" at 12.

¶18-110 Persons within 2 degrees of blood relationship are relatives

Relatives are associated persons. The relatives test has 3 limbs.

The first limb of the relatives test provides that spouses and de facto or civil union partners are relatives: s YB 4(1)(a).

The second limb of the test provides that blood relations, including adopted children, within 2 degrees of relationship are relatives. This test is more limited than the test under the previous rules of association, which measured relatives to the fourth degree. This means that the blood relationships limb of the relatives extends to grandparents and siblings but not to nephews and nieces (third degree) and cousins (fourth degree): s YB 4(1)(b), (3).

The third limb provides that 2 persons are also associated if one person is within 2 degrees of blood relationship to the other person's spouse, civil union partner or de facto partner: s YB 4(1)(c). This means that persons are associated with their in-laws and step-children.

A limitation to the first and third limbs of the general relatives associated persons test provides that this test does not apply for the purposes of the land provisions, defined in s YA 1. Instead, for the purposes of the land provisions, persons are associated because of a blood relationship only if one is the infant child of the other: s YB 4(2).

An adopted child is treated as the child of its adoptive parents, not its birth parents for the purposes of the two relatives test: s YB 4(3).

The first and third limbs of the association test do not apply to ss EB 13 (low-turnover valuation) and EC 5 (transfer of livestock because of self-assessed adverse event).

However, no association will exist for the relatives test if the person cannot reasonably be expected to know that:

- the other person exists, and
- the other person is within 2 degrees of relationship: s YB 4(4).

¶18-120 A person is associated with a trustee for relative

A person (first person) and a trustee of a trust under which a relative (as defined in s YB 4) of the first person has benefited or is eligible to benefit will be associated persons: s YB 5(1). See ¶18-130.

An association between a person and a relative's trustee does not apply for the purposes of the land provisions: s YB 5(2).

Unless the trusts in question have a common settlor, any association with a trustee is limited to an association with that trustee in that trustee's capacity as the trustee of the trust: s YA 1 ("trustee"). Where there are multiple trustees, the association with the trustees is limited to those trustees' capacity as trustees of the trust in question.

Example

Person and trustee for relative: exception for the purposes of the land provisions

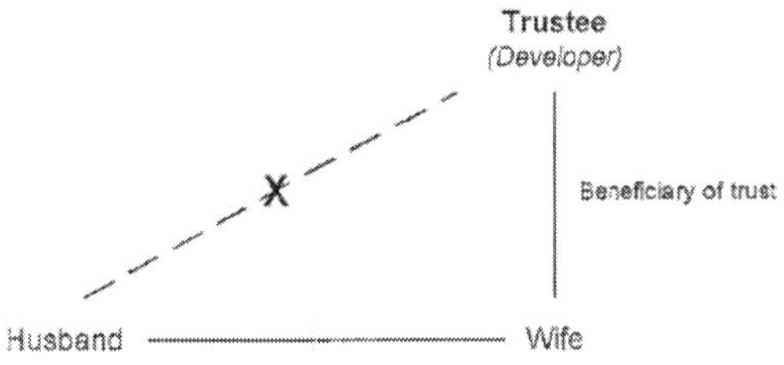

Because the trustee for relative test does not apply for the purposes of the land provisions, the husband would not be associated with the trustee of the trust under which his wife is a beneficiary. Under the previous trustee for relative test in former section YB 12, the husband would have been associated with the trustee for the purposes of the land provisions.

A special report from the Policy Advice Division of Inland Revenue, 15 October 2009: New definitions of "associated persons" at 15.

¶18-130 A trustee and beneficiary are associated

A trustee of a trust and a person who has benefited or is eligible to benefit under the trust are associated persons: s YB 6. This section does not apply to charitable organisations: s YB 16(2). See ¶18-150.

This test of association will not apply for the purposes of the land provisions.

A person has benefited under a trust if the person has received a distribution under the trust.

A person is "eligible to benefit" if the person is either:

- named as a beneficiary, or
- can be identified as a member of a class of beneficiaries, for example, "the children of ...".

A person is not eligible to benefit only because that person could be appointed as a beneficiary under a power of appointment. See *Tax Information Bulletin* ¶79-127 Vol 7, No 9, February 1996 at 25.

Example

Garth is the settlor of the Queen's Trust. The beneficiaries in the deed of trust are defined as Garth, the settlor's spouse, and any person appointed by the trustees. Garth's wife, Denise, is eligible to benefit from the Queen's Trust because, although not named as a beneficiary in the deed, she is a member of a class of beneficiaries comprising "the Settlor's spouse".

John is the settlor of the Sword Shape Trust. He has the power of appointment of beneficiaries and, under this power, can appoint any natural person as a beneficiary. His civil union partner, George, is not named as a beneficiary of the Sword Shape Trust and, therefore, is not eligible to benefit from it.

A person who is eligible to benefit under a trust does not need to have actually received a distribution (s HC 14) under the trust to qualify as a beneficiary.

An exception to this test provides that a trustee will not be associated with the beneficiaries of certain employee trusts: s YB 15.

¶18-140 Two trustees are associated with a common settlor

A trustee of a trust and a trustee of another trust are associated persons if the same person is a settlor of both trusts: s YB 7.

A settlor for the purposes of s YB 7 is defined in s HC 27 (see Chapter 2 – *Settlors*) but does not include a person who provides services to a trust for less than market value: s YB 10. This means that a professional advisor who provides services to a trust at no charge will not be treated as a settlor of the trust.

Importantly, a settlor can include beneficiaries with a current balance that is more than $25,000. See further at Chapter 2 – *Settlors*.

Two persons who are married, in a civil union or de facto relationship are treated as the same single person for the purposes of s YB 7: s YB 7(2). This means that persons with mirror trusts cannot avoid association.

Example

Two trustees with common settlor: mirror trusts

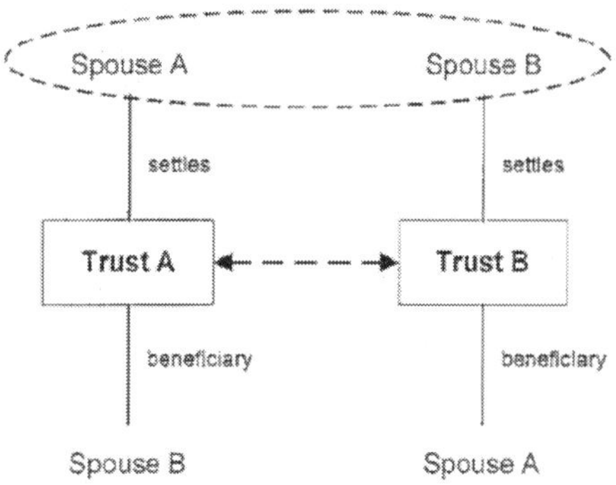

In this example spouse A settles a family trust (Trust A) for the benefit of spouse B and spouse B settles another family trust (Trust B) for the benefit of spouse A. Without the provision in the two trustees with common settlor test treating two persons who are married, in a civil union, or in a de facto relationship as the same single person, the trustees of Trust A and Trust B would not be associated despite the close community of interests.

The trustees of Trust A and Trust B are associated under new section YB 7 because Spouse A and Spouse B are treated as the same single person and therefore the trustees of Trust A and Trust B have a common settlor.

A special report from the Policy Advice Division of Inland Revenue, 15 October 2009: New definitions of "associated persons" at 19.

There is an exception to the two trustees with a common settlor test for certain employee trusts: s YB 15.

¶18-150 Trustee is associated with a settlor

A trustee of a trust and a settlor of the trust are associated persons: s YB 8. "Settlor" for the purposes of s YB 8 is defined in s YB 10.

A settlor for the purposes of s YB 8 is defined in s HC 27 but does not include a person who provides services to a trust for less than market value: s YB 10.

Section YB 8 does not apply to certain employee trusts: s YB 15.

Example

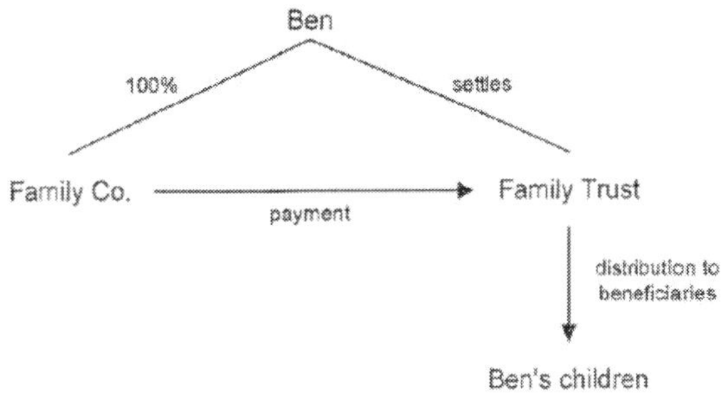

In this example, Family Co. makes a payment to Family Trust. Ben is the sole shareholder of Family Co and the settlor of Family Trust.

Without a trustee and settlor test in the associated persons definition, the payment from Family Co. to Family Trust is not caught as a dividend despite the close community of interests. This is because Family Trust would not be associated with Ben who is the sole shareholder of Family Co.

Under the new trustee and settlor test in section YB 8, Ben and Family Trust are associated persons as Ben is the settlor of Family Trust. The payment from Family Co. to the Family Trust is accordingly treated as a dividend because Family Co. has made a payment to an associated person (Family Trust) of its shareholder (Ben) in terms of section CD 6(1)(a)(ii).

Example

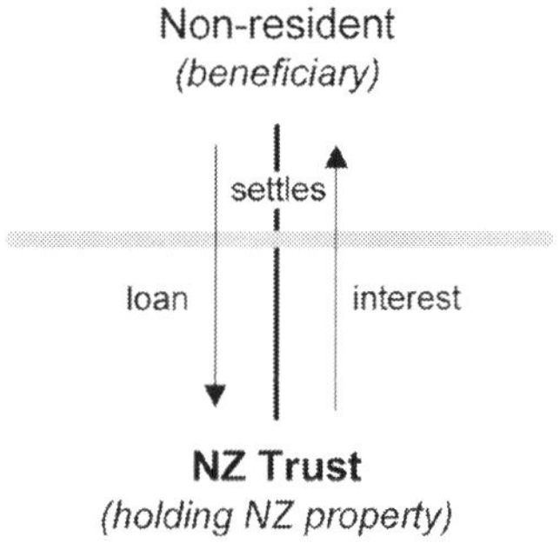

In this example, a non-resident settles a New Zealand trust (with a New Zealand-incorporated company as trustee) which owns New Zealand land and buildings. This investment by the trustee is funded by a loan from the non-resident settlor. If the non-resident is not associated with the New Zealand trustee, then the interest paid on this loan qualifies for the AIL of 2% instead of being subject to the higher NRWT rate.

The previous associated persons definition used in the AIL rules was generally deficient in relation to arrangements involving trusts. In this example in particular, without a trustee and settlor test of association, the interest would qualify for AIL treatment despite the in-substance association between the two parties.

> The new trustee and settlor test in section YB 8 would associate the non-resident with the New Zealand trustee. Accordingly, the interest derived by the non-resident from New Zealand would be subject to a higher rate of NRWT instead of AIL at 2%, which is the appropriate treatment.

A special report from the Policy Advice Division of Inland Revenue, 15 October 2009: New definitions of "associated persons" at 20.

There is no association between a trustee and the settlor of a charitable trust: s YB 8(2). This exception to s YB 8 prevents donors to a charitable trust being associated with each other. However, this exception only applies to registered charitable trusts, that is, charitable trusts that do not pay income tax: s YA 1 ("charitable organisation").

¶18-160 Settlors are associated with beneficiaries

A settlor of a trust and a person who has benefited or is eligible to benefit under the trust will be associated persons: s YB 9. A settlor for the purposes of s YB 9 is defined in s HC 27 but does not include a person who provides services to a trust for less than market value: s YB 10.

This test does not apply for the purposes of the land provisions, defined in s YA 1.

The comments above (¶18-130) under the trustee and beneficiary test heading in relation to the definition of settlor and the meaning of when a person is eligible to benefit under a trust also apply to the settlor and beneficiary associated persons test.

An exception to this test for certain employee trusts is contained in s YB 15. A further exception provides that this section does not apply to charitable organisations: s YB 16(2).

¶18-170 A trustee is associated with a person with power of appointment

A trustee of a trust and a person who has a power of appointment or removal of the trustee (unless the exemption is s YB 11(2)(b) applies) will be associated persons: s YB 11.

A person with a power of appointment, regardless of whether the person is called an appointor, a protector or some other identifier, includes:

- a person who holds the power jointly with another person, and
- a person who holds a power to appoint or remove trustees only with the consent of another person.

A person with a power of appointment does not include a person whose power of appointment is contingent on a future event or a person who only holds a power to veto the appointment or removal of a trustee: A special report from the Policy Advice Division of Inland Revenue, 15 October 2009: New definitions of "associated persons", at 22–23).

However, an exemption in s YB 11(2), provides that a person with a power of appointment or removal of a trustee is exempt from association with a trustee if the appointor is a professional who is subject to the professional code of conduct and disciplinary processes of an approved organisation.

This exemption was enacted by the Taxation (Livestock Valuation, Assets Expenditure, and Remedial Matters) Act 2013 to ensure that those who receive a power of appointment or removal of a trustee in their professional capacity are not associated with the trustee of the trust.

To be an approved organisation, the organisation's natural person members must be subject to a professional code of conduct and to disciplinary processes in accordance with that code (among other requirements). The New Zealand Law Society, Chartered Accountants Australia and New Zealand and STEP (Society of Trust and Estate Practitioners) are approved organisations.

See *Tax Information Bulletin* ¶267-121 Vol 26, No 7, August 2014.

Care is required to monitor who holds the power of appointment and whether any nominations have been made by that person or persons.

¶18-180 A partner is associated with a partnership

A partnership and a partner in the partnership will be associated persons: s YB 12. This test is not modified in any way for partnerships of trusts.

¶18-185 An owner of an interest in a look-through company can be associated with a look-through company

A person will be associated with a look-through company (LTC) if the person is a look-through owner and a director or an employee of the company: s YB 13. A trustee who is both a director and a look-through owner will be associated with the LTC.

¶18-190 Two persons are associated if each person is associated with the same third party

Any two persons are associated if each person is associated with the same third person: s YB 14. This is known as the tripartite test. The tripartite test significantly extends the scope of the associated persons tests and makes the associated persons definition as a whole more difficult to circumvent.

For the tripartite test to associate two persons, each of these persons must be associated, other than under the tripartite test itself, with the same third person. The requirement that the two persons cannot be associated with the same third person under the tripartite test itself is necessary to prevent the tripartite test operating in a reiterative manner.

However, there will be no association between persons A and B only if they are each associated with a third person (C) under different tests of association linking them to companies: ss YB 2, YB 3.

The following examples illustrate how the tripartite test prevents the other associated persons tests being circumvented by arrangements involving the interposition of relatives, companies and trusts.

Example

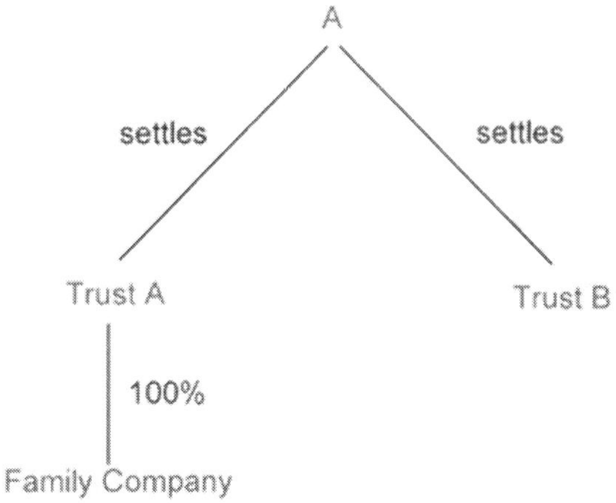

A settles two family trusts: Trust A and Trust B. Trust A in turn owns all the shares in Family Company. The issue is whether Family Company is associated with Trust B. Without the tripartite test in new s YB 14, Family Company and Trust B would not be associated, despite the close community of interests between them. However, Family Company and Trust B would be associated under the tripartite test, in conjunction with the test in new s YB 3 associating a company and a person other than a company (company-individual test) and the two trustees-common settlor test in new s YB 7. In particular, Family Company is associated with Trust A under the company-individual test, and Trust A is associated with Trust B under the two trustees-common settlor test. Therefore, Family Company and Trust B would be associated under the tripartite test.

Example from Taxation (International Taxation, Life Insurance, and Remedial Matters) Bill, Commentary on the Bill, at 87.

Example

Application of the tripartite test and the aggregation rule

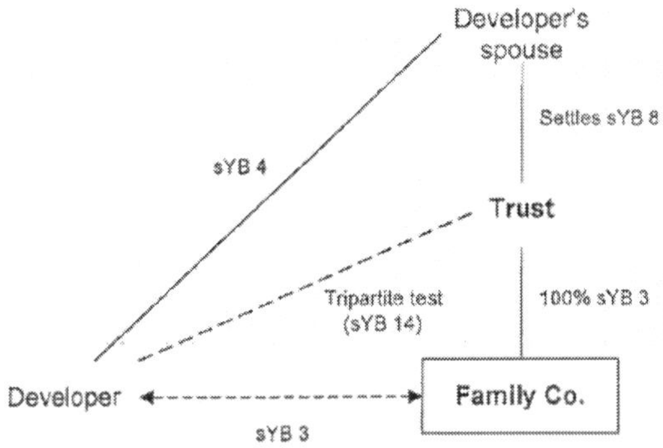

> In this example, Developer's spouse settles Trust, which in turn owns all the shares in Family Co. The issue is whether Developer is associated with Family Co. under the test associating a company and a person other than a company in section YB 3.
>
> Developer would be associated with Family Co. under the company and person other than a company test because of the application of the aggregation rule in that test, in conjunction with the tripartite test. In particular, Developer would be treated for the purposes of the company and person other than a company test as holding all the shares held by Trust in Family Co. This is because Trust is associated with Developer under the tripartite test: Developer is associated with his spouse under the relatives test (section YB 4) and Developer's spouse is associated with Trust under the trustee and settlor test (section YB 8), which means that Developer is associated with Trust under the tripartite test.
>
> Without the tripartite test in section YB 14 and the rule in the company and person other than a company test aggregating interests held by associated persons, Developer would not be associated with Family Co. even though there is a large community of interest between them.

A special report from the Policy Advice Division of Inland Revenue, 15 October 2009: New definitions of "associated persons", at 27.

¶18-200 Exceptions from rules of association for certain trusts

Lines trusts established under the Energy Companies Act 1992, often known as energy consumer trusts, are excluded from the trustee relative test (s YB 5) and the trustee beneficiary test (s YB 6). These exceptions prevent beneficiaries from energy consumer trusts from being associated with each other: s YB 16(1).

¶18-210 Rules of association apply for RLWT purposes

Where a vendor and purchaser are associated persons, for the purposes of the residential land withholding tax rules (RLWT), the liability for RLWT falls on the purchaser. See ss RL 3, YB 1 and ¶19-100.

Also see Inland Revenue an officials' issues paper "Residential land withholding tax", August 2015.

¶18-220 When calculating Family Scheme income for WFF tax credits any associations with companies need to be identified

When calculating "companies income" for the purposes of calculating family scheme income, it is necessary to identify any company in which the trustee and associated persons of the trustee hold voting interests of 50% or more. See s MB 7.

¶18-230 Rules of association apply for GST purposes

Specific rules of association determine the value of supplies and limit input tax credits between associated persons for the purposes of the GST Act. See ¶25-050, ¶25-060 and ¶25-065.

¶18-240 There is inconsistency between the rules of association that apply for Income Tax and GST purposes

The following table is adapted from Sybrand van Schalkwyk "GST and associated person rules – Need for reform" CCH, *New Zealand Tax Planning Report* (16 February 2016) and compares the rules of association from the Income Tax Act and the GST Act with respect to trust-based relationships.

Comparison of Associated Person Rules in Income Tax and GST Acts			
Associated Person Rule	Associated under GST Act?	Income Tax Act – Land	Associated under Income Tax Act (Other)?
Trustee and relative of beneficiary	Yes	No	Yes
Trustee and beneficiaries	Yes	No	Yes
Settlor and beneficiary	Yes (via tri-partite test)	No	Yes
Trustee and settlor	Yes	Yes	Yes
Two trustees with same settlor	Yes	Yes	Yes
Tri-partite test	Yes	Yes	Yes
Trustee and person with power of appointment	No	Yes	Yes

¶18-250 Legislation

Income Tax Act 2007

CB 7 DISPOSAL: LAND ACQUIRED FOR PURPOSES OF BUSINESS RELATING TO LAND

CB 7(1) INCOME

An amount that a person (**person** A) derives from disposing of land is income of person A if–

(a) both the following apply:

(i) at the time person A acquired the land they, or an associated person, carried on a business of dealing in land; and

(ii) person A acquired the land for the purpose of the business; or

(b) both the following apply:

(i) at the time person A acquired the land they, or an associated person, carried on a business of developing land or dividing land into lots; and

(ii) person A acquired the land for the purpose of the business; or

(c) all the following apply:

(i) at the time person A acquired the land they, or an associated person, carried on a business of erecting buildings; and

(ii) person A acquired the land for the purpose of the business; and

(iii) before or after acquiring the land person A, or the associated person, made improvements to it.

CB 7(2) EXCLUSIONS

Subsection (1) is overridden by the exclusions for residential land in section CB 16 and for business premises in section CB 19.

CB 8 DISPOSAL: LAND USED FOR LANDFILL, IF NOTICE OF ELECTION

An amount that a person derives from disposing of land is income of the person if–

(a) the person uses the land as a landfill before disposing of the land; and

(b) at the time of disposal, the land is not being used as a landfill; and

(c) the person acquiring the land is not an associated person; and

(d) the person notifies the Commissioner of an election that the land be subject to this section by the day that is the later of the following:

(i) the day that is 12 months after the day on which the person acquires the land:

(ii) 24 June 2006; and

(e) the person makes an election under paragraph (d) for all land that the person acquires and uses as a landfill; and

(f) any person associated with the person makes an election under paragraph (d) for all land that the associated person acquires and uses as a landfill.

CB 9 DISPOSAL WITHIN 10 YEARS: LAND DEALING BUSINESS

CB 9(1) INCOME

An amount that a person derives from disposing of land is income of the person if–

(a) they dispose of the land within 10 years of acquiring it; and

(b) at the time they acquired the land, they carried on a business of dealing in land, whether or not the land was acquired for the purpose of the business.

CB 9(2) INCOME: ASSOCIATED PERSON IN BUSINESS OF DEALING IN LAND

An amount that a person (**person** A) derives from disposing of land within 10 years of acquiring it is income of person A if a person (**person** B) associated with them at the time the land was acquired carried on a business of dealing in land, whether or not–

(a) person A carried on a business of dealing in land; or

(b) the land was acquired for the purpose of person B's business.

CB 9(3) EXCLUSIONS

Subsection (2) is overridden by the exclusions in sections CB 15C and CB 15D, for bodies linked or associated with a local authority and for companies in the same wholly-owned group as Kāinga Ora-Homes and Communities, and subsections (1) and (2) are overridden by the exclusions in sections CB 16 and CB 19, for residential land and for business premises.

CB 10 DISPOSAL WITHIN 10 YEARS: LAND DEVELOPMENT OR SUBDIVISION BUSINESS

CB 10(1) INCOME

An amount that a person derives from disposing of land is income of the person if–

(a) they dispose of the land within 10 years of acquiring it; and

(b) at the time they acquired the land, they carried on a business of developing land or dividing land into lots, whether or not the land was acquired for the purpose of the business.

CB 10(2) INCOME: ASSOCIATED PERSON IN BUSINESS OF DEVELOPING OR SUBDIVIDING LAND

An amount that a person (**person** A) derives from disposing of land within 10 years of acquiring it is income of person A if a person (**person** B) associated with them at the time the land was acquired carried on a business of developing land or dividing land into lots, whether or not–

(a) person A carried on a business of developing land or dividing land into lots:

(b) the land was acquired for the purpose of person B's business.

CB 10(3) EXCLUSIONS

Subsection (2) is overridden by the exclusions in sections CB 15C and CB 15D, for bodies linked or associated with a local authority and for companies in the same wholly-owned group as Kāinga Ora-Homes and Communities, and subsections (1) and (2) are overridden by the exclusions in sections CB 16 and CB 19, for residential land and for business premises.

CB 11 DISPOSAL WITHIN 10 YEARS OF IMPROVEMENT: BUILDING BUSINESS

CB 11(1) INCOME

An amount that a person derives from disposing of land is income of the person if they dispose of the land and–

(a) within 10 years before the disposal, the person or an associate of the person completed improvements to the land; and

(b) at the time the improvements were begun,–

  (i) the person carried on a business of erecting buildings:

  (ii) an associate of the person carried on a business of erecting buildings.

CB 11(2) PERSON OR ASSOCIATE

Subsection (1) applies whether or not the land was acquired for the person's business or an associate's business.

CB 11(3) EXCLUSIONS

Subsection (1)(b)(ii) is overridden by the exclusions in sections CB 15C and CB 15D, for bodies linked or associated with a local authority and for companies in the same wholly-owned group as Kāinga Ora–Homes and Communities, and subsections (1) and (2) are overridden by the exclusions in sections CB 16 and CB 19, for residential land and for business premises.

CB 12 DISPOSAL: SCHEMES FOR DEVELOPMENT OR DIVISION BEGUN WITHIN 10 YEARS

CB 12(1) INCOME

An amount that a person derives from disposing of land is income of the person if the amount is derived in the following circumstances:

(a) an undertaking or scheme, which is not necessarily in the nature of a business, is carried on; and

(b) the undertaking or scheme involves the development of the land or the division of the land into lots; and

(c) the person, or another person for them, carries on development or division work on or relating to the land; and

(d) the development or division work is not minor; and

(e) the undertaking or scheme was begun within 10 years of the date on which the person acquired the land.

CB 12(2) EXCLUSIONS

Subsection (1) is overridden by the exclusions for residential land in section CB 17, for business premises in section CB 20, for farm land in section CB 21, and for investment land in section CB 23.

CB 13 DISPOSAL: AMOUNT FROM MAJOR DEVELOPMENT OR DIVISION AND NOT ALREADY IN INCOME

CB 13(1) INCOME

An amount that a person derives from disposing of land is income of the person if–

(a) the amount is not income under any of sections CB 6A to CB 12, CB 14, and CZ 39 (Disposal within 5 years: bright-line test for residential land: acquisition on or after 29 March 2018); and

(b) the amount is derived in the following circumstances:

  (i) an undertaking or scheme, which is not necessarily in the nature of a business, is carried on; and

  (ii) the undertaking or scheme involves the development of the land or the division of the land into lots; and

  (iii) the person, or another person for them, carries on development or division work on or relating to the land; and

  (iv) the development or division work involves significant expenditure on channelling, contouring, drainage, earthworks, kerbing, levelling, roading, or any other amenity, service, or work customarily undertaken or provided in major projects involving the development of land for commercial, industrial, or residential purposes.

CB 13(2) EXCLUSIONS

Subsection (1) is overridden by the exclusions for residential land in section CB 17, for business premises in section CB 20, for farm land in section CB 21, and for investment land in section CB 23.

CB 13(3) RELATIONSHIP WITH SECTION DB 27

Section DB 27 (Amount from major development or division and not already in income) deals with a deduction for the value of the land.

[...]

CB 15 TRANSACTIONS BETWEEN ASSOCIATED PERSONS

CB 15(1) INCOME

An amount that a person (the **transferee**) derives from disposing of land is income of the transferee if–

(a) the land has been transferred to the transferee from another person (the **transferor**); and

(b) the transferor and the transferee are associated persons at the time of the transfer; and

(c) the amount derived is more than the cost of the land to the transferee; and

(d) the amount derived would have been income of the transferor under any of sections CB 6 to CB 14 if the transferor had retained and disposed of the land.

CB 15(1B) EXCLUSION FOR KĀINGA ORA–HOMES AND COMMUNITIES AND WHOLLY-OWNED GROUP

Subsection (1) is overridden by section CB 15D.

CB 15(2) DATE ON WHICH SOME TRANSFEREES ACQUIRE LAND

For the purposes of sections CB 7 to CB 12 and CB 14, if a person (the **transferor**) transfers land to a person (the **transferee**) who is an associated person at the time of the transfer, the transferee is treated as acquiring the land on the date, other than under this subsection, on which the transferor acquired the land.

CB 16 RESIDENTIAL EXCLUSION FROM SECTIONS CB 6 TO CB 11

CB 16(1) EXCLUSION

Sections CB 6 to CB 11 do not apply if–

(a) the person (**person** A)–

 (i) acquired the land with a dwellinghouse on it; or

 (ii) acquired the land and erected a dwellinghouse on it; and

(b) the dwellinghouse was occupied mainly as a residence by,–

 (i) person A:

 (ii) if members of person A's family live with them, person A and members of person A's family living with them:

 (iii) if person A is a trustee, 1 or more beneficiaries of the trust.

CB 16(2) WHAT EXCLUSION APPLIES TO

The exclusion applies to the land that has the dwellinghouse on it. It also applies to land related to the land that has the dwellinghouse on it if the total area of the related land is–

(a) 4,500 square metres or less; or

(b) more than 4,500 square metres, if the larger area is required for the reasonable occupation and enjoyment of the dwellinghouse.

CB 16(3) EXCEPTION

The exclusion does not apply when–

(a) section CB 6(1) applies to the disposal; and

(b) person A has engaged in a regular pattern of acquiring and disposing of land described in subsection (1).

CB 16(4) REGULAR PATTERNS UNDERTAKEN BY GROUPS OF PERSONS

For the purposes of subsection (3), in relation to land described in subsection (1), person A includes a group of persons if the requirements of subsection (5) are met.

CB 16(5) MEANING OF GROUP OF PERSONS

For the purposes of subsection (4), a **group of persons**–

(a) means 2 or more persons when together all of the persons occupy, or have occupied, land described in subsection (1); and

(b) includes a person other than a natural person (the **non-natural person**), if another person referred to in paragraph (a) has significant involvement in, or control of, the activities of the non-natural person. For the avoidance of doubt, if the other person is able to direct, alone or as part of a group, the activities of the non-natural person, they have significant involvement in, or control of, the activities of the non-natural person.

[...]

CD 6 WHEN IS A TRANSFER CAUSED BY A SHAREHOLDING RELATIONSHIP?

CD 6(1) GENERAL TEST

A transfer of company value from a company to a person (the **recipient**) is caused by a shareholding in the company if–

(a) the recipient at any relevant time–

  (i) holds shares in the company; or

  (ii) is associated with a shareholder; and

  (iii) *(repealed)*

(b) the company makes the transfer because of that shareholding of the relevant shareholder.

CD 6(2) INDICATION THAT TEST MET

One indication that a transfer is caused by a shareholding is if the terms of the arrangement that results in the transfer are different from the terms on which the company would enter into a similar arrangement if no shareholding were involved.

[...]

YA 1 DEFINITIONS

[...]

trustee,–

(a) for a trust,–

  (i) means the trustee only in the capacity of trustee of the trust; and

  (ii) includes all trustees, for the time being, of the trust:

[...]

SUBPART YB – ASSOCIATED PERSONS AND NOMINEES

YB 1 WHAT THIS SUBPART DOES

YB 1(1) ASSOCIATED PERSON RULES AND NOMINEE RULES

This subpart sets out the rules that–

(a) define when 2 persons are associated persons; and

(b) determine how nominees are treated.

YB 1(2) OTHER REFERENCES

If a rule in this subpart states that 2 persons are associated persons for 1 or more provisions in this Act, a reference in the relevant provision to persons who are associated with each other includes those persons.

YB 1(3) TESTS

The tests of association are categorised as follows:

(a) two companies, *see* section YB 2:

(b) a company and a person other than a company, *see* section YB 3:

(c) two relatives, *see* section YB 4:

(d) a person and a trustee for a relative, *see* section YB 5:

(e) a trustee and a beneficiary, *see* section YB 6:

(f) trustees with a common settlor, *see* section YB 7:

(g) a trustee and a settlor, *see* section YB 8:

(h) a settlor and a beneficiary, *see* section YB 9:

(i) a trustee and a person with a power of appointment or removal, *see* section YB 11:

(j) a partnership and a partner, *see* section YB 12:

(k) two persons who are each associated with the same third person, *see* section YB 14.

YB 1(4) APPLICATION

The sections in this subpart relating to associated persons apply for the purposes of the whole Act unless a section expressly states otherwise.

YB 1(5) LOSS-ATTRIBUTING QUALIFYING COMPANIES AND SHAREHOLDERS

(repealed)

YB 1(6) LOW-TURNOVER TRADERS

A special rule applies for the purposes of subpart EB (Valuation of trading stock (including dealer's livestock)) to determine when a low-turnover trader is associated with a company, *see* section EB 13(2) (Low-turnover valuation).

YB 1(7) CONTROL INTERESTS IN FOREIGN COMPANIES

A special rule applies for the purposes of section EX 3 (Control interests: total of direct, indirect, and associated person interests) to determine when a New Zealand resident is associated with a non-resident relative, *see* section EX 4(1) (Limits to requirement to include associated person interests).

YB 1(8) SUPPLEMENTARY DIVIDEND HOLDING COMPANIES

(repealed)

YB 2 TWO COMPANIES

YB 2(1) COMMON VOTING INTERESTS

Two companies are associated persons if a group of persons exists whose total voting interests in each company are 50% or more.

YB 2(2) COMMON MARKET VALUE INTERESTS

Two companies are associated persons if–

(a) a market value circumstance exists for either company; and

(b) a group of persons exists whose total market value interests in each company are 50% or more.

YB 2(3) COMMON CONTROL BY OTHER MEANS

Two companies are associated persons if a group of persons exists who control both companies by any other means.

YB 2(4) GENERAL AGGREGATION RULE

For the purposes of subsections (1) to (3), if a person (**person** A) and another person (**person** B) are associated under any of sections YB 4 to YB 14, person A is treated as holding anything held by person B.

YB 2(5) AGGREGATION RULE FOR LAND PROVISIONS

For the purposes of subsections (1) to (3), if a person (**person** A) and another person (**person** B) are associated under any of sections YB 4(1)(b) and (2) to (4), YB 7, YB 8, and YB 10 to YB 14, person A is treated as holding anything held by person B.

YB 2(6) EXCEPTION FOR CERTAIN GOVERNMENT ENTITIES

Subsection (3) does not apply to 2 companies if either or both are–

(a) a state enterprise:

(ab) a mixed-ownership enterprise:

(b) a Crown Research Institute:

(c) a Crown health enterprise:

(d) a company that is part of the same group of companies as an entity referred to in any of paragraphs (a) to (c).

YB 2(7) EXCEPTION FOR INTERNATIONAL TAX RULES

In the international tax rules, 2 companies are not associated persons if 1, but not both, is a non-resident.

YB 2(8) EXCEPTION FOR MANAGED FUNDS

For the purposes of the land provisions, 2 companies are not associated persons if 1 is a portfolio investment entity or an entity that qualifies for PIE status.

YB 3 COMPANY AND PERSON OTHER THAN COMPANY

YB 3(1) COMPANY AND 25% VOTING INTEREST HOLDER

A company and a person other than a company are associated persons if the person has a voting interest in the company of 25% or more.

YB 3(2) COMPANY AND 25% MARKET VALUE INTEREST HOLDER

A company and a person other than a company are associated persons if–

(a) a market value circumstance exists for the company; and

(b) the person has a market value interest in the company of 25% or more.

YB 3(3) GENERAL AGGREGATION RULE

For the purposes of subsections (1) and (2), if a person (**person** A) and another person (**person** B) are associated under any of sections YB 4 to YB 14, person A is treated as holding anything held by person B.

YB 3(4) AGGREGATION RULE FOR LAND PROVISIONS

For the purposes of subsections (1) and (2), if a person (**person** A) and another person (**person** B) are associated under any of sections YB 4(1)(b) and (2) to (4), YB 7, YB 8, and YB 10 to YB 14, person A is treated as holding anything held by person B.

YB 3(5) PERSON OTHER THAN COMPANY

(repealed)

YB 4 TWO RELATIVES

YB 4(1) DEGREE OF RELATIONSHIP

Two persons are associated persons if–

(a) they are within 2 degrees of blood relationship:

(b) they are married, in a civil union, or in a de facto relationship:

(c) 1 person is within 2 degrees of blood relationship to the other person's spouse, civil union partner, or de facto partner.

YB 4(2) EXCEPTION: BLOOD RELATIONSHIPS

For the purposes of the land provisions and sections EB 13 (Low turnover valuation) and EC 5 (Transfer of livestock because of self-assessed adverse event), subsection (1)(a) and (c) does not apply, and persons are associated persons because of a blood relationship only if 1 is the infant child of the other.

YB 4(3) TREATMENT OF ADOPTION

For the purposes of this section, a child by adoption is treated as a natural child of the adoptive parents and not as a natural child of the birth parents.

YB 4(4) EXCEPTION

A person is not associated with another person under this section if the person cannot reasonably be expected to know that–

(a) the other person exists:

(b) the person is within 2 degrees of blood relationship to the other person.

YB 5 PERSON AND TRUSTEE FOR RELATIVE

YB 5(1) ASSOCIATION

Two persons (**person** A and **person** B) are associated persons if person A is the trustee of a trust under which a person associated under section YB 4 with person B has benefited or is eligible to benefit.

YB 5(2) LAND PROVISIONS

This section does not apply for the purposes of the land provisions.

YB 6 TRUSTEE AND BENEFICIARY

YB 6(1) ASSOCIATION

A trustee of a trust and a person who has benefited or is eligible to benefit under the trust are associated persons.

YB 6(2) LAND PROVISIONS

This section does not apply for the purposes of the land provisions.

YB 7 TWO TRUSTEES WITH COMMON SETTLOR

YB 7(1) ASSOCIATION

A trustee of a trust and a trustee of another trust are associated persons if the same person is a settlor of both trusts.

YB 7(2) TREATMENT OF SPOUSES AND PARTNERS

For the purposes of this section, 2 persons who are married, in a civil union, or in a de facto relationship are treated as the same single person.

YB 8 TRUSTEE AND SETTLOR

YB 8(1) ASSOCIATION

A trustee of a trust and a settlor of the trust are associated persons.

YB 8(2) EXCLUSION

This section does not apply if the trust is a charitable trust.

YB 9 SETTLOR AND BENEFICIARY

YB 9(1) ASSOCIATION

A settlor of a trust and a person who has benefited or is eligible to benefit under the trust are associated persons.

YB 9(2) LAND PROVISIONS

This section does not apply for the purposes of the land provisions.

YB 10 WHO IS A SETTLOR?

For the purposes of sections YB 7 to YB 9, settlor has the meaning set out in section HC 27 (Who is a settlor?) but does not include a person who provides services to a trust for less than market value.

YB 11 TRUSTEE AND PERSON WITH POWER OF APPOINTMENT OR REMOVAL

YB 11(1) ASSOCIATION

A trustee of a trust and a person who has a power of appointment or of removal of the trustee are associated persons.

YB 11(2) EXCLUSION

This section does not apply if the person—

(a) holds the power as a provider of professional services; and

(b) is subject to a professional code of conduct, and disciplinary process intended to enforce compliance with the code, of an approved organisation as that term is defined in section 3(1) of the Tax Administration Act 1994, for such providers of professional services; and

(c) has not benefited from the trust; and

(d) is not eligible to benefit from the trust.

YB 12 PARTNERSHIP AND PARTNER

YB 12(1) ASSOCIATION

A partnership and a partner in the partnership are associated persons.

YB 12(2) LIMITED PARTNERSHIPS

Subsection (1) does not apply if the partner is a limited partner. Instead a limited partnership and a limited partner are associated persons if the limited partner has a partnership share of 25% or more in a right, obligation, or other property, status, or thing of the limited partnership.

YB 12(3) LIMITED PARTNERSHIPS: GENERAL AGGREGATION RULE

For the purposes of subsection (2), if a person (**person** A) and another person (**person** B) are associated under any of sections YB 2 to YB 11 and YB 14, person A is treated as holding anything held by person B.

YB 12(4) LIMITED PARTNERSHIPS: AGGREGATION RULE FOR LAND PROVISIONS

For the purposes of subsection (2), if a person (**person** A) and another person (**person** B) are associated under any of sections YB 2, YB 3, YB 4(1)(b) and (2) to (4), YB 7, YB 8, YB 10, YB 11, and YB 14, person A is treated as holding anything held by person B.

YB 13 LOOK-THROUGH COMPANIES AND OWNERS OF INTERESTS

YB 13(1) ASSOCIATION

A look-through company and a person who has a look-through interest for the look-through company (an owner) and who is a director or employee for the look-through company are associated persons.

YB 13(2) SOME OWNERS

If subsection (1) does not apply to a look-through company and an owner, then they are associated persons if the owner has effective look-through interests of 25% or more in a right, obligation, or other property status, or thing of the look-through company.

YB 13(3) SOME OWNERS: GENERAL AGGREGATION RULE

For the purposes of subsection (2), if a person (**person** A) and another person (**person** B) are associated under any of sections YB 2 to YB 11 and YB 14, person A is treated as holding anything held by person B.

YB 13(4) SOME OWNERS: AGGREGATION RULE FOR LAND PROVISIONS

For the purposes of subsection (2), if a person (**person** A) and another person (**person** B) are associated under any of sections YB 2, YB 3, YB 4(1)(b) and (2) to (4), YB 7, YB 8, YB 10, YB 11, and YB 14, person A is treated as holding anything held by person B.

YB 14 TRIPARTITE RELATIONSHIP

YB 14(1) TEST

Two persons (**person** A and **person** B) are associated persons if–

(a) person B is associated with a third person (**person** C) under any of sections YB 2 to YB 13; and

(b) person C is associated with person A under any of sections YB 2 to YB 13, excluding the section under which person B is associated with person C.

YB 14(2) EXCEPTION: COMPANIES TESTS

Subsection (1) does not apply if–

(a) person B is associated with person C under section YB 2; and

(b) person C is associated with person A under section YB 3.

YB 14(3) ASSOCIATION FOR PURPOSES OF RESEARCH AND DEVELOPMENT TAX CREDITS

(repealed)

YB 14(4) APPLYING TEST TO LIMITED PARTNERSHIP

For the purpose of applying subsection (1), a limited partnership is treated as being a company.

YB 15 EXCEPTIONS FOR EMPLOYEE TRUSTS

YB 15(1) BENEFICIARIES

Section YB 6(1) does not apply if–

(a) the trust is only for the benefit of employees of an employer; and

(b) neither the beneficiary nor any person associated with the beneficiary directly or indirectly controls the trust.

YB 15(2) NON-CORPORATE SETTLORS

For a settlor that is not a company, sections YB 7, YB 8, and YB 9(1) do not apply if–

(a) the settlor settles property on the terms of the trust only for the benefit of employees of the settlor; and

(b) neither the settlor nor any person associated with the settlor directly or indirectly controls the trust.

YB 15(3) CORPORATE SETTLORS

For a settlor that is a company, sections YB 7, YB 8, and YB 9(1) do not apply if–

(a) the settlor settles property on the terms of the trust only for the benefit of its employees; and

(b) none of the following directly or indirectly controls the trust:

   (i) the settlor:

   (ii) a person associated with the settlor:

   (iii) an executive of the settlor:

   (iv) a director of the settlor:

   (v) a person holding a direct voting interest of 25% or more in the settlor:

   (vi) if a market value circumstance exists for the settlor, a person holding a direct market value interest of 25% or more in the settlor.

YB 15(4) PERSONS WITH POWER OF APPOINTMENT OR REMOVAL

Section YB 11 does not apply if–

(a) the trust is only for the benefit of employees of an employer; and

(b) neither the person (**person** A) who has a power of appointment or of removal of a trustee nor a person associated with person A directly or indirectly controls the trust.

YB 16 EXCEPTIONS FOR CERTAIN TRUSTS AND CHARITABLE ORGANISATIONS

YB 16(1) TRUSTEE AND BENEFICIARY AND TRUSTEE FOR RELATIVE TESTS: CERTAIN TRUSTS

Sections YB 5 and YB 6(1) do not apply to a trustee and another person if the trust is–

(a) a lines trust established under the Energy Companies Act 1992:

(b) an approved unit trust referred to in clause 2 of the Income Tax Act (Exempt Unit Trusts) Order 1990.

YB 16(2) TRUSTEE AND BENEFICIARY AND SETTLOR AND BENEFICIARY TESTS: CHARITABLE ORGANISATION

Sections YB 6(1) and YB 9(1) do not apply to a trustee and a beneficiary or a settlor and a beneficiary if the beneficiary is a charitable organisation.

Part V

ADMINISTRATION

CHAPTER 19

Administration

¶19-010 Operating principle

In addition to maintaining core documents (as defined in the Trusts Act 2019, s 45), including trust accounts appropriate to the value and complexity of the trust property and other trust records in accordance with the terms of the trust, a trustee must also comply with any statutory record-keeping obligations. Trustees must also appraise themselves of the various taxing provisions that can apply differently where an asset (particularly land) is owned by a trust. Also see the trustees' disclosure obligations in Chapter 20 – *Disclosure Obligations.*

¶19-020 The trust must have an IRD number if a trustee derives any income

If a trust earns any income, it must have an IRD number. The application for an IRD number is made in the name of the trust, not the trustee. The form used is IR 596 (www.ird.govt.nz).

If a trust owns land, it should have an IRD number even if the land in question is only the family home. Trustees must provide the trust's IRD number when any land is transferred or received. See further at ¶19-090. It would, therefore, generally be prudent for trusts without an IRD number to obtain one. If the trust has income of less than $200 per year, a non-active trust declaration can then be filed. See ¶19-030.

¶19-030 A trust that derives income must file a tax return

A trustee deriving income must file an annual tax return (unless the income is de minimis, see the exemption in s 43B of the Tax Administration Act 1994) on form IR6 (Form IR 6B "Estate or trust beneficiary details" should also be attached).

When 2 or more persons act as co-trustees, one return is filed jointly. Only income derived by the trust must be returned; non-trust income derived by a trustee in a personal capacity is taxed separately. The trustee is liable for tax on all trust income as if the trustee were beneficially entitled to that income. See ¶21-030.

In the trust's tax return, the trustee will calculate the tax on the beneficiaries' income and pay the tax on that income as agent of the beneficiary. The net income is then paid to the beneficiary.

When a trust furnishes a return of income for a non-standard income year (ie a year with an annual balance date other than 31 March) and any of the income derived by the trustee in that income year is also beneficiary income during the same income year, the beneficiary is deemed to have derived that income during the same tax year that corresponds to the trust's income year: s HC 6, ¶3-150.

A beneficiary must include their share of any beneficiary income or taxable distribution in the beneficiary's own return of income. The beneficiary income must be included in the tax return for the same income year in which the trust included the beneficiary income in its tax return.

Direct assessment of a beneficiary does not relieve the trustee of the responsibility to furnish a return of income for the trust's other income. Nor does it relieve the trustee of the liability to pay any tax owing, should the beneficiary default.

If the trust is carrying on a taxable activity, the trust must register and account for GST. See Chapter 25 – *Goods and Services Tax*.

There is an exemption in s 43B of the Tax Administration Act that allows non-active trusts that are currently required to file nil income tax returns to apply to be exempted from the obligation to file.

Trusts that are non-active will no longer be required to file annual income tax returns if:

- throughout the tax year the trust is a non-active complying trust, and
- the trustee of the trust has filed a declaration that the trust is non-active (and the trust has not become active since making the declaration).

A trust will be non-active if it has:

- not derived or been deemed to have derived any income
- no deductions, and
- not been a party to, or perpetuated or continued with, any transactions with assets of the trust in the tax year, which give rise to income in any person's hands or fringe benefits to any employee or to any former employee.

Minimal amounts of income or deductions can be ignored in determining whether a trust is non-active. These include:

- bank charges or other minimal administration costs that total $200 or less in the tax year
- reasonable fees paid to professional trustees to administer the trust
- up to $200 of interest earned on trust assets in a bank account during the tax year, and
- insurance, rates, and other expenditure incidental to the occupation of a dwelling owned by the trust and incurred by the beneficiaries of the trust.

To obtain an exemption from filing income tax returns, the trustee must file a non-active trust declaration (IR 633) declaring that the trust is a non-active trust and that a trustee of the trust will inform the Commissioner if the trust ceases to be non-active.

¶19-040 Trustees have specific record-keeping obligations

A trust that carries on a business has the same record-keeping obligation as any other person: Tax Administration Act 1994, s 22.

In addition to this general obligation, if a trustee has had a debt forgiven in consideration of natural love and affection (ss EW 44, EZ 39), the trustee must keep records of the amounts forgiven and any amounts distributed to beneficiaries: Tax Administration Act, s 22B(1).

Records of debt forgiveness must be stored safely and retained for the life of the trust: Tax Administration Act, s 22B(2).

Resident trustees of foreign trusts must keep and retain detailed records. See ¶20-040 and ¶20-070.

Note that these record-keeping obligations should be considered an adjunct to the core document obligations set out in s 45 of the Trusts Act. See ¶19-050 below.

¶19-050 A trustee should maintain complete trust records independent of its tax record-keeping obligations

Trustees are obliged under s 45 of the Trusts Act to keep, so far as is reasonable, core trust documents for every trust the trustee acts for. Where there is more than one trustee, the trustee's obligations under s 45 are met where one trustee holds all of the core documents and the other trustees hold at least the trust deed and any variations of trust. The core documents are:

"(a) the trust deed and any other document that contains terms of the trust:

(b) any variations made to the trust deed or trust:

(c) records of the trust property that identify the assets, liabilities, income, and expenses of the trust and that are appropriate to the value and complexity of the trust property:

(d) any records of trustee decisions made during the trustee's trusteeship:

(e) any written contracts entered into during that trustee's trusteeship:

(f) any accounting records and financial statements prepared during that trustee's trusteeship:

(g) documents of appointment, removal, and discharge of trustees (including any court orders appointing or removing trustees):

(h) any letter or memorandum of wishes from the settlor:

(i) any other documents necessary for the administration of the trust:

(j) any documents referred to in paragraphs (a) to (i) that were kept by a former trustee during that person's trusteeship and passed on to the current trustee".

Other documents, information or records not specifically referred to in s 45, but that should also be retained, include:

- contact details of all the trustees and the person or persons with the power to appoint and remove trustees. See ¶18-170.
- contact details of any person with the power to vary the trust deed
- contact details of any person with the power to appoint or remove beneficiaries
- contact details of all beneficiaries
- a gifting schedule
- each beneficiary's IRD number
- each beneficiary's date of birth
- periods of occupation of residential trust property
- records of dividend imputation credits or resident withholding credits available for allocation and details of how these were allocated, and
- all tax returns.

Trustees should also maintain records of all settlements onto the trust and all distributions so that they can meet their reporting obligations under ss 59BA and 59BAB of the Tax Administration Act. These reporting obligations were enacted by the Taxation (Income Tax Rate and Other Amendments) Act 2020, which was introduced on 2 December 2020 and enacted on 7 December 2020 following Royal Assent. The Commentary to the Taxation (Income Tax Rate and Other Amendments) Bill explains the new disclosure requirements at 18 to 19 as follows:

> "Detailed analysis
>
> ***Information required to be provided***
>
> The Bill would require financial accounting information to be provided by trustees on an ongoing basis. This would include:
>
> - profit and loss statements
> - balance sheet items, and
> - other information to be specified by the Commissioner (for example any transfers to the trust by associated persons).
>
> The Commissioner would prescribe additional information relevant to trusts which must be provided as part of the return information, such as loans to or by related parties.
>
> Trustees would also be required to provide information on distributions and settlements made during the income year and include that in their return.
>
> *Distributions*
>
> For distributions, the information required would include identifying information for beneficiaries such as their name, IRD number and date of birth. This is set out in proposed section 59BA(2)(d) [of the Tax Administration Act 1994].

The information required for distributions is similar to the information Inland Revenue collects about beneficiaries as part of the current tax return process, where there is an allocation of income to the beneficiary.

The Commissioner may require other information relating to distributions to be reported, which could include, for example, the source of the distribution.

[...]

Other relevant persons

Proposed section 59BA(2)(e) would require trustees to provide information on those with the power under the trust to appoint or dismiss a trustee, to add or remove a beneficiary, or to amend the trust deed.

Requiring this information is necessary as 'appointers' or those with power to amend the trust deed would not be disclosed otherwise. The reference to the power arising 'under the trust' is intended to ensure this does not capture beneficiaries where they have one of the above powers only if all beneficiaries agree.

This would form part of a trustee's annual return requirements and therefore existing penalty provisions would apply as appropriate, if the information is not provided or false information is provided. No additional or specific penalty is proposed."

¶19-060 The RWT regime has special rules that apply to trustees

Unless an exception applies or the recipient holds an exemption certificate, any person, including a trustee who makes a payment of resident passive income, or a payment that includes such income, must deduct resident withholding tax (RWT) from the payment: ss RE 2, RE 5(3), RE 7–RE 9, YA 1 ("resident passive income").

Resident passive income comprises interest, dividends, taxable Māori authority distributions or a replacement payment paid to a person under a share-lending arrangement. RWT is imposed at source at the time the interest or dividend income is paid. However, in most cases, it is only a withholding tax, and the tax deducted is credited against any final income tax liability of the taxpayer deriving dividends and interest.

When a trustee receives resident passive income, the trustee must deduct RWT if the payer has not done so.

A trustee is not required to make a deduction from dividends that are non-cash dividends. Instead, the trustee must pay the Commissioner an amount equivalent to the RWT that would have been deducted if the dividend had been a cash dividend.

When a trust is issued with an RWT exemption certificate in relation to the carrying on of a taxable activity:

- the certificate is in the name of the trust
- changes in trustees do not have effect so far as RWT is concerned except that trustees are jointly and severally liable and that liability continues until the Commissioner is notified of a change of trustee in writing: s RE 30.

¶19-070 A tax charity has record-keeping obligations but is not required to file a return

A charitable trust that is fully exempt from income tax is not required to file an income tax return. However, accurate records must be kept, and a charitable trust must keep sufficient records to enable the Commissioner to ascertain the source of donations made to the organisation and the application of its funds, whether in New Zealand or overseas: Tax Administration Act, s 32.

The Commissioner may request that the charity provide a return of funds derived and/or received during the income year showing the source and application of those funds: Tax Administration Act, s 58. The Commissioner may advise the Minister of Finance when she believes that funds are not being applied in accordance with the charitable objects of the particular charity.

Charitable trusts have financial reporting obligations under the Charities Act 2005. See Chapter 30 – *Charitable Trusts*.

¶19-080 Residential land can be subject to a bright-line property rule

The bright-line property rule, also referred to as the bright-line test, applies to residential property that was acquired:

- on or after 27 March 2021 and sold within the 10-year bright-line period
- between 29 March 2018 and 26 March 2021 and sold within the 5-year bright-line period
- between 1 October 2015 and 28 March 2018 and sold within the 2-year bright-line period.

The 10-year bright-line test was introduced on 23 March 2021 by way of a Supplementary Order Paper that was included in the Taxation (Annual Rates for 2020–21, Feasibility Expenditure, and Remedial Matters) Act 2021 referred to above. The 10-year bright-line test, which taxes the gains from the disposal of residential property, will apply to residential properties acquired on or after 27 March 2021 and sold within 10 years of that date. See Taxation (Annual Rates for 2020-21, Feasibility Expenditure, and Remedial Matters) Bill (273–2), s CB 6A.

The changes to the bright-line test resulting from the Supplementary Order Paper are extremely far-reaching. While the bright-line property rule has limited specific application to trusts, it applies to trustee property owners in the same way as it does to any other property owners.

The rules that determine when a property is acquired and disposed of, and from which the bright-line period is taken, have not changed. However, there is a concession that applies to irrevocable agreements made by the purchaser before 23 March 2021 where the offer could not be withdrawn before 27 March 2021. In those instances, the 5-year bright-line test can still apply. See Taxation (Annual Rates for 2020–21, Feasibility Expenditure, and Remedial Matters) Bill, s CB 6A(2) and cl 5A of the Supplementary Order Paper to the Taxation (Annual Rates for 2020–21, Feasibility Expenditure, and Remedial Matters) Bill *Commentary on the proposed amendments to: extend the residential property bright-line test, and loosen the loss continuity rules* at 11.

Main home use

The main home exclusion to the bright-line test (see further below) still applies provided the home was used by the owner as the main home for the entire period it was owned. See Taxation (Annual Rates for 2020–21, Feasibility Expenditure, and Remedial Matters) Bill, s CB 6A(2).

A new change-of-use rule now applies if a property is not used as the main home (eg it is rented out) for periods greater than 12 months during the time of ownership. Where the change-of-use rule applies, the owner will have to pay tax on a proportion of the increase in value of the property during the period of ownership. The Commentary on the Supplementary Order Paper notes at 17 that:

> "any period of up to 12 months that the property is not used as the person's main home is counted as a main home period, provided the period is immediately before or after a period during which the property was used as their main home".

It will be very important to ensure good record-keeping and that evidence is retained for any agreements made that the concessionary period applies to. This means that trustees need to carefully record the use and occupation of residential trust property so that the application of the bright-line test can be properly managed.

Inland Revenue has provided the following formula to determine the profit made through the property increasing in value during the period of ownership:

- subtract the purchase price from the sale price
- subtract the cost of capital improvements the owner has made
- subtract the costs to buy and sell the property, and
- multiply the result by the proportion of time the property was not being used as the owner's main home.

See *Fact sheet – Proposed changes to the bright-line test*, Inland Revenue, March 2021.

The change-of-use rules will not apply to residential properties acquired on or after 29 March 2018 and before 27 March 2021 which are subject to the 5-year bright-line test. Where this is the case, the all-or-nothing main home exemption will apply if the property was used for most of the bright-line period as the main home.

New builds

New builds do not fall within the extended bright-line test. However, what qualifies as a new build has not yet been finalised and will be the subject of consultation. A new build is intended to include properties that are acquired within a year of receiving their code compliance certificate under the Building Act 2004. Following consultation, the Government has indicated that there will be retrospective legislation so that new builds acquired on or after 27 March 2021 will continue to be subject to a 5-year bright-line period.

Short-stay accommodation

Previously the definition of residential land applicable to the bright-line test provided an exclusion for business premises. This exclusion has now been removed to the extent that where residential property is used to provide short-stay accommodation in a dwelling that is not the owner's main home, it will be subject to the bright-line test.

Practical considerations

It is very important to retain details of any negotiations and evidence of the agreement between the parties that may have taken place before 23 March 2021 as they may indicate that the acquisition took place before 27 March 2021 and the 5-year bright-line test will apply.

Remember the importance of historical title searches in establishing when transfers took place.

Examples

Inland Revenue has provided a number of examples to show how the new bright-line rules will apply. These are not trust specific, but can have equal application to trustees:

Main home to rental property

Manaia buys a property in 2022 for $800,000. It is not a new build. The property is used as her main home until 2028 when she moves overseas and rents it out.

In 2030 she sells the property for $1.1 million. She did not make any improvements to the property.

Manaia owned the property for 8 years. Because it was not a new build the applicable bright-line period is 10 years. Because she sold it within 10 years of buying it, the bright-line test applies.

The property was Manaia's main home for the 6 years she lived in it (2022 to 2028) so she will pay tax for the remaining 2 of the 8 years she owned the property. Her additional taxable income in the year she sells the property is $75,000 – being 2/8ths of the $300,000 ($1.1 million – $800,000) profit. Manaia will need to add this to her income in her tax return and pay tax on it accordingly.

Rental property to main home

Joseph buys a new build house in 2025 for $1 million and immediately lists it for rent on a short-stay accommodation website. The property is used for short-stay accommodation until 2027 when Joseph moves in and uses it as his main home. He spends $100,000 on double glazing and a new deck.

Joseph sells it 2 years later (in 2029) for $1.2 million.

Joseph owned the property for 4 years. Because it was a new build the applicable bright-line period is 5 years. Because he sold it within 5 years of buying it, the bright-line test applies.

The property was Joseph's main home for the 2 years he lived in it (2027 to 2029) so he will pay tax for the remaining 2 of the 4 years he owned the property. His additional taxable income in the year he sells the property is $50,000 – being 2/4ths of the $100,000 ($1.2m – $1m – $100,000) profit. Joseph will need to add this to his income in his tax return, and pay tax on it accordingly.

Rental interval

Jermain buys a property in 2023 for $600,000. It is not a new build. The property is used as his main home until 2026 when he rents it out. He spent $40,000 adding a bedroom. Jermain moves back into the property in 2028, before selling it in 2031 for $800,000.

Jermain owned the property for 8 years. Because it was not a new build the applicable bright-line period is 10 years. Because he sold it within 10 years of buying it, the bright-line test applies.

Jermain used the property as his main home for the 6 years he lived in it (2023 to 2026 and 2028 to 2031), so he will pay tax for the remaining 2 of the 8 years he owned the property. His additional taxable income in the year he sells the property is $40,000 – being 2/8ths of the $160,000 ($800,000 – $600,000 – $40,000) profit. Jermain will need to add this to his income in his tax return, and pay tax on it accordingly.

Property sold within 12 months of change-of-use

Lilly acquires a property in 2022 which she uses as her main home. In 2025 she buys a new property and moves into it. It takes 9 months to sell the old property.

As Lilly was already living in her new home, there has been a change-of-use for the old property during the 9 months it took to sell – it is no longer her main home.

Because the time between the change-of-use and date the property was sold is less than 12 months, Lilly does not need to pay tax on any gain in value.

Property acquired before 27 March 2021

Junior bought a property in 2020 for $500,000, which he used as his main home for 1 year. He then rented out the property for 3 years before he sold it in 2024 for $600,000. He made no capital improvements to it.

Because Junior acquired the property before 27 March 2021 (and after 29 March 2018), the applicable bright-line period is 5 years, and the change-of-use rule does not apply. Because he sold it within 5 years of buying it, the bright-line test applies.

Junior used the property as his main home for 1 out of the 4 years he owned it. Under the bright-line test for properties acquired before 27 March 2021 this does not qualify as his main home, as it was not his main home for most of the time he owned it. Under those same bright-line rules, Junior's additional taxable income in the year he sells the property is the full $100,000 profit (the difference between the purchase and sale price: $600,000 – $500,000). Junior will need to add this to his income in his tax return, and pay tax on it accordingly.

Source: *Fact sheet – Proposed changes to the bright-line test*, Inland Revenue, March 2021.

When a property is acquired

For tax purposes, a property is generally acquired on the date a binding sale and purchase agreement is entered into (even if some standard conditions, like getting finance or a building report, still need to be met). See "questions we've been asked" QB 17/02: "Income tax – date of acquisition of land, and start date for 2-year bright-line test", which still has application (subject to a carve out that applies to the 10-year bright-line test.

The date property is acquired determines whether the bright-line period is 2, 5 or 10 years.

The date of acquisition also determines which set of rules relating to the main home exclusion and change-of-use will apply.

In most cases, the bright-line period is measured from the date of registration of the transfer and ends upon entry into a binding sale and purchase agreement to sell the property.

There is a limited carve-out for property acquired on or after 27 March 2021 if the purchase was the result of an offer the purchaser made on or before 23 March 2021 that could not be withdrawn before 27 March 2021. In this case, the 5-year bright-line test applies.

The bright-line test was first introduced to improve compliance with the current land rules around buying land with the intention of disposal. The test provides that income tax is payable on gains from the disposal of residential property acquired and disposed of within 2, 5 or 10 years (depending on the date of acquisition and whether the property is a "new build". There are exceptions to the bright-line test, the main exception relating to the sale of the main family home (see below).

For background to the bright-line test, see Inland Revenue's Special Report from Policy and Strategy *Bright-line test for residential land* (November 2015) and *Tax Information Bulletin* ¶281-115 Vol 28, No 1, February 2016.

The bright-line test applies only to "residential land", which is defined in s YA 1 as:

- land that has a dwelling on it
- land for which the owner has an arrangement to build a dwelling on it, or
- bare land that may be used for building a dwelling under the relevant operative district plan, but

does not include land that is:

- used predominantly as business premises, or
- farmland.

"Farmland" is defined in s YA 1 as land that:

- is being worked in the farming or agricultural business of the land's owner, or
- because of its area and nature is capable of being worked as a farming or agricultural business.

Exclusions from the bright-line test

There are 3 key exclusions from the bright-line test:

- the main home exemption (discussed above and below)
- transfers and disposals relating to a deceased estate (see ¶26-145)
- transfers and disposals in accordance with a relationship property agreement.

See ss CB 6A, (6) and CB 16A.

Acquisition date

The 10-year period for the bright-line test runs from the date of registration to the date of disposal (the bright-line date).

There are special rules about when the 10-year period for the bright-line test in s CB 6A starts. The start date for the bright-line test is generally not the same date as the date that land is acquired under the general rules in s CB 15B.

The start of the bright-line test period is generally as set out below:

Type of acquisition	Start of the bright-line period
Standard purchase of land	When the land transfer is registered, and you get the legal title.
Where no title registered to you before disposal	When you acquire the estate or interest in the land you are disposing of.
If you acquired the land "off the plans"	The date that you entered into the contract to acquire the land.
If you acquired land and subsequently subdivided it	Whatever the start date would have been for the original undivided piece of land.
Lease with perpetual right of renewal converted into freehold title	The date you were first granted the leasehold estate.

Based on the table from PUB00220 "Income tax – date of acquisition of land" at [8].

It is important for trustees to appreciate that the acquisition date of land varies depending on which land taxing provision is being applied. This means that trustees must retain all the relevant documents that relate to the purchase of land, including the agreement for sale and purchase and any deeds of nomination as the bright-line test is not the only taxing provision that can apply to the sale of land by trustees.

Bright-line date or date of disposal

The date for the disposal of the property for the purposes of the bright-line test is the earlier of:

- the date of entry into an agreement for sale and purchase
- the date of a gift of the residential land

- the date on which residential land is compulsorily acquired under any Act by the Crown, a local authority, or a public authority
- the date of a mortgagee sale.

If none of the above applies, the date on which the estate or interest in the residential land is disposed of. See s CB 6A(7).

The following table from *Tax Information Bulletin* ¶281-115 Vol 28, No 1, February 2016 summarises the date of disposal for different types of property transactions as follows:

Type of disposal	End date of bright-line period
Standard purchase of land	Date of entry into agreement for sale
Gift	Date of gift (generally registration of title)
Compulsory acquisition	Date of compulsory acquisition
Mortgagee sale	Date land disposed of by mortgagee
Other disposals where no contract to sell	Date of disposal according to ordinary rules

There is no specific provision for distributions from inter vivos trusts. Accordingly, trustees will need to take special care where distributions of residential property are made to beneficiaries to ensure that the trustees recognise what the date of disposal will be for the purposes of the bright-line test.

Although a distribution to a beneficiary is not a gift, if residential property is transferred to a beneficiary (otherwise than under an agreement for sale and property), the end date for the bright-line period will likely be determined in the same way as for a gift, that is, the date the trustees transfer the residential land, rather than, say, the date of a trustees' resolution to make a distribution of the residential property.

See the following example from *Tax Information Bulletin* ¶281-115 Vol 28, No 1, February 2016:

Example: Gift

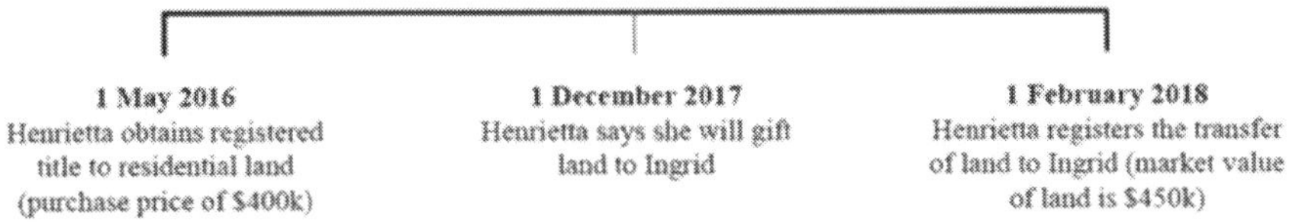

The start date for the bright-line period is 1 May 2016 (the date Henrietta acquired registered title) and the end date is 1 February 2018 (the date Ingrid acquired registered title). Henrietta will be subject to the bright-line test for her gift of land.

Under ordinary tax rules, gifts of land are treated as if they are transferred at market value.

As a result, Henrietta will be deemed to have transferred the land to Ingrid at market value and the $50k gain will be taxable.

It is important that each transfer of residential property is assessed on its own facts and trustees would be prudent to seek advice before making distributions of property to which the bright-line property rule might have application.

Deductions and losses

Deductions can be claimed for property subject to the bright-line test according to ordinary tax rules. However, losses from deductions that are claimable solely against bright-line income (bright-line deductions) are ring-fenced so that they may only be used to offset taxable gains arising under the land sale rules.

The amount of bright-line deductions allowed in any income year is limited to the amount of bright-line income and net land income for that year. Net land income is the amount of net income for the year as if the person's only income they derived was from the disposal of land under ss CB 6 to CB 14.

Any excess deductions not allocated to the income year will be treated as the cost of revenue account property and carried forward to the next income year (subject to the usual restrictions around continuity of losses).

There is also an anti-avoidance provision to the bright-line test in s GB 53. See ¶22-040.

Main home exemption

As noted above, there are exemptions from the bright-line test. The main home exemption will have relevance for many dispositions of residential land owned by trustees where the family home is owned by a trust. The main home exemption is in s CB 16A, which provides that:

> "*Main home exclusion*
>
> (1) Section CB 6A does not apply to a person (person A) who disposes of residential land if, for all of the days in the bright-line period, the land meets the criteria in subsection (2).
>
> *Criteria*
>
> (2) For the purposes of subsection (1) and subsection (6), the criteria are that the land has been used for the relevant period predominantly for a dwelling that was the main home for 1 or more of the following people:
>
> (a) person A:
>
> (b) a beneficiary of a trust, if person A is a trustee of the trust and–
>
> (i) a principal settlor of the trust does not have a main home; or
>
> (ii) if a principal settlor of the trust does have a main home, it is that main home which person A is disposing of.
>
> *When this section does not apply*
>
> (3) The exclusion in subsection (1) does not apply to person A if–
>
> (a) the exclusion has been used by person A 2 or more times within the 2 years immediately preceding the bright-line date for the residential land:

(b) person A has engaged in a regular pattern of acquiring and disposing of residential land described in subsection (2).

[...]

Special rule: counted days

(6) For the purposes of subsection (1) and the definition of **excluded day** in section CB 6A(14)(b), a day that is in the bright-line period is treated as meeting the criteria under subsection (2) (the **criteria**) if–

(a) the residential land meets the criteria at some time in the bright-line period; and

(b) there is a continuous period within the bright-line period for which the criteria are not otherwise met (a **continuous period**); and

(c) the beginning or the end of the continuous period adjoins a period within the bright-line period that meets the criteria; and

(d) the whole of the continuous period is 365 days or less; and

(e) the day is in that continuous period, within the bright-line period.

A definition

(7) In this section, and in sections CZ 40 and EL 9 (which relate to the main home exclusion), **principal settlor** means, for a trust, a settlor whose settlements for the trust are the greatest or greatest equal, by market value."

Note that the main home exemption will not apply if the exemption has been used 2 or more times within the "2 years immediately preceding the bright-line date for the residential land", or the vendor has "engaged in a regular pattern of acquiring and disposing of residential land". See s CB 16A(3).

To be the main home, the dwelling must be the one dwelling (as defined in s YA 1) that:

- is mainly used as a residence by the person, and
- the person has the greatest connection with.

A main home means then, the one dwelling that is mainly used as a residence and with which the person has the greatest connection, if the person has more than one home. Factors to determine the greatest connection include:

- where the person's immediate family live
- whether the person's personal property is in the dwelling
- the time the person occupies the dwelling
- where the person's social ties are strongest, and
- whether the person has employment, business interests and economic ties to the area where the dwelling is located.

Where the main home is owned by trustees, the main home must have been the main home of a beneficiary of the trust and the principal settlor of the trust must not have a main home; or if the principal settlor has a main home, it must be the house being sold. A trust cannot use the main home exclusion when a principal settlor of the trust has another main home. This rule is to ensure that people cannot get the main home exclusion multiple times through the use of a trust.

Example: Trusts – student flat

Dave has two properties, a family home which he lives in, and a student flat which his son lives in while studying. Dave settles the student flat on a trust and makes his son a discretionary beneficiary of the trust.

The trust cannot use the main home exclusion because the principal settlor of the trust (Dave) has another main home.

Example from *Tax Information Bulletin* ¶281-115 Vol 28, No 1, February 2016.

"Principal settlor" is a defined term introduced in 2015 for the purposes of the bright-line test and means the settlor whose settlements for the trust are the greatest or greatest equal, by market value. See ¶5-050. If there are multiple settlors who have provided the greatest equal value to the trust, each of these settlors are "principal settlors" for the purpose of the bright-line test. A person's settlements do not include the provision of services at below market value, or any transfer at value unless the transferor is:

- a beneficiary
- a trustee
- a person with the power of appointment or removal of trustees
- a person with a contingent interest in the trust property, in the case that the trust fails, or
- a decision-maker under the trust.

See definition of "settlement" in s YA 1.

There is no guidance as to who "a decision-maker under the trust" might be. However, it should be presumed that this will include protectors, advisory trustees and any other person in a role that gives the person any power over the trustees or the ability to exercise what would otherwise be trustee powers. A person with the ability to determine a trustee dispute or disagreement might also be a decision-maker under a trust. Accordingly, care should be taking when drafting deeds of trust to avoid inadvertently providing that a person is or could be a principal settlor of a trust.

A person is not a principal settlor if they have provided a "no-strings attached" gift to the trust – see *Tax Information Bulletin* ¶281-115 Vol 28, No 1, February 2016.

To be able to determine who the principal settlor is, the trustees will need to ensure adequate records of gifting and settlements onto the trust by all settlors (as defined for tax purposes), not just the settlors named in the deed of trust. The definition of "settlement" is modified for the purposes of s CB 16A(3) by the definition of "settlement" in s YA 1.

Example

Freda and Brenda settle a trust that owns their family home. The trustees are Freda, Brenda and a corporate trustee of which their solicitor is the director. Brenda's mother, Sandra (who is not a beneficiary, final beneficiary, contingent final beneficiary, appointor or otherwise a decision maker of the trust), has provided an interest-free loan to the trustees to assist with the purchase of the family home. The loan is repayable on demand.

The family home, which is unsuitable for Freda and Brenda, is sold 18 months later. Can the trustees claim the main family home exemption?

The family home has been the main home for Freda and Brenda who are the principal settlors having settled equal amounts on the trust. Sandra is not a principal settlor. Her loan to the trust is not a settlement because the exception to the definition of settlement in s YA 1 applies.

¶19-090 Land Transfer Tax Statements

All land sales require the registered proprietor (transferor) and purchaser (transferee) to each complete a Land Transfer Tax Statement. This requirement was introduced by the Land Transfer Amendment Act 2015 and is part of the package of reforms to ensure the implementation of the bright-line test.

This means that all land-owning trusts (including non-active trusts) must have an IRD number. Note that where the transferor or transferee is acting as an executor or administrator of an estate, there is no requirement to provide an IRD number for the Land Transfer Tax Statement.

The transferor and transferee must each complete a Land Transfer Tax Statement and certify that each answer is true (see www.linz.govt.nz/).

Where the transferor or transferee are trustees, the IRD number used is that of the trust, not the IRD number of the individual trustees. Each trustee must complete a Land Transfer Tax Statement.

The Land Transfer Tax Statement (once completed by the transferor or transferee) is provided to the lawyer or conveyancer who is acting on the transaction.

Non-residents must have a New Zealand bank account before they can get a New Zealand IRD number. Non-resident buyers and sellers must also provide their tax identification number from the country or jurisdiction that they are tax resident in.

¶19-100 Residential land withholding tax

The residential land withholding tax (RLWT) regime is designed to ensure that tax payable on account of the bright-line test (see ¶19-080) is paid by providing a collection mechanism where the seller is offshore. From 1 July 2016, RLWT applied when an "offshore RLWT person" disposes of residential land subject to the bright-line property rules.

The RLWT rules are set out in Subpart RL of the Income Tax Act. Under s RL 1, for RLWT to apply to a particular disposal, there must be:

- a disposal of residential land located in New Zealand, and
- the relevant residential land purchase amount would be income of the vendor under s CB 6A or CZ 39 (which relate to the bright-line test for residential land) ignoring ss CB 6A(13), CB 16A, CZ 39(8) and CZ 40 (which relate to the bright-line test), and
- the vendor must be an offshore RLWT person.

Note that vendors who are co-owners will be treated as disposing of separate residential land on the basis of an appropriate split of the underlying residential land and the consideration for its disposal.

RLWT will not apply when the vendor holds an RLWT certificate of exemption that applies for the disposal of the relevant residential land.

RWLT is calculated by reference to the "residential land purchase amount", which excludes deposits and part-payments (as long as all deposits and part-payments, in total, are less than 50% of the purchase price for the land). This rolling aggregate is to ensure that part-payments are not used to circumvent the application of the RLWT.

Example

Elizabeth agrees to sell her house to Rebecca for $500,000. The contract requires Rebecca to pay a 10% deposit of $50,000, with the remaining $450,000 to be paid upon settlement. The $50,000 deposit is not a residential land purchase amount, but the $450,000 paid upon settlement is a residential land purchase amount.

Example from "Taxation (Residential Land Withholding Tax, GST on Online Services, and Student Loans) Bill: Commentary on the Bill", Policy and Strategy, Inland Revenue, November 2015.

Offshore RLWT persons

Significantly, the vendor must be an "offshore RLWT person" for RLWT to apply. "Offshore RLWT person" is defined in s YA 1 and covers both individuals and non-individuals, such as companies or trusts.

An individual is an "offshore RLWT person" if they are:

- a New Zealand citizen who is outside New Zealand and has not been in New Zealand within the last 3 years
- the holder of a New Zealand residence class visa granted under the Immigration Act 2009 and is outside New Zealand and has not been in New Zealand within the last 12 months, or
- not a New Zealand citizen and does not hold a New Zealand residence class visa granted under the Immigration Act.

A non-natural person is considered to be an "offshore RLWT person" if any of the following conditions are met:

- the person is incorporated outside New Zealand
- the person is not a natural person and is registered outside New Zealand

- the person is constituted under foreign law
- the person is a company or a partner in a limited partnership and more than 25% of the company's directors or of the limited partnership's general partners are offshore RLWT persons
- the person is a company and more than 25% of the company's shareholder decision-making rights are held directly or indirectly by offshore RLWT persons, or
- the person is a partner in a limited partnership or an owner of an effective look-through interest in a look-through company (LTC), and more than 25% of the partnership's partnership shares or of the LTC's effective look-through interests are held directly or indirectly by offshore RLWT persons.

A trust is considered an "offshore RLWT person" if any of the following are met:

- more than 25% of the trustees of the trust are offshore RLWT persons
- more than 25% of the people that have the power to appoint or remove a trustee of the trust, or to amend the trust deed, are offshore RLWT persons
- all natural person beneficiaries and all natural person discretionary beneficiaries of the trust are offshore RLWT persons
- all beneficiaries and all discretionary beneficiaries of the trust are offshore RLWT persons
- a beneficiary, including a discretionary beneficiary, that is an offshore RLWT person has received a distribution from the trust in one of the last 4 years before the relevant disposal of residential land and, if the beneficiary is a natural person, the total distributions to the beneficiary for the relevant year are more than $5,000, or
- the trust has disposed of residential land within 4 years before the relevant disposal of residential land and the trust has a beneficiary, including a discretionary beneficiary, that is an offshore RLWT person.

Example

Debbie and Greg are the settlors and trustees of a family trust. They are both New Zealand citizens and live in New Zealand. Dan and Natalie are discretionary beneficiaries of the trust and are also New Zealand citizens. Dan lives in New Zealand, but Natalie has lived in Australia for the past five years and has not been back to New Zealand.

The trust property consists of the family home in New Zealand as well as some shares and money held in a savings account. Each year, Dan and Natalie receive around $1,000 each in distributions from the trust.

Debbie and Greg as trustees of the trust are not offshore RLWT persons, because they themselves are not offshore RLWT persons and, of the two beneficiaries, only Natalie is an offshore RLWT person, but she has not received more than $5,000 in distributions from the trust in any of the previous four years.

Example from *Tax Information Bulletin* ¶286-104 Vol 28, No 6, July 2016.

The broad definition of "offshore RLWT person" for a trust is intended to ensure that gains do not escape tax through manipulation of the trust. Given the wide-ranging scope of the definition, trustees will need to take care to ensure that the trustees are aware of where beneficiaries are resident at all times and to monitor distributions to non-resident beneficiaries.

Example

Matilda and Madeline are natural persons who are also offshore RLWT persons. They are the only natural person beneficiaries of a trust. A New Zealand charity is appointed as a discretionary beneficiary of the trust. The settlor and trustees of the trust are not offshore RLWT persons. The trustees are treated as offshore RLWT persons for the purposes of the RLWT rules, because all natural person [individual] beneficiaries of the trust (Matilda and Madeline) are offshore RLWT persons.

Example from *Tax Information Bulletin* ¶286-104 Vol 28, No 6, July 2016.

A corporate trustee will be able to qualify for the non-offshore exemption if it meets both the company and trust criteria above.

The vendor's solicitor or conveyancer is required to pay RLWT

The vendor is liable to pay an amount of RLWT, but the vendor's conveyancer is treated as the vendor's agent in relation to the RLWT and must provide returns and satisfy the vendor's liability (s RL 2). That is, the vendor's conveyancer is the "paying agent" in relation to RLWT. If the vendor does not have a conveyancer, the purchaser's conveyancer will be the paying agent. If neither the vendor nor purchaser has a conveyancer, the purchaser will be the paying agent.

If the vendor and purchaser are associated persons, the vendor is not liable to pay RLWT and instead the purchaser (as the withholding agent) will have the withholding tax obligation. The date the associated persons test is applied is the date on which a residential land purchase amount is paid, and test of association is that determined under the general association rules (see Chapter 18 – Associated Persons) rather than the narrow version that is applied for land disposals.

Amount of RLWT

There are 3 calculation methods for RLWT, with the amount of RLWT payable being the lesser of the amounts calculated under these methods.

In most cases, the RLWT payable will be the lesser of the amounts calculated under the first 2 methods. The third method is not available where the paying agent is the purchaser's conveyancer or the purchaser themselves.

First method — s RL 4(2)

The first of the three calculation methods is as follows:

RLWT rate × (current purchase price – vendor's acquisition cost) where:

- **RLWT rate** is the top individual marginal tax rate (39%) or, if the vendor is a company that is not acting as a trustee, the company tax rate (28%)
- **current purchase price** is the purchase price agreed by the vendor and purchaser
- **vendor's acquisition cost** is the purchase price paid by the vendor on acquisition.

It is expected that the vendor's acquisition cost will generally be available from Quotable Value.

Second method — s RL 4(4)

The second calculation method is as follows:

$$0.10 \times \text{current purchase price}$$

Example

Virginia is an offshore RLWT person who agrees to sell her residential property in Tauranga to Thomas. Thomas pays a $100,000 deposit and another $400,000 upon settlement. In determining Virginia's RLWT liability, the "current purchase price" is $500,000. Virginia originally acquired the residential property for $350,000. The "vendor's acquisition cost" for the purposes of determining Virginia's RLWT liability is $350,000.

Virginia does not have a mortgage on the property and she has no outstanding rates.

RLWT calculated using the formula in section RL 4(2) is 33% × ($500,000 – $350,000), or $49,500. RLWT calculated using the formula in section RL 4(4) is 10% × $500,000, or $50,000. Therefore the amount of RLWT payable is $49,500.

Example from *Tax Information Bulletin* ¶286-104 Vol 28, No 6, July 2016.

Third method — s RL 4(6)

RLWT will generally be paid before other disbursements. However, a vendor may have a mortgage secured over the residential land being disposed of and the mortgagee may require the vendor's mortgage obligation to be discharged before the title to the residential land can be released. In most cases, this should not be a problem, but, in some situations, the amount of RLWT payable calculated using the 2 methods outlined above may result in insufficient funds to discharge the vendor's mortgage.

The third calculation method under s RL 4(6) is only available when the vendor or vendor's conveyancer is the person who must pay the RLWT. The amount is the greater of zero and the amount calculated as follows:

$$\text{current purchase price} - \text{security discharge amount} - \text{outstanding rates}$$

where:

- **current purchase price** (which has the same meaning as above)
- **security discharge amount** is the total of the amounts required by licensed security holders to discharge their mortgages or other securities over the residential land, or zero
- **outstanding rates** is the amount of local authority rates outstanding.

For these purposes:

- **licensed security holder** means a New Zealand registered bank or a licensed non-bank deposit taker (as defined in s 4 of the Non-bank Deposit Takers Act 2013) holding a mortgage or other security over the residential land.

The obligation to retain/withhold and pay RLWT is intended to arise upon settlement when, in most cases, the bulk of the purchase price will be paid by the purchaser to the vendor via a conveyancer. At this point, the RLWT paying or withholding agent should retain or withhold RLWT from the funds being paid.

¶19-110 Legislation

Income Tax Act 2007

CB 6A DISPOSAL WITHIN 10 YEARS: BRIGHT-LINE TEST FOR RESIDENTIAL LAND

CB 6A(1) DISPOSAL WITHIN 10 YEARS

Subject to subsection (6), an amount that a person derives from disposing of residential land is income of the person if the bright-line date for the residential land is within 10 years of–

(a) the date on which the instrument to transfer the land to the person was registered–

  (i) under the Land Transfer Act 2017; or

  (ii) under foreign laws of a similar nature to the Land Transfer Act 2017, if the land is outside New Zealand; or

(b) their date of acquisition of the land, if an instrument to transfer the land to the person is not registered on or before the bright-line date.

CB 6A(2) SUBDIVISION

Subject to subsection (6), and despite subsection (1), an amount that a person derives from disposing of residential land that results from the person subdividing other land (the **undivided land**) is income of the person if the bright-line date for the residential land is within 10 years of–

(a) the date on which the instrument to transfer the undivided land to the person was registered–

  (i) under the Land Transfer Act 2017; or

  (ii) under foreign laws of a similar nature to the Land Transfer Act 2017, if the land is outside New Zealand; or

(b) their date of acquisition of the undivided land, if the land is not registered as described in paragraph (a) at the bright-line date.

CB 6A(3) LEASES WITH PERPETUAL RIGHT OF RENEWAL

Subject to subsection (6), and despite subsection (1), an amount that a person derives from disposing of a freehold estate in residential land, acquired as the owner of a leasehold estate with a perpetual right of renewal, is income if the bright-line date for the freehold estate is within 10 years of the grant of the leasehold estate.

CB 6A(4) ESTATE OR INTEREST ACQUIRED UPON COMPLETION OF LAND DEVELOPMENT OR SUBDIVISION

Subject to subsection (6), and despite subsection (1), an amount that a person derives from disposing of an estate or interest in residential land, acquired as the result of the completion of a land development or subdivision, is income if the bright-line date for the estate or interest is within 10 years of the person entering into the agreement under which they acquired the estate or interest upon the completion of the land development or subdivision.

CB 6A(5) BEGINNING OF 10-YEAR PERIOD FOR TRANSFERS BY REGISTRATION IF TRUSTEES CHANGE

If the person referred to in subsection (1)(a) or (2)(a) is a trustee of a trust who has been transferred the land or undivided land from a trustee of the trust, the date on which the instrument was registered is treated as occurring on,–

(a) for subsection (1)(a),–

- (i) the earliest date (the **first date**) on which an instrument to transfer the land to a trustee of the trust was registered under the relevant law referred to in the subsection, if there has been no intervening transfer to a person who is not a trustee; or
- (ii) the first date following the intervening transfer, if there has been an intervening transfer to a person who is not a trustee:

(b) for subsection (2)(a),–

- (i) the earliest date (the **undivided date**) on which an instrument to transfer the undivided land to a trustee of the trust was registered under the relevant law referred to in the subsection, if there has been no intervening transfer to a person who is not a trustee; or
- (ii) the undivided date following the intervening transfer, if there has been an intervening transfer to a person who is not a trustee.

[...]

CB 6A(12) EXCEPTION: DISPOSAL OF LAND BY EXECUTOR, ADMINISTRATOR, OR BENEFICIARY

This section does not apply to an amount that an executor or administrator described in section FC 1(1)(a) (Disposals to which this subpart applies), or a beneficiary described in section FC 1(1)(b), derives from disposing of residential land that was transferred to them on the death of a person.

CB 6A(13) RELATIONSHIP WITH SUBJECT MATTER

This section applies if none of sections CB 6 to CB 12 apply.

[...]

CB 15B WHEN LAND ACQUIRED

CB 15B(1) GENERAL RULE

For the purposes of this subpart except sections CB 6A and CZ 39 (Disposal within 5 years: bright-line test for residential land: acquisition on or after 29 March 2018), a person acquires an estate, interest, or option that is land (the **land**) on the date that begins a period in which the person has an estate or interest in, or an option to acquire, the land, alone or jointly or in common with another person.

CB 15B(2) FIRST EXCEPTION: ACQUISITION OF LAND BY COMPANY TO BE FORMED

If a person, on behalf of a company to be formed, enters an agreement under which the company will have land, the company is treated, for the purposes of this subpart in relation to the land, as existing from when the person enters the agreement.

CB 15B(3) SECOND EXCEPTION: LAND FROM EXERCISE OF OPTION

A person that exercises an option to acquire land and acquires the land, is treated as acquiring the land at the time when they exercise the option.

CB 15B(4) RELATIONSHIP WITH SUBPARTS FB AND FC

Subsections (1) to (3) are overridden, for a transaction, by a provision in subpart FB or FC (which relate to transfers of property) providing for the timing of the transaction.

CB 16A MAIN HOME EXCLUSION FOR DISPOSAL WITHIN 10 YEARS

CB 16A(1) MAIN HOME EXCLUSION

Section CB 6A does not apply to a person (**person** A) who disposes of residential land if, for all of the days in the bright-line period, the land meets the criteria in subsection (2).

CB 16A(2) CRITERIA

For the purposes of subsection (1) and subsection (6), the criteria are that the land has been used for the relevant period predominantly for a dwelling that was the main home for 1 or more of the following people:

(a) person A:

(b) a beneficiary of a trust, if person A is a trustee of the trust and–

  (i) a principal settlor of the trust does not have a main home; or

  (ii) if a principal settlor of the trust does have a main home, it is that main home which person A is disposing of.

CB 16A(3) WHEN THIS SECTION DOES NOT APPLY

The exclusion in subsection (1) does not apply to person A if–

(a) the exclusion has been used by person A 2 or more times within the 2 years immediately preceding the bright-line date for the residential land:

(b) person A has engaged in a regular pattern of acquiring and disposing of residential land described in subsection (2).

CB 16A(4) REGULAR PATTERNS UNDERTAKEN BY GROUPS OF PERSONS

For the purposes of subsection (3)(b), in relation to residential land described in subsection (2), person A includes a group of persons if the requirements of subsection (5) are met.

CB 16A(5) MEANING OF GROUP OF PERSONS

For the purposes of subsection (4), a **group of persons**–

(a) means 2 or more persons when together all of the persons occupy, or have occupied, residential land described in subsection (2); and

(b) includes a person other than a natural person (the **non-natural person**), if another person referred to in paragraph (a) has significant involvement in, or control of, the activities of the non-natural person. For the avoidance of doubt, if the other person is able to direct, alone or as part of a group, the activities of the non-natural person, they have significant involvement in, or control of, the activities of the non-natural person.

CB 16A(6) SPECIAL RULE: COUNTED DAYS

For the purposes of subsection (1) and the definition of **excluded day** in section CB 6A(14)(b), a day that is in the bright-line period is treated as meeting the criteria under subsection (2) (the **criteria**) if–

(a) the residential land meets the criteria at some time in the bright-line period; and

(b) there is a continuous period within the bright-line period for which the criteria are not otherwise met (a **continuous period**); and

(c) the beginning or the end of the continuous period adjoins a period within the bright-line period that meets the criteria; and

(d) the whole of the continuous period is 365 days or less; and

(e) the day is in that continuous period, within the bright-line period.

CB 16A(7) A DEFINITION

In this section, and in sections CZ 40 and EL 9 (which relate to the main home exclusion), **principal settlor** means, for a trust, a settlor whose settlements for the trust are the greatest or greatest equal, by market value.

CB 16 RESIDENTIAL EXCLUSION FROM SECTIONS CB 6 TO CB 11

CB 16(1) EXCLUSION

Sections CB 6 to CB 11 do not apply if–

(a) the person (**person** A)–

  (i) acquired the land with a dwellinghouse on it; or

  (ii) acquired the land and erected a dwellinghouse on it; and

(b) the dwellinghouse was occupied mainly as a residence by,–

  (i) person A;

  (ii) if members of person A's family live with them, person A and members of person A's family living with them:

  (iii) if person A is a trustee, 1 or more beneficiaries of the trust.

CB 16(2) WHAT EXCLUSION APPLIES TO

The exclusion applies to the land that has the dwellinghouse on it. It also applies to land related to the land that has the dwellinghouse on it if the total area of the related land is–

(a) 4,500 square metres or less; or

(b) more than 4,500 square metres, if the larger area is required for the reasonable occupation and enjoyment of the dwellinghouse.

CB 16(3) EXCEPTION

The exclusion does not apply when–

(a) section CB 6(1) applies to the disposal; and

(b) person A has engaged in a regular pattern of acquiring and disposing of land described in subsection (1).

CB 16(4) REGULAR PATTERNS UNDERTAKEN BY GROUPS OF PERSONS

For the purposes of subsection (3), in relation to land described in subsection (1), person A includes a group of persons if the requirements of subsection (5) are met.

[...]

EW 44 CONSIDERATION WHEN DEBT FORGIVEN FOR NATURAL LOVE AND AFFECTION

EW 44(1) WHEN THIS SECTION APPLIES: FIRST CASE

This section applies when–

(a) a person is a debtor; and

(b) the creditor is a natural person; and

(c) the creditor forgives the debtor's debt because of the natural love and affection the creditor has for the debtor.

EW 44(2) WHEN THIS SECTION APPLIES: SECOND CASE

This section also applies when–

(a) a trust is a debtor; and

(b) the trust was established mainly to benefit 1 or both of the following:

  (i) a natural person for whom the creditor has natural love and affection:

  (ii) an organisation or a trust whose income is exempt under section CW 41 (Charities: non-business income) or CW 42 (Charities: business income); and

(c) the creditor is a natural person; and

(d) the creditor forgives the debtor's debt.

EW 44(3) TWO POINTS ABOUT SUBSECTIONS (1) AND (2)

For the purposes of subsections (1) and (2),–

(a) the debtor's debt includes an amount accrued and unpaid at the time of the forgiveness; and

(b) the means by which the debt is forgiven, whether in a will or otherwise, is immaterial.

EW 44(4) CONSIDERATION

The debtor is treated as having paid the debt on the date on which the creditor forgives it.

EZ 39 FORGIVENESS OF DEBT

EZ 39(1) [When a debt is treated as forgiven]

In determining the income or expenditure under the base price adjustment in section EZ 38, an amount owing under a debt, including an amount accrued and unpaid at the time of the forgiveness, is treated as paid when forgiven under the old financial arrangements rules if–

(a) the creditor is a natural person who forgives the debt, whether in a will or otherwise, because of the natural love and affection the creditor has for the debtor; or

(b) the creditor is a natural person who forgives the debt owing by a trust, whether in a will or otherwise, and the trust was established primarily to benefit–

  (i) a natural person for whom the creditor has natural love and affection; or

  (ii) an organisation or a trust whose income is exempt under section CW 41 or CW 42; or

  (iii) a natural person that meets paragraph (b)(i) and an organisation or a trust that meets paragraph (b)(ii).

EZ 39(2) [Distributions to non natural persons]

Subsection (3) applies when a trustee makes a distribution, including a distribution of beneficiary income, to a beneficiary that is neither–

(a) a natural person for whom the creditor has natural love and affection; nor

(b) an organisation or a trust whose income is exempt under section CW 41 or CW 42.

EZ 39(3) [Distributions to other trusts]

Subsection (4) does not apply when a trustee of a trust (**trust A**) to which subsection (1)(b) applies makes a distribution to another trust (**trust B**) if–

(a) trust B is a trust described in subparagraph (i), (ii), or (iii) of subsection (1)(b); and

(b) subsection (1)(b) would apply to trust B if, at the time the distribution is made, the creditor of trust A were a creditor of trust B, and the creditor had forgiven a debt owing by trust B.

EZ 39(4) [Treatment of distributions]

A distribution to the beneficiary is income derived by the trustee–

(a) in the income year in which the distribution is made; and

(b) to the extent that the distribution is less than or equal to the total amount of debts forgiven by the creditor.

EZ 39(5) [Income deemed not to be beneficiary income]

If subsection (4) applies, the income derived by the trustee is not income for the purposes of the **beneficiary income** definition.

EZ 39(6) [Value of debts forgiven is reduced by the amount taxable distributions]

For the purposes of subsection (4), the total amount of debts forgiven by the creditor is reduced by the amount of each distribution that is income derived by the trustee.

EZ 39(7) [Rule applies to distributions made after 20 May 1999]

Subsection (4) applies to a distribution made on or after 20 May 1999.

RE 2 RESIDENT PASSIVE INCOME

RE 2(1) INTEREST, DIVIDENDS, AND CERTAIN DISTRIBUTIONS

Resident passive income means an amount paid to a person to the extent to which it consists of–

(a) interest:

(b) a dividend:

(c) a taxable Maori authority distribution other than a retirement scheme contribution:

(d) a replacement payment paid to a person under a share-lending arrangement.

RE 2(2) EXCLUSIONS AND INCLUSIONS

Subsections (3) to (5) override subsection (1).

RE 2(3) EXCLUSIONS FROM INTEREST

The following amounts are excluded from interest under this section:

(a) exempt interest:

(b) interest derived by a person who has RWT-exempt status under section RE 27:

(c) interest that is non-resident passive income:

(d) interest derived from outside New Zealand by a non-resident:

(e) interest that is exempt income under section CW 27 (Certain income derived by transitional resident):

(f) interest paid by a company and derived by another company when both companies are part of the same group of companies at the time of the payment:

(g) interest paid to an intermediary–

    (i) by a client in relation to the operation of a tax pooling account; or

    (ii) by the Commissioner under section RP 18 (Deposits in tax pooling accounts):

(h) interest payable under section 120D or Part 7 of the Tax Administration Act 1994:

(i) interest arising because section EI 2 (Interest from inflation-indexed instruments) applies to an inflation-indexed instrument.

RE 2(4) INCLUSIONS IN INTEREST

For the purposes of this section, the following amounts are treated as interest and not as a dividend:

(a) a dividend that a building society pays to a member in relation to a withdrawable share in the society:

(b) a dividend that a friendly society pays to its member in relation to a share in the society.

RE 2(5) EXCLUSIONS FROM DIVIDENDS

The following amounts are excluded from a dividend under this section:

(a) a dividend that is exempt income–

    (i) through the application of either of sections CW 9 and CW 10 (which relate to income from equity); or

(ii) under section CW 27 (Certain income derived by transitional resident):

(iii) *(repealed)*

(b) an amount–

(i) of an association rebate that is excluded from being a dividend by section CB 34(5)(a) (Amounts derived by members from mutual associations); or

(ii) that is payable to a person by a company and is treated as being a dividend by sections GB 23 to GB 25 (which relate to excessive remuneration):

(bb) a dividend from a portfolio investment entity:

[...]

(d) a dividend derived by a person who has RWT-exempt status under section RE 27:

(e) a dividend that is non-resident passive income:

(f) a dividend derived by a non-resident other than a dividend that has a source in New Zealand:

(fb) a dividend paid by a company and derived by another company, if the dividend is fully imputed and the paying company chooses to exclude the dividend from being resident passive income:

(g) a dividend paid by a company and derived by another company when both are part of the same group of companies at the time of the payment, other than a dividend referred to in section CW 10(3):

(gb) an amount treated as a dividend under section CB 32C (Dividend income for first year of look-through company):

(h) a dividend that is excluded income under section CX 50B (Contributions to retirement savings schemes) or would be excluded income under that section in the absence of subsection (2)(a) and (b):

(i) a dividend other than a non-cash dividend that–

(i) has an imputation ratio of 30/70 or more; and

(ii) is paid by a unit trust or group investment fund (or RWT proxy on their behalf) that has not withheld RWT from any earlier dividend:

(j) a dividend treated as derived by a person under section GB 1(3) (Arrangements involving dividend stripping).

RE 2(6) BENEFICIARY INCOME

If a person derives an amount described in this section in their capacity as trustee and the amount is beneficiary income, the amount is treated as not derived by the trustee.

RE 2(7) TRUSTEES' RWT SUBSTITUTION PAYMENT

A trustee may pay an amount of money (the **RWT substitution payment**) to the relevant beneficiary that is equal to or less than the amount of RWT withheld for an amount to which subsection (6) applies (the **RPI beneficiary income**).

RE 2(8) EFFECT OF RWT SUBSTITUTION PAYMENT

The RWT substitution payment is treated as an amount of resident passive income that is beneficiary income, with the same nature as the RPI beneficiary income. There is no liability or obligation to withhold RWT in relation to the RWT substitution payment.

RE 30 WHEN UNINCORPORATED BODIES HAVE RWT-EXEMPT STATUS

RE 30(1) WHEN THIS SECTION APPLIES

This section applies when–

(a) an unincorporated body that is carrying on a taxable activity has RWT-exempt status; and

(b) the exemption relates to the carrying on of the taxable activity.

RE 30(2) TREATMENT OF PAYMENTS MADE BY UNINCORPORATED BODIES

For the purposes of the RWT rules, a payment that the body makes in the course of carrying on the taxable activity is treated as a payment made by the body and not by a member of the body. This subsection overrides subsection (7).

RE 30(3) TREATMENT OF PAYMENTS TO MEMBERS OF UNINCORPORATED BODIES

For the purposes of the RWT rules, a payment made to a member of the body in their capacity as a member and in the course of carrying on the taxable activity of the body is treated as a payment made to the body and not to the member.

RE 30(4) JOINT AND SEVERAL LIABILITY FOR AMOUNTS OF TAX

Each member of the body is jointly and severally liable for the RWT that the body is required to pay for as long as the member remains part of the body.

RE 30(5) NATURAL PERSONS, PARTNERSHIPS, JOINT VENTURES, TRUSTEES

For the purposes of subsection (4),–

(a) if the member is a natural person, their estate is liable after their death for an amount payable that remains unpaid:

(b) if the body is a partnership, joint venture, or the trustees of a trust, a member continues as a member until the date the Commissioner is notified of a change of membership.

RE 30(6) MEMBERS AND COMMITTEES

Subsection (7) applies to an unincorporated body other than a partnership, joint venture, or the trustees of a trust, when the business of the body is managed by the members or a committee of its members.

RE 30(7) RESPONSIBILITY OF COMMITTEE OFFICERS AND MEMBERS

If something is required to be done under the RWT rules by or on behalf of the body, each member holding office as president, chair, treasurer, secretary, or a similar office is jointly and severally responsible. In default, each member holding office bears the responsibility. Action taken by 1 officer or committee member is sufficient.

RE 30(8) JOINT AND SEVERAL LIABILITY FOR ACTIONS REQUIRED

If something is required to be done under the RWT rules by or on behalf of the body, each member is jointly and severally liable to do it. However, action taken by 1 member is sufficient. Subsection (7) overrides this subsection.

RE 30(9) CHANGES IN MEMBERSHIP

A change in membership of the unincorporated body has no effect for the purposes of the RWT rules. Subsection (5)(b) overrides this subsection.

RE 30(10) SOME DEFINITIONS

In this section,–

member means a partner, joint venturer, a trustee, or a member of a body.

YA 1 DEFINITIONS

[...]

settlement–

(a) means–

[...]

(c) in the definition of **principal settlor** in section CB 16A[(7)] (Main home exclusion for disposal within [10] years), does not include either services provided to a trust for less than market value, or a transfer of value except if that value is transferred by 1 or more of the following:

- (i) a beneficiary:
- (ii) a trustee:
- (iii) a person with power of appointment or removal of trustees:
- (iv) a person with a contingent interest in the trust property, in the case that the trust fails:
- (v) a decision-maker under the trust.

[Note: At the time of writing, the definition of "settlement" in the Income Tax Act had not yet been amended by replacing in para (c), the words "section CB 16A(3)" with "section CB 16A(7)" and "5 years" with "10 years".]

Tax Administration Act

22B FURTHER RECORDS REQUIRED

22B(1) [Retention of records by trustee]

A trustee to whom either section EW 44 or EZ 39 of the Income Tax Act 2007 applies must keep, in English or te reo Maori, records of–

(a) the amounts of debt forgiven by creditors; and

(b) amounts distributed to the trust's beneficiaries.

22B(2) [Safe custody]

A trustee required to retain records must–

(a) take all reasonable precautions for the safe custody of those records; and

(b) retain those records for as long as the trust exists.

[...]

32 RECORDS OF SPECIFIED CHARITABLE, BENEVOLENT, PHILANTHROPIC, OR CULTURAL BODIES

32(1) [English language]

All gift-exempt bodies must keep in New Zealand sufficient records in the English language to enable the Commissioner to determine both the sources of donations made to them and the application, within New Zealand or within a country or territory outside New Zealand, of their funds.

32(2) [Exceptions]

Despite subsection (1), on application by a gift-exempt body, the Commissioner may notify the body that they are authorised to keep the records in a language other than English.

[...]

33 RETURNS OF INCOME

33(1) [Annual returns of income]

In each tax year, a person must file a return of income for a tax year in the form and with the particulars prescribed by the Commissioner.

33(1B) [Return of income where taxable Maori authority distribution received]

In an income year, a trust, society or institution to which section CW 41 or CW 42 of the Income Tax Act 2007 applies, may furnish to the Commissioner a return of income in the prescribed form for the preceding tax year, together with such other particulars as may be prescribed if the trust, society or institution receives a taxable Maori authority distribution.

[...]

58 RETURNS OF SPECIFIED CHARITABLE, BENEVOLENT, PHILANTHROPIC, OR CULTURAL BODIES

Every gift-exempt body must, when notified by the Commissioner, furnish a return of its funds derived or received in any tax year and showing the source and application of those funds, together with such other particulars as may be required by the Commissioner.

CHAPTER 20

Disclosure Obligations

¶20-010 Operating principle

Disclosure and reporting obligations, initially targeting foreign trusts now also apply to complying trusts. While not strictly relating to the taxation of trusts, international tax requirements and policy decisions to defend the tax base have been significant drivers behind the trend for increased disclosure, followed by concerns to mitigate tax avoidance in the wake of the defence between the trustee tax rate of 33% and the top personal marginal tax rate of 39%.

¶20-020 Annual return for trusts

With effect from 1 April 2021, trustees of complying trusts who derive assessable income (and where no exception applies) must file a tax return and provide the following information:

"(a) a statement of profit or loss and a statement of financial position:

(b) the amount, and nature, of each settlement that–

(i) is not the provision to the trustee, at less than market value, of minor services incidental to the activities of the trust; and

(ii) is made on the trust in the income year:

(c) the name, date of birth, jurisdiction of tax residence, and tax file number and taxpayer identification number, of each settlor who makes a settlement on the trust in the income year or whose details have not previously been supplied to the Commissioner:

(d) for each distribution made by the trustee of the trust in the income year,–

(i) the amount of the distribution:

(ii) the name, date of birth, jurisdiction of tax residence, and tax file number and taxpayer identification number, of the beneficiary who receives the distribution:

(e) the name, date of birth, jurisdiction of tax residence, and tax file number and taxpayer identification number, of each person having a power under the trust to appoint or dismiss a trustee, to add or remove a beneficiary, or to amend the trust deed:

(f) the other information required by the Commissioner."

The information set out above is not required if:

"(a) the trustee is excluded from the requirement to make a return by section 43B (which relates to non-active trusts):

(b) the trustee is required to make a return by section 59D (which relates to foreign trusts):

(c) the trustees of the trust are incorporated as a board under the Charitable Trusts Act 1957:

(d) the trust is a charitable trust registered under the Charities Act 2005:

(e) the trustee is eligible under section HF 2 of the Income Tax Act 2007 to choose under section HF 11 of that Act to become a Maori authority:

(f) the trust is a widely-held superannuation fund, as defined in section YA 1 of the Income Tax Act 2007:

(g) the trust is an employee share scheme that is an exempt ESS, as defined in section YA 1 of the Income Tax Act 2007:

(h) the trustee is a debt funding special purpose vehicle, as defined in section YA 1 of the Income Tax Act 2007:

(i) the trustee is a lines trust established under the Energy Companies Act 1992."

See Tax Administration Act 1994, s 59BA. The Commissioner can also request information for the period from the 2013–14 income year that is in the knowledge, possession or control of the trustee. See Tax Administration Act 1994, s 59BAB.

The reporting required by s 59BA is expected to be in the same form as is currently required for foreign trusts. See ¶20-110. This had not been confirmed by Inland Revenue at the time of writing this book.

These reporting obligations were introduced by the Taxation (Income Tax Rate and Other Amendments) Act 2020, which was introduced on 2 December 2020 and enacted on 7 December 2020. The Commentary to the Taxation (Income Tax Rate and Other Amendments) Bill explained the new disclosure requirements at 18 to 19 as follows:

"Detailed analysis

Information required to be provided

The Bill would require financial accounting information to be provided by trustees on an ongoing basis. This would include:

- profit and loss statements
- balance sheet items, and
- other information to be specified by the Commissioner (for example any transfers to the trust by associated persons).

The Commissioner would prescribe additional information relevant to trusts which must be provided as part of the return information, such as loans to or by related parties.

> Trustees would also be required to provide information on distributions and settlements made during the income year and include that in their return.
>
> *Distributions*
>
> For distributions, the information required would include identifying information for beneficiaries such as their name, IRD number and date of birth. This is set out in proposed section 59BA(2)(d) [of the Tax Administration Act 1994].
>
> The information required for distributions is similar to the information Inland Revenue collects about beneficiaries as part of the current tax return process, where there is an allocation of income to the beneficiary.
>
> The Commissioner may require other information relating to distributions to be reported, which could include, for example, the source of the distribution.
>
> *Settlements*
>
> The information required for settlements over the year would include identifying information for settlors such as name, IRD number and date of birth, as well as the amount and nature of each settlement. In addition, it is intended that for the 2021–22 return year, trustees provide names and details of settlors from prior years. This is achieved in proposed section 59BA(2)(c) by requiring details for those settlors whose details have not previously been supplied to the Commissioner.
>
> Inland Revenue does not currently collect information on subsequent settlements on a trust. This is an information gap which means that Inland Revenue is not capturing information on the true settlor. This is a key piece of information, as New Zealand has a settlor-based trust taxation regime.
>
> *Other relevant persons*
>
> Proposed section 59BA(2)(e) would require trustees to provide information on those with the power under the trust to appoint or dismiss a trustee, to add or remove a beneficiary, or to amend the trust deed.
>
> Requiring this information is necessary as 'appointers' or those with power to amend the trust deed would not be disclosed otherwise. The reference to the power arising 'under the trust' is intended to ensure this does not capture beneficiaries where they have one of the above powers only if all beneficiaries agree.
>
> This would form part of a trustee's annual return requirements and therefore existing penalty provisions would apply as appropriate, if the information is not provided or false information is provided. No additional or specific penalty is proposed."

The new reporting obligations for complying trusts are in addition to the presumption that trustees will give trust information to beneficiaries on request that was introduced by the Trusts Act 2019, which came into full force and effect on 30 January 2021. The practical import of the Trusts Act disclosure presumption and the Tax Administration Act reporting obligations is that the administrative burden of trustees will be significantly increased and trustees need to be mindful of their obligations and how these must be fulfilled.

¶20-025 A settlor must make disclosure where there is no resident trustee

A resident settlor must disclose information of any settlement made onto a trust after 17 December 1987 if there is no resident trustee:

- at the time of settlement, or
- at any time after the settlement.

If there is no resident trustee at the time of settlement, disclosure must be made within 3 months of the date of settlement.

If there is a resident trustee at settlement, but at any time after that there is no resident trustee, disclosure must be made within 3 months of the date on which the trust ceased to have a resident trustee.

Disclosure is also required if a person who is a New Zealand resident makes a settlement on a trust as nominee for another person and there is no resident trustee at settlement. Where a settlement is made by a nominee, disclosure must be made within 3 months of the date of settlement.

Disclosure is made on form IR 462, "Settlors of trusts disclosure" (www.ird.govt.nz). See Appendix at ¶20-110.

These disclosure obligations do not apply to superannuation funds.

See Tax Administration Act 1994, s 59.

Also see ¶20-070 regarding proposed reform relating to foreign trust disclosure.

¶20-030 Disclosure considerations

Where disclosure relates to land, the Commissioner requires the legal description and location of the property. If the property includes shares, details of the number, type, and name of the company and the country of incorporation are required. If the property includes financial arrangements, details of the parties to the financial arrangement, interest rate and term must be supplied. If the property includes services, the nature of the service and the consideration paid must also be disclosed: *Tax Information Bulletin* ¶74-107 Vol 7, No 4, October 1995 at 10.

Where settlements onto a trust do not have a monetary value, for example, where a guarantee is not called up, valuation may not be straight-forward. However, guidance is available with respect to valuing settlements that arise where a right to demand payment is not exercised (see ¶2-030).

Consideration will also be necessary when determining the value of the amount of a distribution on account of non-financial distributions such as the use and occupation of trust residential property.

If disclosure is not made, in addition to any penalties for failure to comply, the Commissioner can determine the amount of trustee income for an income year: Tax Administration Act, s 93B. See further at ¶20-060.

Also see ¶20-070 regarding foreign trust disclosure.

¶20-040 Resident trustees of foreign trusts have disclosure obligations

A resident foreign trustee must also disclose information about the foreign trusts for which that trustee acts. For these purposes, a resident foreign trustee is a New Zealand tax resident who acts as a trustee of a foreign trust that is not registered under the Charities Act 2005.

Foreign trusts must be registered with Inland Revenue and the application must disclose:

- the name of the foreign trust
- the date, amount, settlor and nature of each settlement on the trust
- the name and contact particulars, including tax residence, of each settlor, appointor, person with powers of control, trustee and beneficiary with fixed interests
- the name, age and taxpayer identification details of each minor beneficiary of a fixed trust
- if a resident foreign trustee claims to be a qualifying resident foreign trustee
- if a resident foreign trustee has been appointed by another resident foreign trustee as an agent, the names of the agent trustee and the appointing trustee.

Section 59B(3) of the Tax Administration Act.

Disclosure by a resident foreign trustee is made on form IR 607 "Foreign trust disclosure": www.ird.govt.nz. See Appendix at ¶20-110.

Section 59B also provides for the appointment of a contact trustee who is responsible for making an application to be registered as a foreign trust and is also required to advise of additions or amendments to the provided information: Tax Administration Act, s 59B(3) and (5).

If the trustee is a company, it will be a qualifying resident foreign trustee if there is a New Zealand resident director or other individual in a position allowing significant influence over the management or administration of that company, and that person is a member of an approved organisation.

A resident trustee for a foreign trust must keep records disclosing the history of the trust's administration: Tax Administration Act, s 22(7)(d). The records to be retained include:

- a record of assets and liabilities of the trust and details of all amounts received and expended by the trustee, and
- if the trust carries on a business, records of the accounting information system.

If there is more than one resident foreign trustee, each resident foreign trustee is responsible for the performance of the registration and disclosure obligations and may appoint one of themselves as agent for record-keeping purposes (Tax Administration

Act, s 22(2C)) and for disclosure purposes (Tax Administration Act, s 59B(7)). A resident foreign trustee may apply for permission to keep records offshore, or in a language other than English: Tax Administration Act, s 22(2).

Also see ¶20-070 regarding proposed reform relating to foreign trust disclosure.

¶20-050 Time limits for registration and for returns to be filed by a resident trustee of foreign trust

Resident foreign trustees, were required to apply to the Commissioner for registration and provide the required information for existing foreign trusts at the time the Taxation (Business Tax, Exchange of Information, and Remedial Matters) Act 2017 received the Royal assent and subsequently within 30 days, unless a grace period applies: Tax Administration Act, s 59C.

Subsequent changes must be notified to the Commissioner within 30 days, s 59C(2).

A deferral of the registration and disclosure requirement may apply to certain trustees who are not in the business of providing trustee services and who assume New Zealand residence after 1 October 2006: Tax Administration Act, s 59C(3).

Also see ¶20-070 regarding proposed reform relating to foreign trust disclosure.

¶20-060 There are penalties for non-disclosure

A penalty is imposed on all persons, including settlors and trustees, who knowingly do not provide information about a trust or keep proper records: Tax Administration Act, s 143A.

The penalty for non-disclosure or knowingly giving false information is a fine of up to $50,000. Given the broad definition of settlor, see ¶2-030, care is required to ensure all settlors are identified and meet their disclosure obligations.

A New Zealand resident trustee of a foreign trust that fails to disclose or keep records may also be taxed in New Zealand on the trust's worldwide income. This is because the exemption for foreign-sourced income of a trust that has no New Zealand-resident settlor will not apply to the trust's resident foreign trustee. See s HC 26(1):

A foreign trust can avoid the possibility of taxation on the trust's worldwide income by becoming a qualifying resident foreign trustee, see ¶20-040, or appointing a person to act as such a trustee. See *Tax Information Bulletin* ¶185-120 Vol 18, No 5, June 2006 at 110.

The Commissioner's stated policy is that penalties for failure to make disclosure will not apply if a resident foreign trustee is unaware of the disclosure obligations:

> "If a resident foreign trustee has failed to comply with the new rules but was not aware of these rules, sanctions will not apply. As a matter of practice, if Inland Revenue is aware of the name and contact particulars of a resident foreign trustee, it will notify the trustee of his or her tax responsibilities as a trustee of a foreign trust, seek the required information

disclosure and outline the recordkeeping requirements. Whether the trustee is aware of his or her tax responsibilities will be a question of fact to be determined on a case-by-case basis, although it can be reasonably assumed that 'professional trustees' and those trustees in the business of providing trustee services will be aware of the new requirements.

If a resident foreign trustee has failed to comply with the new rules and the trustee knew or ought to have known about his or her tax responsibilities as a trustee of a foreign trust, the trustee will be in breach of section 143A and, if convicted, will be subject to a monetary fine and/or imprisonment."

See *Tax Information Bulletin* ¶185-120 Vol 18, No 5, June 2006 at 110.

Also see ¶20-070 regarding proposed reform relating to foreign trust disclosure.

¶20-070 Foreign trust disclosure background

The disclosure obligations for the trustees of complying trusts resulted from the release of a large number of documents obtained in 2016 from Panamanian law firm, Mossack Fonseca, which came to be known as the "Panama papers". This led to New Zealand's foreign trust regime coming under close political scrutiny. The Government subsequently initiated an Inquiry into Foreign Trust Disclosure Rules. This Inquiry resulted in a number of recommendations for tightening the foreign trust regime.

As a consequence, the Government introduced a Bill to Parliament that was subsequently enacted as the Taxation (Business Tax, Exchange of Information, and Remedial Matters) Act 2017. This Act amended the Tax Administration Act to implement many of the changes to disclosure requirements for foreign trusts recommended by the Inquiry into Foreign Trust Disclosure Rules. It required resident trustees of a foreign trust to apply for registration of the trust (for existing foreign trusts by 30 June 2017 and for new foreign trusts within 30 days of existence). See ss 59B–59E.

Specific changes introduced in the Act included:

(1) The requirement for foreign trusts to formally register with Inland Revenue. As part of this registration process, each trust is required to declare that:

- the person establishing the foreign trust; and
- the settlor(s); and
- the trustees

have all been advised of, and have agreed to comply with, the applicable requirements in the Tax Administration Act 1994, the Anti-Money Laundering and Countering Financing of Terrorism Act 2009 (and regulations), and Automatic Exchange of Information (AEOI) requirements provided for in the Bill in accordance with the G20/OECD standard).

(2) On registration, the name, email address, foreign residential address, country of tax residence, and taxpayer identification number of all of the following must be provided to Inland Revenue:

- the settlor(s):
- the protector (if there is any):

- non-resident trustees:
- any other natural person who has effective control of the trust:
- beneficiaries of fixed trusts, including the underlying beneficiary where a named beneficiary is a nominee.

The amendments also require the trust deed of the trust to be filed with the registration form, and that discretionary trusts are required to describe in the registration any class of beneficiary not listed in the trust deed. This will enable the identity of a beneficiary to be established at the time of a distribution or when vested rights are exercised.

(3) The registration requirement applies to all trusts formed after enactment of the enabling legislation. Existing foreign trusts were required to meet the new information requirements by 30 June 2017.

(4) The amendments required foreign trusts to file annual returns with Inland Revenue. The proposed amendments require the return to include:

- any changes to the information provided at registration:
- the trust's annual financial statement:
- the amount of any distributions paid or credited and the names, foreign address, taxpayer identification number, and the country of tax residence of the recipient beneficiaries.

(5) When a foreign trust qualifies to be exempt from New Zealand tax. Foreign trusts are not taxable under current law. The Act provided that a foreign trust would lose its exemption from New Zealand tax if it did not register with Inland Revenue and fulfil its associated disclosure obligations. This means that a foreign trust that fails to meet these requirements will be taxable in New Zealand on its worldwide income.

(6) A qualifying resident foreign trustee safe harbour. This means that if a trustee of a foreign trust is convicted of an offence of not providing information requested by Inland Revenue, the foreign trust stands to lose its exemption from New Zealand tax and become subject to New Zealand tax on its worldwide income.

(7) Register of foreign trusts shared with law enforcement agencies. The amendments require Inland Revenue to share information contained in the foreign trusts register for law enforcement purposes with the Department of Internal Affairs and the New Zealand Police.

(8) The Act requires foreign trusts to pay a registration fee of $270 and annual filing fee of $50 to Inland Revenue. The amount of the fees may be adjusted through an Order in Council.

See Government Inquiry into Foreign Trust Disclosure Rules: Report (Released 27 June 2016). See Appendix at ¶20-110 for High Level Overview and Executive Summary.

See Taxation (Business Tax, Exchange of Information, and Remedial Matters) Act 2017.

Also see Regulatory impact statements – Taxation (Business Tax, Exchange of Information, and Remedial Matters) Bill (taxpolicy.ird.govt.nz/publications/2016/2016-ris-bteirm-bill). The same level of disclosure now applies to the trustees of complying trusts, unless a specific exemption applies.

¶20-080 FATCA

The United States' Foreign Account Trust Compliance Act, commonly known as FATCA, was enacted by the United States Government to provide a mechanism to collect information for the United States tax office to enable it to more effectively enforce the United States tax regime, which is based on citizenship, and to discourage tax evasion through the use of offshore vehicles. The Act provides for a punitive 30% withholding tax on payments to non-United States financial institutions (FFIs) as an incentive to comply with FATCA requirements through participation.

The key component of FATCA is an information-gathering regime facilitated through a series of intergovernmental agreements. Under these agreements, foreign governments agree to incorporate FATCA provisions into their respective domestic laws. Consequently, all FFIs within each foreign jurisdiction must comply with the registration and compliance-reporting requirements prescribed under FATCA. The positive aspect for FFIs in countries entering into intergovernmental agreements with the United States is that the agreement versions of FATCA are considerably more concise than the full United States legislation, due diligence obligations are simplified and an FFI need only report to its domestic tax authority, rather than the IS Internal Revenue Service.

The New Zealand Government responded to FATCA by entering into an intergovernmental agreement signed on 12 June 2014. The legislative requirements were implemented by way of the Taxation (Annual Rates, Employee Allowances and Remedial Matters) Act 2014, which received Royal Assent on 30 June 2014, immediately before FATCA coming into effect from 1 July 2014. This recognised the intergovernmental agreement as a form of Double Tax Agreement and inserted a new Pt 11B into the Tax Administration Act 1994. Among the reasons given for New Zealand's participation in FATCA were the interpretation that New Zealand financial institutions could not voluntarily comply with FATCA without breaching New Zealand law (including the Privacy Act 1993); New Zealand direct investment in the United States would be affected; New Zealand financial institutions would likely face significant compliance costs that could affect the public through higher funding costs; and the reputational risk if New Zealand were not to participate.

Among the amendments to the Tax Administration Act were the following:

- Provision for FFIs to elect between alternative compliance categories or "permitted choices" (s 185F)
- FATCA-specific record keeping and due diligence requirements (s 185H)
- Requirements for information reporting to Inland Revenue (s 185I)

- Nullification of agreements intended to avoid FATCA compliance (s 185L, since replaced by s 185R), and
- Offences for failure to register (ss 143(1)(ab) and 143A(1)(ab)).

Effect of FATCA on New Zealand trusts

Under the intergovernmental agreement, all New Zealand resident trusts have a FATCA classification, regardless of the size or the nature of the trust's activities. The classification determines what obligations the trust may have under FATCA. The classification system divides New Zealand resident entities into New Zealand financial institutions (NZFIs), which in turn will either be reporting or non-reporting; and non-financial foreign entities (NFFEs), which in turn may be active or passive. Reporting NZFIs will have full obligations under the intergovernmental agreement, while non-reporting NZFIs are deemed to be compliant and will generally have limited FATCA obligations. NFFEs do not have FATCA obligations; although, under some circumstances, they may need to provide information to financial institutions with which they do business.

For FATCA purposes, some trusts may be reporting NZFIs. This will be the case if they are either custodial institutions or investment entities (there are other classifications as well, but these are much less likely to apply to trusts).

A custodial institution holds financial assets for the account of others. This must be a substantial portion of its business. The definition of investment entity is much broader in scope. Activities of an investment entity are defined to include trading in financial and money market instruments, individual or collective portfolio management and otherwise investing, administering or managing funds on behalf of others. These are in turn divided into those trusts that are investment entities because that is the nature of their own activities, or those deemed to be investment entities because they are managed by an entity that is in the business of being an investment entity. Accordingly, most New Zealand family trusts will not be investment entities on account of their activities, but could be deemed to be investment entities if managed by a professional manager, such as a professional trustee company in the role of trustee or a professional fund manager delegated to manage an investment portfolio with wide-ranging discretions.

Reporting NZFIs are obliged by the intergovernmental agreement to register their FATCA status with the United States IRS (which may be done online), must perform the prescribed due diligence to identify United States Reportable Accounts (including United States tax residents, specified United States entities or Passive NFFEs with United States Controlling Persons). All Reporting NZFIs are deemed to have "accounts" and "account holders". Account holders will include settlors, trustees, mandatory beneficiaries, discretionary beneficiaries that have received a distribution during a reporting period and any other person exercising control over the trust.

There are a number of alternative bases for a trust to be non-reporting if it is deemed to be a NZFI. These include "Trustee Documented Trusts" where the trustee is a reporting NZFI and reports all necessary information disclosure with respect to any United States

Reportable Accounts held by the trust; and "Sponsored Investment Entities" where a third party undertakes FATCA compliance on a trust or other entity's behalf.

Any trust that is not an NZFI will automatically be deemed to be an NFFE. NFFEs may be either "Active" or "Passive". Whether an NFFE is an Active NFFE will depend on whether it has passive income, and the level of that income, or else whether it comes within certain specified categories, such as charities. Accordingly, the primary issue is the nature of passive income. For New Zealand purposes, this is defined as income, such as interest, dividends or royalties. Passive NFFEs may still have reporting obligations where they have United States citizens in positions of control.

See *Tax Information Bulletin* ¶267-111 Vol 26, No 7, August 2014. Also see the Agreement between the Government of New Zealand and the Government of the United States of America to Improve International Tax Compliance and to Implement FATCA (available from ird.govt.nz/international-tax/exchange-of-information/fatca/inland-revenue-role-in-fatca/the-shift-to-automatic-exchange-of-information-between-tax-administrations). Associated documents include a Memorandum of Understanding; Additional terms; and Competent Authority Arrangements (including a specific Competent Authority Arrangement for trusts). See also FATCA Registration Guidance Notes and the *FATCA Trusts Guidance Notes* published by Inland Revenue (ird.govt.nz/international-tax/exchange-of-information/fatca/registration-and-reporting). Also see *Tax Information Bulletin* ¶267-111 Vol 26, No 7, August 2014.

¶20-090 International Information Exchange Developments

The information sharing regime instigated as a consequence of FATCA has since been extended further following New Zealand's ratification of the Convention on Mutual Administrative Assistance in Tax Matters (amended) on 21 November 2013. The Convention on Mutual Administrative Assistance in Tax Matters is a convention that was developed by the OECD and the Council of Europe and is open to members of both organisations. The convention provides the legal basis for regulating the mutual information exchange between participating states regarding tax matters. The convention is also open to other states to participate on an invitation basis and 58 states have ratified the convention to date (in all, 73 states are signatories).

Based on FATCA and its associated implementation agreements, the Convention is implemented through participation of member states in a data exchange protocol using the Standard for Automatic Exchange of Financial Account Information (commonly known as the Common Reporting Standard or CRS). The CRS is also sometimes referred to as "GATCA", referring to a globalised version of FATCA. The CRS is an information standard for the automatic exchange of information (AEoI). This information standard covers requirements for due diligence, automated reporting and associated definitions. Trusts are referred to as Non-Reporting Financial Institutions. Due diligence requirements with respect to trusts or corresponding types of entity may cover settlors, trustees, protectors and beneficiaries with a particular focus on aspects of control and mandatory entitlements (such as to distributions).

The following excerpt from interpretation statement IS 18/01, "Taxation of trusts – income tax" in *Tax Information Bulletin* ¶307-103 Vol 30, No 7, August 2018 sets out further relevant reporting obligations:

> "13.33 From 1 July 2017 trusts that are Reporting New Zealand financial institutions must commence CRS due diligence reviews and thereafter an annual reporting regime commences.
>
> 13.34 If a trust is not a financial institution, but is a type of passive entity (known as a passive non-financial entity) that holds an account with a financial institution, it may be asked by that institution to confirm who its controlling persons are (ie, when that financial institution is carrying out its own due diligence on the trust's account). The trust's controlling persons are the settlors, trustees, protectors, beneficiaries, and any other natural person that controls the trust.
>
> 13.35 For more guidance on AEOI/CRS obligations for trusts that are financial institutions refer to *Tax Information Bulletin* Vol 29, No 4 on the Taxation (Business Tax, Exchange of Information and Remedial Matters) Act 2017. Inland Revenue has also published two comprehensive guides (see Inland Revenue Department NZ, *Is the trust a reporting NZFI under CRS? (IR1052)* (August 2017) and Inland Revenue Department NZ, *Family trust obligations under the CRS (IR1053)* (August 2017)). The guides deal with the AEOI standard and the implementation legislation at a detailed technical level.
>
> 13.36 Inland Revenue has also published guidance on the operation of the FATCA framework as it applies to trusts in Inland Revenue Department NZ, Trust guidance notes: *Foreign Account Tax Compliance Act (FATCA) (IR1087)* (October 2017)."

¶20-100 Land Transfer Tax Statements

With effect from 1 October 2015, trustees must disclose residency and tax information for transfers of real property. See further at ¶19-090.

¶20-110 Appendix

Form IR 462 "Settlors of trusts disclosure" (July 2019)

Inland Revenue
Te Tari Taake

IR462
July 2019

Settlors of trusts disclosure

Tax Administration Act 2004

Please read the notes on the back before completing this form.

1. Trust's name

2. Trust's IRD number — (8 digit numbers start in the second box. *1 2 3 4 5 6 7 8*)
If the trust does not have an IRD number, complete an *IRD number application - non-individual (IR596)* and return it with this form.

3. Trust's address
Street address
Town or city

4. Settlor's name
Settlor's IRD number
Settlor's address
Street address
Town or city
Date trust settled — Day Month Year
Attach a copy of the trust deed and any amendments made.

5. Full description of the nature and date of the settlement (see note 5)
If there is not enough space, please use a separate sheet of paper and staple it to this form.

6. Names and addresses of trustees
If there is not enough space, please use a separate sheet of paper and staple it to this form.
Trustee's name
Trustee's address
Trustee's name
Trustee's address
Trustee's name
Trustee's address

Important: You must attach a copy of the trust deed and any amendments that may alter the nature of the trust and/or the beneficiaries. For more information please call us on 0800 377 774.

*IR462

7. Names and addresses of beneficiaries
If there is not enough space, please use a separate sheet of paper and staple it to this form.

Beneficiary's name

Beneficiary's address

Beneficiary's name

Beneficiary's address

Declaration

To be made by the settlor, nominee settlor or nominal settlor.

I declare that the information given on this form is true and correct.

Name of person completing this form

State whether settlor, nominee settlor or nominal settlor

Signature

/ /

Date

RESET FORM

Notes about disclosures

1. Who has to make a disclosure and when

The following people must make a disclosure.

(i) Anyone who makes a settlement to a trust on or after 17 December 1987 and is resident in New Zealand at the time of settlement, and either:

- no trustee was resident in New Zealand at the time of settlement, or
- there was a resident trustee at settlement and at any time thereafter the trustee became non-resident.

A disclosure in this situation must be made within three months of the date of settlement or of the date on which there is no trustee of the trust resident in New Zealand.

(ii) Anyone who makes a settlement to a trust on or after 17 December 1987 and is resident in New Zealand at the time of settlement, and

- the settlement is made as a nominee for another person or is of a nominal amount, made at the request of another person, and
- no trustee was resident in New Zealand at the time of settlement.

In this case, the disclosure is required within three months of the date of settlement.

2. Settlements

A settlement is any transaction, action or failure to act that makes a person a settlor.

3. Settlors

A settlor is a person who:

- makes any disposition, or
- makes any property available (including financial assistance), or
- provides any service for the benefit of a trust for less than market value. This includes any person who acquires the use of any property or services from the trust for greater than market value.

If a settlement is made by a person:

- as a nominee for any other person, or
- at the request of any other person and is of a nominal amount,

the other person is treated as the settlor.

4. Documents to send

Attach a copy of the trust deed and any amendments that may alter the nature of the trust and/or the beneficiaries.

5. Details to disclose

At Question 5 on the front page, please give full details of the property or services and the transaction (disposal, making available, providing or acquiring) that makes the person a settlor under section YA 1 of the Income Tax Act 2007. This includes:

- date of original and subsequent settlements
- the market value of the property transferred
- consideration paid or received.

If a settlement includes land, shares, financial arrangements or providing services for less than market value, the disclosure must include:

- for land - the legal description and the location of the property
- for shares - the number, type, company name and country of incorporation
- for financial arrangements - the holder and issuer, interest rate and term
- for services - nature of service and consideration paid.

6. Number of disclosures

Please use a separate disclosure form for each trust in respect of which a settlement has been made.

7. Election to change category of trust for tax purposes

An election can be made to pay tax on trustee income of a foreign or non-complying trust if this would not otherwise be required. An election can also be made by new residents who have settled a trust before coming to New Zealand. Making an election may enable the trust to become a complying trust. This means that distributions that would otherwise be taxable will not be taxed in the hands of beneficiaries. If you want to know more about making an election, request an *Election to pay income tax on trustee income (IR463)* form. You can view a copy on our website at **www.ird.govt.nz**

8. When a trust owes an amount to a beneficiary of the trust, the beneficiary does not become a settlor when either:

- the trust pays the beneficiary a market interest rate equal to or greater than the prescribed rate of interest, or
- the amount retained in the beneficiary's current account at the end of the income year is not more than $25,000.

If you live in:

Northland	Auckland	other North Island areas	the South Island
send this form to	send this form to	send this form to	send this form to
Inland Revenue PO Box 3753 Christchurch Mail Centre Christchurch 8140	Inland Revenue PO Box 761 Waikato Mail Centre Hamilton 3240	Inland Revenue PO Box 39010 Wellington Mail Centre Lower Hutt 5045	Inland Revenue PO Box 3753 Christchurch Mail Centre Christchurch 8140

Form IR 607 New Zealand foreign trust registration (April 2021)

Inland Revenue
Te Tari Taake

New Zealand foreign trust registration

IR607
April 2021

This registration form must be completed by the contact trustee of a foreign trust with one or more New Zealand resident trustees.
Please read the notes before completing the form. Remember to sign the declaration.
The contact trustee must also complete a **New Zealand foreign trust connected persons schedule – IR607A** and a **New Zealand foreign trust settlements and distributions schedule – IR900A** when applying for registration.

1. **Trust details**

a. Full name of the foreign trust

b. IRD number (if known)

c. Date trust established
Day Month Year

d. Date New Zealand resident trustee first appointed
Day Month Year

e. Balance date
See 'Trust details' in the notes
Day Month

f. Is this your first foreign trust? Yes No
See 'Trust details' in the notes

2. **Contact trustee details**

a. Full name of the contact trustee

b. IRD number

c. Address of the contact trustee
Street address or PO Box number
Suburb or RD Town or city Postcode

d. Phone number and email address
Phone number
Email address

3. Are all the New Zealand resident trustees natural persons and not in the business of providing trustee services?
Yes - go to question 5
No - go to question 4

4. Have you paid the registration fee to Inland Revenue? Yes No
(See 'Fees and how to pay' in the notes)
Date paid or credited 20
Day Month Year

5. Please provide the following details if the trust has any discretionary beneficiaries or classes of discretionary beneficiaries

Full names of discretionary beneficiaries	Names of classes of discretionary beneficiaries

6. Please ensure you have attached the following:
   - Copy of the trust deed and any amending or supplementary documents
   - Completed **New Zealand foreign trust connected persons schedule - IR607A**
   - Completed **New Zealand foreign trust settlements and distributions schedule - IR900A**

Declaration

Full name

Designation or title (i.e. trustee, or director of trustee company)

Signature

I declare that the information given on this form is true and correct.

Day/Month/Year

RESET FORM

IR607
April 2021

Notes

Purpose of the form

The contact trustee uses this form to register a foreign trust with a New Zealand resident trustee. If the trust is not registered or the details are not provided, the trust will not be eligible for the exemption on foreign-sourced income.

Definitions

A "foreign trust" is a trust that meets the requirements of section HC 11 of the Income Tax Act 2007. Essentially, it is a trust which has not had a New Zealand tax resident settlor after 17 December 1987.

A trust can be both a foreign trust and a complying trust. A "complying trust" is one that has paid tax in New Zealand on all its income and met all its New Zealand tax obligations (HC 10 of the Income Tax Act 2007). In these circumstances the trust is known as a "dual-status trust". These trusts may also need to file income tax returns.

Registration requirements

At the time of registration, the contact trustee must also provide the names and details of everyone who is connected to the trust. This information is collected on the **New Zealand foreign trust connected persons schedule - IR607A**.

In addition, the contact trustee must provide details of historical settlements on the trust. This information is collected on the **New Zealand foreign trust settlements and distributions schedule - IR900A**.

The contact trustee must also provide the trust deed and any amending or supplementary documents as well as any functional equivalents.

Trust details

If the trust does not have a balance date, the default date is 31 March.

Contact trustee details

Please ensure the address on this form is the one we should use to contact you. Please note you are required to disclose your details as a trustee on a **New Zealand foreign trust connected persons schedule - IR607A**.

The address in the case of the IR607A is your physical residential or business address.

Fees and how to pay

If all the New Zealand resident trustees are natural persons and not in the business of providing trustee services, you do not have to pay a registration fee.

If payment is required, registration fees must be paid into Inland Revenue's account with Westpac - 03-0049-0001100-27. The fee for registration is NZ $270.

Use the following details when making a direct credit payment to us:

Particulars	Your IRD number. If you have an 8-digit IRD number put a 0 at the beginning
Payee Code	FTR
Reference	Leave blank

Go to **ird.govt.nz/pay** to find out about paying by:

- direct debit
- credit or debit card
- internet banking.

Discretionary beneficiaries

For a discretionary trust, please complete the table at Question 5, listing all individual discretionary beneficiaries and classes of discretionary beneficiaries.

If a beneficiary receives a distribution during a return year, their full details must be provided with the annual return for that year. These details must be provided on the **New Zealand foreign trust connected persons schedule - IR607A**.

Changes

The contact trustee must provide details of any additions or alterations to the information provided within 30 days of becoming aware of the changes.

You may need to complete a **New Zealand foreign trust connected persons schedule - IR607A** and/or a **New Zealand foreign trust settlements and distributions schedule - IR900A** to provide details of the changes.

If you anticipate ceasing to be the contact trustee you must advise:

- the anticipated date when you will cease to be the contact trustee;
- your email address and the physical residential address after the anticipated date; and
- the name, email address and physical residential or business address of the new contact trustee after the anticipated date.

Where to send the form

Registration can be completed in myIR.

You can also email the forms and attachments to **nzforeigntrusts@ird.govt.nz**

Alternatively, you can post them to:

International Revenue Strategy
Inland Revenue
PO Box 2198
Wellington 6140

More information

For more information, please visit **ird.govt.nz/international-tax/foreign-trusts-nz-resident-trustees**

Government Inquiry into Foreign Trust Disclosure Rules: Report

High-level overview

The issue

Media reports and commentaries on the Panama Papers assert that New Zealand foreign trusts are being used extensively by wealthy individuals in structures that facilitate–

- tax evasion
- aggressive tax planning
- money laundering and hiding of assets.

Potential reputational damage

New Zealand's reputation as a country that cooperates with other countries to counter money laundering, abusive tax practices and other illicit activities may be tarnished.

Perception internationally that New Zealand has weak laws around due diligence and reporting and is generally a 'soft touch'.

New Zealand being cited as a tax haven.

Undermines confidence of compliant New Zealand taxpayers in the integrity of the tax system and leads to comments such as 'Why should I pay more taxes when the wealthy are dodging their taxes through shonky structures shrouded in secrecy?'

Remedies

a) Where the assertions and/or perceptions are not justified: explanation, education and communication.

b) Where the assertions and/or perceptions are justified: change the rules around

   - *tax disclosures* – primary deterrent to tax-related concerns
   - *anti-money laundering* – primary deterrent to money-laundering concerns, but tax disclosures will also assist.

Options for reform where the assertions are justified

Option 1 Some increase in information required to be disclosed by foreign trusts (details of settlor and beneficiaries as listed in trust deed).

Option 2 Significant increase in information required to be disclosed (details of settlor, persons with effective control, non-resident trustees, beneficiaries, trustees, trust deed) coupled with an annual return, expanded application of the AML laws and a register of foreign trusts, searchable (but not by the public).

Option 3 As for 2, but foreign trust register is publicly available.

Option 4 Amend the foreign trust tax regime to repeal the exemption from tax on foreign source income.

Inquiry's recommendation

Adopt Option 2 – Significant increase in information disclosure requirements.

Part 1 Executive Summary

Purpose of Inquiry

1.1 The Inquiry is required to examine New Zealand's foreign trust disclosure rules and to report on whether the rules, and the enforcement of them, are sufficient to ensure New Zealand's reputation is maintained when considered alongside the country's commitment to various OECD and other international agreements. In short, are the rules fit for purpose?

Conclusions

1.2 The Inquiry concludes that the existing foreign trust disclosure rules are inadequate. The rules are not fit for purpose in the context of preserving New Zealand's reputation as a country that cooperates with other jurisdictions to counter money laundering and aggressive tax practices.

1.3 The Inquiry considers that a significant increase in information disclosed when a foreign trust sets up, annual reporting and increased enforcement, will satisfactorily address the issues identified. Banning foreign trusts or removing the current tax exemption is not considered to be necessary or justified.

1.4 In theory, New Zealand's existing tax disclosure and exchange of information arrangements should be sufficient to deter tax abuse, and its anti-money laundering rules should ensure that funds held by foreign trusts are from legitimate sources. However, under current law and enforcement practices the risk of detection by authorities is low. The Inquiry considers that the disclosure requirements can be justifiably described as light-handed.

1.5 Strengthened disclosure requirements should act as a deterrent to offshore parties looking to use New Zealand foreign trusts for illicit purposes.

1.6 The Panama Papers have not been released publicly by the journalists who have them and were not available to the Inquiry. There has been no direct evidence of illicit funds being hidden in New Zealand foreign trusts, or of tax abuse. However, based on the work undertaken, including a review of IRD files, the Inquiry considers it is reasonable to conclude that there are cases where foreign trusts are being used in this way. The current legislation, regulations and practice that govern disclosures by foreign trusts present both the potential and the environment for this to occur.

1.7 Publicity around the Panama Papers has the potential to cause reputational damage both to New Zealand and to many other countries. The Inquiry considers that any significant adverse impact on New Zealand internationally is unlikely if appropriate action is taken to tighten the disclosure rules.

1.8 Foreign trusts, like domestic trusts, are a legitimate vehicle used primarily to manage family wealth. New Zealand is an attractive location in which to base a foreign trust as it offers stable political, judicial and legislative settings and respect for property rights and privacy. The supporting services industry is significant, and generally comprises skilled and efficient professionals.

1.9 Allowing foreign trusts to establish in New Zealand is consistent with the Government's policy of maintaining an open economy which welcomes foreign investment and an active financial services sector.

1.10 The tax treatment of foreign trusts follows New Zealand's long established and principled policy of not imposing New Zealand tax on foreign source income derived by non-residents. It does not result in New Zealand being a tax haven under established OECD criteria. However, the Inquiry notes that the classification tax haven is an ambiguous label that is now of historic relevance. It is best not used as a basis for decision making without much deeper inquiry.

1.11 New Zealand has a strong and well-deserved reputation as an active member of OECD and other international bodies working to clamp down on global corruption, money laundering, financing of terrorism and tax abuse. It is also regarded as a country that leads by example and it rates well in international peer reviews. Actions to increase disclosure requirements would be consistent with New Zealand's commitment to global transparency initiatives, and can be expected to be well regarded by other countries, particularly those in our tax treaty network.

1.12 Before the Inquiry began, the Government had introduced legislation to counter the use of Look Through Companies (LTCs) in foreign trust and other structures to derive foreign source income in excess of a low amount. While the Inquiry was underway the impending introduction of phase 2 of the Anti-Money Laundering (AML) rules was announced. This is expected to be enacted in 2017 and will result in lawyers and accountants being required to apply the AML rules. The Inquiry supports these initiatives and thinks that they will reduce the scope for inappropriate use of foreign trusts.

1.13 The foreign trust regime does not appear to be inconsistent with any specific obligations under current international agreements to which New Zealand is a party. However, as there is a reasonable likelihood that the regime is facilitating the hiding of funds or evasion of tax in some instances, the Inquiry considers that New Zealand's tax treaty partners would have a legitimate expectation that some action will be taken.

1.14 The recommendations in this report are designed to achieve a balance between allowing foreign trusts to continue in New Zealand and materially reducing the scope for foreign trust structures being used for illicit purposes such as hiding illegal funds or evading tax. If adopted, the changes may result in a reduction in the number of foreign trusts, in particular those that rely on non-disclosure to achieve their effectiveness.

Recommendations

1.15 The Inquiry recommends that–

Registration process

1.16 Foreign trusts be required to register on establishment using an expanded version of the current disclosure form, IR 607.

1.17 A register of foreign trusts, searchable only by regulatory agencies, be maintained.

1.18 The registration document include a signed declaration that the person establishing the foreign trust, the settlor(s) and the trustees have been advised of and have agreed to provide the information to comply with–

- the record keeping requirements in the Tax Administration Act
- the Anti-Money Laundering and Countering Financing of Terrorism Act and Regulations
- the Automatic Exchange of Information/Common Reporting Standard requirements (once enacted).

1.19 The registration requirement apply to all trusts formed after enactment of the enabling legislation.

1.20 A transitional rule that requires existing foreign trusts to register, and to supply the information required, by 30 June 2017.

1.21 The registration process be the responsibility of IRD initially. This to be reviewed in the context of the rapidly expanding reporting requirements imposed by international agreements to which New Zealand is a signatory. It is possible that another agency such as the Companies Office (within the Ministry of Business, Innovation and Employment) may be better placed to act as the registering and supervisory agency.

Strengthened disclosure on registration

1.22 The information required to be disclosed to IRD when a foreign trust registers be expanded from the current IR 607 disclosures to include the name, email address, foreign residential address, country of tax residence and Tax Identification Number of–

- the settlor or settlors
- the protector (if there is any)
- non-resident trustees
- any other natural person who has effective control of the trust (including through a chain of control or ownership)
- beneficiaries of fixed trusts, including the underlying beneficiary where a named beneficiary is a nominee.

1.23 For discretionary trusts, any class of beneficiary not listed in the trust deed be listed on the registration form.

1.24 The trust deed be required to be filed with the registration form.

Ongoing tax obligations

1.25 The exemption from New Zealand tax on foreign source income apply only to a foreign trust that has registered and fulfilled the associated disclosure obligations at that time.

1.26 Foreign trusts be required to file an annual return with IRD that includes–

- any changes to the information provided at registration
- the trust's annual financial statements
- the amount of any distributions paid or credited and the names, foreign address, Tax Identification Number and country of tax residence of the recipient beneficiaries.

1.27 The annual return requirement to apply to foreign trusts formed after the enactment date and to all foreign trusts from the income year commencing 1 April 2017.

1.28 The basis for foreign trusts that have a *qualifying* resident foreign trustee being exposed to lesser sanctions than other foreign trusts be reviewed to determine whether it should remain.

Registration and annual filing fee

1.29 Foreign trusts be required to pay a registration and annual filing fee to recover the costs to the Crown of administering the foreign trust regime. The Inquiry considers a fee of $500 at registration and an annual fee of the same amount would be reasonable.

Expansion of scope and application of AML rules

1.30 For services provided to foreign trusts, consideration be given to the removal by Order in Council in the short term (prior to 31 December 2016) of the regulation that excludes lawyers and accountants from AML reporting requirements. The proposed removal of this exclusion when phase 2 of the AML regime is implemented, as announced by the Government in May 2016, will address this recommendation but may not be effective until towards the end of 2017 or later.

1.31 The AML legislation or regulations be revised to include a mandatory requirement to verify in all cases the underlying source of funds or wealth settled on a foreign trust.

1.32 Expanded guidelines be issued explaining the scope of customer due diligence required in establishing and verifying beneficial ownership, effective control and source of funds in complex multi-layered trust structures. These should include a series of detailed worked examples.

Suspicious transaction reporting

1.33 The legislation or regulations that govern suspicious transaction reporting to the Financial Intelligence Unit of the New Zealand Police be revised to facilitate the reporting of actual or proposed transactions that have not or will not necessarily go through a New Zealand bank.

1.34 Greater profile, coupled with training recommendations, be given to the obligation on trust service providers to report suspicious transactions.

Information sharing

1.35 A review be undertaken of the current legislative arrangements for the sharing of information between the three agencies (IRD, FIU and DIA) with supervisory responsibility for disclosures by foreign trusts (and other entities). The purpose of the review, which could coincide with the introduction of phase 2 of the AML regime, would be to determine the financial and efficiency gains and other implications (including secrecy considerations) of sharing strategic intelligence and other information between agencies.

Other observations

1.36 In determining the effectiveness of New Zealand's laws in preventing illegal funds being housed in foreign trusts and tax evasion, the tax disclosure rules and the information required to be provided under the anti-money laundering regime cannot be considered in isolation. Disclosures required to be made to IRD can be expected to improve the effectiveness of the anti-money laundering regime. A key objective of the recommendations is to introduce a deterrent or signal sending effect, which the current rules lack.

1.37 A significant majority of the 23 written submissions to the Inquiry, including from the foreign trust industry and its advisors, support some expansion of the existing disclosure rules. One submission recommended that foreign trusts should be banned or subjected to New Zealand tax.

1.38 The Inquiry noted one local media statement that New Zealand's reputation had suffered a 'huge blow' as a consequence of the Panama Papers, and other statements suggesting long-term reputational damage has occurred. The Inquiry's review of international media on the topic does not support that conclusion. With the exception of a small number of articles in the Australian media, references to New Zealand in the international press appear to have been cursory.

1.39 The Inquiry considers that greater reputational damage has occurred domestically as a result of the Panama Papers debate. In part this has been caused by the incorrect conclusion that wealthy New Zealanders can use foreign trusts established in New Zealand to avoid or reduce their tax. The foreign trust regime cannot be used in this way. However, suggestions to the contrary cause legitimate questions to be raised over the fairness of the tax system.

1.40 The Inquiry was struck by the rapidly expanding number and scope of international agreements to which New Zealand is a signatory that are designed to counter, on a global basis, corruption, crime, money laundering, tax evasion and aggressive tax practices. These overlap government agencies. Issues that arise from this are–

a) The increased reporting in respect of international transactions, ranging from simple bank transfers to complex cross-border structures, will be significant. Education, training and communication of the reasons for these changes will be pivotal to achieving buy-in from New Zealanders, and compliance.

b) There is potential for duplication. For example, the Automatic Exchange of Information/Common Reporting Standard requirements may result in some duplication of information required under the Anti-Money Laundering/ Countering Financing of Terrorism rules.

c) Consideration might be given to having a single government agency assigned an overall coordination role to ensure these initiatives, and the resulting disclosure requirements, are implemented as efficiently as possible.

1.41 Globalisation, coupled with major groupings such as the G20 moving at speed to advocate and implement measures to clamp down on tax evasion and money laundering, is having a significant impact on tax policy and administration. Developed nations are becoming increasingly intolerant of corruption and of avenues through the international financial system that can be a route to financing terrorism. One consequence is a sharp increase in the amount of information that regulators around the world are collecting and sharing. Developments in technology allow the collection, sharing and matching of data at levels and within timeframes not previously thought possible. Another consequence is a proliferation of measures designed better equip countries to tax highly mobile profits in the digital era. This 'new world' can be expected to result in fundamental changes to the way individuals and businesses structure their international dealings.

(The full report can be found at: treasury.govt.nz/sites/default/files/2016-06/report-giftdr-27jun2016.pdf).

¶20-120 Legislation

Tax Administration Act 1994

22 KEEPING OF BUSINESS AND OTHER RECORDS

[...]

22(7) [Definition of records]

[...]

(d) in the case of a foreign trust, other than for the period for which section 59C(3) applies,–

- (i) *(repealed)*
- (ii) *(repealed)*
- (iii) a record of–
  - (A) the assets and liabilities of the foreign trust; and
  - (B) all entries from day to day of all sums of money received and expended by the trustee in relation to the foreign trust and the matters in respect of which the receipt and expenditure takes place; and

(C) if the trust carries on a business, the charts and codes of accounts, the accounting instruction manuals, and the system and programme documentation which describes the accounting system used in each income year in the administration of the trust:

[...]

59 DISCLOSURE OF TRUST PARTICULARS

59(1) [Disclosure of trust details when no resident trustee]

Where any person resident in New Zealand at the time of settlement makes a settlement on or after 17 December 1987 to or for the benefit of a trust or on the terms of a trust and–

(a) at the time of the settlement there was no trustee of that trust resident in New Zealand; or

(b) if at the time of the settlement there was a trustee of the trust resident in New Zealand, on any subsequent date there is no trustee of the trust resident in New Zealand,–

that person shall disclose to the Commissioner in the prescribed form and within 3 months of the date of settlement or of the date on which there is no trustee of the trust resident in New Zealand the fact of that settlement, the name and address of the trustee and the beneficiary of the trust, and such further details as may be required by the Commissioner.

59(2) [Nominee to disclose details of deemed settlor]

Where any person resident in New Zealand at the time of settlement would be treated as having made a settlement to or for the benefit of a trust or on the terms of a trust but for the application of section YB 21 of the Income Tax Act 2007, and where at the time of settlement there was no trustee of that trust resident in New Zealand, that person shall disclose to the Commissioner in the prescribed form within 3 months of the date of settlement the fact of that settlement, the name and address of the person who is deemed to be the settlor of the trust under section YB 21 of that Act, and such further details as may be required by the Commissioner.

59(3) [Trustee to furnish return of all income]

(repealed)

59(4) [Non-application to superannuation fund]

Nothing in subsections (1) and (2) or in section 93B shall apply to any trust that is a superannuation fund, or to any person in respect of a superannuation fund.

[...]

59BA ANNUAL RETURN FOR TRUSTS

59BA(1) [Trustees who derive income must file a return]

A trustee of a trust who derives assessable income for a tax year must file a return for the tax year of all income derived in the corresponding income year by the trustee as trustee of the trust.

59BA(2) [Information required in a return for a tax year]

A trustee who is required to file a return for a tax year under subsection (1) and does not meet the requirements of subsection (3) must make the return in the form prescribed by the Commissioner and include, unless otherwise required by the Commissioner,–

(a) a statement of profit or loss and a statement of financial position:

(b) the amount, and nature, of each settlement that–

  (i) is not the provision to the trustee, at less than market value, of minor services incidental to the activities of the trust; and

  (ii) is made on the trust in the income year:

(c) the name, date of birth, jurisdiction of tax residence, and tax file number and taxpayer identification number, of each settlor who makes a settlement on the trust in the income year or whose details have not previously been supplied to the Commissioner:

(d) for each distribution made by the trustee of the trust in the income year,–

  (i) the amount of the distribution:

  (ii) the name, date of birth, jurisdiction of tax residence, and tax file number and taxpayer identification number, of the beneficiary who receives the distribution:

(e) the name, date of birth, jurisdiction of tax residence, and tax file number and taxpayer identification number, of each person having a power under the trust to appoint or dismiss a trustee, to add or remove a beneficiary, or to amend the trust deed:

(f) the other information required by the Commissioner.

59BA(3) [Trustees not required to file returns under 59BA(2)]

A trustee of a trust who is required to file a return for a tax year under subsection (1) is not required to file a return in the form required by subsection (2) if–

(a) the trustee is excluded from the requirement to make a return by section 43B (which relates to non-active trusts):

(b) the trustee is required to make a return by section 59D (which relates to foreign trusts):

(c) the trustees of the trust are incorporated as a board under the Charitable Trusts Act 1957:

(d) the trust is a charitable trust registered under the Charities Act 2005:

(e) the trustee is eligible under section HF 2 of the Income Tax Act 2007 to choose under section HF 11 of that Act to become a Maori authority:

(f) the trust is a widely-held superannuation fund, as defined in section YA 1 of the Income Tax Act 2007:

(g) the trust is an employee share scheme that is an exempt ESS, as defined in section YA 1 of the Income Tax Act 2007:

(h) the trustee is a debt funding special purpose vehicle, as defined in section YA 1 of the Income Tax Act 2007:

(i) the trustee is a lines trust established under the Energy Companies Act 1992.

59BA(4) [Settlor responsible if trustees non-resident]

If the trustee of a trust is a non-resident, a settlor of the trust who is a New Zealand resident is responsible for ensuring the performance of the obligations imposed on the trustee by this section.

59BA(5) [Commissioner may vary requirements]

The Commissioner may vary the requirements set out in subsection (2) for a trustee or class of trustees.

59BA(6) [Commissioner's variation deemed to be secondary legislation]

A variation under subsection (5) is secondary legislation (see Part 3 of the Legislation Act 2019 for publication requirements).

59BAB COMMISSIONER MAY REQUIRE TRUST INFORMATION FOR PERIOD AFTER 2013–14 INCOME YEAR

59BAB(1) [Commissioner may require information]

The Commissioner may require a trustee of a trust to provide, in the prescribed form and by the specified date, information that—

(a) relates to the trust and a period beginning after the end of the 2013–14 income year and ending before the beginning of the 2021–22 income year; and

(b) would be required to be provided under section 59BA if the period began after the end of the 2020–21 income year; and

(c) is in the knowledge, possession, or control of the trustee.

59BAB(2) [Commissioner may issue notice to trustees]

The Commissioner may issue a notice requiring the trustee of each trust having the characteristics specified in the notice to provide, in the prescribed form and by the specified date, information—

(a) that is described in subsection (1) and is specified in the notice; and

(b) is for each period that is specified in the notice and begins after the end of the 2013–14 income year and ends before the beginning of the 2021–22 income year.

59BAB(3) [Settlor is responsible for compliance if trustee is non-resident]

If the trustee of a trust is a non-resident, a settlor of the trust who is a New Zealand resident is responsible for ensuring the performance of the obligations imposed on the trustee by this section.

59BAB(4) [Commissioner's notice deemed to be secondary legislation]

A notice under subsection (2) is secondary legislation under the Legislation Act 2019.

59B FOREIGN TRUST WITH RESIDENT FOREIGN TRUSTEE: REGISTRATION AND DISCLOSURE

59B(1) [Commissioner may register a foreign trust]

The Commissioner may register a foreign trust if the foreign trust has a resident foreign trustee and a trustee pays the prescribed fee.

59B(2) [Resident foreign trustees must apply for registration]

Resident foreign trustees of a foreign trust must apply to the Commissioner for registration of the foreign trust and pay the prescribed fee.

59B(3) [Information provided with application]

A trustee applying for registration of a foreign trust (the **contact trustee**) is responsible for communicating with the Commissioner for the trust and must provide, with the application and fee,–

(a) the name of the trust:

(b) the date, amount, settlor, and nature of each settlement on the trust that is not a provision to the trustee at less than market value of minor services incidental to the activities of the trust and is made in the period of time ending with the application and beginning with–

(i) the date on which the trust is formed, if a trustee is not a natural person or is in the business of providing trustee services; or

(ii) the later of the date on which the trust is formed and 30 June 2013, if subparagraph (i) does not apply and a trustee becomes required to register the trust on the date on which the Taxation (Business Tax, Exchange of Information, and Remedial Matters) Act 2017 receives the Royal assent; or

(iii) the later of the date on which the trust is formed and the date that is 4 years before the earliest date on which a trustee becomes required to register the trust, if subparagraphs (i) and (ii) do not apply:

(c) the name, email address, physical residential or business address, jurisdiction of tax residence, taxpayer identification number, and connection with the trust of–

(i) each settlor who makes a settlement referred to in paragraph (b):

(ii) each person with a power to appoint or dismiss a trustee, to amend the trust deed, or to add or remove a beneficiary:

(iii) each person with a power to control the exercise of a power referred to in subparagraph (ii):

(iv) each person with a power to control a trustee in the administration of the trust:

(v) each trustee:

(vi) for a fixed trust, each beneficiary that is not a minor and each nominee for a beneficiary:

(vii) for a fixed trust and a beneficiary who is a minor, the parent or guardian of the beneficiary:

(d) for a fixed trust and a beneficiary who is a minor, the name, age, and taxpayer identification number of the beneficiary:

(e) for a discretionary trust, details of each beneficiary or class of beneficiary sufficient for the Commissioner to determine, when a distribution is made under the trust, whether a person is a beneficiary:

(f) a copy of the trust deed and of each document that amends or supplements the trust deed, and a copy of each document that is the functional equivalent of a trust deed or amending or supplementing document.

59B(4) [When disclosure must be made if s 59B(3) does not apply]

The contact trustee must provide a signed declaration that each person referred to in subsection (3)(c)(i) to (vii)–

(a) is deceased; or

(b) despite the efforts of the contact trustee detailed in the declaration, cannot be located by the contact trustee; or

(c) has been informed of, and has agreed to provide the information necessary for compliance with, the requirements relating to the provision of information relating to the trust and persons connected with the trust imposed by all of–

(i) the Tax Administration Act 1994:

(ii) the Anti-Money Laundering and Countering Financing of Terrorism Act 2009:

(iii) the regulations made under the Anti-Money Laundering and Countering Financing of Terrorism Act 2009.

59B(5) [Contact trustee must provide details of additions or alterations]

A contact trustee must provide to the Commissioner the details of an addition or alteration to a particular to which subsection (3) refers and any signed declaration under subsection (4) required as a consequence of the addition or alteration.

59B(6) [When contact trustee anticipates ceasing to act]

A contact trustee who anticipates ceasing to be the person communicating with the Commissioner for the trust must provide to the Commissioner the details of–

(a) the anticipated date on which the trustee ceases to be the contact trustee for the foreign trust:

(b) the email address and physical residential address of the trustee after the anticipated date:

(c) the name, email address, and physical residential or business address of the replacement contact trustee for the foreign trust after the anticipated date.

59B(7) [Obligations if more than one resident trustee]

If a foreign trust has more than 1 resident foreign trustee, each resident foreign trustee is responsible for the performance of the obligations imposed on a trustee relating to registration of the trust, disclosure of information, annual returns, financial statements, and payment of fees.

[...]

93B TRUSTEE INCOME: COMMISSIONER'S POWER TO ASSESS

93B(1) [Person failing to disclose details or provide information]

This section applies when a person–

(a) fails to disclose details of a trust under section 59; or

(b) fails to provide information that the Commissioner has asked for under section 17 in relation to a trust; or

(c) is unable to obtain sufficient information to calculate the amount of trustee income in an income year.

93B(2) [Commissioner may determine amount of income]

The Commissioner may determine in a fair and reasonable manner the amount of trustee income for the income year.

143 ABSOLUTE LIABILITY OFFENCES

[...]

143(1B) [When resident foreign trustee excluded from liability – documents]

No person who is a resident foreign trustee may be convicted of an offence against subsection (1)(a) for not keeping documents required to be kept under section 22 if the person proves that–

(a) the person did not know of the requirements of section 22:

(b) another resident foreign trustee has been appointed under section 22(2C) as agent of the resident foreign trustees for the purposes of section 22 and the Commissioner has been notified of the appointment.

[...]

Part 11B

Foreign account information-sharing agreements

185E PURPOSE

185F(1) [Purpose of this Part]

The purpose of this Part is to give effect to and implement foreign account information-sharing agreements.

[...]

185F PERMITTED CHOICES IN RELATION TO FATCA AGREEMENT

185F(1) [Application]

This section applies for a person, as described in the FATCA agreement (the **agreement**), if–

(a) the agreement describes or contemplates a choice or a course of action or inaction (a **permitted choice**) in relation to them:

(b) a choice made by the New Zealand government under the agreement allows, as described or contemplated in the agreement, the person a permitted choice.

185F(2) [Person authorised to make permitted choice]

The person is authorised to make, do, or not do, as described or contemplated by the agreement, the permitted choice, and to do or not do anything necessarily incidental to giving effect to the permitted choice.

185F(3) [Modification of obligations]

The obligations in this Part are modified to the extent necessary to give effect to anything authorised by subsection (2) (*for example:* a permitted choice, authorised by subsection (2), as to using 1 of 2 due diligence procedures contemplated by the agreement means that the chosen procedure would be part of the required due diligence procedures for the purposes of section 185H).

185F(4) [Notice of choice must be published]

The Commissioner must publish an appropriate notice of a choice made or revoked by the New Zealand government under the agreement in a publication chosen by the Commissioner.

185F(5) [Choices treated as part of agreement]

A person's permitted choice and a choice made by the New Zealand government under the agreement are treated as part of the agreement for the purposes of this Part and section BH 1 of the Income Tax Act 2007.

185F(6) [Non-application of subs (2)–(5) to excluded choice]

Subsections (2) to (5) do not apply to a choice or course of action or inaction listed in subsection (7) (an excluded choice).

185F(7) [Excluded choices]

For the purposes of subsection (6), the following are excluded choices:

(a) an election to report on accounts under Annex 1.II.A of the foreign account information-sharing agreement:

(b) an election to report on accounts under Annex 1.III.A of the foreign account information-sharing agreement:

(c) an election to report on accounts under Annex 1.IV.A of the foreign account information-sharing agreement:

(d) an election to report on accounts under Annex 1.V.A of the foreign account information sharing agreement.

185G OBLIGATIONS RELATED TO FATCA AGREEMENT: REGISTRATION

A person, as described in the FATCA agreement (the **agreement**), is required to comply with the relevant registration requirements described or contemplated in the agreement.

185H OBLIGATIONS RELATED TO FATCA AGREEMENT: DUE DILIGENCE

A person, as described in the FATCA agreement (the **agreement**), is required to apply the relevant due diligence procedures described or contemplated in the agreement.

185I OBLIGATIONS RELATED TO THE FATCA AGREEMENT: INFORMATION FOR NZ COMPETENT AUTHORITY

185I(1) [Information that must be obtained and provided]

A person, as described in the FATCA agreement (the **agreement**), must obtain and provide information to the New Zealand competent authority if that information and its providing and obtaining is described or contemplated in the agreement in relation to the person, and including obtaining and providing–

(a) the information that the New Zealand competent authority is obliged to obtain and exchange with a foreign competent authority:

(b) other information that the person is authorised to obtain and provide to the New Zealand competent authority.

185I(2) [Conditions for obtaining and providing information]

Information described in subsection (1) must be obtained and provided in accordance with–

(a) the agreement; and

(b) regulations made by Order in Council by the Governor-General for the purposes of this Part under section 224.

185J OBLIGATIONS RELATED TO FATCA AGREEMENT: INFORMATION FOR THIRD PARTIES

185J(1) [Foreign competent authority]

A person, as described in the FATCA agreement (the **agreement**), must obtain and provide information to a foreign competent authority if that information and its providing and obtaining is described or contemplated in the agreement in relation to the person, and it is validly requested from the person by the foreign competent authority.

185J(2) [Third party]

A person, as described in the agreement, must obtain and provide information to a third party if that information and its providing and obtaining is described or contemplated in the agreement in relation to the person, and the person is authorised to obtain and provide it to the third party (*for example:* an agreement may contemplate a choice to provide certain information to a third party. If the person chooses to provide that information, section 185F applies to authorise that choice. The person would then have to provide that information to the third party in accordance with their choice and the agreement).

185J(3) [Conditions for obtaining and providing information]

Information described in subsections (1) and (2) must be obtained and provided in accordance with–

(a) the agreement; and

(b) regulations made by Order in Council by the Governor-General for the purposes of this Part under section 224.

185K INFORMATION PROVIDED IN FORM PRESCRIBED BY COMMISSIONER

The information in section 185I(1)(a) and (b) must be provided to the New Zealand competent authority in the prescribed form or electronic format.

185L FOREIGN ACCOUNT INFORMATION-SHARING AGREEMENTS: ANTI-AVOIDANCE

(repealed)

185M TIMEFRAMES NOT SPECIFIED

185M(1) [Period to which information must relate]

If an instrument described in section 185I(2)(a) and (b) does not specify, or is discretionary as to, the period to which the information in section 185I(1)(a) and (b) must relate, then the information must relate to a tax year.

185M(2) [Timeframe when information must be provided]

If an instrument described in section 185I(2)(a) and (b) does not specify, or is discretionary as to, a time when the information in section 185I(1)(a) and (b) must be provided, then the information must be provided within 3 months of the end of the period that the information relates to.

CHAPTER 21

Trustee's Liability for Tax

¶21-010 Operating principle

A trustee is personally liable to meet a trust's income tax and GST obligations. Where there is more than one trustee, the liability is joint and several.

¶21-020 A limitation of liability in a deed of trust does not apply between a trustee and Inland Revenue

A trust does not have legal personality independently of its trustees and, except to the extent of any indemnity available, a trustee is personally liable for the consequences of the trustee's actions as if the trustee had acted personally on the trustee's own account.

Although it is common for a deed of trust to limit a trustee's liability to the assets of the trust, such limitations of liability do not protect a trustee from third party creditors such as Inland Revenue or legislative provisions that determine liability. Accordingly, trustees are personally liable to creditors, including Inland Revenue. In *AMP General Insurance Ltd* v *Macalister Todd Phillips Bodkins* [2006] NZSC 105; (2007) 23 NZTC 21,086; (2006) 1 NZTR ¶16-017, the Supreme Court summarised the relevant principles at [42] as follows:

> "In imposing personal liability the tax statutes do no more than recognise the general principle that liabilities incurred by a trustee in relation to a trust are always the personal liabilities of the trustee. This is an aspect of the nature of a trust, which is not a person but an equitable obligation to deal with property for the benefit of beneficiaries. A creditor has a personal right to sue a trustee and to get judgment and make the trustee bankrupt".

¶21-030 A trustee is liable for a trust's income tax

A trustee is personally liable for tax on trustee income: s HC 24. Where there are 2 or more trustees, the liability is joint and several: s HC 2(2). This means that Inland Revenue can seek to recover a tax debt from any trustee, and it is then up to that trustee to seek reimbursement from the trust or any co-trustee(s).

Note that any entitlement to indemnification out of the trust's assets is only available in respect of liabilities properly incurred in the administration of the trust. See *Bayer* v *Balkins* 95 ATC 4609. Also see *Spencer* v *Spencer* [2013] NZCA 449; (2013) 3 NZTR ¶23-014 and *FAI Money Ltd* v *Crawley* [2016] NZCA 219; (2016) 4 NZTR ¶26-006, where a trustee was held personally liable for a debt entered into by his attorney under a power of attorney. The Court of Appeal noted at [31] and [32] that:

> "[31] ... We are satisfied Mr Crawley had no appreciation of his responsibilities as a trustee of the Trusts and took no steps to fulfil his responsibilities in that respect. He was obliged to familiarise himself with the affairs of the Trusts, to take care of their assets, and to act in the best interests of the beneficiaries. Specifically in relation to the matters at issue, he was obliged to ensure he was kept informed about the intention to borrow money from FAI, to satisfy himself this was in the best interests of the beneficiaries, and to verify the accuracy of the details in the statement of position before executing or authorising the execution of the loan documents containing the warranty relied upon by FAI....
>
> [32] As the Judge noted, unlawful behaviour between donor and donee will not prevent the creation of an obligation between donor and a third party dealing with the agent in good faith: *National Australia Finance Ltd* v *Fahey*. It follows that the terms of the loan agreement and the guarantees bind Mr Crawley despite the power of attorney being exercised outside its terms".

The liability for income tax does not differentiate between a trustee that can also benefit from the trust as a beneficiary and an independent or professional trustee who cannot.

Although not explicitly stated in the Income Tax Act, the trustee's personal liability can extend to any taxes that arise from a trading activity, including PAYE, Employer ACC premiums and FBT: *Macalister Todd Phillips Bodkin* v *AMP General Insurance Ltd* (2005) 1 NZTR ¶15-004 at [14]. See further at Chapter 9 – *Trading Trusts*.

¶21-035 Trustees can be imputed with each other's knowledge

If a property is purchased with the intention of resale, the proceeds of sale can be income for income tax purposes. Where there are regular sales and purchases, the question of whether a taxable activity is being carried on for income tax purposes must also be considered.

In *Case* 5/2013 [2013] NZTRA 05; (2013) 26 NZTC ¶2-004, the TRA held that the proceeds of sale derived by trustees that bought and sold 11 properties over 12 years was income, the TRA finding that the properties were acquired for the purpose of intention of sale. The TRA also held that the Trust was in the business of erecting buildings and that the residential land exemption did not apply. The TRA found that the Trust was deemed to be registered for GST and accordingly the Trust was also liable for GST. Also see ¶25-030.

In addition, penalties were applied on the basis of the Trust's gross carelessness for failing to correctly identify the Trust's tax position. The trustees (including the independent professional trustee later replaced with a trustee company) were jointly and severally liable for the income tax, GST and the shortfall penalties.

The independent trustee denied any intention of resale the question for the court required an assessment of whether the trustees can make a collective decision when one trustee is not involved in the decision making. As noted in the decision:

> "[81] The unanimous decision requirement in the Trust Deed requires that the Trustees are unanimous as to the action or decision to be taken which in this case, involved the purchase of land. However, I accept the Commissioner's submission that it does not necessarily follow that the Trustees have to be unanimous as to their intention for the future use of that land for example for resale or development. There may be situations where Trustees have different intentions.
>
> [82] In the present case where there was no unanimous decision the Commissioner argues that Ms X subsequently ratified the various transactions. Resolutions were produced which were signed ratifying some of the transactions. As a number of the conveyancing files have been destroyed, it is not possible to say that a resolution was signed in respect of every transaction however Ms X processed the transactions and in my view, by her actions, she ratified each sale and purchase. Mr Beck submits that there can be no ratification without sufficient knowledge of the transaction. This again is to confuse the decision to purchase with Mr and Mrs B's intentions. For the reasons set out below, I have found that Mr and Mrs B had the intention to sell at the time they entered into the relevant sale and purchase agreement.
>
> [83] Even if that approach is not correct, Ms X knew that Mr and Mrs B were entering into agreements for sale and purchase and building contracts on a regular basis. It was her evidence that she even raised with Mrs B the risk of a tax liability because of the frequency of these transactions. She allowed her co-trustees to enter into these transactions and in my view, she is now estopped from denying that she sanctioned or approved the decisions of Mr and Mrs B.
>
> [84] In the decision of *Boanas*, Dobson J noted that there may be situations where Trustees' intentions are different where for example, there has been a breach of fiduciary obligations. In the present case I have found that Mr and Mrs B entered into the agreements for sale and purchase within their capacities as Trustees of the Trust with the requisite purpose or intention of resale. Ms X adopted a passive role and permitted her co-trustees to operate as decision makers for the Trust and as a consequence, Ms X may have had a different intention. However, a passive trustee cannot delegate their responsibilities in this fashion and I am of the view that in these circumstances, it is the intention of the co-trustees which becomes the intention of the Trust and Ms X cannot set up a different intention from that of her co-trustees.
>
> [85] In any case, I consider that it would be an extraordinary outcome if a trust can simply ignore the unanimous trustee decision requirement in its day to day operation and then be able to take advantage of that requirement when considering its tax obligations. In the present situation I am of the view that Ms X cannot plead her own ignorance of her co-trustees' intentions when she has simply maintained a passive role and permitted Mr and Mrs B to effectively run the Trust particularly knowing as she did, that Mrs B did not understand her responsibilities as a trustee and saw Ms X as simply having a rubber stamping role.
>
> [86] For these reasons I am satisfied that the purpose or intention to sell can be attributed to the Trust".

The exemption in s CD 1(3) of the Income Tax Act 1994 (the applicable Act now for houses occupied "primarily or principally" as family residences) did not apply as the homes were only occupied for a temporary period to enable the homes to be finished, marketed and sold.

¶21-040 The trustee is liable as an agent to pay tax on beneficiary income and taxable distributions

Although a beneficiary is liable to file a tax return, the trustee is generally liable to pay the tax on beneficiary income and taxable distributions as agent of the beneficiary: s HC 32. The beneficiary can claim a credit for the tax paid on the beneficiary's behalf by the trustee.

When the beneficiary is a non-resident, the trustee's liability as an agent is limited to income the beneficiary derives from New Zealand.

If the trustee fails to meet a beneficiary's tax obligations and the beneficiary is a New Zealand resident, the liability for tax falls on the beneficiary: s HD 4.

Beneficiaries of certain community trusts are accountable for their own tax on distributions from community trusts, rather than the trustee being liable for the tax as agent of the beneficiaries. This applies to those community trusts originally established by the Trustee Banks Restructuring Act 1988 due to the restructuring of the trustee bank group: Community Trusts Act 1999, s 4.

Distributions from these community trusts are exempt in the hands of tax-exempt beneficiaries and taxable to other beneficiaries at the beneficiaries' marginal rates of tax. However, taxable beneficiaries of a community trust must account for their own tax on distributions rather than the trustee of the community trust being accountable for the tax as agent of the beneficiaries: s HD 12(1).

¶21-050 A settlor can be liable for income tax as the trustee's agent if there is no resident trustee

A resident settlor (or a deemed settlor, see Chapter 2 – *Settlors*) has a residual liability for income tax if there is no resident trustee. A settlor who is liable for income tax is liable, subject to a number of exceptions, as the trustee's agent. Where there is more than one settlor, liability is joint and several. However, a settlor is not liable for income tax in respect of which the trustee is liable only as an agent under ss HC 29, HC 32. See ¶8-060.

¶21-060 A trustee–shareholder of a qualifying company is liable for the company's income tax

A trustee–shareholder of a qualifying company that elected to be personally liable for the company's income tax before 1 April 2011 is liable for income tax in proportion to the trustee–shareholder's shareholding. However, this rule is modified for trustee–shareholders who are not beneficiaries so that liability for those shareholders is limited to the assets of the trust: ss HA 5, HA 8, HA 28. (See ¶16-250.)

¶21-065 A trustee–shareholder of a look-through company is liable for the company's income tax

A trustee–shareholder of a look-through company ("LTC") that is the owner of look-through interests that elected into the LTC regime is liable for income tax in proportion to the trustee–shareholder's shareholding: ss CB 32B, HB 1, HB 13. See ¶16-130.

¶21-070 A trustee is liable for GST

A trustee is personally liable for unpaid GST. As with income tax, this liability applies equally to trustees who can benefit from the trust and independent or professional trustees. See *Selkirk* v *McIntyre* [2013] NZHC 575; (2013) 26 NZTC ¶21-008.

Although the liability for GST is limited to GST debts incurred while the person is a trustee, liability continues, regardless of whether a person has retired as a trustee, until the person notifies the Commissioner of Inland Revenue in writing that that person is no longer a trustee: Goods and Services Tax Act 1985 (GST Act), s 57. See ¶25-130.

Example

Joseph retired as one of the 3 trustees of the Holly Wear Trust (the Trust) 3 years ago. Alice was appointed as a new trustee on Joseph's retirement under a deed of retirement and appointment of trustee. Joseph telephoned Inland Revenue to advise that he had retired as a trustee. Following Joseph's retirement, the business owned and operated by the Trust has not been well-managed, the Trust's debts now exceed its assets and there are insufficient funds to meet a significant GST liability that was incurred after Joseph's resignation.

Who is liable for the outstanding GST?

A trustee is liable jointly and severally with the co-trustees for any GST liability arising while still a trustee and until that person advises the Commissioner in writing that the person has retired as a trustee.

As Joseph did not advise the Commissioner in writing that he has retired as a trustee, Joseph will be jointly and severally liable with the trustees for the outstanding GST. Although Joseph can seek to be indemnified from the Trust's assets, if the Trust is insolvent, this may not assist Joseph.

¶21-075 A trustee who meets a trust tax liability personally has a right of equitable contribution

When a trustee incurs liability, that trustee can then sue to recover a proportionate share (and, in limited cases, all of the cost) from any co-trustees. The ability to recover from a co-trustee arises from the concept of "equitable right to contribution", which enables any parties who share a liability to share equally in the payment of that liability. This reflects the unfairness that would otherwise be the case should the trustee who happens to be sued be fully liable for the entire amount. Relevantly, in this regard, the comparative culpability of each trustee is not generally a relevant factor.

In the case of *Selkirk* v *McIntyre* [2013] NZHC 575; (2013) 26 NZTC ¶21-008, Mr Selkirk, who personally paid a GST debt owing by a trust, sought to recover the entirety of the GST debt from his co-trustee. Although the normal position is one of equal contribution, there are limited circumstances where one trustee must fully indemnify another. Where this is the case, the paying trustee is entitled to recover the full amount paid from a co-trustee.

The circumstances in which a trustee will be entitled to a full indemnity can arise:

- if one of the trustees is a solicitor, a co-trustee who has relied on that trustee's advice can claim an indemnity from the solicitor-trustee (the **solicitor-trustee rule**)
- where a trustee receives a personal benefit from a breach of trust from which the other trustee(s) did not participate, the trustees are entitled to an indemnity from the defaulting trustee. However, the indemnity is limited to the amount of personal benefit received (the **personal benefit rule**)
- a fraudulent trustee must indemnify any innocent co-trustees – but not any other fraudulent trustees (the **fraudulent trustee rule**)
- a trustee who is also a beneficiary who benefits from a breach of trust is not entitled to an indemnity from any co-trustees to the extent of the trustee-beneficiary's interest (the **trustee-beneficiary rule**). Note that there are divergent views on how the trustee-beneficiary's beneficial interest is accounted for.

Accordingly, to be entitled to an indemnity, a trustee must have acted innocently and reasonably, and there must have been a breach of trust by a co-trustee. A trustee will not be entitled to a full indemnity if the trustee has:

- participated in any breach of trust
- abdicated responsibilities and a breach occurred due to a co-trustee's erroneous actions.

Mr Selkirk sought a full indemnity due to his own lack of culpability, his role as a "passive trustee" and the fact that he had diligently "chased" his co-trustee to get the trust's accounts in order. While it might be argued that a 4-year lapse in addressing the matter mitigated against such diligence (during which time the debt owed to Inland Revenue grew from $93,480.36 to $518,027.94), nothing turned on this point.

Given the evidence available to the Court, the Court could not identify any rule that would ground a full indemnity for Mr Selkirk. The result was that, while his co-trustee was liable to share the cost, Mr Selkirk remained liable for half.

¶21-080 The director and shareholders of a corporate trustee can be liable for income tax and GST

Directors and controlling shareholders are liable for a company's GST and income tax where an arrangement is entered into in relation to a company and an effect of that arrangement is that a company cannot meet income tax and GST liabilities: s HD 15; GST Act, s 61. For a director to be liable in these circumstances, the director must have either known about the arrangement or have derived a benefit from the arrangement. Shareholders can be liable as the company's agent. However, the liability for a shareholder is limited to the greater of the shareholder's interest or the value derived by the shareholder.

Directors of related companies can incur liability for reckless trading when the interests of a related trust are preferred over those of a company. See ¶24-060.

¶21-090 A trustee has no right of indemnity where the trustee has acted in breach of trust

It is a fundamental principle of trust law that a trustee has a right to be indemnified for costs properly incurred in the administration of the trust: *Worrall* v *Harford* (1802) 8 Ves 4; 32 ER 250. Therefore, a trustee who has incurred a personal tax liability can seek indemnification from the trust. For a comprehensive consideration of the principles relating to the trustee's right of indemnity see *Custom Credit Corp Ltd* v *Ravi Nominees Pty Ltd* (1992) 8 WAR 42 at 52, *Lemery Holdings Pty Ltd* v *Reliance Financial Services Pty Ltd* (2008) NSWLR 580 at 553–554.

This right of indemnity is expressed in s 81 of the Trusts Act, which expressly defers to the rules of common law and equity.

However, where the trustee has incurred costs through that trustee's breach of trust, there is no right of indemnity and the trustee is personally liable until the breach of trust has been repaired: *Knott; Bax* v *Palmer* (1887) 56 LJ Ch 318.

Where there is more than one trustee, each trustee is potentially entitled to an indemnity from the trust. This means that even if one trustee has lost the right of indemnity due to that trustee's breach of trust, another trustee's right may remain intact: *In re Firth*; *Newton* v *Rolfe* [1902] 1 Ch 342.

¶21-095 A trustee cannot avoid liability through retirement

Liability already incurred as a trustee cannot be voided through the trustee's retirement. In *Anderson* v *FC of T* 2015 ATC ¶10-387; [2015] AATA 167, a trustee of a family trust owned land that was subdivided in the course of a commercial development project. After the project ran into difficulties, the trustee sold 2 lots from the project and paid the sale proceeds directly to a mortgagee to whom the trustee had given a personal guarantee. The sales were settled on 13 October 2009 and 18 November 2009. The trustee then retired on 9 December 2009. GST was not returned. The taxpayer could not escape liability by virtue of having retired, as the retirement was after the sales were settled.

¶21-100 Legislation

Income Tax Act 2007

HC 2 OBLIGATIONS OF JOINT TRUSTEES FOR CALCULATING INCOME AND PROVIDING RETURNS

HC 2(1) WHAT THIS SECTION APPLIES TO

This section applies for the purposes of the obligations imposed by section BB 2 (Main obligations) on 2 or more persons who derive income jointly as trustees of a trust.

HC 2(2) SINGLE PERSON

The trustees of the trust are treated in that capacity as if they were a notional single person and are jointly and severally liable to satisfy the obligations imposed by section BB 2 on the notional single person.

HC 2(3) RESIDENCE

If no election under section HC 33 is made for the trust, the notional single person referred to in subsection (2) is–

(a) a New Zealand resident when 1 or more of the trustees is resident in New Zealand:

(b) a non-resident when none of the trustees is resident in New Zealand.

[...]

HC 24 TRUSTEES' OBLIGATIONS

HC 24(1) LIABILITY AS INDIVIDUAL FOR TRUSTEE INCOME

A trustee must satisfy the income tax liability for their taxable income as if they were an individual beneficially entitled to the trustee income.

[...]

HC 24(3) BENEFICIARY INCOME OF MINORS

Section HC 35 applies to treat beneficiary income derived by a minor as if it were trustee income.

[...]

HC 29 SETTLORS' LIABILITY TO INCOME TAX

HC 29(1) WHEN THIS SECTION APPLIES

This section applies to a person who makes a settlement to or for the benefit of a trust after 17 December 1987, and the settlor is resident in New Zealand in an income year. It applies whether or not they settled property on the trust on or before that date. Subsections (3) and (4) override this subsection.

HC 29(2) LIABLE AS AGENT

If a trustee of the trust derives trustee income in the income year, the settlor is liable as agent of the trustee for income tax payable by the trustee. For a trust with more than 1 settlor, the liability is joint and several. However, this subsection does not apply to income tax that the trustee is liable for as agent under section HC 32.

HC 29(3) EXCLUSION: RESIDENT TRUSTEE

This section does not apply if the trust has a resident trustee for the full income year or, if the first settlement on the terms of the trust is made during the income year, from the day on which the settlement is made to the end of the income year.

HC 29(4) EXCLUSION: TRUST TYPES

This section does not apply to the settlor of–

(a) a charitable trust; or

(b) a superannuation fund; or

(c) a trust to the extent to which trustee income is derived from the settlor's remitting an amount under a financial arrangement to which section EW 31 or EZ 38 (which relate to base price adjustments) applies.

HC 29(5) EXCLUSION: SETTLOR NOT RESIDENT AT TIME OF SETTLEMENT

This section does not apply if the settlor is a natural person who, unless they make an election under section HC 33,–

(a) is not resident in New Zealand at the time of any settlement on the trust; and

(b) had not after 17 December 1987 previously been resident in New Zealand.

HC 29(6) EXCLUSION: OTHER SETTLOR MORE APPROPRIATELY LIABLE

This section does not apply to the extent to which the settlor establishes, through full disclosure to the Commissioner of the settlements made, that another person who has settled property on the trust should be liable, having regard to the respective settlements made.

HC 29(7) LIMITED EFFECT OF DISCLOSURE

Subsection (6) does not apply to determine whether the tax obligations in relation to the trustee's income tax liability are met for the purposes of section HC 10(1)(a) and (ab) and meeting the requirements for a complying trust.

[...]

HC 32 LIABILITY OF TRUSTEE AS AGENT

HC 32(1) WHEN THIS SECTION APPLIES

This section applies in an income year when a beneficiary of a trust derives an amount of beneficiary income or a taxable distribution.

HC 32(2) EXCLUSION

Subsection (1) does not apply to a person who derives an amount from a community trust.

HC 32(3) AGENCY

In their capacity as agent, the trustee must satisfy the income tax liability of the beneficiary for their beneficiary income and taxable distributions derived.

[...]

HD 4 TREATMENT OF PRINCIPALS

Despite section HD 3,–

(a) a principal remains liable for their tax obligations, and is not released from them merely through the existence of the agency; and

(b) if the Commissioner agrees, the principal and the agent may decide that the principal is to undertake the duties set out in section HD 3(2).

[...]

HD 12 TRUSTS

HD 12(1) BENEFICIARY INCOME AND TAXABLE DISTRIBUTIONS

If a beneficiary of a trust, other than a beneficiary of a community trust, derives an amount of beneficiary income or taxable distribution in a tax year, the trustee of the trust is treated under section HC 32 (Liability of trustee as agent) as the agent of the beneficiary.

HD 12(2) SETTLORS

If a trustee of a trust, other than a charitable trust, derives trustee income in a tax year, and a settlor of the trust is resident in New Zealand in the tax year, the settlor is treated under section HC 29 (Settlors' liability to income tax) as the agent of the trustee for income tax payable by the trustee (but not for income tax that the trustee is liable for as agent).

Goods and Services Tax Act 1985

57 UNINCORPORATED BODIES

[...]

57(3) [Liability of ex-members for tax]

Despite this section, a member is jointly and severally liable with other members for all tax payable by the unincorporated body during the taxable periods, or part of taxable periods as the case may be, the person is a member of the body, even if the person is no longer a member of the body.

57(3A) [Liability of ex-member's estate for tax]

When an individual member dies, the member's estate is severally liable in due course of administration for tax payable by the unincorporated body to the extent that it remains unpaid, whether or not the individual was a member on the date of their death.

57(3B) [Notice to Commissioner]

For the purpose of subsections (3) and (3A), a member does not stop being a member of the unincorporated body until the date on which the Commissioner is notified of a change in membership of the body.

[...]

Trusts Act 2019

81 TRUSTEE'S LIABILITY FOR EXPENSES AND LIABILITIES INCURRED, AND TRUSTEE'S RIGHT TO INDEMNITY

81(1) [Trustee liability is personal]

A trustee is personally liable for an expense or a liability incurred by the trustee when acting as a trustee.

81(2) [Reimbursement or payment from trust property for reasonably incurred expenses]

However, a trustee who incurs an expense or a liability when acting reasonably on behalf of the trust is entitled,—

(a) if the trustee has paid the expense or discharged the liability out of the trustee's own funds, to reimbursement from the trust property; or

(b) in any other case, to pay the expense or discharge the liability directly from the trust property (or to have it paid or discharged by a remaining trustee).

81(3) [Rules of Common law and equity indemnities apply to indemnities]

The operation and enforcement of the indemnity in this section is governed by the rules of the common law and equity relating to trusts.

81(4) [Common law and equitable indemnities not limited]

This section does not limit any indemnity available at common law or in equity.

[...]

Part VI

AVOIDANCE

CHAPTER 22

Avoidance

¶22-010 Operating principle

Whenever a tax advantage arises through the interpolation of a trust, care should be taken to assess the application of the anti-avoidance provisions.

¶22-020 Obtaining a tax advantage can amount to tax avoidance

Trusts allow income that might otherwise be taxed at the trustee rate, or to a beneficiary on the highest marginal rate (currently 39% while the trust rate is a flat 33%), to be diverted to a beneficiary on a lower marginal rate. This is the case whether the trust is actively trading or a passive investor. When the top marginal rate is higher than the trustee rate, trusts allow the amount of income tax payable in respect of any income derived by the trust to be capped at the trustee rate (rather than the rate applicable to beneficiaries on a higher marginal rate).

Accordingly, the anti-avoidance provisions of the Income Tax Act 2007 are an important element in tax-planning considerations. See further Chapter 24 – *Asset Planning.*

The general anti-avoidance provision has 2 components. The first provides for a tax avoidance arrangement (s YA 1) to be voided against the Commissioner for income tax purposes (s BG 1) and the second allows for any tax advantage under the arrangement to be counteracted: s GA 1.

The general anti-avoidance measure is complemented by specific tax regimes that have the effect of re-characterising any arrangement in contravention of those provisions to a transaction that is conducted at arm's length: Subparts GB, GC. These general and specific anti-avoidance provisions, neither of which override the other, work in tandem.

The Goods and Services Tax Act 1985 has its own general anti-avoidance provision in s 76 of that Act. See Chapter 25 – *Goods and Services Tax.*

Separately, when the 39% marginal rate was reintroduced in 2020, the Government also enacted new reporting obligations for trustees. See Chapter 20 – *Disclosure and Reporting Obligations.* In the media statement that accompanied the re-introduction of the 39% tax rate, Revenue Minister David Parker said:

> "the Government is aware that some people may seek to escape the higher tax rate and shelter their income in trusts, and commentators often make such comments when changes to the top tax rate are proposed.

'This bill includes powers to collect information from trustees to test compliance and the effective operation of the 39 per cent tax rate and to further understand what trustees do with trust assets and income,' David Parker said.

'If trusts are used for the sole purpose of paying a lower tax rate, it is unfair to all those New Zealanders that pay the right amount of tax. If there is evidence of this type of behaviour we will move on it'."

¶22-030 Tax avoidance is defined broadly

For the purposes of the Income Tax Act, a "tax avoidance arrangement" is defined in s YA 1 as an arrangement that has tax avoidance as:

- its purpose or effect, or
- one of its purposes or effects, whether or not any other purpose or effect is referable to ordinary business or family dealings, if the tax avoidance purpose or effect is not merely incidental.

"Tax avoidance" is defined in s YA 1 to include directly or indirectly:

- altering the incidence of income tax
- relieving any person from liability to pay income tax
- avoiding, reducing or postponing any liability to income tax.

The breadth of the definition makes it difficult to determine with any certainty the demarcation between acceptable "tax planning" and unacceptable "tax avoidance" that is subject to anti-avoidance provisions.

¶22-040 The general anti-avoidance provisions are complemented with specific provisions

Specific anti-avoidance provisions complement the specific tax regimes contained elsewhere in the Income Tax Act. Specific anti-avoidance provisions that have application to a trustee include the following:

- Section GB 5, which provides that where there is a change in the beneficiaries of a trust under an arrangement that has a purpose or effect of defeating the intent and application of any of the continuity provisions, there is a deemed disposition by the trustee of the share or option to an unrelated third party and an immediate reacquisition.
- Section GB 22, which operates to prevent a trustee from transferring property or providing services or benefits to a person other than a beneficiary to avoid the beneficiary receiving beneficiary income. Where s GB 22 applies, the property, services or benefits are deemed to be received by the beneficiary.
- Attribution rules that apply to attribute personal services income back to the person who carries out the services when an interposed entity such as a trust is the contracting party: ss GB 27–GB 29; also see Chapter 23 – *Attribution*.

- Section GB 31, which operates to avoid circumventing the FBT rules, can have application where a trustee employs a beneficiary. In such situations, care must be taken when a beneficiary employed by a trust can receive distributions that would otherwise be a fringe benefit, to determine whether the distribution should more correctly be characterised as a fringe benefit.
- Section GB 53, which provides an anti-avoidance provision with respect to the use of trusts with a purpose or effect of defeating the intent and application of the bright-line test for residential land by providing that the trustees are treated as disposing of the trust residential land for an amount of consideration equal to the market value of the land at the time of the change.
- Section GB 55, which provides for the Commissioner to reduce a tax credit for charitable or other public benefit gifts when an arrangement has a purpose or effect of defeating the intent and application of s LD 1.

¶22-050 There is no specific anti-avoidance provision that re-characterises a below market salary

The Commissioner has broad powers to treat excessive salary or wages or share of profits as income in the hands of the recipient and to treat certain payments as a dividend for tax purposes: s GB 23. However, although there is no corollary position that allows a below market salary to be re-characterised where a below market salary is paid, the general anti-avoidance provision may have application. See ¶22-060.

¶22-060 Application of anti-avoidance provisions to trusts

The point at which permissible tax planning becomes tax avoidance can be difficult to discern as each case will turn on its own facts.

Until recently, different outcomes from seemingly similar arrangements make it difficult to form clear guidelines regarding when an arrangement involving a trust will amount to tax avoidance: *Penny* v *C of IR*; *Hooper* v *C of IR* (2009) 24 NZTC 23,406, *Case* W33 (2004) 21 NZTC 11,321, *Case* V20 (2002) 20 NZTC 10,233, *C of IR* v *Penny and Hooper* [2010] NZCA 231; (2010) 24 NZTC 24,287, *White* v *C of IR* (2010) 24 NZTC 24,600. However, in *Penny and Hooper* v *C of IR* [2011] NZSC 95; (2011) 3 NZTR ¶21-014, the Supreme Court stated clearly that even if specific anti-avoidance provisions are complied with, it is the totality of the arrangement that must be considered. So, for example, low salaries or low charges would be more likely to constitute a tax avoidance arrangement if they departed from ordinary business practice or were more than merely incidental to the wider context of the arrangement.

That said, the decided cases do highlight the matters that are taken into consideration.

As a general proposition, the divide between tax planning and tax avoidance is at risk of being crossed when a business is established or restructured for tax reasons. This risk is increased where the arrangement cannot be justified in the context of ordinary family or business dealings. In *Mangin* v *C of IR* 70 ATC 6001, the restructure of a farming operation that involved a different paddock being leased to a family trust each year amounted to tax avoidance. In *Ashton* v *C of IR* (1975) 2 NZTC 61,030 (PC), the interpolation of a trust into an existing trading structure by an accounting firm was also found to be tax avoidance.

Case W33 (supra) (earlier reported as *Case* V20 (supra)) is another example where a restructure was found to be tax avoidance. However, in this case, it was accepted that the restructure could have been effected in an acceptable manner, from an avoidance perspective. In *Case* W33, a dentist who practiced in partnership with another dentist, restructured his practice. The dentist settled a trust and sold his share of the practice to the trust. The dentist then entered into an employment contract with the trust and was paid an annual salary of $80,000, which was significantly less than his past years' earnings. The income derived by the trust was distributed among the beneficiaries, which resulted in tax savings.

Although the amount of tax savings was not significant, the arrangement was found to have a purpose or effect of tax avoidance. The tax avoidance arose because the income tax that would have been paid by the dentist had been altered and his liability for income tax had been relieved in part as his income had been reduced by the arrangement.

In the course of its final judgment, the TRA said at 11,329–11,330 [41] that:

> "It must be possible for the dentist to reconstruct his trading partnership into a structure of his choice for the reasons of severing his business relationship from his dentistry partner and for the reason of general asset protection. That seems to have come down to a choice between operating as a dentist in sole practice, or incorporation of his dental practice, or establishing a trading trust (which is a combination of incorporation and establishment of a trust, and indeed, incorporation probably would have involved a family trust also) to own his dental practice. However, any reconstruction needs to have been on a sensible and normal, or ordinary, business or family basis. Fundamental to that is payment to the dentist of a market salary (in relation to all the circumstances) upon his becoming an employee".

Penny and Hooper v *C of IR* (supra) involves an arrangement where orthopaedic surgeons who were each conducting their own practice restructured their affairs with a result that through the payment of significantly reduced salaries the taxpayers' former incomes were largely diverted to family trusts. No reasons were given by the trustees or companies to explain the payment of significantly reduced salaries following the restructure.

Initially, both Mr Penny and Mr Hooper had conducted practices on their own account. Subsequently, each set up a company to purchase their practice. The majority interest in each company was owned by a family trust. Mr Penny and Mr Hooper were each paid a substantially lower salary following the new arrangement with the balance of the practice income in each case being treated as company income and paid by way of shareholder dividend to the family trusts.

The Commissioner considered that improper advantage was made of the difference between the company tax rate of 33 cents in the dollar and the higher marginal tax rate of 39 cents in the dollar applicable at the time.

The High Court concluded that the arrangement as a whole was not one that had the purpose or effect of tax avoidance or, if it did, any such purpose or effect was merely incidental to the purpose of adopting the corporate form of practice. The Court accepted the taxpayers' case that the formal structures adopted by the taxpayers were a legitimate choice for the conduct of their businesses. Accordingly, the Court found that the arrangement was not contrary to the scheme and purpose of the Income Tax Act 1994 and that the allocation of a commercially realistic salary was not a concept recognised by the Act.

On appeal the majority of the Court of Appeal found that the avoidance of tax was more than a merely incidental purpose or effect of the arrangement. The salaries adopted were so far removed from commercial reality as to be contrived and artificial and could not be regarded as within the acceptable limits of commercial practice. The Court said that it could not have been within the contemplation of Parliament that a company director/employee could adopt a salary of less than one-fifth of a proper commercial salary and thereby secure significant tax advantages while still receiving, in practical terms, the benefit of the company's entire income for himself and his family.

The Supreme Court agreed with the finding of the Court of Appeal and favoured looking at the wider context of the arrangement. It said that even if specific anti-avoidance provisions are complied with, the wider arrangement may still involve avoidance. In this case, the artificially low salaries were more likely to constitute a tax avoidance arrangement because they departed from ordinary business practice and also were more than merely incidental to the wider context of the arrangement.

By contrast in *White* v *C of IR* (supra), over-turning the TRA decision reported as *Case* Z24 (2010) 24 NZTC 14,354, the High Court found that an arrangement whereby an anaesthetist could entirely offset her salary against orchard losses was not tax avoidance. A doctor being employed by a company involved in an orchard enterprise in circumstances where no salary could be paid to the doctor was not tax avoidance.

In *White*, the Court distinguished the decision in *Penny and Hooper* on the basis that, in *Penny and Hooper*, there were funds to pay a salary. However, in *White*, no salary was paid because the interposed "employer" company had no funds to do so, Dr White's income having been diverted to pay real, not contrived, debts.

As can be seen from the decided cases, every case will fall to be determined on its own merits, the legitimacy of the arrangement and the steps that comprise each arrangement being assessed both individually and together.

¶22-065 There is no specific anti-avoidance provision that re-characterises loan advances

Loans to a beneficiary are a common feature of trusts. However, it is possible for a loan advance to be re-characterised as a tax avoidance arrangement if the loan can be reconstructed as income.

In *Krukziener* v *C of IR (No 3)* (2010) 24 NZTC 24,563, a taxpayer property investor and developer who operated through a group of companies and trading trusts unsuccessfully argued that undocumented advances to him of over $5 million were loans and did not comprise a tax avoidance arrangement. The Commissioner considered that the funds were part of a tax-avoidance arrangement and should be reconstructed as income, rendering the taxpayer liable for both income tax and penalties.

The High Court found that the ever-increasing level of advances, coupled with the relative lack of repayments over a long period of time, suggested a deliberate plan that there would be no requirement for the taxpayer to repay the advances unless and until there was a capital distribution available to apply for that purpose. The pattern of advances and repayments pointed to an arrangement and examining each year in isolation did not change this.

¶22-070 Case law assists in developing factors that will indicate avoidance

Clearly the topic of tax avoidance, and the application of a general anti-avoidance provision to any particular fact situation, is a notoriously difficult area of tax law.

Although care must be taken to avoid focusing on "judicial gloss" rather than the wording of the anti-avoidance provisions, a review of the leading anti-avoidance cases allows the development of some guiding principles and propositions:

- A scheme and purpose approach does not simply require the court to focus on the specific provision in isolation of wider considerations. This wider approach was seen to follow from normal principles of statutory construction and could take into account, for example, the commercial nature of the transaction or whether the taxpayer had suffered the economic burden of the expenditure: *Ben Nevis Forestry Ventures Ltd* v *C of IR*; *Accent Management Ltd* v *C of IR* [2008] NZSC 115; (2009) 24 NZTC 23,188.
- An arrangement includes all its steps and the related transactions by which the arrangement is carried out. Tax avoidance can be found in individual steps or a combination of steps. However, even if no individual step amounts to tax avoidance, the combination of steps can amount to tax avoidance: *Ben Nevis*.
- Ascertaining when an arrangement crosses the line between a permissible arrangement and tax avoidance is firmly grounded in the statutory language. The correct approach involves an objective application of a process of statutory construction rather than subjective impressions of morality: *Ben Nevis*.
- The general anti-avoidance provision cannot be used to strike down arrangements only because they involve appropriate use of specific provisions. However, there is a point at which the permissible use of specific provisions ends and tax avoidance begins: *Ben Nevis*.
- Where the use of a specific provision has altered the incidence of tax in a way that cannot have been within Parliamentary contemplation when it enacted the provision, the arrangement will be a tax avoidance arrangement: *Ben Nevis*.

- It is necessary to assess whether the arrangement, viewed in a commercially and economically realistic way, makes use of the specific provision in a manner that is consistent with Parliament's purpose: *Ben Nevis*, *White* v *C of IR* (supra). Also see *Case* 5/2019 [2019] NZTRA 5; (2019) 29 NZTC ¶5-004 at [58], where Sinclair J noted that "there would appear to be no commercial or family purpose for three trusts to subsequently be settled and for the income rights to be transferred successively from one trust to the next as has occurred".
- The structure represents a suitable structure within which to operate a viable business. There is no suggestion that the trust was a sham: *Case* Z22 (2010) 24 NZTC 14,305.
- The general anti-avoidance provision does not limit the matters that may be taken into account when determining whether a tax avoidance arrangement exists. Factors considered could include:
    - the manner in which the arrangement is carried out
    - the economic and commercial effects
    - the duration of the arrangement, or
    - the nature and extent of financial consequences: *Ben Nevis.*
- A classic indicator of use that is outside Parliamentary contemplation is an arrangement where advantage is taken of a specific provision in an artificial or contrived way. Other indicia of tax avoidance include:
    - artificial arrangements that have tax induced features outside the realm of normal practice: *C of IR* v *BNZ Investments Ltd* (2001) 20 NZTC 17,103 (CA)
    - elements of pretence: *C of IR* v *Challenge Corporation Ltd* (1986) 8 NZTC 5,219 (PC)
    - planned measures that degrade the tax base: *AMP Life Ltd* v *C of IR* (2000) 19 NZTC 15,940
    - absence of commerciality, for example, external borrowings attracting interest at commercial rates being advanced interest free to a beneficiary. See *Krukziener* v *C of IR (No 3)* (supra).
- The technical legality of the constituent parts of the arrangement will not prevent a finding of avoidance: *Glenharrow Holdings Ltd* v *C of IR* [2008] NZSC 116; (2009) 24 NZTC 23,236.
- It is not the function of s BG 1 to supplement the specific provisions by preventing arrangements that are objectively within the scheme and purpose of the legislation, but which are contrary to some other subjective notion of morality: *Penny* v *C of IR*; *Hooper* v *C of IR* (2009) 24 NZTC 23,406; (2009) 2 NZTR ¶19-015.

However, also see the decision of the Supreme Court on appeal in *Penny and Hooper* v *C of IR* [2011] NZSC 95; (2011) 3 NZTR ¶21-014.

¶22-080 The difference between the trustee tax rate and lower marginal tax rates means trusts are vulnerable to anti-avoidance consideration

An income-producing structure that includes a trust should be assessed in light of the anti-avoidance provisions due to the inherent ability to manipulate and cap the applicable tax rate.

Every case will turn on its facts and, accordingly, it is important to appreciate that there is no "fail-safe structure". Particular care is required to review arrangements in light of the relevant legislation, while taking consideration of the guidance provided by the decided cases.

Inland Revenue has issued a QWBA ("questions we've been asked" QB 15/11: "Income tax – Scenarios on tax avoidance – 2015", which can be found in *Tax Information Bulletin* ¶2710-107 Vol 27, No 10, November 2015) and which provides guidance as to whether a trustee exercising a discretion to distribute trustee income (that would be taxed at the trustee rate of 33% if retained by the trustee) to a beneficiary on a lower tax rate, a beneficiary with tax losses or a beneficiary to whom the income will be tax exempt can represent tax avoidance.

While finding that the scenarios in the QWBA are not avoidance arrangements for the purposes of the Income Tax Act, the QWBA also provides some useful guidance as to arrangements involving trusts that could be considered tax avoidance. In this regard, the points made in the QWBA are that arrangements that might invite speculation as to whether "in commercial and economic reality" the trustees have distributed income to a beneficiary.

Points to consider include:

- timing of addition and removal of beneficiaries
- how and when income is distributed
- any facts that indicate that the trustees have retained the use and benefit of the income, and
- any facts indicating whether there is a realistic prospect of beneficiaries ever benefitting from the income.

As noted in QB 15/11:

> "95. On their own there may be nothing inherently wrong with any one of these factors. For instance, the fact that in any income year the trustees have resolved to pay beneficiary distributions by credit to account and retain the funds for use within the trust would not, on its own, indicate Parliament's purposes for the distribution of beneficiary income were not being given effect. However, in some cases, a combination of the above facts may raise doubts as to whether, in commercial and economic reality, the trustees have made a distribution of income to a beneficiary.
>
> 96. Although argued under provisions other than the trust rules, *Krukziener* v *CIR (No 3)* (2010) 24 NZTC 24,563 (HC) is an example of where, in the context of s BG 1, a court

> clearly considered that the commercial and economic reality of an arrangement was that the use and benefit of income distributed by trustees was enjoyed by a person other than the beneficiaries nominated to receive the distributions".

Given the number of family trusts where beneficiary current accounts are retained for long periods of time (and where beneficiaries may not even know they have current accounts), the third and fourth points above may give some trustees pause – and perhaps correctly so.

¶22-090 Consequence of tax avoidance

Where tax avoidance occurs, the Commissioner of Inland Revenue has the power to adjust assessable income, deductions and available net losses so as to counteract any tax advantage: s GA 1.

For a more comprehensive discussion and analysis of tax avoidance, see James Coleman *Tax Avoidance Law in New Zealand* (Edition 2, CCH, Auckland, 2013).

¶22-100 There is no specific anti-avoidance regime that applies to trusts in the context of child support

Where a liable parent's level of earnings subject to a formula assessment are reduced due to the interpolation of a trust, this can give grounds for a departure order:

> "The evidence is conclusive that the [father] has deliberately undertaken a course of action designed to reduce his liability for child support".

See *EJV* v *AJCB* [2013] NZCA 100; (2013) 26 NZTC ¶21-012, *B* v *X* (2011) 25 NZTC ¶20-034. See also Child Support Act 1991, ss 104–107.

The Commissioner of Inland Revenue may also initiate a review of a formula assessment of child support under Pt 6B of the Child Support Act if an investigation into a liable parent's affairs shows that the assessment does not accurately reflect the parent's ability to provide financial support to his or her children. In the case of *Kelly* v *C of IR* [2013] NZFC 4248, a partially successful Commissioner-initiated review was carried out where substantial assets were owned in trust. However, the liable parent declared no income.

¶22-110 There is no specific anti-avoidance regime that applies to trusts in the context of the minor beneficiary rules

The minor beneficiary rule, which requires distributions to minors to be taxed at the trustee rate, unless an exemption applies, is an anti-avoidance measure that was introduced to avoid income splitting between parents and children.

Where arrangements that defeat the application of the minor beneficiary rule are made, consideration should be given to the application of the general anti-avoidance provisions.

Arrangements that might come under the scope of these provisions could include:

- multiple trusts being settled, each making annual distributions of $1,000 or less to the same minor beneficiaries
- treating distributions to minor beneficiaries as loans for accounting purposes and making an income distribution once the minor beneficiary rule no longer applies to cancel out the overdrawn current account and "repay" the earlier loans.

See ¶10-060, ¶10-250.

¶22-120 Elements of avoidance may need to be considered in the context of sham transactions

The concept or doctrine of sham is long-standing and has been developed by courts over time. In his article, "Sham, trusts and mutual intention" [2008] NZLJ 227, Matthew Conaglen observes:

> "For well over two hundred years, the courts have refused to permit sham transactions – transactions which were created as "a mere cloak or screen for another transaction" (*Yorkshire Railway Wagon Co* v *Maclure* (1882) 21 ChD 309 at 318) – to conceal the truth. They have asserted a jurisdiction to "see through" (ibid) such transactions to get at "the real truth of the matter" (*Re Watson* (1890) 25 QBD 27 at 33).
>
> ...
>
> The jurisdiction to ignore sham transactions is a jurisdiction of general application".

The New Zealand case law on sham was summarised by the Supreme Court in *Ben Nevis* (supra). In *Ben Nevis*, the Supreme Court stated at [33]:

> "There is no need for us to engage in any extended discussion of what constitutes a sham for present purposes. In essence, a sham is a pretence. It is possible to derive the following propositions from the leading authorities. A document will be a sham when it does not evidence the true common intention of the parties. They either intend to create different rights and obligations from those evidenced by the document or they do not intend to create any rights or obligations, whether of the kind evidenced by the document or at all. A document which originally records the true common intention of the parties may become a sham if the parties later agree to change their arrangement but leave the original document standing and continue to represent it as an accurate reflection of their arrangement".

Also see *Snook* v *London & West Riding Investments Ltd* [1967] 2 QB 786, *Paintin and Nottingham Ltd* v *Miller Gale and Winter* [1971] NZLR 164, *NZI Bank Ltd* v *Euro-National Corporation Ltd* [1992] 3 NZLR 528 (CA) and *Clayton* v *Clayton (Vaughan Road Property Trust)* [2016] NZSC 29; (2016) 4 NZTR ¶26-002.

Where a sham exists – such that the legal rights and obligations created by the documents that evidence the sham and that are intended to mislead third parties – any tax consequences that might result due to avoidance or similar also need to be considered. When considering allegations of sham, the courts are concerned with the parties' subjective intentions, and not with the economic substance or commercial reality of the transaction.

In *Ben Nevis* v *C of IR* (supra), the Court emphasised that the character of the transaction as being determined by the "true meaning of all provisions" of the documents, not the labels adopted in those documents. The Court stated at [48] that:

> "... it is the true meaning of all provisions in a contract that will determine the character of a transaction rather than the label given to it. The label "licence premium" is accordingly not what is important in the present case, but rather the true contractual nature of the legal rights for which payment is to be made and the effect of applying the tax legislation to a payment of that character".

For further discussion on the interpretation of contractual documents, see: *Vector Gas Ltd* v *Bay of Plenty Energy Ltd* [2010] NZSC 5; (2010) 9 NZBLC 102,874, *Yoshimoto* v *Canterbury Golf International Ltd* [2000] NZCA 350, *Boat Park Ltd* v *Hutchinson* [1999] 2 NZLR 74 (CA).

Sham is not the same as tax avoidance. This was emphasised by the Supreme Court in *Ben Nevis*, where the Court noted at [34] that:

> "It is important to keep firmly in mind the difference between sham and avoidance. A sham exists when documents do not reflect the true nature of what the parties have agreed. Avoidance occurs, even though the documents may accurately reflect the transaction which the parties intend to implement, when, for reasons to be discussed more fully below, the arrangement entered into gives a tax advantage which Parliament regards as unacceptable".

The fact the transactions concerned involved or facilitated tax avoidance does not mean they were shams. Similarly, in *Accent Management Ltd* v *C of IR* [2007] NZCA 230; (2007) 23 NZTC 21,323, the Court of Appeal held that the concepts of sham and tax avoidance are not correlatives.

This means that a transaction can be a "tax avoidance arrangement" under s BG 1 without being a sham. Similarly, a transaction can be a sham without being a "tax avoidance arrangement". If a transaction involves tax avoidance, but the documents reflect the true nature of what the parties have agreed, the Commissioner can only challenge it under s BG 1 (or any other anti-avoidance provision).

See interpretation guidelines IG 12/01: "Goods and Services Tax; Income Tax – 'Sham'" and *Tax Information Bulletin* ¶247-102 Vol 24, No 7, August 2012.

It is important to consider contemporary views as to what can constitute a sham or a transaction or transactions that obfuscate true intentions. The judgment in *Full-Circle Staffing, LLC, Watchman Investment Trust, Financial & Tax Services, Inc, Trustee, Tax Matters Partner, et al v Commissioner of Internal Revenue* Docket Nos 12883-15, 17279-15, 17280-15, 17281-15, 17282-15, 21187-15, 5053-16. Filed May 17, 2018 (Full Circle) is a consolidated judgment of the United States Tax Court that warrants consideration in light of how taxing authorities can view arrangements, particularly in the context of restructuring. The background facts of Full Circle can be summarised as follows:

- Mr and Mrs Pudlo restructured their freight forwarding business interests on advice following an Inland Revenue Service audit. It was later determined that they were naïve, but not dishonest with respect to paying income tax on business income that was given to charity (as to 11%) with the balance reinvested in the business.

- The structure included a limited partnership, an irrevocable trust (Watchman) and a charitable trust (Lighthouse).
- Watchman was a discretionary trust settled by a nominee settlor with a third party corporate service provider acting as trustee. The Pudlos were initially named as beneficiaries; subsequently the sole beneficiary was Lighthouse (described in the decision as a vehicle through which the Pudlos could make anonymous charitable donations).
- Watchman was funded by the Pudlos.
- Watchman's trustee was expressly prohibited from participating in Limited (the business in which it was a 94% shareholder).
- Watchman did not have a bank account and so funds to be paid to it were paid by way of cheque from Limited, which would be endorsed to Lighthouse.

The structure adopted was tax effective. During the years in question $900,000 (11% of reported income) was paid to charity. However, no tax was paid in respect of the charitable distributions or the income from the freight forwarding business.

The decision in Full Circle could be considered simply by reference to its tax effects, it is of interest that the sham findings were largely attributable to the control retained by the Pudlos. However, given the relatively recent decision in *JSC Mezhdunarodniy Promyshlenniy Bank* v *Pugachev* [2017] EWHC 2426 (Ch), which related to 5 New Zealand foreign trusts, whether intention can be considered entirely separately to retention of absolute control, such that a trust where absolute control is retained remains valid because a trust is intended, may warrant re-visiting.

In the Full-Circle decision, the United States Tax Court approached the question of sham from a tax perspective by reference to whether:

- the taxpayer's relationship to the property transferred to the trust materially changed after the trust's creation
- the trust has an independent trustee
- an economic interest passed to other trust beneficiaries, and
- the taxpayer feels bound by the restrictions imposed by the trust agreement or the law of trusts. See *Markosian* v *Commissioner* (1980) 73 TC 1235 at 1243–1244.

If a trust lacks economic substance apart from tax considerations, the trust is a sham and is not recognized for Federal tax purposes. See Full-Circle, at 29. However, a trust can be a sham for tax purposes, but remain valid at law. See Full-Circle, at 28.

To establish whether a trust has economic substance, the relevant consideration is whether the [settlor's] relationship to the property transferred to the trust materially changes. See Full-Circle, at 29 and 30 where it is noted that:

> "For purposes of the economic substance of a trust, the Court looks to the economic realities of the trust arrangement to determine who is the true creator, grantor, or settlor of the trust; we look beyond the named settlor to the true settlor. Zmuda v. Commissioner, 79 T.C. at 720–721".

The absence of an independent trustee was significant, in that there was no one to protect the beneficiaries' interests.

Note: From a Commonwealth perspective, this aspect of the test essentially references the inherent jurisdiction of the [High Court] to protect beneficiaries' interests and the question as to whether a trust is intended.

The practical aspects of the decision echo the judgment in *Rosebud Trustee*, where matters such as inappropriate interpolation of family members, lack of a bank account and third-party control were indicia of a sham.

The ability to loan trust principal or income without adequate security or other consideration indicated that the taxpayer was not bound by the restrictions imposed by the trust. This echoes the true effects arguments raised in *Mezhprom Bank v Pugachev*. An observation further underscored by the tax judges need to review any factors that shed light on the "parties' true intent" including "... the parties' agreement, their conduct in the agreement's execution, their statements, the testimony of disinterested persons, the relationship of the parties, their respective abilities and capital contributions, the actual control of income, the purposes for which the income is used...": Full Circle, at 36.

¶22-125 Property settlements onto trust can be deemed to be trustee income

An effective anti-avoidance provision in s HC 7(3) provides that settlements onto a trust that have the effect of avoiding a tax impost are deemed to be trustee income.

Property settled on to a trust from the trustee of another trust is deemed to be trustee income in the hands of the recipient trustee to the extent that the property would represent beneficiary income or a taxable distribution if distributed to a New Zealand resident beneficiary (s HC 4(3)).

Property settled on to a trust for which the settlor is allowed a deduction is also deemed to be trustee income (s HC 4(4)) as is property settled on to a trust that would, but for the settlement, have constituted settlor income, whether the settlor is resident in New Zealand. See s HC 4(5)(a) and (c)).

Property settlements that are deemed to be trustee income are treated as income derived by the trustee in the income year corresponding to the settlement and are excluded from the definition of corpus.

When a settlement is excluded from corpus, it is included in trustee income for the income year in which the settlement occurred, unless the income is distributed to a beneficiary in the same income year. If the trustee distributes this income as beneficiary income or a taxable distribution in the same income year, the amount of trustee income for a settlement excluded from corpus will be reduced by the amount of that distribution.

¶22-130 Legislation

Income Tax Act 2007

BG 1 TAX AVOIDANCE

BG 1(1) AVOIDANCE ARRANGEMENT VOID

A tax avoidance arrangement is void as against the Commissioner for income tax purposes.

BG 1(2) RECONSTRUCTION

Under Part G (Avoidance and non-market transactions), the Commissioner may counteract a tax advantage that a person has obtained from or under a tax avoidance arrangement.

[...]

GA 1 COMMISSIONER'S POWER TO ADJUST

GA 1(1) WHEN THIS SECTION APPLIES

This section applies if an arrangement is void under section BG 1 (Tax avoidance).

GA 1(2) COMMISSIONER'S GENERAL POWER

The Commissioner may adjust the taxable income of a person affected by the arrangement in a way the Commissioner thinks appropriate, in order to counteract a tax advantage obtained by the person from or under the arrangement.

GA 1(3) COMMISSIONER'S SPECIFIC POWER OVER TAX CREDITS

The Commissioner may–

(a) disallow some or all of a tax credit of a person affected by the arrangement; or

(b) allow another person to benefit from some or all of the tax credit.

GA 1(4) COMMISSIONER'S IDENTIFICATION OF HYPOTHETICAL SITUATION

When applying subsections (2) and (3), the Commissioner may have regard to 1 or more of the amounts listed in subsection (5) which, in the Commissioner's opinion, had the arrangement not occurred, the person–

(a) would have had; or

(b) would in all likelihood have had; or

(c) might be expected to have had.

GA 1(5) RECONSTRUCTED AMOUNTS

The amounts referred to in subsection (4) are–

(a) an amount of income of the person:

(b) an amount of deduction of the person:

(c) an amount of tax loss of the person:

(d) an amount of tax credit of the person.

GA 1(6) NO DOUBLE COUNTING

When applying subsection (2), if the Commissioner includes an amount of income or deduction in calculating the taxable income of the person, it must not be included in calculating the taxable income of another person.

GA 1(7) MEANING OF TAX CREDIT

In this section, **tax credit** means a reduction in the tax a person must pay because of–

(a) a credit allowed for a payment by the person of an amount of tax or of another item; or

(b) another type of benefit.

[...]

GB 5 ARRANGEMENTS INVOLVING TRUST BENEFICIARIES

GB 5(1) WHEN THIS SECTION APPLIES

This section applies when–

(a) a share in a company or option over a share in a company is held by a trustee; and

(b) a change occurs in the beneficiaries of the trust; and

(c) a purpose or effect of the change is to defeat the intent and application of a continuity provision.

GB 5(2) TRUSTEE TREATED AS DISPOSING OF SHARE OR OPTION

The trustee is treated as having disposed of the share or option to an unrelated person at the time of the change in beneficiaries, and as having reacquired it immediately afterwards.

GB 5(3) LIMITED APPLICATION OF SUBSECTION (2)

Subsection (2) applies only for the purposes of the application of the rules in sections YC 2 (Voting interests) and YC 3 (Market value interests) in the case of the continuity provisions.

[...]

GB 22 ARRANGEMENTS INVOLVING TRUST BENEFICIARY INCOME

GB 22(1) WHEN THIS SECTION APPLIES

This section applies when–

(a) an arrangement involves a trustee transferring property, or providing services or other benefits, to a person other than a beneficiary of the trust; and

(b) the arrangement has the effect of defeating the intent and application of sections HC 17 to HC 23 (which relate to the income of beneficiaries) in relation to the beneficiary; and

(c) the trust is not a Maori authority.

GB 22(2) APPLICATION OF SECTIONS HC 17 TO HC 23

The beneficiary is treated, for the purposes of sections HC 17 to HC 23, as receiving the property or enjoying the services or benefits.

[...]

GB 31 FBT ARRANGEMENTS: GENERAL

GB 31(1) WHEN THIS SECTION APPLIES

This section applies when–

(a) 2 or more persons enter into an arrangement; and

(b) a purpose or effect of the arrangement is to defeat the intent and application of any of the FBT rules; and

(c) the purpose or effect is not merely incidental.

GB 31(2) FBT RULES TREATED AS APPLYING

For the purposes of the FBT rules, the Commissioner may treat–

(a) a party to the arrangement (the **provider**) as the employer of a person (the **recipient**) of whom the Commissioner notifies the provider:

(b) the recipient as the employee of the provider:

(c) a benefit as being provided by the provider to the recipient through the employment of the recipient.

GB 31(3) ACTUAL OR LIKELY BENEFIT

The Commissioner may apply subsection (2)(c) only in the case of a benefit that,–

(a) is in fact provided by the provider to the recipient; or

(b) had the arrangement not occurred, the recipient–

 (i) would have obtained; or

(ii) would in all likelihood have obtained; or

(iii) might be expected to have obtained.

[...]

YA 1 DEFINITIONS

[...]

tax avoidance includes–

(a) directly or indirectly altering the incidence of any income tax:

(b) directly or indirectly relieving a person from liability to pay income tax or from a potential or prospective liability to future income tax:

(c) directly or indirectly avoiding, postponing, or reducing any liability to income tax or any potential or prospective liability to future income tax

tax avoidance arrangement means an arrangement, whether entered into by the person affected by the arrangement or by another person, that directly or indirectly–

(a) has tax avoidance as its purpose or effect; or

(b) has tax avoidance as 1 of its purposes or effects, whether or not any other purpose or effect is referable to ordinary business or family dealings, if the tax avoidance purpose or effect is not merely incidental

[...]

CHAPTER 23

Attribution

¶23-010 Operating principle

A specific anti-avoidance rule, referred to as the attribution rule, applies to prevent higher income earners from using trusts to divert personal services income so as to avoid the highest personal tax rate (39% at the time of writing compared with the 33% flat rate that applies to trustees).

¶23-020 Income derived by a trustee from personal services can be attributed to the person who carried out the work

Taxpayers may choose to supply personal services through an associated trust. The buyer of the services deals with the trust, which derives the income from the services provided. However, it is the taxpayer (the working person) who carries out the work.

The use of an interposed trust can be for legitimate commercial or other reasons. However, where the use of an interposed trust reduces the overall tax liability, the attribution rule can apply to counteract any reduction in tax liability. When the rule applies, income derived by the trust is attributed to the working person: ss GB 27–GB 29.

The legislation does not specifically provide that the working person for the purposes of the attribution rule is limited to natural persons. However, the words "services are personally performed" in s GB 27(1)(a) indicate that the application is limited to natural persons: *Tax Information Bulletin* ¶1212-132 Vol 12, No 12, December 2000. This is reiterated in the *Tax Information Bulletin* ¶334-106 Vol 33, No 4, May 2021 at 8 and the current interpretation statements IS 19/02, "Income tax – Attribution rule for income from personal services" and IS 21/02, "Income tax – Calculating income from personal services attributed to a working person".

Although the rule also applies to companies and partnerships, the rule is only discussed here in the context of an interposed trust.

For the rule to apply, the trust must be associated with the working person. Association is determined in accordance with Subpart YB. See Chapter 18 – *Associated Persons.*

The attribution rule applies only for the purposes of income tax. The parties' transactions remain unaffected in other legal or commercial contexts.

As the top marginal rate increased from 33% (the trustee rate) with effect from 1 April 2021, and in line with new reporting obligations that apply from the 2021–22 tax year (see Chapter 1 – *Introduction to Trusts and Overview*) greater scrutiny regarding trust distributions should be anticipated as a result.

¶23-030 There is a threshold for application of the attribution rule

The threshold for application of the attribution rule requires that:

- 80% or more of the associated trust's income from personal services is derived from a single buyer or a person associated with that buyer
- 80% or more of the associated trust's total assessable income from personal services is derived through services personally performed by the associated working person or a relative of that person
- the working person's net income, including fringe benefits provided by the associated trust, exceeds the threshold for the top marginal tax rate after attribution in accordance with the rule, and
- substantial business assets are not a necessary part of the business structure used to derive the personal services income: s GB 27(2).

The 80% threshold is an arbitrary figure set to provide a basis for distinguishing unrelated employer–employee relationships: *Tax Information Bulletin* ¶334-106 Vol 33, No 4, May 2021.

Two buyers are not associated if the buyers are public authorities or if the working person could not be expected to know that the buyers were associated other than by making specific enquiry.

For the purposes of the rule, 2 persons are relatives (s YA 1) when one person:

- is within the second degree of blood relationship to the other person
- is in a marriage, civil union or de facto relationship with the other person, or in a marriage, civil union or de facto relationship with a person who is within the second degree of blood relationship to the other person
- is the adopted child of the other or is a child of a person who is within the first degree of relationship to the other person.

If there is more than one person to whom income must be attributed, the amount to be attributed is apportioned on the basis of the value of the services personally performed by each. There is no guidance given as to how the value of each person's services is determined. Appropriate methods could include pro-rating by reference to the proportion of each person's market value salaries, or a percentage based on output. Whatever basis is used, it must be reasonable in the circumstances.

Substantial business assets are defined as depreciable property that is not for private use and cost more than $75,000 or at least 25% of the associated trust's total assessable income from services for the income year: s GB 28(6).

However, depreciable property subject to private use will still meet the definition of substantial business assets if 20% or less of the property's use is private: s GB 28(8).

In determining whether the 20% threshold is exceeded for property subject to the FBT rules, the required calculation measures the proportion that the number of days for which FBT is payable bears to the total days in the income year in which the property is owned or is subject to a specified lease, a finance lease or a hire purchase agreement. For other property, the calculation is based on the proportion that non-deductible expenditure incurred in respect of the property bears to all expenditure incurred in the income year: s GB 28(9).

The substantial business assets test recognises that when substantial business assets are required to perform the services, a portion of the fee for services relates to a return on capital. Accordingly, when substantial assets are required, the return should reflect the assets employed in the business activity as well as the supply of services: *Tax Information Bulletin* ¶334-106 Vol 33, No 4, May 2021.

¶23-040 There are exceptions to the attribution rule

The attribution rule does not apply if the working person and the associated trust are both non-resident during the whole of the trust's income year.

There is no requirement to attribute net income to the extent that the services personally performed are essential support for a product supplied by the associated entity.

There is also a de minimis exception whereby if the amount of net income that would be attributed to the working person does not exceed $5,000, the attribution rule will not apply: s GB 27(3).

¶23-050 Interposed trust must attribute net income to the working person unless an exception applies

If the attribution rule applies, net income derived by the trust that has contracted to provide the personal services is attributed to the working person: s GB 29(1).

When calculating the net income of the associated trust as if the trust's only income came from personal services, a marginal cost approach is taken. In other words, for expenses incurred in deriving both personal services and non-personal services income, for example, accounting fees, salaries or wages, and Companies Office fees, no apportionment is required. See *Tax Information Bulletin* ¶334-106 Vol 33, No 4, May 2021 at 12.

The amount attributed is deductible to the associated trust in the income year in which the amount is attributed: s DC 8.

¶23-060 Amount of income to attribute is determined by calculation

Income attributed in accordance with the attribution rule is allocated to the income year in which it is attributed: s CE 8.

When attribution is required, the attributed amount is the lowest of the associated trust's net income for:

- the corresponding tax year calculated as if the only income came from personal services
- the corresponding tax year
- the corresponding tax year offset by any net loss from a previous year arising from personal services: s GB 29(1).

When determining the trust's income, the trustee is treated as not having made a distribution of beneficiary income, whether this is the case.

The associated trust can deduct the following items provided to the working person in the tax year:

- employment income, and
- the taxable value of fringe benefits and the related FBT on those benefits.

After calculating the amount to attribute in accordance with s GB 29, the net income to be attributed to the working person is further reduced by any beneficiary income that the working person has derived from the associated trust.

If the amount attributed would result in the attributing trust having a tax loss, the amount of beneficiary income is reduced to the extent necessary to achieve no trust income: s GB 29(6).

If the figure calculated is a negative amount, no attribution of income needs to be made.

Example

Munira is an IT consultant. She provides her services to clients through a family trust, of which she is a beneficiary. Munira is the sole provider of personal services. The trust is contracted to only one customer and no substantial business assets are owned by the trust. Munira is paid a salary by the trust of $62,000 during the relevant tax year. The trust has also distributed income of $10,000 to Munira during the same tax year and distributions to 2 other beneficiaries of the trust amount to $5,000 ($3,000 to Jack and $2,000 to Bob). The trust's net income for the tax year is $30,000 (after the deduction of Munira's salary and distributions made to beneficiaries).

The income attributed to Munira for the tax year is calculated as follows:

	$
Net income of trust	30,000.00
Add beneficiary income distributed to beneficiaries	15,000.00
	45,000.00

less beneficiary income distributed to Munira	10,000.00
attributed income	35,000.00

However, if $35,000 is attributed to Munira, the trust will have a net loss for the income year of $5,000 ($30,000–$35,000). The trust's beneficiary income for the tax year must therefore be reduced so that the trust's taxable income is zero and the beneficiary income distributed to beneficiaries other than Munira must be reduced in proportions determined by the trustees or according to the proportion of beneficiary income derived by each beneficiary to the total amount of beneficiary income. Munira's beneficiary income will not be reduced. The beneficiary income of the other beneficiaries (collectively) will be reduced by $5,000 (the net loss of the trust).

Munira's taxable income for the tax year is:

	$
Salary	62,000.00
Beneficiary Income	10,000.00
Attributed Income	35,000.00
	107,000.00

The trust's tax position for the tax year is:

	$
Gross income ($62,000 + $15,000 + $30,000)	107,000
less salary paid to Munira	62,000
less income attributed to Munira	35,000
	10,000

less beneficiary income distributed to:

	Munira	10,000.00	
	other beneficiaries*	nil	10,000
Net income			nil

* Beneficiary income adjustments

beneficiary	*distribution*	*adjustment*	*adjusted distribution*
	$	$	$
Munira	10,000	?	10,000
Jack	3,000	3,000[1]	nil
Bob	2,000	2,000[2]	nil
	15,000	5,000	10,000

[1] $3,000/$5,000 x $5,000

[2] $2,000/$5,000 x $5,000

Application of the rule can be effectively avoided by paying the income from services as a salary or beneficiary income.

¶23-070 Provisional tax is treated as being paid by the person to whom the income is attributed

If the interposed trust pays provisional tax on income from personal services in excess of the working person's residual income tax liability, all or part of that excess may be credited to the working person. The allocation may be made to the extent that provisional tax paid by the recipient of the allocated amount is less than his or her residual income tax for the year. The provisional tax is treated as if it was paid by the person to whom it has been allocated. See s RC 34.

¶23-080 Diverting personal service income can be avoidance

Diverting personal services income by structuring revenue-earning activities through an associated entity such as a trust can also amount to tax avoidance.

Although Inland Revenue accepts that there are legitimate reasons for using trusts, where taxpayers arrange to divert personal services income to take advantage of the lower marginal income tax rates, the arrangement may be viewed as tax avoidance.

For factors to take into account in the context of personal services income, see interpretation statement IS 19/02, "Income tax – Attribution rule for income from personal services", which provides guidance on when the attribution rule for income from personal services in ss GB 27 to GB 29 will apply, makes minor amendments to and replaces interpretation statement IS 18/03, "Income Tax – attribution rule for income from personal services", published in *Tax Information Bulletin* ¶309-10 Vol 30, No 9, October 2018.

Also see Chapter 22 – *Avoidance*.

¶23-085 Look-through companies are not treated as transparent for the attribution rules

A look-through company is treated as an associated entity, not a transparent entity, for attribution rule purposes. See *Tax Information Bulletin* ¶315-106 Vol 31, No 5, June 2019.

¶23-090 Legislation

Income Tax Act 2007

CE 8 ATTRIBUTED INCOME FROM PERSONAL SERVICES

CE 8(1) WHEN THIS SECTION APPLIES

This section applies when, under sections GB 27 to GB 29 (which relate to the attribution rule), a person is required to attribute an amount to another person.

CE 8(2) INCOME

The amount attributed is income of the person to whom it is attributed.

CE 8(3) TIMING OF INCOME

The amount is allocated to the income year in which it is attributed.

[...]

DC 8 ATTRIBUTION OF PERSONAL SERVICES

DC 8(1) WHEN THIS SECTION APPLIES

This section applies when, under sections GB 27 to GB 29 (which relate to the attribution rule for income from personal services), an amount of income of a person (the **associated entity**) is attributed to another person (the **working person**).

DC 8(2) DEDUCTION

The associated entity is allowed a deduction for the amount attributed.

DC 8(3) TIMING OF DEDUCTION

The deduction is allocated to the income year in which the amount is attributed to the working person.

DC 8(4) LINK WITH SUBPART DA

This section supplements the general permission and overrides all the general limitations.

[...]

GB 27 ATTRIBUTION RULE FOR INCOME FROM PERSONAL SERVICES

GB 27(1) APPLICATION OF SECTION GB 29

An amount of income in an income year of a person (the **associated entity**) is attributed to another person (the **working person**) under section GB 29 for the working person's corresponding tax year if,–

(a) during the income year, a third person (the **buyer**) acquires services from the associated entity, and the services are personally performed by the working person; and

(b) the working person is associated with the associated entity; and

(c) the threshold test in subsection (2) is met; and

(d) none of the exemptions in subsection (3) applies.

GB 27(2) THRESHOLD FOR APPLICATION OF ATTRIBUTION RULE

The attribution occurs only if–

(a) 80% or more of the associated entity's total income from personal services during the income year is derived from the supply of services to the buyer, a person associated with the buyer, or a combination of them; and

(b) 80% or more of the associated entity's income from personal services during the income year is derived through services personally performed by the working person, a relative of the working person, or a combination of them; and

(c) the working person's net income for the income year, assuming section GB 29 applies in relation to the associated entity and working person, is more than $70,000; and

(d) substantial business assets are not a necessary part of the business structure that is used to derive the total income referred to in paragraph (a).

GB 27(3) EXEMPTIONS

The attribution does not occur–

(a) if both the associated entity and the working person are non-residents at all times during the associated entity's income year:

(b) if the associated entity is a natural person and is neither a partner of a partnership nor a trustee of a trust:

(c) to the extent to which the services personally performed by the working person are essential support for a product supplied by the associated entity:

(d) if the total amount to be attributed to the working person, for the associated entity and the income year, is less than $5,000, unless–

  (i) the application of this paragraph would prevent income being attributed to the working person for the income year in relation to another associated entity:

  (ii) the associated entity is a CFC and a person who holds an attributing interest in the CFC files, after the date (the **Royal assent date**) on which the Taxation (Annual Rates for 2015–16, Research and Development, and Remedial Matters) Act 2016 receives the Royal assent, a return of income in which the amount of income attributed to the working person is determined under this section:

(e) if the associated entity is a CFC and–

  (i) the amount gives rise to attributed CFC income under section CQ 2(2B) (When attributed CFC income arises) or attributed CFC loss under section DN 2(2) (When attributed CFC loss arises) for a person who holds an attributing interest in the CFC; and

(ii) the person who holds the attributing interest in the CFC files, after the Royal assent date, a return of income in which the amount attributed to the working person is determined under section EX 20B (Attributable CFC amount).

[...]

GB 28 INTERPRETATION OF TERMS USED IN SECTION GB 27

GB 28(1) WHEN THIS SECTION APPLIES

This section applies for the purposes of section GB 27.

GB 28(2) ASSOCIATED PERSONS

A person is treated as being associated with another person if they are associated at the time the services are personally performed by the working person.

GB 28(3) NON-ASSOCIATED BUYERS

For the purposes of section GB 27(2)(a), a buyer is not treated as being associated with another buyer if either–

(a) both buyers are public authorities; or

(b) the working person cannot be reasonably expected to know that a particular buyer is associated with another buyer, other than by making a specific enquiry.

GB 28(4) RELATIVES

For the purposes of section GB 27(2)(b), a person is a relative of the working person only if the person is a relative at the beginning of the relevant income year of the working person.

GB 28(5) FRINGE BENEFITS INCLUDED

For the purposes of section GB 27(2)(c), the working person's annual gross income includes the taxable value of a fringe benefit, as determined under sections RD 25 to RD 63 (which relate to fringe benefit tax), provided or granted by a person associated with the working person.

GB 28(6) MEANING OF SUBSTANTIAL BUSINESS ASSETS

Substantial business assets means depreciable property that–

(a) at the end of the associated entity's corresponding income year, has a total cost of more than either–

  (i) $75,000; or

  (ii) 25% or more of the associated entity's total income from services for the income year; and

(b) is not for private use.

GB 28(7) ASSETS SUBJECT TO FINANCE LEASE, HIRE PURCHASE AGREEMENT, OR SPECIFIED LEASE

For the purposes of subsection (6)(a), the cost of depreciable property includes–

(a) the consideration provided to the lessee in the case of property subject to a finance lease or a hire purchase agreement, including expenditure or loss incurred by the lessee in preparing and installing the finance lease asset for use, unless the lessee is allowed a deduction for the expenditure or loss, other than a deduction for an amount of depreciation loss:

(b) the cost price, in the case of property subject to a specified lease.

GB 28(8) PRIVATE USE OF ASSETS

Subsection (6)(b) does not apply to depreciable property if 20% or less of the property's use is for private use.

GB 28(9) CALCULATION OF PRIVATE PROPORTION OF USE

For the purposes of subsection (8), the percentage of a property's use for private purposes for an income year is calculated according to–

(a) the proportion that the number of days for which fringe benefit tax is payable by the associated entity in relation to the property bears to the total number of days in the income year in which the property is owned by or is subject to a finance lease, hire purchase agreement, or specified lease, involving the associated entity, if the property is subject to the FBT rules:

(b) the proportion that the expenditure incurred in relation to the property, for which a deduction is denied to the associated entity, bears to all expenditure incurred by the associated entity in relation to the property in the income year, if the property is not subject to the FBT rules.

GB 29 ATTRIBUTION RULE: CALCULATION

GB 29(1) AMOUNT ATTRIBUTED

A working person is treated as deriving income in an income year equal to the least of the following amounts:

(a) the associated entity's net income for the corresponding tax year, calculated as if their only income were derived from personal services:

(b) the associated entity's net income for the corresponding tax year:

(c) if and to the extent to which the associated entity is a company or a trust that has a loss balance to be carried forward under section IA 4 (Using loss balances carried forward to tax year) arising from a business or a trading activity of supplying personal services, the associated entity's net income for the corresponding tax year after subtracting the loss balance carried forward from an earlier corresponding tax year.

GB 29(1B) ASSOCIATED ENTITY'S NET INCOME CALCULATED BEFORE ATTRIBUTION

For the purposes of calculating the associated entity's net income for the corresponding tax year in the application of subsection (1), section DC 8 (Attribution of personal services) is ignored.

GB 29(2) CALCULATION FOR TRUSTEE OR PARTNERSHIP

For the purposes of calculating the associated entity's net income for the corresponding tax year in the application of subsection (1),–

(a) if the associated entity is a trustee of a trust, the trustees are treated as not having made a distribution of beneficiary income out of the year's income:

[...]

(c) if the associated entity is a look-through company, the associated entity is treated as a taxpayer and section HB 1 (Look-through companies are transparent) does not apply.

GB 29(3) SALARY PAID OR FRINGE BENEFITS TREATED AS DEDUCTIONS

For the purposes of calculating the associated entity's net income for the corresponding tax year in the application of subsection (1),–

(a) the associated entity is allowed a deduction for employment income paid to the working person during the income year:

(b) the associated entity is allowed a deduction for the taxable value of a fringe benefit provided or granted by the associated entity to the working person during the income year, and for the fringe benefit tax payable on the fringe benefit.

GB 29(4) REDUCTION OF ATTRIBUTABLE INCOME FOR DISTRIBUTIONS

For the purposes of calculating the associated entity's net income for the corresponding tax year in the application of subsection (1), the amount of net income of the associated entity for the corresponding tax year is reduced by–

(a) in the case of a trustee of a trust, the amount of beneficiary income derived by the working person from the trust in the income year:

[...]

GB 29(6) REDUCTION OF BENEFICIARY INCOME WHEN RULE RESULTS IN TRUST HAVING TAX LOSS

If the associated entity is a trustee and the amount attributable would cause the associated entity to have a tax loss for the corresponding tax year, for the purposes of this Act,–

(a) beneficiary income from the trust for the income year must be reduced to the extent to which the associated entity's taxable income for the corresponding tax year is zero; and

(b) the reduction in beneficiary income must be divided among the beneficiaries other than the working person–

(i) according to proportions determined by the trust's trustees:

(ii) if the trustees do not make the determination, according to the proportion that each beneficiary's beneficiary income bears to the total beneficiary income from the trust for the income year.

GB 29(7) ATTRIBUTION TO MORE THAN 1 WORKING PERSON

If the amount attributable is to be attributed to more than 1 working person, the share attributed to each working person must reflect the respective value of the services personally performed by each working person.

[...]

RC 34 ATTRIBUTION RULE FOR INCOME FROM PERSONAL SERVICES

RC 34(1) WHEN THIS SECTION APPLIES

This section applies for the purposes of the provisional tax rules and Part 7 of the Tax Administration Act 1994 for provisional tax paid for income from personal services to which section GB 27 (Attribution rule for income from personal services) may apply. The references in this section to **working person** and **associated entity** reflect the terminology used in section GB 27.

RC 34(2) ASSOCIATED ENTITY TRANSFERRING AMOUNT TO WORKING PERSON

If, in a tax year, the associated entity pays an amount of tax that is more than the provisional tax payable for the tax year, the entity may transfer some or all of the overpayment to the working person to the extent to which the amount of provisional tax paid by the person is less than their residual income tax for the tax year.

RC 34(3) WORKING PERSON TRANSFERRING AMOUNT TO ASSOCIATED ENTITY

If, in a tax year, the working person pays an amount of tax that is more than the provisional tax payable for the tax year, they may transfer some or all of the overpayment to the associated entity to the extent to which the amount of provisional tax paid by the entity is less than their residual income tax for the tax year.

RC 34(4) WHEN TRANSFER MADE

The associated entity and the working person may transfer an amount under subsection (2) or (3), as applicable, on or after the later of–

(a) the day on which the overpayment of provisional tax is paid by the entity or person, as applicable:

(b) the day on which the instalment of provisional tax payable for the tax year becomes payable by–

(i) the person, if the entity is making the transfer; or

(ii) the entity, if the person is making the transfer.

RC 34(5) NOTICE

The Commissioner must be notified of a transfer under subsection (2) or (3) in a notice that–

(a) names the person to whom a transfer is made, and the amount to be transferred; and

(b) states the date on which the overpayment is treated as transferred to the associated entity or working person, as applicable; and

(c) is provided within the time for filing a return of income for the tax year for the person to whom the transfer is made, or an extended time allowed by the Commissioner.

RC 34(6) WHEN TRANSFER MADE AND HOW TRANSFER TREATED

For the purposes of this section, –

(a) a transfer under subsection (2) or (3) is treated as made on the day stated in the notice; and

(b) provisional tax transferred by the associated entity to the working person for a tax year is treated as provisional tax paid by the working person and not by the associated entity; and

(c) provisional tax transferred by the working person to the associated entity is treated as provisional tax paid by the associated entity and not by the working person.

CHAPTER 24

Asset Planning

¶24-010 Operating principle

At the simplest level, trusts represent one of the ways in which property or businesses can be owned. Alternatives to trusts include a personal ownership, a company or a partnership.

¶24-020 No form of asset ownership is perfect

The most appropriate form of ownership will depend, amongst other things, on:

- the reasons for the acquisition and management of assets
- flexibility to adapt to changing business or family dynamics and circumstances, and
- whether the structure adopted can be administered appropriately.

The history of trusts in New Zealand is complex. Some relevant background considerations have been:

- the abolition of estate duty
- ACC legislation precluded personal injury claims
- use of trusts to reduce assets levels for means testing purposes to qualify for a residential care subsidy (after age 65)
- progressive lowering of marginal rates of tax followed by a more recent increase in the top marginal tax rate
- trust commoditisation
- the abolition of gift duty in 2011: see Chapter 13 – *Gift Duty*
- anti-avoidance provisions in various laws and under common law actions: see *Penny* v *C of IR*; *Hooper* v *C of IR* (2009) 24 NZTC 23,406
- use and abuse of corporate trustees: see, for example, *C of IR* v *Newmarket Trustees Ltd* [2012] NZCA 351; (2012) 25 NZTC ¶20-139 and *Rosebud Corporate Trustee Ltd* v *Bublitz* [2014] NZHC 2592 and also see *Jacomb* v *Jacomb* [2020] NZHC 1764; (2020) 5 NZTR ¶30-010 and *Legler* v *Formannoij* [2021] NZHC 1271
- amendments to the Property (Relationships) Act 1976 to increase the application to de facto partners and provisions that strictly relate to trusts

- widening definition of property for relationship property purposes meaning that certain powers in respect of trusts can be valued for relationship property purposes: see *Clayton* v *Clayton (Vaughan Road Property Trust)* [2016] NZSC 29; (2016) 4 NZTR ¶26-002
- challenges to trust validity: see *JSC Mezhdunarodniy Promyshlenniy Bank* v *Pugachev* [2017] EWHC 2426 (Ch) and *Webb* v *Webb* [2020] UKPC 22; (2020) 5 NZTR ¶30-011
- the increased requirement of financial transparency worldwide following the Panama papers and the subsequent introduction of Foreign Account Tax Compliance Act (FATCA), Common Reporting Standard (CRS) and Anti-Money Laundering/Combating the Financing of Terrorism (AML/CFT)
- the introduction of the Trusts Act 2019 following 2 decades of trust law review.

Although trusts are often a default option for structuring family wealth in New Zealand, there are alternative and complementary options to achieve some of the objectives for which trusts are often set up. These can include the following:

- Family Investment Holding Companies, which are private family owned companies (sometimes referred to as Family Offices) that invest rather than trade. In particular, such a company holds the family's long-term investments (eg share portfolios or property) and the shareholders and directors are typically members of the family.
- Family Partnerships are a type of arrangement in which family members pool money to run a business project. Each family member buys units or shares of the business and can profit in proportion to the number of shares they own, as outlined in the partnership operating agreement.
- A Family Charter is a "treaty-like" document that clearly defines and guides a family business into the future. Contained within a Family Charter is the definition of the family business and the relationship of individual family members to the entity.
- An Option Agreement is a legally binding contract between 2 entities outlining each counterparty's responsibilities to the other. It can be used for estate planning in situations in which a family member is living in a home owned by a trust or a testator and it is intended that he or she should ultimately receive the property for a price that is appropriate to the circumstances.
- Insurance Policies can be a useful way to manage risk and create liquidity to transfer value between family members on death or incapacity.
- Golden Shares can be used to grant veto power in the governance and management of family businesses. They can be used to allow family members who are working in the business to have more control over those who are not.
- Redeemable Preference Shares are a type of preference share that can be useful in succession planning. A company issues them to shareholders and later redeems them. This means the company can buy back the shares at a later date. Non-redeemable preference shares cannot be redeemed.

- Family Share Schemes are similar to an Employee Share Scheme except the shares are issued to family members and there are mechanisms within the scheme documents to enable exit and transfers between family members.
- Loans (Secured/Unsecured) can be used to manage risks to family wealth. A secured loan is one that is connected to a piece of collateral – something valuable like a car or a home. An unsecured loan is not protected by any collateral. If you default on the loan, the lender cannot automatically take your property.
- Testamentary Trusts can be written into a will and appoint a trustee to manage the assets of the deceased. These are sometimes used when the beneficiary or beneficiaries are children or disabled.
- Wills can be used instead of trusts as a more certain way to apportion assets following the death of the testator.
- Enduring Powers of Attorney can also be used to manage risk to family wealth arising from incapacity. There are various types of power of attorney. The most common type is the enduring power of attorney (EPA), which is flexible and will allow the person you have named to continue acting even if you are no longer able to make decisions for yourself.
- Relationship Property Agreements provide certainty as to how property will be divided on the relationship ending.
- Contracts for Difference are contracts that enable 2 parties to enter into an agreement for the acquisition of any type of property. If the current asset price is lower at the exit price than the value at the contract's exchange, the seller, rather than the buyer, will benefit from the difference. These can be used in intra-family financing arrangements.
- Property Sharing Agreements are a contract between 2 or more owners of a property. They are intended to cover both the parties existing arrangements regarding the property and also to provide for what may happen in the future with the property. These can be used where family members co-invest.
- Joint Tenancies arise when 2 or more people are buying a property and the shares are undivided and neither person owns a defined share. When one of the owners dies, the survivor inherits the property automatically.
- Family Finance Companies (Savings, Loans and Insurance) are private entities set up and run by a family to provide financial services only to members of the family. These are frequently used by family offices.

Even where a trust is the most appropriate means for asset ownership, if not managed and operated properly, the trust can be vulnerable to allegations of sham or other challenges, which, if proven, can result in the trust's assets reverting back to the ownership of the erstwhile trust's settlor or settlors. In which case, the putative trust assets will be available to the settlor's creditors. See *Davis* v *White* [2016] NZHC 1626; (2016) 4 NZTR 26-012. It is also important to ensure that any assets that are transferred to a trust (or any other ownerships structure) are assets that can properly be dealt with. See *Hamilton* v *Kirwan* [2020] NZHC 2149, where the transfer of land (which the settlor had led his daughter to believe she would later gain an interest in) to a trust was held to be null and void due to a successful claim of proprietary estoppel.

¶24-025 Trusts with limited assets

Trusts are often the centrepiece of a New Zealand family's asset plan. However, it is not uncommon in New Zealand for assets to be held in trust in circumstances where the benefit from the trust is very limited, for example, where the trust's sole asset is a family home. In such cases, while the trustees can make a non-active trust declaration (see ¶19-020), the existence of the trust may just add unnecessary complexity and expense to people's lives. This observation is compounded by the tax implications of residential property owned by trusts that might come under the bright-line test, and the importance of considering the likely tenure of ownership and utilisation of property. See Special report on the new legislation included in the Taxation (Annual Rates for 2020–21, Feasibility Expenditure, and Remedial Matters) Act 2021, first published on 9 April 2021 and a corrected updated report published on 28 April 2021. Key considerations that relate to trusts are:

- The main home exclusion is available to properties held in trust (where the requirements for the exclusion are met). However, the main home exclusion cannot be used for more than one property, where a trust owns multiple properties.
- As the bright-line test is an income tax, consideration regarding the flat trustee rate compared with marginal rates requires consideration.
- Residential land withholding tax is payable on sales of property that come under the bright-line test if there is a connection with an offshore person. Where the sale is by a trust, this can be the case if a non-resident beneficiary has received a distribution of an amount of $5,000 or more within the last 4 years. Similarly, a non-resident trustee will be an offshore person.

¶24-030 Trust specific factors

A trust provides long-term inter-generational asset ownership. Once assets are in trust solution, those assets are protected, not just from the original asset owner's creditors but from creditors of any person who would, but for the trust, otherwise become a subsequent personal owner of that asset. In this way, the protective benefits of a trust are conveyed to subsequent generations.

Where assets are owned in trust solution, those assets are immunised from the settlor's creditors to the extent that any debts owing have been forgiven and to the extent that any transfers of assets for value are not voidable: *Regal Castings Ltd* v *Lightbody* [2008] NZSC 87; (2008) 2 NZTR ¶18-018. In the context of creditors, it is important to consider not just trade creditors but litigious parties and personal liabilities that can be assumed though trade or other exposure, for example, reckless trading as a director. This proposition needs to be considered now in light of the Supreme Court decision in *Clayton* v *Clayton (Vaughan Road Property Trust)* [2016] NZSC 29; (2016) 4 NZTR ¶26-002, which has extended the definition of property for the purposes of the Property (Relationships) Act 1976 to include certain trust powers and rights.. Also consider *Webb* v *Webb* [2020] UKPC 22; (2020) 5 NZTR ¶30-011, where Mr Webb reserved such broad powers to himself that he failed to make an effective disposition of the property that was attributed to the trusts in question. As a result, property that would otherwise have been protected by a trust was available to his former wife and a tax debt incurred during the relationship was treated as unenforceable in the Cook Islands and so was not taken into consideration in the division of property between Mr Webb and his former wife.

Subject to any dispositions to defeat interests in relationship property, assets in trust ownership can also be protected from spouses and de facto or civil union partners. However, following the dissolution of a marriage, the Court has a discretionary power to modify nuptial settlements where the parties' original expectations are altered due to the dissolution of the marriage. See the Family Proceedings Act 1980, s 182, *Clayton* v *Clayton (Claymark Trust)* [2016] NZSC 30; (2016) 4 NZTR ¶26-003, *Little* v *Little* [2020] NZHC 2612; (2020) 5 NZTR ¶30-022 and *Ward* v *Ward* [2009] NZCA 139; (2009) 2 NZTR ¶19-009.

Assets in trust are not affected by a settlor's death and, accordingly, inter-generational ownership can continue without the decimation that can result when indivisible assets are required to be distributed following death. Assets that have been transferred to a trust do not comprise part of a settlor's estate and so are not subject to claims under s 4 of the Family Protection Act 1955. See *Thurston* v *Thurston* [2014] NZHC 2267 and *Pension* v *Forbes* [2014] NZHC 2160. However, this must be now be considered in light of the current review of succession law in New Zealand and the potential in-roads that may strain the limits of testamentary freedom. See, for example, *Hamilton* v *Kirwan (supra)*, *Rule* v *Simpson* [2017] NZHC 2154; (2017) 4 NZTR ¶27-017, *A* v *D* [2019] NZHC 992; (2019) 5 NZTR ¶29-027 and *A* v *D* [2019] NZHC 1891.

Trust income can be retained or distributed at the trustee's discretion. Where all income is paid to the beneficiary or beneficiaries on the lowest marginal rates, care is required to consider if this is a proper exercise of the trustees' discretion and powers. Although this is technically permissible, a prudent trustee would be wise to consider all the beneficiaries and to sacrifice certain tax savings so as to demonstrate that a trust structure served purposes other than tax minimisation and effective income-splitting. See ¶3-140. Also see ¶2-060.

Historically, trusts have been used successfully to avoid tainting by association for a party who undertakes land dealings. In light of the amended associated persons' provisions, any structure that can avoid association should be assessed for tax avoidance, given the clear policy statements that income from targeted land dealings is to be held on revenue account. See Chapter 18 – *Associated Persons*.

¶24-040 Trust control factors should be carefully thought out

It is common for a modern trust to have a settlor or other related party who retains a power to remove and appoint trustees and often also beneficiaries. These indicia of control, considered in some contexts as indicia of invalidity, should be carefully considered so as to ensure a structure that can be operated in accordance with accepted principles of trust law. Where a single person has significant control over a trust, the effect of this control on the separation of the person and the trust should be considered in the context of the structure. See, for example, *Grant* v *Grant* [2011] NZHC 1237; (2011) 3 NZTR ¶21-003 and *Clayton* v *Clayton (Vaughan Road Property Trust)* (supra).

Excessive control, or a failure to exercise any control, by the alleged trustee can be indicia of sham. Accordingly, care is required when both drafting the terms of a trust and managing a trust, to ensure appropriate control mechanisms. See *Rosebud Corporate Trustee Limited* v *Bublitz* [2014] NZHC 2018; (2014) 3 NZTR ¶24-025, where a trust, settled to allow a bankrupt to effectively carry on a property development venture, was found to be a sham; the Judge noting that "[a]ll of this suggests that there was no intention at the outset to create a valid trust.... the intention was to set up a structure behind which Mr Nielsen could carry on a business venture, notwithstanding his bankruptcy, and without his name being in the public domain". See also *JSC Mezhdunarodniy Promyshlenniy Bank* v *Pugachev* [2017] EWHC 2426 (Ch), where the conclusion that the trusts were a sham (if the true effect of each trust was not that Mr Pugachev had retained beneficial ownership) was reached because at all material times Mr Pugachev regarded all the assets in the trusts as belonging to him and intended to retain ultimate control over such assets. The point of the trusts was not to cede control of his assets to someone else; it was to hide his control of them. In other words, Mr Pugachev intended to use the trusts as a pretence to mislead other people by creating the appearance that the property did not belong to him when really it did.

However, note that following *Clayton* v *Clayton (Vaughan Road Property Trust)* (supra), a finding of sham is unlikely where the "three certainties" are met (ie there is intention to settle a trust, trust property and trust objects).

Also see ¶22-120.

¶24-045 Trust obligations beyond liability for tax should also be carefully thought out

A controversial aspect of the Trusts Act 2019 is the new presumption that trustees will make "basic trust information" available to every beneficiary. In New Zealand, it is (regrettably) common for not all (or sometimes any) beneficiaries to be properly engaged with trustees and often beneficiaries are unaware of trusts under which they may have an interest. As a general principle, the new law requires there to be at least a basic level of reporting to all the adult beneficiaries and to the parents/guardians of all the minor beneficiaries.

In New Zealand, many domestic trusts are governed by people (including many lawyers and accountants) who are not well versed in the law relating to trusts. Accordingly, the interests of the class of beneficiaries as a whole being can be subordinate to the interests of the people who set up the trust. This is plainly wrong, and it is a stated aim of the Trusts Act to raise standards of governance and administration.

An issue that trustees increasingly face is how to deal with a beneficiary's request for trust information. The Trusts Act provides a presumption that the trustee will make available basic trust information to every beneficiary and every representative of a beneficiary. This applies to existing trusts and new trusts.

That basic trust information is:

- the fact that a person is a beneficiary of a trust
- the name and contact details of the trustee(s)
- the occurrence of, and details of, each appointment, removal, and retirement of a trustee as it occurs, and
- the right of the beneficiary to request a copy of the terms of the trust or trust information.

The provision of information, including tax and accounting information, may be confronting for some trustees. However, moving forward disclosure obligations may be as important as tax and tax-related reporting obligations. See Chapter 20 – *Disclosure*. Also see *Lambie Trustee Ltd* v *Addleman* [2021] NZSC 54, *Jacomb* v *Jacomb* [2020] NZHC 1764; (2020) 5 NZTR ¶30-010 and *Erceg* v *Erceg* [2017] NZSC 28; (2017) 4 NZTR ¶27-003.

¶24-050 Structuring is less risky than restructuring

If an acceptable structure is adopted in the first instance, it should never be necessary to defend the tax savings that will result when an ineffective structure is altered. In this regard, it is noted that, although Barber DCJ criticised the Commissioner of Inland Revenue in *Case* V20 (2002) 20 NZTC 10,233, for drawing such a distinction, it still stands to reason that the criticism referred to supports the proposition of getting it right first time. See also *Penny and Hooper* v *C of IR* [2011] NZSC 95; (2011) 25 NZTC ¶20-073 as an example of a restructuring where tax savings were found to be a tax avoidance arrangement. With a top tax rate that is now above the flat trustee rate of 33%, this means that earlier trust structures will have an aspect of validity that is not fixed on particular tax effectiveness. Also see Chapter 22 – *Avoidance*.

¶24-060 Commercial reality is imperative

A trading trust offers creditor protection and flexible profit distribution. However, these considerations must be demonstrably real. It is difficult, for example, to support an argument that a structure is designed to provide creditor protection if other valuable assets remain in personal ownership.

In the spirit of commercial reality, deviation from commercial salaries should be considered very carefully. Although decisions go both ways on whether this amounts to tax avoidance (*Case V20* (supra), *Penny and Hooper* v *C of IR* (supra), *White* v *C of IR* [2010] NZHC 1826; (2010) 24 NZTC 24,600), prudence would dictate a salary at least relevant to the taxpayer's lifestyle, if not at a realistic benchmark of a discounted market salary.

Debts between trading entities should be at commercial rates unless there is a supportable reason to deviate from this. The utility of debts that cannot be called up for substantial periods of time or where interest rates are non-commercial should be carefully considered. See *Krukziener* v *C of IR (No 3)* [2010] NZHC 1714; (2010) 24 NZTC 24,563.

¶24-065 Liability can be incurred by directors when a company trades on behalf of a trust

Care is required when interposing corporate structures into a trading trust. In *Owens* v *Shaw* [2016] NZHC 1400, the trustees of a trading trust, also traded through a company (on behalf of the trust) on account of one supplier who was unhappy dealing with a trust. The supplies made to the company were on-supplied to the trust. The company did not have a bank account, but filed nil GST returns to show the "pass through". After a supply dispute, the company via its directors released the trust from its informal agreement to fund the company's purchases. A statutory demand against company lead to its liquidation. The liquidators pursued the trustees unsuccessfully. The Court being of the view that there was no breach of obligation by the trustees to pay the company as the agreement was at an end. However, the directors of the company did not fare so well. The Court finding that, in agreeing to release the trust from its obligations, the directors acted recklessly and breached s 135 of the Companies Act 1993. As a result, the directors were liable for the company's loss, including liquidation costs. Brown J noting at [65] that:

> "The Company went into liquidation because Mr and Mrs Shaw decided to prefer the interests of the beneficiaries of the Trust over the Company and its creditors. The liquidation of the Company was a likely consequence of the abandonment of the purchase and supply agreement. I do not consider that in the circumstances of this case the recovery for the creditors should be diluted by the liquidators' costs and disbursements".

¶24-070 Structural integrity is important

Contracts, agreements and letterheads should all reflect the correct entity. This is particularly important where a business is restructured. If the taxpayer who previously acted on his or her own account is now employed by a company, invoices should be issued in the company's name. Telephone directories, service and utility contracts should also be amended or assigned to reflect the correct contracting party. Income should be banked into the correct entity's bank account. Transfers between entities and employees should all be documented and the basis for any transfer clearly identified, for example, salary, drawings and advance as appropriate. Also see *Rosebud Corporate Trustee Ltd* v *Bublitz* (supra).

All facets of a structure should operate independently and should be able to be shown to do so.

It is also important to appreciate that the structure adopted cannot later be resiled from should it become inconvenient. In *Glover No 2 Ltd* v *The Glover Trust Ltd* [2013] NZCA 608; (2013) 3 NZTR ¶23-028, the Court of Appeal upheld the High Court decision in *Glover Trust Ltd* v *Glover Trust Corp Ltd* [2013] NZHC 545 that prevented the parties from denying the trust arrangement adopted.

The case involved a hastily prepared distribution of trust assets to a new trust, together with a deed of bare trust declaring that the properties in question were held on a bare trust for the existing proprietor.

The logic behind the arrangement derived from the fact that the (original) trust was GST-registered (the case pre-dated compulsory zero rating) and any disposition would have negative tax-consequences. Accordingly, to quote Allan J "the Deed of Bare Trust was created for the purpose of production to the revenue authorities as required".

What was intended, was an outright transfer of trust assets for the ultimate benefit of one party to the relationship. However, it was structured to look in part as if nothing had happened to avoid tax consequences.

The question for the Court was, whether the deed of bare trust was valid, despite its design characteristics of a "ruse". The Court took the position that just because the deed was a ruse, it does not follow that it is invalid or ineffective. The reason for this was that as the bare trust had been effective (the tax liability was avoided), it met its purpose.

The result was that the trustees of the new trust were required to return the properties to the first trust, to which they remained subject.

This decision was upheld on appeal. In the appeal decision, the Court of Appeal referred to the fact the trust's settlor was seeking to impugn the validity of a document prepared in accordance with her instructions, noting at [29] that:

> "On this approach, Ms Sparks' interests would be able to profit from her own wrong given that she executed the documents on behalf of the settlor and trustee. That is because a finding of a sham would likely result in the trust property reverting back to the settlor but allowing it to be retained rather than being available for creditors. Such a result would be inequitable".

The Supreme Court denied leave to appeal the Court of Appeal decision (see *Glover No 2 Ltd* v *The Glover Trust Ltd* [2014] NZSC 54).

The importance of structural integrity is also highlighted in *JF and MF* v *Hexagon Investments Limited* FSD 7 of 2014 (ASCJ) where an off-shore trust structure put in place by New Zealand immigrants was found to be ineffective due to the absence of extrinsic evidence of intention to alienate beneficial interests.

¶24-080 Legal form of trust relationships must be recognised

In *Brown* v *C of IR* [2014] NZHC 1599, deductions for interest paid by the taxpayer on behalf of the trustee borrower were denied because there was no nexus between the taxpayer's income-earning activity and the interest liability incurred by the trust. The taxpayer's argument that he expected to be reimbursed for his payments and that such reimbursement would be taxable income in the taxpayer's hands was unsuccessful. The following diagram outlines the structure adopted.

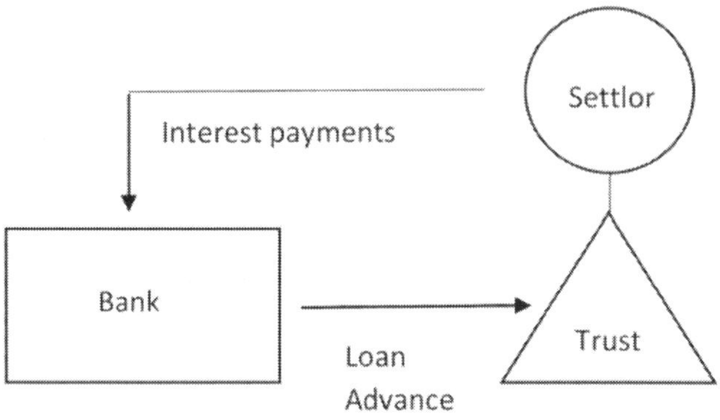

An argument that the taxpayer had a right of indemnity from the trust for the interest paid was also unsuccessful. There was no written agreement between the trust and the taxpayer recording the arrangement. There was no agreement, written or oral, that the trust would repay the taxpayer. There was no contractual obligation on the trust to pay the taxpayer the amount of the interest that he had paid on its behalf. A resolution of the trustees could not create a legally enforceable right on the part of the taxpayer to be reimbursed.

Also see *Brown* v *C of IR* [2014] NZHC 1600.

¶24-090 Relationship property distributions involving trusts

Care is required when dealing with trusts in the context of related party transfers to ensure that no inadvertent tax consequences arise.

Section FB 21 of the Income Tax Act 2007 provides for concessionary treatment where depreciable property is transferred on a "settlement of relationship property". A "settlement of relationship property" is defined in s FB 1B of the Income Tax Act as a transaction *between*

- a person who is a party to the relationship agreement or is associated with a party to the agreement, and
- another person who is a party to the relationship agreement or is associated with a party to the agreement.

This provision was amended by the Taxation (Annual Rates for 2015–16, Research and Development, and Remedial Matters) Act 2016 in situations where "the transfer of property occurs between one of the parties to the agreement and a third party (say, a family trust)". However, care is required to appreciate where such concessionary treatment is available and where it is not.

Part VII

GOODS AND SERVICES TAX

CHAPTER 25

Goods and Services Tax

¶25-010 Operating principle

A trust must register and account for GST if the trust makes taxable supplies in excess of the registration threshold.

Although this seems a straight-forward proposition, trusts can be particularly vulnerable to exceeding the registration threshold due to a failure to correctly recognise and correctly value taxable supplies. Trusts must also be careful to identify supplies made to or by an associated person, as different valuation rules and entitlements to input tax credits can apply.

¶25-020 Statutory focus is the trust not the trustees

A trust does not have legal personality. However, for the purposes of the Goods and Services Tax Act 1985 (GST Act), a trust is an unincorporated body and it is the trust, not its trustee or trustees, that registers for GST: GST Act, ss 2(1) ("unincorporated body"), 57(2)(a).

The main implications of this approach can be summarised as follows:

> "1. A trust and not its beneficiaries, is the jurisdictional focus for GST purposes when considering a trust relationship. Indeed, a trust and its beneficiaries are legally separate and distinct persons for GST purposes which is why a transaction between a trust and a beneficiary will often be a 'supply' which is subject to GST requirements in the ordinary way, as illustrated in *The Trustee, Executors and Agency Company New Zealand Limited & Ors* v *Commissioner of Inland Revenue* (1997) 18 NZTC 13,076 (HC). This case involved a sale of a farm to a major beneficiary of the trust. Sometimes, a transaction between a trust and a beneficiary will, for GST purposes, be between 'associated persons' thereby giving rise to valuation and other issues in terms of ss 10, 10(3A) AND 10(3AB) of the GST Act. These latter rules, however, apply to transactions between 'associates' and are not trust-specific.
>
> 2. Conventional legal and trust principles applying to the trust relationship are trumped by the deeming rules in s 57, at least to the extent that they regulate certain statutory outcomes.

3. Supplies made by, and acquisitions received by, a trust relationship are made and received for GST purposes by the trust, not the trustees or the beneficiaries in that relationship.

4. It is the trust which carries on the taxable activity, not the trustees or the beneficiaries; and anything done by an individual trustee is done for GST purposes by the trust, at least to the extent that it is done by the trustee in his or her capacity as trustee of the trust and as part and parcel of carrying on the trust's taxable activity. Put another way, for GST purposes there are only activities conducted by a trust within the GST tax-base, at least in respect of the things being undertaken on behalf of and as part of that trust's GST registered taxable activity.

5. A trustee of a trust is, along with his or her fellow trustees and the trust, are jointly and severally liable for all GST payable by the trust, and remain so until they have retired and notified the Commissioner of the fact of that retirement."

See *Case* Z12 (2009) 24 NZTC 14,142 at [30].

¶25-030 Taxable supplies made by a trust can be less obvious than supplies made in the way of other business activities

A taxable activity can be carried on, regardless of whether or not for a pecuniary profit. Key components of the definition require only that there is continuous or regular activity and a supply of goods or services for consideration: GST Act, s 6(1)(a).

The definition of supply is an inclusive one that does not rely on any formal supply agreement: GST Act, s 5(1). The ease with which supplies can be made, and the casual relationships that can exist between trustees, beneficiaries and other related parties can conceal a taxable activity carried on by a trading trust.

Although a trading trust is often considered to be a trust with a corporate trustee, any trust that carries on business activity is a trading trust. Here the terminology is used to clarify that the comments about trusts and GST do not generally apply to a trust that does not carry on any business activity.

In *Case 5/2013* [2013] NZTRA 05; (2013) 26 NZTC ¶2-004, the trustees were deemed to be registered for GST, as the trustees were found to have been carrying on a taxable activity that exceeded the GST registration threshold; notwithstanding that the trustees had not collectively agreed or acknowledged that they were buying properties with an intention of re-sale. The relevant test for GST was not whether the Trust acquired property with the intention of re-sale but whether the activity involved, or was intended to involve, the supply of goods and services to another person for consideration, which was the case.

See further at ¶21-035.

¶25-035 Taxable supplies made by trustees of a bare trust can require particular consideration with respect to GST

A bare trust is a trust where the trustee's only duties are to hold the trust property, take reasonable care of it; and transfer the property to or as directed by the trust's beneficiary. The duties of a bare trustee are passive (unlike the "normal" position where trustees have positive duties to manage and exercise their discretions and powers).

Bare trustees can arise as part of a commercial arrangement or where, through circumstance, property is held pending direction.

One practical consideration is what liability the bare trustee has for taxation and, in particular, GST. While as legal owner of trust property, the trustee is normally liable for tax, including GST; where the trustee is a bare trustee, the relationship can be more akin to that of agency, in which case, the specific agency provisions of the GST Act can have application. See, for example, *Trident Holdings; Collins* v *The Queen* (2002) GTC 314 (TCC) and Butler (ed) *Equity and Trusts in New Zealand* (2nd ed, Thomson Reuters, Wellington, 2009). Also see *Priest* v *Ross Asset Management Ltd (in liq)* [2016] NZHC 1803.

That said, it is important to consider each case on its facts. It is also important to ensure that clear responsibility for GST is taken so that a game of "hot potato" does not result between the trustee and the beneficiary. In "questions we've been asked" QB 16/03: "Goods and Services Tax – GST treatment of bare trusts" *Tax Information Bulletin* ¶285-108 Vol 28, No 5, June 2016 at 16, the Commissioner confirmed that the relationship between a beneficiary and a bare trustee acting on the directions of the beneficiary is predominantly an agency relationship. This means any supplies of trust property made by the trustee are deemed to be made by the beneficiary and the taxable activity carried on by the bare trustee is deemed to be carried on by the beneficiary.

The following examples from QB 16/03 explore relevant considerations of bare trusts.

Example 1 – Bare trustee enters into lease agreements on behalf of beneficiaries

Starlight Nominees Ltd is the legal owner of three commercial rental properties as bare trustee on behalf of two business partners, Greg and Rhonda. Greg and Rhonda take care of the day-today activities of the rental business and instruct Starlight to enter into all leases and other contracts as required. There is no written agreement between Starlight and Greg and Rhonda under s 60(1B). In this case, Starlight is both bare trustee and agent for Greg and Rhonda. The supply of the properties for rent is treated as a supply made by Greg and Rhonda: s 60(1), *Case R1* [(1994) 16 NZTC 6,001] and [*C of IR* v *Campbell Investments* (2004) 21 NZTC 18,559 (HC)].

Example 2 – Bare trustee transfers trust property to third party

Greg and Rhonda decide to sell one of the properties and instruct Starlight to enter into an agreement for sale and purchase of real estate with the purchaser and to transfer the property to the purchaser on settlement. In this case also, Starlight is both trustee and agent for Greg and Rhonda. The supply of the property to the purchaser is treated as a supply made by Greg and Rhonda: s 60(1), *Case R1* and *Campbell Investments*.

Example 3 — Bare trustee transfers properties to beneficiaries

Greg and Rhonda now decide to hold the legal title to the remaining properties in their own names. They instruct Starlight to transfer the legal title in the properties to them. The transfer of the legal title to Greg and Rhonda is not a supply to them for GST purposes, because Greg and Rhonda already own the properties beneficially.

Also see interpretation statements IS 21/01, "GST and Agency" (*Tax Information Bulletin* ¶332-108 Vol 33, No 2, March 2021) and IS 19/04, "Income tax – distributions from foreign trusts" (*Tax Information Bulletin* ¶321-112 Vol 32, No 1, February 2020, at [188]–[195].

¶25-040 Supply is interpreted extremely widely and can include distributions from testamentary and inter vivos trusts

It is often understood that "GST is a tax on transactions". See, for example, *Simunovich Fisheries Ltd* v *C of IR* (2002) 20 NZTC 17,456 at [4] per Richardson P for the full bench of the Court of Appeal. However, with no disrespect to the learned judge, GST is no more, and no less, than a tax on supplies.

In practice it is the lack of an apparent transaction inherent in certain supplies made by a trust that can obscure GST obligations. Examples of supplies made by a trading trust that can have GST implications include:

- distributions made under a will where the deceased carried on a taxable activity before death
- trust resettlements
- capital distributions, and
- supplies of trust property to associated persons for less than market value.

¶25-050 Trustees and beneficiaries are associated persons for GST purposes

GST is imposed by reference to the value of a supply: GST Act, s 8(1). Special rules determine the value of certain supplies between trusts and associated persons.

Although it is the trust rather than the trustee that registers for GST, for the purposes of the GST Act, association is determined by reference to the trustee.

A trustee of a trust is associated with:

- a person who has benefited or is eligible to benefit, other than where the trustee is a charitable or non-profit body: GST Act, s 2A(1)(f)
- a settlor, other than where the trustee is a charitable or non-profit body: GST Act, s 2A(1)(g)

- a trustee of another trust if the trusts have a common settlor: GST Act, s 2A(1)(h)
- a person holding a power of appointment and removal of the trustee (but not if the person holding the power is a professional, subject to a code of professional conduct, has not benefitted from the trust and is not eligible to do so: GST Act, s 2A(1)(hb)
- two persons who are both associated with a third person: GST Act, s 2A(1)(i).

A person is eligible to benefit from a trust if that person is named as a beneficiary or is part of a class of beneficiaries.

Example

Constance is the eldest daughter of Gerald and Rosanne, the settlors of the Lamplight Trust. Constance is eligible to benefit from the Lamplight Trust because she is a member of the class of beneficiaries: "the children of the Settlors".

However, a person is not eligible to benefit from a trust only because that person could be appointed as a beneficiary.

For the purposes of the definition of associated persons in the GST Act, "settlor" has the same wide definition as that in Income Tax Act 2007, s YA 1: GST Act, s 2A(7). This means that a reference to settlor can extend beyond the person named in the deed of trust.

Correctly determining the value of a supply is important not just to ensure that the correct amount of any GST is returned but also, where a trust is unregistered, to establish whether the registration threshold will be exceeded. See further at ¶25-120.

The valuation rules mean that where a supply is made from a trading trust to an unregistered beneficiary, GST will need to be accounted for at market value (GST Act, s 10(3)) regardless of whether any consideration is made for the supply.

¶25-060 The test of association is particularly broad due to it being a tripartite test

The tripartite nature of part of the test of association means that care is required when dealing with third parties that can be an associated person for GST purposes due to an interposed relationship: GST Act, s 2A(1)(i).

For the purposes of the definition of associated persons, a person acting as a trustee will be treated as acting in a different capacity from that person's personal capacity; and from the trustee of any other trust: QB 07/03 "Trustees in the Context of the Goods and Services Tax Act 1985: Does a Separate Trustee Capacity and Personal Capacity Exist and do separate Trustee Capacities Exist for Trustees of Multiple Trusts?".

Example

A is a trustee of a trust. A's wife (C) is a shareholder of a company, (B), and has a 25% voting interest in Ormiston. C is also a beneficiary of the trust. The trust sells property to the company. When determining the time of supply of the property under section 9(2)(a), a factor to consider is whether or not the parties are associated with each other. The question is whether the trust and the company are associated. To determine association, it is necessary to consider section 2A(1)

> …
>
> Section 2A(1)(i) is a test for association in a tripartite situation such as this, and provides that two people will be associated under section 2A(1)(i) if they are each associated with a third person under any one of paragraphs (a) to (hb), being the remaining paragraphs of section 2A(1). The trust (represented by A, the trustee) and the company will be associated under section 2A(1)(i) if they are each associated with a third person under any one of the remaining paragraphs of section 2A(1).
>
> A's wife (C) holds a voting interest of 25% in the company (B). This means that C and B are associated by virtue of section 2A(1)(b)(i).
>
> The issue to then be determined is whether A and A's wife (C) are associated. If they too are associated under any of the paragraphs (a) to (hb) of section 2A(1), then the company and the trust will be associated persons.
>
> Because A is a trustee of the trust, he is regarded as having two capacities, a trustee capacity and a separate personal capacity. In this case the transaction involves trust property being sold to the company, with A acting in his trustee capacity. Because A is viewed only in his capacity as trustee of a trust, there is no association between A and A's wife (C) under section 2A(1)(c)(ii), which associates two people through marriage. Consequently, the trust and the company cannot be associated through A's marriage to C. However, as C is a beneficiary of the trust, and is, therefore, associated with A under section 2A(1)(f), the trust and the company are associated.
>
> Furthermore, in this scenario, it is worth noting that section 2A(4) results in A being treated as holding a 25% interest in company B.

This example is taken from QB 07/03.

¶25-065 Associations can also arise for GST purposes through the application of the "control by any other means" test

The tests of association include a backstop test where a group of persons *"has control of each of those companies by any other means whatsoever"*.

Where 2 companies have the same director and ultimate shareholder through intervening companies, the question of "control by any other means" is satisfied. This can also be the case where one of the interposed companies is a corporate trustee and the legal owner does not represent the entire beneficial ownership. Note that in the context of control by any other means whatsoever, the means of control do not need to be the same for each of the companies in question. See *Concepts 124 Ltd* v *C of IR* [2014] NZHC 2140; (2014) 3 NZTR ¶24-031 at [81].

In *Concepts 124 Ltd* v *C of IR*, the High Court upheld the TRA's decision in *Case* 11/2013 (2013) 26 NZTC ¶2-010 that the GST input credits the taxpayer company, Concepts 124 Ltd (Concepts 124), was entitled to deduct in relation to the purchase of a property from another company (Ormiston) was limited to the tax included in the original cost of the property to Ormiston, as Concepts 124 and Ormiston were found to be "associated persons" in terms of s 2A(1)(a)(i) and (iii).

Background facts

Mr Cummings was the sole director of Concepts 124. The shares in Concepts 124 were wholly owned by Working Concepts Limited (Working Concepts) and Mr Cummings was the sole shareholder and director of Working Concepts. Mr Cummings was also the sole director of Ormiston. The shares in Ormiston were wholly owned by Flatbush Holdings Limited (Flatbush). Mr Cummings was the sole shareholder and director of Flatbush. Flatbush held 75% of the equity in Ormiston for the benefit of the Flatbush Holdings Trust and 25% for the benefit of Mr Cummings.

On 29 October 2004, Working Concepts Limited purchased a property as 3 lots for a total purchase price of $847,000. This included GST of $94,111.12. In 2006, Working Concepts nominated Ormiston as the purchaser of the property. Ormiston began to develop the property into an apartment block complex. On 10 July 2008, Ormiston and the taxpayer entered into a sale and purchase agreement for the property. The purchase price was $8,034,750, to be paid in 18 instalments of $423,000 with a final instalment of $420,750 to be paid on settlement. This agreement was signed by Mr Cummings, as director, on behalf of Ormiston and by Mr A, as director, on behalf of the taxpayer. Up to 23 July 2008, Ormiston had incurred costs of $3,009,296 in acquiring and developing the property.

The structure can be represented as:

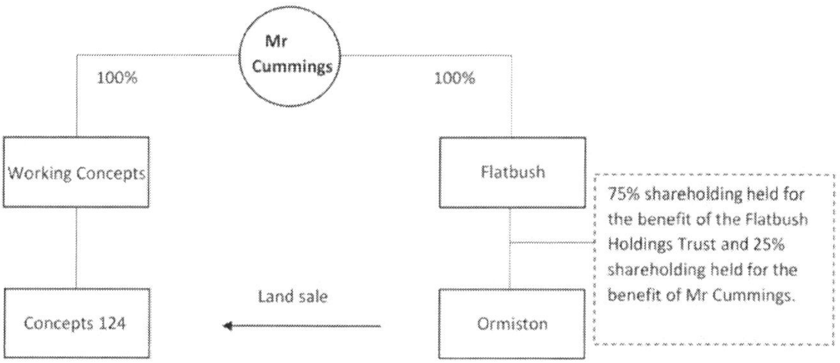

During the GST tax periods between July 2008 and October 2009, the taxpayer paid 17 instalments of the purchase price to Ormiston by way of book entry. The taxpayer claimed GST input deductions in respect of those instalment payments.

The Commissioner considered that the taxpayer and Ormiston were associated companies because they were both controlled by Mr Cummings under s 2A(1)(a)(iii).

It was not disputed that the supply of the property from Ormiston (which was not registered for GST) to the taxpayer was the supply of a "secondhand good" for the purposes of the Act. It was also not in dispute that the taxpayer (which was registered for GST at all relevant times) was entitled to deduct input tax on the purchase of the property. What was in dispute between the Commissioner and the taxpayer was the quantum of the input tax.

If the taxpayer and Ormiston were not associated persons at the time, the quantum of the input tax credit was the tax fraction of the consideration as claimed by the taxpayer in terms of s 3A(3)(e). If the companies were associated persons, s 3A(3)(a) provided that the amount of the input tax was the lesser of:

- the tax included in the original cost of the goods to the supplier
- the tax fraction of the purchase price, and
- the tax fraction of the open market value of the supply.

The lesser of the 3 amounts in this case was the tax included in the original cost of the goods to the supplier. The original cost of the goods (being the land) to Ormiston was $847,000. The GST included in the original supply was $94,111.12.

The Commissioner considered that because the taxpayer and Ormiston were associated persons, the taxpayer was entitled to an input tax deduction of $94,111.12 (the GST included in the original supply) and assessed the taxpayer accordingly.

It was accepted that Mr Cummings was deemed to have a 100% voting interest in the Concepts 124. Mr Cummings also had a 100% voting interest in Ormiston. The issue for determination was whether for the purposes of s 2A(1)(a)(iii), Mr Cummings had control of Concepts 124 and Ormiston by any other means whatsoever. The Taxation Review Authority found that he did.

This decision was upheld by the High Court that also found that Concepts 124 and Ormiston were associated persons in terms of s 2A(1)(a)(i) because Mr Cummings, a "group of persons", was to be treated as having, through Working Concepts and Flatbush respectively, 100% of the voting interests in each of Concepts 124 and Ormiston. In coming to this conclusion, the High Court analysed the history and intention of the relevant sections and found that in determining the voting interests held in a company, corporate shareholders can be "looked through", even where that shareholder company is holding the shares as a trustee.

In support of this, the High Court noted that although there is a rule precluding corporate trustees being "looked through" for the purposes of the continuity rules for loss and imputation credit purposes (s YC 9 of the Income Tax Act 2007 discussed further below), no such rule precludes corporate trustees being "looked through" in a GST context.

With Flatbush being "looked through" to Mr Cummings (as its shareholder), Mr Cummings constituted a person with a voting interest of more than 50% in each of Concepts 124 and Ormiston. As a result of the association, Concepts 124 was only entitled to claim the lesser amount of the original GST input tax. The GST Act makes no reference, directly or indirectly, to shares held on trust. This is correct in accordance with the general law of trusts in that trustees act personally and not as some separate trustee personality. For the purposes of the GST Act, "held" is not qualified, in that definition, by reference to whether the shares in question are owned legally only (as when held on trust) or legally and beneficially (as when held personally). Further, as a matter of basic company law, a share is held by the person registered as its holder for the time being in the company's share register. Company law requires companies to ignore trust interests. That is the basis upon which questions of control of companies have also been determined in the tax context.

This is confirmed by the continuity provisions in the Income Tax Act, which has the policy intent of ensuring that the future benefit of tax losses is enjoyed by the economic owners of the company at the time the underlying economic losses were incurred. Section YC 9, which means attribution is not to be made to individual shareholders where there is an interposed company holding shares on trust, further confirms this.

Section YC 4 does not contemplate that voting interests are to be traced through a corporate trustee to its shareholders. Rather, s YC 9 means that such tracing does not occur where voting interests are determined in the context of the continuity provisions. Where control is being determined, there is no reason not to attribute control to the (personal) shareholders of a company that holds shares in another company on trust.

Importantly, s YC 4 does not deem the shareholders of a corporate trustee to be the economic owners of the company: rather it deems them to be, through the shareholding interests held by the corporate trustee, the controllers of the company. That is a different concept.

The case shows how the use of corporate trustees can provide unexpected results and the importance of carefully considering the appropriate ownership and management structure for a corporate trustee.

Also see *Staithes Drive Development Ltd* v *C of IR* [2015] NZHC 2593; (2015) 27 NZTC ¶22-028 and Sybrand van Schalkwyk "GST and associated person rules – Need for reform" CCH, New Zealand Tax Planning Report (16 February 2016), which compares the rules of association from the Income Tax Act and GST Act (also see the table at ¶18-240).

¶25-070 The market value rules do not apply to supplies to associated persons who are GST-registered

An exception to s 10(3) of the GST Act applies to any supply to an associated person who is GST-registered and applies the goods or services for the purposes of making taxable supplies: GST Act, s 10(3A).

Where the exception applies, the market valuation rules do not apply.

Example

The trustee of the Croft Trust has resolved to distribute a parcel of farming land owned by the Croft Trust to Bruce, a beneficiary of the trust. Bruce is associated with the trustee of the Croft Trust: GST Act, s 2A(1)(f). Both the Croft Trust and Bruce are GST-registered. Bruce already carries on a farming activity and will apply the distributed parcel of land to that activity.

The market value rules will not apply to the supply of the farming land as both parties are GST-registered and the land will be applied to Bruce's taxable activity.

¶25-080 The time of supply is varied for associated persons

The time of supply is varied for associated persons. Unless the time of supply is triggered in the normal way, by payment or issue of an invoice, the time of supply will be deemed to occur:

- once goods are supplied or made available, or
- in the cases of services, unless deemed to be supplied in New Zealand, when the service is performed: GST Act, s 9(2)(a)(iii).

¶25-090 Input tax credits can be limited for supplies between associated persons

When a seller and purchaser are associated persons, any input tax credit is limited to the lesser of the tax included in the original cost of the goods to the supplier, the tax fraction of the purchase price, and the tax fraction of the open market value of the supply. GST Act, s 3A(3)(a).

Secondhand goods credits are subject to the same limitation: GST Act, s 3A(2), (3). See *Case* 3/2011 (2011) 25 NZTC ¶1-003.

Example

Tracey is the registered proprietor of a block of bare land she purchased in 1980 for $200,000. In 2009 Tracey, who has never been GST-registered, sells this block of land to the trustee of Caitlin's Trust, a GST-registered trust of which Tracey is the settlor. The sale price is market value of $1.3 million.

The trustee of Caitlin's Trust is associated with Tracey: GST Act, s 2A(1)(g). Accordingly, the secondhand goods credit available to the trust is the lesser of the tax fraction of the purchase price, the tax fraction of open market value or the tax included in the price when the land was purchased by Tracey.

As the land was a pre-GST asset, Caitlin's Trust cannot claim a secondhand goods credit.

¶25-100 There is no requirement that a zero-rated supply be for consideration

The zero-rating provisions apply to trustees without modification regardless of whether the supply is to an associated person. Accordingly, any supply between trustees, from or to a trustee, which meets the requirements for the supply of a going concern or a zero-rated supply of land, can be zero-rated: GST Act, ss 2(1) ("going concern"), 11(1)(m), 11(1)(mb), 78F.

The absence of consideration does not prevent zero-rating, as there is no requirement that the supply of a going concern be for consideration.

Example

The trustees of the Hohepa Trust own a business that is transferred to the trustees of the Napier-Robertson Trust under a deed of resettlement. No consideration is made for the supply. Each trust is GST-registered.

The deed of resettlement contains a clause that provides that the resettling and recipient trustees agree that the supply is the supply of a going concern.

The trustees of the Napier-Robertson Trust will continue to carry on the business.

The supply can be zero-rated as the supply of the going concern, presuming all the requirements of a going concern are met, despite there being no consideration.

Where the zero-rating requirements cannot be met, the supply will be a taxable supply.

¶25-110 A deed of acknowledgment of debt is consideration for the purposes of the GST Act

The definition of consideration for the purposes of the Act is sufficiently broad to include a deed of acknowledgment of debt: GST Act, s 2(1).

This means that where the purchase price for a sale is met by an acknowledgment of debt, an input tax credit can be claimed where the relevant requirements are met.

The time at which an input tax credit can be claimed will depend on whether the trust is registered on an invoice, payments or hybrid basis. This will be the case regardless of whether the lender subsequently forgives the debt in part or in whole.

Example

The trustees of a trust have agreed to purchase a valuable painting from an associated party, the price of which includes $50,000 GST. The trust is registered for GST on a payments basis. The full purchase price, supported by an independent valuation, is being settled by way of a deed of acknowledgment of debt. The associated vendor is also registered and is aware that GST of $50,000 will be payable on the sale.

As the purchase price is settled by a deed of acknowledgment of debt, is this treated as being a valid purchase in the period in which the deed is entered into so that a GST input tax credit can be claimed?

Yes, presupposing the other requirements of an input tax credit are met, Inland Revenue accepts that payment prima facie occurs via an acknowledgment of debt in the form of a deed that is separate from the sale and purchase agreement, and which is consistent with the sale and purchase agreement and any other documentation.

See *Tax Information Bulletin* ¶511-102 Vol 5, No 11, April 1994 at 1.

¶25-120 The registration threshold is not different for a trust

The registration threshold is the same for trusts, whether charitable or not, as for any other person or unincorporated body.

Arrangements involving family trusts and associated parties are often more informal than arrangements with third parties. Arrangements can develop over time and commonly are not recorded in writing. This can lead to difficulties in determining the exact nature of agreements and, for example, the amount of consideration for a supply.

A useful example of the risks of informal arrangements is demonstrated in *The Trustee, Executors and Agency Company New Zealand Ltd* v *C of IR* (1997) 18 NZTC 13,076. In that case, the rental paid did not exceed the registration threshold. However, as the lessee was also liable to meet the trustee landlord's local body rates obligation, this payment represented additional consideration for the supply of the lease and, as such, meant that the total consideration paid was in excess of the registration threshold. In a decision upheld by the High Court, the TRA noted in *Case* R29 (1994) 16 NZTC 6,155 at 6,161 that:

> "I accept that because of the family nature of this lease, its terms were not committed to writing. It was suggested to me that the family nature of things was a proper explanation for there being no written lease. I accept that this is often the case but it is not good practice for family arrangements to be treated in a different manner from normal business arrangements. It is important that all business arrangements, whether family in nature or not, be committed to writing".

Where the registration threshold is exceeded, a trust, as is the case for any other person, is deemed to be registered for GST.

Example

The trustee of the Pepper Pot Trust leases a commercial property to Coco, an associated person. Although the annual rental paid is $35,000, the market rental is above the registration threshold and so the trustee of the Pepper Pot Trust will be deemed to be registered for GST and will be liable to return GST on the lease to Coco, regardless of whether GST can be recovered from Coco.

¶25-130 Trustee is liable for trust's GST despite registration being in the name of the trust

The trustee, or if more than one, the trustees jointly and severally, is liable for a trust's GST during the taxable periods, or part thereof, that relate to a particular trustee's appointment. This is the case regardless of whether the trustee can benefit from the trust. See *Selkirk* v *McIntyre* [2013] NZHC 575, where Mr Selkirk, personally paid the entire GST debt owing by a trust and then obtained a court order for an equal contribution from his co-trustee (but not full reimbursement). See further at ¶21-075.

A trustees' liability continues until that trustee advises Inland Revenue in writing that the trustee has retired as a trustee: GST Act, s 57(3B), *Chester Trustee Services Ltd* v *C of IR* (2002) 20 NZTC 17,725.

There is no prescribed form of notice regarding retirement as a trustee. However, good practice would be to include a copy of the deed of retirement with the letter advising the retirement.

Example

On 27 July Fred gave notice to Inland Revenue that he was retiring as trustee of the William Tell Family Trust. Subsequently, Inland Revenue reassessed the GST payable for the taxable period ending 30 June.

Fred remains personally liable for the amount of the original assessment as well as the additional GST assessed.

If a trustee dies, the trustee's liability continues until the trustee's executor advises Inland Revenue that the trustee has died.

If a trustee is adjudicated bankrupt and then retires as a trustee, the trustee will remain liable for any GST obligation incurred before resignation.

Subject to the terms of the trust, there is no requirement for a bankrupt trustee to retire. However, a trustee who does not resign is not automatically released from any GST liability upon the trustee's discharge from bankruptcy and there are circumstances where that liability can survive bankruptcy: *Duncan* v *C of IR* [2007] NZCA 235; (2007) 23 NZTC 21,380.

¶25-135 Liability for GST cannot be avoided through retirement

Corporate trustees are a common feature of modern trading trusts. The basic rationale is that the use of a company means that any liability that would otherwise accrue – say to a natural person trustee – accrues instead to the company; and provided the directors do not breach the duties owed under the Companies Act 1993, in the event of insolvency, there is no loss to the Trust. Corporate trustees used in these circumstances generally have no assets.

Not all support the use of such companies as a trustee. Ford stated in "Trading Trusts and Creditor's Rights" (1981) 13(1) *Melbourne University Law Review* 1 that "[t]he fruit of this union of the law of trusts and the law of limited liability companies is a commercial monstrosity".

Arguably, *Commissioner of Inland Revenue* v *Robertson* [2017] NZHC 31; (2017) 4 NZTR ¶27-002, where Robertson unsuccessfully sought summary judgment that the Commissioner's claim against him to recover $159,910.58 of GST refund paid by mistake to a trustee company of which he was the liquidator, supports Ford's views.

The facts of *C of IR v Robertson* are not entirely straight-forward, and as the matter was heard on a summary judgment basis there are still facts not in evidence.

Simply put the relevant facts for the purposes of this discussion are:

- The trading trust (WBR Trust) settled by Mr Brown was a property trader.
- The deed for the WBR Trust provided for an appointor, but no appointor was named.
- The trustee was Hukatere Coastal Trustee Limited (Hukatere).
- Hukatere was insolvent due to GST arrears.

- Mr Brown purported to remove Hukatere and appointed RVB Corporate Trustee Ltd (RVB) as trustee of the WBR Trust on or about 29 March 2010. Note that Mr Brown did not have a power of appointment and Hukatere was not party to the deed removing it as a trustee.
- On 14 April 2010, Hukatere was placed into liquidation. Mr Robertson was the liquidator.
- In September 2010, Mr Robertson, as liquidator, receives GST refunds since argued by the Commissioner to have been paid in error, totalling $159,910.58.
- In December 2010, Mr Robertson pays $152,387.89 to RVB's accountant. That sum was then later paid to RVB's accountant who paid it to the trustee (Shakespeare Trustees Limited) of the Napier Investments Trust. No evidence was given that Shakespeare Trustees Limited was a trustee (or beneficiary) of the WBR Trust.
- The Commissioner says the money was paid in error and wants it back.
- Mr Robertson's position is that he is not required to return the funds to the Commissioner.

In considering the matter, the Court sets out a number of general propositions at [29] that usefully canvass the often-underappreciated issue as to what trustee is liable for what, when there has been a change of trustee:

- A trust is not an independent entity.
- A trustee who incurs liability is personally liable for the debt – this includes tax debts.
- A trustee has a right of indemnity for liability incurred as a trustee, which is secured by an equitable lien over trust assets – this right includes rights of realisation, retention, exoneration and reimbursement from trust assets.
- Trust assets vest in new trustees when a trustee is removed or retired – see s 47 of the Trustee Act 1956 (since repealed, now see Trusts Act 2019, s 116).
- Retirement does not extinguish any liability incurred before retirement or impose liability on the new trustee for those debts, but the new trustee takes the trust assets subject to the former trustee's rights of indemnity for that liability.
- On liquidation, a company's assets are controlled by the liquidator, but they are not the liquidator's property.
- A trustee's liability for GST does not cease on retirement but continues until the Commissioner is notified of the retirement.

One of the issues in the case in hand relates to when Hukatere was removed as a trustee and whether this was before its liquidation. This is important as different outcomes are possible depending on when the trusteeship ended.

It is difficult to see how it can be argued that a sole trustee can be removed by a deed to which it is not a party in circumstances where a power of appointment has not been exercised. This is because s 43(1) of the Trustee Act provides that where there is no appointor who can act, it is the trustee that has the power (exercisable by deed) to appoint a new trustee. This matter will be considered further at the substantive hearing. It does highlight (again) the need to review deeds of appointment and removal against trust deeds, and in some cases the Trustee Act, to ensure and effective deed.

The case raises important fact specific considerations about when (or whether) a trustee is entitled to a tax refund in circumstances where there has been a change of trustee, and the rights between retiring and new trustees. The case also considers when assets vest in a new trustee. Again, the matter is fact specific. However, the decision is a useful resource that also contains helpful examples and reference to other decided cases on the matters raised.

¶25-140 GST registration ceases at death

When a GST-registered person dies, that person's taxable period ends on the date of death. The trustee of the estate is deemed to be registered from the date of the trustee's appointment in the capacity of agent of the deceased: GST Act, s 58. The trustee, as a specified agent, must give notice within 21 days of the date of the appointment.

The trustee is liable to file returns from the date of deemed registration and can file returns on behalf of the deceased up until the date of death. See *Tax Information Bulletin* ¶23-116 Vol 2, No 3, October 1990, Appendix B at 4.

> **"Example 1**
>
> Mele is a sole trader. She owns and operates a florist business trading as "Blooming Good". She is registered for GST on the invoice basis and files returns two-monthly. Her taxable periods end on the last day of February, April, June, August, October, and December. Mele employs her only sister Tala.
>
> Mele dies suddenly on 3 April. When Mele first went into business she made a will. Her will provides that all her property passes to her spouse, Tom. The will appoints Tom and Tala as Mele's executors. Tom and Tala agree that in the short term it would be prudent for Tala to carry on the business as she knows all the customers and is familiar with how it operates. Following Mele's death the florist shop is closed for a week. Tala reopens the shop on 10 April. Tala wonders what she must do to continue to meet the business's GST obligations, and contacts her local Inland Revenue office.
>
> Tala is told to provide formal notification in writing that she is now carrying on Mele's taxable activity, i.e., the florist business as Mele's personal representative, and the date of Mele's death. Inland Revenue advises that she must do so before 25 April, i.e., 21 days from, but not including, 3 April. Under the GST legislation, Tala is now deemed to be a registered person carrying on Mele's taxable activity. Tala is told that she is personally liable for the GST obligations and liabilities of the florist business incurred on and after 3 April while she continues to carry on the business as Mele's personal representative.
>
> Inland Revenue staff remind Tala that she will need to file a return for the March/April taxable period ending 30 April. This return is due by 31 May. This will involve making two returns: one for the period 1 March to 3 April, the other for the period 4 April to 30 April."

Example 1 from the *Tax Information Bulletin* ¶76-107 Vol 7, No 6, December 1995 at 14.

The trustee of an estate will charge GST on any supplies made as is the case for any other GST-registered person. The associated person provisions will apply as relevant as for the trustee of an inter vivos trust. See ¶24-040.

The trustee of an estate is personally liable for GST from the date of death, but is not liable for any GST liability that arose before the date of death. The trustee can also obtain unclaimed input tax credits that relate to the period before death. However, the Commissioner can set off any entitlement to an input tax credit against any liability that arose before death: GST Act, s 46(7).

For a more comprehensive analysis of the GST Act, see A McKenzie *GST – A Practical Guide* (Edition 9, CCH, Auckland, 2012).

¶25-150 Legislation

Goods and Services Tax Act 1985

2 INTERPRETATION

2(1) [Definitions]

[...]

"**consideration**", in relation to the supply of goods and services to any person, includes any payment made or any act or forbearance, whether or not voluntary, in respect of, in response to, or for the inducement of, the supply of any goods and services, whether by that person or by any other person; but does not include any payment made by any person as an unconditional gift to any non-profit body

[...]

"**going concern**", in relation to a supplier and a recipient, means the situation where–

(a) there is a supply of a taxable activity, or of a part of a taxable activity where that part is capable of separate operation; and

(b) all of the goods and services that are necessary for the continued operation of that taxable activity or that part of a taxable activity are supplied to the recipient; and

(c) the supplier carries on, or is to carry on, that taxable activity or that part of a taxable activity up to the time of its transfer to the recipient

[...]

"**unincorporated body**" means an unincorporated body of persons, including a partnership, a joint venture, and the trustees of a trust

[...]

2A MEANING OF ASSOCIATED PERSONS

2A(1) [Associated persons defined]

In this Act, **associated persons** or persons associated with each other are–

(a) two companies if a group of persons–

(i) has voting interests in each of those companies of 50% or more when added together; or

(ii) has market value interests in each of those companies of 50% or more when added together and a market value circumstance exists in respect of either company; or

(iii) has control of each of those companies by any other means whatsoever:

(b) a company and a person other than a company if the person has–

(i) a voting interest in the company of 25% or more; or

(ii) a market value interest in the company of 25% or more and a market value circumstance exists in respect of the company:

(bb) a person, or a branch or division of the person that is treated as a separate person under section 56B, and another branch or division of the person that is treated as a separate person under section 56B:

(c) two persons who are–

(i) connected by blood relationship:

(ii) connected by marriage, civil union or de facto relationship:

(iii) connected by adoption:

(iv) *(repealed)*

(cb) a trustee of a trust and another person (**person** A), if–

(i) person A is associated with another person (the **relative**) under paragraph (c); and

(ii) the relative is associated with the trustee under paragraph (f):

(d) a partnership and a partner in the partnership:

(e) *(repealed)*

(f) a trustee of a trust and a person who has benefited or is eligible to benefit under the trust, except if, in relation to a supply of goods and services,–

(i) the trustee is a charitable or non-profit body with wholly or principally charitable, benevolent, philanthropic, or cultural purposes and the supply is made in carrying out these purposes; or

(ii) the person is a charitable or non-profit body with wholly or principally charitable, benevolent, philanthropic, or cultural purposes and the supply enables them to carry out these purposes:

(g) a trustee of a trust and a settlor of the trust, except if the trustee is a charitable or non-profit body with wholly or principally charitable, benevolent, philanthropic or cultural purposes:

(h) a trustee of a trust and a trustee of another trust if the same person is a settlor of both trusts, except if, in relation to a supply of goods and services,–

(i) either trustee is a charitable or non-profit body with wholly or principally charitable, benevolent, philanthropic, or cultural purposes; and

(ii) the supply is made in, or enables, the carrying out of the charitable, benevolent, philanthropic, or cultural purposes:

(hb) A trustee of a trust and a person who has a power of appointment or of removal of the trustee, except if the person–

(i) holds the power as a provider of professional services; and

(ii) is subject to a professional code of conduct, and disciplinary process intended to enforce compliance with the code, of an approved organisation as that term is defined in section 3(1) of the Tax Administration Act 1994, for such providers of professional services; and

(iii) has not benefited from the trust; and

(iv) is not eligible to benefit from the trust:

(i) a person (person A) and another person (person B) if–

(i) person B is associated with a third person (person C) under any one of paragraphs (a) to (hb); and

(ii) person C is associated with person A under any one of paragraphs (a) to (hb).

[...]

2A(7) [Settlor defined]

For the purpose of subsection (1)(g) and (1)(h), **settlor** has the meaning set out in section YA 1 of the Income Tax Act 2007.

[...]

9 TIME OF SUPPLY

9(1) [Time of supply]

Subject to this Act, for the purposes of this Act a supply of goods and services shall be deemed to take place at the earlier of the time an invoice is issued by the supplier or the recipient or the time any payment is received by the supplier, in respect of that supply.

9(2) [Time of supply in certain circumstances]

Notwithstanding anything in subsection (1), a supply of goods and services shall be deemed to take place–

(a) if the supply is an associated supply,–

(i) in the case of a supply of goods which are to be removed, at the time of the removal; and

(ii) in the case of a supply of goods which are not to be removed, at the time when they are made available to the recipient; and

(iii) in the case of a supply of services, at the time the services are performed, unless subparagraph (iv) applies; and

(iv) in the case of a supply of services that is treated by section 8(4B) as being made in New Zealand, at the end of the taxable period that includes the date that is 2 months after the first balance date of the recipient that follows the completion of the performance of the services:

provided that this paragraph shall not apply in any case where an invoice is issued, or any payment is made, in respect of that supply, on or before the last day for furnishing the return in relation to the taxable period during which, but for this proviso, that supply would have been made:

[...]

10 VALUE OF SUPPLY OF GOODS AND SERVICES

[...]

10(3) [Associated supplies]

Subject to subsections (3A), (3AB), (3B), (3C), (3D) and (8), the consideration for a supply is treated as being the open market value of the supply if–

(a) the supply is made by a person for no consideration or for a consideration that is less than the open market value of the supply; and

(b) the supply is an associated supply; and

(c) the supply is not a fringe benefit that the supplier has, or is deemed to have, provided or granted under the FBT rules of the Income Tax Act 2007 to the recipient, being a person employed under a contract of service by the supplier.

[...]

10(3AB) [Non-application of section 10(3)]

Subsection (3) does not apply to a supply of goods and services if the recipient–

(a) acquires the supply for no consideration; and

(b) from the time of the supply, applies the goods and services for the purpose of making taxable supplies.

[...]

11 ZERO-RATING OF GOODS

11(1) [Zero-rated goods]

A supply of goods that is chargeable with tax under section 8 must be charged at the rate of 0% in the following situations:

[...]

(m) the supply to a registered person of a taxable activity, or part of a taxable activity, that is a going concern at the time of the supply, if–

(i) the supplier and the recipient agree that the supply is the supply of a going concern, and their agreement is recorded in a document; and

(ii) the supplier and the recipient intend that the supply is of a taxable activity, or part of a taxable activity, that is capable of being carried on as a going concern by the recipient; or

(mb) the supply wholly or partly consists of land, being a supply–

(i) made by a registered person to another registered person who acquires the goods with the intention of using them for making taxable supplies; and

(ii) that is not a supply of land intended to be used as a principal place of residence of the recipient of the supply or a person associated with them under section 2A(1)(c); or

[...]

51 PERSONS MAKING SUPPLIES IN COURSE OF TAXABLE ACTIVITY TO BE REGISTERED

51(1) [Liability to register]

Subject to this Act, every person who, on or after 1 October 1986, carries on any taxable activity and is not registered, becomes liable to be registered–

(a) at the end of any month where the total value of supplies made in New Zealand in that month and the 11 months immediately preceding that month in the course of carrying on all taxable activities has exceeded $60,000 (or such larger amount as the Governor-General may, from time to time, by Order in Council declare):

provided that a person does not become liable to be registered by virtue of this paragraph where the Commissioner is satisfied that the value of those supplies in the period of 12 months beginning on the day after the last day of the period referred to in the said paragraph will not exceed that amount:

[...]

57 UNINCORPORATED BODIES

[...]

57(2) [Members of an unincorporated body]

Where an unincorporated body that carries on any taxable activity is registered pursuant to this Act,–

(a) the members of that body shall not themselves be registered or liable to be registered under this Act in relation to the carrying on of that taxable activity; and

(b) any supply of goods and services made in the course of carrying on that taxable activity shall be deemed for the purposes of this Act to be supplied by that body, and shall be deemed not to be made by any member of that body; and

(c) any supply of goods and services to, or acquisition of goods by, any member of that body acting in the capacity as a member of that body and in the course of carrying on that taxable activity, not being a supply to which paragraph (b) applies, shall be deemed for the purposes of this Act to be supplied to or acquired by that body, and shall be deemed not to be supplied to or acquired by that member; and

(d) that registration shall be in the name of the body, or where that body is the trustees of a trust, in the name of the trust; and

(e) subject to subsections (3) to (3B), any change of members of that body shall have no effect for the purposes of this Act.

57(3) [Liability of ex-members for tax]

Despite this section, a member is jointly and severally liable with other members for all tax payable by the unincorporated body during the taxable periods, or part of taxable periods as the case may be, the person is a member of the body, even if the person is no longer a member of the body.

57(3A) [Liability of ex-member's estate for tax]

When an individual member dies, the member's estate is severally liable in due course of administration for tax payable by the unincorporated body to the extent that it remains unpaid, whether or not the individual was a member on the date of their death.

57(3B) [Notice to Commissioner]

For the purpose of subsections (3) and (3A), a member does not stop being a member of the unincorporated body until the date on which the Commissioner is notified of a change in membership of the body.

57(4) [Service of notice]

For the purposes of this Act, any notice served in accordance with this Act which is addressed to an unincorporated body by the name in which it is registered pursuant to this Act, shall be deemed to be served on that body and on all members of that body.

57(5) [Liability of members for statutory requirement]

Subject to subsection (6), where anything is required to be done pursuant to this Act by or on behalf of an unincorporated body, it shall be the joint and several liability of all the members to do any such thing:

provided that any such thing done by 1 member shall be sufficient compliance with any such requirement.

57(6) [Office holders liable]

Notwithstanding anything in this section, but subject to subsections (3) to (3B), where anything is required to be done pursuant to this Act by or on behalf of an unincorporated body, not being a partnership, joint venture, or trustees of a trust, the affairs of which are managed by its members or a committee or committees of its members, it shall be the joint and several responsibility of–

(a) every member holding office as president, chairman, treasurer, secretary, or any similar office; or

(b) in default of any such member, every member holding office as a member of a committee:

provided that if it is done by any official or committee member, referred to in paragraph (a) or paragraph (b), that shall be sufficient compliance with any such requirement.

58 PERSONAL REPRESENTATIVE, LIQUIDATOR, RECEIVER, ETC

58(1) [Definitions]

In this section and sections 46 and 55–

"**agency period**" means the period beginning on the date on which a person becomes entitled to act as a specified agent carrying on a taxable activity in relation to an incapacitated person and ending on the earlier of–

(a) the date on which some person other than the incapacitated person or the specified agent is registered in respect of the taxable activity; or

(b) the date on which there is no longer a person acting as a specified agent in relation to the incapacitated person

"**incapacitated person**" means a registered person who dies, or goes into liquidation or receivership, or becomes bankrupt or incapacitated

"**specified agent**" means a person carrying on any taxable activity in a capacity as personal representative, liquidator, or receiver of an incapacitated person, or otherwise as agent for or on behalf of or in the stead of an incapacitated person.

58(1A) [Specified agent carrying on taxable activity]

Despite sections 5(2) and 60, a person who becomes a specified agent is treated as being a registered person carrying on the taxable activity of the incapacitated person during the agency period, and the incapacitated person is not treated as carrying on the taxable activity during the period.

58(1B) [Specified agent carrying on part of taxable activity]

If a person becomes a specified agent and has been appointed to carry on part of the incapacitated person's taxable activity only, subsection (1A) applies only to the part of the taxable activity the person has been appointed to carry on.

58(1C) [Reduction for supplies made before agency period]

Subject to section 46(7), a specified agent may deduct an amount under section 20(3) relating to supplies made before the agency period if the incapacitated person is entitled to, and has not previously deducted, the amount.

58(1D) [Specified agent not personally liable]

A specified agent is not personally liable for any liabilities incurred under this Act by the incapacitated person on or before the date the agency period starts.

[...]

58(3) [Notice to Commissioner]

Any person who becomes a specified agent, or who as a mortgagee in possession carries on any taxable activity of the mortgagor, shall, within 21 days of becoming a specified agent or commencing that taxable activity of the mortgagor, notify the Commissioner of that fact and of the date of the death or of the liquidation or receivership or bankruptcy or mortgagee taking possession of any land or other property previously mortgaged by the mortgagor, or of the nature of the incapacity and the date on which it began.

Part VIII

DEATH

CHAPTER 26

Deceased Estates

¶26-010 Operating principle

Transfers of property in the tax base at death are disposals and acquisitions for tax purposes. The tax treatment of these transfers is determined in accordance with asset transfer rules.

¶26-020 Testamentary trust can arise following assent

By operation of a will or the Administration Act 1969, the assets of a deceased person's estate are held by the deceased's executor(s) or personal representatives (also referred to as administrators). No trust arises until assent whereupon the deceased's executor(s) or personal representatives hold the property of the estate as a trustee or trustees. Such assent can be express or inferred from the circumstances. See interpretation statement IS 19/04, "Income tax – distributions from foreign trusts" (*Tax Information Bulletin* Vol 32, No 1, February 2020, at [41]). Guidance on the transition from executor to trustee is provided in *IRC* v *Smith* [1930] 1 KB 713, where the Lord Judge notes that "The property which on the death of the testator vests in the executor does not remain vested in him for ever. So soon as he assents to the dispositions of the will becoming operative and to the trusts taking effect, the estate vested in him as executor is divested and vests under the dispositions of the will in the trustees of the will".

¶26-030 Executor or administrator takes place of the deceased and winds up the deceased person's affairs

Following a person's death, that person's estate vests in the deceased person's personal representative as trustee of the deceased's estate. The personal representative is either the executor(s) (where the deceased has left a will) or the administrator (where the deceased dies intestate, that is, without a will). For convenience, both are referred to here as the trustee who winds up that person's affairs and in whom the deceased person's estate vests. This vesting of property in the trustee is referred to as a transmission of property from the deceased to the trustee, rather than a transfer. The different terminology reflecting that the property vests under law rather than a transaction between parties. See further at *Tax Education Office Newsletter* No 95, December 1994, at 1, "Taxation Consequences of Death".

The beneficiaries of an estate have no beneficial or proprietary interest in the assets of the estate during the course of administration, although these beneficiaries do have the right to ensure that the estate is properly administered. See *Rauch* v *Maguire* [2010] NZHC 1109; (2010) 3 NZTR ¶20-016. Also see the Trusts Act 2019.

The trustee is responsible for ensuring that assets are dealt with in accordance with the deceased's will or, on intestacy, the Administration Act. The trustee of an estate has the same rights and owes the same obligations as the trustee of an inter vivos trust.

For practical guidance on the administration of deceased estates, see Cordelia Thomas *Forsyth's Guide to Trusts and Estate Practice* (Ed 7, CCH, Auckland 2014).

¶26-040 There are 3 stages of an estate

For taxation purposes, death is treated variously as cessation or disposal of assets and, for taxation purposes, has 3 effective stages:

- death
- the period that the trustee manages the estate, and
- distribution to beneficiaries.

The trustee is responsible for the tax obligations relating to both the deceased person for the estate and any taxation consequences from the distribution of assets.

¶26-050 Return is prepared for the period to the date of death

The trustee is responsible for preparing and filing a return covering the period from the deceased taxpayer's last balance date to the date of death. The return must be prepared on the same basis as that adopted by the deceased while alive and include all income derived during this period. However, if the deceased would not have been required to file a return, there is no requirement for the trustee to file a return on the deceased's behalf: Tax Administration Act 1994, ss 33A (has application only until the 2016–17 year after which it was repealed), 43.

When completing the deceased person's tax return, it is necessary to determine what income is accounted for on account of the deceased and what income is to be accounted for by the estate in its return.

This is the case even if the whole of the estate may pass immediately to beneficiaries who are absolutely entitled in possession to the capital and income of the estate: ss CV 12, HC 8.

Income derived before death is accounted for by the deceased. Income derived after death is accounted for by the estate. Accordingly, it is necessary to correctly establish when different sources of income are derived.

Salary, wages, bonuses, holiday pay, long service leave, directors' fees, superannuation, pensions, annuities, beneficiary income are derived on receipt or when credited to an account or dealt with on the recipient's behalf.

Interest income that accrues on a day-to-day basis before death is derived by the deceased and accounted for as the deceased's income. Other interest that is accrued at the date of death but paid following death is treated as being derived after death and is trustee income. Interest derived after the date of death that relates to a period after that date is treated as trustee or beneficiary income, depending on the terms of the will.

Dividends are derived when paid or credited to the shareholder or the shareholder's trustee. Dividend income relating to a period that spans the date of death is apportioned over that period. When an apportionment is made, the income allocated to the period before the date of death is treated as trustee income if it was not derived by the deceased before death. Dividend income allocated to the period after the date of death is treated as trustee or beneficiary income, depending on the terms of the will: s HC 8.

Example

Bill is a retired farmer holding shares in XYZ Ltd. His income year ends on 30 June. Bill dies on 1 April. On 30 June, XYZ Ltd declares a dividend of $600. The dividend is stated to relate to the period 1 November to 30 April. The dividend is apportioned as follows:

	$
To date of death	500
Balance of dividend period	100
	600

The $100 balance of dividend is treated as trustee income because it was not derived by Bill during his lifetime.

Rental income is derived when received and is allocated on the same basis as interest income.

Personal services income or fees (earned other than as an employee):

- in relation to those professionals who return income on a cash basis (barristers and doctors), is derived when received
- in relation to other professional taxpayers, is derived on an accruals basis.

Business income is derived on an accruals basis.

Deductions are available for expenses incurred in the derivation of income by the deceased person and the trustee.

Fixed charges, such as rates, insurance, interest and depreciation, can be deducted on a proportionate basis according to the number of days covering the period from the beginning of the income year to the date of death.

For other expenses not of a fixed nature, such as repairs and maintenance and legal expenses, the deduction is available to the deceased person only if the liability for the expenses has been incurred on or before the date of death. This is the case whether the expense is actually paid by the trustee after the date of death.

¶26-060 Trustee must register the estate as a new taxpayer

The trustee must register the estate as a taxpayer and apply for a new IRD number in the name of the estate. These returns are filed on an IR6: Income tax return: Estate or trust. The trustee does not use the deceased person's IRD number for the estate's return.

¶26-070 Income derived after death is trustee or beneficiary income

Income derived after death is trustee or beneficiary income depending on the terms of the deceased's will.

Income derived from property bequeathed as a specific legacy is taxed as beneficiary income from the date of death to the time of distribution to the beneficiary. A specific legacy is a gift of a defined item of property. For example, "I give all my AMP shares to my friend Byron France".

Income derived from residuary gifts before distribution is taxed as trustee income: *Doctor Barnardo's Homes* v *IR Commrs* (1921) 7 TC 646, *Marie Celeste Samaritan Society of London Hospital* v *IR Commrs* (1926) 11 TC 226. Residuary gifts refers to all the property of the estate after payment of debts and specific legacies.

Income derived by an estate pending determination of the residue is taxed as trustee income: *Corbett* v *IR Commrs* [1938] 1 KB 567.

Fees for work completed by or on behalf of the trustee after the date of death should be returned in the estate return of income for the tax year in which an account was rendered.

The Income Tax Act overrides the common law principle that income earned, but not derived for tax purposes, by a deceased person before death is capital in the hands of a beneficiary of that person's estate. Accordingly, any amount received by the trustee is assessable income to the trustee in the year of receipt if the income:

- is not included in the deceased person's return to the date of death, but
- would have been taxable to the deceased had the deceased been alive when it was received: s HC 8.

Income that has been included in the assessable income of the deceased taxpayer or their trustee and that is subsequently written off as a bad debt is deductible:

- firstly, against any trustee income derived in the year in which the debt is written off
- secondly, against any income derived by or in trust for a beneficiary who has a vested interest in the capital of the estate, to the extent that the loss is chargeable against the capital of that beneficiary, and
- thirdly, any balance is carried forward to subsequent income years and offset against trustee and beneficiary income according to the rules outlined above: s DB 32.

¶26-080 Ascertaining beneficiary income of deceased estate depends on the terms of the deceased person's will and the nature of the estate

A will may specifically state that no apportionment is to be made between income and capital. In such cases, income accrued to date of death would be trustee income or beneficiary income depending on whether the income vests absolutely in the interest in the beneficiaries.

A deduction is allowed for bad debts if they have previously been included in the income of the deceased or in trustee income and the debts are written off. The deduction is allowed against trustee income with the balance, if any, deducted from the income of a beneficiary to the extent that the loss is chargeable against the capital of that beneficiary. When income is insufficient to absorb the loss, the loss may be carried forward and deducted in the next tax year on the same basis: s DB 32.

Should the debt subsequently be recovered, it would be treated as trustee income. The exception is if the debt was written off against the income of a particular beneficiary. In such a case, it would be treated as income in the hands of that beneficiary: s CG 3.

If the trustee purchases depreciable assets for deriving income or carrying on a business for the purpose of deriving income, the trustee is entitled to claim depreciation.

Net losses incurred by a taxpayer in one income year are generally available for carry-forward and offset against net income in subsequent income years. However, such net losses are lost upon death and unable to be carried forward against income derived by a taxpayer's deceased estate. This is because, for tax purposes, the estate is a different taxpayer. See *Tax Information Bulletin* ¶72-124 Vol 7, No 2, August 1995 at 31.

When the trustee has the power to carry on a business, any loss arising out of that business is a loss to the trustee and not to the beneficiaries. The resulting net loss may be carried forward and deducted from trustee income derived in a future income year. See ¶11-030.

When an estate incurs a loss, that loss is considered by the Commissioner to have been incurred by the trustee and not by the beneficiaries. See *Tax Information Bulletin* ¶71-117 Vol 7, No 1, July 1995 at 19.

However, if the beneficiary has a vested share in the year the loss is sustained, the loss may be carried forward and offset against beneficiary income. The same treatment may also apply when the trustee carries on the business as a bare trustee, that is, not under authority of the will but with agreement of the beneficiaries after the point of distribution. In some instances, the trustee is authorised to recoup losses from future beneficiary income. When the trustee exercises any such power, the beneficiary is taxed on net income for the year after deduction of the loss recouped by the trustee.

Income derived by the trustee from estate assets held for the benefit of any charitable trust or other similar charitable organisation is exempt from tax in the hands of the executor: s CW 43.

¶26-090 Trustee is liable for income tax

The trustee is liable for income tax owed by the deceased as well as any income tax liability incurred by the trustee.

However, the trustee's liability for income tax in respect of income derived by the deceased before their death is limited to the net assets of the estate. This includes tax that may be assessed as a consequence of Inland Revenue reopening previous year assessments. The Commissioner may write off outstanding tax if a taxpayer's estate has been distributed: Tax Administration Act, s 177C(2).

A final return must be prepared at the time the estate is wound up and the assets are distributed to the beneficiaries. If the period of the estate spans more than one tax year, a return will be due at the end of each intervening tax year as well.

Before the final distribution of estate assets or trust income is made, the trustee should ensure that sufficient funds have been reserved to meet all tax obligations that will or may prove to be payable either in the trustee's own right or as agent of the beneficiaries as the trustee may be liable for any shortfall. See *The Public Trustee* v *Flower* [1990] NZHC 555; (1991) 13 NZTC 8,042 where the trustee obtained judgment against the residuary beneficiary when a tax liability of the deceased was identified after the estate has been distributed. Note that while judgment was made against the beneficiary, the trustee was found to have been negligent, although no loss had arisen as the debt was a bona fide debt of the estate.

¶26-100 There is a deemed disposal and acquisition at market value when the deceased's tax-base property is transferred to the trustee

Subject to specific exceptions for close relationships, transfers of property in the tax base following a person's death, as well as in-kind distributions of property by trusts and companies, and gifts of property, will be treated as disposals and acquisitions at market value: s FC 2(1). See further at Chapter 33 – *Resettlement*.

The effect of the asset transfer rules is that unless an exemption applies, there are 2 market value transfers following a death. The first is at the time of the deceased person's death and the second is on the subsequent distribution of the estate to the beneficiaries. See *Tax Information Bulletin* ¶177-111 Vol 17, No 7, September 2005 at 41.

¶26-110 Asset transfer rules only apply to property in the tax base

The asset transfer rules only apply to property in the tax base.

Property in the tax base is property of the following types (s FC 1(2)):

- revenue account property
- an attributing interest in a FIF

- a financial arrangement (excluding a financial arrangement in respect of which the deceased or a trustee of the deceased was a cash basis person), and
- depreciable property.

¶26-120 Asset transfer rules do not apply to transfers to a spouse or partner

The asset transfer rules do not apply to a disposal of property in the tax base under the terms of a will or intestacy to the surviving spouse, civil union or de facto partner.

Transfers of such property are treated as a transfer under a relationship agreement, that is, the assets are transferred at tax book value: s FC 3. This means that the tax consequences are not realised until the transferee disposes of the inherited property. When property is transferred as if under a relationship agreement, the transferee effectively assumes the depreciation profile of the transferor. Depreciation recovery income is not recognised on the transfer: s FB 21. The policy behind this treatment is the view that it is appropriate that the outcome is the same whether property is transferred under a relationship agreement or following death.

This same treatment applies to the transmission to the trustee and on the distribution to the beneficiary.

For this exemption to apply, all the deceased person's tax-base assets must be distributed to the surviving spouse or partner or a close relative.

A close relative is a surviving spouse or civil union or de facto partner or a person within the second degree of relationship: s FC 1(2).

¶26-130 Asset transfer rules do not apply to simple estates

What is commonly referred to as a simple estate is an estate where:

- there are no life interests
- the terms of the deceased's will or intestacy do not require that any property is held in trust (other than for the period in which the property is subject to administration or executorship), and
- for the duration of the estate, the net income of the estate is distributed beneficially to the maximum extent that is legally allowable: s FC 4(1).

The asset transfer rules do not apply to a disposal of property from a simple estate to a tax charity (see ¶30-100) or to a close relative of the deceased: s FC 4(2).

Transfers from applicable simple estates are also treated as a transfer under a relationship agreement, that is, the assets are transferred at tax book value. This same treatment applies to the transmission to the trustee and on the distribution to the beneficiary.

Example

Joe (a widower) died on 5 October. Tony is the trustee of Joe's estate. Included in the assets in the estate are a residential rental property (the only property in Joe's tax base), $5,000 cash and a valuable collection of antiques (Joe collected antiques as a hobby when he was alive). The final beneficiaries of Joe's estate are his son, Andy, his niece, Adele, and the Red Cross. Tony makes the final distribution of Joe's estate on 28 March of the following year. Under the terms of Joe's will, Tony distributes the residential rental property to Andy, the $5,000 cash to the Red Cross and the collection of antiques to Adele. Joe's will does not establish any life interest or require any of Joe's property to be held in trust.

Although Adele, a relative of Joe who is not within the second degree of relationship, is included in Joe's will as a final beneficiary, the exception for the final distribution of a simple estate still applies. This is because no property that is in Joe's tax base is distributed to a beneficiary who is not within the second degree of relationship to Joe. Accordingly, the transfer of the residential property from Tony to Andy will be made at the tax book value of the estate. Any tax consequences of the transfer will be realised when Andy subsequently disposes of the property.

If instead the residential rental property is distributed to Adele and the collection of antiques is distributed to Andy, the exception will not apply. There will be a deemed disposal and acquisition at market value of the residential rental property distributed to Adele.

A person who receives depreciable property by way of a bequest under the asset transfer rules can use the market value of the asset determined in accordance with those rules as the cost base to calculate that person's depreciation loss on the asset.

Example

Jessica inherits a rental property from her great aunt, who is not within the second degree of relationship with Jessica. Jessica decides to keep the property as an investment. Under the asset transfer rules, the transfer of the property from Jessica's great aunt's estate to Jessica is treated as a transfer at market value. The estate must include in its final tax return any depreciation recovery income or depreciation loss arising on the transfer of the rental property. Jessica will be allowed to calculate the depreciation loss on the rental property based on the market value at which it was transferred to her.

¶26-140 Ten-year rule does not apply to simple estates

The distribution of land that would have been subject to tax under "the ten-year rule" (ss CB 9–CB 14) if it had been sold by the deceased will not be taxable under that rule, provided the land is distributed to a surviving spouse or partner or a person within the second degree of relationship to the deceased: s FC 5. This exception applies when the property is transferred from the deceased person to the trustee and also when the final distribution is made to beneficiaries.

Briefly, "the ten-year rule" is the disposal of land by:

- a land dealer or a land developer within 10 years of acquiring it
- a builder within 10 years of completing improvements to it, or

- a person who has disposed of land within 10 years of acquisition for more than its cost, and at least 20% of the excess received is due to various rules or zoning changes that relate to that land.

If there is no relief from the application of the 10-year rule, a deduction is allowed to the executor or administrator or the final beneficiary for:

- the cost of the land to the deceased person, and
- all other costs incurred by the deceased person and the executor or administrator or the beneficiary that have not previously been deducted.

¶26-145 Deceased estates are exempted from the bright-line test

Deceased estates to which s FC 1(1)(a) or (b) apply are exempted from the "bright-line" test in s CB 6A. Also see s FC 9(2), which provides that the bright-line test does not apply to any intervening transfer to an executor or administrator. However, the "bright-line" test will apply to the recipient who adopts the deceased's acquisition cost and date of acquisition. See ss FB 3A and FC 3.

See further at ¶19-080.

¶26-147 Deceased estates are a non-notifiable transfer for land transfer tax statements

A land transfer tax statement must be completed for all transfers of freehold, leasehold, life estates, stratum estates, licences to occupy and other specified estates in land as defined in s 77 of the Land Transfer Act 2017.

However, executors and administrators of a deceased's estate are exempt from providing tax details as a transfer by the executor or administrator for a deceased's estate is a non-notifiable transfer. See the Land Transfer (Land Information and Offshore Persons Information) Exemption Regulations 2015.

See further at ¶19-090.

¶26-150 Exemption to the asset transfer rules applies for the distribution of forestry rights

The transfer of property that is timber, standing timber or the right to take timber is made at tax book value if the property is disposed of to a surviving spouse or partner or a person within the second degree of relationship to the deceased: s FC 6. This applies when the property is transferred from the deceased person to the trustee and also when the final distribution is made to beneficiaries.

¶26-160 An exemption to the asset transfer rules applies for unexpired prepayments

The transfer of unexpired prepayments by a deceased estate to the executor or administrator of the estate or on final distribution of the estate is made at cost. The date of valuation is the end of an income year: s FC 7.

¶26-170 Financial arrangements can be distributed at cost if the deceased was a cash basis person

The transfer of a financial arrangement by a deceased estate to the trustee or on final distribution of the estate is made at cost, provided that the trustee of the estate is a cash basis person: ss EW 60, FC 8.

¶26-180 Tax losses are lost at death

Net losses incurred by a taxpayer in one income year are generally available for carry-forward and offset against net income in subsequent income years. However, such net losses are lost upon death and unable to be carried forward against income derived by a taxpayer's deceased estate. This is because, for tax purposes, the estate is a different taxpayer. See *Tax Information Bulletin* ¶72-124 Vol 7, No 2, August 1995 at 31. See Chapter 11 – *Losses*.

¶26-190 Death does not result in additional use of money interest

Additional use of money interest (UOMI) is not charged in the year of death so long as all of the deceased person's provisional and terminal tax payments are made by the due date: Tax Administration Act, s 120C(1)(f). This is a concessionary measure, which ensures that a trustee will not incur UOMI where a tax liability arises due to the taxpayer's death.

¶26-200 Shareholder continuity is not affected by death

The death of a shareholder will not affect the shareholder continuity requirements that must be met by companies to enable the carry-forward of losses, imputation and FDP credits. Where a person has acquired shares, or share options, as a beneficiary or trustee under the will or on intestacy of a deceased person, the beneficiary or trustee is deemed to have acquired the shares on the date on which the shares were acquired by the deceased person and to have held them since that time: s YC 8. See ¶17-060.

If the deceased is a shareholder in a qualifying company, the qualifying company elections will be revoked upon the death, and the company will cease to be a qualifying company from the first day of the income year in which the shareholder died. A grace period applies to allow a new election.

If the deceased is the shareholder in a look-through company ("LTC"), there is no automatic revocation of LTC elections by events such as the death of a shareholder: s HB 1. Also see Chapter 16 – *Closely Held Companies*.

¶26-202 When the owner of a LTC dies there is a deemed disposal of the underlying property

When an owner of an interest in a LTC dies, subpart FC applies and the owner will be treated as disposing of his or her shares in the LTC at market value immediately before his or her death, unless asset transfer rules do not apply: see ¶26-120.

If the asset transfer rules apply and no threshold exclusion applies (see ¶26-203–¶26-209), for tax purposes the disposal of underlying property must be accounted for.

Also see *Tax Information Bulletin* ¶231-111 Vol 23, No 1, February 2011 at 54, 55.

¶26-203 There is a $50,000 threshold before tax that may need to be accounted for following the death of a shareholder in a LTC

Where an interest in a LTC is disposed of it is only necessary to account for tax on the deemed sale of shares if the amount of the disposal proceeds exceeds the total net tax book value of the owner's share of the LTC property (less any liabilities under generally accepted accounting practice) by more than $50,000. When shares in the same LTC have been sold within a 12-month period, all sales are taken into account for the purposes of the threshold. See s HB 5.

¶26-205 There is a $3 million turnover threshold before a revenue account adjustment is necessary following the death of a shareholder in a LTC

Where an interest in a LTC is disposed of, a revenue account adjustment for trading stock is not required if the LTC's total annual turnover is $3 million or less. See s HB 1(5).

¶26-207 There is a $200,000 historical cost threshold before depreciation recovery is necessary following the death of a shareholder in a LTC

Where an interest in a LTC is disposed of, it is not necessary to account for depreciation recovery or loss on the exiting owner's share of any depreciable tangible asset if the historical cost of the asset is $200,000 or less. See s HB 7.

¶26-208 Base price adjustments are not always required after the death of a shareholder

Where an interest in a LTC is disposed of, it is not necessary to perform a base price adjustment for the exiting owner's interest in a financial arrangement if:

- the LTC is not in the business of deriving income from financial arrangements, and
- the financial arrangement has been entered into as a necessary and incidental purpose of the LTC's business.

Exiting owners do not have to account for tax on financial arrangements and excepted financial arrangements described in s EW 5(10). See s HB 8.

¶26-209 Exceptions also apply to short-term sale and purchase agreements and some livestock

Where an interest in a LTC that comprises interests in a short-term sale and purchase agreement is disposed of, the consideration received is excluded income.

If the LTC property consists of livestock that includes female breeding livestock that is valued using the national standard cost scheme or the cost price method, the entering owner may furnish a return of income choosing to apply s EC 26B. The entering owner is treated as if they had originally purchased and held the livestock, not the exiting owner. This is designed to reduce compliance costs for the LTC. Unless asset transfer rules do not apply, there will be a deemed disposal of the property by the deceased at market value, triggering any tax consequences of the sale.

See ss HB 9, HB 10.

¶26-210 Taxable activity ceases on death

The date of death of a GST-registered person is deemed to be the last day of that person's taxable period: Goods and Services Tax Act 1985 (GST Act), s 15E. A GST return must be prepared up to this date and filed, together with any payment, on or before the last day allowed for the filing of the return: GST Act, ss 16, 23.

A GST return must also be prepared covering the period from the date of death to the end of the deceased taxpayer's normal taxable period.

The deceased person's trustee is deemed to be a registered person carrying on the taxable activity of the deceased person in the capacity of agent of the deceased: GST Act, s 58. This means that output tax is not payable on the assets "transferred" to the executor on the death of the registered person. However, this agency status ceases at the end of the executorship. Accordingly, the transfer of estate assets used in the taxable activity to a testamentary trust or the distribution of those assets to the beneficiaries of the estate will constitute a taxable supply for GST purposes and will be subject to GST. See *Tax Information Bulletin* ¶410-119 Vol 4, No 10, May 1993 at 12.

The supply will be zero-rated where the estate assets are transferred or distributed as a going concern and the recipient is GST-registered.

The trustee must advise the Commissioner in writing of the death of the taxpayer and of the trustee's appointment as the specified agent of the deceased within 21 days of the date of death. As the trustee is deemed to be personally carrying on the taxable activity of the deceased, the trustee is liable for any GST payable.

However, the trustee is not personally liable for any liabilities incurred by the taxpayer before their death: GST Act, s 58(1D).

¶26-220 Legislation

Income Tax Act 2007

CV 12 TRUSTEES: AMOUNTS RECEIVED AFTER PERSON'S DEATH

To the extent to which section HC 8 (Amounts received after person's death) applies to an amount that a trustee of an estate of a deceased person receives in an income year, the amount is income of the trustee.

EW 60 TRUSTEE OF DECEASED'S ESTATE

EW 60(1) WHEN TRUSTEE OF ESTATE IS CASH BASIS PERSON

A trustee of a deceased's estate is a cash basis person for financial arrangements in the estate in the circumstances described in subsection (2) for the period described in subsection (3).

EW 60(2) CIRCUMSTANCES

The circumstances are that, at the time of the deceased's death,–

(a) the deceased is a cash basis person; and

(b) the financial arrangements in the deceased's estate meet the requirements of section EW 54(1)(a) and (b).

EW 60(3) PERIOD

The period is the income year in which the deceased dies and in each of the 4 following income years. However, if at any time in those 5 income years the financial arrangements in the deceased's estate cease to meet the requirements of section EW 54(1)(a) and (b), the trustee ceases to be a cash basis person for financial arrangements in the estate and cannot again be a cash basis person for them.

EW 60(4) MODIFICATIONS TO BE READ IN

For the purposes of this section, sections EW 54 and EW 55 are read with the modifications necessary to make them refer to the case of a deceased estate.

FC 4 PROPERTY TRANSFERRED TO CHARITIES OR TO CLOSE RELATIVES AND OTHERS

FC 4(1) WHEN THIS SECTION APPLIES

This section applies in the circumstances described in section FC 1(1)(b) when tax-base property is transferred on a person's death if–

(a) each beneficiary of the deceased person is described in subsection (2); and

(b) no life interest in the property is created; and

(c) no trust over the property is created, other than a trust to execute the will and administer the estate; and

(d) the net income of the estate is distributed as described in subsection (3).

FC 4(2) BENEFICIARIES OF DECEASED

A beneficiary of the deceased person must be–

(a) a close relative of the deceased person:

(b) a person exempt under section CW 41, CW 42, or CW 43 (which relate to exempt income of charities).

FC 4(3) INCOME FROM ESTATE MUST BE DISTRIBUTED

While the administration of the estate is continuing, the net income of the estate is distributed to the extent allowed–

(a) under the will or the rules governing intestacy; and

(b) by the trustee's legal obligations.

FC 4(4) TRANSFER SUBJECT TO SUBPART FB

The transfer is treated as a transfer of property on a settlement of relationship property under subpart FB (Transfers of relationship property).

FC 5 LAND TRANSFERRED TO CLOSE RELATIVES

FC 5(1) WHAT THIS SECTION APPLIES TO

This section applies in the circumstances described in section FC 1(1)(a) or (b) when land is transferred on a person's death to a close relative of the person.

FC 5(2) LAND

Sections CB 9 to CB 11 and CB 14 (which relate to the disposal of land) do not apply to the transfer of land, including any intervening transfer to an executor or administrator that, if it had been disposed of by the deceased person, would have resulted in income under any of those sections.

FC 5(3) COST OF LAND

If the land is transferred to a person who disposes of it within 10 years of its acquisition by the deceased person, and the person derives income under any of sections CB 9 to CB 11 and CB 14, the cost of land to the person is–

(a) the cost of the land incurred by the deceased person; and

(b) all other expenditure incurred by the person, the deceased person, or the administrator or executor of the deceased person, as applicable, for which no deduction has been allowed.

[...]

HB 4 GENERAL PROVISIONS RELATING TO DISPOSALS

HB 4(1) RELATIONSHIP BETWEEN DISPOSAL UNDER THIS SECTION, DISPOSAL SAFE HARBOURS, AND SUBPART FB

This section overrides sections HB 5 to HB 9. This section does not apply, and sections HB 5 to HB 9 do not apply, for disposals of owners' interests under transactions to which subpart FB (Transfers of relationship property) applies or is treated as applying.

HB 4(2) ELECTION FOR SPECIFIED LIVESTOCK DISPOSED OF TO NEW OWNER

Section HB 10 applies for an entering owner if the entering owner furnishes a return of income that applies the section.

HB 4(3) PERMANENT CESSATION

A person is treated as disposing of all of their owner's interests for a look-through company to a single third party for a payment equal to the interests' market value, if the look-through company ceases to exist as an entity through liquidation, court order, or otherwise.

HB 4(4) CAPITAL REDUCTION

A person is treated as disposing of all of their owner's interests for a look-through company to a single third party for a payment equal to the interests' market value to the extent to which an owner's capital is reduced by a cancellation or a buy-back by the look-through company that is not pro rata for all owners.

[...]

HC 8 AMOUNTS RECEIVED AFTER PERSON'S DEATH

HC 8(1) WHEN THIS SECTION APPLIES

This section applies when a trustee of an estate of a deceased person receives an amount in an income year that is not income that the person derived during their lifetime, but would have been included in the person's income had they been alive when it was received.

HC 8(2) INCOME

The amount is treated under section CV 12 (Trustees: amounts received after person's death) as income derived by the trustee in the income year.

Part IX

SPECIAL CASES

CHAPTER 27

Gaming Trusts

¶27-010 Operating principle

Gross proceeds from gaming machines operated by gaming trusts for an authorised purpose are exempt from income tax.

¶27-020 Gaming machines must be owned and operated by a gaming trust

Gaming machines that operate outside casinos may be owned and operated by a corporate society, which may include gaming trusts: Gambling Act 2003.

A gaming trust is a trust that operates gaming machines, distributing the proceeds into the community by way of grants.

Widely known gaming trusts include the NZ Community Trust, Pub Charity, The Lion Foundation, The Trusts Community Foundation, Trillian Trust and The Southern Trust.

¶27-030 Licenced gaming-machine operator

To become a licenced gaming-machine operator, a gaming trust is required to apply or distribute net proceeds only to or for an authorised purpose. The term "authorised purpose" includes both a charitable purpose and a non-commercial purpose that is beneficial to the whole or a section of the community.

Example

The promotion of amateur sport is a non-commercial purpose that is beneficial to the community.

The Gambling Commission oversees the adherence of gaming trusts and other corporate societies holding class 4 licences with respect to expenditure. In order to maximise net proceeds available for distribution, licensees are required to incur only costs that are "actual, reasonable and necessary" in conducting gambling activities, for the purpose of compliance with s CW 48(b) of the Income Tax Act: see Letter from Department of Internal Affairs, Key Messages from The Southern Trust (GC10/10) and The Trusts Charitable Foundation (GC11/10) Gambling Commission Appeals, 5 July 2010. Also see the New Zealand Gambling Law Guide, which publishes Gambling Commission Decisions at gamblinglaw.co.nz/Gambling-Commission-Decisions/decision-contents.aspx.

¶27-040 Gaming trusts do not need to register as tax charities to obtain income tax exemption

Gaming trusts do not need to register with the Charities Registration Board to become a tax charity. A gaming trust's gross gambling proceeds will be exempt income if the gaming trust is licensed in accordance with the Gambling Act, and the net proceeds are applied or distributed to the community: s CW 48.

The specific tax exemption that applies to gaming trusts reflects concern expressed during the select committee stage of the Charities Bill, subsequently enacted as the Charities Act 2005, regarding the fact that gaming trusts, which are already subject to a regulatory regime imposed by the Department of Internal Affairs, would be the subject of a second tier of supervision by the then Charities Commission (now the Charity Services arm of the Department of Internal Affairs, including the independent Charities Registration Board) if registration was required to obtain an exemption from income tax.

¶27-050 No exemption from GST

The GST Act applies to gaming trusts. However, there are special provisions that apply in respect of the meaning and value of a gambling supply for the purposes of that Act.

¶27-060 Legislation

Gambling Act 2003

4 INTERPRETATION

4(1) [Definitions]

[...]

authorised purpose means,–

(a) for class 1 gambling, class 2 gambling, and class 3 gambling, any of the following purposes:

 (i) a charitable purpose:

 (ii) a non-commercial purpose that is beneficial to the whole or a section of the community:

 (iii) promoting, controlling, and conducting race meetings under the Racing Industry Act 2020, including the payment of stakes:

 (iv) an electioneering purpose:

(b) for class 4 gambling, any of the purposes specified in paragraph (a)(i) to (iii)

[...]

corporate society means 1 society that is–

(a) incorporated under the Incorporated Societies Act 1908; or

(b) incorporated as a board under the Charitable Trusts Act 1957; or

(c) a company incorporated under the Companies Act 1993 that–

  (i) does not have the capacity or power to make a profit; and

  (ii) is incorporated and conducted solely for authorised purposes; or

(d) a working men's club registered under the Friendly Societies and Credit Unions Act 1982

[...]

31 REQUIREMENTS FOR CLASS 4 GAMBLING

Class 4 gambling may be conducted only by a corporate society that holds–

(a) a class 4 operator's licence for the gambling; and

(b) a class 4 venue licence for the place where the gambling is conducted.

[...]

50 APPLICATION FOR CLASS 4 OPERATOR'S LICENCE

(1) A corporate society may apply to the Secretary for a licence to conduct class 4 gambling.

[...]

65 APPLICATION FOR CLASS 4 VENUE LICENCE

(1) A corporate society may apply to the Secretary for a class 4 venue licence.

[...]

Goods and Services Tax Act 1985

5 MEANING OF TERM SUPPLY

[...]

5(10) [Supply of gambling services]

For the purposes of this Act, an amount of money paid by a person to participate in gambling (including a New Zealand lottery) or in a prize competition is treated as a payment for a supply of services by the following:

(a) for gambling, by the person, society, licensed promoter, or organiser who under the Gambling Act 2003 conducts the gambling:

(b) for a prize competition, by the person who conducts the prize competition.

[...]

10 VALUE OF SUPPLY OF GOODS AND SERVICES

[...]

10(14) [Consideration for supply of gambling services]

If a supply of services is treated as having been made under section 5(10), the consideration for the supply is calculated using the formula–

amounts received – prizes

where–

(a) **amounts received** is the total of all amounts in money received in relation to the supply–

  (i) for gambling, by the person, society, licensed promoter, or organiser who under the Gambling Act 2003 conducts the gambling:

  (ii) for a prize competition, by the person who conducts the prize competition:

(b) **prizes** is the total amount of all prizes paid and payable in money in relation to the supply, reduced by the total amount of input tax for supplies for which the prizes are treated as being consideration.

10(15) [Gambling and New Zealand lottery defined]

For the purposes of subsection (14), the terms **gambling** and **New Zealand lottery** have the meanings set out in section 4(1) of the Gambling Act 2003.

[...]

Income Tax Act 2007

CW 48 INCOME FROM CONDUCTING GAMING-MACHINE GAMBLING

An amount of income derived by a person that is gross gambling proceeds from gaming-machine gambling is exempt income if–

(a) the person is authorised to conduct the gaming-machine gambling under the Gambling Act 2003 by a gaming-machine operator's licence and a gaming-machine venue licence; and

(b) the person complies with the Gambling Act 2003 in applying and distributing the net gambling proceeds from the gaming-machine gambling.

CHAPTER 28

Funeral Trusts

¶28-010 Operating principle

Income derived by the trustee of a compliant funeral trust is exempt income.

¶28-020 Trusts for funeral expenses

Funeral trusts may be established by private individuals (they are offered as a service by most of the statutory trustee companies) or they may be established by companies or businesses. In the latter case, funeral trusts are settled for the sole purpose of meeting funeral expenses for an employer's employees and the employee's spouse or partner and dependants. The contributions to the fund of a funeral trust can be made by the employer or the employee.

A deposit of up to $10,000 in a funeral trust is an exempt asset for means testing purposes. See Residential Care and Disability Support Services Act 2018, sch 2, pt 2, s 4(d).

¶28-030 Interest and dividend income derived by the trustee of a funeral trust is exempt income

Interest and/or dividend income derived by the trustee of a funeral trust established to benefit employees of a company or business is exempt income if (s CW 45):

- at least 10 employees can benefit from the fund
- the sole purpose of the fund is to pay expenses associated with the funerals of:
  - employees
  - employees' spouses, civil union partners, de facto partners, and dependants, and
  - deceased employees' surviving spouses, civil union partners, de facto partners, and surviving dependants
- all beneficiaries have equal entitlements from the fund
- all contributions are made by the employer or the employee, and
- the fund is approved by the Commissioner.

Income other than interest or dividend income derived by the trustee of a funeral fund is not exempt income.

Example

Big Wine Company Limited employs 300 staff. The Big Wine Company Funeral Trust pays $3,000 towards the funeral expenses of any present or past employee. Big Wine Company Limited is the sole contributor to the Big Wine Company Funeral Trust, which has been approved by the Commissioner as a funeral trust.

The Big Wine Company Funeral Trust derives $25,000 of interest income and $38,000 of rental income.

The interest income is exempt income. However, the rental income is taxable as the exemption in s CW 45 is limited to interest and dividend income.

¶28-040 Legislation

Income Tax Act 2007

CW 45 FUNERAL TRUSTS

Interest or a dividend derived by a trustee in trust for a fund is exempt income if, when the interest or dividend is derived by the trustee,–

(a) the sole purpose of the fund is the payment of the expenses associated with the funerals of–

(i) employees of an employer:

(ii) spouses, civil union partners, de facto partners, and dependants of employees of the employer:

(iii) surviving spouses, civil union partners, de facto partners, and surviving dependants of deceased employees of the employer; and

(b) the employer has at least 10 employees; and

(c) all persons eligible for benefits from the fund are eligible equally for benefits from the fund; and

(d) no contributions to the fund are made by a person who is not the employer or an employee of the employer; and

(e) the fund is approved by the Commissioner.

CHAPTER 29

Unit Trusts

¶29-010 Operating principle

A unit trust is treated as a company for taxation purposes. Accordingly, unit trusts are taxed at the company rate and not at the trust tax rate. Distributions to beneficiaries are deemed to be dividends and are taxed accordingly.

¶29-020 Unit trust defined

A unit trust is a scheme or arrangement in the form of a trust that allows the participants to share in the unit trust's income in proportion to each participant's respective interest: s YA 1 "unit trust". Unit trusts are not created by any specific legislation, although the treatment of unit trusts for specific purposes (such as managed investments) has been subject to legislative controls.

Given the very distinct treatment of unit trusts for tax purposes, it is important to emphasise that the law applying to trusts and to trustees generally still applies to unit trusts. In its *Review of the Law of Trusts* (NZLC R130, 2013), the Law Commission determined that general trust principles should apply to unit trusts except in specific circumstances such as where other regulatory bodies (such as the Financial Markets Authority) have overriding statutory authority. This was borne out in the Trusts Act 2019, which makes no exclusion for unit trusts so that, for purposes other than taxation, the wider law of trusts applies to unit trusts.

The income of a unit trust may be of a capital or revenue nature.

The participants benefit as beneficiaries under a trust. However, the amounts paid to each beneficiary are treated as dividends for tax purposes.

Exclusions from the definition of a "unit trust" include:

- a trust for the benefit of debenture holders
- the Common Fund of the Public Trust or any group investment fund established by the Public Trust
- the Common Fund of the Māori Trustee
- a group investment fund established under the Trustee Companies Act 1967
- a registered friendly society
- a superannuation fund

- an employee share purchase scheme, and
- funeral trusts.

Accordingly, the Trusts Act 2019 does apply to unit trusts, as the characteristics of a unit trust are also the characteristics of an express trust. As noted in the *Review of the Law of Trusts* (NZLC R130, 2013) at 3.46:

> "One of the reasons identified for using the trust form is the management standards that apply with trustees being bound to act prudently, preserve trust property and act impartially between beneficiaries: '[t]his approach can be attractive for investment vehicles such as unit trusts, superannuation trusts and so on'."

However, the trust rules under the Income Tax Act do not apply to unit trusts: s HC 1(2)(a). Moreover, although not expressly excluded from the new reporting obligations that apply to complying trusts, subject to our comments below, it is understood that unit trusts will not be subject to the new reporting obligations contained in s 59BA of the Tax Administration Act 1994 (Annual return for trusts).

¶29-030 Discretionary trusts are rarely unit trusts

Traditional discretionary family trusts will not usually be subject to the unit trust regime because they are discretionary, and beneficiaries do not subscribe, purchase or contribute to their entitlement to distributions from the trust. However, trusts that provide for settlors to benefit in a fixed way can, sometimes inadvertently, come within the unit trust definition.

This is more likely to occur in relation to trusts, particularly trading trusts, established outside of the family context by more than one unrelated party. It is not possible to opt out of the unit trust regime, which is proscriptive, such that if an arrangement involving a trust meets the definition of a unit trust, the trust rules will not apply and the trust will be taxed as a company.

¶29-040 Features of a unit trust

In public binding ruling BR Pub 95/5A (since expired), the Commissioner stated that to constitute a unit trust for tax purposes, an entity must meet the following requirements (there was also a requirement that there not be a single unit holder). However, the Commissioner's views here have been subsequently modified (see below):

- The entity must be a trust. It cannot be in the form of a partnership or a joint venture, presuming it does not involve a trust, as in those entities, management and control are in the hands of the member. In contrast, in a trust situation, the management and control of the property settled are with the trustees.
- The trust must have subscribers, purchasers, or contributors who are beneficiaries under the trust. In contrast, a family trust is not a unit trust because beneficiaries of a family trust do not subscribe, purchase, or contribute for their entitlement to distributions from the trust.
- Unit holders must have a facility to participate in any income or gains arising from the investments that are the subject of the trust. For example, a subscriber

for units that carry a nil return would not count for the purposes of the definition.

Example

Arnold, Beatrice and Crystal decide to establish a business together using a trading trust (the ABC Trust). Arnold settles $25,000 on the ABC Trust and Beatrice and Crystal each settle $12,500 upon the ABC Trust.

The ABC Trust has a corporate trustee and the beneficiaries are Arnold, Beatrice and Crystal.

ABC's trust deed provides that the beneficiaries receive distributions in the following predetermined ratio:

Arnold is entitled to 50% of the trust's total income, and

Beatrice and Crystal are each entitled to 25% of the trust's total income.

The ABC Trust meets the definition of a unit trust. Arnold, Beatrice and Crystal have contributed to the trust and participate in the income and gains earned by the trust based on their contributions.

The trust rules will not apply to the ABC Trust, which will be taxed as a company.

Note that the Unit Trusts Act 1960 was repealed on 1 December 2014 by s 4(1)(e) of the Financial Markets (Repeals and Amendments) Act 2013. Unit trusts as vehicles for managed investments are now governed by the Managed Investment Scheme provisions of the Financial Markets Conduct Act 2013.

In 2016 the Commissioner issued an interpretation statement IS 16/02, "Income Tax – Unit trusts – When a unit trust can have a single unit holder" indicating that the Commissioner's view with respect to whether a unit trust may have a single member has altered and that an objective analysis is required when a unit trust has only a single unit holder/beneficiary.

The interpretation statement observes that other legislative provisions assume that a unit trust will have more than one beneficiary or unit holder but considers that this was not based on any actual analysis. For example, ss HM 3(1)(b)(iii) and HM 9(c) (both since repealed) concerning the portfolio investment entity (PIE) rules used the plural term "subscribers". However, this more accurately reflected the nature of the PIE regime than the technical considerations of what constitutes a unit trust. The repeal of those 2 provisions appears to have more explicitly aligned with the interpretation that a unit trust could have a single beneficiary/unit holder.

In the interpretation statement, the Commissioner concludes that whether a sole beneficiary of a trust is the sole unit holder of a unit trust is an issue of objective and intention that will most likely be reflected in whether the Trust Deed provides "facilities" for multiple unit holders. The Commissioner expresses the view that "the essential feature of a 'unit trust' is the provision of the facilities for subscribers to participate, and that is not altered by there being only one subscriber".

Other factors discussed in the interpretation statement that a court might consider in determining whether such a trust is a unit trust might include the nature of the structure, whether it may have previously had multiple unit holders (eg whether a unit trust may have been subject to a takeover leaving a single holder with all of the units in the trust), or whether there is the prospect of more holders subscribing to units in future.

Given that this represents a change from the position set out in BR Pub 95/5A, the Commissioner proposed a transitional arrangement until 31 March 2018 so that those who have ordered their affairs in reliance on the previous position may change. In particular trusts with only one unit holder but with facilities in the trust deed for multiple unit holders may transition by either adding subscribers or by amending the trust deed to ensure they are not a unit trust and their present status will apply from the tax year ended 31 March 2017. Trusts that have taken the view they are unit trusts even though they have a single unit holder but do have facilities for multiple subscribers are in line with the Commissioner's position.

¶29-050 Unit trusts are excluded from the trust and qualifying company regimes

Unit trusts are excluded from the trust regime in subpart HC: s HC 1(2)(a). A unit trust is taxed instead as a company, the definition of which includes a unit trust: s YA 1 ("company").

However, the trustee is treated as the agent of the unit trust in relation to income derived by the unit trust: s HD 13.

If a trust is a unit trust and a complying trust, the unit trust rules prevail and the trust will be taxed as a company. This view, expressed in public binding ruling BR Pub 95/5A, has been confirmed as still representing the Commissioner's position: *Tax Information Bulletin* ¶125-103 Vol 12, No 5, May 2000 at 4.

Unit trusts do not qualify for the qualifying company regime, which specifically excludes unit trusts: s HA 2.

¶29-060 Unit trusts must maintain an imputation credit account

New Zealand unit trusts must maintain an imputation credit account in the same way as any other company: s OB 1. Tax paid by the unit trust is credited to its imputation credit account. Resident unit holders are entitled to imputation credits to the extent to which they are allocated to income distributions.

When the manager of a unit trust, or a person nominated by the manager, redeems units from unit holders in the ordinary course of business, the dividend derived does not include any imputation credits attached to the dividend to the extent it constitutes a recovery of the purchase price: s CD 16.

¶29-070 Redemption of a unit is not always a dividend

An amount paid by the manager of a unit trust on the redemption of a unit may not be a dividend. As with companies, unlisted unit trusts must apply either the ordering rule or the slice rule to ascertain the amount of available subscribed capital which may be attributed to a redeemed unit. If the ordering rule does not apply, the proceeds of the redemption will not be a dividend: ss CD 22(4), CZ 13.

For further commentary on the taxation of unit trusts, see *Tax Information Bulletin* ¶79-113 Vol 7, No 9, February 1996 at 7. See also Tony Lines "Corporate tax regime for unit trusts now permanent" CCH, *New Zealand Tax Planning Report* (No 1, March 1996) at 5.

In the regulatory impact assessment released in conjunction with the Taxation (Income Tax Rate and Other Amendments) Act 2020, which introduced a higher 39% top marginal personal income tax rate, the rationale for maintaining the top PIE rate with that of unit trusts and companies was discussed and the concern expressed that if the top PIE tax rate were the same as the top personal tax rate "taxpayers would use unit trusts ... and avoid dividend taxation at their personal rate by having the managers of the unit trusts buy back their units. Buy-back arrangements like this are not treated as dividends and the taxpayer's profit from the buyback is usually a non-taxable capital gain".

¶29-080 Bonus issues by foreign unit trusts can be taxable

A bonus issue made to a unit holder in a unit trust that is a foreign company is a taxable bonus issue if the bonus issue is made instead of causing a beneficial interest in money or property of the unit trust to vest absolutely in the unit holder: s CD 10.

¶29-090 Special rules apply to public unit trusts to reduce compliance costs

Public unit trusts are unit trusts that meet certain criteria regarding the number of unit holders and include retail unit trusts, whose units are offered to the public and that which have a hundred or more unit holders, and certain wholesale unit trusts, whose units are held by widely held investment vehicles such as other unit trusts or superannuation funds. For the purposes of determining the number of unit holders and other percentage interests referred to in the definition in s YA 1, persons associated with one another are treated as one person. To reduce the compliance costs of determining whether unit holders are associated, unit holders must disclose their associations to the trustee on request. Unless there are reasonable grounds for believing the disclosure is not correct, the trustee is entitled to rely on the disclosure: Tax Administration Act 1994, s 32D.

¶29-100 Unit holders in public unit trusts treated as a single notional person

All unit holders in a public unit trust are treated as a notional single person. This avoids the need to keep track of the unit-holding changes: s YC 12(2).

¶29-110 Public unit trusts that invest in other public unit trusts can elect to transfer expenditure between funds

Public unit trusts that invest in other public unit trusts or group investment funds incur expenditure on administration and management. However, the only income received is in the form of dividends that are usually fully imputed. Special provisions allow public unit trusts ("member funds") that invest in other public unit trusts or group investment funds deriving category A income (defined as "master funds" but sometimes referred to as "funds of funds") to elect to transfer expenditure to the master fund: ss DV 5–DV 7.

All expenditure other than expenditure on revenue account property and expenditure on financial arrangements other than those denominated in New Zealand dollars and for which expenditure is allocated using the yield to maturity method, can be transferred.

The master fund is able to deduct the expenditure, and the expenditure is treated as not having been incurred by the member fund. The master fund cannot deduct more than its taxable income for the year in which the income is transferred, less all non-resident passive income derived by the master fund in that year. Expenditure that cannot be deducted by the master fund may be carried forward by the member fund as an available net loss and transferred to the master fund in a later year. If, after the date it has filed its return, the master fund is able to deduct more than the amount actually deducted, the Commissioner may allow a member fund to transfer expenditure to the extent of the difference to the master fund after the return has been filed. The member fund and the master fund must agree that the expenditure be transferred to the master fund and expenditure may only be transferred to the extent that the member fund has a net loss. In order for expenditure to be transferred, the member fund must have funds invested in the master fund at all times between the date on which the member fund incurs the expenditure and the last day of the tax year in which the expenditure is deducted by the master fund. In the income year in which the member fund stops investing in the master fund, neither the member fund nor the master fund can deduct the expenditure and the member fund must treat the expenditure as an available net loss. See also ss IA 2(4)(a), IA 7(4).

Any amount paid to the member fund by the master fund for the expenditure transferred is not income or a dividend for tax purposes. See *Tax Information Bulletin* ¶1311-116 Vol 13, No 11, November 2001 at 39.

The expenditure transferred gives rise to a credit in the master fund's imputation credit account on 31 March of the tax year in which the expenditure is deducted. Similarly, the expenditure transferred gives rise to a debit in the member fund's imputation credit account on 31 March of the tax year in which the expenditure is transferred. If the debit to the member fund's imputation credit account in these circumstances results in a debit balance, there is no requirement to pay further income tax on the debit arising on transfer of the expenditure. See ss OB 19, OB 46, OB 65.

¶29-120 Legislation

Income Tax Act 2007

HD 13 UNIT TRUSTS

A trustee of a unit trust is treated as an agent of the unit trust in relation to income derived by the unit trust.

[...]

YA 1 DEFINITIONS

[...]

company–

[...]

(b) includes a unit trust:

[...]

public unit trust means–

(a) a unit trust that has 100 or more unit holders, treating all associated persons as 1 person, who are–

- (i) unit trust managers who hold units in the ordinary course of their activities in relation to the unit trust; or
- (ii) persons with an interest of 25% or less in the unit trust, treating all associated persons as 1 person; or
- (iii) persons with an interest of 25% or more in the unit trust, treating all associated persons as 1 person, if their interest is 25% or more because of unusual or temporary circumstances, such as the recent establishment or forthcoming termination of the unit trust, and if the unit trust would meet the requirements of any of paragraphs (b), (c), (d), and (e); or

(b) a unit trust whose unit holders are any 1 or more of the following:

- (i) a public unit trust as described in paragraph (a) or this paragraph:
- (ii) a group investment fund:
- (iii) a life insurance company:
- (iv) a superannuation fund:
- (v) a unit trust manager, trustee, or person nominated by the manager or the trustee who holds units in the ordinary course of management activities in relation to the unit trust:
- (vi) a person with an interest of 5% or less in the unit trust, treating all associated persons as 1 person:

(vii) a person with an interest of 5% or more in the unit trust, treating all associated persons as 1 person, if their interest is 5% or more because of unusual or temporary circumstances, such as the recent establishment or forthcoming termination of the unit trust, and if the unit trust would meet the requirements of any of paragraphs (a), (c), (d), and (e); or

(c) a unit trust that has less than 100 unit holders if it could reasonably be regarded as a widely-held investment vehicle for direct investment by members of the public despite its number of unit holders or investors; or

(d) a unit trust that has less than 100 unit holders if it has less than 100 unit holders or investors because of unusual or temporary circumstances, such as its recent establishment or forthcoming termination, and if it would otherwise meet the requirements of any of paragraphs (a), (b), (c), and (e); or

(e) a unit trust that has less than 100 unit holders if it could reasonably be regarded as a vehicle mainly for investment by widely-held vehicles for direct investment that are 1 or more of the following:

(i) unit trusts; or

(ii) group investment funds; or

(iii) life insurance companies; or

(iv) superannuation funds; or

(v) portfolio investment entities

[...]

unit trust—

(a) means a scheme or arrangement that is made for the purpose or has the effect of providing facilities for subscribers, purchasers, or contributors to participate, as beneficiaries under a trust, in income and capital gains arising from the property that is subject to the trust; and

(b) does not include—

(i) a trust for the benefit of debenture holders:

(ii) the Common Fund of Public Trust:

(iii) a group investment fund established by Public Trust:

(iv) the Common Fund of the Maori Trustee:

(v) a group investment fund established under the Trustee Companies Act 1967:

(vi) a friendly society registered under the Friendly Societies and Credit Unions Act 1982:

(vii) a superannuation fund:

(viii) an employee share purchase scheme:

(ix) a fund that meets the requirements of section CW 45 (Funeral trusts):

(x) any other trust of any specified kind that is declared by the Governor-General, by Order in Council, not to be a unit trust for the purposes of section HD 13 (Unit trusts)

unit trust manager is defined in section CD 16(4) (Certain dividends not increased by tax credits) for the purposes of that section.

YC 12 PUBLIC UNIT TRUSTS

YC 12(1) APPLICATION BY PUBLIC UNIT TRUST

Subsections (2) to (4) apply in relation to a public unit trust if the public unit trust chooses to apply them.

YC 12(1B) APPLICATION BY SUBSIDIARIES

A person in which a public unit trust holds an ownership interest may choose, when determining the holders of ownership interests in the person, to treat section YC 4 as not applying to the public unit trust as a shareholder company for the person and to treat the ownership interest as being held in the way described in subsection (2).

YC 12(2) UNIT HOLDERS TREATED AS NOTIONAL SINGLE PERSON

The unit holders' shares in the unit trust are treated as held by a notional single person that–

(a) is not a company; and

(b) exists as long as the unit trust exists; and

(c) holds nothing other than the shares in the unit trust.

[...]

YC 12(4) NOTIONAL SINGLE PERSON TREATED AS ALWAYS EXISTING

The notional single person is treated as having accumulated and as having always existed in relation to the balances, at the start of the 2001–02 tax year, of the unit trust's–

(a) imputation credit account:

(b) *(repealed)*

(c) loss balances.

CHAPTER 30

Charitable Trusts

¶30-010 Operating principle

Exemptions from income tax are available to registered charitable trusts that derive income for charitable purposes.

¶30-020 The differences between charitable trusts and private trusts extend beyond taxation benefits

A charitable trust has features in addition to the entitlement to exempt income (if registered) that are different to those of other express trusts, such as a discretionary family trust.

A charitable trust (whether or not registered), unlike a non-charitable trust, can continue indefinitely. This is because the maximum duration of up to 125 years that applies to the majority of express trusts, does not apply to a charitable trust. See the Trusts Act 2019, s 16. This means that a trust for charitable purposes need not vest at the end of the maximum duration that otherwise applies but can continue indefinitely.

Charitable trusts are public trusts that are enforceable by the Attorney-General rather than by the trust's beneficiaries, which is otherwise the case. This is true even if there are natural persons who can benefit from the charitable trust: *Re Belling (dec'd)* [1967] Ch 425.

¶30-030 A charitable trust must have a charitable purpose

The main difference between a charitable trust and other express trusts that exist for the benefit of the trust's beneficiaries, is that a charitable trust is a trust that has charitable purposes, rather than identifiable beneficiaries or classes of beneficiaries. Accordingly, distributions from a charitable trust are made in respect of, or in the furtherance of, the trust's purposes, rather than to a specified beneficiary or beneficiaries.

¶30-040 Charitable purpose is a defined term

The definition of charitable purpose is codified in the Income Tax Act 2007 and the Charities Act 2005. The definitions in these Acts commence with a restatement of the common law definition of charitable purposes, which defines charitable purpose as including "every charitable purpose, whether it relates to the relief of poverty, the advancement of education or religion, or any other matter beneficial to the community": s YA 1 "charitable purpose", Charities Act, s 5(1). In doing so, the definitions repeat what are referred to as the 4 heads of charity, which can be traced back to the preamble to the Statute of Charitable Uses 1601 (43 Elizabeth I c.4).

The legislative definition also includes an amendment to the common law to reflect the development and evolution of charitable purpose in New Zealand and the place of tribal and bloodline affiliations in Māori culture. See ¶30-060.

The definition of "charitable purpose" in the Charities Act was amended in 2012 to include the promotion of amateur sport, if it is the means by which a charitable purpose is pursued.

As the definition of charitable purpose is inclusive rather than exclusive, there is no single test that determines whether any particular purpose is charitable. For this reason, every charitable purpose must be reviewed against the principles developed at common law to determine whether a purpose or purposes are charitable. See *Re Greenpeace of New Zealand Incorporated* [2014] NZSC 105; (2014) 3 NZTR ¶24-013, where the majority of the Supreme Court noted at [56] that:

> "The very fact that s 5, and the Act as a whole, assumes the common law approach to charities (as the Select Committee report makes clear) points away from codification. Reference in statutes to the common law without more is to the common law as it develops from time to time ...".

¶30-050 A purpose other than the relief of poverty must contain an element of public benefit

Although not clearly stated in the legislation, an element of public benefit is a necessary pre-requisite for valid charitable purposes other than the relief of poverty. See *Molloy* v *C of IR* (1981) 5 NZTC 61,070 (CA). This is also the case in accordance with common law principles.

Therefore, once it is established that the purpose of a trust is charitable in character, it must also be established that the trust will benefit an appreciable sector of the public. *Travis Trust* v *Charities Commission* [2008] NZHC 1912; (2008) 2 NZTR ¶18-030.

¶30-060 The public benefit test is met when a trust exists for an appreciable section of the community

Determining whether there is a sufficient element of public benefit requires a 2-fold test: first, are the purposes of the trust such as to confer a benefit on the public or a section of the public; and second, does the class of persons eligible to benefit constitute the public or a sufficient section of it? See *New Zealand Society of Accountants* v *C of IR*; *New Zealand Law Society* v *C of IR* (1986) 8 NZTC 5,205 (CA).

This test can be restated as requiring a determination as to whether a charity's purposes benefit a private segment of the community rather than purposes that could more properly be considered to benefit a wider community. The precise nature of the test changes depending on which head of charity is under consideration.

As a general principle, it is accepted that a charity can meet the public benefit test if it must exist for the benefit of the community or an appreciably important section of the community. Although this generally means that a charity will not meet the public benefit test if the charity exists for the benefit of particular individuals, that is not the case if the purpose would satisfy the public benefit requirement apart from the fact that the beneficiaries of the trust, or the members of the society or institution, are related by blood: s YA 1 "charitable purpose", Charities Act, s 5(2).

This legislative amendment to the common law reflects the development and evolution of charitable purpose in New Zealand and the place of tribal and bloodline affiliations in Māori culture. See further discussion of blood relationship in the Inland Revenue issues paper IP3168 issued in February 2000.

At the same time, the blood relationship exemption was incorporated in legislation. Marae were defined as having a charitable purpose if both of the following conditions are satisfied:

- the physical structure of the marae is situated on land that is a Māori reservation referred to in Te Ture Whenua Maori Act 1993 (Maori Land Act 1993), and
- the funds of the marae are used only for the administration and maintenance of the land and of the physical structure of the marae or some other charitable purpose. See Charities Act 2005, s 5(2)(b).

Also see *Foundation for Anti-Aging Research* v *Charities Registration Board* [2015] NZCA 449, a decision largely concerned with the procedure for appealing registration decisions that reiterates the need to evidence sufficient public benefit.

¶30-070 Historically the public benefit requirement would not be met if a trust had a political purpose

Historically, a trust with charitable purposes could not meet the public benefit requirement if it also had a political purpose. This was because it had long been the position that a court cannot judge whether any political purpose is for the public benefit. See *Bowman* v *Secular Society Ltd* [1917] AC 406 at 442, *National Anti-Vivisection Society* v *IR Commrs* [1948] AC 31, *IR Commrs* v *Temperance Council of the Christian Churches of England and Wales* (1926) 136 LT 27, *Re Draco Foundation (NZ) Charitable Trust* [2011] NZHC 368; (2011) 25 NZTC ¶20-032, and *Re Greenpeace of New Zealand* [2011] NZHC 77; (2011) 25 NZTC ¶20-045.

Following the Supreme Court decision in *Re Greenpeace of New Zealand Incorporated* [2014] NZSC 105; (2014) 26 NZTC ¶21-088, this is no longer the case in New Zealand. The majority of the Supreme Court in *Greenpeace* held (considering whether Greenpeace's political nuclear disarmament activities should preclude it from registration as a charity) that:

- A "political purpose" exclusion should no longer be applied in New Zealand. Political and charitable purposes are not mutually exclusive. The inquiry should be whether a purpose is for a public benefit that the law recognises as charitable.
- Section 5 of the Act provides an exemption for non-charitable activities if ancillary.

The Supreme Court also held that although illegal activity may disqualify an entity from registration, such activity will not necessarily justify removal from the charities register. Following this decision, the Charities Board reconsidered Greenpeace NZ's application but again declined it determining that Greenpeace NZ's purposes included advocating its own views on environmental issues and on peace, nuclear disarmament and the elimination of weapons of mass destruction and it could not be established that these purposes were of public benefit and charitable. It also considered that Greenpeace NZ had an illegal purpose that disqualified it from charitable status. This decision was successfully appealed to the High Court, where Mallon J concluded at [176] that:

> "I consider the Board was in error in declining Greenpeace NZ's application for charitable status. Greenpeace NZ's main activity is to advocate for the protection of the environment. It does that mainly by advocating for measures to mitigate climate change, for sustainable fishing for the protection of the ocean environment and for improving the quality of New Zealand's freshwater. There is a charitable public benefit in that advocacy, as it contributes to the broad-based support and effort necessary for the end goal of protecting the environment. The advocacy takes a variety of forms. Where it involves commissioning independent scientific research that it makes available on its website, it also advances education. Greenpeace NZ's purpose to promote peace, nuclear disarmament and the elimination of weapons of mass destruction is ancillary and therefore not disqualifying. It does not have an illegal purpose."
>
> See *Re Greenpeace of New Zealand Inc* [2020] NZHC 1999; (2020) 5 NZTR ¶30-012; (2020) 29 NZTC ¶24-071.

Greenpeace's date of registration was subsequently backdated to the date it had made a properly completed application for registration in June 2008: *Greenpeace of New Zealand Inc* v *Charities Registration Board* [2020] NZHC 2993; (2020) 29 NZTC ¶24-083.

Also see *Family First New Zealand* v *Attorney-General* [2020] NZCA 366; (2020) 29 NZTC ¶24-074, where the majority of the Court of Appeal found that:

> "[146] Most basically, the fact that Family First favours, to use the Board's phrase, the 'traditional family' does not in our view mean that its advocacy for family and marriage as important and valuable institutions loses the necessary advancement of a public, charitable, benefit. We acknowledge there is in New Zealand, consistent with our tradition of pragmatic and progressive social theory and legislation, a recognition and acceptance of alternative forms of family, including as based on de facto relationships, civil unions and same-sex marriages. Nevertheless we can take judicial notice of the fact that by far the larger part of the social groups constituting families in contemporary New Zealand, at least in the nuclear family sense, are those based on civil or religious marriages between men and women.

> [147] It would be curious if promotion of what the Board called the 'traditional family' would cease to be of public benefit because there is a growing acceptance of other forms of stable family life, including within whānau and hapū relationships.
>
> [148] And to be fair, Family First recognised the contribution non-traditional forms of family life can make. As it says in its Statement of Principles:
>
>> We acknowledge the tremendous contribution made by single, adoptive and step-parents and extended whānau in society. We wish to ensure they receive appropriate levels of assistance, without denying the clear empirical evidence that the best environment in which to raise children is the biological two-parent, husband-wife family.
>
> [149] Thus far, and recognising the possible significance of Family First's advocacy of specific legal recognition of certain forms of family and marriage over others, we are satisfied that Family First's purposes and principles are ones which promote a public benefit in a manner analogous with public charitable benefits as recognised in New Zealand over time."

The majority of the Court of Appeal also found that the extent of Family First's advocacy was no more than ancillary (so as not to outweigh its charitable purpose). However, a warning was issued (see [176] regarding Family First's priorities and activities for the future).

¶30-080 No absolute test determinative of public benefit

The absence of a recognised test as to what will constitute public benefit is highlighted in the decision of Bleby J in the South Australian Supreme Court case of *Strathalbyn Show Jumping Club Inc* v *Mayes* [2001] SASC 73 Bleby J noting at 75 that:

> "Public benefit is an elusive quality. It is not always open to sound reason, but it is a quality often plainly recognised when it exists".

As noted in the Court of Appeal decision in *Family First* at [136] "... The assessment of whether there is public benefit in a charitable sense therefore requires consideration of the end promoted and the means and manner of that promotion". In the absence of a definitive test, whether a purpose is of public benefit is determined on a case-by-case basis.

Example

Income derived by the trustees of a fund created for the benefit of retired ministers of the Presbyterian Church was exempt from tax. The benefits conferred on retired ministers were sufficiently connected with the advancement of religion and in sufficient numbers to meet the public benefit element of the charitable purposes test *Presbyterian Church of New Zealand Beneficiary Fund* v *C of IR* (1994) 16 NZTC 11,185.

Example

By contrast in *Hester* v *C of IR* (2004) 21 NZTC 18,421 (HC) and *Hester* v *C of IR* (2005) 22 NZTC 19,007 (CA) where the trustees of the Church of Jesus Christ of Latter Day Saints provided a defined benefit and contributory superannuation to employees of the church, there was no public benefit. In that case, it was held that there was an insufficient nexus between the benefits provided to the employees of the church by the plan and the charitable activities of the church and that it was not appropriate to equate the charitable purposes of the church with the purposes of the plan when applying the "natural and probable consequences" test from the Presbyterian Church Fund. The purpose of the plan in Hester was to benefit the employees of the church. That was a private benefit inconsistent with the charitable purpose claimed by the trustees of the plan. Leave to appeal to the Supreme Court was dismissed in *Hester* v *C of IR* (2005) 22 NZTC 19,194.

In New Zealand, freemasonry was held not to have an exclusively charitable purpose because any public benefit from an organisation that sought to achieve its aims by making its members better people was too remote: *Re the Grand Lodge of Antient Free and Accepted Masons in New Zealand* (2010) 24 NZTC 24,590.

In *Re Family First New Zealand*, in determining whether Family First's role is of benefit to the public, the High Court noted that:

> "[86] ... the Charities Board should refer to analogous cases. In doing so, however, it is essential the Charities Board not undertake its analogical assessment by seeking to carefully match Family First's purposes with organisations that have achieved recognition as charitable entities. Doing so would risk undermining the Supreme Court's recognition, for the first time, that political purposes are not excluded from being classified as charitable.
>
> [...]
>
> [88] ... I am not suggesting the Charities Board must accept Family First's purposes are for the benefit of the public when it reconsiders Family First's case.
>
> [89] I am saying, however, that the analogical analysis which the Charities Board must undertake should be informed by examining whether Family First's activities are objectively directed at promoting the moral improvement of society. This exercise should not be conflated with a subjective assessment of the merits of Family First's views. Members of the Charities Board may personally disagree with the views of Family First, but at the same time recognise there is a legitimate analogy between its role and those organisations that have been recognised as charities. Such an approach would be consistent with the obligation on members of the Charities Board to act with honesty, integrity and in good faith."

¶30-082 Promotion of sport and leisure for its own sake will not generally meet the public benefit requirement

Traditionally, the promotion of sports or leisure activities for their own sake has not been held to be charitable. This view was revisited and confirmed in *Travis Trust* v *Charities Commission* (supra), which concerned a trust that sponsored a horse race. In this case, Joseph Williams J held that although the law of charities could and should develop in light of changing social patterns (regarding whether support of sports should be charitable), he did not accept that the promotion of horse racing was charitable or that, in public benefit terms, an appreciable section of the community benefited. See ¶30-040 regarding amateur sport.

¶30-084 The advancement of education is presumed to be of public benefit

The advancement of education is generally presumed to be for the public benefit. However, the presumption is a rebuttable presumption that the court will determine based on the evidence presented to it: *Re Education New Zealand Trust* (2010) 24 NZTC 24,354 at [24], [26].

Helpful guidance is provided by the High Court in *Re Family First New Zealand* (supra) at [91] where the court state that "[t]o be a charitable education activity, the entity must, in addition to conferring a public benefit, promote learning which may be undertaken through a variety of means such as training programmes, conferences or by carrying out or disseminating research that improves knowledge about a particular issue".

¶30-086 The advancement of religion is presumed to be of public benefit

Public benefit is also presumed in respect of the advancement of religion to avoid the courts being in a position of judging between religions. Accordingly, the threshold before the presumption of public benefit is rebutted is high. See *Liberty Trust* v *Charities Commission* [2011] NZHC 577; (2011) 3 NZTR ¶21-004 for a consideration of the charitable nature of the advancement of religion.

¶30-088 Public benefit must be expressly shown where the claimed purpose of the trust is to benefit the community

Where the purpose of a trust is to benefit the community, the benefit need not be for all of the public. However, it must be for a significant part: *Oppenheim* v *Tobacco Securities Trust Co Ltd* [1951] AC 297, *Molloy* v *C of IR* (1981) 5 NZTC 61,070 (CA), *Canterbury Development Corp* v *Charities Commission*; *Canterbury Development Corp Trust* v *Charities Commission*; *CEDF Trustee Ltd as Trustee of the Canterbury Economic Development Fund* v *Charities Commission* [2010] NZHC 331; (2010) 24 NZTC 24,143, *Foundation for Anti-Aging Research* v *Charities Registration Board* (supra).

¶30-090 A declaration of trust under s 24B of the Maori Trust Boards Act can entitle a charitable trust that does not meet the charitable purpose or public benefit test to an income tax exemption

Section 24B of the Maori Trust Boards Act 1955 allows Māori Trust Boards to establish charitable trusts that can be entitled to the income tax exemptions in ss CW 41 and CW 42.

For the exemptions from income tax to be available when a Māori Trust Board executes a declaration that property of a trust is held for charitable purposes:

- the purposes must be purposes specified in s 24 or 24A of the Maori Trust Boards Act

- the Commissioner must be satisfied that notwithstanding that the charitable purposes may not be charitable at common law or may not meet the public benefit test, all other requirements of charitable status are met
- the declaration of trust has been approved by the Commissioner, and
- the trust meets the essential requirements for registration as a charitable entity under s 13 of the Charities Act.

See public binding ruling BR Pub 08/02, "Maori Trust Boards: Declaration of trust for charitable purposes made under section 24B of the Maori Trust Boards Act 1955 – Income tax consequences", July 2008 in *Tax Information Bulletin* ¶208-107 Vol 20, No 8, September 2008.

¶30-100 Exemptions from income tax that were previously available to any charity are now limited to charities that are registered as tax charities

Before 1 July 2008, although charities could and often did seek confirmation of entitlement to tax exemptions, it was not necessary to do so as a charity could self-assess its entitlement to exemption from income tax. This is no longer the case and, from 1 July 2008, unless a specific exemption applies, exemptions from income tax and RWT only apply to charities that are registered with the Charities Registration Board (the Board), or previously with the Charities Commission, or applied to register before 1 July 2008: Taxation (Personal Tax Cuts, Annual Rates, and Remedial Matters) Act 2008 (see s CW 41(5)(b)).

However, as registration with the Board is voluntary, a trust can be charitable at common law but nevertheless subject to tax on its income. Some charities may elect to forego registration and the tax benefits that flow from this to preserve privacy and the reporting obligations and the scrutiny that can otherwise apply to a registered charity.

For tax purposes, a registered charity is referred to as a tax charity: s CW 41(5).

A tax charity is exempt from income tax in respect of any non-business income. Non-business income includes investment income such as interest or dividends: s CW 41.

A tax charity is exempt from income tax in respect of its business income if no person with some control over the business is able to benefit from that position of control: s CW 42.

For the purposes of the trust rules, a trust is a charitable trust in respect of an income year if all income derived by that trust is held for charitable purposes and any income derived in the year is tax-exempt business or non-business income: s HC 13.

Enjoyment of charitable status before the enactment of the Charities Act and the requirement for registration as a charity does not of itself ensure registration as a tax charity. *Re the Grand Lodge of Antient Free and Accepted Masons in New Zealand* (supra) involved a Grand Lodge that had previously enjoyed charitable status in New

Zealand for over 50 years. However, the High Court held that the Charities Act 2005 did not change the tests for determining a charity, it only changed the decision-maker, and that if existing status was to have been protected, the Act would have said so.

¶30-105 Requirements to be an officer of a registered charity

A person is not generally able to be an officer of a registered charity if the person has been convicted of tax evasion or a similar offence under s 143B of the Tax Administration Act 1994 and sentenced for that offence within the last 7 years.

There is a range of other factors that may prevent someone from being qualified as an officer under the Charities Act 2005, for example, if they are under 16 years old, an undischarged bankrupt, or have been convicted for a crime involving dishonesty.

The Charities Act 2005 may define officers differently to the way a charity's rules define them. An officer can be a person or a body corporate.

If a charity is a trust, its officers are all the current trustees.

¶30-110 A charity is only entitled to a certificate of exemption for RWT if the charity is a registered charity

Tax charities are also exempt from RWT. Certificates of exemption from RWT, previously available to any charity, are no longer issued to any charity that is not a tax charity. Applications for exemption are made using the Inland Revenue form IR 451: "Application for exemption from RWT on interest and dividends". If a registered charity has had RWT deducted incorrectly, for example, if an interest payer deducted RWT from interest earned after a charity was registered, but before its certificate of exemption was issued, it is not necessary to file a tax return to obtain the refund. The refund can be obtained by completing an IR 454 form: "Resident withholding tax – refund request".

¶30-120 The Charities Registration Board was established to provide for the registration of charities

Initially, the administration of the Charities Act 2005 (the Act) and, in particular, the process for registering, monitoring and deregistering charitable entities was vested in the Charities Commission (the Commission). The Commission was disestablished from 1 July 2012 and, since then, the Act has been administered by the Board as a separate, independent office within the Department of Internal Affairs.

In addition to providing a charities register that can be searched free of charge by the public, functions of the Board include:

- promoting public trust and confidence in the charitable sector
- encouraging and promoting the effective use of charitable resources
- educating and assisting charities in matters relating to good governance and management
- making appropriate information available to assist persons to apply for registration as charitable entities
- receiving, considering and processing annual returns submitted by charitable entities (registered entities must file an annual return in a prescribed form within 6 months after the entity's balance date), and
- monitoring charitable entities and their activities to ensure that registered charitable entities continue to be qualified for registration.

Charities that no longer meet the requirements for registration; engage in serious wrongdoing; or significantly and persistently fail to comply with the Charities Act can be deregistered by the Board: Charities Act, ss 31–36.

The Charities register can be searched at charities.govt.nz.

¶30-130 Registration can be backdated

Registration as a charitable entity may be backdated if the Board is satisfied that the entity was qualified for registration as a charitable entity at all times during the period between the effective registration time and the time that the entity actually became registered as a charitable entity. The effective date of registration cannot be earlier than:

- in the case of a charitable trust created or established by a gift made after a date to be set by Order in Council and that was exempt from gift duty, the time that the gift was made, and
- in any other case, the time at which the Board received a properly completed application for registration as a charitable entity. See Charities Act, s 20 and *Greenpeace of New Zealand Inc* v *Charities Registration Board* [2020] NZHC 2993; (2020) 29 NZTC ¶24-083.

The backdating of registration applies for the purposes of the Charities Act and the Income Tax Act.

For an overview of the Charities Act, see further at CCH, *New Zealand Tax Updater*, No 4, May 2005 and in the *Tax Information Bulletin* ¶177-123 Vol 17, No 7, September 2005 at 58–61.

Also see *In re National Council of Women of New Zealand Incorporated*; *National Council of Women of New Zealand Incorporated* v *Commissioner of Inland Revenue (No 2)* [2014] NZHC 3200; (2014) 26 NZTC ¶21-116, where the High Court held that where the Charities Registration Board did not have the discretion to back-date registration decisions under s 20 of the Charities Act, the High Court had wider powers under s 61 of the Charities Act. In the case of National Council of Women of New Zealand

Incorporated, the High Court concluded that an order backdating NCW's registration was justifiable (given that the overall purpose of the Charities Act is to encourage and promote the effective use of charitable resources) and backdated the National Council of Women of New Zealand Incorporated registration.

¶30-140 Registration partway through an income tax year

If a charity registers with the Board partway through a tax year, the charity's income will only be tax exempt for the portion of the year that the charity is a tax charity. See s CW 41.

¶30-150 Tax consequences of deregistration

Rules were introduced by the Taxation (Annual Rates, Employee Allowances, and Remedial Matters) Act 2014 to address the tax consequences that arise for entities that are removed (or deregistered) from the charities register. These rules apply whether deregistration is voluntary.

These rules clarify when a deregistered charity should commence as a taxpayer, how the charity should treat its assets and liabilities when it becomes a taxpayer, and what tax provisions should apply in the future. The rules also clarify the tax consequences for donors that have made donations to these entities.

The tax consequences of de-registration were highlighted in an officials' issues paper, "Clarifying the tax consequences for deregistered charities", which was released in July 2013.

Before amendment, the tax rules that applied meant that it was possible for a charity to be deregistered and to face retrospective tax liabilities even if it had been fully compliant with its rules. The nature and extent of the potential tax consequences ultimately depended on the underlying reason why the charity was deregistered. These consequences were more onerous (and involved retrospective tax liabilities) if the deregistered charity was found never to have had a "charitable purpose" or had ceased being charitable in purpose at some time in the past, compared with the situation in which a deregistered charity had simply failed to file the required annual return.

The rules, which had general application from 14 April 2014, clarify the applicable tax law so that deregistered charities and their donors have greater certainty about their tax obligations. The key features of the rules around deregistration can be summarised as follows:

- Section HR 11, which prescribes how a deregistered charity should establish its initial tax base – such as the opening values of its assets and consideration for its financial arrangements.
- Section CW 41 provides that entities that are removed from the charities register will continue to be tax-exempt either until the day on which the entity does not comply with its rules (as these appear on the charities register) or the "day of final decision".

- "Day of final decision" as defined in s YA 1 is the later of the day the entity is removed from the charities register or the day on which all reasonably contemplated administrative appeals and Court proceedings, including appeal rights, are finalised or exhausted in relation to the charity's charitable status.
- Section HR 12 imposes a tax on net assets of the entity which are held 12 months after the day the entity is no longer exempt from tax under s CW 41 or CW 42.
- Section CV 17 provides that any amount of income arising under s HR 12 will be income of the entity for the income year, that is, 12 months after the day of final decision.
- The definition of "charitable organisation" in s YA 1 also includes an entity that has been removed from the charities register but only for a specified period. This amendment ensures that deregistered charities can, in certain circumstances, still qualify for an FBT exemption, even if that entity is later deregistered.
- Monetary gifts that meet the requirements of a "charitable or other public benefit gift" in s LD 3(1) made to registered charities can still qualify for donations tax relief even if that entity is later deregistered.

The following examples from *Tax Information Bulletin* ¶267-112 Vol 26, No 7, August 2014 illustrate how and when the tax base calculations are to be undertaken.

Example 1: Depreciable property

Charity A was registered as a charitable entity in 2008. That same year, Charity A purchased office furniture for $50,000 (GST exclusive) during the first month of the 2008 tax year. In 2013, Charity A was deregistered because it was found by Charities Services to have been non-compliant with its rules. This non-compliance has been occurring since 2008. Charity A still owns the office furniture at the date of deregistration. The depreciation rate for office furniture is 19.2%.

Charity A must file an income tax return for each year starting from the 2008 year.

Under new section HR 11(2), the cost of premises, plant, equipment and trading stock is the value that would be used at the "date of cessation" under the general tax rules if section CW 41 or CW 42 never applied. Under the general tax rules, office furniture must be depreciated each year it is used in the business of Charity A. Therefore, the cost of office furniture for each year from 2008 to the present day is as follows:

Year	2008	2009	2010	2011	2012	2013
Opening value ($)	50,000	40,400	32,643	26,376	21,312	17,220
Depreciation ($)	9,600	7,757	6,267	5,064	4,092	3,306
Year-end balance ($)	40,400	32,643	26,376	21,312	17,220	13,914

Charity A will introduce the asset into the tax base at $50,000 and recognise a depreciation charge of $9,600 in its 2008 income tax return.

Example 2: Financial arrangement rules

Assuming the deregistration facts as above, Charity A had loaned $100,000 to person X in 2008. The loan was repayable on demand and interest was 10% per annum, compounding. No loan repayments were made.

Under new section HR 11(3), Charity A is required to account for this loan under the financial arrangement rules in each of the years that it had ceased to meet the requirements of section CW 41 or CW 42. It must also calculate an opening value using the formula in new section HR 11(4). The calculations are as follows:

Year	2008	2009	2010	2011	2012	2013
Opening value ($)	100,000	110,000	121,000	133,100	146,410	161,051
Interest ($)	10,000	11,000	12,100	13,310	14,641	16,105
Year-end balance ($)	110,000	121,000	133,100	146,410	161,051	177,156

In 2008 the opening value would be $100,000 and the closing value would be $110,000. Charity A would account for $10,000 accrued interest income in its 2008 income tax return.

Example: Taxation of tax-exempt accumulation

Charity A's date of deregistration is 1 June 2014. Charity A did not dispute its deregistration, and so this is also its day of final decision. The balance sheet for Charity A at 1 June 2014 is shown below.

Assets	
Cash	$50
Inventory	$300
Land (donated)	$3,000
Liabilities	
Loan	$200
Equity	
Shareholders' equity	$3,150

The net assets calculation will be $3,150 less the value of the donated land and less any relevant adjustments such as assets and income distributed for charitable purposes or in accordance with the entity's rules within 12 months of the date of deregistration. The net assets value will be $150 ($3,150 less $3,000). Assume Charity A has a July balance date for tax purposes. Charity A would include $150 as income in its 2015 income tax return.

¶30-160 Certain unregistered charities are included in the definition of tax charity

In addition to charities registered under the Charities Act, tax charity is also defined to include (s CW 41(5)):

- a trust that carries out its charitable purposes outside New Zealand, and which is approved as a tax charity by the Commissioner in circumstances where registration as a charitable entity under the Charities Act is unavailable, and
- a charity removed from the register but qualifying under the transitional rules (see ¶30-150).

¶30-170 Exemptions from income tax do not extend to PAYE or GST

Any exemption from income tax does not extend to PAYE on payments to employees or GST, which must still be accounted for by any charity that is registered or is required to be registered for GST. See Chapter 25 – *Goods and Services Tax*.

However, supplies of donated goods by non-profit bodies are exempt supplies. The definition of a non-profit body will include a tax charity, provided that the governing rules prevent any distributions for private benefit: Goods and Services Tax Act 1985, ss 2(1) ("non-profit body"), 14(1)(b).

There is also a specific exclusion in the definition of associated persons in the Goods and Services Tax Act that can apply where trustees of 2 trusts, one of which is a charitable trust, would otherwise be associated through a common settlor. See *Tax Information Bulletin* ¶221-109 Vol 22, No 1, February 2010 at 38, 39.

Also see Exposure Draft QWB00078 "Goods and Services Tax – Non-profit bodies – Registration, accounting for GST, and deregistration", which draws attention to matters a non-profit organisation must take into consideration when registering for GST. The QWBA considers the requirements (and the compliance costs) for a non-profit body with 2 buildings used for different purposes when:

- registering for GST
- accounting for GST
- cancelling GST registration.

¶30-180 Charities are generally exempt from paying FBT on any benefits provided to employees in furtherance of the charity's charitable purpose

Charities are generally exempt from FBT. The FBT rules exclude benefits provided by a charitable organisation, including a charitable trust, to its employees. However, this exemption is limited to employment in relation to the charity's charitable purposes: s CX 25(1). See public binding ruling BR Pub 17/06: "Fringe benefit tax – charitable and other donee organisations and fringe benefit tax".

> "**Example 1**
>
> A non-profit organisation has the principal purpose of providing education through a private school. The organisation is a charitable organisation for the purposes of the FBT rules because it is not carried on for the private gain of any individual and its funds are applied wholly or mainly for the advancement of education within New Zealand.
>
> The organisation charges tuition fees for the education it provides and has had surpluses of income over expenditure for the last three income years. It provides a car to its school principal for work and private use.

> The organisation is not liable for FBT on the benefit arising from the private use or availability for the private use of the car provided to the principal. This is because the benefit is provided by a charitable organisation to an employee who is employed in an activity that is within the charitable organisation's benevolent, charitable, cultural or philanthropic purposes. The employee is not employed in a business activity that is carried on by the charitable organisation outside its benevolent, charitable, cultural or philanthropic purposes."

Example 1 from BR Pub 17/06.

The exclusion does not apply to a benefit that comprises a short-term charge facility, if the value of the benefit is more than the lesser of 5% of the employee's salary or wages or $1,200 for a tax year: s CX 25(2), (3).

It is important to note that, for the purposes of the exemption from FBT, a charity (s YA 1 "charitable organisation") is defined by reference to recipients of charitable or public benefit gifts, previously referred to as donee organisations, (s LD 3) and charitable organisations listed in sch 32, not by whether the charity is registered on the Charities Register. Universities, local and public authorities are expressly excluded from the definition.

¶30-190 Tax credits for charitable or public benefit gifts

A charitable or other public benefit gift means a gift of money of $5 or more that is paid to a society, institution, association, organisation, trust, or fund described in s LD 3(2).

However, the definition of a charitable or other public benefit gift expressly excludes a testamentary gift. See s LD 3(1)(c). Accordingly, an amount left to a charity in a will is a testamentary gift and will not qualify as a charitable or other public benefit gift and therefore not qualify for a tax credit.

Also, a forgiveness of debt is not a "charitable or other public benefit gift" under s LD 1 of the Income Tax Act 2007. See s LD 3 and *C of IR* v *Roberts* [2019] NZCA 654; (2019) 29 NZTC ¶24-026 for the position before this amendment to s LD 3 of the Income Tax Act effective 1 April 2020. Section LD 3(2) was amended to confer donee status on an entity registered on the Charities Register to ensure that donors have a greater level of certainty that their donations tax relief will not ordinarily be reversed in circumstances when they have made a *bona fide* monetary gift and the entity they have donated to is later deregistered.

A person who makes a donation to a charitable organisation (that meets the requirements of a public benefit gift as defined in s LD 3(1)) has a tax credit for the tax year equal to the amount calculated using the formula:

$$\text{total gifts} \times 33\ 1/3\%.$$

A "public benefit gift" is a monetary gift of $5 or more to a charity as defined in s LD 3(2) that (with some exemptions) is required to apply its funds "wholly or mainly to charitable, benevolent, philanthropic, or cultural purposes within New Zealand": s LD 3(2)(a).

With effect from 1 April 2019, an anti-avoidance provision has applied to arrangements involving tax credits under s LD 1. Section GB 55 provides that the Commissioner can reduce the amount of a tax credit under s LD 1 when a person has entered into an arrangement that has a purpose or effect of defeating the intent and application of that section. See Income Tax Act, ss LD 1–LD 3, sch 32 and the Tax Administration Act, s 41A.

¶30-195 Wholly or mainly safe harbour

In September 2018, the Commissioner released an interpretation statement IS 18/05, "Income tax: donee organisations – meaning of wholly or mainly applying funds to specified purposes within New Zealand", and fact sheet, "Applying the 'safe harbour' approach" (*Tax Information Bulletin* ¶3010-104 Vol 30, No 10, November 2018 at 25). The statement applies from the beginning of the 2019–20 income year.

The Commissioner had previously accepted in some cases that "wholly or mainly" could mean as little as a bare majority, that is, more than 50%. In the statement, the Commissioner concludes that "wholly or mainly" in this context requires considerably more than a bare majority, but that it is not possible to interpret the expression with any greater certainty. However, to bring greater certainty, the Commissioner proposed an administrative safe harbour. If an organisation meets or exceeds the minimum safe harbour percentage, the Commissioner will generally accept that the organisation meets the "wholly or mainly" requirement without further enquiry. The Commissioner has set the safe harbour percentage at a minimum of 75%.

Other interpretative conclusions reached in the statement include the following:

- The most appropriate meaning of "funds" is "cash on hand", which includes cash and other highly liquid assets available to meet commitments. "Funds" is accepted as equating to the accounting concepts of "cash" and "cash equivalents".
- "Applied" means "devoted to" or "put to use". Funds can be applied by being spent or accumulated, that is, set aside for future spending or investment.
- The expression "funds are applied" suggests:
    - The application of funds arises as a result of the organisation either spending money or undertaking some affirmative act to invest or set aside the money for future spending for some purpose or purposes.
    - The affirmative act is the decision to accumulate funds that has been made at the appropriate level in the organisation for decisions of that type according to its established management practices.
    - The decision to accumulate funds will need sufficient detail to be able to characterise that application of funds as advancing charitable, benevolent, philanthropic, or cultural purposes within New Zealand.

- It is the specified purposes that must be "within New Zealand" not the application of funds. This means the location where funds are spent is not relevant.
- The enquiry in regard to the application of funds is to identify objectively whether a sufficient relationship exists between the purposes served by the actual or proposed activity and advancing specified purposes within New Zealand. The connection needs to be sufficiently direct, although not necessarily an immediate connection.
- Where funds have been applied to more than one purpose, apportionment may be necessary. Apportionment issues can be approached on a similar basis to apportionment arising under s DA 1 (the general permission).

The statement also includes a large number of examples to help an organisation decide how much of its total funds are accumulated or spent for specified purposes within New Zealand.

Safe harbour approach

The safe harbour approach comprises determining an organisation's safe harbour percentage for a financial year. Calculating an organisation's safe harbour percentage involves 3 steps:

- Use the organisation's statement of cash flows in its financial statements or statement of receipts and payments in its performance report to find the organisation's "total funds". "Total funds" is the sum of the cash on hand at the end of a year and the cash spent during the year (ie, all cash outflows whether capital or revenue).
- Find the amount of the organisation's "funds applied to specified purposes within New Zealand". This is a combination of the cash spent, invested or set aside entirely for specified purposes within New Zealand and amounts reasonably apportioned to those purposes.
- Divide the cash spent or set aside for specified purposes within New Zealand (as per the second step) by the organisation's "total funds" (as per the first step) and express this as a percentage.

If the figure is below 75% in any year, the cumulative total of its funds applied over the current and preceding 2 years can be used (including years before the commencement of the statement). This allows some year-on-year variation for exceptional years. However, it is not expected that under the rolling 3-year cumulative safe harbour calculation an organisation would devote 50% or less of its funds to specified purposes within New Zealand in any particular year.

The statement states that if the rolling 3-year cumulative safe harbour percentage is below 75% or the figure in any year is 50% or below, the organisation should contact Inland Revenue as soon as possible.

The statement includes a worked example of the safe harbour calculation.

Change in practice

Charities that are unable to satisfy the "wholly or mainly" requirement can:

- seek to be added to sch 32 of the Income Tax Act as an overseas donee organisation approved by Parliament (this option is not available if an organisation is established for the principal purpose of fostering or administering any religion, cult or political creed)
- establish and maintain a separate fund exclusively for specified purposes within New Zealand (in which case only gifts to that fund would be eligible for donation tax benefits).

Companies and Māori authorities are not entitled to a tax credit, but can claim a deduction for donations made to charitable organisations: ss DB 41, DV 12. This deduction is limited to the company's net income before the deduction is taken into account so that the deduction available cannot put them into a loss position.

New Zealand-based charities that apply some or all of their funds for overseas purposes and who want donors to receive tax benefits in connection with any donations received, are required to be named as a donee organisation on the list of recipient of charitable or other public benefit gifts in the Income Tax Act 2007.

With effect from 1 April 2020, for a gift of money to be a charitable gift to one of the above entities, the entity must be on the list published by the Commissioner. This does not apply to community housing entities, Boards of Trustees or tertiary education institutions. In addition, if an entity qualifies for registration under the Charities Act 2005, it has to register to qualify for donee status.

The list of funds and institutions that qualify for the credit (both those listed in sch 32 and those Inland Revenue has approved as satisfying the criteria in s LD 3(2)) is regularly updated on the Inland Revenue website (ird.govt.nz – search keyword: donee organisation).

Also see "question we've been asked", QB 19/10: "Donations: What is required to establish and maintain a fund under s LD 3(2)(c) of the Income Tax Act 2007?" (*Tax Information Bulletin* ¶317-105 Vol 31, No 7, August 2019 at 23), which considers what is required to establish and maintain a fund so that it qualifies as a donee organisation. ED0207a, "Charities and donee organisations: Part 1: Charities" and ED0207b, "Charities and donee organisations: Part 2: Donee organisations" set out how Inland Revenue and Charities Services will monitor and advise charitable entities of the requirements for income tax exemption and donee status.

¶30-200 Non-business income derived by a tax charity is exempt income

Non-business income, also referred to as passive income, includes interest and dividend income.

Non-business income derived by tax charities for charitable purposes is exempt income. This is the case whether the charitable purposes are limited to New Zealand.

Inland Revenue policy provides that registration as a tax charity is sufficient to ensure the non-business income exemption applies. See operational statement OS 06/02 "Interaction of Tax and Charities Rules, Covering Tax Exemption and Donee Status", issued 14 November 2006 with effect from 1 February 2007.

However, the non-business income exemption does not apply to a charity that is not registered, or where transitional legislation applies, has not applied to register: s CW 41(5).

The non-business income exemption does not extend to council-controlled organisations: s CW 41(4). A council-controlled organisation (s YA 1) includes an entity, not being a company, which operates a trading undertaking for the purpose of making a profit and in respect of which one or more local authorities have a majority control interest.

The non-business income exemption does not extend to any business carried on by, or for, the benefit of a tax charity: s CW 41(3). It is clear from this exemption that for non-business income to be exempt, the income must be derived directly by the tax charity.

¶30-210 A charitable trust does not have to have exclusively charitable purposes

Trusts are treated less restrictively than societies and institutions for the purposes of establishing entitlement to tax exemptions. Charities other than trusts must have exclusively charitable objects to meet the requirements for the exemption from income tax.

If the purposes of a charitable trust are not exclusively charitable, the charity can still be entitled to the non-business income exemption if a segregated part of its income has been received and must be applied exclusively for charitable purposes. See *Latimer* v *C of IR* (2002) 20 NZTC 17,737 (CA) regarding the interpretation of s CB 4(1)(c) of the Income Tax Act 1994, an earlier version of s CW 41. Upheld on appeal to the Privy Council: *Latimer (Trustees for the Crown Forestry Rental Trust)* v *C of IR* (2004) 21 NZTC 18,470.

Where a non-charitable purpose is not an independent purpose but is ancillary, subordinate or incidental to a charitable purpose, its presence does not negate the charitable purpose. See *C of IR* v *New Zealand Council of Law Reporting* (1981) 5 NZTC 61,053 (CA). These remarks were later interpreted in a slightly narrower vein to mean that all independent purposes, as well as the fundamental purpose, must be of a charitable nature for the exemption to apply. See *Cowey Mills & Co Ltd* v *C of IR* (1982) 5 NZTC 61,172, *C of IR* v *NTN Bearing-Saeco (New Zealand) Ltd* (1986) 8 NZTC 5,039.

Section 5(4) of the Charities Act provides that a non-charitable purpose is ancillary to a charitable purpose if the non-charitable purpose is:

- ancillary, secondary, subordinate, or incidental to a charitable purpose of the trust, society or institution, and
- not an independent purpose of the trust, society or institution.

Example

The primary purpose of a trust was to ensure the continuance of education fell within the criteria established as constituting a trust for the advancement of education. The trust's schools were open to any member of the public prepared to meet the fees and expenses and, therefore, an element of public benefit was present. The fact that parents and the school may gain an advantage was of a secondary nature and did not negate the trust's charitable purpose: *Educational Fees Protection Society Incorporation* v *C of IR* (1991) 13 NZTC 8,203.

As stated by the Supreme Court in *Re Greenpeace of New Zealand Incorporated* [2014] NZSC 105; (2014) 3 NZTR ¶24-013, the inclusion of a non-charitable purpose ("for example, advocacy") does not prevent registration as a charity if it is "merely ancillary to a charitable purpose of the trust" and how much of an ancillary purpose is sufficient to outweigh a charitable purpose is determined on a case-by-case basis. In *Re Education New Zealand Trust* (2010) 24 NZTC 24,354, a trust that promoted New Zealand educational institutes to fee-paying students, it was established that approximately 30% of the students attracted ended up in profit-making institutions. This 30% private benefit was sufficient to outweigh the public benefit and did not comprise an ancillary purpose. It is important to appreciate that nothing turns on the 30% figure in and of itself and that the relationship between public and private benefits is determined both quantitatively and qualitatively on a case by case basis.

In *Re the Grand Lodge of Antient Free and Accepted Masons in New Zealand* (supra), it was only after the necessary expenditure in running freemasonry had been incurred that the balance was expended on charity. Here the charitable purposes were found to be ancillary and lacked a quantitative component. See also ¶30-080.

¶30-220 Donations are not income

Donations or koha are not non-business income. Donations and koha are gifts.

No income tax liability will arise in respect of a donation that has been voluntarily made and where there is no consideration for that donation. For further information in determining whether koha is a gift, see the Inland Revenue publication IR 278 "Payments and gifts in the Maori community".

A record must be kept regarding the source of any donations to a charitable trust or public benefit gift recipient together with information regarding how the funds have been used, both within New Zealand, and if relevant, overseas. See also ¶19-070 and ¶30-290.

However, a donation must not be consideration for a service or supply. See *C of IR* v *Church of Jesus Christ of Latter-Day Saints Trust Board* [2020] NZSC 102; (2020) 29 NZTC ¶24-077, where the Supreme Court dismissed the Commissioner's application for leave to appeal the Court of Appeal decision that all payments made to the Church of Jesus Christ of Latter-Day Saints Trust Board by donors were gifts for the purposes of s LD 1 of the Income Tax Act, notwithstanding that the payments made by the taxpayers to the Trust were made when a missionary connected to the taxpayers was chosen to perform the Church's services abroad.

¶30-230 Different sources of funds can have different tax treatment

In addition to obvious donations or income, a charity can receive subscriptions, grants, subsidies, bequests and the proceeds from the sale of donated goods, which are generally not liable for income tax, whether or not a charity is registered. However, other commercial receipts, such as a suspensory loan, admission fees and income from the sale of purchased goods, will generally be taxable if no exemption applies. See the Inland Revenue publication IR 255 "Charitable and donee organisations" at 35.

The correct tax treatment may not always be obvious from the name of a receipt and so care must be taken to correctly determine how to account for different receipts.

¶30-235 Charitable and donee organisations and fringe benefit tax

In 2017, following an earlier consultation, Inland Revenue released public ruling BR Pub 17/06 "Fringe benefit tax – charitable and other donee organisations and fringe benefit tax" (*Tax Information Bulletin* ¶295-104 Vol 29, No 5, June 2017).

The item replaces an earlier public ruling (BR Pub 09/03). BR Pub 09/03 will continue to apply for a further 3 years to arrangements entered into before an initial draft ruling was published on 22 November 2016.

The Explanatory Fact Sheet issued alongside PUB00229 outlines what it is about as follows:

> "Essentially, a qualifying organisation does not pay FBT on benefits provided to an employee where their employment is in an activity carried on within the organisation's benevolent, charitable, cultural, or philanthropic purposes. An example of this would be where a person is employed by an organisation to carry out the benevolent, charitable, cultural, or philanthropic purposes of the organisation (ie, the 'good works') and is provided with a car.
>
> However, a qualifying organisation may have to pay FBT on any benefits provided to an employee to the extent their employment is in a business activity carried on outside the organisation's benevolent, charitable, cultural, or philanthropic purposes. An example of this would be where an organisation runs a business unrelated to the purposes of the organisation and provides an employee in that business with a car. This is the case even if the business's profits from that unrelated business are used to fund the organisation's 'good works'.
>
> Some qualifying organisations may need to apportion fringe benefits where employees are engaged in business activities both inside and outside the organisation's benevolent, charitable, cultural, or philanthropic purposes. This is a change in the Commissioner's view."

¶30-240 Business income derived for charitable purpose is exempt income if there is no element of personal benefit

Income derived by a business carried on by a tax charity for charitable purposes is exempt from income tax if no related party can benefit from the business: s CW 42.

See *Trustees of the Auckland Medical Aid Trust* v *C of IR* (1979) 4 NZTC 61,404, *Cowey Mills & Co Ltd* v *C of IR* (1982) 5 NZTC 61,172, *C of IR* v *NTN Bearing-Saeco (New Zealand) Ltd* (1986) 8 NZTC 5,039.

If a business is not carried on in trust for charitable purposes, a subsequent disposition of income to a charity does not make it "charitable". See *MK Hunt Foundation Ltd* v *C of IR* [1961] NZLR 405.

The derivation of business income can be direct or indirect. This means that, unlike non-business income, the income can be derived by a business that is carried on for the benefit of the charitable trust, but not necessarily by the charitable trust itself.

Although an entity such as a company that carries on a business for the benefit of a tax charity is not required to register itself as a tax charity, it can do so if it complies with the requirements of registration, including having a charitable purpose. If an entity that carries on business for the benefit of a tax charity is not registered as a charitable trust, the entity will need to ensure that Inland Revenue recognises that the income has been derived for a tax charity and is tax exempt.

To attract the business income exemption, the real or fundamental purpose of the business, and any independent purpose, must be of a charitable nature. That is, regardless of what type of business, the proceeds from the business must be applied to the charity's purposes.

However, the exemption is not lost if income earned is not applied immediately for the charitable purposes, that is, the income may be held in reserve in the course of carrying on the business: *Calder Construction Co Ltd* v *C of IR* (1963) 13 ATD 214. That said, although yet to be determined definitively, there must be a point at which the income reserves are applied to the charity's purposes.

¶30-250 Business income tax exemption is lost where a person with control over the business can benefit

Unless a specific exemption applies (see ¶30-260), the business income exemption is not available if a person with some control over the business can obtain a personal benefit as a result of an association with the charity of the business, often referred to as the related party benefit.

The purpose of this control exception is to prevent situations in which a person carries on a business through the medium of a charitable trust or a company owned by a charitable trust in circumstances where it is likely that the person would have carried on that business in a personal capacity.

A person is a related party treated as having some control over the business if the person is:

- the settlor or trustee of the trust that carries on the business
- a shareholder or director of the company carrying on the business

- a settlor or trustee of a trust that is a shareholder of the company carrying on the business
- a person associated with a settlor, trustee, shareholder or director as noted above: s CW 42(5)(b).

However, simply having a person in a position of control is insufficient to lose the business exemption. To fall within the exclusion to the business income exemption, there must be a connection between the person having control and the benefit or advantage received. This connection requires that the person is able to materially influence the nature or amount of the benefit or income or the circumstances in which it is to be received by reason of the relationship to the trust or business: s CW 42(5)(a).

For the purposes of this limitation, a person is deemed to be a settlor of the trust and to gain a benefit or advantage in the carrying on of a business of the trust when that person has disposed of any asset to the trust that is used by the trust in the carrying on of that business, and when that person retains or reserves an interest in that asset or when that asset will revert to that person: s CW 42(6).

The concept of a business is given an extended meaning for the purposes of the business income exemption and includes the situation in which the trustee derives rental income from an asset that will revert back, or there is a reservation of an interest in the asset to the person who disposed of it to the trust: s CW 42(3).

In such a situation, the holding of the asset for the derivation of rental income is deemed to constitute the carrying on of a business by the trustee. In the absence of any such specific provision, it would be arguable that the mere holding of rental property does not amount to the carrying on of a business and, in this way, the control exemption could be circumvented.

The definition of "benefit or advantage" for the purposes of the business income exemption is extensive and applies, in addition to the derivation of income under ordinary concepts (s CA 1(2)), to any benefit or advantage, whether in money or money's worth. For the purposes of this exclusion, benefit or advantage includes (s CW 42(8)):

- income from business or trade
- property obtained by theft
- income from the disposal of land
- income from financial instruments
- royalties
- dividends
- income from employment
- attributed income
- benefits, pensions, compensation, and government grants
- repayment of bad debts

- attributed controlled foreign company income
- FIF income
- retaining or reserving an interest in an asset where the person has disposed of the asset to the trust or the asset will revert to them.

If a trust fails to satisfy the related party benefit test for any reason in an income year, the whole of the trust's business income for that year must be returned as trustee income: s CW 42(9). No regard is had to the quantum of the benefit, so that the exemption is lost no matter how large or small the benefit. The tax exemption is lost because a person is able to arrange a benefit or advantage through association with the charity. That is, whether the person actually receives the benefit is irrelevant – it is the possibility of a benefit that is determinative: *C of IR* v *Dick* (2001) 20 NZTC 17,396.

See also Chapter 18 – *Associated Persons*.

¶30-260 Some limited benefits are excluded from the related party benefit test

The exemption continues to be available, despite the benefit to the related party, if the benefit is:

- in the form of interest on a loan made at current commercial rates, bearing in mind the nature and term of the loan: s CW 42(8)(d)
- income from providing professional services to the charity or business, for example, legal and accounting services, when the services were given in the course of the carrying on of a professional public practice: s CW 42(7). This exclusion applies when this income is the only benefit received. Therefore, if a benefit was received or was capable of being received in some other capacity, the exemption would be lost.

¶30-270 The business income exemption does not apply to the extent that a charity has charitable purposes overseas

Business income, in terms of the exemption, is exempt only to the extent that it is derived for charitable purposes within New Zealand. However, the exemption is not lost if the charitable purposes are not limited to New Zealand. Where income is derived from a business operated for a charity with charitable purposes both in New Zealand and overseas, the income is apportioned such that the exemption is only available in respect of that part applicable to charitable purposes within New Zealand: s CW 42(4).

Example

The AIDS Trust is a registered charitable trust that operates a publishing business. The profits from the business are applied to the Trust's charitable purposes within New Zealand and overseas. For the financial year ended 31 March, the Trust had a trading profit of $5 million, of which $2 million was applied to foreign purposes.

No person with any position of control can benefit from the Trust.

Only business income applied to the Trust's charitable purposes in New Zealand will be exempt from income tax. Therefore, the trustee will be liable for tax on the $2 million of income applied for foreign purposes.

¶30-280 An exemption from income tax applies to income derived from an estate that is held for charitable purposes

Income derived by the executor or administrator from a charitable bequest is tax exempt from the date of death to the end of the income year following the year in which death occurred: s CW 43. However, other income earned by the estate will still be taxable.

After the end of the income year following the year of death, the exemption will continue to apply only if the charitable beneficiary is a tax charity.

¶30-290 Record-keeping

Charities must register with Inland Revenue regardless of whether the charity is registered with the Board.

However, a charitable trust that is exempt from all income tax is not required to file an income tax return.

Whether a tax return is required, accurate records must be kept and the trust must maintain sufficient records, in New Zealand, to enable the Commissioner to ascertain the source of donations made to the trust and the application of its funds, whether in New Zealand or overseas. On application to the Commissioner, records may be kept in a language other than English: Tax Administration Act, s 32.

The Commissioner may request that a trust provide a return of funds derived and/or received during the tax year, the return showing the source and application of those funds: Tax Administration Act, s 58. The Commissioner may also advise the Board if he/she believes funds are not being applied in accordance with the trust's charitable objects.

A charitable trust that is a member of a Māori authority may file a tax return to claim a refund of Māori authority credits attached to a distribution received from the Māori authority: Tax Administration Act, s 33(1B).

¶30-295 External reporting obligations

The Financial Reporting Act 2013 provides for the External Reporting Board (XRB) to develop an accounting framework for New Zealand. The XRB has implemented a new Accounting Standards Framework. This applies to all accounting periods commencing after 1 April 2015.

All registered charities are now required to prepare annual financial statements in accordance with accounting standards. The mandatory auditing requirements set out that Charities with annual expenditure:

- of $1 million or more must have their financial statements audited by a qualified accountant
- between $500,000 and $1 million must have their financial statements reviewed by a qualified accountant
- less than $500,000 can choose to have their financial statements reviewed or audited, or do neither.

The accounting standards framework has a tiered approach that will apply based on the charity's level of expenditure:

- Tier 1 – over $30 million (or public accountability – receives investment funds) – full standards apply
- Tier 2 – $2 million to $30 million – reduced disclosure regime
- Tier 3 – $125,000 to $2 million – simple format report with accrual accounting
- Tier 4 – operational payments under $125,000 – simple format report with only cash accounting required.

Ninety-five percent of charities in New Zealand are Tier 3 or Tier 4. Tier 3 and Tier 4 charities can choose a simple format template report or develop a tailored report. Charities can choose a higher tier – but if a charity changes a tier, the reporting standard must change by the third year.

All registered charities must also file an annual return with Charities Services together with a copy of their financial statements.

The standards that apply determine the content and form of the financial statements that a charity must file together with its annual return. These statements will be available to the public on the Charities Register website.

¶30-300 Practical matters for a trustee to consider before making a distribution to a charitable beneficiary

Before making any distribution to a charitable beneficiary, a trustee should establish whether the charity is registered on the Charities Register.

If an income distribution is to be made to a charitable beneficiary, the trustee will only have an income liability as agent for the beneficiary if the charity is not a tax charity.

If a capital distribution is to be made to a charitable beneficiary from a trust where debts owing by a trustee have been previously forgiven, care must be taken to establish whether the beneficiary is a tax charity. This is because where debts owing by a trustee have been forgiven, income can arise under the financial arrangements rules if a capital distribution is made to an unregistered charity. See ¶4-110 and Chapter 14 – *Forgiveness of Debt.*

Example

A registered charitable trust makes significant payments to various charities from its non-business income each year. Charities are discretionary beneficiaries of the trust. The payments are treated as distributions of beneficiary income by the trustee. Is the trustee liable to pay tax on income distributions to charities if the funds are not used within New Zealand?

Assuming the income from the trust is passive income, such as income derived from interest, dividends or royalties, the distribution to the charities will be non-business income and exempt from tax under s CW 41. This is because income retains its character in the hands of a beneficiary.

However, if the distribution was not exempt income, for example, if it was business income applied to purposes outside of New Zealand, the trustee would be liable for the beneficiaries' income tax liability.

¶30-310 Legislation

Charities Act 2005

5 MEANING OF CHARITABLE PURPOSE AND EFFECT OF ANCILLARY NON-CHARITABLE PURPOSE

5(1) [Inclusive definition of charitable purpose]

In this Act, unless the context otherwise requires, charitable purpose includes every charitable purpose, whether it relates to the relief of poverty, the advancement of education or religion, or any other matter beneficial to the community.

5(2) [Blood relatives and marae]

However,–

(a) the purpose of a trust, society, or institution is a charitable purpose under this Act if the purpose would satisfy the public benefit requirement apart from the fact that the beneficiaries of the trust, or the members of the society or institution, are related by blood; and

(b) a marae has a charitable purpose if the physical structure of the marae is situated on land that is a Maori reservation referred to in Te Ture Whenua Maori Act 1993 (Maori Land Act 1993) and the funds of the marae are not used for a purpose other than–

  (i) the administration and maintenance of the land and of the physical structure of the marae:

  (ii) a purpose that is a charitable purpose other than under this paragraph.

5(2A) [Promotion of amateur sport]

The promotion of amateur sport may be a charitable purpose if it is the means by which a charitable purpose referred to in subsection (1) is pursued.

5(3) [Ancillary non-charitable purpose does not prevent registration]

To avoid doubt, if the purposes of a trust, society, or an institution include a non-charitable purpose (for example, advocacy) that is merely ancillary to a charitable purpose of the trust, society, or institution, the presence of that non-charitable purpose does not prevent the trustees of the trust, the society, or the institution from qualifying for registration as a charitable entity.

5(4) [Ancillary non-charitable purpose defined]

For the purposes of subsection (3), a non-charitable purpose is ancillary to a charitable purpose of the trust, society, or institution if the non-charitable purpose is–

(a) ancillary, secondary, subordinate, or incidental to a charitable purpose of the trust, society, or institution; and

(b) not an independent purpose of the trust, society, or institution.

Goods and Services Tax Act 1985

2(1) DEFINITIONS

non-profit body means any society, association, or organisation, whether incorporated or not,–

(a) which is carried on other than for the purposes of profit or gain to any proprietor, member, or shareholder; and

(b) which is, by the terms of its constitution, rules, or other document constituting or governing the activities of that society, association, or organisation, prohibited from making any distribution whether by way of money, property, or otherwise howsoever, to any such proprietor, member, or shareholder

[...]

14 EXEMPT SUPPLIES

14(1) [Exempt Supplies]

The following supplies of goods and services shall be exempt from tax:

[...]

(b) the supply by any non-profit body of any donated goods and services:

[...]

Income Tax Act 2007

CW 41 CHARITIES: NON-BUSINESS INCOME

CW 41(1) EXEMPT INCOME

The following are exempt income:

(aa) an amount of income derived by a person who is removed from the register of charitable entities (the **register**) under the Charities Act 2005, if it is derived in the period starting with the day they are registered on the register and ending with the earlier of the following days:

(i) the day on which the person does not comply with the person's rules contained in the register:

(ii) the day of final decision:

(a) an amount of income derived by a trustee in trust for charitable purposes:

(b) an amount of income derived by a society or institution established and maintained exclusively for charitable purposes and not carried on for the private pecuniary profit of any individual.

CW 41(2) EXCLUSION: TRUSTEES, SOCIETY, OR INSTITUTION NOT REGISTERED

This section does not apply to an amount of income if, at the time that the amount of income is derived, the trustee or trustees of the trust, the society, or the institution is not, or are not, a tax charity.

CW 41(3) EXCLUSION: BUSINESS INCOME

This section does not apply to an amount of income derived from a business carried on by, or for, or for the benefit of a trust, society, or institution of a kind referred to in subsection (1).

CW 41(4) EXCLUSION: COUNCIL-CONTROLLED ORGANISATION INCOME

This section does not apply to an amount of income derived by–

(a) a council-controlled organisation, other than a council-controlled organisation operating a hospital as a charitable activity:

(b) a local authority from a council-controlled organisation, other than from a council-controlled organisation operating a hospital as a charitable activity on behalf of the local authority.

CW 41(5) DEFINITION

Tax charity means,–

(a) a trustee, a society, or an institution, registered as a charitable entity under the Charities Act 2005:

(b) a trustee, a society, or an institution (the **entity**), that–

(i) has started, before 1 July 2008, to take reasonable steps in the process of preparing an application for registering the entity as a charitable entity under the Charities Act 2005; and

(ii) intends to complete the process of preparing an application described in subparagraph (i); and

(iii) has not been notified by the Commissioner that the entity is not a tax charity:

(c) a trustee, a society, or an institution, that is or are non-resident and carrying out its or their charitable purposes outside New Zealand, and which is approved as a tax charity by the Commissioner in circumstances where registration as a charitable entity under the Charities Act 2005 is unavailable:

(d) a person who is removed from the register, in the period starting with the day they are registered on the register and ending with the earlier of the following days:

(i) the day on which the person does not comply with the person's rules contained in the register:

(ii) the day of final decision.

CW 42 CHARITIES: BUSINESS INCOME

CW 42(1) EXEMPT INCOME

Income derived directly or indirectly from a business carried on by, or for, or for the benefit of a trust, society, or institution of a kind referred to in section CW 41(1) is exempt income if–

(aa) the entity carrying on the business is, at the time that the income is derived, registered as a charitable entity under the Charities Act 2005; and

(a) the trust, society, or institution carries out its charitable purposes in New Zealand; and

(b) the trustee or trustees of the trust, the society, or the institution is or are, at the time that the income is derived, a tax charity; and

(c) no person with some control over the business is able to direct or divert an amount derived from the business to the benefit or advantage of,–

(i) if subparagraph (ii) does not apply, a person other than the trust, society, or institution except for a purpose of the trust, society, or institution:

(ii) if a trust, society, or institution (the **operating entity**) is carrying on the business for or for the benefit of another trust, society, or institution (the **controlling entity**), a person other than the operating entity or the controlling entity except for a purpose of the operating entity or the controlling entity.

Subsections (3) to (8) expand on this subsection.

CW 42(2) EXCLUSION

This section does not apply to an amount of income derived by–

(a) a council-controlled organisation, other than a council-controlled organisation operating a hospital as a charitable activity:

(b) a local authority from a council-controlled organisation, other than from a council-controlled organisation operating a hospital as a charitable activity on behalf of the local authority.

CW 42(3) CARRYING ON A BUSINESS: TRUSTEE

For the purposes of subsection (1), a trustee is treated as carrying on a business if–

(a) the trustee derives rents, fines, premiums, or other revenues from an asset of the trust; and

(b) the asset was disposed of to the trust by a person of a kind described in subsection (5)(b); and

(c) either–

 (i) the person retains or reserves an interest in the asset; or

 (ii) the asset will revert to the person.

CW 42(4) CHARITABLE PURPOSES IN NEW ZEALAND AND OVERSEAS

For the purposes of subsection (1)(a), if the charitable purposes of the trust, society, or institution are not limited to New Zealand, income derived from the business in a tax year is apportioned reasonably between those purposes in New Zealand and those outside New Zealand. Only the part apportioned to the New Zealand purposes is exempt income.

CW 42(5) CONTROL OVER BUSINESS

For the purposes of subsection (1)(c) and section CW 42B(2)(c) and (4) for an income year, a person is treated as having some control over the business, and as being able to direct or divert amounts from the business if, in the tax year,–

(a) they are, in any way, whether directly or indirectly, able to determine, or materially influence the determination of,–

 (i) the nature or extent of a relevant benefit or advantage; or

 (ii) the circumstances in which a relevant benefit or advantage is, or is to be, given or received; and

(b) their ability to determine or influence the benefit or advantage arises because they are–

 (i) a settlor or trustee of the trust by which the business is carried on; or

(ii) a shareholder or director of the company by which the business is carried on; or

(iii) a settlor or trustee of a trust that is a shareholder of the company by which the business is carried on; or

(iv) a person associated with a settlor, trustee, shareholder, or director referred to in any of subparagraphs (i) to (iii).

CW 42(6) CONTROL: SETTLOR ASSET DISPOSED OF TO TRUST

For the purposes of subsection (5) and section CW 42B(2)(c) and (4), a person is treated as a settlor of a trust, and as gaining a benefit or advantage in the carrying on of a business of the trust, if–

(a) they have disposed of an asset to the trust, and the asset is used by the trust in the carrying on of the business; and

(b) they retain or reserve an interest in the asset, or the asset will revert to them.

CW 42(7) NO CONTROL

For the purposes of subsection (1)(c) and section CW 42B(2)(c) and (5), a person is not treated as having some control over the business merely because–

(a) they provide professional services to the trust or company by which the business is carried on; and

(b) their ability to determine, or materially influence the determination of, the nature or extent of a relevent benefit or advantage arises because they–

(i) provide the services in the course of and as part of carrying on, as a business, a professional public practice; or

(ii) are a statutory trustee company; or

(iii) are Public Trust; or

(iv) are the Maori Trustee.

CW 42(8) BENEFIT OR ADVANTAGE

For the purposes of subsection (1)(c) and section CW 42B(2)(c) and (6), a benefit or advantage to a person–

(a) may or may not be something that is convertible into money:

(b) unless excluded under paragraph (d), includes deriving an amount that would be income of the person under 1 or more of the following provisions:

(i) section CA 1(2) (Amounts that are income):

(ii) sections CB 1 to CB 23 (which relate to income from business or trade-like activities):

(iii) section CB 32 (Property obtained by theft):

(iv) sections CC 1 (Land), CC 3 to CC 8 (which relate to income from financial instruments), and CC 9 (Royalties):

(v) section CD 1 (Dividend):

(vi) sections CE 1 (Amounts derived in connection with employment) and CE 8 (Attributed income from personal services):

(vii) section CF 1 (Benefits, pensions, compensation, and government grants):

(viii) section CG 3 (Bad debt repayment):

(ix) sections CQ 1 (Attributed controlled foreign company income) and CQ 4 (Foreign investment fund income):

(c) includes retaining or reserving an interest in an asset in the case described in subsection (3), if the person has disposed of the asset to the trust or the asset will revert to them:

(d) does not include earning interest on money lent, if the interest is payable at no more than the current commercial rate, given the nature and term of the loan.

CW 42(9) NON-EXEMPT BUSINESS INCOME

If an amount derived from the carrying on of a business by or for a trust is not exempt income because of a failure to comply with subsection (1)(c), the amount is trustee income.

[...]

CW 43 CHARITABLE BEQUESTS

CW 43(1) EXEMPT INCOME

An amount of income derived by a deceased's executor or administrator is exempt income to the extent to which the requirements of subsections (2) and (3) are met, having regard to all relevant matters including–

(a) the terms of the deceased's will, including the rights of annuitants, legatees, and other beneficiaries; and

(b) the nature and extent of the debts and liabilities of, and other charges against, the estate and their likely effect on the income and assets available for distribution to the beneficiaries; and

(c) the shares and prospective shares of the beneficiaries in the income and assets of the estate.

CW 43(2) GIFT TO CHARITY

The first requirement is that the amount arises from or is attributable to assets of the estate that have been left to a trust, society, or institution of a kind referred to in section CW 41(1).

CW 43(3) EXEMPT IN HANDS OF CHARITY

The second requirement is that the amount, if derived by the trust, society, or institution or by a business carried on by, or for, or for the benefit of it, would be exempt income under section CW 41 or CW 42.

CW 43(4) TIMING OF REGISTRATION AS CHARITABLE ENTITY

An amount of income derived by a deceased's executor or administrator that is derived during the period beginning on the deceased's date of death and ending at the end of the income year that follows the income year in which the deceased died is not prevented from being exempt income under this section merely because the trustee or trustees of the trust, the society, or the institution is not, or are not, a tax charity.

CW 43(5) REQUIREMENTS OF SECTIONS CW 41 AND CW 42 DISREGARDED

For the purposes of subsection (4), until the end of the income year that follows the income year in which the deceased died, the requirements of sections CW 41 and CW 42 for the trustee or trustees of the trust, the society, or the institution to be a tax charity must be disregarded when applying those sections for the purposes of this section.

CW 43(6) AMOUNTS DERIVED AFTER END OF CERTAIN PERIOD

This section does not apply to an amount of income derived after the end of the income year that follows the income year in which the deceased died if, at the time that the amount of income is derived, the trustee or trustees of the trust, the society, or the institution is not, or are not, a tax charity.

[...]

CX 25 BENEFITS PROVIDED BY CHARITABLE ORGANISATIONS

CX 25(1) WHEN NOT FRINGE BENEFIT

A charitable organisation that provides a benefit to an employee does not provide a fringe benefit except to the extent to which–

(a) the employee receives the benefit mainly in connection with their employment; and

(b) the employment consists of the carrying on by the organisation of a business whose activity is outside its benevolent, charitable, cultural, or philanthropic purposes.

CX 25(2) WHEN EMPLOYER PROVIDES CHARGE FACILITIES

Subsection (1) does not apply, and the benefit provided is a fringe benefit, if a charitable organisation provides a benefit to an employee by way of short-term charge facilities and the value of the benefit from the short-term charge facilities for the employee in a tax year is more than the lesser for the tax year of–

(a) 5% of the employee's salary or wages:

(b) $1,200.

CX 25(3) MEANING OF SHORT-TERM CHARGE FACILITIES

For the purposes of the FBT rules, a **short-term charge facility** means an arrangement that–

(a) enables an employee to obtain goods or services that have no connection with the employer or its operations by–

(i) buying or hiring the goods or services:

(ii) charging the cost of the goods or services to an account:

(iii) providing consideration other than money for the goods or services; and

(b) requires the employer to provide some or all of the payment or other consideration for the goods or services; and

(c) is not a fringe benefit under section CX 10.

[...]

HC 13 CHARITABLE TRUSTS

In the trust rules, a trust is a **charitable trust** in an income year if–

(a) all income derived or accumulated by the trustee in that or in any earlier income year is held for charitable purposes; and

(b) any income derived by the trustee in the income year is exempt income under either section CW 41(1) (Charities: non-business income) or CW 42(1) (Charities: business income).

[...]

LD 3 MEANING OF CHARITABLE OR OTHER PUBLIC BENEFIT GIFT

LD 3(1) MEANING

For the purposes of sections DB 41 and DV 12 (which relate to deductions for gifts of money), and this subpart, a charitable or other public benefit gift–

(a) means a gift of money of $5 or more that is paid to a society, institution, association, organisation, trust, or fund (the entity), if–

(i) the entity is described in subsection (2)(a), (ab), (b), (c), or (d), and the name of the entity is on the list published by the Commissioner under section 41A(14) to (16) of the Tax Administration Act 1994:

(ii) the entity is described in subsection (2)(ac), (bb), or (bc):

(iii) the name of the entity is listed in schedule 32 (Recipients of charitable or other public benefit gifts):

(b) includes a subscription of $5 or more paid to an entity only if the subscription does not confer any rights arising from membership in that entity or any other society, institution, association, organisation, trust, or fund:

(c) does not include–

(i) a testamentary gift:

(ii) a gift made by forgiving some or all of a debt.

LD 3(2) DESCRIPTION OF ORGANISATIONS

The following are the entities referred to in subsection (1)(a) and (b):

(a) a society, institution, association, organisation, or trust that is not carried on for the private pecuniary profit of an individual, and whose funds are applied wholly or mainly to charitable, benevolent, philanthropic, or cultural purposes within New Zealand:

(ab) an entity that, but for this paragraph, no longer meets the requirements of this subsection, but only for the period starting on the day it fails to meet those requirements and ending on the later of–

(i) the day the entity is removed from the register of charitable entities under the Charities Act 2005:

(ii) the day on which all reasonably contemplated administrative appeals and Court proceedings, including appeal righ^ts, are finalised or exhausted in relation to the person's charitable status.

(ac) a community housing entity, if the gift is made at a time the entity is eligible to derive exempt income under section CW 42B (Community housing trusts and companies):

(a) a public institution maintained exclusively for any 1 or more of the purposes within New Zealand set out in paragraph (a):

(bb) a board that is constituted under subpart 5 of Part 3 of the Education and Training Act 2020 and is not carried on for the private pecuniary profit of any individual:

(bc) a tertiary education institution:

(c) a fund established and maintained exclusively for the purpose of providing money for any 1 or more of the purposes within New Zealand set out in paragraph (a), by a society, institution, association, organisation, or trust that is not carried on for the private pecuniary profit of an individual:

(d) a public fund established and maintained exclusively for the purpose of providing money for any 1 or more of the purposes within New Zealand set out in paragraph (a).

[...]

YA 1 DEFINITIONS

[...]

charitable organisation–

(a) means, for a quarter or an income year, an association, fund, institution, organisation, society, or trust to which section LD 3(2) (Meaning of charitable or other public benefit gift) or schedule 32 (Recipients of charitable or other public benefit gifts) applies–

(i) in the quarter; or

(ii) in the income year, if fringe benefit tax is payable on an income year basis under section RD 60 (Close company option); and

[...]

(b) does not include a local authority, a public authority, or a university

[...]

charitable purpose includes every charitable purpose, whether it relates to the relief of poverty, the advancement of education or religion, or any other matter beneficial to the community, and–

(a) the purpose of a trust, society, or institution is charitable under this Act if the purpose would meet the public benefit requirement apart from the fact that the beneficiaries of the trust, or the members of the society or institution, are related by blood:

(b) a marae has a charitable purpose if–

(i) the physical structure of the marae is situated on land that is a Maori reservation referred to in Te Ture Whenua Maori Act 1993 (the Maori Land Act 1993); and

(ii) the funds of the marae are not used for a purpose other than the administration and maintenance of the land and of the physical structure of the marae, or are used for a purpose that is a charitable purpose

charitable trust is defined in section HC 13 (Charitable trusts) for the purposes of the trust rules

tax charity is defined in section CW 41(5)

Maori Trust Boards Act 1955

24B TRUSTS FOR CHARITABLE PURPOSES

(1) Any Board may from time to time, in its discretion, execute under its seal a declaration of trust declaring that it shall stand possessed of any of its property, whether real or personal, upon trust for charitable purposes.

(2) Any income derived by the Board from any property to which the declaration relates shall be applied for such purposes referred to in section 24 or section 24A as may be specified in the declaration of trust; and, for the purposes of the Income Tax Act 2007, any such income shall be deemed to be income derived by trustees in trust for charitable purposes.

(3) No declaration of trust under this section shall have any force or effect unless it has been approved by the Commissioner of Inland Revenue.

CHAPTER 31

Community Housing Trusts

¶31-010 Operating principle

Income derived by the trustee of a community housing trust is exempt income.

¶31-020 Community housing trusts

The Income Tax Act 2007 was amended in 2014 to provide that income derived by community housing entities, including trusts and companies, is exempt income. The purpose of this exemption is to encourage increased investment in housing on a non-profit basis to provide accommodation for low income earners. Accordingly, the Act provides limits for the number of beneficiaries or clients, applying on a means tested basis, who exceed prescribed levels of income or assets.

A further amendment in 2016 (which applied retrospectively from 30 June 2014) clarified that, for it to qualify, an entity must be a registered community housing provider under the Public and Community Housing Management Act 1992, so that if an entity meets the definition, it need not be registered as a charity (s CW 42B(2)(aa)). This overcame the uncertainty regarding the position of many community housing trusts following the de-registration of the Queenstown Lakes Community Housing Trust (see *Re Queenstown Lakes Community Housing Trust* [2011] NZHC 617; (2011) 25 NZTC ¶20-059).

¶31-030 Income derived by the trustee of a community housing trust is exempt income

Income derived by the trustee of a community housing trust may be exempt income. In order to qualify (s CW 42B):

- the entity must be a registered community housing provider
- it must not carry on activities for the private pecuniary profit of any individual
- all profits of the trust must be applied to either:
    - community housing entities that qualify under s CW 42B
    - beneficiaries or clients of the trust

- tax charities, or
- any other persons for whom distributions would be deemed charitable purposes

- no individual exercising a degree of control over the trust's activities may divert funds derived from the activities to the benefit of:
  - a person other than the trust itself unless for a purpose of the trust or a charitable purpose; or
  - if the trust is carrying on activities for a community housing entity, a person who is not acting for the operating or controlling entity or, otherwise, for a charitable purpose
- the definition of control is the same as that applying to other charities under s CW 42 of the Income Tax Act and likewise the factors that would indicate a person should not be treated as exerting control; and
- similarly, the nature of a benefit or advantage for the purpose of the section is that applying to other charities under s CW 42(8).

Community housing entity, as defined, does not include a trustee or company if more than 15% of the beneficiaries exceed the relevant means tested entry threshold, which threshold is set out in sch 34 of the Income Tax Act (and which may be periodically adjusted), or if the nature of the assistance provided to beneficiaries with income or assets below the threshold is substantially different from that provided to beneficiaries whose assets or income exceed the threshold.

See further *Tax Information Bulletin* ¶267-113 Vol 26, No 7, August 2014.

¶31-040 Legislation

Income Tax Act 2007

CW 42B COMMUNITY HOUSING TRUSTS AND COMPANIES

CW 42B(1) EXEMPT INCOME

An amount of income derived by a community housing entity is exempt income.

CW 42B(2) DEFINITION

In this section and section LD 3 (Meaning of charitable or other public benefit gift), **community housing entity** means a trustee or company (the **entity**) whose activities involve the provision of housing or housing assistance (the **activities**), and–

(aa) the entity is a registered community housing provider under the Public and Community Housing Management Act 1992; and

(a) the activities are not carried on for the private pecuniary profit of any individual; and

(b) all profit is retained by the entity, or distributed or applied to–

(i) community housing entities that meet the requirements to derive exempt income under this section:

(ii) beneficiaries or clients of the entity:

(iii) tax charities:

(iv) persons to whom distributions would be in accordance with charitable purposes; and

(c) no person with some control over the activities is able to direct or divert an amount derived from the activities to the benefit or advantage of,–

(i) if subparagraph (ii) does not apply, a person other than the entity except for a purpose of the entity or a charitable purpose:

(ii) if the entity (the **operating entity**) is carrying on the activities for or for the benefit of a community housing entity or charity (the **controlling entity**), a person other than the operating entity or the controlling entity except for a purpose of the operating entity or the controlling entity or for a charitable purpose.

CW 42B(3) DEFINITION: EXCEPTION

Despite subsection (2), **community housing entity** does not include a trustee or company (the entity) if–

(a) more than 15% of the people who become beneficiaries or clients of the entity on a date that is or is after 14 April 2014 have, on that date, income or assets exceeding a value (the **entry threshold**) set out in schedule 34 (Community housing trusts and companies: income and assets of beneficiaries and clients) that is relevant to the beneficiary or client:

(b) the provision of housing or housing assistance to a beneficiary or client who has income and assets not exceeding the entry thresholds is substantially different from the provision of housing or housing assistance to a beneficiary or client who has income or assets exceeding an entry threshold.

CW 42B(4) CONTROL OVER ACTIVITIES

For the purposes of subsection (2)(c), for an income year, a person is treated as having some control over the activities, and as being able to direct or divert amounts from the activities if, in the tax year, they are described in section CW 42(5)(a) and (b) and (6) (Charities: business income).

CW 42B(5) NO CONTROL

For the purposes of subsection (2)(c), a person described in section CW 42(7)(a) and (b) is not treated as having some control merely because of the factors in section CW 42(7)(a) and (b).

CW 42B(6) BENEFIT OR ADVANTAGE

For the purposes of subsection (2)(c), a benefit or advantage to a person includes a benefit or advantage included under section CW 42(8).

Part X

VARIATION, RESETTLEMENT AND WINDING UP

CHAPTER 32

Variation

¶32-010 Operating principle

A trust can be varied without tax consequences. However, there may be tax consequences where the extent of variation is so significant that a new trust results.

¶32-020 Variation is not a defined term

> "While the general rule is that trusts, once established, cannot be varied, changes in law, taxation rules and family circumstances can mean that trust deeds need to be modified to enable the trust property to be dealt with or the trust administered in a different way. The law has long recognised that there are circumstances where trusts should be able to be varied, brought to an end (revoked) or resettled onto new trusts."

Law Commission *Review of the Law of Trusts – A Trusts Act for New Zealand* (NZLC R130, 2013) at Chapter 10 – *Revocation and Variation.*

Where variation is required, a trust may be varied by the trustees if the deed of trust contains a power of variation; or, in the absence of an express power, if all the beneficiaries are of age and consent to the variation: generally referred to as the rule in *Saunders* v *Vautier* (1841) Cr & Ph 240; 41 ER 482 (now codified in the Trusts Act 2019: s 122). See also *Philips New Zealand Ltd* v *Philips New Zealand Ltd* (1996) 1 NZSC 40,368 and *Gough* v *Strahl* [2013] NZHC 3184.

The extent of any power of variation depends on the terms of the deed that contains the power: *Kearns* v *Hill* (1990) 21 NSWLR 107 (CA), *Chief Commissioner of Stamp Duties* v *Buckle* (1998) 151 ALR 1 (HCA).

A trust can also be varied under a statutory power of variation (Trusts Act 2019, s 124) or the court's inherent jurisdiction: *Chapman* v *Chapman* [1954] 1 All ER 798 (HL).

See *Clarkson* v *Brady* [2013] NZHC 437, where applications were brought under s 64A of the Trustee Act (since repealed by the Trusts Act) to vary trusts that were "near mirror in nature" for reasons that included expansion of the classes of beneficiaries; ability to assist a family trust experiencing financial difficulties; and tax benefits.

The judgment in *Clarkson* v *Brady* (supra) provides a useful guide to the matters taken into consideration in a case that is described as "rather more sophisticated" than earlier mirror trust decisions. As with *Tatham* v *Tatham* [2010] NZHC 2315; (2010) 3 NZTR ¶20-043 (discussed at ¶32-030), the prospect of a tax benefit was not a negativing factor from the court's perspective.

In *Argus* v *Barber* [2013] NZHC 3010, the Court approved variations under s 64A of the Trustee Act (since repealed by the Trusts Act), including a variation to the distribution date that was sought due to concerns that the trust no longer met the definition of a "complying trust" due to minor changes in the definition of complying trusts introduced when the term "qualifying trusts" was replaced with "complying trusts". The variation did not address the definitional issue (this is being addressed separately and the trust's accountant advised that a legislative change might be required to resolve the matter), but it did give the trustees time so that the matter might be resolved.

When considering whether to approve a variation, the Court's standpoint was whether the variation is in the interests of the beneficiaries who cannot by reason of age, infirmity or contingency, provide their own consent. The Court did not consider external factors, such as whether the variation might not be in the best interests of, say, Inland Revenue.

The court did not have a power to approve a variation of trust under s 64A of the Trustee Act if the variation might be detrimental to the beneficiary on whose behalf the approval was sought. Section 124 of the Trusts Act is not so circumscribed and provides the court with a greater discretion. The principles that now apply, as modified by s 124 of the Trusts Act, are set out in *Gavin* v *Gavin* [2021] NZHC 550 at [15] as follows:

(a) The power to approve a variation is discretionary.

(b) The court may, on behalf of any beneficiary described in s 124(2) who has an interest in the property of a trust, consider any proposal to terminate, vary or resettle a trust.

(c) The court's discretion is to be exercised with reference to the factors identified in s 124(4), including the intentions of the settlor, to the extent these can be ascertained.

(d) The court can approve a scheme which conflicts with the intentions of the settlor but should not do so lightly.

(e) The court considers the trust provisions afresh if circumstances have arisen which were not foreseen or may not have been foreseeable at the time the trust was established.

(f) The court is able to approve an arrangement to the detriment of any person on whose behalf the court is giving consent, provided the effect of the orders would not reduce or remove a vested interest in the trust property.

(g) The court is to take a wide approach to benefits and detriment and arrangements and must consider the arrangements as a whole in a practical and business-like way. Indirect and intangible benefits and detriments are relevant, including the welfare and honour of the family.

(h) Difficulties may be met by amendments to the proposal or covenants by persons benefitting to make good losses to the disadvantage of other beneficiaries.

(i) An order approving a proposed variation may be conditional.

Although variations are common in practice, the taxation consequences, which are not addressed in the Trusts Act, can be unclear and accordingly a considered approach is necessary.

¶32-030 Tax consequences of variation

Variations run from changes to deeds of trust for administrative reasons or to reflect legislative amendment, to changes that affect beneficial interests.

The consequences of a variation depend on the extent of variation. A variation of a minor nature, such as a change of the trust's name, will not have tax consequences because there is no alteration to the rights or obligations under the trust.

However, where a fundamental variation of trust occurs, such that there is in fact a new trust or trusts, it is necessary to consider the tax consequences of the variation. In this regard, a distinction can be made between a variation of dispositive powers and a variation of administrative powers in a trust. Variations to dispositive powers will include, for example, changes to beneficial interests, or the manner in which a beneficiary might benefit. Such variations may cause a change in taxation. An administrative change will usually relate to the administration of a trust and such variations will likely be neutral – unless, for example, the residence of the trustee changes as a result.

A general power to vary trust powers usually only includes variation of administrative powers. However, a power to resettle will involve dispositive powers.

Regardless of these general guidelines, difficulty lies in determining the nature of a variation at trust law so that any tax law consequences can be correctly identified. These tax consequences arise, not from the fact of the variation, but owing to the disposition of property in the tax base.

Generally, these are the consequences that arise from a loss of continuity of a trust or from any disposition of property onto new trustees as is the case in a resettlement. See Chapter 33 – *Resettlement.*

Other variations may have no effect on the trust structure but can have a tax effect because of a resultant impact on tax revenue following the variation. Where this is the case, although a court will not decline to approve a variation because of a loss of revenue to Inland Revenue (see *Dalziell* v *Dalziell* (2008) 27 FRNZ 276, where a variation to the trust period prevented the realisation of a tax liability before the trust would have the ability to meet the tax impost), the trustee would be wise to assess any avoidance risk. See Chapter 22 – *Avoidance.*

In the case of *Tatham* v *Tatham* (supra), which followed *Dalziell* v *Dalziell*, it was noted that although no issue was taken as to the possibility that the circumstances might fall within the ambit of a "tax avoidance arrangement", the Court was of the view that it was appropriate to specifically consider that possibility, McKenzie J stating:

> [14] I consider that the fact that the proposed variation might be part of an arrangement which falls within the scope of the definition of the term "tax avoidance arrangement" does not affect the propriety of the exercise by the Court of its power of approval. The law is clear that the Court is concerned with the interests of the beneficiaries or other persons

> on whose behalf the Court's approval is sought. It is not concerned with the consequences to the revenue. That general principle is not, in my view, affected by the existence of the anti avoidance provisions in the Income Tax Act. I do not consider that the Court is required to embark on the difficult exercise of considering whether the granting of approval might engage those provisions.
>
> [15] It is however desirable to state that the approval of the Court to a variation of Trust will not alter the nature of the arrangement. If the overall circumstances in which the variation of Trust is effected are such that the arrangement falls within the spirit, as well as the letter, of the term "tax avoidance arrangement", then that consequence will not be avoided simply because, in implementing that arrangement, the approval of the Court has been necessary. The approval of the Court will not give the arrangement an *imprimatur* so far as possible tax avoidance is concerned.
>
> [16] In one respect however, I consider that the possibility that the variation might involve a tax avoidance arrangement is a relevant consideration for the Court. The Court must consider whether the variation is in the interests of those persons on whose behalf the sanction of the Court is necessary. In this case, the lessening of the tax liability is relied upon as a benefit to the persons with whose interests the Court is concerned. If there were a significant risk that the benefit might not be achieved, that is clearly a material consideration for the Court, when considering their interests.

In assessing that risk, the Court found that the appropriate way to look at the question was as it was put by Danckwerts J in *Re Cohen's Will Trusts* [1959] 3 All ER 523 at 524:

> ... if it is a risk that an adult would be prepared to take, the court is prepared to take it on behalf of an infant.

The Court then went on in *Tatham* to find that as the trustees had sought their own advice that the arrangement was not tax avoidance for the purposes of the Income Tax Act, that was sufficient for the Court to be satisfied that the variation sought should be allowed. That said, this approach does not advance any assistance regarding when a variation will amount to a resettlement.

The following statement from the report of the Australian Review of Business Taxation: A Tax System Redesigned: More Certainty, Equitable and Durable, July 1999, at 479 usefully summarises the uncertainty that prevails regarding the consequences of variation:

> An existing trust may cease and a new trust may be created as the result of changes to a trust deed, changes to the substance or nature of a beneficiary's interest in the trust or changes to the operation of a trust. Such changes can give rise to the resettlement of a trust for some legal purposes. However, neither trust law nor taxation law is clear about exactly what changes to a trust deed constitute the creation of a new trust.

¶32-040 Whether a variation effects a new trust is a matter of scale and degree

In the absence of any formal guidelines, it is often unclear whether a variation has merely altered the terms of the trust without tax consequence, or whether a fundamental change has resulted such that the variation has effected a termination of the trust and a settlement or resettlement onto new terms.

The difficulty in matters of variation is to identify the point where changes are such that a new trust estate comes into existence as a consequence of a loss of continuity of the beneficial interests in the former trust.

Although it is accepted that a fundamental variation can result in a new trust, as each case will turn on its own facts, the exact nature of change that may cause a new trust to come into existence is not always clear.

The uncertainty surrounding variation has troubled trustees for many years. Although the question has been before various courts, the jurisprudence on the subject does not provide clear guidelines. For example, in *Re Ball's Settlement Trusts* [1968] 1 WLR 899 Megarry VC states that:

> If an arrangement changes the whole substratum of the trust, then it may well be that it cannot be regarded as varying the trust.

That said, what comprises the substratum has not been the subject of a definitive definition. In *Lock* v *Westpac Banking Corp* (1991) 25 NSWLR 593, a case concerning the variation of a superannuation trust deed, Waddell CJ said at 606–607:

> The substratum is to be determined as a matter of construction of the deed and having regard to the circumstances. If the amendment is a matter of construction within the power, it cannot be an infringement of the substratum.

See also Law Commission *Perpetuities and The Revocation and Variation of Trusts: Review of the Law of Trusts: Third Issues Paper* (NZLC, IP22, April 2011) at [5.14] where the Law Commission states that in its view:

> Using the elusive concept of the "substratum" of a trust to distinguish between resettlements and variations, as Megarry J did in *Re Ball*, is problematic.... the only justification for attributing weight to such a concept would be to ensure that there remained some adherence to the settlor's original purpose in determining the terms of the trust.

The validity of any doctrine of substratum is comprehensively considered in the Court of Appeal for Bermuda Civil Appeal in *Grand View Private Trust Company Ltd* v *Wong* Civil Appeal 5A of 2019. This decision highlights the conflation of powers and the purposes of a trust.

A more relevant exploration to determine whether a new trust will arise is to consider the changes that the variation will bring about. In *FCT* v *Clark* [2011] FCAFC 5; 2011 ATC ¶20-236, the Full Federal Court takes a somewhat concessional approach as to what will constitute a loss of continuity. The reasoning in *Clark* and other contemporary decisions, such as *FC of T* v *Commercial Nominees of Australia Ltd* [2001] HCA 33; 2001 ATC 4336, *Commissioner of State Revenue (Vic)* v *Lam & Kym Pty Ltd* [2004] VSCA 204; 2004 ATC 5058, *Chief Commissioner of Stamp Duties (NSW)* v *Buckle* [1998] HCA 4; 98 ATC 4097, *Commissioner of State Revenue (WA)* v *Serana Pty Ltd* [2008] WASCA 82; 2008 ATC ¶20-017, have been heard in the context of matters arising from specific transactions. The prevailing theme is the importance of being able to identify a continuum of property and membership. As noted at [88] in *Clark*:

> "Such an approach [the continuum of property and membership] is consistent with the position at general law in relation to the four essential indicia of the existence of a trust: the trustee, trust property, the beneficiary and an equitable obligation

annexed to the trust property: JD Heydon & MJ Leeming: Jacobs' Law of Trusts in Australia (2006) 7th ed, at [104]–[110]. In *Commercial Nominees* both the Full Court, at [49] of its reasons, and the High Court, at [35] of its reasons, pointed out that there was nothing in Pt IX, nor in the 1936 Act generally, which imposed some statutory requirement of continuity for determining when there is a sufficient identity of the trusts involved ...".

However, as the matter is often disregarded, even when the court is approving a variation, care is required to make appropriate enquiries on a case-by-case basis. See, for example, *McKnight* v *Craig* [2010] NZHC 1086; (2010) 3 NZTR ¶20-019, where the Court approved a substantial variation of 2 mirror trusts resulting in a single new trust where no consideration was given as to whether the variation was in fact a resettlement and, if so, the nature of the tax consequences (if any). Also see *Shanks* v *Shanks* (2010) 3 NZTR ¶20-021, and *De Bernardo* v *De Bernardo* (2010) 3 NZTR ¶20-011 – the subject of a similar application involving a trust valued at $17 million where again no consideration was given as to whether the variation was in fact a resettlement.

¶32-050 A variation in the class of beneficiaries may result in a new trust

Identifiable beneficiaries are a pre-requisite of a valid trust (see ¶1-080). Although it is common for the beneficiaries of any trust to change over time, a variation of trust that results in a change of beneficial owner can represent the termination of a trust and the establishment of a new trust for different objects.

The extent of variation of a beneficial interest required to effect a new trust is unclear. Although some decisions suggest that there can be no resettlement without a change of beneficial interest (*Wedge* v *Acting Comptroller of Stamps (Vic)* (1941) 64 CLR 75) what is less clear is the corollary position of how much the class of beneficiaries can change before a fundamental variation is effected.

Some guidance is provided by *FC of T* v *Commercial Nominees of Australia Ltd* [2001] HCA 33; 2001 ATC 4336 (see ¶17-080) where the High Court of Australia considered whether changes to a trust, including the introduction of a new class of beneficiaries, resulted in the creation of a new trust in the context of continuity of a superannuation fund. In that case, the addition of a new class of beneficiaries did not terminate the original trust, as it was accepted that the identity of the persons entitled to benefit under the trust would be likely to change over time, as new members came into the scheme and others left.

Although the case could be considered limited authority other than in respect of superannuation funds, it is useful in that it highlights the importance of context. Accordingly, *Commercial Nominees* could be used to support the proposition that for a variation to amount to a fundamental change, the variation must effect a change not contemplated by the original deed of trust; or be so significant that there is no relationship between the original class of beneficiaries and the amended class of beneficiaries. Arguably, it might be said that in the case of a fully discretionary trust where any beneficiary has no more than an expectancy, the only change to the class of beneficiary that would effect a termination of the trust would be a change to the final beneficiary in whom the residue of the trust property will eventually vest. This aligns with the definition of an express trust in the Trusts Act and the requirement for certainty as to the beneficiaries or the class of beneficiaries. See the Trusts Act 2019, s 15. In *Grand View Private Trust*, the Court of Appeal of Bermuda rejected the arguments put forward that if a power of removal and appointment was used in a manner that was destructive of the substratum (whatever precisely that means) this was fundamentally inconsistent with the purpose of the trust.

Further at [185] in *Grand View Private Trust*, the Court of Appeal of Bermuda specifically rejected "the proposition that there is some absolute rule which, whatever the terms of the power or the circumstances of the trust, [that] prohibits the exercise of specific powers of addition and exclusion of beneficiaries from altering the substratum of the trust – a metaphorical term the characteristics of which it may be difficult to define, and which may not necessarily exist".

¶32-060 Altering the vesting date will not generally result in a new trust

It is common for a trustee to have a power to vary the trust period.

Unless the term of a trust is an essential feature of the trust, a variation to trust that either brings forward or extends the term of the trust will not of itself generally result in a new trust: *IR Commrs* v *Holmden* [1968] AC 685; [1968] 1 All ER 148.

When extending the maximum duration of a trust, even in situations when no new trust estate arises, it will be essential to consider the tax consequences for the parties whose interests would have vested in possession on the now varied termination date. The extension of the term could amount to a disposal of these reversionary interests.

In *Dalziell* v *Dalziell* (2008) 27 FRNZ 276, although not specifically addressed, it is clear from the orders made and the context of the matter that there was no question of whether the variation to extend the vesting date had the effect of terminating the trust. Also see *Dalziell* v *Dalziell (supra)*, *Argus* v *Barber* (supra), *Hensman* [2015] NZHC 1004.

¶32-070 Changes in trust property are not generally a variation of trust

The creation of a trust through a nominal settlement and the later addition of further property is a long-standing accepted practice: *Truesdale* v *FC of T* 70 ATC 4056.

For tax purposes, trustees may treat subsequent settlement on the same terms as a single settlement: s HC 3.

Therefore, unless a trust was established for the express purpose of holding a particular asset, it is unlikely that a change of trust property would effect a fundamental variation of trust.

¶32-080 Variations of an administrative nature will not generally give rise to a new trust

It is common practice for the terms of a trust to be varied in accordance with a power of variation. Although there is no clear legal principle that can be applied, as a general proposition, where a variation relates only to matters of administration and there is no alteration to the beneficiaries' rights or the terms on which the trust property is held, the resulting variation will not give rise to a new trust.

An example of a change of an administrative nature would be a variation whereby the minimum number of trustees was increased or decreased. A variation of a defined term that does not alter beneficial rights is another example of a variation of an administrative nature.

See further D Barnett, *Resettlement: finding the new charter of rights* (2006) 80 ALJ 254, 263.

¶32-090 A settlement onto a trust on new terms can bring about a new trust

Where a new settlement onto a trust requires that the terms of the trust are altered in respect of that settlement, the settlement may in fact represent a new trust. However, as the existing trust terms are not necessarily varied, the existing trust may not come to an end, as is the case where there is a fundamental variation. In such cases, determining whether a new trust results will require consideration in the context of the particular circumstances: *Hart (Inspector of Taxes)* v *Briscoe* [1978] STC 89.

¶32-100 A change of trustee is not a variation of trust

Although a change of legal ownership of trust property results, the retirement or appointment of a trustee is not of itself a variation of trust: *Massereene & Ferrard* v *IR Commr* [1900] 2 IR (Irish) 138, 147. In the normal course of events following the retirement and appointment of a trustee, the trust property vests in the new trustee who assumes the rights and obligations of the retiring trustee and the trust continues.

However, if the change of trustee is part of an arrangement where the trust property is to be held by a new trustee on new terms, the trustee should assess the effect of that variation on the continuity of the trust. Tax consequences should also be considered whenever non-resident trustees are appointed in jurisdictions where the trustee's residence determines the taxation of a trust, such as in the United Kingdom. As a matter of prudence, advice should always be sought before the appointment of a non-resident trustee so as to confirm this point.

¶32-110 A variation can have tax consequences even if it does not amount to a resettlement

Where there is a fundamental variation of a fixed trust such that a new class of beneficiaries arises, any dispositions of property effected by the variation will likely be subject to the same tax consequences as a resettlement: *Swires (HMIT)* v *Renton* [1991] BTC 363, *IR Commrs* v *Holmden* [1968] AC 685; [1968] 1 All ER 148; *Chief Commissioner of Stamp Duties* v *Buckle* (1998) 151 ALR 1.

However, the variation need not amount to a resettlement. The tax treatment is only the same because a fundamental variation, like a resettlement, results in a disposition for tax purposes together with the requisite consequences.

¶32-120 Legislation

Income Tax Act 2007

HC 3 MULTIPLE SETTLEMENTS

For the purposes of this subpart, if a settlement is made on a trust and further settlements are made on the same terms, a trustee of the trust may treat all the settlements as 1 trust.

CHAPTER 33

Resettlement

¶33-010 Operating principle

Resettlement occurs when all or some of the property of a trust is resettled onto a different trust. The taxation consequences of a resettlement are those that arise on the transfer of property or following a loss of continuity.

The assets of a trust can be resettled, in whole or in part, onto the trustees of another trust.

¶33-020 Resettlement is not a defined term

In addition to a formal resettlement where all or some of the property subject to a trust is transferred to another trust, a resettlement can occur where a trust is varied such that even though a formal resettlement does not occur, the consequences are that the trust property is subject to a new trust. See ¶32-040. A resettlement can also occur with the unanimous consent of the beneficiaries under s 122 of the Trusts Act 2019, by power of the court under s 124 of the Trusts Act, under a power of resettlement contained in the deed of trust or under the statutory power of advancement: Trusts Act 2019, s 64.

As a resettlement at is most elemental level is merely a disposition of trust assets, care must be taken to recognise the attendant tax consequences.

For convenience, the term resettlement is used to cover both a formal resettlement and the consequences of a termination in an existing trust.

¶33-030 Distributions under a resettlement are treated as occurring at market value

Generic rules were enacted in 2005 for the tax treatment of the transfer of property in certain situations, including resettlements. See ¶26-100. When property is resettled onto another trust, no consideration is paid by the recipient trustee. However, for tax purposes, the property transferred is valued at market value.

The same value is used by both the resettling and the recipient trustee: s FC 2.

The effective date of the transfer is the date of the resettlement: s FC 2(1).

Example

A family trust (Trust A) owns a variety of investments, some of which are FIF interests. Partway through the year, Trust A was wound up and settled on another trust (Trust B). How is the resettlement treated for tax purposes?

The resettlement will be treated as a disposal by Trust A and an acquisition by Trust B of the overseas equities at market value. The deemed disposal and acquisition is treated as occurring on the date of the resettlement.

Trust A's tax liability will calculated in accordance with the FIF rules. See ¶7-050.

¶33-040 Depreciable property that is distributed under a resettlement has a tax book value for the recipient trustee

The deemed market value means that the resettling trustee must account for any depreciation recovery income in respect of depreciable property. This means that the resettling trustee must account for any depreciation recovery income, although the transfer was not made for consideration. See ss EE 44–EE 52.

The recipient trustee is deemed to have acquired the property at market value: s FC 2(1).

¶33-050 Resettled land is transferred at market value

A resettlement of land that is subject to the land disposal provisions is treated as a disposal of the land at its market value: ss FC 1(1)(f), FC 2. This may require the trustee to recognise income on the resettlement.

The recipient trustee is treated as having a cost of acquisition that is the same as the trustee's disposal value. That will provide a cost base for the recipient trustee, if the recipient trustee holds the land on revenue account.

Income from the sale of land distributed under a resettlement and later sold by the recipient trustee can give rise to income in the hands of the recipient trustee if the sale proceeds would have been taxable to the resettling trustee: s CB 15.

Where ss CB 7 to CB 12 and CB 14 apply, the recipient trustee will be treated as having acquired the land on the date on which the land was first acquired by the resettling trustee: s CB 15(2)). See ¶18-040.

Note that with very limited exceptions (eg if s FB 1B applies (settlement of relationship property)), a resettlement of residential land will have the effect of "resetting" the bright-line date for the purposes of s CB 6A.

¶33-060 Financial arrangements are resettled at market value

Where a financial arrangement is resettled, the transfer will be at market value for tax purposes: ss FC 1(1)(f), FC 2. This is the case even though there will be no consideration for the resettlement.

Financial arrangements include outstanding debts and fixed interest securities. The financial arrangements rules tax the economic benefit associated with financial arrangements. When a financial arrangement is transferred, a wash-up calculation referred to as a base price adjustment occurs. The base price adjustment requires a calculation that compares the consideration received and paid in respect of the financial arrangement and provides that the difference is treated as income or expenditure.

¶33-070 Outstanding debts can be novated or repaid on a resettlement

If any debts are owing when a trust is resettled, the outstanding debts can be repaid or novated.

A novation effects an assignment so that the debt remains but the recipient trustee accepts the liability for the debt.

¶33-080 Debt forgiveness income can arise on a resettlement if the exception to s EW 50 does not apply

If the resettling trustee has had debts forgiven, income can arise to the resettling trustee, up to the amount of the debt forgiven, if the beneficiaries of the recipient trustee are neither persons other than those for whom the creditor has natural love and affection nor registered charities: s EW 50.

This would be the case if a resettlement was made from a trust where the only beneficiaries were the creditor's children, onto a trust that had corporate beneficiaries. When this is the case, the previously forgiven amounts are income to the trustee of the resettling trust in the income year of the resettlement: s EW 50(6). See Chapter 14 – *Forgiveness of Debt*.

Example

Elaine advanced $200,000 to Elaine's Trust. The debt was progressively forgiven. The beneficiaries of Elaine's Trust are her grandchildren and the SPCA, a registered tax charity. Elaine's Trust has been resettled onto Peggy's Trust, a trust of which the sole beneficiary is the SPCA. No income is incurred by the trustee of Elaine's trust in respect of the resettlement as the exception in s EW 50 will apply.

Also see ¶34-030.

¶33-090 A resettlement may result in a loss of continuity

There are no modifications to the continuity provisions for companies that apply to resettlements. Accordingly, if 49% continuity is not maintained following a resettlement, any tax losses will be forfeited in companies other than look-through companies. See ¶17-030.

Further, if 66% continuity is not maintained in a company (other than a qualifying company), any imputation credits will be lost. See ¶17-110.

However, if the company whose shares are being resettled is in a position to declare an imputed dividend, some or all of the credits may be utilised before the resettlement.

Example

The majority shareholder in a company is a trust, holding 998 of 1000 shares. The shares have been resettled on a new trust. The beneficiaries of the new trust are the same as the beneficiaries of the old trust. There is no intention of avoiding or defeating the imputation legislation by resettling the trust. Does this constitute loss of continuity for imputation credits?

Yes, shareholder continuity of 66% or more for imputation credits will not be satisfied. The resettlement of the shares will affect the company's ability to carry forward any pre-existing losses and will give rise to forfeiture of the imputation credits. However, the imputation credit problem may easily be overcome by way of a taxable bonus issue or a dividend before resettlement.

¶33-100 GST must be accounted for on any taxable supplies that are made under the resettlement

A supply under a resettlement may be a supply for GST purposes. Accordingly, if the resettling trust is GST-registered, GST must be accounted for on the supply of any assets that comprise the trust's taxable activity.

Although a supply under a resettlement will not be made for consideration, if the recipient trust is associated with the resettling trustee, but not GST-registered, the supply will be deemed to be made at market value: GST Act, s 10(3).

Where both the resettling and recipient trusts are GST-registered, the market value provisions will not apply.

If the recipient trust is also GST-registered, it may be possible to zero-rate any taxable supplies that are not compulsorily zero-rated as a going concern. The fact that there will be no consideration made for a supply under a resettlement does not affect the ability to zero-rate a supply, consideration not being a requirement for zero-rating: GST Act, ss 11(1)(m), (mb), 78F. See ¶25-100.

If the recipient trustee is GST-registered and the resettling trustee is not, a secondhand goods credit is unlikely to be available, as the secondhand goods provision effectively requires that there be payment: GST Act, s 3A(3). Also see A McKenzie *GST – A Practical Guide* (Edition 9, CCH, Auckland, 2012) at 1306.

¶33-110 Tax losses will be forfeited if the resettling trust is wound up

Losses cannot be resettled onto another trust. Where a resettling trust retains some assets, it will retain any losses. However, if the resettling trust resettles all its property onto the recipient trust, the resettling trust will cease to exist and, accordingly, the tax losses will be forfeited. See ¶34-070.

¶33-120 Legislation

Income Tax Act 2007

EW 50 INCOME WHEN DEBT FORGIVEN TO TRUSTEE

EW 50(1) WHEN THIS SECTION APPLIES

This section applies when–

(a) a trust is a debtor; and

(b) the trust was established mainly to benefit 1 or both of the following:

 (i) a natural person for whom the creditor has natural love and affection; or

 (ii) an organisation or a trust whose income is exempt under section CW 41 (Charities: non-business income) or CW 42 (Charities: business income); and

 (c) the creditor is a natural person; and

 (d) the creditor forgives the debtor's debt; and

 (e) a trustee of the trust makes a distribution, including a distribution of beneficiary income, to a beneficiary; and

 (f) the beneficiary is–

  (i) not a natural person for whom the creditor has natural love and affection; and

  (ii) not an organisation or a trust whose income is exempt under section CW 41 or CW 42; and

 (g) the distribution is made on or after 20 May 1999.

EW 50(2) EXCLUSION

This section does not apply when–

(a) a trust (**trust** A) is a debtor; and

(b) trust A was established mainly to benefit 1 or both of the following:

  (i) a natural person for whom the creditor has natural love and affection; or

  (ii) an organisation or a trust whose income is exempt under section CW 41 or CW 42; and

(c) the creditor is a natural person; and

(d) the creditor forgives the debtor's debt; and

(e) a trustee of the trust makes a distribution to another trust (**trust B**); and

(f) at the time the distribution is made, trust B is also established mainly to benefit 1 or both of the following:

  (i) a natural person for whom the creditor has natural love and affection; or

  (ii) an organisation or a trust whose income is exempt under section CW 41 or CW 42.

EW 50(3) TWO POINTS ABOUT SUBSECTIONS (1) AND (2)

For the purposes of subsections (1) and (2),–

(a) the debtor's debt includes an amount accrued and unpaid at the time of the forgiveness; and

(b) the means by which the debt is forgiven, whether in a will or otherwise, is immaterial.

EW 50(4) DISTRIBUTION IS INCOME OF TRUSTEE

The distribution is income of the trustee, under section CC 3(2) (Financial arrangements), to the extent to which it is less than or equal to the total amount of the debts of the trust forgiven to it by the creditor.

EW 50(5) DISTRIBUTION SUBTRACTED FROM TOTAL AMOUNT FORGIVEN

The distribution is subtracted from the total amount of the debts of the trust forgiven to it by the creditor as the total amount stands at the time of the distribution.

EW 50(6) TIMING

The income is derived by the trustee in the income year in which the distribution is made.

[...]

FC 1 DISPOSALS TO WHICH THIS SUBPART APPLIES

FC 1(1) TYPES OF DISTRIBUTIONS AND GIFTS

This subpart provides a value for property that is disposed of under the [following] transactions...:

[...]

(f) the transfer of property on a settlement by the trustee of a trust on the trustee of another trust, if authorised under–

  (i) a trust instrument as a power of advancement or resettlement:

  (ii) section 64 of the Trusts Act 2019 as the payment or application of capital money or other capital assets.

[...]

FC 2 TRANSFER AT MARKET VALUE

FC 2(1) MARKET VALUE

The transfer of property in circumstances described in section FC 1(1) is treated as a disposal by the transferor and an acquisition by the transferee at the market value of the item for the transferor. The disposal is treated as occurring on the date of the transaction.

[...]

CHAPTER 34

Winding Up

¶34-010 Operating principle

There are no specific taxation provisions that apply when a trust is wound up. Accordingly, the treatment of any distribution of trust assets on a winding up is no different to that which applies during the life of the trust.

¶34-020 All of the trust assets and/or income are distributed when a trust is wound up

A trust is wound up following the termination of a trust when all of the trust's assets are distributed onto its beneficiaries or onto another trust by way of resettlement. Although certain formalities are required to record the end of the trust, these are practical rather than legislatively prescribed when the existing trusts are extinguished.

Section 124 of the Trusts Act 2019 provides that the court has the power to approve the termination of a trust.

The taxation consequences contingent on winding up a trust are those that apply to the distribution of the trust's assets regardless of the circumstances of the termination and winding up of the trust.

¶34-030 Certain distributions on a winding up can result in trustee income

If debts have been forgiven during the life of the trust, distributions on a winding up to persons, other than tax charities, for whom the settlor does not have natural love and affection, will result in income to the trustees: s EW 50.

A trust with both debts owing and debts owed can, to the extent permitted by the deed of trust, enter into a debt defeasance to cancel out any debts.

Example

Trust A, which the trustees wish to wind up, has capital of $50,000 and a debt owed to it by Trust B of $162,000. The trustees of Trust A are indebted to that trust's settlor to the amount of $112,000.

Trust A can enter into a debt defeasance with the trustees of Trust B for the debt's original face value of $112,000. Trust A will need to perform a base price adjustment in relation to the debt defeased. The consideration will be the financial arrangement's market value, which should be the face value of the debt, leaving Trust A in a tax-neutral position. Trust B will be treated as being in the same position as Trust A before the debt defeasance.

The remaining capital can be distributed in accordance with the terms of the deed of trust for Trust A.

¶34-040 Where a loss of continuity occurs due to a trust being wound up consequences are the same as for any loss of continuity

The continuity rules for shareholding do not contain any exceptions that address a loss of continuity because a trust is wound up. See Chapter 17 – *Continuity*.

¶34-050 Distributions of corpus on a winding up will be tax-free if the distribution would have been tax-free if made before winding up

Distributions of corpus made on winding up the trust are treated as any other capital distribution and will be tax-free to the same extent as would have been the case for an earlier capital distribution. See Chapter 6 – *Beneficiary Distributions*.

¶34-060 Deductions may not be available for the income year in which a trust is wound up

When a trust is wound up, current year income must necessarily be paid as beneficiary income. This means that deductions cannot be offset against the income as would be the case if the income was retained as trustee income.

¶34-070 Any losses are lost when a trust is wound up

Any losses retained on winding up will be lost. There are no provisions that allow tax losses to be distributed to the beneficiaries when a trust is wound up.

Example

A complying trust is being wound up. The final distribution includes a distribution of corpus and current year net income, the trustees have before year tax losses that exceed the current income. All beneficiaries are resident in New Zealand and no beneficiaries are minor beneficiaries. How will this final distribution be treated for income tax purposes?

For the purposes of determining the trustee's allowable deductions, any beneficiary income is deemed to be trustee income.

Any current year income distributed to beneficiaries will be taxed as beneficiary income, unless the beneficiaries are non-resident or minor beneficiaries, and will have the effect of reducing the amount of trustee income against which previous year losses can be offset.

Any losses not offset against trustee income will be lost.

¶34-080 Winding up the trust will cause the cessation of a taxable activity

If the trust is GST-registered, there will be a cessation of the taxable activity on or before the winding of the trust. The relevant matters to consider are the same as for the cessation of any business. See Chapter 25 – *Goods and Services Tax*.

¶34-090 There are practical matters for a trustee to attend to when winding up a trust

The act of winding up the trust itself is normally under a resolution and there are no legal formalities attached. However, there will be notices to be made. For example:

- registration of any property transfers should be confirmed
- the trustee should seek confirmation from Inland Revenue that there are no outstanding tax matters
- the trust's bankers should be notified that the trust has been wound up and the trust's bank accounts closed
- final accounts will be prepared so that the trustees can make final accounts to the beneficiaries
- a final tax return should be filed
- if the trust is GST-registered, it will need to de-register before the trust is wound up
- Inland Revenue should be notified that the trust has been wound up.

It is also prudent to ensure that all of the relevant trust documents have been prepared, executed and appropriately stored. Documents that might be required as a precursor to winding up a trust may include, but are not limited to:

- letters of advice
- deed of distribution
- deeds of indemnity
- trustee resolutions
- deed to bring forward the vesting date.

Beneficiaries' rights to request trust documents do not cease when a trust is wound up. See *Erceg* v *Erceg* [2015] NZHC 594; (2015) 4 NZTR ¶25-010 and *Erceg* v *Erceg* [2016] NZCA 7; (2016) 4 NZTR ¶26-001.

¶34-100 A trustee's liability for tax is not extinguished when a trust is wound up

The trustee will remain liable for the trust's tax liabilities following the winding up of a trust. Once the trust's assets are fully distributed, the trustee's right to indemnity from the trust's assets is practically limited. Accordingly, a prudent trustee may seek personal indemnification from the final beneficiaries for any shortfalls or liabilities in respect of any tax or other obligations, before making the final distribution of the trust's assets. Where a beneficiary will not provide a satisfactory indemnity, the trustee can apply to the court for directions in this matter under s 66 of the Trustee Act. See, for example, *Worn* v *Buxton* HC Auckland M 125-SD01, 17 June 2002.

A trustee is also liable for any outstanding tax if the trust has not been formally wound up, but the trust's assets have been distributed. See *Selkirk* v *McIntyre* [2013] NZHC 575; (2013) 3 NZTR ¶23-002 where the professional trustee was liable for a trust's unpaid GST. See further at ¶25-130 and ¶21-070.

¶34-110 Legislation

Trusts Act 2019

124 POWER OF COURT TO APPROVE TERMINATION, VARIATION, OR RESETTLEMENT OF TRUST

124(1) [Approval by the court]

The court may, on behalf of any of the beneficiaries described in subsection (2) who has an interest in the property of a trust, approve the termination, variation, or resettlement of the trust.

124(2) [Beneficiaries on whose behalf the court may make order]

The beneficiaries are–

(a) a beneficiary who lacks capacity:

(b) a person who may acquire a beneficial interest at a future date or on the happening of a future event or on becoming a member of a certain class of persons:

(c) a future person who may acquire a beneficial interest.

124(3) [Who may apply]

An application for an order of approval may be made by–

(a) the trustees or any one of them:

(b) any person with a beneficial interest in the trust property.

124(4) [Factors for the court]

On an application for an order of approval, the court must take into account each of the following factors:

(a) the nature of any person's interest in the trust property and the effect of the proposed order on that interest:

(b) the benefit or detriment that may result to any person with an interest in the trust property if the court makes or refuses to make the proposed order:

(c) the intentions of the settlor of the trust in settling the trust, if it is practicable to ascertain those intentions.

124(5) [Order must not reduce vested interest]

The court must not make an order of approval if its effect would be to reduce or remove any vested interest in the trust property.

124(6) [Order to be binding]

An order of approval binds the person on whose behalf it is made and takes effect without any further step.

Case Table

The case citations used as examples or as references in this book are listed below in alphabetical order.

Paragraph

C

D

E

Paragraph

J

K

L

M

Legislation Finding List

INCOME TAX ACT (EXEMPT UNIT TRUSTS) ORDER 1990

INCOME TAX ASSESSMENT ACT 1936 (AUST)

INHERITANCE TAX ACT 1984 (UK)

LAND TRANSFER ACT 2017

LAND TRANSFER (LAND INFORMATION AND OFFSHORE PERSONS INFORMATION) EXEMPTION REGULATIONS 2015

LEGISLATION ACT 2019

Index

Made in United States
Orlando, FL
04 November 2026

90205877R00334